GOD IN TRANSLATION

God in Translation

Deities in Cross-Cultural Discourse
in the Biblical World

Mark S. Smith

William B. Eerdmans Publishing Company
Grand Rapids, Michigan / Cambridge, U.K.

First published 2008 by Mohr Siebeck, Tübingen,
as volume 57 of the Forschungen zum Alten Testament series

This edition published 2010 by
Wm. B. Eerdmans Publishing Co.
2140 Oak Industrial Drive N.E., Grand Rapids, Michigan 49505 /
P.O. Box 163, Cambridge CB3 9PU U.K.

Printed in the United States of America

16 15 14 13 12 11 10   7 6 5 4 3 2 1

Library of Congress Cataloging-in-Publication Data
Smith, Mark S., 1955-
God in translation: deities in cross-cultural discourse in the biblical world /
Mark S. Smith.
p.   cm.
Originally published: Tübingen: Mohr Siebeck, c2008.
(Forschungen zum Alten Testament; 57)
Includes indexes.
ISBN 978-0-8028-6433-8 (pbk.: alk. paper)
1. Gods in the Bible. 2. Intercultural communication —
Religious aspects — History. I. Title.

BS680.G57S65   2010
202′.1109394 — dc22

2010023317

www.eerdmans.com

To my wife, Liz Bloch-Smith,

always,

and to our children,

Benjamin,

Rachel,

&

Shula,

stars shining within

Contents

Preface

As the new millennium unfolds, the world seems to be experiencing increasing religious conflict. Whether abroad or at home, religious extremism appears to be on the rise. From what we see in the news, it is sometimes difficult to escape the impression that the world is retreating into religious camps, each with its own religious and political absolutism justified by its own version of the truth sponsored by its own divinity. Several parts of the world appear intensely polarized along religious lines. Battle lines are being drawn across continents and within societies. The savage part of this conflict involves how religious intolerance translates into political and military violence.

It was not always so. The twentieth century, especially in the decades following the Second World War, witnessed a profound shift in the attitude of world religions towards one other. In fits and starts, the so-called major religions of the world engaged in serious dialogues over their religious differences and shared values.[1] It may be said with justification that this period represented the greatest time of constructive inter-religious engagement since antiquity. Yet this seems to be passing. We now live at a point, perhaps a particularly dangerous flash-point, when the struggle over what major religions do and do not share is shifting towards a conviction that there is less and less basis or reason for discussing the matter. Indeed, reason seems to have little to do with what is presently transpiring among religions and cultures.

This study undertakes an exploration of intercultural contact over three major periods in what I am broadly calling the "biblical world" (both Hebrew Bible and New Testament). These are the ancient Near East during the Late Bronze Age (Chapter One); ancient Israel during the monarchy and afterwards (Chapters Two, Three and Four); and Judea and the other cultures of the Mediterranean basin following the death of Alexander the Great (Chapters Five and Six). In this book I am going to tell the story of

---

[1] See Eric J. Sharpe, "Dialogue of Religions," *ER* 4.2342–45 (with bibliography). For dialogue within Christianity in the twentieth century (up through the mid-1980s), see the 1987 survey by a major figure in the field of ecumenical dialogue, Robert McAfee Brown, "Ecumenical Movement," *ER* 4.2683–91.

what has been called "translatability" of deities, namely how deities of various cultures were identified or recognized by name across cultural boundaries.

This story was not always about successful cross-cultural understanding. In antiquity, translatability could function as the arm of empire power, a point crucial for being sensitive to religious particularity in the face of dominant "western" culture today. Then as in modern times, translatability potentially serves as an insidious instrument of political oppression, at times quite oblivious to, or even intolerant of, the cultural traditions of others. Thus, contrary to some modern academic authors, ancient translatability is not a proper model for encouraging tolerance of others or for overcoming religious particularity. It has also been claimed that traditional forms of monotheism, for example in Judaism and Christianity, lead to intolerance and violence. However, the ancient record shows that this was not so. Monotheism in antiquity was not itself the mechanism of intolerance or even violence. Indeed, it was often the opposite, a strategy for resisting imperial power and maintaining local cultural traditions. Thus in its quest for understanding across cultures, humanity will be well served by maintaining respect for its specific traditions and by cultivating humility.

As I hope this study shows, the ancient story anticipates aspects of the situation in the world today. It is my hope that by reflecting on the ancient situation, we might be able to understand our world and ourselves better. Otherwise, there is the risk of something of our humanity – and perhaps of our divinity – getting lost in translation.

Acknowledgements

This study is due in no small measure to Ron Hendel. It was he who first drew my attention to the work of Jan Assmann on cross-cultural recognition of deities, and it was he who encouraged me to take a closer look at this subject. He also provided helpful consultation at later stages of this work. For these reasons, I happily begin with profound thanks to Ron. I am also grateful for two visits with Jan Assmann, which helped me to understand better his intellectual project on translatability of deities.

Several colleagues read a chapter or more of this work. For their great help I am deeply appreciative: Paul Aspan, Dominic Boyer, John Collins, Dan Fleming, Alan Kierkeslager, Beate Pongratz-Leisten, John Meier, Seth Sanders, Peter Schäfer and Peter Spitaler, as well as my daughters, Rachel and Shula Smith, and my student Cory Peacock. I thank a number of other scholars whom I consulted on particular points: Moshe Bernstein, Elizabeth Bloch-Smith, Joel Burnett, David Carpenter, David Carr, Billie Jean Collins, Avery Cardinal Dulles, Dan Fleming, Ogden Goelet, Kathryn Hellerstein, Christoph Levin, Peter Machinist, Martti Nissinen, Douglas Oakman, Ann Roth, Larry Schiffman, Gregory Sterling, and Karel van der Toorn. It should be clear from this roster of names that the sections on Assyriological and Egyptological literature and on the Greco-Roman period and New Testament received extensive help from these colleagues. I would be remiss if I failed to single out the particularly important aid provided by Beate Pongratz-Leisten on the Assyriological material and by Peter Spitaler on the New Testament discussion. This work also benefited from discussions with students in several courses taught at NYU, in particular a directed readings course with an undergraduate student, Marina Mogilevskaya (now an employee of Goldman Sachs).

Various chapters were presented in a number of academic forums in 2006 and 2007 (in order): the Department of Theology at Fordham University; the Pacific Northwest regional meeting of the American Academy of Religion and the Society of Biblical Literature; the international meeting of the Catholic Biblical Association of America; a seminar at Cornell University, made possible thanks to Seth Sanders and Dominic Boyer; a symposium on "Revolutionary Monotheism," held at Princeton University, organized by Beate Pongratz-Leisten; the meeting of the Canadian Society of Biblical Studies; and the Notre Dame-New York University Joint Program: Jewish and Christian Scholars on Judaism and Christianity in Antiquity. Finally, visits to the theological faculties of Ludwig-Maximilians-Universität München and Eberhard-Karls-Universität Tübingen in June, 2007 provided amenable settings for further reflection and work. My hosts, in particular Christoph Levin at Munich, and Herbert Niehr and Bernd Janowski at Tübingen, provided the opportunity to deliver lectures and to discuss aspects of this research. The trip was underwritten very generously by Mohr Siebeck, and for this aid I am indebted to the head of the house, Georg Siebeck, and his editorial director, Henning Ziebritzki. I am grateful to the scholars of these societies and groups for their responses and encouragement. In view of the many debts noted here and cited in the chapters that follow, it should be clear that this study largely constitutes an effort at synthesis. For all of the wonderful help that I have received, I add the important caveat that all errors remain my own.

This work was accepted graciously into the Forschungen zum Alten Testament series. For their good counsel and help, I wish to thank my cherished colleagues on the series' editorial board, Bernd Janowski and Hermann Spieckermann, as well as the series director, Henning Ziebritzki. I also wish to thank Tanja Mix of Mohr Siebeck for her wonderful work in producing and correcting the page-proofs for publication. My acknowledgments end with my family, to whom this book is dedicated with the greatest of gratitude and affection.

August 15, 2007   Mark S. Smith
The Feast of the Assumption

Abbreviations and Sigla

AB	The Anchor Bible
ABD	*Anchor Bible Dictionary*. Ed. David Noel Freedman. Six volumes. Garden City, NY: Doubleday, 1992.
ABRL	Anchor Bible Reference Library
AD	Dates after the traditional date of the birth of Christ (= CE)
AOS	American Oriental Series/Society
AP	A. E. Cowley, *Aramaic Papyri of the Fifth Century B. C.* Oxford: Clarendon, 1923; reprinted ed., Osnabrück: Otto Zeller, 1967.
AJA	*American Journal of Archaeology*
ANEP	*The Ancient Near East in Pictures Relating to the Old Testament.* Ed. James B. Pritchard. Princeton: Princeton University, 1954.
ANET	*Ancient Near Eastern Texts Relating to the Old Testament.* Ed. James B. Pritchard. Third edition with supplement. Princeton: Princeton University, 1969.
AOAT	Alter Orient und Altes Testament
ARM	Archives royale de Mari
BASOR	*Bulletin of the American Schools of Oriental Research*
BBB	Bonner Biblische Beiträge
BC	Before Christ (= BCE)
BCE	Before the Common Era (= BC)
BDB	Francis Brown, S. R. Driver, and C. A. Briggs, *Hebrew and English Lexicon of the Old Testament*. Oxford: Clarendon, 1907.
BH	Biblical Hebrew
BHS	*Biblia Hebraica Stuttgartensia*. Ed. K. Elliger and W. Rudolph et al. Fifth revised edition. Stuttgart: Deutsche Bibelgesellschaft, 1997.
BIOSCS	*Bulletin of the International Organization for Septuagint and Cognate Studies*
BM	British Museum number
bT.	Babylonian Talmud
BZ	*Biblische Zeitschrift*
BZAW	Beihefte zur Zeitschrift für die alttestamentliche Wissenschaft
CAD	*The Assyrian Dictionary of the Oriental Institute of the University of Chicago*. Chicago: The Oriental Institute; Glückstadt: J. J. Augustin, 1956–.
CANE	*Civilizations of the Ancient Near East*. Ed. Jack M. Sasson. Four volumes. New York: Charles Scribner's Sons, 1995.

CAT   *The Cuneiform Alphabetic Texts from Ugarit, Ras Ibn Hani and
           Other Places (KTU: second enlarged edition).* Ed. Manfried Diet-
           rich, Oswald Loretz and Joaquín Sanmartín. Abhandlungen zur
           Literatur Alt-Syrien-Palästinas und Mesopotamiens 8. Münster:
           Ugarit, 1995. Texts cited by number.
CBQ   *The Catholic Biblical Quarterly*
CBQMS   The Catholic Biblical Quarterly Monograph Series
CD   Damascus Document (from the Cairo Geniza)
CE   Common Era (= AD)
CHANE   Culture and History of the Ancient Near East
COS   *The Context of Scripture.* Ed. W. W. Hallo and K. Lawson
           Younger. Three volumes. Leiden/Boston: Brill, 1997, 2000, 2002.
CT   Cuneiform Texts from Babylonian Tablets in the British Museum
CTH   Emmanuel Laroche, *Catalogue des textes hittites.* Paris: Klinck-
           sieck, 1971.

DDD   *Dictionary of Deities and Demons in the Bible (DDD).* Ed. Karel
           van der Toorn, Bob Becking, and Pieter W. van der Horst. Second
           edition. Leiden: Brill, 1999.
DJD   Discoveries in the Judaean Desert series. Oxford: Clarendon,
           1955-
DN(s)   divine name(s)
DNWSI   *Dictionary of the North-West Semitic Inscriptions.* Ed. J. Hoftijzer
           and K. Jongeling. Two volumes. Leiden/New York/Köln: Brill,
           1995.
DSS   Dead Sea Scrolls
DSSSE   *The Dead Sea Scrolls Study Edition.* Ed. Florentino García Mar-
           tínez and Eibert J. C. Tigchelaar. Two volumes. Leiden/Boston/
           Köln: Brill; Grand Rapids, MI/Cambridge, UK: Eerdmans, 1997,
           1998.

EA   El Amarna texts, numbering as found in William L. Moran, *The
           Amarna Letters.* Baltimore/London: Johns Hopkins University,
           1992; and Shlomo Izre'el, *The Amarna Scholarly Tablets.* Cunei-
           form Monographs 9. Groningen: Styx, 1997.
EPRO   Études préliminaires aux religions orientales dans l'empire romain
ER   *Encyclopedia of Religion.* Second edition. Ed. Lindsay Jones.
           Fifteen volumes. Detroit: Thomson Gale, 2005.

FAT   Forschungen zum Alten Testament
FRLANT   Forschungen zur Religion und Literatur des Alten und Neuen
           Testaments

GDR   German Democratic Republic (the former East Germany)

HSM   Harvard Semitic Monographs
HSS   Harvard Semitic Studies
HTR   *Harvard Theological Review*

ICC	The International Critical Commentary
JAOS	*Journal of the American Oriental Society*
JBL	*Journal of Biblical Literature*
JNES	*Journal of Near Eastern Studies*
JQR	*Jewish Quarterly Review*
JSJ	*Journal for the Study of Judaism in the Persian, Hellenistic and Roman Periods*
JSOTSup	Journal for the Study of the Old Testament Supplement series
KAI	Herbert Donner and Wolfgang Röllig, *Kanaanäische und aramäische Inschriften.* Third edition. Wiesbaden: Harrassowitz, 1971–1976. Cited by text number.
KAR	Erich Ebeling, *Keilschrifttexte aus Assur religiösen Inhalts.* Leipzig: J. C. Hinrichs, 1919–23.
KUB	Keilschrifturkunden aus Boghazköi
LCL	Loeb Classical Library
LXX	Septuagint (Greek translation of the Hebrew Bible)
MT	Masoretic Text (text of the Bible in Jewish tradition)
NAB	New American Bible translation
NJBC	*The New Jerome Biblical Commentary*
NJPS	*TANAKH The Holy Scriptures: The New JPS Translation According to the Traditional Hebrew Text.* Philadelphia/New York/Jerusalem: The Jewish Publication Society, 1988.
OB	Old Babylonian period (used also as a phase of Akkadian language)
OBO	Orbis biblicus et orientalis
OEAE	*The Oxford Encyclopedia of Ancient Egypt.* Ed. Donald B. Redford. Three volumes. Oxford/New York: Oxford University, 2001.
OLA	Orientalia Lovaniensia Analecta
OTL	Old Testament Library
OTPS	*The Old Testament Pseudepigrapha.* Ed. James H. Charlesworth. Two volumes. Garden City, NY: Doubleday, 1985.
PDMT	Magical Texts in Demotic Papyri, in *PGMT.*
PE	*Preparatio evangelica,* written by Eusebius
PGM	Karl Preisendanz, ed. *Papyri Graecae Magicae: Die griechischen Zauberpapyri.* Berlin, 1928. Second edition. Two volumes. Ed. A. Henrichs. Stuttgart: B. G. Teubner, 1973–1974. Cited by textual number.
PGMT	Hans Dieter Betz, ed. *The Greek Magical Papyri in Translation including the Demotic Spells.* Second edition. Chicago/London: University of Chicago, 1992. Cited by page number.
PMLA	*Publications of the Modern Language Association of America*

PRU IV	Jean Nougayrol. *Le palais royal d'Ugarit. Volume IV*. Mission de Ras Shamra IX. Paris: Imprimerie Nationale/Librairie C. Klincksieck, 1956.
RB	*Revue biblique*
RdQ	*Revue de Qumran*
RHA	*Revue hittite et asianique*
RS	Ras Shamra (number of object found at the site of Ras Shamra – Ugarit)
RNAB	Revised New American Bible translation
SAA	State Archives of Assyria
SBLDS	Society of Biblical Literature Dissertation Series
SBLMS	Society of Biblical Literature Monograph Series
SBLRBS	Society of Biblical Literature Resources for Biblical Study
SBLTT	Society of Biblical Literature Texts and Translations
SBLWAW	Society of Biblical Literature Writings from the Ancient World
SED	Sozialistische Einheitspartei Deutschlands (Socialist Unity Party of the GDR)
SNTSMS	Society for New Testament Studies Monograph Series
SP	Samaritan Pentateuch
STDJ	Studies on the Texts of the Desert of Judah
TDOT	*Theological Dictionary of the Old Testament*. Ed. G. Johannes Botterweck and Helmer Ringgren. Trans. John T. Willis. Revised edition. Grand Rapids, MI: Eerdmans, 1977–.
TSAJ	Texte und Studien zum Antiken Judentum
TUAT	Texte aus der Umwelt des Alten Testaments
UF	*Ugarit-Forschungen*
UNP	*Ugaritic Narrative Poetry*. Texts and Translations by Mark S. Smith, Simon B. Parker, Edward L. Greenstein, Theodore J. Lewis and David Marcus. Ed. Simon B. Parker. SBLWAW 9. Atlanta: Scholars, 1997.
VT	*Vetus Testamentum*
VTSup	Vetus Testamentum Supplements
WUNT	Wissenschaftliche Untersuchungen zum Neuen Testament
ZAW	*Zeitschrift für die alttestamentliche Wissenschaft*
ZDPV	*Zeitschrift des deutschen Palästina-Vereins*
ZThK	*Zeitschrift für Theologie und Kirche*
1QM	Serek ha-Milḥamah (The War Scroll) from Cave 1 at Qumran
1QS	Serek ha-Yaḥad (The Rule of the Community) from Cave 1 at Qumran
3Q	Text(s) from Cave Three at Qumran

4Q	Text(s) from Cave Four at Qumran
11Q	Text(s) from Cave Eleven at Qumran
11QPs[a]	Psalms Scroll "a" from Cave Eleven at Qumran
G-stem	Basic verbal stem in Semitic languages corresponding to the Qal stem in Hebrew
D-stem	Verbal stem with doubled second root-letter corresponding to the Hebrew Piel
N-stem	Verbal stem corresponding to the Hebrew Niphal

A Note on Transliteration and Citation

I have decided to use approximate transliteration of ancient foreign words. I have not put in diacritical marks for vowels. Despite this simplification, I trust that it will be clear to scholars to what words in the original texts the transliterations refer. In order to make this work more accessible, I have spelled out the full names of the books of the Bible, even for citations of specific verses.

Timeline: Periods, Events and Writings

BCE   Before the Common Era (= BC, "before Christ")
CE   Common Era (= AD, "in the year of the Lord")
ca.   Latin circa, meaning approximately or around

Middle Bronze Age (ca. 2000 BCE – 1550 BCE)

Old Babylonian period in Mesopotamia,
Roughly equivalent to Middle Kingdom and Second Intermediate Period in Egypt

Late Bronze Age (ca. 1550 BCE – 1200 BCE)

Roughly equivalent to the Middle Babylonian (Middle Assyrian) period in Mesopotamia

Late 1500s	Consolidation of the Hurrian kingdom of Mitanni
ca. 1539–1075	Egyptian New Kingdom
ca. 1500–1375	Hittite Middle Kingdom
1390–1352	Reign of Amenophis (Amenhotpe) III
	El Amarna letters of Amenophis III
ca. 1375–1175	Hittite New Kingdom
	Heyday of Ugarit, cosmopolitan city-state on the Syrian coast
1352–1336	Reign of Amenophis (Amenhotpe) IV (Akhenaten)
	El Amarna letters of Amenophis IV (Akhenaten)
1349	Amenophis changes his name to Akhenaten and establishes new cult center at El Amarna
1336–1327	Reign of Tutankhamun
	Last of the El Amarna letters
1279–1213	Reign of Ramesses II
1275	Battle of Qadesh
1258	Peace treaty of Ramesses II and Hattusili III
ca. 1250–1200 (?)	Early traditions of Israel
1213.1203	Reign of Merneptah
ca. 1208	Merneptah stele (with the earliest known extra-biblical reference to Israel)
ca. 1180	End of the Hittite Empire and the destruction of Ugarit

Iron I Period (1200 BCE – 1000 BCE): premonarchic period

ca. 1200–1000	Premonarchic Israel
ca. 1100–1000	Basic body of the poem of Judges 5 and some sayings in Genesis 49 (?)

	Early inscriptions (e. g., personal names on arrowheads)
ca. 1030–1010	Saul as king over "Gilead, the Ashurites (?), Jezreel, Ephraim and Benjamin" (2 Samuel 2:9)

Iron II Period (ca. 1000 BCE – 540 BCE): period of the monarchy and "Exile"

ca. 1010–970	David as king of Judah and Israel ("United Monarchy"), treaty with Tyre, hegemony over other neighbors
ca. 970–930	Solomon as king of Judah and Israel ("United Monarchy"), treaty and trade network with Tyre, and diplomatic relations with Egypt
ca. 960s	Jerusalem Temple built
ca. 930	Death of Solomon, decoupling of the northern kingdom (Israel) and the southern kingdom (Judah)
ca. 930–913	Jeroboam I, first king of the northern kingdom (Israel)
925	Pharaoh Shishak invades Judah
ca. 900s-800s (?)	The Gezer Calendar inscription
	Early royal psalms (e. g., sections of Psalm 18 = 2 Samuel 22)?
	The "Yahwist" ("J") text/source (?)
876–869	Omri, king of northern kingdom of Israel, establishes new capital at Samaria, pays tribute to Assyria
869–850	Ahab, king of north (Israel), coalition with Tyre via marriage to Jezebel
853	Battle of Qarqar: Levantine coalition, including Ahab, holds off Assyrian encroachment
mid-800s	The prophet Elijah in the northern kingdom in reign of Ahab
	The "Elohist" ("E") text/source (?)
842–815	Jehu overthrows Omride dynasty and rules as king of north
mid/late-800s	The prophet Elisha (disciple of Elijah) in the north
early 700s	Kuntillet Ajrud inscriptions (in the Sinai)
786–746	Reign of Jeroboam II, last flowering of Israel before the Assyrian conquest of the Levant
770s	Samaria Ostraca inscriptions (years 9, 10, 15 and 17 of Jeroboam II, 786–746)
ca. 750s	Prophecy of Amos during reign of Jeroboam II in Israel
745–727	Tiglath-pileser III, king of Assyria, conquers the Levant
ca. late 740	Prophecy of Hosea in Israel,
– early 730s	Core of Deuteronomy 12–25 written (?)
ca. 734–732	Isaiah delivers oracles of consolation to King Ahaz of Judah, including "Immanuel oracles" of Isaiah 7 and 9, to support the king during the war waged against Judah by Israel and Syria ("Syro-Ephraimite War")
732	Assyria comes to the aid of the Judah
732–724	Hoshea, last king of Israel and vassal of Assyria

722	Assyrian conquest of the north, twenty-seven thousand taken as captives, northern refugees flee to Judah, Israel incorporated into the Assyrian empire as provincial territory
ca. 727/715	Beginning of the reign of Hezekiah as king of Judah
late 700s	Khirbet el-Qom burial inscription (in Judah)
ca. 705–701	Hezekiah prepares for Assyrian invasion of Judah, fortifies the walls of Jerusalem and extends its water-works
	The Siloam tunnel inscription reflecting Hezekiah's work
701	Assyrians under Sennacherib invade, lay siege to Jerusalem, take over two hundred thousand Judeans to Assyria, with Judah remaining as vassal to Assyria
	Isaiah's prophecy to Hezekiah during Sennacherib's invasion, as reported in Isaiah 36–39 = 2 Kings 18–19
	First edition of the Books of Kings, produced during Hezekiah's reign inspired by "victory" over Assyrians
	Core of Proverbs brought into the southern court by "men of Hezekiah" (cf. Proverbs 25:1)
ca. 698/687	End of Hezekiah's reign in Judah
689/687–642	Manasseh as king of Judah, vassal to Assyria
640–609	Josiah as king of Judah
627–582	Jeremiah's career as prophet
late 620s	Assyrian withdrawal from the Levant, Judah as small regional power
ca. late 620s–610s	Revision of Kings in time of Josiah (?)
	So-called "discovery" of the Torah (some form of "Deuteronomy"?) in Jerusalem Temple reported in 2 Kings 22
	So-called reforms of Josiah
ca. 610–586	Prophecy of Jeremiah in Jerusalem
late 610s	Collapse of Assyrian empire, rise of Babylonian empire
604–562	Nebuchadnezzar II of Babylon
597	Conquest of Jerusalem by the Babylonians under Nebuchadnezzar II, about three thousand Judeans taken to Babylonia (2 Kings 24; Jeremiah 52:28)
593–563	The priest Ezekiel serves as prophet in Babylonia
587–586	Further conquest of Jerusalem by the Babylonians
	About eight hundred Judeans taken to Babylonia (Jeremiah 52:29)
	Destruction of Jerusalem and Temple (2 Kings 25)
586–538	Captivity of members of Judean elite in Babylonia
582	Babylonian incursion into Judah, with further captivity of approximately 750 Judeans (Jeremiah 52:30)
ca. late 580s	Book of Lamentations and Psalm 74 composed in Jerusalem
	Psalm 137 composed in Babylonia
	Amos 9:11–15 and Isaiah 11:1–9 added (following demise of Davidic dynasty, perhaps later)

ca. 561	King Jehoiachin released from prison in Babylon (2 Kings 25:27–30)
559	Cyrus comes to the throne of Persia
ca. 550s	Production of "Deuteronomistic History" and supplements to Kings (e. g., 2 Kings 25:27–30)
556–539	Nabonidus, last king of Babylon

Persian Period (540 BCE–333 BCE): Yehud as a Persian province

539	Conquest of Babylonia by Cyrus the Persian
538	Edict of Cyrus granting permission for some captive peoples to return to their homelands
	Isaiah 40–55, composed in Babylonia, celebrating prospect of return to Judah; Psalm 126, anticipating return
	First group of Judeans return to the province of Yehud (Judah), under the leadership of Sheshbazzar, first governor (Ezra 5:14)
530–522	Reign of Cambyses
525	Persian capture of Egypt
522	Revolt within Persian empire following the death of Cambyses
	Darius assumes office as Persian king, consolidates power through 521
522–486	Darius I as king of Persia
ca. 520–518	Rebuilding of Jerusalem Temple led by Zerubbabel, second governor of Yehud, and the priest Jeshua, religious leader of Yehud, with prophecy of Haggai and Zechariah 1–6
late 500s–(?)	Priestly arrangement of the Torah (Pentateuch)
	Post-exilic expansions to the "Deuteronomistic History" (e. g., 1 Kings 8)
	New preface added to Deuteronomy (Deuteronomy 1:1–4:43)
	Isaiah 56–66
	The book of Job in its present form (?)
late 500s–early 300s	Documents of Judeans written from Elephantine (in southern Egypt)
ca. late 440s	Nehemiah as Persian governor of Yehud, leads rebuilding of Jerusalem's walls
ca. 440–416	Murashu documents (from Nippur in Mesopotamia)
ca. 419	"Passover letter" from Elephantine
ca. 409	Elephantine letter about rebuilding Elephantine temple
mid-400s	Mission of Ezra to Jerusalem (?), religious reforms said to be undertaken
400s	Song of Songs?
	Qohelet (also known as Ecclesiastes)?
300s (before 333)	I and II Chronicles
	Court-tales of Daniel 2–6
	The book of Esther
	The Levitical compilation of the book of Psalms (?)

Hellenistic Period (333 BCE – 164 BCE): Judea as contested territory

333	Alexander the Great conquers Egypt and the Levant
ca. 330	Conflicts in the priestly ranks in Jerusalem leads to Samaritan Jewish priestly establishment, with continued relations with Jerusalem priesthood
323	Death of Alexander, his empire split among his generals, issuing in four regional dynasties, including Egypt (Ptolemies) and Syria (Seleucids)
ca. 312–200	Judea under control of Egyptian Ptolemies, growing Jewish community in Alexandria (Egypt)
late 300s-200s	Zechariah 9–14
ca. 200–165	Control of Judea by Syrian Seleucids
ca. 180	Ben Sira (also known as Sirach or Ecclesiasticus) written
175–164	Antiochus IV Epiphanes (Seleucid ruler)
171	Murder of the priest, Onias III
168–164	Judean revolt against Seleucids and their Jewish priestly and upper class allies led by the Maccabees
167	Seleucid dedication of the Jerusalem Temple to Zeus (1 Maccabees 1)
ca. 167	Apocalyptic visions of Daniel 7–12 against Seleucids
164	Death of Antiochus IV Epiphanes
200s-100s	Torah, Historical Books, Prophets and Psalms recognized as authoritative Scriptures, with many of these biblical works circulating in multiple forms

Maccabean Monarchy (164 BCE – 63 BCE): Judea independent

167–164	Maccabean revolt
164	Maccabean victory over the Seleucid armies, Restoration of the Jerusalem Temple (1 Maccabees 4–6)
164–160	Judas Maccabeus rules Judea
160–142	Jonathan (brother of Judas) rules Judea, battles Nabateans, fortifies Jerusalem
ca. 154	The Jewish priest Onias IV permitted to build a temple in Leontopolis in Egypt, sign of division in priestly ranks
ca. 150	Further split in priestly ranks, signaled by the first references to Essenes and by the establishment of Dead Sea Scroll movement/ community, and perhaps by the first references to Pharisees
142–134	Simon rules Judea, gains recognition of Judean independence by Seleucids, later defends against Seleucid incursions
134–104	John Hyrcanus rules Judea
103–76	Alexander Janneus expands boundaries of Judean state

Roman Period (63 BCE – 395 CE/AD): Judea as Roman territory

63 BCE	Roman general Pompey establishes Roman control over Judea
44 BCE	Assassination of Julius Caesar

37–4 BCE	Herod ("the Great") rules Judea under Roman patronage, rebuilds the Jerusalem Temple, builds Caesarea, Masada and Herodium
31 BCE	Victory of Octavius (Augustus Caesar) at the battle of Actium
27 BCE – 14 CE	Reign of Augustus Caesar
ca. 20 BCE – 20 CE	Hillel
4 BCE – 6 CE	Herod Archelaus rules Judea, Samaria and Idumea as ethnarch under the Romans
4 BCE – 39 CE	Herod Antipas rules Galilee and Perea as tetrarch under the Romans
ca. 4 BCE – 30 CE	Life of Jesus
26–36 CE	Pontius Pilate, Roman governor of Judea
ca. 50–120 CE	New Testament works written
66–73 CE	First Jewish revolt and Roman subjugation under Vespasian
67 CE	Roman conquest of Galilee
68 CE	Roman destruction of Qumran
70 CE	Romans recapture Jerusalem and destroy the Temple
73 CE	Capture of Masada
75–79 CE	Josephus writes *Jewish War*
93 or 94 CE	Josephus completes *Antiquities*
ca. 100	Death of Josephus
115–117 CE	Jewish revolts in the Diaspora
132–135 CE	Second Jewish Revolt in the land
ca. 200 CE	The redaction of the Mishnah
200–300s CE	Jewish and Christians canons of the Hebrew Bible
ca. 390 CE	The Jerusalem Talmud completed
ca. 500 CE	The Babylonian Talmud completed

Introduction

The Subject of Translatability of Deities

1. The Rationale for this Study

Understanding ancient cultures entails a series of intellectual operations mediating or "translating" between antiquity and the present. Scholars of ancient societies are required to delve into details. Some of these involve issues of language and thus translation in a literal sense. Words also contain traces of cultural realities lying within the ancient texts.[1] Translating words thus requires an effort at translating ancient conceptions and perceptions presented in the texts. Archaeological and pictorial sources also help us to understand ancient cultures. Studying details in these various ancient media is thus crucially important and central to the task of translating the ancient world as best we can. Thus serious researchers follow a scholarly version of the admonition given by the brilliant early church figure, Origen: "Observe each detail which has been written. For, if one knows how to dig into the depth, he will find a treasure in the details, and perhaps also, the precious jewels of the mysteries lie hidden where they are not esteemed" (*Homily on Genesis* VIII).[2]

Cultural Translation in Anthropology

At a general level, the operation of translation involves a coordination of cross-cultural understandings, a task particularly familiar to anthropologists. Clifford Geertz reflected on the problem of cross-cultural translation

---

[1] The translation of texts has been an important field historically, and there is a very rich secondary literature on this subject. See Lawrence Venuti, *The Translator's Invisibility: A History of Translation* (London/New York: Routledge, 1995). Venuti (pp. 308–9) reflects on the tension between the imposition of the translator's culture and its tendency to assimilate the translated and treating the translated as culturally "other," thus alien and culturally deformed or devalued. See also the essays in: *Interculturality and the Historical Study of Literary Translations* (ed. Harald Kittel and Armin Paul Frank; Göttinger Beiträge zur Internationalen Übersetzungsforschung 4; Berlin: E. Schmidt, 1991); and Jeremy Munday, *Introducing Translation Studies* (London/New York: Routledge, 2001). For these latter references, I wish to thank Kathryn Hellerstein.

[2] Origen, *Homilies on Genesis and Exodus* (trans. Ronald E. Heine; The Fathers of the Church 71; Washington, DC: Catholic University of America, 1982) 136 (Genesis Homily VIII).

in these terms: "It involves learning how, as a being from elsewhere with a world of one's own, to live with them."[3] Talal Asad characterized the field as largely a matter of cultural translation: "the phrase 'the translation of cultures' … increasingly since the 1950s has become an almost banal description of the distinctive task of social anthropology."[4] In support of this view, he cites an essay by Edmund Leach that views social anthropologists as "establishing a methodology for the translation of cultural language."[5] Asad further invokes Max Gluckman as support for the notion that "cultural translation" is an acceptable way to describe the task of social anthropology.[6] Asad himself writes in a similar vein: "the anthropologist's translation is not merely a matter of matching sentences in the abstract, but of *learning to live another form of life* and to speak another kind of language."[7]

Anthropological translation is practiced according to Asad along the following lines: " 'Cultural translation' must accommodate itself to a different language not only in the sense of English as opposed to Dinka, or English as opposed to Kabbashi Arabic, but also in the sense of a British, middle class, academic game as opposed to the modes of the 'tribal' Sudan."[8] For Asad, cultural translation is analogous to but differs from language translation in a number of respects: "One difference between the anthropologist and the linguist in the matter of translation is perhaps this: that whereas the latter is immediately faced with a specific piece of discourse produced within the society studied, a discourse that is *then* textualized, the former must construct the discourse *as* a cultural text in terms of the meanings *implicit* in a range of practices."[9] The distinction is useful and it might be expanded. After exploring the inequalities of language between the western academy and third-world cultures, Asad concludes: "the process of 'cultural translation' is inevitably enmeshed in conditions of powers – professional, national, international."[10] Translation requires a sensibility to the power relations embedded in the process. In the end both language and cultural translation require knowledge of both language and culture; one cannot do

---

[3] Geertz, in a lecture in the series entitled *A Life of Learning* (Charles Homer Haskins Lecture for 1999; American Council of Learned Societies Occasional Paper, No. 45; np: American Council of Learned Societies, 1999) 14.

[4] Asad, "The Concept of Cultural Translation in British Social Anthropology," in: *Writing Culture: The Poetics and Politics of Ethnography* (ed. James and Clifford and George E. Marcus; A School of American Research Advanced Seminar; Berkeley/Los Angeles/London: University of California, 1986) 141 (reference courtesy of Kathryn Hellerstein).

[5] Cited by Asad, "The Concept," 142.

[6] Cited by Asad, "The Concept," 143.

[7] Asad, "The Concept," 149. Asad's italics.

[8] Asad, "The Concept," 159.

[9] Asad, "The Concept," 160. Asad's italics.

[10] Asad, "The Concept," 163.

without the other. In the hands of the best practitioners of this double-form of translation, knowledge and experience of language and culture inform one another.[11]

Cultural Translation in Autobiography

Somewhat analogous to anthropology with respect to cultural translatability are personal memoirs that chart an author's cross-cultural translation from one society to another. Eva Hoffman's autobiographical work, *Lost in Translation: A Life in a New Language,* offers a dramatic account of her family's migration from Poland to North America in the late 1950s.[12] For her, translation in language and culture assumes a central role in her narrative of her experience, as she moves first to Vancouver and later to Cambridge and New York. Such memoirs render the writer's life as a study in cross-cultural experience. Memoirs seem quite different in nature from anthropological study. As a field, anthropology involves methods and practices designed to minimize or contain the role of the investigator, while memoirs place the writer at the center of the narrative. Yet sometimes the memoirist experiences herself as "an anthropologist of the highly detached variety."[13] Moreover, anthropology (like most fields) is hardly without personal involvement or prejudice. Indeed, it is clear from the history of many academic fields that personal perspective is impossible to contain or restrain entirely, and it is here that the place of the examiner in both anthropology and autobiography may converge.

Although their methodologies differ enormously, anthropology and autobiography of the sort represented by Hoffman's work may be quite similar, as it is the examiners and their experiences that mediate between cultures and their understandings.[14] Both require what Hoffman calls

---

[11] See G. Witherspoon, "Language in Culture and Culture in Language," *International Journal of American Linguistics* 46/1 (1980) 1–13, cited and discussed by Alec Basson, *Divine Metaphors in Selected Hebrew Psalms of Lamentation* (FAT 2/15; Tübingen: Mohr Siebeck, 2006) 37–38.

[12] Hoffman, *Lost in Translation: A Life in a New Language* (New York: Penguin, 1989). I thank Kathryn Hellerstein for bringing this work to my attention. See also Hoffman's essay, "The New Nomads," in: *Letters of Transit: Reflections on Exile, Identity, Language, and Loss* (ed. André Aciman; New York: The New Press, 1999) 35–63. I am very grateful to Rachel E. Smith for bringing this work to my attention and for providing me with a copy of this book.

[13] Hoffman, *Lost in Translation,* 131.

[14] In mediating between Polish and English, between the experience of her old life and her new one, Hoffman (*Lost in Translation,* 107) describes herself: "I am becoming a living avatar of structuralist wisdom." However, "the problem is that the signifier has become severed from the signified" (*Lost in Translation,* 106). In this narrative, language and cultural translation is at once an experience of personal, emotional violence.

"double vision,"[15] the first component being their own original culture and the second the "other," the new culture that they experience distinctly as not their own. Here Hoffman's language echoes the comments of Geertz and Asad noted above about the double life or double language involved by anthropological study. Finally, Hoffman's comments on the asymmetry of her experience also resonate with Asad's critique of British anthropology and the third world cultures that it studies. For Hoffman, her experience from her old country cannot stand up to the overwhelming context of new country.[16] Perhaps most fundamentally, it is interesting to note how language translation functions as a basic idea for both cultural anthropology and for memoirs (at least, in Hoffman's case). Memoirs of this sort are also a reminder that cross-cultural translation seems to becoming an increasing part of human life in this era of heightened mobility, which stems from both voluntary and involuntary conditions. What we see in these fields of endeavor is the interrelation between the translation of language and the translation of culture; one is impossible without the other.[17]

Cultural Translation and Antiquity

The task of translating cultures of the past in the present is in some respects a more difficult task than either anthropology or autobiography. The challenge to "translate translatability" across cultures in antiquity into modern terms is doubly daunting: it involves coordinating both ancient and modern understandings of cultural features, as well as an assessment of their differences and their similarities.[18] Bearing in mind the observations of anthropologists and memoirists, we may ask: how does this double-task of translatability succeed where the distance involved is not only spatial but also temporal? To use Geertz's image, how, if at all, can modern investigators live in the culture of the past in any meaningful sense? Hoffman, too, captures this problem involving her experience of moving from Polish to English. She describes her experience of her loss of language: "Polish is becoming a dead language, the language of the untranslatable past."[19] How much more so for those who study the distant past, and not simply the past within the compass of their lifetimes? We may immerse ourselves in the

---

[15] Hoffman, *Lost in Translation,* 132.

[16] Hoffman, *Lost in Translation,* 210.

[17] For various literary reflections on culture and language, see the essays in: *Letters of Transit: Reflections on Exile, Identity, Language, and Loss* (ed. André Aciman; New York: The New Press, 1999).

[18] This constellation of issues is insightfully raised in different ways by the essays in Part I of *Inventing Ancient Culture: Historicism, Periodization, and the Ancient World* (ed. Mark Golden and Peter Toohey; London/New York: Routledge, 1997).

[19] Hoffman, *Lost in Translation,* 120.

features of ancient cultures, these signals from the past, and we may provide our educated guesses how best to understand them. In trying to communicate these signals from the past, translation can hardly be perfect. Again, in Hoffman's words, "In order to translate a language, or a text, without changing its meaning, one would have to transport its audience as well."[20] For ancient cultures, this is clearly impossible.

The Herculean task of translating ancient cultures to our modern context involves a further investigation into how cross-cultural translation operated within antiquity itself. One important area involving translation across cultures in the ancient world is religion. While the study of religion across cultures is a hallmark of the modern study of religion, theoretical consideration of the cross-cultural relations in the area of ancient religion has received less attention.[21] One facet of ancient cross-cultural relations concerns how people around the eastern Mediterranean world expressed themselves about the deities of other cultures that they encountered. Many ancient texts recognize deities belonging to foreign lands. This study examines cases of cross-cultural recognition of deities in the "biblical world," particularly Syria-Palestine (or the Levant) from the Late Bronze Age and well into the Roman period.

Cultural Translation and Divinities in Antiquity

This work builds on research on deities by students of Egypt and the ancient Near East. Expressions of cross-cultural recognition of deities have been noted for decades.[22] In recent years, the question has been raised anew by Jan Assmann, most notably in his book, *Moses the Egyptian: The*

---

[20] Hoffman, *Lost in Translation,* 273.

[21] The essays on religion in the volume edited by Sanford Budick and Wolfgang Iser, *The Translatability of Cultures: Figurations of the Space Between* (Stanford: Stanford University, 1996) are limited to those by Jan Assmann, "Translating Gods: Religion as a Factor of Cultural (Un)Translatability" (pp. 25–36), and Moshe Barasch, "Visual Syncretism: A Case Study" (pp. 37–54). No essays are devoted to religion in: *The Translatability of Cultures: Proceedings of the Fifth Stuttgart Seminar in Cultural Studies, 03.08.14.08.1998/ Stuttgart Seminar in Cultural Studies* (Stuttgart: Metzler, 1999). The Cultural Translation Project of the University of Wisconsin at Madison has not taken an interest in religious phenomena thus far, at http://polyglot.lss.wisc.edu/ctp/. A rather fine consideration of the issues of cultural translation (albeit restricted to modern religion) is provided by Kwasi Wiredu, "Identity as an Intellectual Problem," in: *Identity and the Politics of Scholarship in the Study of Religion* (ed. José Ignacio Cabezón and Sheila Greeve Davaney; London/ New York: Routledge, 2004) 209–28.

[22] For example, see John Wilson, "The Egyptians and the Gods of Asia," in: *Ancient Near Eastern Texts Relating to the Old Testament* (ed. James B. Pritchard; Princeton: Princeton University, 1950; third edition with supplement, 1969) 249 (henceforth *ANET*).

Memory of Egypt in Western Monotheism.[23] Other scholars working in the
ancient Near East, particularly Alfonso Archi, have drawn on this notion.[24]
Assmann's presentation tends to accent the cross-cultural identification or
equation of specific deities. At the same time, his understanding of what he
calls "translatability" of deities involves more. The evidence discussed by
Assmann suggests various notions of translatability of divinity well beyond
such identifications or equations. In his notion of "translatability" of divinity, Assmann additionally points to broader cross-cultural recognition of
other people's deities. In many cases, the texts show the recognition that
the deities of other cultures function in ways like its own deities. Sometimes
these cultures relate the deities of other cultures to their own deities. In this
intercultural "god-talk," people in one culture, most commonly at a highly
elite level, explicitly recognize that the deities of other cultures are as real
as its own. A term used by Assmann that captures the international and
intercultural context of this discourse is "the idea of an *ecumene.*"[25] For
Assmann, intercultural "god-talk" is a fundamental feature within a larger
international, political ecumenism. We should be alert to the fact that here
a term from the Greco-Roman context is used somewhat anachronistically
for the Bronze Age. Indeed, this term does not truly capture social identity
in the Bronze Age or in the Iron Age, which was based on the family and
tribe as well as the city. In sum, translatability involves specific equations or
identifications of deities across cultures and the larger recognition of deities
of other cultures in connection to one's own deities.

It is important to be clear about what translatability is not in Assmann's
work. It is not the importation of deities, or the influence of foreign religious ideas or concepts about divinity. Religious importation of deities[26]

---

[23] Assmann, *Moses the Egyptian: The Memory of Egypt in Western Monotheism*
(Cambridge, MA/London: Harvard University, 1997) 3, 28, 44–54. For further details,
see Chapter One below.
[24] See Archi, "Hurrian Gods and the Festivals of the Hattian-Hittite Layer," in: *The Life
and Times of Ḫattušili III and Tutḫaliya IV: Proceedings of a Symposium in Honour of
J. De Roos, 12–13 December, 20003, Leiden* (ed. Theo P. J. van den Hout, with the assistance
of C. H. van Zoest; Leiden: Nederlands Instituut voor het Nabije Oosten, 2006) 147–63.
[25] Assmann, *Akhanyati's Theology of Light and Time* (The Israel Academy of Sciences and Humanities Proceedings, vol. VII No. 4; Jerusalem: The Israel Academy of
Sciences and Humanities, 1992) para. 2.2. The Greek term, *oikumene,* is used by Rodolfo
Ragionieri, "The Amarna Age: The International Society in the Making," in: *Amarna Diplomacy: The Beginnings of International Relations* (ed. Raymond Cohen and Raymond
Westbrook; Baltimore/London: Johns Hopkins University, 2000) 42–53, esp. 49.
[26] For Asiatic deities in Egypt, the classic study is Rainer Stadelmann, *Syrisch-palästi-
nische Gottheiten in Ägypten* (Probleme der Ägyptologie 5; Leiden: Brill, 1967). See also
Raphael Giveon, "New Material Concerning Canaanite Gods in Egypt," in: *Proceedings of the Ninth World Congress of Jewish Studies: Division A. The Period of the Bible*
(Jerusalem: World Union of Jewish Studies, 1986) 1–4; Donald Redford, *Egypt, Canaan,
and Israel in Ancient Times* (Princeton: Princeton University, 1992) 43–48, 116–18, 228,

may help to induce cross-cultural recognition of deities. Similarly, the expression of translatability is sometimes affected by cultural migration or importation of religious culture.[27] However, such accompanying factors do not belong to Assmann's core notion of translatability. Likewise, Assmann's account would not include particular terms of divinity in themselves, such as *'elohim* ("gods, God"), Persian and Greco-Roman period titles like "lord of heaven" and "god of heaven," or Greco-Roman concepts including *logos* ("word"), or even specific forms of divinity, such as monotheism (or "one-god" worldviews) and dualism (e. g., "Persian dualism"). It is true that these may be shared cross-culturally by religions and may accompany instances of translatability, but shared titles or concepts of divinity do not constitute the core notion of translatability in Assmann's account. At various points in this study, these sorts of features related to translatability are mentioned, as they indicate aspects of the cultural contours of the phenomenon as well as the cultural sensibilities about it in different contexts. Still, this work maintains a focus on translatability.

One major question in Assmann's discussion of "translatability" of divinity involves what he calls the Bible's "Mosaic distinction" (as in the title of his book, *Die Mosaische Unterscheidung*).[28] For Assmann, this "Mosaic distinction" suggests a fundamentally different religious situation compared with other religious expressions of the ancient Near East and Egypt. In contrast to the rest of the ancient Near East, where translatability of deities across cultural lines seemed to be the norm, Assmann writes in these terms about "the Mosaic distinction":

We may call this new type of religion "counter-religion" because it rejects and repudiates everything that went before and what is outside itself as "paganism."

231–33; and Christiane Zivie-Coche, "Dieux Autres, Dieux des Autres: Identité Culturelle et Alterité dans l'Egypte Ancienne," *Israel Oriental Studies* XIV (1994) = *Concepts of the Other in Near Eastern Religions* (ed. Ilai Alon, Ithamar Gruenwald and Itamar Singer; Leiden/New York/Köln: Brill, 1994) 56–78.

For the importation of Syro-Mesopotamian deities into Hatti, see Itamar Singer, " 'The Thousand Gods of Hatti': The Limits of an Expanding Pantheon," *Israel Oriental Studies* XIV (1994) = *Concepts of the Other in Near Eastern Religions* (ed. Ilai Alon, Ithamar Gruenwald and Itamar Singer; Leiden/New York/Köln: Brill, 1994) 91; Alfonso Archi, "Kizzuwatna Amid Anatolian and Syrian Cults," in: *Anatolia Antica: Studi in memoria di Fiorella Imparati* (ed. Stefano de Martino and Franca Pecchioli Daddi; Eothen 11; Florence: LoGisma, 2002) 47–53.

[27] Archi has discussed translatability in connection with this phenomenon. See Archi, "Hurrian Gods and the Festivals of the Hattian-Hittite Layer," 147–63. For this issue, see Chapter One. For a useful discussion of cross-cultural transmission of cultural material, see Jacke Phillips, "A Question of Reception," in: *Archaeological Perspectives on the Transmission and Transformation of Culture in the Eastern Mediterranean* (ed. Joanne Clarke; Levant Supplementary Studies 2; Oxford: Oxbow, 2005) 39–47.

[28] Assmann, *Die Mosaische Unterscheidung: Oder der Preis des Monotheismus* (München/Wien: C. Hanser, 2003).

It no longer functioned as a means of intercultural translation; on the contrary, it functioned as a means of intercultural estrangement. Whereas polytheism, or rather "cosmotheism," rendered different cultures mutually transparent or compatible, the new counter-religion blocked intercultural translatability. False gods cannot be translated.[29]

In other words, translatability did not become prevalent in the Bible because of its "Mosaic distinction" between the one true God and all other false deities. When it comes to ancient Israel, Assmann's "Mosaic distinction" is expressed not so much in historical terms as in conceptual categories. In Assmann's case, the lack of historical particulars is perhaps due in large measure to his approach, one that is disinterested in historical context as such; it focuses instead on the history of cultural memory. His inattention to historical particulars may also be in part a matter of academic discipline; Assmann is an Egyptologist and not a scholar of the Bible.

The historical particulars involving ancient Israel and the Hebrew Bible come into focus as we move into discussions by biblical scholars. In the wake of Assmann's work, two biblical scholars have addressed the topic as it pertains to ancient Israel. Ronald Hendel and I have raised the issue of translatability in the Bible with rather different results.[30] In his 2005 book, *Remembering Abraham,* Hendel largely follows Assmann's lead, as it begins with the premise of a lack of translatability for ancient Israel. In my own book, *The Memoirs of God,* that appeared in 2004, I suggested that the history of ancient Israelite religion involved both translatability and its eventual rejection. In our works, neither Hendel nor I devote much discussion to the question of translatability. Indeed, the relative brevity of Assmann's discussions of translatability points to the need for greater discussion of the topic. The three of us have left unexplored a number of seminal questions. Apart from relatively brief discussions, we have not examined the different forms or expressions of translatability, attested in the Late Bronze Age (ca. 1550–1200 BCE/BC) and monarchic Israel (ca. 1000–586 BCE/BC),[31] or in the Greco-Roman period (ca. 332 BCE/

---

[29] Assmann, *Moses the Egyptian,* 3. See also his article, "Monotheismus und Ikonoklasmus als politische Theologie," in: *Mose: Ägypten und das Alte Testament* (ed. Eckart Otto; Stuttgarter Bibelstudien 189; Stuttgart: Katholisches Bibelwerk, 2000) 121–39.

[30] Hendel, *Remembering Abraham: Culture, Memory, and History of the Hebrew Bible* (Oxford/New York: Oxford University, 2005) 3–6, especially 5; and Smith, *The Memoirs of God: History, Memory, and the Experience of the Divine in Ancient Israel* (Minneapolis: Fortress, 2004) 4–5, 113.

[31] Designations of periods and the dates given for them are in large measure conventions resulting from the academic study of the past. The questions posed to the past often predispose scholars to prioritize types of changes and thereby issue in the periods informed by particular sorts of historical understandings (for example, political events and royal reigns versus broader religious or social history and traditions or economic tends). In the wake of the *Annales* school, made famous by the work of Fernand Braudel, it is evident

BC–135 CE/AD).[32] The following section lays out my general goals for the chapters of this book.

---

that multiple periodizations could be devised based on short-term (*l'histoire événemen-tielle*) versus long-term change (*la longue durée*) and some middle-range changes posited in-between. In recent years, the place of social history or women's history in construct-ing periodization has been raised for ancient history, for example for Rome (e. g., see the survey of Phyllis Culham, "Did Roman Women Have an Empire?" in: *Inventing Ancient Culture: Historicism, Periodization, and the Ancient World* [ed. Mark Golden and Peter Toohey; London/New York: Routledge, 1997] 192–204); I am unaware of any comparable reconsideration for the ancient Near East. For transmission of traditional religious tradi-tions, I could see an argument for ca. 1400–800 BCE/CE in the Levant as a basic period, with political changes suggesting the bases for subunits within this larger time frame (cf. J. C. Greenfield, "The 'Cluster' in Biblical Poetry," *Maarav* 5–6 [1990] 167), in particular ca. 1200 as a major demarcation on several interrelated fronts (see *The Crisis Years: the 12th Century B. C.: From beyond the Danube to the Tigris* [ed. William A. Ward and Mar-tha S. Joukowsky; Dubuque, Iowa: Kendall/Hunt, 1992]). For an interesting reflection on periodization for ancient Greece ca. 1200–700 BCE/BC, see Ian Morris, "Periodiza-tion and the Heroes: Inventing a Dark Age," in: *Inventing Ancient Culture: Historicism, Periodization, and the Ancient World* (ed. Mark Golden and Peter Toohey; London/New York: Routledge, 1997) 96–131.

[32] The Greco-Roman period as it is used in this study may be divided into the Hellenis-tic period (ca. 332–63 BCE/BC) and the Roman period (ca. 63 BCE/BC–395 CE/AD; cf. Fergus Millar, *The Roman Near East 31 BC–AD 337* [Cambridge, MA/London: Harvard University, 1993]). Here I am following the recent practice of using the Greco-Roman period to refer to the ancient Mediterranean world prior to what has been called Late Antiquity (ca. 250–800 CE/AD); see G. W. Bowersock, Peter Brown and Oleg Grabar, ed., *Late Antiquity: A Guide to the Postclassical World* (Cambridge, MA: Belknap, 1999) ix–x. For this approach to the "Greco-Roman period" generally, see Fritz Graf, "What is Ancient Mediterranean Religion?" in: *Religions of the Ancient World: A Guide* (ed. Sarah Iles Johnston; Cambridge, MA/London: Belknap, 2004) 3–16; and Christopher A. Faraone, *Ancient Greek Love Magic* (Cambridge, MA/London: Harvard University, 1999) 17, with additional secondary literature in favor of this approach. It is evident that Romanization in the eastern part of the empire in large measure meant "Hellenistic" influence. See Ramsay MacMullen, *Romanization in the Time of Augustus* (New Haven: Yale University, 2000). See also the interesting discussion of Garth Fowden, *The Egyptian Hermes: A Historical Approach to the Pagan Mind* (Princeton: Princeton, 1986) 13–22. To be sure, there have been critical assessments as they apply to specific regions. For example, for Egypt, see N. Lewis, " 'Greco-Roman Egypt': Fact or Fiction," in: *Proceedings of the XIIth International Congress of Papyrology* (ed. D. H. Samuel; American Studies in Papyrology 7; Toronto/Amsterdam: Hakkert, 1970) 3–14; and "The Romanity of Roman Egypt: A Growing Consensus," in: *Atti del XVII Congresso internazionale di papirologia* (Naples: Centro internazionale per lo studio dei papyri ercolensi, 1984) 1077–84.

At this point I would add a further clarification: because of its imprecision, I have made an effort to avoid the word, "Hellenism," and I tend to reserve the word, "Hellenistic," as a chronological designation, or as a general label for the eastern Mediterranean world. For helpful cautions about this term, see Barry S. Strauss, "The Problem of Periodiza-tion: The Case of the Peloponnesian War," in: *Inventing Ancient Culture: Historicism, Periodization, and the Ancient World* (ed. Mark Golden and Peter Toohey; London/New York: Routledge, 1997) 165–66. For the pejorative use of term in antiquity, see Polymnia Athanassiadi and Michael Frede, "Introduction," in: *Pagan Monotheism in Late Antiquity*

The Goals of this Study

My first goal is to expand the parameters of Assmann's abbreviated account of translatability in the ancient Near East. In part because Assmann's main aim is to provide a relatively brief inventory of examples of translatability for the various periods, he devotes little consideration to related factors in their cultural contexts. He also provides hardly any discussion involving their change of expression, and the resulting picture is a somewhat static representation of translatability. This study looks at the cultural contexts for expressions of translatability, as well as some of the major developments in the representation of translatability between the Late Bronze Age context and the Greco-Roman world. The cultural contexts develop as we move from the Bronze Age through to the Greco-Roman period. Some account is thus needed for these large-scale changes.

My second goal is to reverse Assmann's claims about the lack of translatability in the Bible, by presenting evidence for translatability in monarchic Israel, with some attention to its larger cultural and hermeneutical dynamics. On this score, my thesis essentially boils down to the following points: (1) in keeping with its scale and relatively local relations with other polities, Israel deployed a form of local translatability during the period of the monarchies, if not earlier; (2) this translatability took the form of a worldview that could recognize other national gods as valid for Israel's neighbors just as Yahweh was for Israel; (3) Israel's loss of translatability represented an internal development that corresponds with its experience of the initial stage of the international age emerging under the Assyrians and the Babylonians; (4) the conceptual shift in this period involved a sophisticated hermeneutic that retained older formulations of translatability within expressions of non-translatability and monotheism; (5) the hermeneutic of theism within ancient Israel and Yehud was an ongoing intellectual project involving various forms of textual harmonization; and (6) if Assmann's "Mosaic distinction" is to be maintained, it would be during the late biblical and post-biblical reception of the Bible than generally the Bible itself (much less ancient Israel) when it comes into focus.

(ed. Polymnia Athanassiadi and Michael Frede; Oxford: Clarendon; New York: Oxford University, 1999) 6–7. For the question of "Hellenism" in the biblical field, see the classic work of Martin Hengel, *Judaism and Hellenism: Studies in their Encounter in Palestine during the early Hellenistic period* (second one-volume ed.; Minneapolis: Fortress, 1991). See also his retrospective essay, "Judaism and Hellenism Revisited," in *Hellenism in the Land of Israel* (ed. John J. Collins and Gregory E. Sterling; Christianity and Judaism in Antiquity Series 13; South Bend, in: University of Notre Dame, 2001) 6–37; and Seth Schwartz, *Imperialism and Jewish Society, 200 B.C.E. to 640 C.E.* (Princeton/Oxford: Princeton University, 2001) 22–31. For further discussion, see Chapter Six.

A third goal involves an effort at uncovering ideas about divinity that the ancients presupposed in their texts, whether in the Hebrew Bible or in other ancient Near Eastern literatures. As we move through documents from various periods, we see the ancients deploying various categories of divinity in their construction of cross-cultural translatability. In order to highlight this aspect of ancient translatability, I have adopted a descriptive approach in this study, in order to bring out the theoretical underpinnings of cross-cultural translation represented in the texts. The descriptive task, at least for this study, will not adopt some modern theory (or meta-theory) for analyzing expressions of cross-cultural translatability in the texts. Deploying a modern theory may run the risk of displacing and obscuring the theoretical operations underlying the ancient texts. Instead, the goal is to identify and examine the theoretical parameters built by the ancients into their expressions of cross-cultural translatability of deities. Accordingly, this study is designed to observe how the language and categories for translation of divinity in one culture are borrowed and used by another.

Excursus: What is a God?

Before explaining the plan of this book, it is important to be clear about divinity in our ancient texts. To help clarify what was meant by "god" or "goddess," we should explore the terms that the ancient writers themselves used for deities. The main rubric is the Hebrew word, *'el,* and its two plural forms, *'elim* and *'elohim* (as well as the singular, *'eloah,* which was secondarily formed from the plural, *'elohim*). Cognate literatures show comparable forms, such as Ugaritic *'il* (plural *'ilm*), and Akkadian *ilu* (plural *ilu, ilanu*).[33] Hebrew and other ancient languages do not have lower and upper case letters. The singular form of these words in Hebrew can be translated as "god" and sometimes "God" as a name. The plural form can be "gods," yet the Hebrew plural form is also used for "God."

---

[33] See Wolfgang Herrmann, "El," *DDD* 274–80; Dennis Pardee, "Eloah," *DDD* 285–88; Karel van der Toorn, "God (I)," *DDD* 352–65; and Joel S. Burnett, *A Reassessment of Biblical Elohim* (SBLDS 183; Atlanta: Society of Biblical Literature, 2001). For discussion of Akkadian *ilu,* see Barbara Nevling Porter, "The Anxiety of Multiplicity: Concepts of Divinity as One and Many in Ancient Assyria," in: *One God or Many? Concepts of Divinity in the Ancient World* (ed. Barbara Nevling Porter; Transactions of the Casco Bay Assyriological Institute, vol. 1; np: np, 2000) 243–48. For consideration of this question in both the ancient Near East and in the Greco-Roman context, see M. L. West, "Toward Monotheism," in: *Pagan Monotheism in Late Antiquity* (ed. Polymnia Athanassiadi and Michael Frede; Oxford: Clarendon; New York: Oxford University, 1999) 21–40. West's survey is instructive, but in surveying biblical references to multiple deities, it omits Israelite monotheistic expressions in the eighth to the sixth centuries BCE and later, much less the possible historical context for this shift. See M. S. Smith, *The Origins of Biblical Monotheism: Israel's Polytheistic Background and the Ugaritic Texts* (Oxford/New York: Oxford University, 2001) 149–94.

Let me explain in a bit more detail. These words all derive from the base *'l,* and they cover a multitude of "divinities" in addition to "Yahweh, your god" (e. g., Exodus 20:2 = Deuteronomy 5:6) or "God," i. e., Yahweh (Exodus 19:3). The plural form is also used regularly as a word or title for Yahweh, namely "God." In the thinking of many Bible readers, the only "gods" besides the true god, the Lord, are false gods. Such false gods are called "other gods" (Exodus 20:3 = Deuteronomy 5:7, Judges 2:11, etc.); "other god" (singular) in Exodus 34:14, or "new gods" (Deuteronomy 32:17), or "their gods," i. e., of other people (Exodus 34:15); gods of the heaven/heavenly court who mated with human women (Genesis 6:1–2), regarded in later literature as sinning angels (e. g., in 2 Peter 2:4, Jude 6); and the *šedim* translated as "demons" by the NJPS and denigrated as "not-gods" in Deuteronomy 32:17 (cf. verse 21). These putatively false gods in some biblical contexts clearly include gods and goddesses (Judges 2:12–13, 3:6–7).[34] As can be seen from these cases, the translations of these passages raise the problem of understanding the various terms for deity, god and goddess.

Despite the general assumption of traditional reading, the biblical usage of these words for god, gods/deities, and God is considerably broader and more complex than most people today recognize when they think of what a god is.[35] When readers look at the question of divinity in the Bible, they are often concerned with the issues surrounding the nature and status of the true God versus other or false gods. However, the various biblical terms for god(s) may refer to a number of additional phenomena. Contrary to the popular view of the Bible, ancient Israel included all sorts of "gods," and not all of these were divided sharply into either God or negative, foreign gods, as suggested by the following sample.[36] For the sake of convenience, I provide a representative range of usage for god, gods and God, including positive, collective usages for divinities other than the so-called one god of Israel. Collective usages of gods include the case of Exodus 15:11, where the speaker asks in a positive manner: "Who is like you among the gods, O Yahweh?" These gods, literally "divine sons," are also said to belong to the heavenly court (e. g., *bene 'elim* in Psalms 29:1, 89:7; cf. *bene ha'elohim*

---

[34] Foreign goddesses are rarely labeled with the masculine term. An exception, "Ashtoreth, the god (*'elohe*) of the Sidonians," appears in a list of the national deities of Israel's neighbors in 1 Kings 11:33.

[35] This is an old question, posed for example by Cicero (*De natura deorum,* 3.17.43–20.52). See H. Rackham, *Cicero. De Natura Deorum. Academica* (LCL; Cambridge, MA: Harvard University; London: W. Heinemann, 1933) 326–37. See also the remarks of Lucio Troiani, "Cicero," *ER* 3.1786–87.

[36] So *BDB* 42–44; Frank M. Cross, " *'ēl,*" *TDOT* 1:242–61; Helmer Ringgren, " *'ĕlōhîm,*" *TDOT* 1:267–84; van der Toorn, "God," *DDD* 352–65; Smith, *The Origins of Biblical Monotheism,* 83–103.

in Job 1:6, 2:1). They work for the chief god/divine king and bow down to this chief god (*'elohim*, Psalm 97:7; cf. Psalm 96:4). They shouted for joy at the time of creation (and parallel to "morning stars," in Job 38:7). Thus the word "god" extends to both a major god such as Yahweh and minor divinities including his divine courtiers.

Some additional phenomena also fall under the rubric of "gods." Some ritual representations of divinity, the divinity's presence or the divinity's emblem-animal, are called "gods," for example, the calves of 1 Kings 12:28 and the so-called "Golden Calf" of Exodus 32:4, 8. Foreign gods likewise have images ("images of its gods," Isaiah 21:9; Psalm 96:5). Jacob calls household figurines (*terapim*, Genesis 31:34, 35) "my gods" (*'elohay*, Genesis 31:30). We find the same interchange of *terapim* and *'elohim* also in Judges 18:17–18, 24. Divinized human ancestors are also called "gods." Isaiah 8:19 refers to the dead in general by *'elohim* (see Isaiah 29:4c). The deceased figure of Saul is characterized as *'elohim* in 1 Samuel 28:13. In this connection, we might note the lack of response from *'elohim* to soothsayers in Micah 3:7,[37] or the "inheritance of *'elohim*" parallel to the "inheritance of the fathers," in 2 Samuel 14:16.[38]

When we turn to the singular form of "god," we also see considerable variation. The singular form of the word applies to the Israelite god rendered "God" in our translations ("God" as opposed to a human, in Isaiah 31:3; Hosea 11:9), but also to a specific god named El (also called El Elyon) in Genesis 14:19–20 and 14:22 (cf. El mentioned more in the poems of Numbers 23–24 than Yahweh). At the same time, the singular form is used as a general noun. For example, it is a term for "a god" (Deuteronomy 32:39, 1 Kings 18:24; Hosea 13:4; Psalm 14:2 = 53:2 = Psalm 10:4), for the chief god ("the god") in 1 Kings 18:21, 27, for the god of an area, "the god of the land" (2 Kings 17:26, 27), or for the "personal god" or "household god" ("the god of my father," Exodus 15:2). We also see the singular form used in the general sense of "the god" with some sort of predication, for example in 1 Kings 18:24: "the god who responds with fire, that one is (the) god." A similar sort of general usage appears in 1 Kings 20:26: "The Arameans have said: 'Yahweh is a god of mountains, but he is not a god of lowlands.'" The word can be used to denote one's god in a neutral fashion, for example in Ruth 1:16: "your god shall be my god." It appears in rather negative terms modifying a non-Israelite/Judean divine name: "Chemosh, your god" (Judges 11:24); "Dagon, our god" (1 Samuel 5:7; cf. "the house of his god" and "the treasury of his god," in Daniel 1:2).

---

[37] Van der Toorn, "God (I)," *DDD* 365.

[38] T.J. Lewis, "The Ancestral Estate (נַחֲלַת אֱלֹהִים) in 2 Samuel 14:16," *JBL* 110 (1991) 597–612; van der Toorn, "God (I)," *DDD* 365.

The singular form of the noun denotes non-anthropomorphic features associated with or emanating from divinity: "a divine fire" (Job 1:16; cf. the divine "name" personified compared to a fire in Isaiah 30:27). Physical locations are associated with divinity (or, "participate" in divinity): e. g., divine mountain (Ezekiel 28:14, 16; Psalm 68:16); "house of divinity" (Judges 18:31). Even the living human king can be labeled as "divine": "your throne, o divine one, is forever and ever," spoken by a royal servant to the king in Psalm 45:7 (cf. Egyptian king addressed by vassals as "my god" in the El Amarna letters 157, 213, 215, 233, 241, 243, 270, 299, 301, 305, 306, 319, 363, 366).[39] Other human figures are occasionally associated with deity: "a man of *'elohim*" (prophet in 1 Samuel 9:6–10; Moses, in Deuteronomy 33:1, Joshua 14:6, Psalm 90:1, etc.). Note that the "man of God," who appears to Manoah's wife in Judges 13:6, to her "looked like a messenger of God, exceedingly fearsome." From this brief listing of usages, we might say that the words for divinity apply to several sorts of beings regarded as "divine, extraordinary."[40] Such powers evidence capacities beyond what normal human beings can do.[41] These include gods in the modern sense as well as a number of extra-human powers lesser in status or rank.

To extrapolate from these usages of the words for "god," one might suggest that divinity in biblical and ancient Near Eastern terms was thought, metaphysically speaking, to be constituted by power: humans and other non-deities characterized as *'elohim* in some respects participate in the power of, or associated with, the divine power recognized as a god. Christian metaphysics in the Middle Ages understood reality in terms of Being and beings. In this worldview, all creatures derive their existence or being from (or, "participate in") Being itself, namely God. In comparison, ancient Levantine cultures largely viewed the use of *'elohim* (and its terms) as a matter of Power and powers.[42] As some uses of *'elohim* indicate, the category

---

[39] For a convenient translation, see William L. Moran, *The Amarna Letters* (Baltimore/London: Johns Hopkins University, 1992).

[40] Van der Toorn, *DDD* 363.

[41] Cf. *'elohim* for "higher" power, analogously applied to Moses relative to others in Exodus 4:16 and 7:1. Psalm 8:6 relates that humanity was created lacking a little relative to *'elohim*.

[42] For further discussion, see Smith, *The Memoirs of God*, 161–62. For the Greek use of "power" (*dunamis*), see Frederick William Danker, ed., *A Greek-English Lexicon of the New Testament and Other Christian Literature* (third ed.; Chicago/London: University of Chicago, 2000) 263, #5. The term in the Greco-Roman period is applied to supernatural spirits and angels. Power is not the only term used in expressing such relationships linking divinity and reality. BH *ruaḥ* (conventionally translated "spirit, wind") serves as another "biblical ontology" (in other words, that which binds humanity or reality to the divine), for example in Psalm 104:29–30 (cf. in verse 4 the divine messengers are represented as *ruaḥ* and *'eš*, "fire"; and in verse 24 the rains represent the divine infusion into the wise order of creation). For discussion of *ruaḥ* in Psalm 104, see Chapter One.

of power is a major constituent of this word, and it is for this reason that a number of scholars have traced the etymology of the words for god, gods and God to the Semitic root, *'yl, "to be first, be powerful," despite some difficulties with this view.[43]

2. The Plan of this Book

Contours and Limitations of this Study

I would like to begin my explanation of the book's structure with a few words about the limits of this study. First, the subject of this book treats translatability of deities mostly as they appear in a representative sample of texts; this is not an exhaustive catalogue. The examples presented extend well beyond what Assmann presents, but this work is not intended to be a comprehensive compilation of possible examples.

Second, the work offers only occasional discussion of translatability as found in art or in archaeological sources.[44] Iconography of one deity associated cross-culturally with the artistic representation of another poses particular difficulties for determining the nature of the influence: does it point to translatability, that the two deities are thought to be identified, equated or at least connected to one another? Or, is the artistic influence a matter of artistic style or preference? Or, are both involved? Some examples of iconography come up over the course of this discussion, but only where translatability can be reasonably posited. At various points in this study, iconography also serves as a helpful indicator of the larger cultural context of translatability.

Third, this study rarely mentions cases of translatability of texts themselves from one culture to another (for example, the well-known case of the adaptation of the Egyptian Words of Amenemope in the Bible, in Proverbs

---

[43] See Marvin H. Pope, *El in the Ugaritic Texts* (VTSup 2; Leiden: Brill, 1955) 16–21; Helmer Ringgren, "*'ělōhîm*," *TDOT* 1:273; Smith, *The Origins of Biblical Monotheism*, 7.

[44] This study draws on several works on the subject, including the important survey of Othmar Keel and Christoph Uehlinger, *Gods, Goddesses, and Images of God in Ancient Israel* (trans. Thomas Trapp; Minneapolis: Fortress, 1998). See also the survey of iconographical studies (with a helpful discussion of methodological issues) in: Theodore J. Lewis, "Syro-Palestinian Iconography and Divine Images," in: *Cult Image and Divine Representation in the Ancient Near East* (ed. Neal H. Walls; American Schools of Oriental Research Books Series 10; Boston: American Schools of Oriental Research, 2005) 69–107, esp. 71–82. In their study, Uehlinger and Keel use grammatical terms for iconography (*Gods*, 12–13, 120, 169). In accord with their usage, a "grammar of iconography" remains an important desideratum for the field. Also needed is further methodological reflection on and documentation of the variation of divine name, meaning, functions and representations, an issue raised in an important way by Keel and Uehlinger (*Gods*, 105–6).

22:17–23:11). These instances are pertinent where translations of texts point up cases of translatability of deities as well. There are a handful of such cases, for example, the Hittite text called "El, Ashertu and the Storm-god,"[45] which substitutes a Sumero-Akkadian ideogram ISHTAR for one of the West Semitic goddesses (discussed in Chapter One); and the substitution of the name of the Israelite god with the Egyptian name of Horus in an Aramaic version of Psalm 20 (written in Demotic script) found in Papyrus Amherst 63 (discussed in Chapter Four). These are rare, however. Throughout this study, the emphasis falls on cross-cultural recognition of deities themselves.

Fourth and finally, there are several issues related to translatability that are mentioned in this study. However, it is impossible to address all of them in a systematic manner, given the scope of this work. The discussion touches on various forms of polytheism and monotheism, both biblical and non-biblical. These include what has been called Christian binitarianism and trinitarianism, as well as Jewish binitarianism (in Chapter Six). Attention is brought briefly to other forms of theism as well. Matters pertaining to the important feature of anthropomorphism also arise over the course of the discussion. As interesting as these topics are, this study maintains its focus on the question of translatability. At the same time, it is important to mention these matters. I would add that in some respects the category of translatability seems little more than an alternative terminology for discussing some well-worn subjects, such as monotheism and polytheism. However, translatability provides some contours for understanding monotheism and polytheism better. Furthermore, it is arguable that in ancient Israel translatability predates clear expressions of monotheism and thus it may have been one of the conditions pre-existing Israelite monotheistic declarations and theologies.

An Overview of the Chapters

We begin in Chapter One with Assmann's account of cross-cultural recognition of deities in the Late Bronze Age (ca. 1550–1200), which was constructed through specific equation of deities across cultural boundaries and by broader cross-cultural representations of deities; this is what he calls "translatability." The survey in this chapter will extend the range of texts under discussion and will address these according to their different genres. In the survey, it will be possible to note some important political and religious features of translatability across the Levant in the Late Bronze Age.

---

[45] *ANET* 519. This text has also been called "Elkunirsha and Ashertu" for example by Harry A. Hoffner, Jr., *Hittite Myths* (SBLWAW 2; Atlanta: Society of Biblical Literature, 1990) 69–70. See similarly Gary Beckman, in: *COS* 1.149. For details to this text, see Hoffner, "The Elkunirsa Myth Reconsidered," *RHA* 23/76 (1965) 5–16.

It is also worthwhile to touch occasionally on earlier material in the Bronze Age. However, beginning with the Late Bronze Age provides a helpful way to focus the discussion. It also serves as a useful means for setting the stage for understanding the "biblical world," which in this study will include the Hebrew Bible or Old Testament as well as the New Testament.

The setting for translatability in the Late Bronze Age is overtly political. For over a century since the discovery of ancient texts in the Middle East, scholars have discussed the nature of relations among the great kingdoms of the ancient Mediterranean and Near Eastern world during the Late Bronze Age. A great deal of energy has been devoted to the study of these ancient texts, in particular international treaties and letters. The results have included new understandings of ancient history and politics as well as religion within these various polities. One of the more important points that Assmann makes and that can be extended involves the political culture informing religious translatability in this period: it was largely a function of ruling powers and scribal elites. In the area of international relations, it has become abundantly clear from research that religion accompanied politics. In international communication between rulers of relatively equal status, parity of power issued in corresponding expressions of parity between the gods and goddesses belonging to the different kingdoms. Likewise, in the relations between an overlord king and his royal vassals, differences in power issued in different expressions of recognition of the divinities of the overlord. Arguably, this is as we might expect, but we also see different forms of the overlord's recognition of the deities of his vassals. Before entering this probing of the ancient world, we cannot help but emphasize the shifting contexts of power and politics that inform these relations and their attendant expressions about divinities.[46] We may characterize this situation broadly as a contrast between empire powers, which set the terms of intercultural discourse, and their vassals, who tried to maintain their own cultural identities in the face of their overlords and their dominant culture. For the purposes of this discussion, we will highlight the empire powers of Hatti and Egypt, and Ugarit will serve as

---

[46] Without engaging in a full-fledged discussion of ideological criticism, this approach has influenced my thinking about the subject of this book. Intellectual religion and its political contexts are highly elitist. For a number of representative authors in this area, in particular Anthony Giddens and John B. Thompson, see Elizabeth A. Clark, *History, Text, Author: Historians and the Linguistic Turn* (Cambridge, MA/London: Harvard University, 2005) 174–75. To recast Thompson's notion that ideology is "meaning in the service of power," we might suggest that divinities as represented in the texts that we will study provide divine sanction for the political values attached to texts in service to their royal patrons' power. At the same time, I would want to guard against highlighting the political at the expense of other basic features of these texts. For a cautionary note in this vein, see Christiane Sourvino-Inwood, "Reconstructing Change: Ideology and the Eleusinian Mysteries," in: *Inventing Ancient Culture: Historicism, Periodization, and the Ancient World* (ed. Mark Golden and Peter Toohey; London/New York: Routledge, 1997) 143.

the parade example of a local power attempting to preserve its own identity in the shadow of the empire powers.

The survey in Chapter One further points to the intellectual categories and outlook presupposed by ancient political powers and their scribal apparatus. I suggest in Chapter One that texts containing expressions of translatability engaged in an intellectual or second-order discourse about deities. (First-order discourse is discourse expressed in religious experience, such as prayer; second-order discourse involves discourse representing intellectual reflection about the content of that experience, as in theology or philosophy of religion or history of religion or comparative religion.) As examples of second-order discourse embedded in texts of this period, some documents, especially treaties, betray implicit categories or typologies of deities. This sort of classification represents an implicit second-order discourse that anticipates the work of modern scholars who study ancient religions. Thus, in addition to charting translatability in the Bronze Age, it is an aim of Chapter One to indicate some of the ways in which the intellectual activity in the ancient world relates to the modern fields of history of religion and comparative religion. We will see how ancient scribes operated with theories of religion. These are often implicit to their writings; they didn't produce abstract treatises on such subjects. However, this does not make their theorizing any less significant for modern researchers who may miss such implicit theorizing embedded in ancient writings. Sometimes scholars take a modern theory of religion and apply it to an ancient text, but this procedure may overlook the fundamental, indigenous theory informing such texts. Part of our modern task is not simply to apply our modern theories to ancient texts, but to understand both their theories and our own, in order to deepen our understanding of the outlooks of both the ancients and ourselves.

In Chapter Two, we will take a look at cases of translatability in the Hebrew Bible. This chapter challenges the view of Jan Assmann and Ronald Hendel that the Bible or ancient Israel essentially rejected translatability of deities. On the contrary, some biblical passages offer fine textual representations of translatability of deities. To be sure, these are not as common as what we find in the Bronze Age record in Chapter One, but this is hardly surprising in view of the fact that later biblical texts largely reject translatability or show no interest in it. Given that a lack of translatability, specifically in the form of the rejection of foreign gods, becomes a norm in biblical literature, it is all the more remarkable that examples of translatability survived at all. In view of the evidence showing translatability, it is problematic to accept the surmise of Assmann and Hendel that a lack of translatability is originally fundamental to the Bible or ancient Israel.

In view of the general shift from translatability to non-translatability in ancient Israel, the situation calls for further probing. Chapter Three looks at the shift to non-translatability and the biblical "one-god" worldview, which clearly worked with Israel's own traditions yet responded to its particular conditions. One central circumstance facing Israel was the new dominance of Mesopotamia and its "one-god" worldviews. (Mesopotamia in the first millennium and its possible significance for understanding the development of divine conceptualization in Judah do not appear in Assman's account.) Some Israelite texts responded to Mesopotamian expressions of human and divine power by generating its own "one-god" worldview that differed sharply from Mesopotamian ideas. Indeed, Israel may be understood as a local power attempting to preserve its own religious and cultural heritage in the face of Mesopotamian empire power. How Israel would pursue this cultural agenda differed in some respects from the strategies evident at Ugarit in the Late Bronze Age. As we will see, one aspect of this difference has in turn to do with the differing natures of the empire that each of them faced. Ugarit knew multiple empires simultaneously, while Israel largely experienced one empire at any given point as it formulated its own "one-god" worldview. The contrasting situations show a comparable result in the area of translatability. We may contrast the first millennium context with the situation of the Late Bronze Age empires. While these generated various forms of translatability of deities, seventh-sixth century Mesopotamia and Israel both stand out by comparison in developing non-translatability of divinity. The "great powers" of the Late Bronze Age produced an intense intercultural discussion that included translatability, while the successive empires of the Iron Age did not generate such a sustained discourse of this sort. In these different imperial situations, the very form of empire informed the degree and nature of translatability

Chapter Three also introduces a refinement for understanding of translatability, specifically between geographical or "horizontal" translatability, on the one hand, and on the other hand, temporal or "vertical" translatability. Like the Late Bronze Age world before it, Israel engaged in translatability across geographical boundaries, an intellectual project that may be called more specifically "horizontal translatability." Yet it also translated its own indigenous tradition of divinity through time, in what may be labeled "vertical translatability": the god(s) of its earliest recalled experience was understood as its national god, despite some rather complex changes in early Israelite divinity.[47] Thus Israel during the monarchy enjoyed forms of both horizontal and vertical translatability. In the course of time, horizontal

---

[47] For a sketch of changes in the configuration of divinity in ancient Israel and the role of collective memory in shaping it, see Mark Smith, *The Memoirs of God: History, Memory, and the Experience of God in Ancient Israel* (Minneapolis: Fortress, 2004).

translatability came to be largely rejected for reasons that we will explore toward the end of Chapter Three and also in Chapter Four.

Chapter Four moves the discussion to textual evidence aimed against translatability in the Hebrew Bible during the post-exilic period, especially in the Greco-Roman context. The discussion of the Persian period is limited compared with other periods, in large measure because it plays no role in Assmann's account. Moreover, the Persian period largely shows considerable continuity in the contours of translatability. This situation changes dramatically in the Greco-Roman period. Within this time frame, biblical censorship serves to "protect" the biblical God from the appearance of horizontal translatability. We will examine two cases of censorship aimed against translatability, Deuteronomy 32:8–9 and Genesis 14:22. By studying the different textual witnesses in the passages, it is possible to identify changes made by scribal censors. These show deliberate choices or alterations designed to protect against the appearance of polytheism. In addition to examining the passages according to standard text-critical methodology, we will also probe these passages for how they were reread and echoed in later biblical passages as well as extra-biblical literature of the Greco-Roman period. In other words, I seek to use the approach of what has been called inner-biblical exegesis to aid my text-critical study of the two passages. Let me explain what I mean.

Usually text-critical study focuses on the attestations of the words in various sorts of biblical manuscripts, such as the Masoretic text (MT), the Septuagint (LXX) and the biblical manuscripts among the Dead Sea Scrolls. We can add to our understanding of the words transmitted in these different manuscript witnesses, by linking their readings to biblical passages that interpret the same verses. It is possible in these cases to connect text-critical readings of a verse with its inner-biblical interpretations. By seeing how these passages were reread between the time of their composition in ancient Israel and the time of their textual witnesses in the Greco-Roman period, we may gain a sense of how the representation of divinity in a passage was being interpreted in the time of its textual witnesses. We may thereby understand better what sorts of understandings of the words were operative at the time of these textual witnesses. The differences among the textual witnesses are thus not simply a matter of scribal error, but in some cases reflective of changes in the conceptualization of divinity.

Chapter Four also undertakes a broader exploration of censorship and its larger place within the intellectual culture of post-exilic Israel. This exploration is particularly informed by the work of Dominic Boyer[48] and

---

[48] Boyer, "Censorship as a Vocation: The Institutions, Practices, and Cultural Logic of Media Control in the German Democratic Republic," *Comparative Studies in History and*

Michael Holquist[49] on modern censorship. In Boyer's studies, censorship is not simply some sort of small-minded, anti-intellectual activity, but fits into a larger cultural context of the intellectual activities devoted to the production of state self-representation. This general point applies to biblical censorship. Like modern censorship, biblical censorship is to be situated more broadly within the larger context of intellectual and political production of texts.

Chapter Five turns to translatability in the wider Greco-Roman world. Assmann has pointed to the pervasive character of translatability in this period. He notes the phenomenon and a number of examples across the Mediterranean basin. This chapter adds to the cases of translatability discussed by Assmann, but it also focuses on the range of genres that deploy it. New genres of translatability include histories and philosophy. These emerge not only out of Greco-Roman centers of learning, from also among local writers; the emphasis in this discussion falls on Levantine authors who deploy history and philosophy to stake their own claims about divinity. Moreover, it is important to discuss the emergent political and cultural realities that affected the translatability in this period, especially compared to what is attested in either the Late Bronze Age Levant or Iron Age Israel. The massive increase in the social settings of translatability and in the mobility of knowledge and knowledge-specialists issues in translatability of divinity as a broad religious expression, well beyond what we see for the Late Bronze Age or the Iron Age. There is also local resistance to the dominant cultural translatability. Just as Ugarit showed cultural resistance to the Late Bronze empire powers and Israel rejected Mesopotamian "one-god" empire ideology during the Iron Age, so too local Levantine elites while drawing on Greco-Roman forms and concepts also resisted the dominant perspective championed by the cultural and political centers.

As in Chapters Three and Four, Chapter Five draws on the distinction between horizontal and vertical translatability. Horizontal translatability is the norm for this period, yet inner-cultural vertical translatability in some corners of the Greco-Roman world serves as a mean to express resistance to the dominant Hellenistic discourse about horizontal translatability. In Chapter Five, we also see how some of the cultural practices that accompany translatability in the Greco-Roman world anticipate modern studies of religion and theology in their discussions of divinity. This general point is raised already with the analysis of Late Bronze Age texts in Chapter One,

---

Society 45/3 (2003) 511–45. See also his book, *Spirit and System: Media, Intellectuals, and the Dialectic in Modern German Culture* (Chicago/London: University of Chicago, 2005) 114–16, 132–147. Chapter Four explores Boyer's work in considerable detail.

[49] Holquist, "Corrupt Originals: The Paradox of Censorship," *PMLA* 109 (January, 1994) 14–25; cited by Boyer, "Censorship as a Vocation," 512 n. 2, 528, 542.

but by comparison the categories and typologies of divinity are considerably more explicit in the Greco-Roman world. Indeed, the range of philosophical and theological debates about divinity in this period as well as the social and political conditions that inform them may strike many readers as anticipating some elements in the intellectual discussions about divinity in the modern context since the Enlightenment.

Chapter Six examines some Jewish and Christian responses to translatability. Horizontal translatability in these sources, compared to what we see in the wider Greco-Roman context in Chapter Five, is relatively rare and qualified. This situation changes rather dramatically in Christian texts as we move into the second century CE, but prior to this point, Jewish and Christian heirs to the Hebrew Bible often but not always rejected horizontal translatability. In short, Jewish and Christian responses fit into the larger pattern of local resistance that can be traced from the Late Bronze Age with Ugarit, through the Iron Age with Israel, and into the Greco-Roman period, with local writers such as Philo of Byblos. At the same time, the Jewish and Christian responses were not altogether monolithic and they are thus deserving of attention. We have a handful of cases of Jewish horizontal translatability. It is also evident that Christian texts of the New Testament sometimes drew on non-Christian notions bearing on divinity in order to build their communication between the Christian gospel and its audiences. To anticipate the course that we will chart over our six chapters, the texts manifest a spectrum rather than entirely sharp options for or against translatability. Rarely, if ever, does a text express a simple translation of deities uninformed by any perspective; similarly, rarely do we find an absolute rejection of any form of translatability. Neither extreme seems to have been the general option taken in antiquity.

This range of viewpoints in the ancient world is manifest in the modern context as well. In the Epilogue, I offer some reflection on Jan Assmann's contributions to our topic as well as a critique of his study. Then I provide some observations about how the intellectual task involved in translatability in the ancient world relates to our own labors as scholars of God. I do not propose to focus on the nature of our task, our methodologies, our theories, the nature of our data sets, or the philosophical underpinnings of our work. Still I will touch on these matters, as the question of ancient translation of divinity holds implications for what we do, or perhaps more accurately, for who are. Although I am not a scholar of modern "knowledge specialists," academic or otherwise, nor a scholar of intellectual production in the context of modern society,[50] I do not think that we can escape the reality

---

[50] For this sort of work for nineteenth and twentieth century Germany, see Dominic Boyer, *Spirit and System: Media, Intellectuals, and the Dialectic in Modern German*

of our own horizons and context, which influence our intellectual projects and shape the resulting intellectual products. To my mind, it is intellectually important to take stock of our own place in the production of studies such as this one, and to recognize not only how our scholarly efforts are devoted to understanding the ancient texts, but also how our studies indicate our own locations as students of this ancient material. International discourse about divinity, then as now, has contours that require our recognition for their strengths and their weaknesses, their visions and their myopias. Recognizing some of these in the past may aid us in our quest to fathom better the dimensions of present academic challenges involved in addressing divinity. As readers will note throughout this study, what the writers of ancient texts did intellectually anticipates to a degree what we modern scholars have been up to. I mention these sorts of issues along the way in this work, as I find them pertinent; and in the Epilogue I return to a general consideration of these matters in light of the study in the chapters that follow. In order to be a bit clearer about what I have in mind, I would like to highlight some of these issues at this point.

3. A Word about Academic Location

The story that I am about to tell about translatability of deities in the biblical world draws not only on the resources of ancient Near Eastern and biblical studies, but also on the perspectives found in scholarly research in the fields of theology and religion (history of religion and comparative religion),[51]

Culture (Chicago/London: University of Chicago, 2005). For the field of sociology in France, see Pierre Bourdieu's book, *Homo Academicus* (trans. P. Collier; Stanford: Stanford University, 1988); see the discussion and critique in: Boyer, *Spirit and System*, 30–31. Of course, a great deal has been written on academia in the United States, but in Boyer's view, there is no comparable study that situates academic work within its larger societal context in the United States. Cf. Bill Readings, *The University in Ruins* (Cambridge, MA: Harvard University, 1986). For these references I am indebted to Boyer.

[51] For a survey of the field of religion, see the series of articles grouped under "Study of Religion," in: *ER* 13.8760–96. For the study of theology, *ER* 13.9125–42 offers two articles, one on comparative theology and another on Christian Theology. In my remarks that follow, I am referring to the latter. The field of religion has come in for some strong critiques in recent years. See Timothy Fitzgerald, *The Ideology of Religious Studies* (New York/Oxford: Oxford University, 2000); and the reviews by Benson Saler, Gustavo Benavides, and Frank Koromo, with a response by Timothy Fitzgerald, in: *Religious Studies Review* 27/2 (April 2001) 103–15. Fitzgerald's basic point is that there is no such phenomenon as religion and concludes that there is no real intellectual basis for a field that goes by that name. Instead, Fitzgerald would prefer departments of "ethnographic cultural studies" or "theoretically informed ethnography." The study of religion would thus belong to culturally and theoretically informed ethnography of American and European societies. For Fitzgerald, religious studies as a field is little more than "a thinly veiled version of

and to a lesser degree literature and history.[52] Unfortunately (to my mind), the fields of theology and religion have historically stood in considerable tension, if not hostility, in relation to one another.[53] Perhaps at the risk of setting up straw men or perpetuating stereotypes, I am concerned that theologians and historians of religion are at times dismissive of the intellectual value of each other's field (this is based on personal experience and not on any scientific survey). This hypothetical sort of historian of religion might champion translatability and the larger intellectual activity involved with it in the wider Mediterranean world over and against the overall biblical position taken against translatability.

Jan Assmann's Presuppositions

This sort of favoritism may be inferred from some of Assmann's remarks as well as the construction of his project as a whole. In view of the scope of *Moses the Egyptian* down through the Enlightenment and Freud, it may be asked whether Assmann's construal of monotheism as an intolerant form of religion represents a polemic against traditional Christianity. The point is arguably clearer from the title of his book, *Die Mosaische Unterscheidung: Oder der Preis des Monotheismus*. The second part of this title makes a claim that monotheism itself has taken a terrible toll. Assmann traces a trajectory to the Deism project of the seventeenth and eighteenth centuries from the translatability of the Late Bronze and Greco-Roman periods.[54] Assmann's own project implicitly aims to locate itself as the endpoint of this trajectory, as this message is represented in the very title of the book's final

---

liberal theology" (as expressed in Korom's review, p. 109). The reviewers in turn question whether a problematic term constitutes a sufficient basis for abandoning the constellations of studies grouped around it. Daniel Dubuisson agrees with Fitzgerald's basic point; see Dubuisson's critique of the field of religion in his book, *The Western Construction of Religion: Myth, Knowledge, and Ideology* (trans. William Sayers; Baltimore/London: Johns Hopkins University, 2003). For him, categories of comparative religion represent a particular intellectual privileging comparable to theology. He is particularly critical of Mircea Eliade's privileging of the "sacred" as a category. For the interesting problem of how personal belief may affects a historian of religion such as Eliade, see the discussion in: Bryan S. Rennie, "Eliade, Mircea [Further Considerations]," *ER* 4.2757–63, esp. 2761, which mentions the issue of Eliade's "latent theological agenda." These critiques suggest interesting tensions in the relationship of the field of religion to theology.

[52] I have been aided in particular by Elizabeth A. Clark's survey of the "culture wars" (or, "theory wars") in her book, *History, Theory, Text*. Note also the reflections by Geertz, *A Life of Learning*, 14–16. I hope that it will be clear to readers, especially from Chapters Five and Six, that the fields of classical studies and late antiquity have informed my consideration of these questions.

[53] See the comments of Mark C. Taylor, "Introduction," in: *Critical Terms for Religious Studies* (ed. Mark C. Taylor; Chicago/London: University of Chicago, 1998) 1–19, esp. 10–11.

[54] Assmann, *Moses the Egyptian*, 47.

chapter, "Abolishing the Mosaic Distinction: Religious Antagonism and Its Overcoming." To be sure, Assmann has engaged in a highly sophisticated recovery of cultural history, but in doing so, he takes sides in the contemporary debate over theism and belief.[55]

Some critics see in Assmann's project a kind of theological claim for tolerant, post-Christian appreciation of world religion, which is inspired by the Enlightenment critique of the Christian churches of Europe as bastions of intolerance, conflict, and persecution.[56] Some evidently view him as a sort of Enlightenment or post-Holocaust theologian, who uses ancient Near Eastern texts as proof-texts[57] for his genealogy of tolerant deism and Freud for his critique of traditional western religion.[58] In his representation of monotheism, Assmann's perspective belongs to a longstanding tradition of modern scholars of religion who regard violence as an inherent feature of monotheism.[59] This side of Assmann's work is arguably a form of modern

---

[55] This is perhaps most explicitly indicated in his essay, "Gottesbilder – Menschenbilder: anthropologische Konsequenzen des Monotheismus," in: *Götterbilder – Gottesbilder – Weltbilder. Polytheismus und Monotheismus in der Welt der Antike. Band II: Griechenland und Rom, Judentum, Christentum und Islam* (ed. Reinhard G. Kratz and Hermann Spieckermann; FAT 2/18; Tübingen: Mohr Siebeck, 2006) 313–29, esp. 326.

[56] In this connection, one may note the subtitle of the book by Tomoko Masuzawa, *The Invention of World Religions: Or, How European Universalism Was Preserved in the Language of Pluralism* (Chicago/London: University of Chicago, 2005).

[57] Assmann's treatment of the ancient evidence has been strongly criticized in discussions by Rolf Rendtorff, Erich Zenger, Klaus Koch, Gerhard Kaiser, and Karl-Josef Kuschel, conveniently collected in: Assmann, *Die Mosaische Unterscheidung*, 193–286. Several of these treatments address Assmann's mishandling of biblical material and a lack of understanding about ancient Israel. See also the critique Gerhard Kaiser, "War der Exodus der Sünderfall? Fragen an Jan Assmann anläßlich seiner Monographie 'Moses der Ägypter'," *ZThK* 98 (2001) 1–24. Kaiser in particular objects to Assmann's analogy between the putatively comparable "monotheisms" of Akhenaten and the Bible. The differences are to be noted. Indeed, whatever connection can be historically traced (see Chapter One) indicates a major series of interpretive alterations such that the two barely resemble one another with respect to content. For this reason, the effort to connect the two appears misplaced.

[58] See the criticism of Assmann's construal of Freud, by Peter Schäfer, "Geschichte und Gedächtnisgeschichte: Jan Assmanns 'Mosaische Unterscheidung'," in: *Memoria – Wege jüdischen Erinnerns: Festschrift für Michael Brocke zum 65. Geburtstag* (ed. Birgit E. Klein and Christiane E. Müller; Berlin: Metropol, 2005) 19–39; and "The Triumph of Pure Spirituality: Sigmund Freud's *Moses and Monotheism*," in: *New Perspectives on Freud's 'Moses and Monotheism'* (ed. Ruth Ginsberg and Ilana Pardes; Tübingen: Max Niemeyer, 2006) 19–43, esp. 35–37. (I thank Professor Schäfer for kindly providing me with a copy of these articles.)

[59] For this idea among historians of religion, see also Theodore M. Ludwig, "Monotheism," *ER* 9.6160. This idea is accepted as a given in other corners of academia. For a rather lengthy example in this vein, see Regina Schwartz, *The Curse of Cain: The Violent Legacy of Monotheism* (Chicago: University of Chicago, 1997). For a critique of Schwartz's views, see R. W. L. Moberly, "Is Monotheism Bad for You? Some Reflections on God, the Bible, and Life in the Light of Regina Schwartz's *The Curse of Cain*," in: *The God of Israel*

theology on his part and certainly an undemonstrated set of assumptions. The theological purpose of Assmann's work is so evident that it motivated a vigorous response from Joseph Cardinal Ratzinger, now Pope Benedict XVI.[60] He is highly concerned with the question of truth and tolerance. At the same time, in some respects Ratzinger's is a rather scholarly response. He assails Assmann for his flat treatment of polytheism: "When we look into the actual history of polytheistic religions, then the picture he sketches – a rather vague one, by the way – appears itself a myth. In the first place, polytheistic religions differ considerably among themselves."[61] Ratzinger is further critical for Assmann's high valuation of polytheism, but not simply on theoretical or theological grounds, but as a matter of historical analysis: "the gods were by no means always peaceful and interchangeable. They were just as often, indeed more often, the reason for people using violence against each other."[62]

The critique of Assmann's correlation of polytheism and non-violence finds resonance in other quarters. Contrary to Assmann's view, Robert Gnuse has recently emphasized[63] that violence in the Bible hardly depends on the concept of monotheism as such for its motivation. Indeed, some recent studies of ethno-political violence do not include forms of divinity as one of the "beliefs that propel groups toward conflict."[64] Perhaps the most

---

(ed. Robert P. Gordon; University of Cambridge Oriental Publications 64; Cambridge, UK/New York: Cambridge University, 2007) 94–112; and see in the same volume the brief remarks by Ronald E. Clements, "Monotheism and the God of Many Names," 48. Cf. the discussion of violence in the Bible in Hector Avalos, *The End of Biblical Studies* (Amherst, NY: Prometheus Books, 2007).

[60] Joseph Cardinal Ratzinger, *Truth and Tolerance: Christian Belief and World Religions* (trans. Henry Taylor; San Francisco: Ignatius, 2004) 210–31. It is to be noted that this is the only essay not published prior to the appearance of this volume (originally published in German in 2003). I wish to thank Avery Cardinal Dulles for bringing Ratzinger's essay to my attention.

[61] Ratzinger, *Truth and Tolerance*, 217. It might appear to some readers that the characterization of monotheism in Ratzinger's hands (see *Truth and Tolerance*, 224; cf. pp. 28–39) reflects a simplification of the same sort for which Ratzinger criticizes Assman on polytheism. In both cases, the forms of theism themselves (and arguably in simplified forms) are given considerable credence by both figures, and in both the historical account of polytheism and monotheism is inadequate. In Ratzinger's case, this might be considered more tolerable since his task is not primarily a historical one, and he is not a historian of ancient religion like Assmann. Both also characterize Israelite monotheism as revolutionary (for Ratzinger on this point, see *Truth and Tolerance*, 35).

[62] Ratzinger, *Truth and Tolerance,* 219. For ancient translatability, see also *Truth and Tolerance,* 25. For a critique of Ratzinger's view, see p. 169 n. 139.

[63] Gnuse, "Intellectual Breakthrough or Tyranny: Monotheism's Contested Implications," *Horizons* 34 (2007) 78–95.

[64] See the studies of Roy J. Eidelson and Judy I. Eidelson, "Dangerous Ideas: Five Beliefs that Propel Groups toward Conflict," *American Psychologist* 58 (2003) 182–92. Roy Eidelson was the executive director of the Solomon Asch Center for Study of Ethnopolitical Conflict at the University of Pennsylvania.

concrete evidence against Assmann's correlations between polytheism and tolerance on the one hand and between monotheism and violence on the other may be seen in the ancient practice of the ban or *ḥerem*. This practice of the warfare destruction of people and property following battle was at home equally among Israel's polytheistic neighbors, for example in Moab, as it was in Israel, in both its earlier, polytheistic and later monotheistic phases.[65] In both contexts, the *ḥerem* was religiously grounded violence. Thus violence is hardly specific to Israel (or much less, its putative monotheism at this point in its history), as Klaus Koch has highlighted in his critical review of *Moses the Egyptian*.[66]

The Hebrew Bible may talk of the servitude of the other nations to the god of Israel, yet violence is not the outstanding trope. To be sure, there are expressions of religiously sanctioned violence in the Bible, which does represent a hermeneutical challenge to modern readers.[67] However, this is not due in particular to monotheism. Israelite monotheism as such shows no particular capacity for violence. In the periods when monotheism is being expressed (to my mind, the seventh and sixth centuries and onwards), Israel is hardly a major force of violence. This is true rather of Mesopotamian state polytheism in this period.[68] Indeed, it may be argued that Israel is on the

---

[65] For the broader context of the *ḥerem* in West Semitic religion including Israel, see Norbert Lohfink, "*ḥārem, ḥerem*," *TDOT* 5. 180–99; Abraham Malamat, *Mari and the Early Israelite Experience* (The Schweich Lectures 1984; Oxford/New York: Oxford University, 1989) 70–79; Philip D. Stern, *The Biblical Herem: A Window on Israel's Religious Experience* (Brown Judaic Studies 211; Atlanta: Scholars, 1991); M. S. Smith, "Anat's Warfare Cannibalism and the Biblical *Ḥerem*," in: *The Pitcher Is Broken: Memorial Essays in Honor of Gösta W. Ahlström* (ed. L. K. Handy and S. Holloway; JSOTSup 190; Sheffield: Sheffield, 1995) 368–86; and Lauren Monroe, "Israelite Moabite and Sabaean War-*ḥerem* Traditions and the Forging of National Identity: Reconsidering the Sabaean Text RES 3945 in Light of Biblical and Moabite Evidence," *VT* 57 (2007) 318–41. For *ḥerem* in more specific biblical contexts, see Joel S. Kaminsky, "Joshua 7: A Reassessment of Israelite Conceptions of Corporate Punishment," in: *The Pitcher is Broken: Memorial Essays for Gösta W. Ahlström* (ed. L. K. Handy and S. Holloway; JSOTSup 190; Sheffield: Sheffield, 1995) 315–46; Richard D. Nelson, "*Herem* and the Deuteronomic Social Conscience," in: *Deuteronomy and Deuteronomic Literature: Festschrift C. H. W. Brekelmans* (ed. Marc Vervenne and Johan Lust; Bibliotheca Ephemerides Theologicae Lovanienses 133; Leuven: University/Peeters, 1997) 39–54; Susan Niditch, *War in the Hebrew Bible: A Study in the Ethics of Violence* (New York/Oxford: Oxford University, 1993) 28–42, 151–52; Christa Schäfer-Lichtenberger, "Bedeutung und Funktion von *ḥerem* in biblisch-hebräischen Texten," *BZ* 38 (1994) 270–75; and Allan Bornapé, "El problema del חרם en el Pentateuco y su dimensión ritual," *DavarLogos* 4 (2005) 1–16. I am grateful to Richard Nelson for providing me with some of these references.

[66] Koch, "Monotheismus als Sündenbock?," *Theologische Literaturzeitung* 124 (1999) 874–84, reprinted in: Assmann, *Die Mosaische Unterscheidung*, 221–38.

[67] See John J. Collins, "The Zeal of Phinehas: The Bible and the Legitimation of Violence," *JBL* 122 (2003) 3–21.

[68] See the comment on the contrast made by Shalom Paul, *Divrei Shalom: Collected Studies of Shalom M. Paul on the Bible and the Ancient Near East 1967–2005* (CHANE

receiving end of such violence over the course of the very period when it generated its monotheistic worldview. The record of the violence done to Israel has been characterized as "post-traumatic stress disorder."[69] In short, ancient Near Eastern cultures, both polytheistic and monotheistic, associate violence with various gods and goddesses. In the history of the ancient Near East, violence is not inherent in either monotheism or polytheism. It is not a function of the form of theism, whether polytheism or monotheism; it is a function of power and the capacity to wield it. In this respect critics of Israel's monotheism tend to view it in the abstract and disembed it from its cultural and political context. For these reasons, it is finally time to put to rest this canard about monotheism and violence.[70]

A comparable difficulty lies in Assmann's correlation of translatability and tolerance. Translatability is hardly a model or forerunner for modern tolerance, as Assmann would have it. Translatability often served empires or empire cultures over and against local cultures, in short in the interests of political and cultural domination. In turn, local cultures expressed their resistance against the empire discourse of translatability, usually in one of two ways. Ancient Israel developed a critique of translatability as an act of resistance against empire (as we will see in Chapters Three and Four). In the Greco-Roman period Levantine writers critiqued versions of translatability offered from the political centers (as discussed in Chapter Five).[71] Thus it may be argued that as long as its underpinnings depend on its empire

---

23; Leiden/Boston: Brill, 2005) 22 (Paul's italics): "Israel's mission is not one of *world conquest*, as in the Mesopotamian inscriptions, but rather one of *world salvation*."

[69] William Morrow, "Post-Traumatic Stress Disorder and Vicarious Atonement in Second Isaiah," in: *Psychology and the Bible. A New Way to Read the Scriptures: Volume 1. From Freud to Kohut* (ed. J. Harold Ellens and Wayne G. Rollins; Westport, CT/London: Praeger, 2004) 167–83.

[70] Eckart Otto notes other problems posed by Assmann's claims. See Otto, *Mose: Geschichte und Legende* (München: C.H. Beck, 2006) 105 (I wish to thank Professor Otto for drawing my attention to his discussion). The main difficulty concerns Assmann's historical and political understanding of ancient Israel and the worldview of Israelite monotheism as clarified through a proper comparison with Assyrian royal ideology. In a sympathetic reading of Assmann's claim, one might try to propose that a "one-god" idea in Mesopotamian and Israel in the seventh-sixth centuries (see Chapter Three for discussion) points to violence in their systems. However, this would be highly misleading. Assyrian and Babylonian state violence is sanctioned not only by their chief gods but also by other deities (for example, Ishtar). As such, this state violence is not monotheistic.

[71] Post-colonial theory offers a helpful avenue for pursuing some of these points. For a recent discussion of post-colonial criticism in the context of local resistance in the Greco-Roman period, see David M. Carr, *Writing on the Tablet of the Heart: Origins of Scripture and Literature* (Oxford/New York: Oxford University, 2005) 196–97, with references to the theoretical literature on the subject. For the application of post-colonial theory to the Roman empire and early Christianity, see Elizabeth A. Clark, *History, Theory, Text: Historians and the Linguistic Turn* (Cambridge, MA/London: Harvard University, 2004) 181–85.

context, translatability does not offer a model of tolerance for the modern world.

Despite this critique of Assmann's view of translatability, it is to his credit that his project helps to show how such ancient developments anticipate modern inter-religious work and study of world religions that are common today. Assmann's work also points to the need for a theory of cultural translation that can be applied to various areas of religious phenomena, both ancient and modern. It seems that relatively little on intercultural translation in the area of ancient religion has been attempted up to this point; Assman is exceptional in this regard. It is one of the aims of this book to extend his intellectual project on intercultural religious translation in the area of deities and divinity more generally.

The Fields of Religion and Theology

Assmann's work highlights a further question regarding the roles of the fields of religion and theology in this type of intellectual project. Both disciplines continue to aim their polemics against each other, sometimes with good reason. History of religion work has been sometimes seen as reductionist in treating sacred sources and traditions. This is Daniel Gold's reflection on the problem as he sees it:

Religionists reduce others' experience to their own terms when they talk about it and may attribute certain aspects of it to hard social-scientific causes. But they also want somehow to maintain the independence of a sphere of religious behavior that moves according to its own imperatives. As in any field, this independence is crucial if the study of religion is to maintain (or in this case establish) itself as a discipline. Nevertheless, religion as object of study presents its own problems of reduction. For, as scholars, we want a rational explanation; but, fascinated by our materials, we do not want totally to lose the allure of the irrational. We want a science of religion that has science and religion, too.[72]

To apply Mircea Eliade's famous category to his own work, the field of religion leaves a "sacred space" for religion that its own descriptions do not and cannot demystify, and perhaps its practitioners do not wish to demystify. Here Gold begins with the basic problem of reductionism on the part of scholars of religion and fans out to a wider problem of the built-in paradox of the study of religion, that its descriptions can never approach the object of their investigation and perhaps are designed not to do so. The questions of potential reductionism and distortion for the field of religion are more involved than what has been raised here, but we can begin to see

---

[72] See the reflections on reductionism on the part of historians of religion offered by Daniel Gold, "The Paradox in Writing on Religion," *HTR* 83 (1990) 332. I return to this question in the Epilogue.

some of the contours of the difficulties. It is important to bear in mind that the contemporary situation in the study of religion follows from a long history of modern western scholarship.[73] Viewed in these terms, the study of religion raises questions about the situatedness of the field within the historical context of modern empires. Thus suspicions about the field of religion are raised for good reason.

Historians of religions sometimes view the work of theology as parochial or privileging the sacred apart from or beyond analysis. (It is with this issue that J. Samuel Preus opens his study, *Explaining Religion,* which is devoted to reviewing modern figures important in the "naturalist" study of religion.[74]) Biblical theologians have been accused of taking little interest in the world beyond the Bible, whether it involves Hebrew Bible (Old Testament) or New Testament. This stance may appear constitutive of the so-called "canonical approach" to the Bible, often associated with the names of Brevard Child and his student, Christopher Seitz.[75] Some biblical theologians operating outside of this approach, such as Walter Brueggemann,[76] also seem to miss the challenges of the biblical witnesses to the wider world,

---

[73] For an important consideration of the modern historical development of the field of religion, see Tomoko Masuzawa, *The Invention of World Religions: Or, How European Universalism Was Preserved in the Language of Pluralism* (Chicago/London: University of Chicago, 2005).

[74] See Preus, *Explaining Religion: Criticism and Theory from Bodin to Freud* (New Haven/London: Yale University, 1987) ix–xxix. The main concern for Preus is descriptive, namely how post-Enlightenment social and psychological paradigms attempt to explain religion's origins; the force of his presentation tends at various points toward the prescriptive (e. g., p. xx). In both the Introduction and Conclusion to the book (see also pp. 203–4), Preus complains of the unwillingness of the theological tradition to submit to naturalistic paradigms for the study of religion; they, in turn, might complain of his unwillingness to submit to theological paradigms, or even to meet them halfway by considering both naturalist and transcendent paradigms in tandem.

[75] See Brevard S. Childs, *Introduction to the Old Testament as Scripture* (London: SCM, 1979); *Old Testament Theology in a Canonical Context* (Philadelphia: Fortress, 1985); Christopher Seitz, *Word Without End: The Old Testament as Abiding Theological Witness* (Grand Rapids, MI: Eerdmans, 1998); and William Ross Blackburn, "The Missionary Heart of Exodus" (Ph. D. dissertation, Saint Andrew's University, 2005). One objection to some of these discussions of the "canonical" approach is not simply the effort to ground its legitimacy on a questionable notion of the "final form" of the biblical text, and not even to do so without examining the attendant historical and theological presuppositions, but to use the notion of "final form" without an adequate defense of the historical and theological bases on which it rests. For issues surrounding the question of the "final form" of the Hebrew Bible, see James A. Loader, "The Finality of the Old Testament 'Final Text'," *Old Testament Essays* 15 (2002) 739–53. Furthermore, the "canonical" approach at times decouples the theological from the historical by ignoring the historical "situatedness" of the text. From a theological perspective, it might be said that to decouple the two is arguably a theological error if Christian Scripture may be regarded, like Jesus Christ, as fully human and fully divine.

[76] Brueggemann, *Theology of the Old Testament: Testimony, Dispute, Advocacy* (Minneapolis: Fortress, 1997).

namely that the gods of the nations did indeed seem real in the context of ancient Israel; and only by taking that sensibility seriously is it possible to deal adequately with biblical texts that address divinity. It seems to me that both extremes (which I do not necessarily take to be the norms of these fields) run the risk of being intellectually short sighted. We need intellectual help wherever we can find it, and to my mind, both sides can aid each other. Historians of religion, despite their differences with those working in theology (in particular, biblical theology and historical theology), may well benefit from their historical research despite differences in approach or evaluations. Historians of religion may appreciate the notion implicit in the perspective of the theologically minded, namely what is culturally specific is necessary for understanding prior to any comparative move. Both theologians and historians of religion can readily defend the importance of studying what is culturally specific. Moreover, both fields can benefit from taking seriously what each other prizes.

There has been a comparable difficulty within biblical studies. It might be argued that some scholars in biblical studies, especially those with theological interests, may take seriously the religious experience informing the ancient texts. Yet with few exceptions,[77] this was often less true of the historical-critical scholars especially in more recent generations.[78] In biblical studies,

---

[77] Perhaps Marvin H. Pope would represent an exception. For the role of imagination in Pope's work, see Mark S. Smith, "Introduction," in: Marvin H. Pope, *Probative Pontificating in Ugaritic and Biblical Studies: Collected Essays* (ed. Mark S. Smith; Ugaritisch-biblische Literatur 10; Münster: Ugarit, 1994) 3–4, 10–11. For an example of Pope's words that reveal a bit of his character, see his "Introduction," to Alan Cooper, "Divine Names and Epithets in the Ugaritic Texts," in: *Ras Shamra Parallels: Vol. III: The Texts from Ugarit and the Hebrew Bible* (ed. Stan Rummel; AnOr 51; Rome: Pontificium Institutum Biblicum, 1981) 335.

[78] For example, note the comment of Frank Moore Cross on the "schizophrenic aspect to my own relation to the Bible," in: "Contrasting Insights of Biblical Giants: BAR Interviews Elie Wiesel and Frank Moore Cross," *Biblical Archaeology Review* 30/4 (July/August 2004) 30. The religious experience of the ancients play little or no role in his comments, a scholarly stance that appears to have been influenced by his own religious experience; one might entertain seeing a contrasting influence in Cross' reference to his father as "to some degree a mystic" (p. 31). Despite strenuous efforts at objective or scientific scholarship, it seems that Cross' background has influenced his own approach to the ancient evidence. Still Cross could appreciate scholars with perspectives other than his own; see his warm appreciation for Pope expressed in his piece, "In Memoriam: Marvin Hoyle Pope (1916–1997)," *ZAW* 110 (1998) 325–26. My point is not that subjectivity is a negative feature to be criticized; on the contrary, each scholar, in both her or his research and personal horizons critically deployed, adds to the great fund of learning. Thus one's own religious experience might arguably add to one's capacity to understand the religious experience of others, including those of the ancient writers of biblical and non-biblical texts. Sometimes it may mar such efforts, but belonging to a larger association of scholars can help to prevent facile equations of past and present religious experience; however, it is no guarantee. This is a primary rationale for professional associations to have the broadest range of horizons possible, including diverse cultural and personal experience.

there seemed to be an unwritten rule that religious experience was to be avoided precisely because it seemed to partake of the confessional, and thus was not an element of serious scholarship.[79] Here I think that theologically informed scholars often do take religious experience seriously and thus may offer a healthy balance in this regard. In turn, theologically minded scholars can benefit from history of religion work. It seems to me that in contrast to the theologically minded, historians of religion are often prepared to take seriously the perspectives of those works that stand outside the Bible, as they are less mindful of the biblical canon. The theologically minded should be able to appreciate what is incarnate in the world, as historians of religion are able to tease it out and contextualize it. In short, theologians are perhaps inclined to take seriously the discourse about divinity inside the Bible, while historians of religion are able to see how works outside of the Bible can help us understand the inside better. Within this overlap, there is an intellectual space between their intellectual efforts.[80] This space affords an intellectual benefit to be gained on both sides in undertaking the study of divinity in the Bible from the perspective of both its inside and outside contexts,[81] and to attending to the dynamics that link these inside and outside contexts; this is for the long-term and mutual benefit of both, not just for understanding the past, but also for the present.

My Double-Lenses

Let me speak to this question of double perspective more directly. In fairness to Assmann, if I suggest a critique of his work for its possible "religious" leanings, then my own project is subject to comparable scrutiny as well. The project of this book expresses my own intellectual "double-lenses," standing within the religious tradition(s) and also analyzing it (them) from outside such boundaries. My personal "double-lenses" are founded on my double personal commitment. On the one hand, I am a Roman Catholic,

---

[79] Compare for the field of New Testament the book by Luke Timothy Johnson, *Religious Experience in Earliest Christianity: A Missing Dimension in New Testament Studies* (Minneapolis: Fortress, 1998).

[80] See the essays in: *Fields of Faith: Theology and Religious Studies for the Twenty-First Century* (ed. David F. Ford, Ben Quash and Janet Martin Soskice; Cambridge, UK / New York: Cambridge University, 2005). Note also the critique of the field of religion from within that field by Daniel Dubuisson, *The Western Construction of Religion*. Dubuisson sees the very term religion as religiously or theologically informed; he prefers the term "cosmographic formations" (see especially pp. 36, 180, 198–213).

[81] For a fine probing of divinity with both theological and historical approaches, see the essays in: *The God of Israel* (ed. Robert P. Gordon; University of Cambridge Oriental Publications 64; Cambridge, UK / New York: Cambridge University, 2007). Given the common tendency to avoid their combination, the nexus between the theological or religious dimensions within the biblical texts on the one hand, and on the other hand, their historical and cultural contexts, remains a major desideratum for the field of biblical studies.

which for me means that I perceive the reality of God through the created order; I am therefore a Christian who senses the divine through creation and not outside of it; I am, so to speak, an "incarnational Christian," who ritually celebrates the mysterious and mediated reality of the divine in the sacraments. On the other hand, my longtime personal experience with Judaism informs and qualifies my sense of Christianity. My religious "dual citizenship" is reflected in a number of my professional positions. I taught in Catholic institutions for a decade (the École Biblique, Saint Paul Seminary, Saint Joseph's University and the Pontifical Biblical Institute). I spent another seven years at Yale, and over the past seven years I have served at New York University in its Department of Hebrew and Judaic studies (I am a Catholic holding a chair on a Jewish studies faculty). Thankfully, being a non-Jewish scholar in a Jewish studies department has been a joy, thanks to the faculty and students at NYU. Indeed, the work of non-Jewish scholars continues to develop as one of the interesting features in the landscape of Jewish studies.[82] My professional duality is reflected in another way, in my work squarely within Bible on the one side, in particular the books of Psalms and Exodus, and on the other side, my research in comparative work and in extra-biblical sources, especially the Ugaritic texts and to a lesser extent, the Dead Sea Scrolls. Duality is a basic feature of my personal and intellectual horizons, perhaps informed by the duality of my childhood education in the Roman Catholic tradition (I continue to identify with the tradition of Christian humanistic study and service fostered by my Benedictine teachers at Saint Anselm's Abbey School in Washington, DC),[83] and by my subsequent personal and professional engagement with Catholicism and Judaism.

Bearing in mind these multiple sets of religious and intellectual duality, I would see my work in part as an effort to point out the complexity of discourse about God within the tradition of the church, in part as a caution against simplification accepted by those both inside and outside the church. In a way, my work is a defense of monotheism, but it is also a brief on behalf of polytheism, in the sense that one can only understand what one is pre-

---

[82] More generally, North America offers quite an open environment, and it does not carry the burden that Jewish studies face elsewhere, especially in Germany. See Peter Schäfer, "Jewish Studies in Germany Today," *Jewish Studies Quarterly* 3 (1996) 146–61. Compare Jacob Neusner, "Three Generations of Post-War Study of Judaism in Germany: Goldberg, Schaefer, Houtman and Becker and the Demolition of Historical Judaism," *Religion* 34 (2004) 315–30.

[83] I do not mean the so-called Renaissance and Cartesian tradition of humanism attacked by Lévi-Strauss for its efforts to turn humanity into "an absolute lord of creation." See Lévi-Strauss, "Claude Lévi-Strauss Reconsiders," 23–24, as discussed by Clark, *History, Theory, Text*, 52. See also the brief but interesting survey of "Humanism," by Lewis W. Spitz in: *ER* 6.4174–78.

pared to probe with the utmost seriousness and sympathy.[84] To my mind, it is the dialectic or tension between translatability and its lack, between outside and inside, between polytheism and monotheism that provides a key to understanding the larger story of divinity in our ancient texts. If the very discourse of translatability sometimes seems reductionist[85] and intellectually inadequate to the ancient texts that lie before us, the solution is not simply to retreat to theology inside the church's walls, but to continue to explore the difficult terrain shared by theology and other fields such as history of religion. Advocates for various sides may sometimes regard the other as claiming special privilege. My own claim is neither. Instead, I advocate a discussion especially – but not only – where and when these fields intersect.

What this brief reflection on my own stance indicates is that my project in this book is no less "constructed" than Assmann's. It is hardly a disinterested or "objective" quest to uncover the past "as it actually happened" (to echo the positivist creedal formula of the nineteenth century Germany historian, Otto Ranke, "wie es eigentlich gewesen").[86] From my comments, I hope it is clear that this study reflects a perspective on "history" or historical narratives more at home in recent thinking among professional historians and scholars of religion, as expressed by Elizabeth A. Clark: "such histories should acknowledge that, as intellectual constructions, they differ from 'the past,' vanished and now available only through 'traces,' and that no historical construction is 'politically innocent' but is driven by the problems and questions set by the historian in the present."[87] In working on this study, I have tried to remain aware of my intellectual horizons in order to take as full advantage of them as possible, to try to see how they help me view the scope of translatability's ancient "traces" (to echo Clark's remark), to correct any misplaced predispositions and to extend my horizons in light of what my scholarly colleagues offer in their studies. I leave it to readers to judge how faithful this study has been to the ancient "traces" of translatability. Further

---

[84] I have discussed this problem in my book, *The Origins of Biblical Monotheism*, 10–14. For reflections by a Catholic scholar on remaining a Catholic while seriously engaging polytheistic literature and religion, see the reflections of Francis X. Clooney, S.J., "Neither Here nor There: Crossing Boundaries, Becoming Insiders, Remaining Catholic," in: *Identity and the Politics of Scholarship in the Study of Religion* (ed. José Ignacio Cabezón and Sheila Greeve Davaney; London/New York: Routledge, 2004) 99–111. While several of Clooney's reflections resonate for me, I recognize the very major difference that his scholarship deals with a polytheistic tradition with living religious personnel and current holy sites.

[85] Cf. the claim of reductionism raised against non-theological approaches to religion, discussed in: Preus, *Explaining Religion*, ix–x. See also the discussion in the Epilogue to this study.

[86] See the discussion of Clark, *History, Theory, Text*, 9–10.

[87] Clark, *History, Theory, Text*, 7.

discussion of these issues at this point would be getting ahead of our story, and we will return to them in the Epilogue. With these matters in mind, let us turn to the beginning of this study, which surveys cross-cultural recognition of deities in the Late Bronze Age.

Chapter One

Empires and Their Deities:
Translatability in the Late Bronze Age

O Sun-goddess of Arinna, queen of all countries!
In the Hatti country you bear the name
of the Sun-goddess of Arinna;
but in the land which you made the cedar
land you bear the name Hebat.
Prayer of the Hittite queen, Puduhepa[1]

1. Introduction to Late Bronze Age Translatability

Modern Accounts of Translatability

For the Bronze Age context of translatability, we may begin with accounts by two well-known Egyptologists, John Wilson and Jan Assmann. Decades ago Wilson made the following observations:

> In earlier history the Egyptians had identified foreign gods with their own deities, so that the goddess of Byblos was a Hat-Hor to them and various Asiatic gods were Seth to them … There were also two cosmopolitan forces at work: a worship of Asiatic gods as such at their shrines in Asia and a domestication of Asiatic gods in Egypt.[2]

Wilson here notes famous identifications of Egyptian and West Semitic deities that resulted from the Egyptian encounter with the religious culture of western Asia.[3] As Wilson's quote indicates, such identifications were based on a perception of function and gender shared by the deities in question.

---

[1] *ANET* 393 (discussed below).

[2] Wilson, "The Egyptians and the Gods of Asia," in: *Ancient Near Eastern Texts Relating to the Old Testament* (ed. James B. Pritchard; Princeton, NJ: Princeton University, 1950) 249 *ANET* 249.

[3] Western Asia in this usage consists of modern day Turkey, Syria, Lebanon, Jordan and Israel (with the disputed territories). The greater part of this area has also been called the Levant, a term used quite frequently in this study. The ancient cultures of the Levant are often called "West Semitic," as the languages that they speak belong to this subdivision of the Semitic language family. In the Bronze Age, the best known West Semitic language is Ugaritic, so named after the site of ancient Ugarit (Ras Shamra), located on the coast of Syria about one hundred miles north of Beirut. For a fine introduction to the site, its ancient history and its material culture, see the book by Marguerite Yon, *The City of Ugarit at Tell Ras Shamra* (Winona Lake, IN: Eisenbrauns, 2006).

His quote also acknowledges two attendant conditions, which signal at this early point in this study the fact that translatability was often related to larger cultural and religious factors.

For another example of translatability, Wilson cites the substitution of divine names in the poem describing Ramesses II's battle of Kadesh known from the Luxor text. The Egyptian king brags, "I was like Seth in his time (of might)." The same poem, as recorded at Abydos, has the name of the god Montu instead of Seth; and a third copy known from a papyrus has Baal.[4] These substitutions show the names of three warrior-gods, two of them Egyptian, Seth and Montu, and a third, Baal, who was a West Semitic import. It is the function for which each god is known that determines his role in these three instances: each is a figure of divine might. Wilson provides a sample of further cases that show the projection of the phenomenon from Egypt into the Levant as it imposed its hegemony there. Overall, Wilson's comments were quite abbreviated and were hardly intended to be a general account of the topic.

Since the time when Wilson made his observations, other scholars of the ancient Near East have also discussed the phenomenon of cross-cultural recognition of deities.[5] In an influential study, Jan Assmann addressed the subject of what he calls "intercultural translation" or "translatability" of deities.[6] Assmann characterizes the concept or quality of translatability in these terms: "The conviction that God or the gods are international was characteristic of the polytheistic religions of the ancient Near East."[7] He adds:

---

[4] *ANET* 201 n. 10. See also the so-called Baal-Seth iconography, discussed by Othmar Keel and Christoph Uehlinger, *Gods, Goddesses, and Images of God in Ancient Israel* (trans. Thomas Trapp; Minneapolis: Fortress, 1998) 76–78, 88, 146 n. 16, 169.

[5] For translatability in Bronze Age Anatolia, see Alfonso Archi, "Hurrian Gods and the Festivals of the Hattian-Hittite Layer," in: *The Life and Times of Ḫattušili III and Tutḫaliya IV: Proceedings of a Symposium in Honour of J. De Roos, 12–13 December, 2003, Leiden* (ed. Theo P. J. van den Hout, with the assistance of C. H. van Zoest; Leiden: Nederlands Instituut voor het Nabije Oosten, 2006) 147–63. For West Semitic translatability, see the comments made by Robert du Mesnil du Buisson, *Études sur les dieux phéniciés héritées par l'empire romain* (EPRO 14; Leiden: Brill, 1970) xvii–xviii.

[6] Assman, *Moses the Egyptian: The Memory of Egypt in Western Monotheism* (Cambridge, MA/London: Harvard University, 1997) 44–54. See also Assmann's accounts in the following works: *Akhanyati's Theology of Light and Time* (The Israel Academy of Sciences and Humanities Proceedings vol. VII No. 4; Jerusalem, 1992) section 2.2; *The Mind of Egypt: History and Meaning in the Time of the Pharaohs* (trans. Andrew Jenkins; Cambridge, MA/London: Harvard University, 2002) 397; "Monotheism and Polytheism," in: *Religions of the Ancient World: A Guide* (ed. Sarah Iles Johnston; Cambridge, MA/London: Belknap, 2004) 24–25; and *Of God and Gods: Egypt, Israel, and the Rise of Monotheism* (The Mosse Lectures, Jerusalem 2004; Madison, WI: University of Wisconsin, 2008) 80–85.

[7] Assman, *Moses the Egyptian,* 45.

… in the context of "high-cultural" polytheisms the deities are clearly differentiated and personalized by name, shape, and function. The great achievement of polytheism is the articulation of a common semantic universe. The gods are given a semantic dimension, by means of mythical narratives and theocosmological speculations. It is this semantic dimension that makes the name translatable. Tribal religions are ethnocentric. The powers worshipped by one tribe are different from the powers worshipped by another tribe. In contrast, the highly differentiated members of polytheistic pantheons lend themselves easily to cross-cultural translation or "interpretation." Well-known cases are the *interpretatio Latina* of Greek divinities and the *interpretatio Graeca* of Egyptian ones. Translation functions because the names have not only a reference, but also a meaning. The meaning of a deity is his or her specific character as it unfolded in myths, hymns, rites, and so on. This character makes a deity comparable to other deities with similar traits. The similarity of gods makes their names mutually translatable. But in historical reality, this correlation has to be reversed. The practice of translating the names of the gods created a concept of similarity and produced the idea or conviction that the gods are international.[8]

Assmann's account begins at the opposite end of the Near East from Wilson. Assmann starts with the Mesopotamian *Listenwissenschaft* of the third millennium (the Fara period).[9] Given the brevity of Assmann's account regarding this important westward cultural shift, it might be useful to provide some background information for this development.

The Role of the Mesopotamian Scribal Curriculum in Translatability

The westward spread of Mesopotamian scribal culture involved a very long process. For a few millennia prior to the Bronze Age, networks of trade connected northern Syria and southern Mesopotamia, as indicated by the clay tokens studied by Denise Schmandt-Besserat.[10] These old trade routes in the second half of the fourth millennium facilitated the movement of cuneiform script as well as the cylinder seal tradition of southern Mesopotamia up the Euphrates River into northern Syria, as witnessed at the sites of Jebel Aruda and Habuba Kabira South (Tell Qannas).[11] By the middle of the

---

[8] Assman, *Moses the Egyptian*, 45. Note also the comments about *interpretatio graeca* made by Garth Fowden, *The Egyptian Hermes: A Historical Approach to the Pagan Mind* (Princeton: Princeton University, 1986) 45. Fowden emphasizes that the phrase is "doubly suspect," insofar as it conveys that Greeks were its authors when Egyptians were involved as well, and that the phrase suggests only translation was involved when in fact it also involved considerable interpretation. The latter qualification is reflected in Assmann's remarks quoted here.

[9] See Anton Deimel, *Schultexte aus Fara* (Die Inschriften von Fara 2; Wissenschaftliche Veröffentlichung der Deutschen Orient-Gesellschaft 43; Leipzig: J.C. Hinrichs, 1923) 1–9.

[10] See her book, *Before Writing* (Austin: University of Texas, 1992); and for a convenient summary, her article, "Record Keeping before Writing," *CANE* 4.2097–2106. For a critique, see Piotr Michalowski, "Tokenism," *American Anthropologist* 95 (1993) 996–99.

[11] See Eva Strommenger, *Habuba Kabira: eine Stadt vor 5000 Jahren* (Sendschrift der Deutschen Orient-Gesellschaft 12; Mainz: Zaben, 1980); and "Habuba Kabira South/Tell

third millennium, the famous Syrian site of Ebla (Tell Mardikh) produced literary tablets as well as bilingual texts.[12] In this period, it is evident that the site of Mari (Tell Hariri) served as a midpoint on the Euphrates for the transmission of Mesopotamian scribal culture to Syria.[13] Contrary to Assmann's rather neat distinction between tribal versus urban cultures and their modes of construing divinity (in the quote provided above), recent studies have shown that urban culture is closely related to and intertwined with tribal culture. As shown by a detailed, important study by Daniel E. Fleming,[14] Mari is a well-known case of a tribally based city, which may be more representative of West Semitic cities than has been appreciated. Family and tribal identity inform royal identity[15] as well as the representation of deities,[16]

Qannas and Jebel Aruda," in: *Ebla to Damascus: Art and Archaeology of Ancient Syria* (ed. Harvey Weiss; Washington, DC: Smithsonian Institution Traveling Exhibition Service, 1985) 83–86. For the broader context, see Harvey Weiss, "Protohistoric Syria and Origins of Cities and Civilization," in: *Ebla to Damascus: Art and Archaeology of Ancient Syria* (ed. Harvey Weiss; Washington, DC: Smithsonian Institution Traveling Exhibition Service, 1985) 77–83. For cylinder seals at these sites ca. 3200–2900, see Beatrice Tessier, *Ancient Near Eastern Cylinder Seals from the Marcopoli Collection* (Berkeley/Los Angeles/London: University of California; Beverly Hills, CA: Summa Publications, 1984) 51–54. For further remarks on writing at these sites, see Hermann Vanstiphout, "Memory and Literacy in Ancient Western Asia," *CANE* 4.2181–96, esp. 2183. Networks of trade arguably set the stage for the northern and westward transmission of Mesopotamian scribal tradition, as may be inferred from the older clay tokens studied by Denise Schmandt-Besserat (see the preceding note)

[12] See Alfonso Archi, "The Archives of Ebla," 72–86, esp. 82–83, and Paolo Matthiae, "The Archives of the Royal Palace G of Ebla," 53–71, in: *Cuneiform Archives and Libraries: Papers Read at the 30e Rencontre Assyriologique Internationale Leiden, 4–8 July 1983* (ed. Klaas R. Veenhof; Istanbul: Nederlands Historisch-Archaeologisch Instituut, 1986). See also Pelio Fronzaroli, ed., *Literature and Literary Language at Ebla* (Florence: Dipartimento di linguistica, Università di Firenze, 1992), especially Manfred Krebernik, "Mesopotamian Myths at Ebla: ARET 5, 6, and ARET 5, 7," 69–149; Piotr Michalowski, "Third Millennium Contacts: Observations on the Relationships between Mari and Ebla," *JAOS* 105 (1985) 293–302, and "Sumerian Literature: An Overview," *CANE* 4.2281; and Lucio Milano, "Ebla: A Third-Millennium City-State in Ancient Syria," *CANE* 2.1219–30.

[13] See Stephanie Dalley, *Mari and Karana: Two Old Babylonian Cities* (London/New York: Longman, 1984); Piotr Michalowski, "Mari: The View from Ebla," in: *Mari in Retrospect: Fifty Years of Mari and Mari Studies* (ed. Gordon D. Young; Winona Lake, IN: Eisenbrauns, 1992) 243–48. See the references to Mari in the texts of Sargon ca. 2380–2335 (e. g., *ANET* 267, 268).

[14] Daniel E. Fleming, *Democracy's Ancient Ancestors: Mari and Early Collective Governance* (Cambridge, UK / New York: Cambridge University, 2004).

[15] See the study of J. David Schloen, *The House of the Father as Fact and Symbol: Patrimonialism in Ugarit and the Ancient Near East* (Studies in the Archaeology and History of the Levant 2; Winona Lake, IN: Eisenbrauns, 2001).

[16] See an initial sketch of the family model in West Semitic religion in: Schloen, *The House of the Father,* 349–57. See also my book, *The Origins of Biblical Monotheism: Israel's Polytheistic Background and the Ugaritic Texts* (Oxford/New York: Oxford University, 2001) 54–66.

and it is out of this context of social and political identity that intercultural engagement and international scribal communication developed.

Cuneiform arrived in the southern Levant ("Canaan") during the middle of the second millennium, in the Middle Bronze Age.[17] Thus the international discourse developed by the Mesopotamian scribal tradition in the ancient Near East, particularly in the Levant, was the outcome of a long process unfolding over the course of a millennium or more.[18] By the middle of the second millennium, the Mesopotamian scribal curriculum and the accompanying use of Akkadian as a *lingua franca* had become the norm in Levantine polities, and also in Hatti to the north (in modern Turkey) and Egypt to the south. The so-called god-lists that Assmann discusses belonged to the list-literature (*Listenwissenschaft*) that moved westward as part of the Mesopotamian scribal curriculum.[19] This material catalogued objects, such as names of animal, plants and trees, metals, textiles and vessels, as well as professions.[20] Lists with god-names are found in Mesopotamia in

---

[17] For a convenient collection of the sources from this period, see Wayne Horowitz and Takayoshi Oshima, with Seth Sanders, *Cuneiform in Canaan: Cuneiform Sources from the Land of Israel in Ancient Times* (Jerusalem: Israel Exploration Society/The Hebrew University of Jerusalem, 2006) 10–15.

[18] For a recent survey of the spread of Mesopotamian scribal culture to the west in this period, see David M. Carr, *Writing on the Tablet of the Heart: Origins of Scripture and Literature* (Oxford/New York: Oxford University, 2005) 17–61. See also the remarks of Karel van der Toorn, *Scribal Culture and the Making of the Hebrew Bible* (Cambridge, MA/London: Harvard University, 2007) 39–73, 112–13; and Ryan Byrne, "The Refuge of Scribalism in Iron I Palestine," *BASOR* 345 (2007) 1–31, esp. 12–17. The spread of Mesopotamian scribal culture through Syria-Palestine is a complex matter lying beyond the scope of this discussion (see below for further information about the Levantine context). As my colleague Daniel Fleming has suggested to me, we should perhaps be speaking of scribal curricula and not a curriculum. While he uses the singular for the Sumero-Akkadian curriculum, for the Iron I Israelite context Byrne ("The Refuge of Scribalism," 1, 3, and see also pp. 7 and 23) refers to curricula rather than a single standard curriculum.

[19] See Hans J. Nissen, "Bemerkungen zur Listenliteratur Vorderasiens im 3. Jahrtausend," in: *La lingua di Ebla: atti del convegno internazionale (Napoli, 21–23 aprile 1980)* (ed. Luigi Cagni; Series minor, Seminario di studi asiatici, 14; Naples: Istituto universitario orientale, Seminario di studi asiatici, 1981) 99–108. For a convenient summary of this material at Ebla, see W. W. Hallo, *Origins: The Ancient Near Eastern Background of Some Modern Western Institutions* (Studies in the History and Culture of the Ancient Near East VI; Leiden/New York/Köln: Brill, 1996) 156–57. For *Listenwissenschaft*, see Wolfram von Soden, "Leistung und Grenze sumerischer und babylonischer Wissenschaft," *Die Welt als Geschichte* 2 (1936) 411–64, 509–57; reprinted, with additions and corrections, in the monographs by Benno Landsberger and Wolfram von Soden, published together as *Die Einbegrifflichkeit der babylonischen Welt/Leistung und Grenze sumerischer und babylonischer Wissenschaft* (Darmstadt: Wissenschaftliche Buchgesellschaft, 1965) 21–133. The term is commonly used by Assyriologists; in addition to the above, see van der Toorn, *Scribal Culture*, 119–20, and his remarks on p. 99 and p. 305 n. 81; and Byrne, "The Refuge of Scribalism," 15 n. 64.

[20] In addition to the references in the preceding note, see Hallo, *Origins*, 85; and Erica Reiner, *Astral Magic in Babylonia* (Transactions of the American Philosophical Society 85/4; Philadelphia: The American Philosophical Association, 1995) 26.

the first half of the second millennium, during the Middle Bronze Age (the Isin-Larsa and Old Babylonian periods).[21] The genre of god-lists spread westward to the Kassites and beyond to Western Asia over the course of the second half of the second millennium. It is in the Kassite period that bilingual lists and its translation of divinity enters the *Listenwissenschaft*.[22] Moreover, it is to be noted that the god-lists are hardly uniform in structure, and in several cases they are not designed as such to provide equations of deities. (They are not, strictly speaking, "god-lists.")

To illustrate the evidence, let us briefly consider two major exemplars of the lists involving deities. According to Richard L. Litke, the two series known as An: [d]A-nu-um and An: Anu ša ameli differ considerably. An: [d]A-nu-um is not a lexical list for giving Sumerian and Akkadian equivalents. It is essentially a Sumerian series of names with a corresponding explanatory column of comments that indicate the offices and relationships of deities.[23] In contrast, An: Anu ša ameli, the text that figures prominently in Assmann's account, is more properly an Akkadian list, and unlike An: [d]A-nu-um, it shows little interest in the status or relationships of the various deities to one another. The first of its three columns list approximately 160 Sumerian gods, the second about 20 deities and the third a series of relationship between the figures named in the first two columns. The relationships sometimes involve concrete objects, while others name an abstract relationship. Thus the entries are statements explaining the roles and places of deities in reality, and generally speaking, they are hardly lists designed for the equations of deities. In view of such differences, we might view the lists involving deities in a broader context as local or regional cases of scribal, intellectual learning aimed at making sense of deities, sometimes in cross-cultural terms.

Assmann's account places considerable importance on these Mesopotamian lists and the migration of the genre westward as the intellectual background for translatability of deities in western Asia during the Bronze Age. His reconstruction of cultural translatability finds its strongest ex-

---

[21] This presentation follows the discussion of the material by Litke, *A Reconstruction of the Assyro-Babylonian God-Lists, An: [d]A-nu-um and An: Anu ša amēli* (Texts from the Babylonian Collection, 3; New Haven: Yale Babylonian Collection, 1998) 2, and with a fuller account of the details on pp. 2–6. Litke provides an edition of the series with comments. See also the abbreviated remarks by Miguel Civil, "Ancient Mesopotamian Lexicography," *CANE* 4. 2311.

[22] For bilingualism more broadly, see Christopher Woods, "Bilingualism, Scribal Learning, and the Death of Sumerian," in: *Margins of Writing, Origins of Cultures: New Approaches to Writing and Reading in the Ancient Near East. Papers from the Symposium Held February 25–26, 2005 (Oriental Seminars)* (ed. Seth Sanders; Chicago: Oriental Institute, 2006) 91–120.

[23] Litke, *A Reconstruction*, 1–18, esp. 6.

pressions as his account moves into the Levant,[24] especially in the genres of treaties and letters, which we will explore below. For Assmann, it is the commercial and political interconnectedness within the Near Eastern and eastern Mediterranean world during the second millennium that induces a comparable interconnectedness in the sphere of divinity.[25] Such international interactions gradually led to a religious concept, whereby deities of different polities, in Assmann's words, "must necessarily be the same as those worshipped by other nations but under different names."[26] Whether the ancients truly thought the gods were "the same" figures worshipped only under different names arguably levels the differences among deities cross-culturally and does not appear to represent the ancients' own sensibilities about their deities.[27] Still Assmann's discussion does point to a new level of international discourse of divinity.

This shared conceptualization was enhanced in part by the common diplomatic language of Akkadian. It served as the central language for international discourse across Western Asia and Egypt.[28] (Notable in this regard,

---

[24] See Jean Bottéro, "Les Étrangers et Leur Dieux, Vus de Mesopotamie," *Israel Oriental Studies* XIV (1994) = *Concepts of the Other in Near Eastern Religions* (ed. Ilai Alon, Ithamar Gruenwald and Itamar Singer; Leiden/New York/Köln: Brill, 1994) 32–34.

[25] A helpful sense of international communication in this context may be gleaned from the survey of Gary H. Oller, "Messengers and Ambassadors in Ancient Western Asia," *CANE* 3.1465–73 (with bibliography). This interconnectedness between royal courts is also reflected by discussions about exchange of personnel, for example, the physician in EA 49 and a diviner in EA 35. See Carlo Zaccagnini, "The Interdependence of the Great Powers," in: *Amarna Diplomacy: The Beginnings of International Relations* (ed. Raymond Cohen and Raymond Westbrook; Baltimore/London: Johns Hopkins University, 2000) 146. See also more broadly his study of mobile crafts personnel, "Patterns of Mobility among Ancient Near Eastern Craftsmen," *JNES* 42 (1983) 245–64. Note also Abraham Malamat, "Musicians from Hazor Sent to Mari," *Qadmoniot* 32 (1999) 43–44 (Heb.); and Nadav Na'aman, "Dispatching Canaanite Maidservants to the Pharaoh," *Ancient Near Eastern Studies* (formerly *Abr-Nahrain*) 39 (2002) 76–82. For an examination of the context from the perspective of trade in luxury goods in this period, see Marian H. Feldman, *Diplomacy by Design: Luxury Arts and an "International Style" in the Ancient Near East, 1400–1200 BCE* (Chicago: University of Chicago, 2006). For the broader context of Bronze Age international relations, see Kristian Kristiansen and Thomas Larsson, *The Rise of Bronze Age Society: Travels, Transmissions and Transformations* (Cambridge, UK: Cambridge University, 2005).

[26] Assman, *Moses the Egyptian,* 47.

[27] For a critique of Assmann on this point, see Joseph Cardinal Ratzinger, *Truth and Tolerance: Christian Belief and World Religions* (trans. Henry Taylor; San Francisco: Ignatius, 2004) 219. Cf. p. 169 n. 139 below.

[28] For the scribal curriculum at Amarna, see Pinchas Artzi, "The Present State of the Amarna Documents," in: *Proceedings of the Ninth World Congress of Jewish Studies (19085). Panel Sessions: Bible and the Ancient Near East* (ed. M. Goshen-Gottstein, assisted by David Assaf; Publications of the Perry Foundation for Biblical Research in the Hebrew University of Jerusalem; Jerusalem: World Union of Jewish Studies, 1988) 3–16; "Studies in the Library of the Amarna Archive," in: *Bar-Ilan Studies in Assyriology Dedicated to Pinhas Artzi* (ed. Jacob Klein and Aaron Skaist; Bar-Ilan Studies in Near

it has been surmised that it was the Hittites and not Mesopotamians who taught Akkadian to the Egyptians.[29]) Along with this international language acquisition went Mesopotamian learning, which included deity-lists, treaties and epistolary conventions. As Shlomo Izre'el shows, the currents of scribal influence across Western Asia and Egypt in this period were complex. He notes that in some texts, the international cuneiform scribal practice was affected by local norms (e.g., the tinted dots, a known Egyptian scribal practice, added to EA 356, 357 and 372[30]). According to Wayne Horowitz and Takayoshi Oshima, a gradual separation of cuneiform tradition took place in Canaan from Mesopotamia over the course of the Middle Bronze Age, and the Late Bronze witnessed a further differentiation between the Akkadian of Syria and Mesopotamia on the one hand and Canaan on the other.[31] They comment:

> In terms of the writing system, the Late Bronze Age tablets exhibit true independence from Mesopotamia. The hand of almost all the tablets show affinities with the hand of the Amarna archives, suggesting close contacts with the scribal traditions of the Egyptian Empire, rather than Kassite Babylonia, Middle Assyria, or even the areas of Syria under Hittite (earlier Hurrian) control … The academic tradition of the materials, on the other hand, show signs of ongoing contact with developments of the Mesopotamian scribal tradition, as well as some more local features.[32]

As the remarks of Horowitz and Oshima suggest, in the west (or perhaps better, southwest), the scribal tradition was affected by the larger international political context. In Assmann's account, scribal activity and political realities worked in tandem in the translatability of divinity.

Before proceeding, it is important to note that translatability largely represents a discourse limited to an extremely limited scribal elite. The *Listenwissenschaft* was a particularly high scholarly achievement, only one of a number of specialities chosen by advanced scribes. Treaties and letters represent the interests of royal elites. Thus these texts reflect notions held

---

Eastern Languages and Culture. Publications of the Bar-Ilan University Institute of Assyriology; Ramat-Gan: Bar-Ilan University, 1990) 139–56; and Shlomo Izre'el, *The Amarna Scholarly Tablets* (Cuneiform Monographs 9; Groningen: Styx, 1997) 9–13. For the Hittite situation, see Gary Beckman, "Mesopotamians and Mesopotamian Learning at Hattusha," *Journal of Cuneiform Studies* 35 (1983) 97–114.

[29] For discussion, see Gary Beckman, "Mesopotamians and Mesopotamian Learning at Hattusha," 112–13; Gernot Wilhelm, "Zur Paläographie der in Ägypten geschriebenen Keilschriftbriefe," *Studien zur altägyptischen Kultur* 11 (1984 = Festschrift Wolfgang Helck) 643–53; and Izre'el, *The Amarna Scholarly Tablets,* 10. Note the Egyptian-Akkadian bilingual at Amarna (EA 368), in: Izre'el, *The Amarna Scholarly Tablets,* 77–81. Izre'el (*The Amarna Scholarly Tablets,* 12 and 22) believes that EA 343 may have been written by a scribe of a Levantine vassal in Egypt.

[30] Izre'el, *The Amarna Scholarly Tablets,* 46–47, 55.

[31] Horowitz and Oshima, *Cuneiform in Canaan,* 14.

[32] Horowitz and Oshima, *Cuneiform in Canaan,* 18.

by the scribal elite and the monarchical circles that they served. The other genres that are discussed below likewise reflect this very elite level. Accordingly, it would appear that translation of deities is not a general feature of the cultures. It belonged to a highly limited political and scribal world.

The Mesopotamian Scribal Curriculum and Deity-Lists at Ugarit

Assmann's discussion tends to accent the translatability of specific deities. To illustrate this specific sort of translatability, let us take a look at some of the best examples available, namely deity-lists discovered on tablets at the cosmopolitan city-state of ancient Ugarit (Ras Shamra).[33] Like the rest of the Levant in this period, Ugarit had assimilated the Sumero-Akkadian scribal curriculum,[34] and deity-lists were part of this tradition. At the same time, the deity-lists were "directly related to sacrificial practice," according to Dennis Pardee.[35] Pardee bases this conclusion on the correspondence between the listing of deities in RS 92.2004 and the order of deities honored in the sacrificial ritual of *KTU/CAT* 1.148. Generally, the lists from Ugarit consist of a single column. Indeed, some of these lists are evidently the same one in different languages. *KTU/CAT* 1.47 and 1.118 (cf. 1.148.1–9) are Ugaritic versions of essentially the same list, corresponding to the Sumero-Akkadian version, RS 20.024.[36] The same is true for the Ugaritic *KTU/CAT* 1.148.23–44 and the Sumero-Akkadian text RS 92.2004.[37] In several cases, the listing of deities as expected is according to type of deity. For purposes of illustration, three cases may suffice[38]:

   1. Ugaritic Shapshu and Sumerian ^{d}UTU appear in the same slot where the lists attest to them.[39] Both are sun-deities. The case is of further interest,

---

[33] As recognized shortly after their publication in 1968, for example, in 1970 by du Mesnil du Buisson, *Études*, xviii.

[34] For discussion, see W.H. van Soldt, "Babylonian Lexical, Religious and Literary Texts and Scribal Education at Ugarit and its Implications for the Alphabetic Literary Texts," in: *Ugarit: Ein ostmediterranes Kulturzentrum im Alten Orient. Ergebnisse und Perspektiven der Forschung. Band I: Ugarit und seine altorientalische Umwelt* (ed. Manfried Dietrich and Oswald Loretz; Abhandlungen zur Literatur Alt-Syrien-Palästinas 7; Münster: Ugarit, 1995) 171–212. For Sumerian and Akkadian texts at Ugarit, see Daniel Arnaud, *Corpus des textes de bibliothèque de Ras Shamra – Ougarit (1936–2000) en sumérien, babylonien et assyrien* (Aula Orientalis – Supplementa 23; Barcelona: Editorial AUSA, 2007).

[35] Pardee, *Ritual and Cult at Ugarit* (ed. Theodore J. Lewis; SBLWAW 10; Atlanta: Scholars, 2002) 11.

[36] For a convenient presentation, see Pardee, *Ritual and Cult at Ugarit,* 14–15. All three cases of equated deities derive from *CAT* 1.118 and RS 20.024.

[37] Pardee, *Ritual and Cult at Ugarit,* 18.

[38] Sometimes no equivalence takes place; instead, a Sumero-Akkadian spelling is provided, e.g., Ugaritic El represented as DINGER^{lum}, or Ugaritic Dagan as ^{d}da-gan.

[39] Pardee, *Ritual and Cult at Ugarit,* 14, slot 22.

as it is one of the few that crosses gender lines.[40] Shaphsu is female while ᵈUTU is masculine (Akkadian Shamash). In this case, the high correlation of function supersedes the otherwise common procedure of equating deities of the same gender, as we see in the next two cases.

2. The Ugaritic goddesses called the Kotharatu, the "skillful females," appear in the same slot in the list[41] as the Akkadian Sassuratu, the womb or mother goddesses.[42] In fact, both sets of goddesses are "womb goddesses": the Kotharatu seem to be involved in human conception as in the Ugaritic story of Aqhat (*CAT/KTU* 1.17 II 24–42), while the Sassuratu are most active in gestation, for example, in the Akkadian narrative of Atrahasis.[43]

3. The deities listed as Kothar and é.a (Ea) share the same slot.[44] Both are wise figures whose dwellings are associated with waters, yet the two gods differ in status and roles. Ea is a major god not known for manufacturing goods, while Kothar is the divine handyman and not a major god as such.[45] (One might have expected instead El correlated with Ea/Enki.[46])

As John Wilson noted with the examples in his account, these three cases point to function and gender as major categories of cross-cultural classification of deities.[47]

---

[40] For another possible example, see Nadav Na'aman, *Canaan in the Second Millennium B. C. E.: Collected Essays. Volume 2* (Winona Lake, IN: Eisenbrauns, 2005) 246–49. Na'aman believes that the four attestations of the writing NIN.URTA in the Amarna letters (EA 74:31; 84:39; 170:36; 290:16) may be understood as the goddess Anat, thanks in part to their shared role as warriors.

[41] Pardee, *Ritual and Cult at Ugarit*, 14, slot 13.

[42] See Pardee, "Kosharoth," *DDD* 491–92. See also Mark S. Smith, "Appendix I: The Kotharat," in: Smith, "Kothar wa-Hasis, the Ugaritic Craftsman God" (Ph. D. dissertation, Yale University, 1985) 466–72; and *CAD Š /II:*146. Note also the speculative study of du Mesnil du Buisson, *Études,* 1–7.

[43] On these views of the two sets of goddesses, see Pardee, "Kosharoth," *DDD* 491–92; Smith, "Appendix I: The Kotharat," in: "Kothar wa-Hasis, the Ugaritic Craftsman God," 469; Karel van der Toorn, *From Her Cradle to Her Grave: The Role of Religion in the Life of the Israelite and the Babylonian Woman* (trans. Sara J. Denning-Bolle; Sheffield: Sheffield, 1994) 86–87; Richard W. Whitekettle, "Human Reproduction in the Textual Record of Mesopotamia and Syria-Palestine during the First and Second Millennia B. C." (Ph. D. dissertation, Yale University, 1995) 393.

[44] Pardee, *Ritual and Cult at Ugarit*, 14 (*KTU* 1.118.15 = RS 20.024.15), slot 16.

[45] See Pardee, "Koshar," *DDD* 490; Smith, "Kothar wa-Hasis, the Ugaritic Craftsman God," 41.

[46] On the similarity between El and Ea, see Jonas C. Greenfield, *'Al Kanfei Yonah: Collected Studies of Jonas C. Greenfield on Semitic Philology* (ed. Shalom Paul, Michael E. Stone and Avital Pinnick; two vols.; Leiden/Boston: Brill; Jerusalem: Magnes, 2001) 2.895.

[47] Only rarely is such identification made on the basis of similarity of name, such as Horus and Hauron; so Kenneth A. Kitchen, *Pharaoh Triumphant: The Life and Times of Ramesses II, King of Egypt* (Warminster, UK: Aris & Phillips, 1982) 161. For the identification of these two gods, see also J. van Dijk, "The Canaanite God Horon and his

One tablet from Ras Shamra consists of three parallel columns of deity names in Sumero-Akkadian, Hurrian and Ugaritic.[48] The list is quite broken, and it is difficult to gain as much insight from it as one might wish. Still the fact that a multi-columned list of deities is involved suggests a recognized principle of translatability. Indeed, this list belongs to a larger group of polyglot lists consisting of common words; just as these words of different languages are equated to one another, so too the names of deities of different cultures. Thus with this list we literally have translation of divinity. In terms of the deities equated, this list is consistent with what we have already noted. For example, we again see the sun-deities equated, as are Kothar and Ea. Thus the principles of organization in the single-columned lists are also at work in the production of this parallel series of deities.[49] In these works, deities of different cultures can be arranged together according to particular perceptions about their natures. In short, Assmann's notion of translatability is explicitly manifest in the multi-columned list and implicit in the single-columned lists.

In the lists from Ugarit, translation operates according to a number of different principles. Deities are generally considered along lines of type. Usually the lists maintain consistency in gender, unless the deities of a given class cross gender lines (e. g., the sun-deities). What we clearly see is an implicit theory of typology of divinity, and thus an indigenous form of analysis corresponding to the classifications of deities found in the modern study of comparative religion.[50] We may also be sensitive to the political or

---

Cult in Egypt," *Göttinger Miszellen* 107 (1989) 59–69, esp. 62–63; and U. Rüterswörden, "Horon," *DDD* 426.

[48] Jean Nougayrol, "Textes suméro-accadiens des archives et bibliothèques privées d'Ugarit," in: *Ugaritica V: Nouveaux texts accadiens, hourrites et ugaritiques des archives et bibliothèques privées d'Ugarit. Commentaires des texts historiques (première partie)* (ed. Claude F. A. Schaeffer; Mission de Ras Shamra XVI; Paris: Imprimerie Nationale/Librairie orientaliste Paul Geuthner, 1968) 247–49.

[49] In the lists, this sort of comparison extends beyond deities to other aspects of divinity, such as the divine mountain of the storm-god (e.g., *KTU/CAT* 1.47.5 and 1.118.4). For discussion, see Klaus Koch, *Der Gott Israels und die Götter des Orients: Religionsgeschichtliche Studien II. Zum 80. Geburtstag von Klaus Koch* (ed. Friedhelm Hartenstein und Martin Rösel; FRLANT 216; Göttingen: Vandenhoeck & Ruprecht, 2007) 133–37.

[50] Early modern work in the study of comparative religion developed a number of types of deities, such as "sky gods," "high gods" or "creator-gods," "mother goddesses," "fertility goddesses," and "dying and rising gods," in other words, deities of various activities or functions (*Sondergötter*). See the account in Jan de Vries, *The Study of Religion: A Historical Approach* (trans. Kees W. Bolle; New York: Harcourt, Brace and World, 1967) 110–28, 134–41. For "sky gods" in the nineteenth and twentieth centuries, see the survey of Lawrence E. Sullivan, "Supreme Beings," in: *ER* 13.8867–81, esp. 8874–79. Several of these types, especially "fertility goddesses" and "dying and rising gods," went essentially unchallenged by scholars of the ancient Near East through most of the twentieth century. For discussion and critique of "fertility goddesses," see Izak Cornelius, *The Many Faces of the Goddess: The Iconography of the Syro-Palestinian Goddesses Anat, Astarte, Qedeshet,*

cultural context for this sort of equation of deities. The dynamic involved may not simply be a matter of equal translation, but may also involve the superimposition of a dominant culture onto local traditions.[51] As the next section indicates, politics is a central feature of translatability in the Late Bronze Age context.

The International Context of Intercultural Discourse

Beyond specific identifications, there were several broader notions of translatability of divinity operative on various levels in the scribal curriculum deployed by ancient Near Eastern cultures of the Late Bronze Age. A

---

and Asherah c. 1500–1000 (OBO 204; Fribourg: Academic/Göttingen: Vandenhoeck & Ruprecht, 2004) 9–12. For a similar critique regarding so-called "dying and rising" gods, see Smith, *The Origins of Biblical Monotheism,* 104–131; "The Death of 'Dying and Rising Gods' in the Biblical World: An Update, with Special Reference to Baal in the Baal Cycle," *Scandinavian Journal of the Old Testament* 12/2 (1998) 257–313.

In contrast, Mircea Eliade, perhaps the best-known scholar of comparative religion in the twentieth century, was considerably less given to such "types" of deities, as his accounts tend to focus on the larger context of the ritual process in which deities function. For Eliade, deities generally speaking are expressive of what he calls "archaic ontology," both in aetiological terms (namely, in the roles that deities play in providing explanations for the origins of such ontology), and in its re-actualization (namely, in their ritual presence which manifests their creative energies). See Eliade, *Cosmos and History: The Myth of the Eternal Return* (trans. Willard R. Trask; New York: Harper & Row, 1959) 3, 6, 7, 14, 21, 28, 32; and *Rites and Symbols of Initiation: The Mysteries of Birth and Rebirth* (trans. Willard R. Trask; New York: Harper & Row, 1965) xii–xiv. At the same time, Eliade would sometimes classify (or perhaps better, "type") deities according to function, for example "the hero" of combat against the "marine monster" (Eliade, *Cosmos and History,* 37) and "Great Mother" (*Rites and Symbols of Initiation,* 112); cf. his reference to "so-called fertility gods" (*Cosmos and History,* 109). In some respects, Eliade's work represents a constructive response to the reductionism often seen in the "typing" of deities, which to my mind is actually "type-casting." Such a representation of deities might be viewed critically as stereotyping, which Roland Barthes regards as "ideology's dominant mode of operation" (as characterized by Clark, *History, Theory, Text,* 175). In this view scholars of religion who type deities implicitly seek domination over the claims of their subject matter. A more sympathetic interpretation might view types as a convenient means for purposes of cross-cultural comparison (just as it was in antiquity). For a current example in the field of comparative religion, see the entries by Theodore M. Ludwig for "Gods and Goddesses" in: *ER* 6.3616–24 and "Monotheism," in: *ER* 9.6156. The more charitable view seems more appropriate, given the increasing sophistication in more recent descriptions of deities.

[51] For this issue of "superimposition," as it applies to the equation of deities in some contexts of cultural contact in the second millennium, see Archi, "Hurrian Gods," 148. As cases in point, Archi cites the equation of Sumero-Akkadian Enlil with West Semitic Dagan in some OB inscriptions form Mari as well as the fusion of Hattian and Hittite tradition in the old Hittite pantheon. For the latter, see the comments of Theo van den Hout, "Another View of Hittite Literature," in: *Anatolia Antica: Studi in memoria di Fiorella Imparati* (ed. Stefano de Martino and Franca Pecchioli Daddi; Eothen 11; Florence: LoGisma, 2002) 857–78, esp. 857, 865–66.

term used by Assmann to capture this international context is "the idea of an *ecumene*."[52] Translatability is arguably only one feature within a larger international political ecumenism. At the same time, we should be alert to the fact that the term ecumene derives from the Greco-Roman context and it is used somewhat anachronistically for the Bronze Age. Indeed, this term does not truly capture social and political identities of people generally in the Bronze Age or in the Iron Age, which were based on the family and tribe as well as the city. As noted above, this level of international discourse was a highly elite phenomenon. Using the term ecumene runs the risk of a second anachronism. For some, such a characterization echoes modern ecumenical efforts between religious groups. Despite these difficulties, the conditions that gave rise to the ancient and modern situations are not without points of comparison (we will return to this point later). As Steven R. David says of the fourteenth century Amarna Age, "it is precisely because the Amarna Age was so different from our own that its similarities are all the more striking."[53] For these reasons, ecumene is used occasionally in this study.

The larger context in the Bronze Age and its numerous types of translatability point to the need for examination beyond the somewhat limited discussions by Assmann.[54] To be fair, there is no indication that Assmann intended his treatments of translatability to be comprehensive. In his book, *Moses the Egyptian*, Assmann uses the concept of intercultural translation largely as a foil to the main interest of the book dealing with the ancient world, namely what he calls "the Mosaic distinction."[55] At this point it seems that a longer account of translatability in the Bronze Age that explores its range, its cultural context and its construction of categories of divinity is in order. Thus, a wider range of genres that attest to translatability is marshaled here. Furthermore, attention is paid in the following discussion to the political context of translatability, specifically its function as a production of the "great powers' club" in the Late Bronze Age. Indeed, as Mario Liverani's important study shows, the discourse discussed by Assmann was found on the exchange of diplomacy, prestige

---

[52] Assmann, *Akhanyati's Theology of Light and Time*, [12] = 154. For further observations on the use of this term, see Rodolfo Ragionieri, "The Amarna Age: The International Society in the Making," in: *Amarna Diplomacy: The Beginnings of International Relations* (ed. Raymond Cohen and Raymond Westbrook; Baltimore/London: Johns Hopkins University, 2000) 42–53, esp. 49.

[53] David, "Realism, Constructivism, and the Amarna Letters," in: *Amarna Diplomacy*, 67.

[54] See n. 6.

[55] For explanation, see the Introduction (under "The Plan of the Book") and the beginning of Chapter Two.

gifts, and diplomacy.[56] These practices played roles in their practices of reciprocal recognition. Or, as Carlo Zaccagnini puts the point, this period is marked by "intensive interaction of great politic-territorial formations, that reciprocally acknowledge their existence."[57] This acknowledgment was cast often in terms of the cross-cultural recognition of the deities of other states, or in other words, translatability of divinity. Translatability between unequal polities in this period also involved the differing and sometimes dialectical interactions between great powers and their vassals. In the discourse among these great powers and their vassals, we gain insight into various forms of translatability. It functioned both as a projection of imperial power and as a means of expressing local identity. In short, it was only in a context of competing peers that inspired such cross-cultural discourse about divinity. In contexts where multiple great powers are not operative (as we will see in the Iron Age), this sort of international discourse is less at work. Finally, further analysis of some texts provides help in uncovering the ancient conceptual categories for translatability and their implications for understanding the ancients' own understanding of religion and religious categories.

At the outset, it is important to note explicitly what intercultural translation or translatability of divinity entails in the texts that we will survey below. It does not simply involve foreign influence of ideas about divinity. Perhaps at its most basic, translatability is evident in the specific equation of individual deities across cultures. It is further manifest as the recognition of various deities of another culture in tandem with one's own or the recognition of a group of deities of another culture. We will also see that in these acts of recognition, the ancients at times translate other deities into their own terms, occasionally even into the names of their own deities, and they use classificatory categories to mediate these sorts of recognition of others' deities. We begin the following section with treaties and letters, the foundations of cross-cultural recognition of deities in the Late Bronze Age. Then we will briefly note some examples of translatability in myths, prayer and rituals.

---

[56] Fundamental here is the study of Mario Liverani, *International Relations in the Ancient Near East, 1600–1100 BCE* (New York: Palgrave, 2001).

[57] Zaccagnini, "The Forms of Alliance and Subjugation in the Near East of the Late Bronze Age," in: *I Trattati nel Monde Antico: Forma, ideologia, funzione* (ed. Luciano Canfora, Mario Liverani and Carlo Zaccagnini; Rome: "L'Erma" di Bretschneider, 1990) 37.

2. Treaties and Letters

Treaties

When we look at translatability in treaties,[58] we see a score of concepts that go beyond identification of individual deities. One of the finer cases identified by John Wilson involves a well-known treaty between Hattusili III and Ramesses II, which was concluded ca. 1269 after years of hostility between the Hittites and the Egyptians.[59] The originals[60] that were written on silver tablets[61] and placed before their respective chief deities have not survived, but we are in the fortunate position of having some fragmentary Akkadian copies as well as Egyptian paraphrases posted around Egypt, with copies surviving from the temple of Amun of Karnak and from the Ramesseum,

---

[58] See the important, older work of Dennis J. McCarthy, *Treaty and Covenant: A Study in Form in the Ancient Oriental Documents and in the Old Testament* (new ed. completely rewritten; Analecta Biblica 21A; Rome: Biblical Institute, 1978).

[59] For the texts, see the basic work of Elmar Edel, *Der Vertrag zwischen Ramses II. von Ägypten und Ḫattušili III. von Ḫatti* (Wissenschaftliche Veröffentlichung der Deutschen Orient-Gesellschaft 95; Berlin: Gebr. Mann, 1997), and his translation in: "Der ägyptisch-hethitische Friedensvertrag zwischen Ramses II. und Ḫattušili III.," vgl. Ḫattušili in: *Rechts- und Wirtschaftsurkunden. Historisch-chronologische Texte, Staatsverträge* (TUAT I, 2; Gütersloh: Mohn, 1983) 135–53 (with bibliography). For a convenient translation, see *ANET* 199–203. For translation of the Akkadian copies with further notes, see Gary Beckman, *Hittite Diplomatic Texts* (ed. Harry A. Hoffner, Jr.; SBLWAW 7; Atlanta: Scholars, 1996) 90–95.
For important discussions, see Anson Rainey and Zipporah Cochavi-Rainey, "Comparative Grammatical Notes on the Treaty between Ramses II and Hattusili III," in: *Studies in Egyptology Presented to Miriam Lichtheim* (ed. Sarah Israelit Groll; two vols.; Jerusalem: Magnes, 1990) 1.796–823; and Ogden Goelet, Jr and Baruch A. Levine, "Making Peace in Heaven and On Earth: Religious and Legal Aspects of the Treaty between Ramasses II and Ḫattušili III," in: *Boundaries of the Ancient Near Eastern World: A Tribute to Cyrus H. Gordon* (ed. Meir Lubetski, Claire Gottlieb and Sharon Keller; JSOTSup 273; Sheffield: Sheffield, 1998) 252–99 (I have particularly benefited from this essay, which Professor Goelet most graciously made available to me). For context, see also McCarthy, *Treaty and Covenant,* 46–48; and Redford, *Egypt, Canaan, and Israel in Ancient Times,* 188–91.

[60] According to Edel, the text was originally executed in Akkadian. Kenneth Kitchen (*Pharaoh Triumphant,* 77) accepts this view, as does Trevor Bryce, who states: "two independent versions were composed ... The Hittite version was originally written in Akkadian, from a first Hittite draft, inscribed on a silver tablet, and then sent to Egypt, where it was translated into Egyptian." See Bryce, *The Kingdom of the Hittites* (new edition; Oxford/New York: Oxford University, 2005) 277. For the opposite view, that "the Egyptian version may represent the 'base text' of this document, rather than a translation of an Akkadian original," see Ogden Goelet, in: Goelet and Levine, "Making Peace in Heaven and On Earth," 262. Beckman (*Hittite Diplomatic Texts,* 91) mentions "the mutual interference of three languages – Hittite, Egyptian, and Akkadian."

[61] This is mentioned in line 14 in the Akkadian text (see Edel, *Der Vertrag,* 6; *ANET* 202) and in the Egyptian text prior to the preamble and in the preamble itself (Edel, *Der Vertrag,* 16–17, 20–21; *ANET* 199).

the funerary temple of Ramesses II on the west bank of Thebes.[62] The end
of the Akkadian version has unfortunately been lost. The extant versions
follow the same basic format of an opening statement (often called the
preamble), a description of prior relations, the various provisions of the
treaty, and its curses and blessings. Each text adds a different introduction
prior to the preamble, and each version is styled further according to local
custom.[63]

The treaty's most famous representation of divinity involves the divine
witnesses and the curses and blessings. The divine witnesses invoked in the
Egyptian version are "a thousand gods of the male gods and of the female
gods of them of the land of Hatti, together with a thousand gods of the male
gods and of the female gods of them of the land of Egypt."[64] Corporately,
the deities of both lands thus serve as equal guarantors of the treaty. This is a
fine example of a general notion of translatability beyond the identification
of specific deities across these cultures.[65] At the same time, we may note that
such an expression assumes a Hittite cultural form, specifically in the expression, "the thousand gods of Hatti,"[66] adopted here to express the larger
corporate body not only of Hatti but also of Egypt. The expression, "the
male gods and of the female gods," is likewise a Hittite formula.[67] We see in
this case not only a very general notion of comparability of divinity between
the two great powers of this period, but also a use of Hittite notions of the
divine corporate for purposes of conveying this international god-talk.

Following this general expression, the treaty goes on to list the names of
specific deities.[68] In the Egyptian version, we first meet "the Re, the lord
of the sky; the Re of the town of Arinna, the Seth, lord of the sky; Seth of
Hatti," etc. The list of Hittite deities in this Egyptian version dominates,
with a relatively brief list of Egyptian deities saved for the end: "Amon; the
Re; Seth."[69] Generally speaking, there seems to be no direct equivalence of
deities made, since the listing of Hittite gods is considerably longer than the
listing of the Egyptian gods, which is in fact quite abbreviated. However,
this presentation shows more. We may note four sorts of conceptual classification. First of all, it is clear that chief deities of both polities are included.
Accordingly, we may say that the relative political status of deities repre-

---

[62] See Beckman, *Hittite Diplomatic Texts*, 91; Redford, *Egypt, Canaan, and Israel in Ancient Times*, 190.
[63] Beckman, *Hittite Diplomatic Texts*, 91.
[64] *ANET* 200–1.
[65] For this point, see Archi, "Hurrian Gods and the Festivals of the Hattian-Hittite Layer," 147.
[66] See Singer, " 'The Thousand Gods of Hatti'," 81.
[67] See Singer, " 'The Thousand Gods of Hatti'," 95, 99.
[68] *ANET* 201; Singer, " 'The Thousand Gods of Hatti'," 99–100.
[69] Singer, " 'The Thousand Gods of Hatti'," 94.

sents an acknowledged category of classification. Second, Hittite texts of the period show "classification of the gods according to several 'functional' categories,'" as nicely put by Itamar Singer.[70] Our treaty provides but one such category, "the gods, the lords of oaths," yet Singer cites more extensive listings of such groupings attested in other texts. For example, the earlier treaty of the Hittite monarch Mursili II (1321–1295) and Tuppi-Tessub of Amurru (ca. 1313–1280) gives the deities of the parties in the following manner: sun-gods and storm-gods; patron-gods; various warrior deities; deities of specific mountains; finally, components of nature, "the mountains, the rivers, the springs, the Great Sea, heaven and earth, the winds and clouds."[71] This classification is hardly unique to this treaty.[72] Third, in the treaty between Hattusili III and Ramesses II, geographical places and entities also serve as categories for listing deities.[73] Fourth and finally, there is generally an effort to keep divine gender straight in such cultural translation, though Singer notes that the scribes are not always consistent in this regard.[74] In short, in the treaty form of this period we meet what is perhaps the first comparative intellectual operation providing various categories for deities. Thus translatability involves not only specific deities, but also categories of deities.

Before passing to the matter of the deities as witnesses to the treaty, we may note a final, salient detail. In the treaty between Hattusili III and Ramesses II, the names of several Hittite deities are Egyptianized: "the Re, the lord of the sky; the Re of the town of Arinna, the Seth, lord of the sky; Seth of Hatti" – these are Hittite deities. The "Re of the town of Arinna" expresses an original Hittite "Sun-goddess of Arinna."[75] Thus the Egyptian version of the treaty does not simply presuppose general translatability of divinity in terms of function, purpose or geography. The treaty also shows the Egyptian recognition that the specific Hittite deities translate into specific Egyptian deities, a cross-cultural process that Egyptian literature and iconography applied to other foreign gods and goddesses, such as West

---

[70] Singer, " 'The Thousand Gods of Hatti'," 90.

[71] *ANET* 205; Beckman, *Hittite Historical Texts*, 58–59.

[72] See also *ANET* 205–6. It is to be noted also that heaven and earth, as well as mountains and valleys, also feature in the Ugaritic lists discussed above (see *CAT* 1.118.11 and 18); see also Koch, *Der Gott Israels und die Götter des Orients*, 134–35. For mountains, rivers and springs in another treaty, see the J. Eidem, "An Old Assyrian treaty from Tell Leilan," in: *Marchands, diplomates et empereurs: Études sur la civilisation mésopotamienne offertes à Paul Garelli* (ed. D. Charpin and F. Joannès; Paris: Editions Recherche sur les civilizations, 19991) 185–208 (information courtesy of Beate Pongratz-Leisten).

[73] Singer, " 'The Thousand Gods of Hatti'," 101.

[74] Singer, " 'The Thousand Gods of Hatti'," 100.

[75] *ANET* 201 n.15.

Semitic deities.[76] Thus, the treaty here takes a further conceptual step in translating foreign deities into Egyptian names.[77]

The treaty provides a further representation of divinity, which has been particularly highlighted by Ogden Goelet, Jr. and Baruch A. Levine. Goelet draws particular attention to the expression, "the God" (*p3 nṯr*) in the Egyptian versions of this text with the same expression in Egyptian wisdom literature not referring to a specific deity, but to "'whatever god you intend,' that is, 'a template deity'."[78] He sees the Akkadian version as following suit in preserving "some notion of *singularity* in the phraseology" (Goelet's italics). In his contribution to this co-authored essay, Levine pays particular attention to the anonymous designation DINGER-lì, "the god," in the Akkadian version of the treaty (line 10), which he considers to be the Akkadian translation of Egyptian *p3 nṯr*.[79] Levine suggests three possible interpretations for the term: (1) the chief god of each party; (2) an impersonal power or quality that governs matters; and (3) a supreme, international unnamed deity who adjudicates between the chief deities of the parties. Levine prefers the third alternative,[80] yet he grants that it is speculative.

---

[76] In this context we should note the classic importation of West Semitic deities and the resulting identification of deities, such as Baal and Seth. For example, the image of Baal on the so-called "400-year Stele" is accompanied by the text in Egyptian identifying the god as Seth. On this particular case, see R. Stadelmann, *Syrisch-Palästinensische Gottheiten in Ägypten* (Probleme der Ägyptologie 5; Leiden: Brill, 1967) 33. For Baal-Seth more generally, see Stadelmann, *Syrisch-Palästinensische Gottheiten in Ägypten,* 32–47; and Herman Te Velde, "Seth," *OEAE* 3.269–70 (with bibliography). For further cases, see in addition to Stadelmann's book, Redford, *Egypt, Canaan, and Israel in Ancient Times,* 43–48, 116–18, 228, 231–33; Linda Carless Hulin, "The Worshippers of Asiatic Gods in Egypt," in: *Papers for Discussion: Presented by the Department of Egyptology, The Hebrew University, Jerusalem: Volume I 1981–1982* (ed. Sarah Groll and H. Emily Stein; Jerusalem: Hebrew University, 1982) 270–77; and Christiane Zivie-Coche, "Dieux Autres, Dieux des Autres: Identité Culturelle et Alterité dans l'Egypte Ancienne," *Israel Oriental Studies* XIV (1994) = *Concepts of the Other in Near Eastern Religions* (ed. Ilai Alon, Ithamar Gruenwald and Itamar Singer; Leiden/New York/Köln: Brill, 1994) 56–78. For iconographic evidence for the importation of Asiatic goddesses into Late Kingdom Egypt, see Cornelius, *The Many Faces of the Goddess;* and K. Lahn, "Qedeschet. Genese einer Transfergottheit im ägyptisch-vorderasiatischen Raum," *Studien zur Altägyptischen Kultur* 33 (2005) 201–37. A comparable importation of Syro-Mesopotamian deities into Hatti is also attested. See Itamar Singer, "'The Thousand Gods of Hatti': The Limits of an Expanding Pantheon," *Israel Oriental Studies* XIV (1994) = *Concepts of the Other in Near Eastern Religions,* 91.

[77] This is not a matter of the original language in which the treaty was composed, but of how the names of the Hittite gods are handled in Egyptian.

[78] Goelet in Goelet and Levine, "Making Peace in Heaven and On Earth," 273, and see further pp. 265, 271–74.

[79] Levine in Goelet and Levine, "Making Peace in Heaven and On Earth," 282–91.

[80] It was also the view of Cyrus H. Gordon that a single god lies behind references to "the god" in Egyptian wisdom literature. See Cyrus Gordon and Gary A. Rendsburg, *The Bible and the Ancient Near East* (fourth ed.; New York/London: W. W. Norton, 1997) 141.

It is to be noted that the explicit attestations for the "supreme god" are relatively rare.[81] They play no role in the other texts relevant to our survey of translatability of deities. Levine's alternative proposal that "the god" is a neutral means for referring to the chief god of each party comports with James Allen's understanding of the Egyptian evidence for "the god" as whatever god the writer has in mind.[82] This alternative would also fit with the larger pattern of texts that tend to correlate deities of two parties according to shared function. In this understanding, "the god" would serve to capture the role of the chief god, perhaps literally as "THE god" from the writer's perspective. In this connection, we may note Akkadian *ilanu* used sometimes for a single deity (e.g., EA 74:57, 84:35), and sometimes for the Egyptian king (e.g., EA 151:1, 198:2; see also 366:11–16), a practice discussed by Joel S. Burnett and Nadav Na'aman.[83] In the majority of these

---

[81] For example, the Hymn to Amun (Papyrus Leiden I 350), chapter 300: "All the gods are three: Amun, the Sun and Ptah, without their seconds. His (the supreme god?) identity is hidden in Amun, his is the Sun as face, his body as Ptah" (*COS* 1.25). Note also Papyrus Chester Beatty IV recto x 2 (cited in *ANET* 372). See Jan Assmann, *The Search for God in Ancient Egypt* (trans. David Lorton; Ithaca, NY/London: Cornell University, 2001) 10–13; and his book, *Of God and Gods: Egypt, Israel, and the Rise of Monotheism* (Madison, WI: University of Wisconsin, 2008) 64–65. Like Gordon and Rendsburg (*The Bible and the Ancient Near East*, 141), Assmann sees the notion of a single god behind the deities in Bronze Age Egyptian religion and in the Greco-Roman period. For Greco-Roman examples for the Greco-Roman period, compare Xenophanes' "true god," who is "One god among gods and men (the) greatest/Neither in form nor in thought resembling human beings," as translated by H.S. Versnel, "Thrice One: Three Greek Experiments in Oneness," in: *One God or Many? Concepts of Divinity in the Ancient World* (ed. Barbara Nevling Porter; Transactions of the Casco Bay Assyriological Institute, vol. 1; np: np, 2000) 93. Cf. the older translation of John Burnet in: *The Portable Greek Reader* (ed. W.H. Auden; New York: Viking, 1948) 69: "One god, the greatest among gods and men, neither in form like mortals nor in thought …". This view of the Egyptian evidence is disputed by James Allen. See also the following note as well as the discussion in Chapter Five, p. 245. This "one-god" representation in Egyptian texts in the Bronze Age is not discussed further in this context, as it is an inner-cultural expression and not a cross-cultural one.

[82] Allen, "Monotheism in Ancient Egypt," in: *Text, Artifact, and Image: Revealing Ancient Israelite Religion* (ed. Gary Beckman and Theodore J. Lewis; Brown Judaic Studies 346; Providence, RI: Brown Judaic Studies, 2006) 320–25. See especially his comments on p. 324. See also John Baines, "Egyptian Deities in Context," in: *One God or Many? Concepts of Divinity in the Ancient World* (ed. Barbara Nevling Porter; Transactions of the Casco Bay Assyriological Institute, vol. 1; np: np, 2000) 56–62.

[83] Burnett, *A Reassessment of Biblical Elohim*, 16; Na'aman, *Canaan in the Second Millennium B. C. E.*, 249–50. Examples of the plural of *ilu* used for singular (e.g., Babylonian Theodicy, lines 49, 82, 219, 241, 295) are noted by W.G. Lambert, *Babylonian Wisdom Literature* (Oxford: Clarendon, 1960; repr., Winona Lake, IN: Eisenbrauns, 1996) 67, and by Burnett, *A Reassessment of Biblical Elohim*, 40–50, esp. 43, who evidently regards the feature as borrowed by Assyrian scribes from the Levant. The plural usage for a single deity has often been used to explain the use of the plural form for *'elohim* ("God") in the Hebrew Bible (see Burnett, *A Reassessment of Biblical Elohim*, 15, 24). Many scholars regard the biblical usage as a "plural of majesty" (so Na'aman among others). Burnett,

instances, the usage seems to apply to the personal god, which might help to explain the application of the plural to the Egyptian kings in letter sent by vassals.[84]

We now turn to the important role that deities play as witnesses to the treaty concluded by Hattusili III and Ramesses II. According to a standard reconstruction of the Egyptian version, the deities "are with me as witnesses [*hearing*] these words."[85] As noted above, the texts of the treaty between Hattusili III and Ramesses II, following their conclusion, were said to be set before important deities of the respective parties. In addition, a subsequent expression of the deities' role in maintaining the treaty is attested. The importance of this role may be witnessed in a letter that was sent following the conclusion of the treaty. The Egyptian queen Nefertiry, in an act of international correspondence rather uncommon for a queen,[86] states to her Hittite counterpart: "Re and the Weather-god (of the Hittites) shall uphold the treaty and Re will make it a prosperous peace, and he shall make excellent the brotherhood between the great king, the king of Egypt, and the great king, the king of Khatte, his brother, forever and ever!"[87] On this statement Redford comments the following: "The gods were as good as Her Majesty predicted: for the remaining lifetime of the Hittite empire the treaty was never broken".[88]

The context of this treaty provides no further information about how the human patrons of the treaty understood the deities to function at the time of making the treaty. For this question we may turn to another Hittite treaty, this one concluded in the third quarter of the fourteenth century between Suppiluliuma II of Hatti (1344–1322) and Shattiwaza of Mitanni (ca. 1340).[89] How the gods function is more explicitly expressed in this treaty:

---

by contrast, sees *'elohim* as a "divine plural," more specifically a " 'concretized' abstract plural."

A particularly distinctive usage deserves mention. EN. DINGER.MEŠ-*nu* ZI-*ka lí-iṣ-ṣur*, "May the Lord God (plural used for singular) guard your life," is used in a Late Bronze Age letter from Taanach sent by Ahiamai to Talwashur (see Horowitz and Oshima, *Cuneiform in Canaan*, 133, 134). This divine representation perhaps anticipates some biblical divine titles, e.g., BH "(my) Lord, my God" (*'adonay 'elohay*) in Psalms 38:16 and 86:12. It also approximates BH "Yahweh [Lord] God (*yhwh 'elohim*), especially with respect to the syntax and the second element used as a singular.

[84] See Lambert, *Babylonian Wisdom Literature*, 67; cf. Burnett, *A Reassessment of Biblical Elohim*, 12 and 46 n. 143.

[85] *ANET* 201; *ANET*'s italics.

[86] Gay Robins, *Women in Ancient Egypt* (Cambridge, MA: Harvard University, 1993) 34.

[87] Cited from Redford, *Egypt, Canaan, and Israel in Ancient Times*, 190.

[88] Redford, *Egypt, Canaan, and Israel in Ancient Times*, 190.

[89] *ANET* 205; Beckman, *Hittite Diplomatic Texts*, 37–49. For the reading Shattiwaza for the standard Kurtiwaza, see Beckman, *Hittite Diplomatic Texts*, 118 n. 67; and Amélie Kuhrt, *The Ancient Near East c. 3000–330* (Routledge History of the Ancient World;

"At the conclusion of the treaty we have called the gods to be assembled and the gods of the contracting parties to be present, to listen and serve as witnesses." After this statement, the Hittite and Hurrian deities are listed, ending in the conclusion that conveys the conceptual reality about these deities: "At the conclusion of the words of this treaty, let them be present, let them listen and let them serve as witnesses."[90] The repeated expression provides insight into the understanding of translatability. The passage not only involves the overall divine corporate sponsors of the two human parties. The making of the treaty is also the occasion for a meeting of the two sets of deities, as it were, in an international divine council, so that they may witness to its terms.[91] For the ritual formalizing of a treaty, statues of deities were sent to serve in their capacity as witnesses.[92] Statues could also travel in order to add divine sanction to other forms of diplomatic communication among allies. EA 164, for example, mentions the gods that Aziru has sent to his ally Tutu for the proper securing of an oath from him.[93]

Treaty-making ritual may take place in a temple or perhaps a palace in the presence of the parties' deities. We may begin with an iconographic representation of treaty ritual. A stele from Ugarit (RS 7.116) depicts two humans facing one another, with treaty documents sitting on a stand between them.

London/New York: Routledge, 1995) 330–31 n. 1. This figure was evidently Kili-Teshub, a son of Tushratta; Shattiwaza seems to be his throne name taken after his installation as king by Suppiluliuma. His dates are unknown. See Kuhrt, *The Ancient Near East,* 253, 292–93; and Marc Van De Mieroop, *A History of the Ancient Near East ca. 3000–323 BC* (Blackwell History of the Ancient World; Malden, MA/Oxford/Carlton, Australia: Blackwell, 2004) 143.

[90] *ANET* 206; cf. Beckman, *Hittite Diplomatic Texts,* 47, 48. As Beckman's translation indicates with its brackets, some of the formulary is reconstructed.

[91] In a vassal treaty, the same phenomenon may only involve a council of the gods of the party of the overlord. For example, in the treaty concluded between Tudhaliyas IV (1237–09) and Ulmi-Teshub of Dattasa (*Keilschrifturkunden aus Boghazköi* IV.10), the list of deities called as witnesses is prefaced by the following statement: "This is the tablet of the treaty that I have made for you. Now then, the thousand gods have been called into council on behalf of this word. Let them attend to the tablet and be witness to it" (translation in McCarthy, *Treaty and Covenant,* 305). For further discussion of divine witnesses with additional examples, see Michael L. Barré, *The God-List in the Treaty between Hannibal and Philip V of Macedonia: A Study in Light of the Ancient Near East Treaty Tradition* (The Johns Hopkins Near Eastern Studies; Baltimore/London: Johns Hopkins University, 1983) 96–99.

[92] The practice underlies the following from Mari letter ARM 26 199, as noted and rendered by van der Toorn (*Scribal Culture,* 112, 309 n. 11): "They keep sending messages proposing peace, and they even send their gods." See Wolfgang Heimpel, *Letters to the King of Mari: A New Translation with Historical Introduction, Notes, and Commentary* (Mesopotamian Civilizations 12; Winona Lake, IN: Eisenbrauns, 2003) 253.

[93] Theodore J. Lewis, "Syro-Palestinian Iconography and Divine Images," in: *Cult Image and Divine Representation in the Ancient Near East* (ed. Neal H. Walls; American Schools of Oriental Research Books Series 10; Boston: American Schools of Oriental Research, 2005) 94.

According to Claude F. A. Schaeffer, this stele "au voisinage du temple de
Baal où elle avait été déposée, rappelle la cérémonie de serment qui a eu
lieu, en pareil cas, en face des deux expéditions de l'accord."[94] For a textual
example, Raymond Westbrook points to EA 74, one of many letters that
Rib-Hadda of Byblos sends to his Egyptian overlord. Rib-Hadda complains
of the alliance of Abdi-Ashirta with troops evidently belonging to another
socio-political group, namely the men of Ammiya. Their agreement was
made in a temple of a West Semitic god identified only by the name of
Ninurta (NIN.URTA).[95] The Mari letters provide another example. In the
temple of Sin at Harran, Yamina and the kings of Zalmaqum take the oath
of alliance.[96]

Westbrook notes further that the treaty may be sealed by a meal. EA
162 alludes to the meal shared by treaty partners, Aziru of Amurru and
the ruler of Qidsha.[97] At this point we pause to note how the practice of treaty/covenant meals continued into the Iron Age, reflected in
both Neo-Assyrian treaty-texts[98] and biblical texts (such as Genesis 31:44–

---

[94] Schaeffer, *Ugaritica III* (Mission de Ras Shamra VIII; Paris: Geuthner, 1958) 92, with
a picture of the stele on plate VI. For another picture, see *ANEP* 608, with the following
description given on p. {322}: "Two male figures, clothed in Syrian costume, stand on
opposite sides of a table with hands extended so that the tips of the fingers touch. The
figure to the right wears a conical hat. The table, which probably has tripod base, holds
four tablet-like objects arranged in two piles. At the upper part of the stela there are two
lotus blossoms." See also Marguerite Yon, ed., *Arts et industries de la pierre* (Ras Shamra
– Ougarit 6; Paris: Editions Recherche sur les civilizations; Lyon: Maison de l'Orient,
1991) 303.

[95] For a translation, see William L. Moran, *The Amarna Letters* (Baltimore/London:
Johns Hopkins University, 1992) 143. For discussion, see Raymond Westbrook, "Interna-
tional Law in the Amarna Age," in: *Amarna Diplomacy: The Beginnings of International
Relations* (ed. Raymond Cohen and Raymond Westbrook; Baltimore/London: Johns
Hopkins University, 2000) 38.

[96] ARM 26 24:10–13, in: J. M. Durand, *Archives épistolaires de Mari I/1* (Paris: Editions
recherches sur les civilizations, 1988) 152–54. For a convenient English translation and
notes, see Heimpel, *Letters to the King of Mari*, 189. The text was brought to my attention
courtesy of Daniel Fleming. For a later example, see the neo-Assyrian vassal treaties of
Esarhaddon, discussed by D. J. Wiseman, *The Vassal-Treaties of Esarhaddon* (London:
British School of Archaeology, 1958) 3–4. See column I, lines 41–42: "The treaty (which)
Esarhaddon, king of Assyria, has made with you, in the presence of the great gods of
heaven and earth" (Wiseman, *The Vassal-Treaties*, 32). As reported by Wiseman (p. 1),
the throne-room where the fragments of these texts were discovered belonged to the
temple of Nabu.

[97] See Moran, *The Amarna Letters*, 249; and Westbrook, "International Law in the
Amarna Age," 38. For the context of EA 162, see Moran, *Amarna Studies: Collected Writings* (ed. John Huehnergard and Shlomo Izre'el; HSS 54; Winona Lake, IN: Eisenbrauns,
2003) 37–38. The practice of depositing a copy of the treaty in a temple likewise suggests
its religious character and perhaps the additional place of the deity as its witness. In addition to the discussion above, see McCarthy, *Treaty and Covenant*, 64.

[98] See the Vassal Treaties of Esarhaddon (VTE), column II, lines 153–154: "you will
not make a treaty by serving food at table, by drinking from a cup"; see D. J. Wiseman,

54[99]), with later reflexes in New Testament accounts of the "Last Supper" (Mark 14:22–25; Matthew 26:26–29; Luke 22:14–20). Simo Parpola and Theodore J. Lewis[100] have compared this New Testament covenant meal with the Neo-Assyrian oracle of Ishtar of Arbela to Esarhaddon: "In your hearts you say, 'Ishtar is slight,' and you will go to your cities and districts, eat (your) bread and forget this covenant. (But when) you drink from this water, you will remember me and keep this covenant which I have made on behalf of Esarhaddon."[101] Parpola and Lewis have also noted that like this oracle, these New Testament texts of the "Last Supper" represent the meal as an act commemorating the figure in whose name the covenant is made.

In this connection, the covenantal symbolization of wine as poured out blood bears mentioning, especially as represented in the Last Supper accounts (Mark 14:24; Matthew 26:28; Luke 22:20; see also 1 Corinthians 11:23–26). The biblical antecedent for this representation seems to be the covenantal meal in Exodus 24, which includes blood poured to be thrown on the altar and the people.[102] Here the connection of the blood poured

---

"The Vassal-Treaties of Esarhaddon," *Iraq* 20 (1958) 40. Note also below the citation of the covenant meal mentioned in the oracle of Ishtar of Arbela to Esarhaddon. Martti Nissinen also points to a neo-Assyrian text dating to 809, which provides the expenditures for the divine council's meal, which includes honey, oil, sesame, barley and wheat. See M. Nissinen, "Prophets and the Divine Council," in: *Kein Land für sich allein: Studien zum Kulturkontakt in Kanaan, Israel/Palästina und Ebirnâri für Manfred Weippert zum 65. Geburtstag* (ed. Ulrich Hübner and Ernst Axel Knauf; OBO 186; Fribourg: Universitätsverlag; Göttingen: Vandenhoeck & Ruprecht, 2002) 16–17. For the text, see L. Kataja and R. Whiting, *Grants, Decrees and Gifts of the Neo-Assyrian Period* (SAA XXII; Helsinki: Helsinki University, 1995) 74.

[99] See Theodore J. Lewis, "Covenant and Blood Rituals: Understanding Exodus 24:3–8 in Its Ancient Near Eastern Context," in: *Confronting the Past: Archaeological and Historical Essays on Ancient Israel in Honor of William G. Dever* (ed. S. Gitin, J.E. Wright and J.P. Dessel; Winona Lake, IN: Eisenbrauns, 2006) 342. See the discussion in Chapter Two, p. 106.

[100] In his note to this passage to the oracle of Ishtar of Arbela to Esarhaddon (cited here), Parpola compares Luke 22:17–20. See Parpola, *Assyrian Prophecies* (SAA IX; Helsinki: Helsinki University, 1997) 25. Lewis ("Covenant and Blood Rituals," 342 n. 8) characterizes the comparison as "stretching." It is unclear why, since in the broader context of his discussion of covenant and meals, Lewis compares Mark 14:24.

[101] For the text of the oracle, see Simo Parpola, *Assyrian Prophecies* (SAA IX; Helsinki: Helsinki University, 1997) 25 (3.4), discussed by Lewis, "Covenant and Blood Rituals," 342; and Nissinen, "Prophets and the Divine Council," 14–15.

[102] For blood in Israelite covenantal ritual including Exodus 24, see Dennis J. McCarthy, SJ, "The Symbolism of Blood and Sacrifice," *JBL* 88 (1969) 166–76, and "Further Notes on the Symbolism of Blood and Sacrifice," *JBL* 92 (1973) 205–10, repr. in McCarthy, *Institution and Narrative: Collected Essays* (Analecta Biblica 108; Rome: Biblical Institute, 1985) 207–12; S. David Sperling, "Blood," *ABD* 1.761–63; and Lewis, "Covenant and Blood Rituals," 341–50. For the purposes of this discussion, it matters little how verses 1–2 and 9–11 (with reference to the meal on the mountain) are related to verses 3–8 (with its references to the blood). Even if the verses would be attributed to different authors, the

out and the people's covenantal commitment is implicit at best. The same is true in Psalm 16:4, which refers somewhat cryptically to "their libations of blood." In this case, the blood poured out may be directed to the dead who share "blood relations" with the living.[103] In contrast with these two biblical texts, the Last Supper account is more explicit about the symbolization of wine as blood. In this respect it finds a helpful though distant antecedent in what may also be called a covenantal context. The so-called "Second Hittite Soldiers' Oath" (KUB 43.38), paragraph 11 (lines 13–16) identifies the wine poured out as the blood of the party involved.[104] In this text, the priest pours

fact that they are linked, even if secondarily, attests to the conceptual association on some level, and this is suggested by other texts such as Psalm 50. The association is evident also in Emar 373, column I, line 34: "After eating and drinking, they rub all the stones with oil and blood." The context is the "sacrificial homage for all of the gods," as stated in line 35. For the text and translation of Emar 373, column 1, lines 34–35, see Daniel Fleming, *Time at Emar: The Cultic Calendar and the Rituals from the Diviner's Archive* (Mesopotamian Civilizations 11; Winona Lake, IN: Eisenbrauns, 2000) 238–39. The statement in column I, line 34, repeats in column I, line 60 (Fleming, *Time at Emar*, 240–41), in column IV, line 167 (partially reconstructed; Fleming, *Time at Emar*, 248–49), and in Emar 375, line 14 (Fleming, *Time at Emar*, 260–61).

[103] This passage is highly charged with polemic, which may obscure the reference to blood, in particular the cultic practice of pouring out blood in honor of deceased relatives. For this view, see Klaas Spronk, *Beatific Afterlife in Ancient Israel and in the Ancient Near East* (AOAT 219; Kevelaer: Butzon & Bercker; Neukirchen-Vluyn: Neukirchener, 1986) 336. Spronk connects this verse to the priestly material in Leviticus 17:14. In this comparison Spronk is followed by Theodore J. Lewis, *Cults of the Dead in Ancient Israel and Ugarit* (HSM 39; Atlanta: Scholars, 1989) 166. While accepting the nature of the cultic practice proposed, Marc Vervenne contrasts the cult of the deceased ancestors with the priestly blood ritual: "Only the cult of the dead and the netherworld stressed blood." See Vervenne, "'The Blood is the Life and the Life is the Blood': Blood as Symbol of Life and Death in Biblical Tradition (Gen. 9,4)," in: *Ritual and Sacrifice in the Ancient Near East* (ed. J. Quaegebeur; OLA 55; Leuven: Peeters, 1993) 459. This may be overstating the contrast. The priestly view of blood in Leviticus 17:14 and in other biblical books (Genesis 9:4; Deuteronomy 12:23) may have represented a priestly counterpoint to domestic practice represented by the blood-libations in Psalm 16:4. Broadly speaking, both draw on the same concept of blood as an expression of kin-relations; one is literal while the other is "fictive kinship," that is by analogy to literal kinship (on this notion, see below). In this connection, it is worth noting the good (though somewhat circumstantial) case for this psalm as a priestly attack against such family practices, proposed by Karel van der Toorn, *Family Religion in Babylonia, Syria and Israel: Continuity and Change in the Forms of Religious Life* (Studies in the History and Culture of the Ancient Near East VII; Leiden/New York/Köln: Brill, 1996) 210–11; and Raymond Jacques Tournay, "À propos du Psaume 16, 1–4," *Revue biblique* 108 (2001) 21–25.

[104] For the metaphorical analogy of of blood as wine, see Isaiah 49:26: "as with wine, with their (own) blood they shall be drunk." The analogy between wine and blood is also reflected in the well-attested characterization of wine as the "blood of the vine/grapes." For West Semitic examples, see *KTU/CAT* 1.4 III 43–44, IV 37–38; Genesis 49:11; Deuteronomy 32:14 (mentioned by Sperling, "Blood," 761); and the Latin transliteration of Punic in Plautus, *Poenulus*, 1142: *neste ien nested um et*, "Let us drink wine; let us drink the blood of the vine," cited in: Charles R. Krahmalkov, *Phoenician-Punic Dictionary* (OLA 90; Studia Phoenicia XV; Leuven: Uitgeverij Peeters en Departement Oosterse

out wine and speaks: "[This] is not w[ine], it is your blood."[105] In both texts, the speech belongs to covenantal ritual. Though not well attested, this motif may have belonged to a longstanding repertoire of covenantal images.

To summarize the Late Bronze Age evidence afforded by the treaties, they show various expressions of what Assmann calls translatability, in some cases of a rather wide-ranging sort. We do not meet only specific cross-cultural identifications of individual deities. We also see the translation of concepts of deities crossing cultural boundaries ("the thousand gods of Hatti") as well as translation of names of other deities into local languages ("the Re of the town of Arinna"). We also have identifications of classes of deities, as well as expressions of deities coming together and working together. Underlying cross-cultural recognition of deities was the cross-cultural expression of the other party as family. Kings, who recognized one another as relative equals, addressed each another as brothers. In a treaty with his nephew and brother-in-law, Shaushga-muwa, who ruled Amurru, the Hittite king Tudhaliya IV writes about his royal peers: "The kings who are my equals in rank are the king of Egypt, the king of Babylonia, the king of Assyria and the king of Ahhiyawa."[106] This international brotherhood of the great kings in turn brought their deities together as well. Such deities can work together in order to help make treaties work. In short, translatability as we have seen thus far is a function of an imperial *ecumene* of relative equals. Where "brothers" fail to subdue or dominate one another, they along with their deities can be brought together in order to help effect a *modus vivendi* between them.

Studies, 2000) 149. In the Tyrian legend of the invention of wine cited by Achilles Tatius (2.2), Dionysius the god of the vine said that wine "is harvest water, the blood of the grape (*haima botrous*)." For further parallels, see É. Lipiński, "Banquet en l'honneur de Baal. *CTA* 3 (VAB), A, 4–22," *UF* 2 (1970) 86–87; J. C. de Moor and P. van Lugt, "The Spectre of Pan-Ugaritism," *Bibliotheca Orientalis* 31 (1974) 14; and J. A. Zamora, *La vid y el vino en Ugarit* (Banco de datos filológicos semíticos nordoccidentales: Monografías 6; Madrid: Consejo de investigaciones científicas, 2000) 599–601. See also the military metaphor of "drinking blood" in Numbers 23:24.

[105] Billie Jean Collins, "The Second Soldiers' Oath," in: *COS* 1.167 (I wish to thank Anne Marie Kitz who brought this text to my attention and Billie Jean Collins for help regarding this text). It would be tempting to link this Hittite soldier's oath to the Greek soldiers' oath sacrifice, described by Xenophon (*Anabasis* 2.2, 9), discussed by McCarthy, "Further Notes on the Symbolism of Blood and Sacrifice," 207 = McCarthy, *Institution and Narrative*, 209. McCarthy regards the Greek material as potentially related to Israelite blood ritual.

[106] See Beckman, *Hittite Diplomatic Texts*, 101. In a third millennium letter from Ebla, this language is extended to corresponding members of royal courts. Ibubu, the steward of the royal palace, writes to an envoy of the ruler of Hamazi: "Thus (says) Ibubu, the steward of the palace of the king to the envoy: 'I am (your) brother and you are (my) brother." Piotr Michalowski, *Letters from Early Mesopotamia* (ed. Erica Reiner; SBLWAW 3; Atlanta, GA: Scholars, 1993) 13 (column i), 14.

Translatability is equally at work in enforcing power over vassals. This is evident in treaties, but also in letters. We now turn to letters to see how translatability of divinity operated in both parity and vassal relations.

Letters from the El Amarna Corpus

A particularly rich source for translatability comes from the Amarna letters, a correspondence that served to maintain international relations within the great political *ecumene* in western Asia and Egypt during the third quarter of the fourteenth century.[107] The correspondence generally dates to the reigns of three kings: Amenophis (Amenhotpe) III; his son Amenophis (Amenhotpe) IV (better known as Akhenaten,[108] whose name means "Beneficial to the Aten"[109]); and perhaps early into the reign of Tutankhamun (or Smenkhare).[110] Many of the letters originated from Egypt's "brother" kings in Babylonia (EA 1–14), Assyria (EA 15–16), Mitanni (EA 17, 19–30), Arzawa (EA 31–32), Alashiya (EA 33–40) and Hatti (EA 41–44), but the vassals of the Egyptians take up the greater part of correspondence (EA 45–382, including copies of some letters originating in Egypt).[111] We begin the following survey with letters governing relations between rulers equal in status and then proceed to letters involving relations between Egyptian overlords and their vassals.[112]

---

[107] For the political dimensions of these letters, see the essay of Mario Liverani, "Political Lexicon and Political Ideologies in the Amarna Letters," *Berytus* 31 (1983) 41–56. Some of Liverani's points are addressed by William L. Moran, "Some Reflections on Amarna Politics," in: *Solving Riddles and Untying Knots: Biblical, Epigraphic, and Semitic Studies Presented to Jonas C. Greenfield* (ed. Z. Zevit, S. Gitin and M. Sokoloff; Winona Lake, IN: Eisenbrauns, 1995) 559–72, reprinted in: Moran, *Amarna Studies,* 327–41. The international political dynamics revealed by the Amarna correspondence are particularly well conveyed by the essays in the volume entitled *Amarna Diplomacy: The Beginnings of International Relations* (ed. Raymond Cohen and Raymond Westbrook; Baltimore/London: Johns Hopkins University, 2000). The essays cover a wide range of topics from geopolitical relations to intelligence gathering. Scholars have generally taken relatively little interest in the conceptualization of divinity in the correspondence.
[108] Or perhaps more accurately, Akhanyati, so Assmann, *Akhanyati's Theology of Light and Time,* [1] = 143.
[109] Or, alternatively, "glorified spirit of the Aten." See Donald B. Redford, *Akhenaten: The Heretic King* (Princeton: Princeton University, 1984) 141.
[110] See Cohen and Westbrook, "Introduction: The Amarna System," in: *Amarna Diplomacy,* 6.
[111] See Moran, *The Amarna Letters,* xiii–xxxix; and Cohen and Westbrook, "Introduction: The Amarna System," 6–9. The following EA citations and translations (with some simplification of the spellings of personal names) come from Moran's translation.
[112] The typologies of letters correspond to those of treaties; see Westbrook, "International Law in the Amarna Age," in: *Amarna Diplomacy: The Beginnings of International Relations* (ed. Raymond Cohen and Raymond Westbrook; Baltimore/London: Johns Hopkins University, 2000) 39. For a discussion of the great kings on par in the Amarna

Deities and Parity

The letters sent by Tushratta of Mitanni offer a particularly rich source for international religious expressions.[113] These include wishes for divine support of prosperity of his relations with Amenophis III (called Nimmureya in the letters). EA 19 expresses three wishes:

"May the gods grant it, and Teshup, my lord, and Aman make *flour[ish]* for evermore, just as it is now, this mutual love of ours"; "may Shaushka and Aman make her the image of my brother's desire"; and "may the gods grant …". The wishes expressed here point to two important concepts. The first is the notion of the collective of "the gods," which to judge from other references to deities include the gods of both Mitanni and Egypt. This case is hardly unique (e. g., EA 20:79). In this way we see the unnamed deities of both parties treated as a single collective. The second feature involves the mention of two specific deities, one from each land of the two parties. These two deities do not translate in any sense of equivalence, as we noted for the god-lists. Instead, two leading deities are named: for the Egyptian side, it is the same god named, Aman (Amun), while the Mitanni deities named vary, Teshup and Shaushka. EA 20, in naming Shaushka and Aman together, calls the first deity, "my mistress" and the second, "the god of my brother." EA 21 expresses the notion with yet another formulation: "May my gods and the gods of my brother protect them." With these specifications, we see the notion of family linked to the naming of deities. In neither instance is there any narrow sense of translatability; instead, there is a larger sense of an international clan with their family-gods.

The same correspondence provides a further insight into the practice of what Assmann calls international political ecumenism. In EA 23, the Hurrian king Tushratta addresses the matter of a statue of the goddess Shaushka that has been taken to Egypt for the benefit of Amenophis III.[114] Following the standard introductory formulas, the letter states how the goddess herself had communicated her desire: "I wish to go to Egypt, a country that I love, and then return." The letter relates the honor that she received from the Egyptians and then expresses the wish that she return. Tushratta then

---

correspondence, see Carlo Zaccagnini, "The Interdependence of the Great Powers," in: *Amarna Diplomacy*, 141–53.

[113] For the political context of this correspondence, see Pinhas Artzi, "The Diplomatic Service in Action," in: *Amarna Diplomacy*, 205–11.

[114] See the remarks by Zaccagnini, "The Interdependence of the Great Powers," in: *Amarna Diplomacy*, 146. Zaccagnini holds that the statue was dispatched "probably to heal the old and suffering Amenhotep III." This view is rejected, mostly for its lack of evidence, by Moran, *The Amarna Letters*, 62, and by Artzi, "The Diplomatic Service in Action," 208. For text, translation and notes to EA 23, see Martti Nissinen, *Prophets and Prophecy in the Ancient Near East* (SBLWAW 12; Atlanta: Society of Biblical Literature, 2003) 182–83.

voices a wish for the goddess' protection for both parties, and ends with the rhetorical question: "Is Shaushka for me alone my god(dess), for my brother not his god(dess)?" In the context of international relations, the goddess or more specifically her statue traveled to the Egyptian court to express and maintain good relations between the two parties.[115] She is accepted as a deity to be honored not only at home, but also abroad. In being honored in both lands, her presence signals the bond between them. Thus what we see about the role of deities in maintaining good relations at the level of rhetoric is conveyed further through the praxis of sending statues of one's deity to another king.

We do not have many examples of cross-cultural praxis of translatability, as it was hardly the norm. Indeed, it was commonly assumed in ancient Near Eastern cultures that a deity's own land was generally the appropriate site for her or his cult.[116] Nonetheless, intercultural praxis occurs some-times, not only at the international level, but also at the regional level where cultures meet. A short detour from the Amarna corpus provides an example on the local level, specifically a small sphinx discovered in the temple of Hathor at Serabit el-Khadem (in the western Sinai desert). The inscription (Sinai 345) on the statue includes an example of old West Semitic alphabetic writing, dated to 1700–1500 BCE/BC by Gordon J. Hamilton.[117] The left base of the sphinx contains the West Semitic title, "the Lady" (*b'lt*), while the right shoulder shows an Egyptian inscription, "beloved of Hathor (*ḥtḥr*), [lady] of turquoise." This sphinx is evidently a votive offering made to Hathor by local West Semitic workers of the turquoise mine at the site. They recognized the Egyptian goddess Hathor in terms of their own god-dess known by the title, "the Lady" (*b'lt*).[118] This case is particularly helpful

---

[115] For traveling statues, see also Theodore J. Lewis, "Syro-Palestinian Iconography and Divine Images," in: *Cult Image and Divine Representation in the Ancient Near East* (ed. Neal H. Walls; American Schools of Oriental Research Books Series 10; Boston: American Schools of Oriental Research, 2005) 93–97.

[116] To mention one example, note the statements made by Mursili II in his prayer: "But in no other country anywhere do they present them [sacrifices] so"; and "Only in Hatti is Mursili the king, your servant, reverent to you." See Albrecht Goetze, *ANET* 396; and Ada Taggar-Cohen, *Hittite Priesthood* (Heidelberg: Winter, 2006) 114, 125.

[117] For this information, see Gordon J. Hamilton, *The Origins of the West Semitic Alphabet in Egyptian Scripts* (CBQMS 40; Washington, DC: The Catholic Biblical As-sociation of America, 2006) 332–35. I thank Professor Hamilton for drawing my attention to this case.

[118] The title is one of the clearer words identified in the inscriptions. For further dis-cussion of the goddess, see Meindert Dijkstra, "Semitic Worship at Serabit el-Khadem (Sinai)," *Zeitschrift für Althebraistik* 10 (1997) 89–97, esp. 90–91 and 95. Dijkstra identi-fies Hathor/Baalat with the goddess Anat, whom he proposes to see in Sinai 527. In general, the readings for the Serabit el-Khadem inscriptions are notoriously difficult, and a number of Dikjstra's interpretations regarding the goddess call for reconsideration in light of Hamilton's epigraphic analysis of the corpus.

for our broader discussion, as it indicates that not only royal courts with international connections, but also workers in an intercultural context could engage in translatability of divinity.

To return to the Amarna correspondence, one of the rare Hurrian letters, EA 24, provides further expressions of international political theology: "As now my brother loves me, as now I love my brother, so may Teshup, Shaushka, Amanu, Shimige, Ea-sharri and all the gods love us in their hearts very, very much"; "… and we, between us, are one, the Hurrian land and the land of Egypt"; and "… and may my gods know, and may the gods of my brother know!" The first quote names deities of both parties within the collective, "all the gods," without differentiating between Hittite and Egyptian deities.[119] And as before, this letter shows family language for the two parties, as brothers, with the expression of divine love for the two parties. Love here is not simply an affective expression, but also a term for communicating good political relations.[120] The second quote shows a conceptualization not seen up to this point in our discussion, and that is the oneness of the lands of the two parties. It is hardly without parallel, as we see in EA 19: "This country is my brother's country, and this house is my brother's house." Thus in EA 24, the two parties are not linked merely by the treaty-relations; these issue further in the linking of their deities and their lands. The third quote echoes expressions that we have met already. It is a variation on the blessings of both parties' deities. It is interesting to note how this particular letter uses three rather different expressions to capture different sides of the international relations involved. Indeed, in looking over the Mitannian letters in the Amarna correspondence, they are notable for different levels of religious expression: basic communication (in the form of blessings); reflections in the form of propositional statements, what moderns might call theological expressions (e.g., the oneness of the lands of the parties); and an example of praxis (in this case, in the matter of the statue).

The Amarna correspondence with Arzawa (in Cilicia) contains a message to the king, but also to the scribe who reads the tablet. The part directed to

---

[119] Cf. the collectivity of deities including Baal Sapon, Athtart, Anat and all the gods of Alashiya invoked in *CAT* 2.42.4–9 for the well-being of the Egyptian king, himself named as *mlk 'lm*, "eternal king," which is evidently a translation of a title of Osiris, or possibly Aten or Resheph (*ḥk 3d̲.t*); for the text, see Dennis Pardee, "Epigraphic and Philological Notes," *UF* 19 (1987) 205, 207; for the divine identifications, see Alan Cooper, "*MLK 'LM:* 'Eternal King' or 'King of Eternity',," in: *Love & Death in the Ancient Near East: Essays in Honor of Marvin H. Hope* (ed. John H. Marks and Robert G. Good; Guilford, CT: Four Quarters, 1987) 2, 3, 6.

[120] See William L. Moran, "The Ancient Near Eastern Background of the Love of God in Deuteronomy," *CBQ* 25 (1963) 77–87; and Jacqueline E. Lapsley, "Feeling Our Way: Love for God in Deuteronomy," *CBQ* 65 (2003) 350–69.

the scribe in EA 32 asks: "May Nabu, the king of wisdom, (and) Ishtanush of the Gateway graciously protect the scribe who reads this tablet, and around you may they graciously hold the(ir) hands. You, scribe, write well to me; put down, moreover, your name. The tablets that are brought here always write in Hittite!" Before the last two sentences (which are taken up with practical scribal matters), the opening expression consists of the sort of blessing that we meet at the beginning of most letters. In this case, though, the expression is couched in terms appropriate to scribes. Nabu is the divine embodiment of the Sumero-Akkadian scribal learning that made its way in the centers throughout western Asia and Egypt in this period. Ishtanush is the Hittite sun-god. Thus we have a pairing of the divine scribal patron with a leading figure of the Hittite pantheon. The two gods are presented jointly as protecting the scribe and linked together in doing so by holding hands. Here there is no comparable function or role or even rank. Thus translatability in the narrow sense of equation or identification is not the point.

Deities and Vassals

As we move into the correspondence to the Egyptian overlord from his vassals, additional expressions of translatability come into play. The vassal, Akizzi of Qatna, conveys his submission by expressing that "I fall at the feet of my lord, my Storm-god, seven times" (EA 52). This usage is perhaps to be viewed against the background of the customary title for the Egyptian king, "the Sun." As Moran notes,[121] the usage of "my Storm-god" recalls the royal title, "My Sun," as found in the opening of many letters (e.g., EA 45, 49, 60, 61, 78, 83, 85; cf. EA 55; *CAT* 2.39.1, 3, 5, etc.), an identification stated explicitly in EA 155:6, 47: "the king is the Eternal Sun."[122] According to Moran, this may be "an adaptation, in local terms," of this common epithet. Thus the title could be, in Moran's terms, adapted for international communication. Moran's view is supported by the fact that the Egyptian royal title, "the Sun," applied also at Ugarit (*CAT* 2.81.19, 30), is also used of the Hittite king in some of the Ugaritic international documents (e.g., *CAT* 3.1.11, 25). Thus divine terms translate cross-culturally, here expressed in the person of the king. In this case, the adaptation or translation moves in the opposite direction of the Egyptian translation of divine names from Hittite into Egyptian that we met above in our discussion of treaties ("the Re, the lord of the sky; the Re of the

---

[121] Moran, *The Amarna Letters*, 123 n. 2.

[122] See Cooper, "*MLK 'LM:* 'Eternal King'," 3; and Pardee, *Les textes para-my-thologiques de la 24e campagne (1961)* (Ras Shamra – Ougarit IV; Éditions Recherche sur les Civilisations, Mémoire no. 77; Paris: Éditions Recherche sur les Civilisations, 1988) 89–91.

town of Arinna, the Seth, lord of the sky; Seth of Hatti"). International translatability thus traveled in both directions.

Akizzi of Qatna writes another letter (EA 55), this time concerning a statue of Shimigi, "the god of my father." The original statue, which had been made in Egypt, had been stolen by the Hittites from Qatna, and Akizzi wishes to have more gold sent from Egypt in order to make another statue of the god. If the Egyptian king sends the gold for the benefit of Shimigi, then "my lord will become, because of Shimigi, *more* famous than before." The case here differs from the case of the statue of Shaushka that we saw in EA 23 or the cases of the statue of the deity in EA 84 and 134. Still the parties in these cases are not the same, which indicates that this praxis in not limited to two particular parties, but functions within the larger international political ecumenism. Moreover, the case in EA 55 does not simply suggest a blessing that issues from the gift of gold, but also links the fame of the Egyptian king to the deity whom he elects to benefit; the benefit then will accrue to the Egyptian king's favor. In the case of EA 84, the concern for the deity (or his statue) follows with a rhetorical question: "Would it be pleasing that he [the king's enemy] had seized Gubla? *[Loo]k*, Gubla is like Hikuptah to my lord!" This expression in a vassal's appeal is perhaps analogous to the appeal of partners in EA about the lands of Mitanni and Egypt being one in EA 19 ("This country is my brother's country, and this house is my brother's house") and EA 24 ("… and we, between us, are one, the Hurrian land and the land of Egypt"). Land is a category of expressing shared identity, paralleled in the praxis represented by statues.

Blessings from Byblos

Many letters of the vassal correspondence from the coastal town of Gubla (Byblos) invoke the local goddess, "the Lady of Gubla," to help the Egyptian king. For example, in EA 68 Rib-Hadda asks: "May the Lady of Gubla grant power to the king, my lord" (see also EA 74, 75, 76, 77, 78, 79, 81, 83, 85, 89, 92, 108; cf. EA 73, and the ending of 83). Such wishes for the king's welfare are common in the openings of vassals' letters. Compared to what we have seen thus far, there is nothing particularly dramatic about such a blessing formula. In EA 77, 87 and 95, the Lady of Gubla is paired with Aman, the sort of feature seen above in the correspondence among "brothers." (We also meet in this correspondence, in EA 86, a wish for help from Aman for an Egyptian official.) Perhaps here, though, the pedestrian nature of the blessings should make us pause, for it is the local deity of the vassal who is invoked to help the overlord.

A general or theoretical statement underlying these expressions of good wishes for the Egyptian king, what might be viewed as a "theological" (or "second order") proposition, is given in EA 137: "The King, my lord, knows that the gods of Gubla are *holy*". This is not simply a statement of "theological" principle; it is an indicator also that the Egyptian king knows this principle about the gods of his vassal polity. Another variation in the blessing formulary of the Byblian correspondence is a request for blessing from the Egyptian king's own god: "May (your personal) god show concern for you and your household" (EA 97, 209, 227, 250).[123] Various deities from different cultures can exercise the role of blessing the Egyptian king. As we saw in the treaties, the role of divine witness applies to the goddess in the Byblian correspondence (EA 77). Thus typology of divinity operative in these letters largely resides in categories of functions and not their natures. In sum, as in the treaty of Mursilis II with Ramesses II, we noted that the deities listed as witnesses combine character and function.

The Egyptian King as Medium of Divine Imagery

The person of the Egyptian king, perhaps not surprisingly in vassal correspondence, occasionally serves as an expression of divinity, sometimes in combination with deities across cultures.[124] In a rather famous instance, Rib-Hadda of Byblos compares the king to two deities (EA 108): "Moreover, is it pleasing to the sight of the king, who is like Baal[125] and Shamash in the sky, that the sons of Abdi-Ashirta do as they please?" Both of these cosmic deities belong to two major categories in the list of divine witnesses in the treaty between Hattusili III and Ramesses II, namely storm-gods and sun-deities. Interestingly, this case invokes two deities neither of whom is Egyptian as such. The king himself is addressed regularly as "the Sun" in this correspondence, while the reference to the storm-god is less common.

The two types of gods appear in a more developed manner in EA 147, which was sent by Abi-Milku of Tyre:

My lord is the Sun who comes forth over all lands day by day, according to the way (of being) of the Sun, his gracious father, who gives life by his sweet breath and

---

[123] These prayers on behalf of the Egyptian king appear to be part of the rhetoric of persuasion by the speaker, Rib-Hadda, apparently as further ingratiation (note also EA 108 cited in the following section). His self-representation as an unrewarded yet unrelentingly loyal vassal to his Egyptian overlord has been discussed by Mario Liverani, "Rib-Adda, giusto sofferante," *Altorientalische Forschungen* 1 (1974) 175–205, translated as "Rib-Hadda, righteous sufferer," in: Liverani, *Myth and Politics in Ancient and Near Eastern Historiography* (ed. Zainab Bahrani and Marc Van De Mieroop; Ithaca, NY: Cornell University, 2004) 97–124; and William L. Moran, "Rib-Hadda: Job at Byblos?" in: *Biblical and Related Studies Presented to Samuel Iwry* (ed. Ann Kort and Scott Morschauser; Winona Lake, IN: Eisenbrauns, 1985) 173–81, reprinted in: Moran, *Amarna Studies,* 307–15.

[124] For discussion, see Joel S. Burnett, *A Reassessment of Biblical Elohim* (SBLDS 183; Atlanta: Society of Biblical Literature, 2001) 16–20.

[125] Or, perhaps: Haddu. See Moran, *The Amarna Letters,* 182 n. 1.

returns with his north wind; who establishes the entire land in peace by power of his arm; who gives forth his cry like Baal, and all the land is frightened at his cry.

This addition to the customary forms for opening letters has been noted often, and it has even been characterized as a hymn to the Pharaoh.[126] The Sun is at home in the Egyptian context, and here the Egyptian king is said to have the divine Sun as "his gracious father." There is oneness of being or reality between the divine and human counterparts. The royal title, "the Sun", expresses the Egyptian king's ontological participation in the "sunness" of his divine father, the Sun. Furthermore, the Sun is here juxtaposed with the correspondingly significant divine figure in the Levantine context, namely the Storm-god. Of supreme importance for the respective parties, the two gods are combined as expressions of the Egyptian king's capacities. It is also worth noting that the scribe who generated this letter was himself an Egyptian who had learned cuneiform.[127] As an Egyptian, this scribe was in a particularly good position to elaborate Egyptian notions in his lavish praise of the Egyptian king. He included Baal/Haddu in this praise, as the the Levantine storm-god was already known in Egyptian circles in this period.

Excursus: Egyptian-Levantine Translatability and Its Influence in Psalm 104

The combination of the imagery of the Sun-god and Storm-god in these sources has been noted in connection with the question of possible Egyptian influence on Psalm 104. The material parallels between the Great Hymn to the Aten known from the court of Amenophis IV (Akhenaten) and Psalm 104 have proven nearly irresistible to Egyptologists and biblical scholars alike.[128] The many topics shared by the two include the rising and

---

[126] See Moran, *The Amarna Letters*, 233.

[127] Albright, *ANET* 484 n. 2.

[128] The modern scholarly literature on the subject goes back at least to James Henry Breasted's 1894 dissertation, "De Hymnis in Solem sub Rege Amenophide IV conceptis," directed by Adolph Erman at Berlin. See also Breasted, *The Dawn of Conscience* (New York: Charles Scribner's Sons, 1933) 281–86. The comparison of the Aten hymns and Psalm 104 has since been common in the scholarly literature. For a representative case from the 1950s, see John A. Wilson, *The Culture of Ancient Egypt* (Chicago/London: The University of Chicago, 1951; Phoenix Books Edition, 1956) 227–29. This trend has continued among subsequent authors, for example, Erik Hornung in his survey, *Akhenaten and the Religion of Light* (trans. David Lorton; Ithaca/London: Cornell University, 1999) 11, 13. For further literature (with good bibliography), see Pierre Auffret, *Hymnes d'Égypte et d'Israël: études de structure littéraires* (OBO 34; Fribourg: Universitätsverlag; Göttingen: Vandenhoeck & Ruprecht, 1981) 133–316; Thomas Krüger, " 'Kosmostheologie' zwischen Mythos und Erfahrung. Ps 104 im Horizont altorientalischer und alttestamentlicher 'Schöpfungs'konzepte," *Biblische Notizen* 68 (1993) 49–78; and Matthias Köckert, "Literargeschichtliche und religionsgeschichtliche Beobachtungen zu Psalm 104," in:

setting of the sun, the specific animals in their environments (especially the birds), as well as ships on the sea[129] (although some of these appear in other hymns).[130] The texts also contain a similar exclamation: "How many are your deeds, Yahweh" (Psalm 104:24)//"How many are your deeds."[131] Commentators have been particularly attentive to the following similarity between Psalm 104 and the Great Hymn of Aten:

Psalm 104:29–30	*Great Hymn to the Aten*
You hide your face, they are troubled	The earth comes into being by your hand, as you made it,
You take away your breath, they die, And return to dust.	When you dawn, they live, When you set, they die.
You send forth your breath, they are created, And you renew the face of the earth.	you yourself are lifetime, one lives by you.[132]

It has been because of these resonances that many scholars have made various cases for influence, whether direct or indirect.

Despite enduring support for the comparison of the two texts, enthusiasm for even indirect influence has been tempered in recent decades. In some quarters, the argument for any form of influence is simply rejected outright.[133] Still some Egyptologists, such as Jan Assmann and Donald Redford, argue for Egyptian influence on both the Amarna correspondence (especially in EA 147) and on Psalm 104.[134] Following the observations of Paul Dion,[135] both scholars note the combination of Sun and Storm in

---

Schriftauslegung in der Schrift (Festschrift für Odil Hannes Steck zu seinem 65. Geburtstag; ed. Reinhard G. Kratz, Thomas Krüger and Konrad Schmid; BZAW 300; Berlin/New York: de Gruyter, 2000) 259–80.

[129] See Meir Weiss, *The Bible From Within: The Method of Total Interpretation* (Jerusalem: Magnes, 1984) 85–87.

[130] See Wilson, *The Culture of Ancient Egypt,* 227. See also Assmann, *Akhanyati's Theology of Light and Time,* esp. [24] (fascicle pagination) = 166 (series pagination).

[131] Miriam Lichtheim, *COS* 1.46. For a handy discussion of the setting of the versions of the great Aten hymn (in the tombs of Any, Apy, Mahu, Meryre I, and Tutu), see William J. Murnane, *Texts from the Amarna Period in Egypt* (ed. Edmund S. Meltzer; SBLWAW 5; Atlanta: Scholars, 1995) 123, 126, 151, 157–59 (with a composite translation) and 190. See also pp. 112–16 for the hymn in the tomb of Ay.

[132] The translation of this section of the Egyptian text comes from Assmann, *Akhanyati's Theology of Light and Time,* [25] = 167. Lichtheim's translation in *COS* 1.46 involves an emendation for the initial line.

[133] Miriam Lichtheim, *Ancient Egyptian Literature: Volume II. The New Kingdom* (Berkeley/Los Angeles/London: University of California, 1976) 100 n. 3.

[134] Assmann, *Akhanyati's Theology of Light and Time,* 24 n. 90; and *The Search for God in Ancient Egypt,* 212–13; Redford, *Egypt, Canaan, and Israel in Ancient Times,* 387.

[135] Dion, "YHWH as Storm-God and Sun-God," *ZAW* 103 (1991) 43–71. For the West Semitic storm-god in this text, see also F. M. Cross, *Canaanite Myth and Hebrew Epic: Essays in the History of Religion of Israel* (Cambridge, MA/London: Harvard University,

Psalm 104 and in EA 147. Redford views the combination seen in EA 147 as the prototype for Psalm 104. In contrast, Assmann is skeptical of this literary relationship. He comments that EA 147 "can no longer serve as a 'missing link' between Akhenaten's hymn and Psalm 104."[136] The issue is not simple. Redford may be right that such a Late Bronze Age reception and adaptation of the Egyptian theology of the king served as a model for what we see in Psalm 104, even if indirectly.

These discussions do not cover all of the available evidence in support of the Levant as a possible point between the Egyptian tradition behind the Aten hymns and Psalm 104. The combination of solar and storm language appears not only in EA 147 but also in EA 108, which would seem to suggest a wider attestation of the combination along the Levantine coast. The ongoing influence of the Egyptian-West Semitic combination may be seen in the eleventh century Egyptian story of Wenamun, which mentions both Amun and Seth as storm-gods. The prince of Byblos, Tjekerbaal, tells Wenamun: "For Amun makes thunder in the sky ever since he placed Seth beside him!"[137] Miriam Lichtheim notes that Seth here is "equated with the Syrian Baal," since "both were storm gods."[138] At a minimum, this speech reflects translatability, in that the two gods, one Egyptian and the other Byblian, are represented together as storm-gods. At the same time, no mere correspondence of functions is being asserted. The assumption of translatability of gods in this context furnishes a way for the parties to argue their claims for the relative preeminence of their own god. In the case of Tjekerbaal, he is asserting a Byblian view of this translatability, which makes Baal-Seth central in the divine scheme of things. Edward F. Wente Jr. comments to this effect: "Tjekerbaal audaciously claims that Amon's purpose in endowing Egypt was for the ultimate benefit of Byblos. Amon is efficacious only after Seth, equivalent to Semitic Baal, was installed beside

---

1973) 150–51. Note also Peter C. Craigie, "The Comparison of Hebrew Poetry: Psalm 104 in the Light of Egyptian and Ugaritic Poetry," *Semitics* 4 (1974) 10–21.

[136] Assmann, *Akhanyati's Theology of Light and Time*, [26] = 167.

[137] For this translation, see Miriam Lichtheim, *Ancient Egyptian Literature. Volume II: The New Kingdom* (Berkeley/Los Angeles/London: University of California, 1976) 227 and *COS* 1.91. For further discussion, see Othmar Keel and Christoph Uehlinger, *Gods, Goddesses, and Images of God in Ancient Israel* (trans. Thomas Trapp; Minneapolis: Fortress, 1998) 114.

[138] Lichtheim, *Ancient Egyptian Literature*, 230 n. 12 and *COS* 1.91 n. 12. The Egyptian view expressed in Wenamun omits the Syrian god in this discussion of Amun's power: "His is the sea, and his the Lebanon ..." (*COS* 1.91). As John Wilson notes (*ANET* 17 n. 27, 27 n. 23), the Egyptian view of the two gods' relationship would be couched with Amun in the clearly superior position. The Egyptian view of the hierarchical relationship between the two gods is expressed by Baal-Seth as the son of Amun, in: "The Contest of Horus and Seth for the Rule" (*ANET* 17 n. 27).

him."[139] In other words, the Levantine expression of translatability here additionally supplies a local interpretation of the Egyptian understanding of Amun. The location for this equation at Byblos[140] dovetails with the Amarna letter from Byblos, EA 108, which is noted above. The translatability in the combination of Egyptian solar divinity and West Semitic storm-god in the various Late Bronze Age Levantine sources then is not restricted to a single text, and it continues into the Iron I period.

The textual evidence points to the coastal Levantine ports of Byblos (EA 108 and Wen-Amun) and Tyre (EA 147), which were under Egyptian hegemony down into the Iron Age, as transmission points for the combination of Egyptian solar god (in various forms) and the West Semitic storm-god. To this Levantine evidence may be added an oval seal from Tell Keisan combining the Egyptian sun-deity with Baal-Seth, according to Keel and Uehlinger.[141] They suggest that the sun-god was replaced frequently by Amun issuing in his combination with Baal-Seth as seen in Wenamun. In this connection, they also note seal amulets bearing the name of Amun (written cryptographically) and the name of Seth. As the intercultural meeting points between the dominant culture of Egypt and local Levantine culture, the Amarna letters from Byblos and Tyre deployed an Egyptian-Levantine form of translatability to express praise of their overlord.

The Amarna letters themselves contain another feature that potentially supports Redford's view that they served as a prototype for the combined solar and storm imagery of Psalm 104, and it is one that has perhaps not received adequate attention in this discussion. This involves the terminology in the Amarna letters for the king's "breath," which functions in a manner quite similar to Biblical Hebrew *ruaḥ* in Psalm 104. One term, Akkadian *šeḫu*, is mentioned several times in EA 147 (in lines 9, 19, 23, 26, 34, 44) and also in EA 146:7 and 155:9.[142] The word is thought to render Egyptian *t3w.f*

---

[139] Wente, "The Report of Wenamon," in: *The Literature of Ancient Egypt: An Anthology of Stories, Instructions, and Poetry* (new edition; ed. William Kelly Simpson; New Haven/London: Yale University, 1973) 149 n. 19.

[140] This identification is the consensus of Egyptologists. For a dissenting view, see Alessandra Nibbi, *Wenamun and Alashiya Reconsidered* (Oxford: DE Publications, 1985) 15, 51, 85, 90–91, 107, and 109. Nibbi proposes an identification instead with the inland site of El Gibali at Lake Timsah, located to the east of the delta.

[141] Keel and Uehlinger, *Gods*, 114–16. They reckon that a replacement of the Egyptian sun god by Amun is involved here.

[142] Moran, *The Amarna Letters*, 173 n. 9. Rainey reads *šeḫu* behind TI in EA 227:9: "And when I heard these words of yours and the coming forth of the life force (TI) of the sun god to me, I rejoiced ...". See Anson Rainey, *Canaanite in the Amarna Tablets: A Linguistic Analysis of the Mixed Dialect used by the Scribes from Canaan* (4 vols.; Leiden: New York/Köln: Brill, 1996) 2.94. This possibility is considered also by Moran, *The Amarna Letters*, 289 n. 2.

ndm[143] meaning, "wind," here more specifically "breath, emanation."[144] Some Amarna letters (such as EA 147:9, 19, 34, 44; 146:7) use the phrase, "sweet breath" (*šeḫu ṭabu*), which is a loan phrase from Egyptian *t3w ndm n 'nh*, "the sweet breath of life," also an Amarna usage.[145] As Moran notes,[146] the word *šeḫu* is concentrated in the letters of Abi-Milku of Tyre. A second term, *šaru* is also used several times for the king's breath (EA 100:36, 40; 141:2, 10, 13, 37, 43; 143:1, 33; 144:2, 6, 8; 145:9, 20; 149:23, 38; 164:13; 281:3; and 297:18). The word occurs in a variety of phrases: "breath of my life" (*šari balaṭiya*, in EA 141:10, 13, 37, 43; 143:1–2, 33; 144:2, 8; *šari ša balaṭiya*, in 144:6–7), and "sweet breath" (*šaru ṭabtu*, in 297:18).[147] A couple of citations may provide a sense of the usage. The king's breath is expression of life for his vassal: "May the breath of the king not depart from us" (EA 100:36).[148] Elsewhere it simply serves as part of the opening address to the king: "my lord, m[y] Sun, my god, the breath of my life" (EA 141:2).[149]

The local West Semitic adaptation of the Akkadian terms may be indicated by the grammar. According to Moran, the nouns are normally masculine, but not in some of instances in the Amarna letters (EA 100:37, 141:15; 297:18). For Moran, this may reflect some West Semitic interference of the feminine noun (he compares the feminine Biblical Hebrew *ruaḥ* used in Psalm 104). If correct, it is possible to see a further thread from the Egyptian usage through the Amarna correspondence and into Psalm 104. The Akkadian terms in their Levantine attestations arguably underlie the use of *ruaḥ* in Psalm 104, as the use of the biblical word in this context somewhat stands out relative to its other attestations in the Bible.[150] The

---

[143] William Foxwell Albright, "The Egyptian Correspondence of Abimilki, Prince of Tyre," *Journal of Egyptian Archaeology* 23 (1937) 198–99; C. Grave, "Northwest Semitic *ṣapānu* in a Breakup of an Egyptian Stereotype Phrase in EA 147," *Orientalia* 51 (1982) 161–82. See also Assmann, *The Search for God in Ancient Egypt*, 213, 256 n. 75. See the entry in: Adolf Erman and Hermann Grapow, *Ägyptisches Handwörterbuch* (fourth ed.; seven vols.; Berlin: Akademie, 1982) 5.532.

[144] *CAD* Š/2:266–67. See also J. A. Knudtzon, *Die El-Amarna-Tafeln* (two vols.; Aalen: O. Zeller, 1964) 2.1520.

[145] Erman and Grapow, *Ägyptisches Handwörterbuch*, 5.532. For help with the Egyptian material involved, I wish to thank Ann Macy Roth.

[146] Moran, *The Amarna Letters*, 173 n. 9.

[147] *Die El-Amarna-Tafeln* (two vols; ed. Jørgen A. Knudtzon; Leipzig: J.C. Hinrichs, 1915); Moran, *The Amarna Letters*, 173 n. 9; *CAD* B:49 and Š/2:139 (cf. the verb *napāšu*, "to breath," in: EA 179:12, as read by Knudtzon, *Die El-Amarna-Tafeln*, 690, and Moran, *The Amarna Letters*, 262 n. 1).

[148] Moran, *The Amarna Letters*, 172. Note also the use of "the kindly breath" (*šara ṭaba*) of the god in the Babylonian Theodicy, line 241 (Lambert, *Babylonian Wisdom Literature*, 84–85).

[149] For this style of address with additional examples from the EA corpus, see Joel S. Burnett, *A Reassessment of Biblical Elohim* (SBLDS 183; Atlanta: Society of Biblical Literature, 2001) 8–9.

[150] Moran, *The Amarna Letters*, 173 n. 9. But see Lamentations 4:20.

proximity in usage involves not only the basic semantics of "breath," but also the religious usage of the term[151] in the sense of the king sustaining the human party (human-divine in the Amarna material, divine in the case of Psalm 104). As this royal rhetoric passed through the filter of its Levantine vassals, its local context in turn contributed to it by combining the Egyptian language of the sun with the imagery of the West Semitic storm, as Dion has observed.

In view of the evidence reviewed thus far, the Levant may be posited as the location for mediating the concept of the divine life-giving breath. This deduction would comport with what is known of the Levantine context in this period. In their important study, Othmar Keel and Christoph Uehlinger characterize the political situation as one of "Egyptian colonialism."[152] The same is true of the textual record. The lavish praise of the Levantine Amarna material conveys the vassal perspective, that the Egyptian king is similar to the great gods of all the lands, since he is after all, as one Ugaritic letter puts the point, "king of kings" (*CAT* 2.81.3, 20). Above we have noted the presence of other Egyptian notions in Ugaritic correspondence, and scholars have noted additional literary features shared between the Amarna correspondence and biblical literature.[153]

The reconstruction for the local Israelite reception of the divine breath might be bolstered by appeal to Iron I iconography. According to Keel and Uehlinger,[154] a number of steatite amulets carry the Egyptian image of the sun, perhaps communicating the idea of the king as the "perfect sun god." These appear in Iron I iconography in the Levant (especially from Philistia, but also Megiddo, Taanach and Tel Tayinat in Syria). One depiction, on a rectangular plaque from Taanach, portrays a striding deity with outstretched arms, which Keel and Uehlinger take to be a gesture of supporting the heavens. The *uraeus* coming from the god's mouth on one side of the plaque shows a scorching breath and on the other side his "reinvigorating breath of life (see Ps 104:29 f.)."[155] As their quote suggests, Keel and Uehlinger are proposing that the plaque depicts the "breath" that we have in Egyptian sources and in Psalm 104. This material represents further

---

[151] Cf. the concept of Hittite *ištanza*, "soul, spirit, mind, will," shared by divinity and humanity, see Ada Taggar-Cohen, *Hittite Priesthood* (Heidelberg: Winter, 2006) 74, 95: "Is the soul of a human and of the gods any different?" (*CTH* 264, col. I, paragraph 2, line 21, written with the Sumerogram ZI; Taggar-Cohen, *Hittite Priesthood*, 41, 95).

[152] Keel and Uehlinger, *Gods*, 49–108.

[153] See Richard S. Hess, "Hebrew Psalms and Amarna Correspondence from Jerusalem: Some Comparisons and Implications," *ZAW* 101 (1989) 249–65. Note also the older study of Anton Jirku, "Kanaʻanäische Psalmenfragmente in der vorisraelitischen Zeit Palästinas und Syriens," *JBL* 52 (1933) 108–20.

[154] Keel and Uehlinger, *Gods*, 136–38.

[155] Keel and Uehlinger, *Gods*, 137.

circumstantial evidence that comports with the path of cultural transmission that I am proposing here. Keel and Uehlinger also point to scarabs that bear the name of Amun-Re or the cryptogram of his name; these are attested down into Iron II Israel.[156]

In the final stage of development, further transformation in the material takes place within Psalm 104 itself, with its own development of the combined solar and storm language to Yahweh. While this combination was inherited, as was its form of the divine *ruaḥ*,[157] Psalm 104 drew on local Israelite idiom as well. Some idioms in this psalm are quite at home in biblical rhetoric, for example the image of hiding the face and the image of the face of the earth (in Psalm 104:29–30, quoted above). It has also been observed by Aloysius Fitzgerald: "the meteorology, which presumes that the agriculture depends on rain, is pure Syro-Palestinian."[158] According to Fitzgerald, the storm imagery in Psalm 104 includes not only the rainstorm, but also the dry east wind (scirocco). In sum, this rhetoric of praise of the divine spirit can be plausibly traced from Late Bronze Egypt to Israel.

On the whole, commentators have noted the relative lack of evidence for this posited path of transmission from Egypt through Levantine coastal cities and into Iron Age Israel, and this is true even when the iconographic record is added to the discussion. On the textual level, this deficiency is perhaps

---

[156] Keel and Uehlinger, *Gods,* 138. Despite the reversal of Egyptian influence in Iron I context, ongoing Egyptian influence evident in the wider archaeological record would comport with this reconstruction. For the archaeological evidence, see the important survey of Elizabeth Bloch-Smith and Beth Alpert Nakhai, "A Landscape Comes to Life: The Iron I Period," *Near Eastern Archaeology* 62 (1999) 83–84, 86–87, and 115. For Egyptian pottery and potters in the Late Bronze Age Canaan, see Ann E. Killebrew, "Cultural Homogenisation and Diversity in Canaan during the 13th and 12th Centuries BC," in: *Archaeological Perspectives on the Transmission and Transformation of Culture in the Eastern Mediterranean* (ed. Joanne Clarke; Levant Supplementary Studies 2; Oxford: Oxbow Books, 2005) 170–75. Killebrew also notes Egyptian-style forms in the Iron I period.

[157] Biblical scholars are often reminded of *ruaḥ 'elohim* in Genesis 1:2, arguably a reflex of the usage in Psalm 104 (cf. the divine spirit or breath used in creating or restoring humanity: Genesis 2:7, 6:17, 7:15, 22; Ezekiel 37:5, 6, 9, 10, 14; Job 33:4; cf. Isaiah 33:11). In this feature Psalm 104 appears typologically prior to Genesis 1. This is true of other features shared by the two passages. For example, the light is presented explicitly in Psalm 104 metaphorically as the god's garment, imagined as a theophanic element (cf. Enuma Elish's presentation of Marduk in tablet I, lines 101–104; see the translations in *ANET* 62, *COS* 1.392, and Jean Bottéro and Samuel N. Kramer, *Lorsque les dieux faisaient l'homme: Mythologie mésopotamienne* [Paris: Gallimard, 1989] 609). Genesis 1:3, in contrast, does not engage in this mode of presentation. Instead, light is placed within the structure of creative acts. In this context, this light provides for the lights of verse 14, themselves markers of priestly calendar. See Jon D. Levenson, *Creation and the Persistence of Evil: The Jewish Drama of Divine Omnipotence* (San Francisco: Harper & Row, 1988) 55.

[158] Fitzgerald, *The Lord of the East Wind* (CBQMS 34; Washington, DC: The Catholic Biblical Association of America, 2002) 167 n. 14.

due in some measure to the different genres involved. At the beginning of this transmission, we have a series of Egyptian royal hymns from the court of Akhenaten and at its end is the hymn of Psalm 104. In-between, all we have for evidence involves letters mediating between Egypt and the Levant. We have no attested body of hymns from the Levant in the Late Bronze Age to confirm this posited path of transmission. In the letters, the full-blown rhetoric of the hymnic material is abbreviated at best. We may suppose that the scribes of these Levantine courts learned, adopted and adapted Egyptian court rhetoric in order to offer praise back to their Egyptian overlord. Psalm 104 appears, from our vantage point, rather developed in its rhetoric, but in fact it may be that some of this rhetoric managed to continue throughout this period in the Levant into the Iron Age. Despite the lack of evidence, the iconography may point to the larger context of transmission. In sum, the iconographic record parallels the meager literary evidence for the cultural transmission of solar imagery from Egypt through the Amarna correspondence and into Iron Age Israel, in particular in Psalm 104.

3. Concepts of Divine Translatability: Family, Shared Resources, Oneness

From the preceding survey of treaties and letters, we see three underlying concepts informing the various expressions of what Assmann regards as translatability. In these cases, all three were transcultural, that is, at home in the cultures of both parties. The first and perhaps most basic is the notion of the various kings as brothers in a single international household. The further expressions of shared resources and oneness are both grounded in the family metaphor. These three major notions expressing cross-cultural relations in international correspondence are treated here in turn, with reference to their attestation in texts beyond the Amarna letters.

Family Relations

The cross-cultural metaphor of family relations is absolutely key for understanding the conceptualization of international discourse in the Late Bronze Age. The language of international brotherhood is ubiquitous in the international correspondence, especially in the Amarna letters.[159] Other letters dating to the Late Bronze Age likewise reflect this political metaphor. In RS 18.54 A, lines 17'–20' (*PRU IV*, pp. 228–29), the speaker

---

[159] See Samuel A. Meier, "Diplomacy and International Marriages," in: *Amarna Diplomacy*, 165–73.

calls his addressee, the king of Ugarit, "my brother". Paul Kalluveettil comments: "The writer … is committed to behave as if they belong to the same family, his possessions really belong to his ally and those of his partner to him."[160] Here the parties are implicitly one, embedded in the notion that their resources are regarded explicitly as a single entity. Before proceeding, it is to be noted that the family metaphor was grounded in the diplomatic practice of international marriages linking the great powers.[161] Thus the metaphor was sometimes enhanced by the actual realities of family. We should also be clear that this metaphorical family did not actually function as family. Indeed, international relations, in the words of Daniel Druckman and Serdar Güner, "were not a 'brotherhood' in the sense of a communal system in which each king acted to secure the welfare and security of the other kingdoms."[162]

The overarching metaphor of family relations became a particularly prominent topic in the scholarly literature beginning in the late 1950s, when studies identified treaty and covenant in international contexts across a wide spectrum of political and economic documents dating to the second and first millennia. Perhaps best remembered by the work of Dennis J. McCarthy,[163] this international treaty language was readily identified in a repertoire of expressions identified in biblical studies under the rubric of covenant.[164] The line of research continues to command wide attention.[165] A great deal

---

[160] Kalluveettil, *Declaration and Covenant: A Comprehensive Review of Covenant Formulae from the Old Testament and the Ancient Near East* (Analecta Biblica 88; Rome: Pontifical Biblical Institute, 1982) 103.

[161] Carlo Zaccagnini, "The Interdependence of the Great Powers," in: *Amarna Diplomacy,* 144–45; Meier, "Diplomacy and International Marriages," in: *Amarna Diplomacy,* 166–67; and Cohen and Westbrook, "Conclusion," in: *Amarna Diplomacy,* 232–33.

[162] Druckman and Güner, "A Social-Psychological Analysis of Amarna Diplomacy," in: *Amarna Diplomacy,* 176.

[163] McCarthy, *Treaty and Covenant.* See also his work, *Institution and Narrative: Collected Essays* (Analecta Biblica 108; Rome: Pontifical Biblical Institute, 1985).

[164] See the listing in: McCarthy, *Treaty and Covenant,* 328–34; Kalluveettil, *Declaration and Covenant,* 219–35.

[165] In addition to Kalluveettil, *Declaration and Covenant,* recent studies include: Michael L. Barré, *The God-List in the Treaty between Hannibal and Philip V of Macedonia;* Cross, *From Epic to Canon: History and Literature in Ancient Israel* (Baltimore/London: Johns Hopkins University, 1998) 3–21; Gary N. Knoppers, "Ancient Near Eastern Royal Grants and the Davidic Covenant," *JAOS* 116 (1996) 670–97; Jacqueline E. Lapsley, "Feeling Our Way: Love for God in Deuteronomy," *CBQ* 65 (2003) 350–69; Robert A. Oden, "The Place of Covenant in the Religion of Ancient Israel," in: *Ancient Israelite Religion: Essays in Honor of Frank Moore Cross* (ed. P.D. Miller, Jr., P.D. Hanson and S.D. McBride (Philadelphia: Fortress, 1987) 427–47; Theodore J. Lewis, "The Identity and Function of El/Baal Berith," *JBL* 115 (1996) 401–23, and "Covenant and Blood Rituals: Understanding Exodus 24:3–8 in Its Ancient Near Eastern Context," in: *Confronting the Past: Archaeological and Historical Essays on Ancient Israel in Honor of William G. Dever* (ed. S. Gitin, J.E. Wright and J.P. Dessel; Winona Lake, IN: Eisenbrauns, 2006)

of treaty or covenant language clearly was family language, by which the parties to the treaty expressed their relations in familial terms, father and son in vassal treaties, brothers in parity treaties. In these instances, treaties established relations between two monarchs who were unrelated in terms of family relations. The larger world of ruling monarchs could be understood as a large family or a series of families, where each king knew his place, either as overlord, equal or vassal. Family was, to use Mary Douglas' expression, a "natural symbol"[166] for expressing these sets of relations. This conceptual usage was not restricted to narrow family terms, but extended to other expressions at home in the family, such as the language of love and familiarity (or literally, "knowledge").

In this scholarly landscape, the familial language and its family settings hardly escaped notice. Scholars of covenants and treaties cited instances of individuals making covenants to establish ties across family lines. In this discussion biblical illustrations were offered as support. David makes a covenant with Abner (2 Samuel 3:12, 13; cf. 21). Rahab makes an alliance with Joshua's scouts via an oath by which they promise to do *ḥesed* to her in return for her help (Joshua 2:12–14).[167] A third case, the covenant between Jonathan and David (1 Samuel 18:3, 20:8, 23:18), often comes to mind in discussions of covenants. It might seem that some language in this case echoes old treaty forms used by kings. Moran notes the expression "to love PN as oneself" in both 1 Samuel 18:3 and in the oath of Assyrian vassals made to Esarhaddon.[168] From these examples, it is evident that such language was operative in various sorts of covenantal relationships, not only at the international level. These cases – and further examples could be brought to bear – indicate that covenantal procedures appear operative on various social levels. It is for this reason that covenant could be readily applied to marriage

---

341–50; Saul M. Olyan, "Honor, Shame, and Covenant Relations in Ancient Israel," *JBL* 115 (1996) 201–18; and S. David Sperling, *The Original Torah: The Political Intent of the Bible Writers* (New York/London: New York University, 1998) 61–74.

[166] Douglas, *Natural Symbols: Explorations in Cosmology* (New York: Pantheon, 1970).

[167] Note Moshe Weinfeld's point that BH *berit* is to be understood as an "obligation bound by oath." See Weinfeld, "*Berît* – Covenant vs. Obligation," *Biblica* 56 (1975) 120–28, esp. 123–25. The oath serves also as the mechanism for establishing the interpersonal covenant in Ruth 1:16–17 (this passage also uses expressions of shared resources as in international royal relations between kings in 1 Kings 22:4 and 2 Kings 3:7). For this point, see Tikva Frymer-Kensky, *Reading the Women of the Bible: A New Interpretation of Their Stories* (New York: Schocken, 2002) 241; and Mark S. Smith, " 'Your People Shall be My People': Family and Covenant in Ruth 1:16–17," *CBQ* 69 (2007) 242–58.

[168] Moran, "The Ancient Near Eastern Background of the Love of God in Deuteronomy," *CBQ* 25 (1963) 77–87, esp. 82 n. 33. See further Ada Taggar-Cohen, "Political Loyalty in the Biblical Account of 1 Samuel xx–xxii in the Light of Hittite Texts," *VT* 55 (2005) 251–68, esp. 258.

(cf. Malachi 2:14; Ezekiel 16:8; Proverbs 2:17).[169] Despite the recognition of such cases, it often escaped scholarly attention that covenant relations could take place at several levels of society and not only in the settings most conspicuous from newly-discovered texts, namely the international relations among royal courts. Covenant/treaty was a mechanism useful for family life to extend relations beyond the family or even to intensify relations within family life (e. g., Genesis 31:44–50).[170] Accordingly, royal treaties are to be seen as monarchic expressions of basic family and clan relations and not the other way around.

This shift in perspective emerged in a fresh way, in part thanks to remarks made by Frank M. Cross in his 1998 volume, *From Epic to Canon*. In an essay entitled "Kinship and Covenant in Ancient Israel," Cross formulated the basic point that covenant is fictive family relations: "Often it has been asserted that the language of 'brotherhood' and 'fatherhood,' 'love,' and 'loyalty' is 'covenant terminology'." In other words, the language of covenant, kinship-in-law, is taken from the language of kinship, kinship-in-flesh."[171] Cross called covenantal relations "kinship-in-law."[172] The implications of this insight had been recognized earlier, already in 1982, by Paul Kalluveettil in his book, *Declaration and Covenant*. A student of Dennis McCarthy, Kalluveettil points to a wide variety of non-royal examples of covenant language. Like Cross' essay, Kalluveettil's volume indicates that covenant is modeled on family and was operative in both non-royal and royal contexts in order to express relations between persons or parties who were otherwise unrelated to one another.[173] Kalluveettil accordingly characterizes covenant as "a fictious extension of kinship,"[174] functional at several levels of society. Kalluveettil concludes: "It is wrong then to tie it down to the political field."[175] It is not family bonds that are simply like international treaties or covenants. Rather, it is covenant/treaty, whether at the local level or on the international level, that is modelled on family in order to establish ties across family lines. Family also fits with the two other theoretical expressions for such relations, shared resources and oneness.

---

[169] Kalluveettil, *Declaration and Covenant*, 6. This usage has been thought to be relatively late. So Sperling (*The Original Torah*, 65–66) remarks: "There can be little doubt that post-exilic Hebrew broadened the semantic range *berît* to include the marriage relation, under the influence of the Akkadian *riksu/rikistu*. Like *berit*, Akkadian *riksu* means 'contract' but used from earliest time for a full range of contractual agreements, from marriage to international treaties."

[170] Kalluveettil, *Declaration and Covenant*, 8, 11–12. See below pp. 104–7.

[171] Cross, *From Epic to Canon*, 11.

[172] Cross, *From Epic to Canon*, 7, 13.

[173] Kalluveettil, *Declaration and Covenant*, 7–16.

[174] Kalluveettil, *Declaration and Covenant*, 205.

[175] Kalluveettil, *Declaration and Covenant*, 15.

Shared Resources and Oneness

Some Late Bronze letters express a notion of reciprocality or mutuality in the form of shared resources. These are less common by comparison with the family language, so for illustration, I would mention the same letter as one mentioned in the preceding discussion of family (RS 18.54 A): "As for me I have said: Everything of my house is yours and everything of your house is mine."[176] Accordingly, the international relations are expressed as a matter of resources shared, as one finds with family households.

Oneness is the last of our three theoretical expressions. Occasionally a letter communicates a notion of oneness of land. In the discussion of the Amarna letters in the preceding section, we noted the case of EA 19. Again, such expressions are not nearly as common as expressions of family terms, so we briefly note some further examples. Mursilis II of Hatti declares to Talmisharruma of Aleppo[177]: "May all of us together and our house be one."[178] An edict of the Hittite monarch Mursilis governing his relations with king of Niqmepa of Ugarit states: "For a long time, the king of Ugarit and the king of Siyannu were one."[179] Finally, a letter to the king of Ugarit, from his servant Parsu, says referring to the kingdoms of Amurru and Ugarit: "Amurru and Ugarit are one."[180] These expressions belong to the discourse of family expressions, like shared resources. The family, in this case international, is regarded as a single unit living on a single land-inheritance and sharing resources.

At the base of all of these expressions is the international family. This understanding works well with Assmann's characterization of such relations as *ecumene,* noted earlier in our discussion.[181] In all these expressions, what we see then is not translatability in any narrow sense. Instead, translatability is arguably a feature of international *ecumene.* The larger political setting of this sort of ecumenism is a function of empires, both in their relations with one another and in their relations with their vassals (and vice-versa). Thus the context is one of international imperium of monarchs supporting the scribe-theologians who construct this international religious worldview and who serve at their behest. Itamar Singer well remarks:

---

[176] Lines 17'–20', in: *PRU IV,* 228–29. For shared resources see p. 116 below and Pirke Abot 5:14.

[177] Ernst F. Weidner, *Politische Dokumente aus Kleinasien: Die Staatsverträge in akkadischer Sprache aus dem Archiv von Boghazköi* (Boghazköi Studien 8–9; Hildesheim/Zürich/New York: G. Olms, 1970 (= reprint of the 1923 ed.; Leipzig): 86–87, text 6, rev. lines 9–10.

[178] Kalluveettil, *Declaration and Covenant,* 102.

[179] RS 17.382 + 380, lines 3–4, in: *PRU IV,* 80.

[180] RS 20.162, lines 17–19, in: *Ugaritica V,* 115.

[181] Assmann, *Akhanyati's Theology of Light and Time,* [12] = 154.

"A basic knowledge of foreign pantheons was not just an intellectual asset of Hittite theologians, but rather an essential requirement for the Hittite 'Foreign Office'."[182]

In the texts that we have surveyed in this chapter, many of the basic terms used for cross-cultural communication about deities belonged already to the various societies across the ancient world of Western Asia and Egypt. The basic language of family, for example, was at home in the different polities of this region just as it was for their deities.[183] In addition, scribes took concepts at home in their own contexts and extended these across political lines in order to express in religious terms the bonds between two parties. Thus we might say that the language of intercultural discourse, in particular the family, arises from specific cultural discourses that were similar. As we saw with the Egyptian version of the treaty between Hattusili III and Ramesses II, these scribes sometimes went further in taking expressions of the international language and translating them into their own local idiom. Yet underlying such translations is the medium or setting of empire, specifically its rulers and their scribal functionaries. This sort of religious, political translation operated geographically across political units that were contemporaneous. For this reason, we might characterize this operation as "horizontal translatability," as opposed to or in tandem with "vertical translatability," which involved translation of divinity through time within a particular culture. (The significance of this distinction will emerge more clearly when we turn to the evidence for ancient Israel in Chapter Two.) Politics was not the only context for expressing translatability in the Late Bronze Age. While treaties and letters provided the mechanisms for inter-cultural discourse about deities, the period also attests to further expressions of translatability, in myths, ritual and prayer.

4. Myths, Ritual and Prayer

International political relations fostered wider inter-religious expressions in myths, prayer and ritual. In a number of the cases discussed in this section, translatability is accompanied by a number of additional features, such as religious influence and literary borrowings.

Myths

Several acts of translatability of divinity can be found in the Late Bronze instances of myths that literally were translated from one language to

---

[182] Singer, " 'The Thousand Gods of Hatti'," 93.

[183] For West Semitic material, see Smith, *The Origins of Biblical Monotheism*, 54–66.

another.[184] In such a case, the names of the deities involved are translated as well, though not always consistently. A good example is a Canaanite myth now attested only in Hittite, sometimes called "El, Ashertu and the Storm-god."[185] This myth survives only as a series of fragments belonging to a single tablet. What remains of the myth opens midcourse with a speech of the well-known West Semitic goddess Ashertu threatening the otherwise unspecified Storm-god. Angered by her words, the Storm-god goes for redress to the watery home of the West Semitic Elkunirsha. This god asks the Storm-god why he has come, and the Storm-god relates his experience at the hands of Ashertu. She had insisted on sleeping with him, but when he refused she threatened him, Elkunirsha responds by telling the Storm-god to sleep with her, though she is his wife. The narrative continues by relating that the Storm-god did so. Afterwards the Storm-god informs Ashertu that he slew her children: "Of your sons I slew 77, I slew 88." As a result, Ashertu initiates mourning for seven years. After a gap, the text seems to open with a speech by the goddess. In response, Elkunirsha tells his wife that he hands over the Storm-god to her to do with as she pleases. Then there appears a new figure named only by an ideogram ISHTAR (otherwise known as a famous Mesopotamian goddess of war and love). She overhears this conversation, thanks to her ability to be transformed into the very cup that Elkunirsha holds and into a bird that can roost on his wall. After Elkunirsha and Ashertu themselves sleep together, ISHTAR flies to the Storm-god to inform him of what she has heard. At this point in the narrative, the tablet breaks off.

The myth is thought to have been Canaanite (or more properly, West Semitic) because two of the divine names in the text correspond to deities known from the West Semitic texts. The first is Elkunirsha, which literally means El, creator of the earth.[186] This is El the creator god known from the Ugaritic texts and identified with biblical El Elyon,[187] called "creator of heaven and earth," known for example in Genesis 14:19, 22. The sec-

---

[184] See the observation on the mobility of myth made by Jan Bremmer, "Ritual," in: *Religions of the Ancient World: A Guide* (ed. Sarah Iles Johnston; Cambridge, MA/London: Belknap, 2004) 43.

[185] *ANET,* 519. See also the name as "Elkurnisha and Ashertu" given by Harry A. Hoffner, Jr., *Hittite Myths* (SBLWAW 2; Atlanta: Society of Biblical Literature, 1990) 69–70. See similarly Gary Beckman, in: *COS* 1.149. For details for this text, see Hoffner, "The Elkunirsa Myth Reconsidered," *RHA* 23/76 (1965) 5–16.

[186] On this divine title, see Patrick D. Miller, "El, Creator of Earth," *BASOR* 239 (1980) 43–46.

[187] See *ANET* 519 n. 1. On this divine title, the older classic study is G. L. della Vida, "'El 'Elion in Genesis xiv:18–20," *JBL* 63 (1944) 1–9. See also Rolf Rendtorff, "The Background of the Title אל עליון in Gen XIV," in: *Fourth World Congress of Jewish Studies: Papers. Volume I* (Jerusalem: World Union of Jewish Studies, 1967) 167–70.

ond is El's spouse, Ashertu, also known as Ugaritic Athirat and Hebrew Asherah.[188] Moreover, some of the motifs in the text correspond to those found in the Ugaritic Baal Cycle, such as the tent of Elkunirsha, the spindle of the goddess, the theme of the Storm-god's hostility toward the children of Ashertu, and the number of her divine children, given in typical West Semitic fashion for parallelism of numerals, 77//88 (compared with 70 in the Baal Cycle).[189] Thus all scholars who comment on this text agree on the Canaanite or at least West Semitic origin of this myth.

As a result of its translation into Hittite, two divine elements were translated from Canaanite or West Semitic into Hittite. Elkunirsha is no simple rendering of the god, El. As Gary Beckman notes, "the Hittite translator has misunderstood the Canaanite phrase, El, Creator of the Earth" as a simple divine name, which he has rendered as Elkunirša."[190] The term for the Storm-god is a generic term, [d]U with Hittite phonetic complements[191]; it is written not as the specific name of either the West Semitic storm-god, Baal (or Baal of Ugarit or Baal Saphon) or the Hittite storm-god (of which there are several).[192] Thus translatability in the case of this divine name takes the form of a generic rendering. The other divine element involves the goddess written as [d]ISHTAR. Given that Anat was a goddess of love and war who flies like a bird, many scholars have surmised that ISHTAR is a translation of the name of the goddess Anat.[193] These cases illustrate that some divine names translate literally in terms of their own West Semitic names, while others are provided with an interpretive lens that makes them more intelligible to the text's Hittite audience. In addition to the translation of specific myths from West Semitic culture to the north, there are several West Semitic myths (or mythemes) that likewise cross cultural boundaries to the south. At the outset of this chapter we noted the translation of deities from the Levant to Egypt in Wilson's account of translatability. This direction of translation also applies to the West Semitic motifs of the warrior-god's military conflict with the cosmic monster (often the Sea) and the desire of the cosmic Sea for the goddess.[194] In these cases, it is the relatively

---

[188] See *ANET* 519 n. 2.

[189] These are noted by Hoffner, "The Elkunirsa Myth Reconsidered," 5–16.

[190] Beckman, *COS* 1.149.

[191] Hoffner, "The Elkunirsa Myth Reconsidered," 6 n. 6. The raised "d" here ("dinger") is a special writing to denote divinity as the class to which the figure belongs.

[192] Because of the West Semitic background of the text, Hoffner and Beckman both render the name of the Storm-god as Baal. See Hoffner, *Hittite Myths,* 69–70; Beckman, *COS* 1.149.

[193] In view of the West Semitic background of the text, Hoffner renders the name of the goddess as Anat-Astarte. See Hoffner, *Hittite Myths,* 69–70. Beckman (*COS* 1.149) renders her name simply as "Astarte."

[194] As noted by Donald B. Redford, "The Sea and the Goddess," in: *Studies in Egyptology Presented to Miriam Lichtheim* (ed. Sarah Israelit-Groll; two vols.; Jerusalem:

less powerful Levantine vassal that supplied mythic features of interest to the empire powers of Hatti and Egypt.

The influence moved in the opposite direction as well, from the great powers to a lesser power. Ugaritic literature shows two cases of foreign influence, which were noted by the great master of Ugaritic studies, H. L. Ginsberg.[195] The first case, from Mesopotamia (perhaps mediated via Mitanni) to Ugarit, involves the mythic hymn of the Mesopotamian moon-goddess Nikkal wa-Ib (*KTU/CAT* 1.24), which relates her marriage to the West Semitic moon-god, Yarikh.[196] The marriage of the two deities suggests an implicit recognition of the category of moon-deities, one foreign and one indigenous to Ugarit.[197] Here, as in treaties and letters, the concept of family provides a means to make the fundamental cross-cultural connection between two parties, in this case two deities who were of comparable type in the eyes of the ancients.

The second case, from Egypt to Ugarit, appears in the Baal Cycle. One of the homes of Kothar wa-Hasis, the Ugaritic craftsman-god, is said to be Hikuptah, literally "the house of the soul (*ka*) of Ptah" (*KTU/CAT* 1.3 VI 15–16; cf. 1. 17 V 20–21).[198] Hikuptah, better known as Memphis, was so named because Ptah was the chief god of the city. As Ginsberg deduced,

---

Magnes, 1990) 2.824–35. See also Redford, *Egypt, Canaan, and Israel in Ancient Times,* 45–46, 232–35; and the older work of Stadelmann, *Syrisch-Palästinensische Gottheiten in Ägypten,* 125–33.

[195] See H. L. Ginsberg, "Two Religious Borrowings in Ugaritic Literature," *Orientalia* 8 (1939) 317–27.

[196] For text and translation, see *UNP* 215–18; and the detailed discussion of Gabriele Theuer, *Der Mondgott in den Religionen Syrien-Palästinas: Unter besonderer Berücksichtigung von KTU 1.24* (OBO 173; Fribourg: Universitätsverlag; Göttingen: Vandenhoeck & Ruprecht, 2000) 135–249. Nikkal wa-Ib is a double-name, which is quite common at Ugarit (cf. Kothar wa-Hasis). The first element of this double-name, Nikkal, literally means "great lady" (ultimately derived from Sumerian nin.gal) and the second, Ib, "fruit" (Akkadian *inbu*). The name Yarikh literally means "moon." For these deities in this text, see Steve A. Wiggins, "What's in a Name? Yariḫ at Ugarit," *UF* 30 (1998) 761–79. From a number of other features in the text, scholars have suggested that the foreign influence involved is specifically Hurrian.

[197] So Pardee, *Ritual and Cult at Ugarit,* 279. As noted below, this goddess also appears in ritual, in 1.41.26 and 1.106.14 (Pardee, *Ritual and Cult at Ugarit,* 54–55, 60, 62. See the following section.

[198] *UNP,* 59 and 119. Prior to Ginsberg, this identification had been made by G. Hoffmann, "Aramäische Inschriften aus Nêrab bei Aleppo. Neue und alte Götter," *Zeitschrift für Assyriologie* 11 (1896) 254. See also W. F. Albright, *Archaeology and the Religion of Israel* (Baltimore: Johns Hopkins University, 1942) 82, and *Yahweh and the Gods of Canaan* (Garden City, NY: Doubleday, 1968; repr., Winona Lake, IN: Eisenbrauns, nd) 137, 225; Theodor H. Gaster, *Thespis: Ritual, Myth and Drama in the Ancient Near East* (New York: H. Schuman, 1950) 156; K. Vine, "The Establishment of Baal at Ugarit" (Ph. D. dissertation, University of Michigan, 1965) 44–45; Michael David Coogan, *Stories from Ancient Canaan* (Philadelphia: Westminster, 1978) 118; Smith, "Kothar wa-Hasis, the Ugaritic Craftsman God," 41; Redford, *Egypt, Canaan, and Israel in Ancient Times,* 40.

this passage presupposes the identification between the Egyptian god, Ptah, and the Ugaritic god. The identification of Kothar with Ptah was based also on some similarity of divine functions: like Kothar, Ptah was associated with arts and crafts.[199] This sort of influence is hardly surprising in view of Egyptian hegemony over Ugarit for a good portion of its history, in particular during the reigns of Amenophis III and Amenophis IV (Akhenaten).[200] Moreover, Memphis was the site of an Asiatic quarter, with temples dedicated to Baal and Astarte.[201] This sort of identification in the Ugaritic material may draw in part on Memphis' reputation as an Egyptian-West Semitic "site of translatability." As noted above, Egyptian motifs, such as an invocation of "Amon and the gods of Egypt," appear in Ugaritic correspondence (*KTU/CAT* 2.23.21–22). Ugarit's material culture, for example in its iconography of deities, likewise reflects a wide array of cross-cultural influences.[202]

The interesting question about foreign influence in Ugaritic literature is why there are not more cases of clear Egyptian, Hittite or Mesopotamian textual translatability, given the notable foreign influence at Ras Shamra,

---

[199] See Jacobus van Dijk, "Ptah," in: *OEAE* 3.74–76, with relevant studies, including the older book by Maj Sandman Holmberg, *The God Ptah* (Lund: C. W. K. Gleerup, 1946).

[200] For the history of relations between Egypt and Ugarit, see the fine survey of Itamar Singer, "A Political History of Ugarit," in: *Handbook of Ugaritic Studies* (ed. W. G. E. Watson and N. Wyatt; Handbuch der Orientalistik 39; Leiden/Boston, 1999) 603–733, esp. 622–27.

[201] See Redford, *Egypt, Canaan, and Israel in Ancient Times* (Princeton, NJ: Princeton University, 1992) 228; and Hulin, "The Worshippers of Asiatic Gods in Egypt," 274.

[202] Various foreign influences on the iconography of deities at Ugarit have been noted. For example, Izak Cornelius mentions the "mixture of Hittite, Egyptian and local traditions" on the Louvre Baal stela (*ANEP* #490). See Cornelius, "The Iconography of Ugarit," in: *Handbook of Ugaritic Studies* (ed. W. G. E. Watson and N. Wyatt; Handbuch der Orientalistik 39; Leiden/Boston, 1999) 589. Another Baal stela (*ANEP* #485) is compared by Cornelius ("The Iconography of Ugarit," 589) with the iconography of Egyptianized Baal (Seth) with a *was*-scepter (but no horns). The depiction of a female figure (usually considered a goddess) flanked by goats, carved on the lid of an ivory round box from Minet el-Bheida (*ANEP* #464), shows Aegean influence (*ANEP* 303, #464). On this piece, see Helene Kantor, "The Aegean and the Orient in the Second Millennium B.C.," *AJA* 51 (1947) 86–89, plate 22. For a broader consideration of this influence, see John F. Healey, "Between the Aegean and the Near East – Ugarit as Point of Contact," in: *'Schnittpunkt' Ugarit* (ed. Manfred Kropp and Andreas Wagner; Nordostafrikanisch-westasiatische Studien 2; Frankfurt am Main et al.: Lang, 1999) 47–57. In the same volume, note also the useful survey of foreign influences at Ugarit by Dagmar Stockfisch, "Ugarit – 'Internationale' Handelsmetropole im Schnittpunkt des vorderasiatisch-ostmediterranen Verkehrsnetzes," 255–70.

whether in the scribal curriculum[203] or even in cult.[204] Translatability did move in two directions, from the greater powers to the lesser and from the lesser powers to the greater powers.[205] Yet interestingly, it is the latter that is better attested. We may illustrate this direction of influence further through some broader literary comparisons of Ugarit, Hatti and Mesopotamia. The tradition of narrative poetry to which the Ugaritic corpus was heir was considerably older than the present Late Bronze Age forms of the Ugaritic texts (ca. 1400–1180). This has been detected through detailed literary comparisons. For example, Moran compared the type-scene of counting months of pregnancy found in the Old Babylonian (Middle Bronze) text of Atrahasis, the Hittite Kumarbi myth and the Ugaritic story of Aqhat (*KTU/CAT* 1.17 II).[206] Based on his study of the type-scene in these three texts, Moran referred to "the west epic tradition." Similarly, Simon Parker regarded the conflict between the warrior-goddess and the human hero in Gilgamesh VI and 1.17 VI as pointing to "a common tradition."[207] Parker also viewed these sorts of parallels across languages as indicative of "traditional oral sources."[208] On the basis of triangulation of sources, Frank H. Polak has offered a similar view. He traces the type-phrase, "to lift up the eyes and look," in Old Babylonian Gilgamesh, Hittite and Ugaritic literary contexts. On the basis of this shared feature across languages, he would posit a shared literary tradition in mythic, epic poetry in the west that goes back to the Old Babylonian period (Middle Bronze Age).[209] In this connection, we may note the older argument of Thorkild Jacobsen that the basic theme of the

---

[203] The cases are few in number. In addition to the cases adduced above, Arnaud, *Corpus des textes de bibliothèque de Ras Shamra – Ougarit (1936–2000),* 201–2, notes the Akkadian text, RS 94.2953 as reflecting the window episode in the Ugaritic Baal Cycle.

[204] In this connection, we might note the different gentilics, including the Hurrian and the Hittite mentioned in the ritual text, *KTU/CAT* 1.40 = RS 1.002. For a convenient text and translation, see Pardee, *Ritual and Cult at Ugarit,* 80, 82–83 (Pardee's Sections V and VI).

[205] See the comments made in this vein by Wilfred G. Lambert, "Interchange of Ideas between Southern Mesopotamia and Syria-Palestine as seen in Literature," in: *Mesopotamien und seine Nachbarn* (ed. H.J. Nissen and J. Renger; Berlin: D. Reimer, 1987) 311–16.

[206] Moran, *The Most Magic Word* (ed. Ronald S. Hendel; CBQMS 35; Washington, DC: The Catholic Biblical Association of America, 2002) 51–52. On this case, see also Parker, *The Pre-Biblical Narrative Tradition* (SBLRBS 24; Atlanta: Scholars, 1989) 103–5. For further examples and discussion of such parallel material in this vein, see Parker, *The Pre-Biblical Narrative Tradition,* 26, 45, 54, 113–17, 140, 220.

[207] Parker, *The Pre-Biblical Narrative Tradition,* 114.

[208] Parker, *The Pre-Biblical Narrative Tradition,* 220.

[209] Polak, "Linguistic and Stylistic Aspects of Epic Formulae in Ancient Semitic Poetry and Biblical Narrative," in: *Biblical Hebrew in its Northwest Semitic Setting* (ed. Steven E. Fassberg and Avi Hurvitz; Jerusalem: Magnes, 2006) 285–304, esp. 287–88. Elsewhere (p. 298) Polak refers to "Northwest Semitic epic poetry."

conflict of the divine hero against the cosmic enemy found in the Mesopotamian classic, Enuma Elish (sometimes called the "Epic of Creation"),
was borrowed from the Levant.[210] This drift from old West Semitic sources
to Mesopotamian culture also appears with the incorporation of the West
Semitic figure of Ddn/Dtn in the genealogy of the Old Babylonian dynasty,
which in turn was incorporated into the Assyrian King List A.[211]

In these cases, the literary features go back to languages that intersect in
northwest Syria in the Middle and Late Bronze Ages. The regional West
Semitic tradition to which Ugarit was heir proved to be a literary source
of some importance for composition in the empire states of Mesopotamia
and Hatti. At the same time, despite its political stature in relation to these
great powers, the city-state of Ugarit managed to generate its own literary
identity over and against the larger Mesopotamian curriculum, which had
penetrated the scribal curriculum at Ugarit. This literary situation was part
and parcel of Ugarit's maintenance of its own local cultural tradition in the
larger context of empire powers to which it was heavily subject. Ugarit
used its local textual traditions in order to maintain its identity in the face of
empire culture.[212] In the case of Ugarit, translatability, or better its relative
lack, played a role in its political and cultural situation.[213]

Ritual and Prayer

Like other genres, ritual is hardly immune from translatability. Ritual texts
mention deities of other lands,[214] but in some of these cases translatability
of the local Ugaritic deity with a foreign divine counterpart is evident. The
Ugaritic parallel ritual-texts, *KTU/CAT* 1.41.25–26//1.87.28–29, list Yarikh
before the Mesopotamian moon-goddess, Nikkal.[215] In the preceding section we noted how the Ugaritic myth *KTU/CAT* 1.24 could connect in narrative terms the Mesopotamian moon-goddess with the Ugaritic moon-god;

---

[210] Jacobsen, "The Battle between Marduk and Tiamat," *JAOS* 88 (1968) 104–8. See
the discussion and further defense of this view in my book, *The Ugaritic Baal Cycle: Volume 1. Introduction with Text, Translation and Commentary of KTU 1.1–1.2* (VTSup 55;
Leiden: Brill, 1994) 108–14. See Chapter Three for further discussion of Enuma Elish.

[211] For documentation and discussion, see Smith, *The Ugaritic Baal Cycle,* 113–14.

[212] See Seth Sanders, "What Was the Alphabet For? The Rise of Written Vernaculars and
the Making of Israelite National Literature," *Maarav* 11/1 (2004) 25–56. See also the comments by William S. Morrow, "Cuneiform Literacy and Deuteronomic Composition,"
Bibliotheca Orientalis 62 (2005) 207–8; and Carole Roche, "Introduction à la civilization
d'Ougarit" in: *La Bible et l'héritage d'Ougarit* (ed. Jean-Marc Michaud; Proche-Orient et
Littérature Ougaritique; Sherbrooke, Canada: Editions GGC, 2005) 39–40.

[213] On this point, Ugarit offers an interesting study in contrast with Israel. Following
Sanders' lead ("What Was the Alphabet For?"), we will address this question in Chapter
Three.

[214] See also Nikkal in 1.106.14 (Pardee, *Ritual and Cult at Ugarit,* 54–55).

[215] Pardee, *Ritual and Cult at Ugarit,* 60, 62.

so too the ritual texts link the two moon deities. Ugaritic rituals also refer to Yarikh (*KTU/CAT* 1.39.14; 1.102.4; see also 1.123.6) in the same lists with "Kassite Yarikh" (assuming the word is to be understood in this manner),[216] in other words the Kassite moon-god (*KTU/CAT* 1.39.19; 1.102.14; see also 1.123.7). These ritual listings seem to recognize implicitly that this Kassite deity was a moon-deity analogous enough to Ugarit's own such that it would label it as "Kassite." Thus within these lists, there is a recognition of the indigenous moon-god of Ugarit, along with the foreign moon-deities. Comparable translatability may be seen also for Baal of Aleppo listed after Baal of Ugarit in RS 24.284.23–24 = *KTU/CAT* 1.130.10–11,[217] or for Baal of Aleppo listed before Baal of Sapan in 1.148.26–27 (cf. 4.728.2–3). The gods of the land of Aleppo have been reconstructed for the offerings-text, *KTU/CAT* 1.148.42–43.[218] Thus some translatability is evident in ritual and cult at Ugarit.[219]

When we move out to other types of texts such as prayer, we meet a range of notions that extend beyond a basic sense of translatability. One case that illustrates the breadth of intercultural discourse comes from Hatti. In a prayer of the prominent Hittite queen Puduhepa (consort of Hattusili[220]), she addresses the Sun-goddess of Arinna:

---

[216] So Gregorio del Olmo Lete and Joaquín Sanmartín, *A Dictionary of the Ugaritic Language in the Alphabetic Tradition: Part One ['(a/i/u)-k]* (Handbuch der Orientalistik I/67; Leiden/Boston: Brill, 2003) 473; Pardee, *Ritual and Cult at Ugarit*, 21. For a different view of the phrase as meaning "Neumond" ("new moon"), see Theuer, *Der Mondgott in den Religionen Syrien-Palästinas*, 33 n. 70, 44, 79 n. 310, 88, 97, 282, 294. The interpretation is based on a presumed contrast with *yrḫ wks'a* as the "full moon," which precedes in 1.123.6–7. Theuer (pp. 121 n. 145, 294 n. 71, 313 n. 29) also suggests an association of this "new moon" god with Shaggar, an old moon-deity (see Karel van der Toorn, "Sheger," *DDD* 761). An etymology for *kty* as "new moon" is not provided by Theuer (cf. *Der Mondgott*, 44–45 n. 126), and the word is otherwise unattested in this meaning in Ugaritic, in contrast with "Kassite" (see del Olmo Lete and Sanmartín, *A Dictionary of the Ugaritic Language in the Alphabetic Tradition*, 473).

[217] See Pardee, *Ritual and Cult at Ugarit*, 32–33.

[218] Pardee, *Ritual and Cult at Ugarit*, 18, 47, 49. These gods are attested in the parallel listing in RS 92.2004.18, as noted by Pardee.

[219] Note also the Hurrian-Ugaritic sacrificial text, 1.110, which lists Hurrian deities along with El and Anat (see also 1.111). The Hurrian god, Thalannni, appears in this text as well as three times in the Ugaritic ritual text, 1.132.4, 18 and 22 (Pardee, *Ritual and Cult at Ugarit*, 97–98). See also the range of deities and places mentioned in 1.100 as well as 1.108.2–3. See also Astarte and Hurrian Tha'uthka in 1.116.

[220] For this queen (also daughter of a priest), see Johan de Roos, "Materials for a Biography: The Correspondence of Puduḫepa with Egypt and Ugarit," in: *The Life and Times of Ḫattušili III and Tutḫaliya IV: Proceedings of a Symposium in Honour of J. De Roos, 12–13 December, 20003, Leiden* (ed. Theo P. J. van den Hout, with the assistance of C. H. van Zoest; Leiden: Nederlands Instituut voor het Nabije Oosten, 2006) 17–26. See also Theo P. J. van den Hout, "Khattushili III, King of the Hittites," in: *CANE* 2.1107–12; and Cem Kerasu, "Some Observations on the Women in the Hittite Texts," in: *Anatolia*

"O Sun-goddess of Arinna, queen of all countries! In the Hatti country you bear the name of the Sun-goddess of Arinna; but in the land which you made the cedar land you bear the name Hebat."[221]

Alfonso Archi notes that the two goddesses were the most important female deities of their respective Hittite and west Hurrian pantheons.[222] At first glance, this utterance might seem to operate with the assumption of god-lists found at Ugarit. However, a closer look would suggest that in addressing the goddess as the Sun-goddess of Arinna, this particular figure is the underlying reality for both the Sun-goddess of Arinna in Hatti and Hebat in the Levant. The expression of translation here is more profoundly an expression of religious imperialism: the goddess thought in the Levant to be Hebat is in fact actually the Sun-goddess of Arinna. Earlier in this chapter I mentioned the possible problem of anachronism in using the term ecumenism for discourse of translatability. Yet in some respects, the type of expression found in the prayer of Puduhepa or in Anzu[223] anticipates some modern religious discourse influenced by theological ecumenism that has been accused of its own theological imperialism.[224]

Translatability of divinity in the Late Bronze is particularly marked in treaties and letters, yet it also makes some appearances in literature, prayer and ritual. These instances are indications of translatability's pervasiveness in the Late Bronze Age not only in cross-cultural discourse, but also in expressions of inner-cultural communal life (e.g., ritual at Ugarit). From a geographical perspective, translatability transpires over long distances through international treaties and correspondence. It also took place in closer quarters, through intercultural contact in polities that allowed for a

---

Antica: Studi in memoria di Fiorella Imparati (ed. Stefano de Martino and Franca Pecchioli Daddi; Eothen 11; Florence: LoGisma, 2002) 419–24, esp. 420–21.

[221] KUB 21.27(+) I 3–6. See *ANET* 393; Singer, "The Thousand Gods of Hatti," 90.

[222] Archi, "Hurrian Gods and the Festivals of the Hattian-Hittite Layer," 148.

[223] This sort of expression appears in the praise at the end of Standard Babylonian version of Anzu, tablet III, lines 131 f.: "In Elam they gave (you) your name Hurabtil, In Susa they speak of you as Inshushinak …". Benjamin R. Foster, *Before the Muses: An Anthology of Akkadian Literature* (third ed.; Bethesda, MD: CDL, 2005) 576. Compare also the Neo-Assyrian hymn to Nanaya, in: Erica Reiner, "A Sumero-Akkadian Hymn of Nanâ," *JNES* 33 (1974) 221–36; and Brigitte Groneberg, "Aspekte der 'Göttlichkeit" in: Mesopotamien: Zur Klassifizierung von Göttern und Zwischenwesen," in: *Götterbilder – Gottesbilder – Weltbilder. Polytheismus und Monotheismus in der Welt der Antike. Band I: Ägypten, Mesopotamien, Persien, Kleinasien, Syrien, Palästina* (ed. Reinhard G. Kratz and Hermann Spieckermann; FAT 2/17; Tübingen: Mohr Siebeck, 2006) 140–41. We will return to the Neo-Assyrian context in Chapter Three.

[224] For example, Karl Rahner's notion of non-Christians as potentially being "anonymous Christians." See Rahner's essay, "Christianity and the non-Christian Religions," in: *Theological Investigations, Volume 5* (Baltimore: Helicon Press, 1966) 115–34 (reference courtesy of Millie Feske). Rahner's piece is based on a lecture delivered on April 28, 1961.

substantial foreign presence (e. g., Memphis and Ugarit) and in zones where different cultures met (e. g., Serabit el-Khadem). The story of translatability takes a dramatic turn as we move into the Iron Age where translatability in the Levant was largely a local matter. Chapter Two offers an account of regional translatability during the period of the Israelite monarchy.

Chapter Two

Translatability and National Gods in Ancient Israel

Do you not possess what Chemosh
your god made you possess?
So we will possess what Yahweh our god
has caused us to possess.
Judges 11:24

1. Claims for the Absence of Biblical Translatability

Between the Bronze Age context, discussed in Chapter One, and the Greco-Roman situation, which we will examine in Chapters Five and Six, is Iron Age Israel. Israel in the Iron I period was a small tribal society based in the central and northern highlands. In the Iron II period, following the reign of Solomon, Israel refers to the northern tribal kingdom while Judah refers to the southern kingdom. (For the sake of convenience, Israel is often used for both the northern and southern kingdoms.) Israel's religious situation differs from the rest of the ancient Near East and Egypt, according to Jan Assmann. While translatability was a common feature of the ancient Near East, Israel introduced what Assmann calls "the Mosaic distinction,"[1] namely a rejection of translatability for Israel's God with other deities.

Assmann did not work out this "distinction" in historical or cultural terms for ancient Israel. Assmann poses "Mosaic distinction" not so much in historical terms as in conceptual categories; his treatment largely passes over historical questions.[2] He cites some biblical texts (e.g., Jeremiah 10; Isaiah 44; Psalm 115, as well as the book of Deuteronomy more broadly)

---

[1] Assmann, *Moses the Egyptian: The Memory of Egypt in Western Monotheism* (Cambridge, MA: Harvard University, 1997) 1–15.

[2] A writer with a somewhat comparable take on the biblical situation, though with even less concern for historical and cultural context, is Yaakov Malkin, in: *His God and Other Literary Characters,* posted at www.culturaljudaism.org/ccj/articles. A selection, "Part II: God and Moses. Chapter II," is published in: *Contemplate: The International Journal of Cultural Jewish Thought* 3 (2005–2006) 27–34. Malkin takes the biblical narrative at face value, in particular Moses' lawgiving as the original moment of Israel's religious identity. His characterization of Israelite religion as Mosaic religion in opposition to all other religions is rather consonant with Assmann's approach. And like Assmann, Malkin blames intolerance on monotheism itself.

as representative of "the Mosaic distinction,"[3] yet all of the texts date from the sixth century or later. If biblical data matter for Assmann's view, then the "Mosaic distinction," especially with the intolerant edge that he gives it, would be a minority report at best. Moreover, his account does not address either the evidence for translatability or the historical or cultural situation in Israel prior to these texts. As a result, there is no discussion of translatability or "the Mosaic distinction" in Israel prior to these texts nor is there any consideration of the shift represented by these texts.

The situation changes as we move into discussions by biblical scholars. Assmann's "Mosaic distinction" is presented in a favorable manner by Ronald S. Hendel in his work, *Remembering Abraham*.[4] In the opening of this book, Hendel takes his point of departure from Assmann based on Numbers 23:9: "Behold, it is a people dwelling apart, not counting itself among the nations."[5] Hendel offers his basic thesis: "Israel was a nation and a culture of the ancient Near East, yet it saw itself as different and somehow incommensurate with the other nations."[6] Hendel follows this proposition by noting that Israel's sense of uniqueness was hardly unique for the ancient world. Then Hendel offers a further comment, connected to the post-biblical development of the Jewish people:

But, on another level, the ancient Israelite claim to uniqueness was more forceful than most peoples' and more central to its self-definition. Indeed, it is arguable that this claim to uniqueness was in some measure self-fulfilling, enabling the Jewish people to outlive all the other cultures of the ancient Near East. By persisting in its claim to uniqueness, and by routinizing this claim in its religious and cultural habits, the Jewish people made that uniqueness a historical reality. The fact of its being alone today, roughly three millennia later, seems to ratify Balaam's perception that this is a people apart.[7]

Hendel casts the situation of early Israel in terms of a lack of translatability. He notes Assmann's observations about translatability, in particular the adoption and equation of foreign deities with one's own in Egypt as well as the standard formulas of treaties calling on various deities of both parties as witnesses:

Although the names, languages, and local practices might differ, there was a consciousness of a basic cultural translatability in the ancient Near East. Ancient Israel seems to have been the exception to the rule. Israelite writings from the earliest

---

[3] Assmann, *Die Mosaische Unterscheidung: Oder der Preis des Monotheismus* (München/Wien: C. Hanser, 2003) 39–47.

[4] Hendel, *Remembering Abraham: Culture, Memory, and History in the Hebrew Bible* (Oxford/New York: Oxford University, 2005) 4.

[5] Hendel, *Remembering Abraham*, 4–5, 124 nn. 5–6.

[6] Translation as it appears in: Hendel, *Remembering Abraham*, 4.

[7] Hendel, *Remembering Abraham*, 4.

period repeatedly sound the theme of non-translatability, of the birth of something new and different.[8]

Before assessing Hendel's view, we may note that his sense of culture in general and of ancient Israel's in particular is sophisticated, especially in noting its shared cultural heritage with the predecessor culture of the Levant. Hendel's case for a lack of translatability is not to be associated with earlier scholars who appear to have operated with an *a priori* assumption that Israelite cultural features essentially differ from the preceding and contemporary Iron Age I culture.[9] Indeed, Hendel himself notes the implications of putting the speech in the mouth of Balaam, a non-Israelite figure known from extra-biblical inscriptional material. He notes that "the fame of Balaam in West Semitic traditions show that Israelite traditions were not unique, that is, they shared a common root and perspective with Israel's neighbors. The voice of Balaam subtly proclaims that Israel was not wholly a nation apart."[10]

Numbers 23:9 as Evidence against Translatability?

Before further discussing Hendel's view, it is to be noted that his discussion of Numbers 23:9 as evidence against translatability is not put forward as a major argument of his book, but serves as its "theme," as he calls it.[11] It sounds the book's opening note about Israel and its culture. It is arguably a rhetorical turn. As such, it is not presented as a sustained discussion of the question of translatability.[12] At the same time, given Hendel's stature in the field, readers may take his position as a historically valid view about early Israel and its general lack of translatability. Thus, it seems necessary to address Hendel's position. We may begin with his use of Numbers 23:9: "A people dwelling apart, not counting itself among the nations."

On a variety of grounds, it is debatable whether the text of Numbers 23:9 constitutes an adequate base of evidence against translatability early Israel. First, there is the matter of its date. Hendel relies on old grammatical

---

[8] Hendel, *Remembering Abraham*, 5.

[9] Hendel's view is arguably not too distant from that of Ziony Zevit; see M. S. Smith, "Review Article of *The Religions of Ancient Israel: A Synthesis of Parallactic Approaches* (Ziony Zevit)," *Maarav* 11/2 (2004) 145–218, esp. 153, 212–18. See further the final footnote to that essay.

[10] Hendel, *Remembering Abraham*, 5.

[11] Hendel, *Remembering Abraham*, 4.

[12] This is clear from a helpful e-mail that Hendel sent to me on 19 May 2006. In it he suggested possible instances of translatability for ancient Israel. Had Hendel wished to provide a more sustained account of translatability, it might have involved the very cases treated in this chapter.

features in the poem to argue for a very early date.[13] In recent years, dating of biblical poems based on grammatical features has been criticized.[14] While scholars may point to old grammatical features in a number of poems, such a procedure hardly guarantees the high antiquity of any given composition, as other factors may be involved as well (regional variation or poetic diction among others). Contrary to Hendel's early dating, Baruch A. Levine had made a case for the early ninth century for Numbers 23:7–10. Levine comments how "the biblical Balaam poems celebrate Israelite power in Moab during the reign of Omri and his successors before the middle of the ninth century B.C.E."[15] While some material in the poems may be traditional and predate Omri's reign, this hardly requires a thirteenth or twelfth century milieu. Second, there is the question of whether the verse would be representative of early Israel even if it were as early as Hendel posits. A single verse arguably does not appear to constitute an adequate base for generalizing about earliest Israel. Instead, a single attestation may simply represent one particular view of the matter. Third and finally, there remains the more basic question as to whether the verse is truly expressive of non-translatability.

With regard to this third point, Levine explores a number of possibilities about the meaning of this verse, but none of them approximates Hendel's view. Two different views in particular deserve notice. According to Stanley Gevirtz, the verse concerns Israel's safety: "The meaning of these words, as recognized by most commentators who point for confirmation to Jer. 49:31, is that the people, Israel, is safeguarded from harm – it is invulner-

---

[13] Hendel's view of the poem's antiquity as well as a discussion of using the verse for Israel's sense of difference may be found in a broad manner in: Peter Machinist, "The Question of Distinctiveness in Ancient Israel: An Essay," in: *Ah, Assyria …: Studies in Assyrian History and Ancient Near Eastern Historiography Presented to Hayim Tadmor* (ed. M. Cogan and I. Eph'al; Scripta Hierosolymitana 33; Jerusalem: Magnes, 1991) 204, 207. To be clear, Machinist cites favorably the approach taken by Abraham Malamat cited below.

[14] See the cautions of Ian Young, "Biblical Texts Cannot Be Dated Linguistically," *Hebrew Studies* 46 (2005) 341–51, esp. 342–43. One need not be as pessimistic as Young, but his points as they apply to the so-called old poetry need to be addressed. He claims for example that feminine singular final -*â* would be -*ati* in any text prior to 1000, and that none of the so-called old poems show such a form. To the contrary, the form is attested. See *zimrat* in Exodus 15:2 (reused in Psalm 118:14 and Isaiah 12:2). Note also the apparently double feminine *'emata* in 15:16 (the form otherwise being *'ema*); and *ḥokmôt* in Judges 5:29 (see H.L. Ginsberg, "Ugaritico-Phoenicia," *Journal of the Ancient Near East Society* 5 [1973 = The Gaster Festschrift] 134 n. 19). In both poems, there are a few cases of feminine singular nouns ending in -*â*, but these could be the result of grammatical updating such as seen in Psalm 18 = 2 Samuel 22 (see below). Young does not mention this possibility in this context, but he does elsewhere, e.g., in: Ziony Zevit, "Symposium Discussion Session: An Edited Transcription," *Hebrew Studies* 46 (2006) 375.

[15] Levine, *Numbers 21–36: A New Translation with Introduction and Commentary* (AB 4A; New York: Doubleday, 2000) 232.

able."[16] Bolstering his claim, Gevirtz points further to the parallelism of *bdd*, "alone," with *bṭḥ*, "secure," in Deuteronomy 33:28. Gevirtz concludes the following from the parallel: "Balaam finds the people of Israel to be safe and secure – invulnerable to harm."[17] Abraham Malamat offers a somewhat different view based on what he sees as a valuable parallel to Numbers 23:9 in the Mari correspondence. Malamat suggests that the biblical verse expresses Israel's self-reliance, an ability to flourish without allies.[18] With the proposals of both Gevirtz and Malamat, Balaam's declaration would express Israel's security or independence, not its basic lack of religious translatability. Thus Hendel's interpretation of Numbers 23:9 with specific reference to translatability is open to question.

Even if one were inclined to follow Hendel's approach to the verse, it could refer to some sort of cultural self-perception that Israel has settled in some sense apart from other nations.[19] However, this need not indicate Hendel's view of the lack of translatability for early Israel. Thus one might agree with Hendel that the verse may suggest – at least for the tradition that produced the verse – early Israel's memory of itself as culturally and socially distinctive from other groups. However, it must be recognized that Hendel is arguing for considerably more, namely for a lack of translatability of divinity. Indeed, early Israel's sense of itself as a cultural entity is not expressed in terms of translatability or its lack, at least not in texts considered to be old.[20]

---

[16] Gevirtz, *Patterns in the Early Poetry of Israel* (Studies in Ancient Oriental Civilization 32; Chicago: University of Chicago, 1963) 58, 60–61.

[17] Gevirtz, *Patterns in the Early Poetry of Israel*, 61.

[18] Malamat, *Mari and the Bible* (Studies in CHANE XII; Leiden/Boston/Köln, 1998) 216–18. The parallel proposed by Malamat is a report of Itur-Asdu to Zimri-Lim: "There is no kinglet who is strong by himself" (Malamat's translation; see William L. Moran, *ANET* 628: "There is no king [*šarru*] who is strong just by himself"). Malamat sees in this message a characterization opposite to Balaam's characterization of Israel in Numbers 23:9.

[19] Cf. Leviticus 13:46 on the matter of someone considered impure from a skin affliction: "he shall dwell apart (*badad yešeb;* outside the camp will be his dwelling." (Note the "bicolon" structure here; with its double-use of *yšb, it approximates poetic parallelism.)

[20] Judges 5:8 has been accepted (sometimes without comment) as old evidence for Israel's sense of "new gods" as not their own (cf. "other gods"). For example, see Robert P. Gordon, "Introducing the God of Israel," in: *The God of Israel* (ed. Robert P. Gordon; University of Cambridge Oriental Publications 64; Cambridge, UK: Cambridge University, 2007) 4–5. The usual translation for Judges 5:8 ("he chose new gods"), has been supported by Kevin J. Cathcart: "the verse conveys that the subsequent warring and weaponlessness of Israel were the result of their choosing gods other than YHWH." See Cathcart, "the 'Demons' in Judges 5:8a," *Biblische Notizen* 21 (1977) 111–12; see also Michael David Coogan, "A Structural and Literary Analysis of the Song of Deborah," *CBQ* 40 (1978) 147. However, this sort of explanation does not fit the context of the verse, which concerns leadership. It is arguable that this sort of modern interpretation fills a textual gap with the sort of deuteronomistic historiography found in the book of Judges.

What translatability of divinity involves is the recognition of others' divinity across (and even despite) cultural boundaries. It is unclear that this verse expresses such a view of non-translatability of divinity for earliest Israel.

The Balaam poems in Numbers 23–24 have in fact been read in a manner that runs counter to Hendel's discussion. For some commentators, the use of multiple divine titles in the Balaam poems suggests an independent tradition of El in addition to Yahweh. Thus Levine notes: "we may conclude that Deuteronomy 32 … must surely have been composed after El was synthesized with YHWH. The Balaam poems [in Numbers 23–24], in contrast, were composed before this synthesis took place, so that they portray El, Elyon and Shadday as independent beings."[21] Thus contrary to the view espoused by Hendel, such figures have been brought together with the figure of Yahweh, arguably implying an early form of translatability between El and Yahweh. A fair reading of the very difficult evidence would suggest that Yahweh was a god secondarily imported into the highlands of Israel from the south (Edom/Paran/Teiman/Seir in Deuteronomy 33:2, Judges 5:4, Psalm 68:8, 18, and Habakkuk 3:3, 7)[22] and that he was identified secondarily at some point

---

Manfred Görg comments: "Die inkriminierte 'Erwählung neuer Götter' erinnert an dtn Sprache, verrät also den beginnenden Monotheismus." Manfred Görg, *Richter* (Die Neue Echter-Bibel: Kommentar zum Alten Testament mit Einheitsübersetzung 31; Würzburg: Echter, 1993) 32.

  Other commentators have sought to read *'elohim* with the immediate context in view. W. Nowack took the word *'elohim* as "Richter." See Nowack, *Richter-Ruth* (Handkommentar zum Alten Testament I/4; Göttingen: Vandenhoeck & Ruprecht, 1900) 45. With the context of leadership in view, Frank M. Cross reads instead, "they chose new leaders." According to Cross, "leaders" was later reread as "gods" (*'lwhym*), a secondary interpretation facilitated by the similar spellings in Hebrew for "chiefs" (*'lym/'ylm*) and "gods" (*'lym*). See Cross, *Canaanite Myth and Hebrew Epic: Essays in the History of the Religion of Israel* (Cambridge, MA/London: Harvard University, 1973) 122–23 n. 34. For *'elim* as a term for leadership, see Exodus 15:15 (see also Job 41:17; Ezekiel 17:13, 32:21). One may ask in addition whether *'elohim* in Judges 5:8 might reflect a rhetorical use for leaders (cf. *'elohim* in Psalm 45:7a applied to the king, not God). In any case, human figures appear to be involved in accordance with the context. It may be that the later interpretation of Judges 5:8 was informed by a verse that addresses the problem of other gods, namely Deuteronomy 32:17, which is hardly pre-monarchic. The discussion returns to this point below, in addressing the conceptual shift marked by Deuteronomy 32:17 in its historiography about other deities.

  [21] Levine, *Numbers 21–36,* 229. For El in early Israelite religion, see also the recent treatment of R. Scott Chalmers, "Who is the Real El? A Reconstruction of the Prophet's Polemic in Hosea 12:5a," *CBQ* 68 (2006) 611–30.

  [22] For discussions of the southern tradition for Yahweh, see Cross, *Canaanite Myth and Hebrew Epic,* 100–2; L.E. Axelsson, *The Lord Rose up from Seir* (Coniectanea Biblica Old Testament Series 25; Lund: Gleerup, 1987); John Day, *Yahweh and the Gods and Goddesses of Canaan* (JSOTSup 265; Sheffield: Sheffield Academic Press, 2000) 15–16; André Lemaire, *The Birth of Monotheism: The Rise and Disappearance of Yahwism* (Washington, DC: Biblical Archaeology Society, 2007) 21–23; and Mark S. Smith, *The Early History of God: Yahweh and the Other Deities in Ancient Israel* (sec. ed.; Grand Rapids, MI/Cambridge, UK: Eerdmans; Dearborn, MI: Dove, 2002) 25,

with the indigenous Canaanite and early Israelite god El.[23] (This would be reflected in later texts that reflect an older distinction between the two gods,

32–33, and 81. For a recent discussion of the literary context for the poetic passages, see Henrik Pfeiffer, *Jahwes Kommen von Süden: Jdc 5; Hab 3; Dtn 33 und Ps 68 in ihrem literatur- und theologiegeschichtlichen Umfeld* (FRLANT 211; Göttingen: Vandenhoeck & Ruprecht, 2005).

In support of an early southern backward for Yahweh in these passages, scholars have drawn attention to an Egyptian list of lands dating to Amenophis (and Ramesses II) that includes "the land of the Shasu, Yhw3" and "land of the Shasu, S'rr." The first has often been conjectured to be a reference to a place named after the god Yahweh (or vice-versa) and the second would be Seir (see also Seir in the summary of the northern wars of Ramesses III, *ANET* 262, and perhaps in EA 288:26; cf. Seir in Deuteronomy 33:2, and parallel with Edom in Judges 5:4); both would be located southeast of Canaan. Representative of this view are Manfred Weippert, "Semitische Nomaden des zweiten Jahrtausends," *Biblica* 55 (1974) 271 (for the historical reconstruction), and 427 and 430 (for the readings of the Egyptian inscriptions); Karel van der Toorn, "Yahweh," *DDD* 911–12; and Lawrence E. Stager, "Forging an Identity: The Emergence of Ancient Israel," in: *The Oxford History of the Biblical World* (ed. Michael D. Coogan; New York/Oxford: Oxford University, 1998) 145. In connection to these place-names, it is to be noted that the place-name of Edom is likewise attested with the Shasu, "the Shasu tribes of Edom," in: "The Report of a Frontier Official," in Papyrus Anastasi VI, *ANET* 258. Like Seir, Edom is mentioned in the old poetic references to Yahweh (Judges 5:4); it might be named for a deity, though this is quite unclear; see *ANET* 250 n. 28, and Ernest Axel Knauf, "Edom," *DDD* 273–74.

Anson Rainey addresses the putative reference to Yahweh in this way: "Is this a reference to Yahweh? No one knows." Rainey then mentions Judges 5:4 and comments: "Perhaps it is only a coincidence, but the most ancient literary tradition we have associated with Yahweh with an area that can quite possibly be equated with a territory occupied by Shasu pastoralists." See Rainey, "Amarna and Later: Aspects of Social History," in: *Symbiosis, Symbolism, and the Power of the Past: Canaan, Ancient Israel, and Their Neighbors – From the Late Bronze Age through Roman Palaestina* (ed. William G. Dever and Seymour Gitin; the AIAR Anniversary Volume; Winona Lake, IN: Eisenbrauns, 2003) 180. If the putative reference to Yahweh were correct, it would suggest that this god originated as a deity from the region of Seir and Edom and not the god of Israel (so van der Toorn, "Yahweh," *DDD* 912, followed by Smith, *The Early History of God,* 32–33 n. 45; see also Day, *Yahweh,* 15–16; and Lemaire, *The Birth of Monotheism,* 21–23).

Christoph Levin has argued that the southern mountain tradition for Yahweh is a late development to be located in relation to the representation of Yahweh and Edom in Isaiah 63. See Levin, "Das Alter des Deboraliedes," in his *Fortschreibungen: Gesammelte Studien zum Alten Testament* (BZAW 316; Berlin/New York: de Gruyter, 2003) 132–35. However, the reference to "Yahweh of Teiman" in the Kuntillet 'Ajrud inscriptions as well as the description of divine theophany in the same corpus would seem to suggest a tradition of the southern theophany that goes back at least to the late eight century; see Othmar Keel and Christoph Uehlinger, *Gods, Goddesses, and Images of God in Ancient Israel* (trans. Thomas Trapp; Minneapolis: Fortress, 1998) 244–45. For "Yahweh of Teiman" in the inscriptions, see F. W. Dobbs-Allsopp, J. J. M. Roberts, C. L. Seow and R. E. Whitaker, *Hebrew Inscriptions: Texts from the Biblical Period of the Monarchy with Concordance* (New Haven/London: Yale University, 2005) 285, 293 and 296; for theophanic language, see p. 287. In favor his view, Levin specifically notes the mention of Edom in 63:1 and the use of *nzlw* in Isaiah 63:19// Judges 5:5a. These comparisons do not speak to the geographical reference to Seir, nor to the different modes of the theophanies in the two passages. Based on literary-critical grounds, Judges 5:4–5 does not appear to be based directly on Isaiah 63. Instead, it might argued that if there is some particular literary rela-

such as the original text of Deuteronomy 32:8–9.[24]) The old southern tradition for Yahweh, over and against the well-attested tradition of El in Canaan (long recognized by many scholars),[25] points to the secondary identification of El and Yahweh, which might constitute the earliest Israelite case of cross-cultural translatability, specifically in their capacities as chief-gods of their respective regions (despite their rather divergent natures).[26] If correct, translatability would lie at the very heart of early Israelite divinity. However, several scholars hold what seems to be a less likely view, namely that Yahweh was originally derived as a title of El.[27] Claims in either direction about the original relationship between these two gods cannot be established with confidence. In either case, the complex history of El and Yahweh in early Israelite religion as well as the lack of evidence for translatability in Numbers 23:9 underscores the difficulty in using this verse to claim that non-translatability was a general feature of early Israel. Indeed, it may be taken to suggest the opposite, that translatability was an early feature of Israelite religion. In contrast, the texts discussed in the following section are quite clear about Israelite translatability during the monarchy.

---

tionship, Isaiah 63 represents an elaboration inspired in part by the old poetic tradition. Moreover, Isaiah 63:7–9 claims to be drawing on older tradition. By the way, one could imagine a specific scribal addition to Judges 5:5a based on Isaiah 63:19, since the phrase is absent from Psalm 68:9.

[23] See Day, *Yahweh,* 13–17, who traces the view to F. K. Movers and cites Otto Eissfeldt and T. N. D. Mettinger. See also Klaus Koch, *Der Gott Israels und die Götter des Orients: Religionsgeschichtliche Studien II. Zum 80. Geburtstag von Klaus Koch* (ed. Friedhelm Hartenstein und Martin Rösel; FRLANT 216; Göttingen: Vandenhoeck & Ruprecht, 2007) 13–20, 171–209; and Mark S. Smith, *The Early History of God,* 32–33, and *The Origins of Biblical Monotheism: Israel's Polytheistic Background and the Ugaritic Texts* (Oxford/New York: Oxford University, 2001) 143–46. This text is discussed in Chapter Four.

[24] So Juha Pakkala, *Intolerant Monolatry in the Deuteronomistic History* (Publications of the Finnish Exegetical Society 76; Helsinki: The Finnish Exegetical Society; Göttingen: Vandenhoeck & Ruprecht, 1999) 227 n. 21. For this text, see Chapters Three and Four. Such an identification issues in the convergence of these gods' divine characteristics in the biblical record, as laid out in: Smith, *The Early History of God,* 7–9, 57–59, 195–202.

[25] Cross, *Canaanite Myth and Hebrew Epic,* 15–75; Day, *Yahweh,* 13–17; Meindert Dijkstra, "El, Yhwh and their Asherah: On Continuity and Discontinuity in Canaanite and Ancient Israelite Religion," in: *Ugarit: Ein ostmediterranes Kulturzentrum im Alten Orient. Ergebnisse und Perspektiven der Forschung. Band I: Ugarit und seine altorientalische Umwelt* (ed. Manfried Dietrich and Oswald Loretz; Abhandlungen zur Literatur Alt-Syrien-Palästinas 7; Münster: Ugarit, 1995) 43–73; Koch, *Der Gott Israels und die Götter des Orients,* 13–20, 171–209; and Lemaire, *The Birth of Monotheism,* 19–28. These scholars regard Yahweh originally as a title of El or a part of one.

[26] As we saw in Chapter One, divergent natures are hardly an impediment to translatability. Leadership roles were at times the operative basis for translatability.

[27] Cross, *Canaanite Myth and Hebrew Epic,* 60–75; Day, *Yahweh,* 13–17; Dijkstra, "El, Yhwh and their Asherah," 43–73, esp. 44–45 and 53–64; Koch, *Der Gott Israels und die Götter des Orients,* 13–20, 171–209; and Lemaire, *The Birth of Monotheism,* 46.

2. Evidence of Translatability in the Hebrew Bible

It is not difficult to be critical of Hendel's interpretation of Numbers 23:9 as a rejection of translatability in Israel. Disproving the view requires mustering evidence of biblical passages that do reflect translatability. A number of biblical texts in fact militate against the view of Assmann and Hendel that a lack of translatability was a basic feature of erliest Israel.[28]

The Context of Translatability in Iron Age Israel

Before surveying biblical cases of Israelite translatability, it is important to note the historical context for Iron Age Israel. Translatability in this period takes place on a more regional or local scale, compared with the intercultural discourse of the great international ages.[29] The biblical cases discussed below involve intercultural contacts between Israelites and their immediate eastern and northern neighbors, not distant allies as in the Late Bronze Age. This difference calls for comment. Early Israel stands between two great international periods of the Late Bronze Age and the end of the Iron Age. In the first of these two international ages, the dominant polities, unable to achieve empire over the others, engaged in an intense construction of international relations and discourse.[30] In this context Israel emerged at the very end of the Late Bronze Age,[31] apparently as some sort of social unit,[32] if the oldest reference to Israel (*ysr'r*) in the "triumph hymn" on the

---

[28] Genesis 14:19–22 might at first glance seem to provide another instance. However, the name Yahweh in verse 22, while present in the MT, Targum and Vulgate, is missing from the Samaritan Pentateuch, LXX and Peshitta; see also 1QapGen, aramaic, col. XXII, line 21. Based on this distribution of witnesses, the divine name has been viewed as a secondary addition to the verse: Emanuel Tov, *Textual Criticism of the Hebrew Bible* (Minneapolis: Fortress; Assen/Maastricht: Van Gorcum, 1992) 282; Michael Astour, "Melchizedek," *ABD* 4:685: "it should be considered a late editorial gloss." This passage is discussed in Chapter Four.

[29] For a helpful discussion of the difference in the situations between the Late Bronze Age empires and Iron I Canaan-Israel, see Ann E. Killebrew, "Cultural Homogenisation and Diversity in Canaan during the 13th and 12th Centuries BC," in: *Archaeological Perspectives on the Transmission and Transformation of Culture in the Eastern Mediterranean* (ed. Joanne Clarke; Levant Supplementary Studies 2; Oxford: Oxbow, 2005) 170–75.

[30] For the picture in the Late Bronze Age, see Chapter One. For the situation in the Greco-Roman world, see Chapters Five and Six.

[31] A full picture for the Iron I period based on texts and archaeology can be found in: Elizabeth Bloch-Smith and Beth Alpert Nakhai, "A Landscape Comes to Life: The Iron I Period," *Near Eastern Archaeology* 62 (1999) 62–92, 101–27. See also Avraham Faust, *Israels's Ethnogenesis: Settlement, Interaction, Expansion and Resistance* (London/Oakville: Equinox, 2006) 113– 27, 170–87, and 227–30.

[32] This is suggested by the people determinative applied to Israel in the Merneptah stela (see the following note) and by the expression, "the people of Yahweh" in Judges

Merneptah stele (line 27) is any indication.[33] It was toward the beginning
of the next great international age when the political kingdoms of Israel

---

5:11 (see also Numbers 11:29; cf. Moab as "the people of Chemosh" in Numbers 21:29
and Jeremiah 48:46). What this older social unit actually comprised is unclear. Biblical
commentators regularly take it as some form of an early tribal Israel, even a ten-tribe or
twelve-tribe league or confederation. However, there is no evidence that such a league or
confederation was constitutive of Israel from the outset (though it was so by the middle or
end of the Iron I period). For a critical consideration of Israel in the Mernepteh stele and
Judges 5, see Kenton L. Sparks, *Ethnicity and Identity in Ancient Israel: Prolegomena to
the Study of Ethnic Sentiments and Their Expression in the Hebrew Bible* (Winona Lake,
IN: Eisenbrauns, 1998) 94–124. Judges 5 may be read not so much as making a strong
claim for a league or confederation as reflecting the problem concerning the nature of
Israel and its composition; in other words, the poem may reflect the lack of supra-tribal
organization. It is to be noted that the idea of Israel as a people in Judges 5 appears only
in the introduction of the poem, in verses 2–13, and not in the body of the poem proper,
in verses 14–30, including its discussion of the social units called to war in verses 14–18.
The word "people" in this latter section is confined to Zebulun in verse 18, which seems
to reflect a different usage in the poem. The introduction reflects an interpretation of the
material gathered in the body of the poem; this interpretation adds the idea of Israel's
"people-hood" to the material represented in the poem's body. On this matter, see Hans
Peter Müller, "Der Aufbau des Deboraliedes," *VT* 16 (1966) 446–59; Pfeiffer, *Jahwes
Kommen von Süden,* 31–34, for levels illustrated via a translation with different fonts,
and 58–69 for discussion of the poem's putative five levels; and Volkmar Fritz, "The
Complex of Traditions in Judges 4 and 5 and the Religion of Pre-state Israel," in: *"I Will
Speak the Riddles of Ancient times": Archaeological and Historical Studies in Honor of
Amihai Mazar on the Occasion of His Sixtieth Birthday* (ed. Aren M. Maier and Pierre
de Miroschedji; two vols.; Winona Lake, IN: Eisenbrauns, 2006) 2.689–98. See also the
survey of Heinz-Dieter Neef, *Deboraerzählung und Deboralied: Studien zu Jdc 4,1–5,31*
(Biblisch-Theologische Studien 49; Neukirchen-Vluyn: Neukirchener, 2002) 54–69. If
the introduction reflects an additional interpretive lens to the material in the body of the
poem (as noted by commentators such as Fritz), then the idea of Israel's "people-hood" in
Judges 5 is not original to the tradition of the poem, but reflects a secondary interpretation,
perhaps though a relatively early one (late pre-monarchic or early monarchic period?).
It is also to be noted that the so-called "old poetic features" in Judges 5 neither require
a pre-monarchic date nor preclude it. Only the apparent positive reference to Amaleq in
verse 14, if authentic, particularly militates for a pre-monarchic setting. Thus the material in the body of the poem, in verses 14–30, may pre-date the monarchy, while most of
the introduction in verses 2–13, as well as the first-person references in the body of the
poem, may not. The debate over dating the poem by its linguistic features is presently
a stalemate. See Michael Waltisberg, "Zum Alter der Sprache des Deborahliedes R. 5,"
Zeitschrift für Althebraistik 12 (1999) 218–32; and Levin, "Das Alter des Deboralieds,"
124–141. See the response by Gary Rendsburg, "Hurvitz Redux: On the Continued
Scholarly Inattention to a Simple Principle of Hebrew Philology," in: *Biblical Hebrew:
Chronology and Typology* (ed. I. Young; London: Continuum, 2003) 104–128. While
I am inclined to view some features as Iron I, the evidence at present does not require
such an early date for any of them. Instead, it is the cultural features in the poem, such
as the positive reference to Amalek in verse 14a, which militate in favor of an early date.
Other possible early features include the military practice involving hair in verse 2; the
antiquity of the theophany tradition as it is appears in verses 4–5 (with the name of
Edom versus its occurrences elsewhere); the form of the rhetorical question in verse 8b;
the heterogenous nature of the tribes named in verse 14–18; and the relatively minor
place of Yahweh or Israel as such in the body of the poem in verses 14–30 (see above).

and Judah succumb. At the risk of gross generalization, from a large-scale perspective on ancient Near Eastern history Israel may be situated within

---

[33] For detailed studies of the text, see Alviero Niccacci, "La stele d'Israël. Grammaire et stratégie de communication," in: *Études Égyptologiques et Bibliques à la mémoire du Père B. Couroyer* (ed. Marcel Sigrist; Cahiers de la Revue Biblique 36; Paris: Gabalda, 1997) 43–107; and Sameh Iskander, "The Reign of Merneptah," (Ph.D. dissertation, New York University, 2002) 69–90, 287–303. For handy translations and discussion of the final section mentioning Israel, see John A. Wilson, *ANET* 378 and James K. Hoffmeier, *COS* 2.40–41. For a photograph of the word, "Israel," see *ANEP* 343. Understanding Israel in this text first depends on the determinative (an indicator of semantic category) written with the name of Israel. It is commonly noted that the determinative for "people" rather than a geographical determinative is applied to Israel, while the other places in this stele bear the determinative used for a foreign country (Wilson, *ANET* 378 n. 18; Hoffmeier, *COS* 1.41). It is also regularly observed that the determinatives are not used consistently by New Kingdom scribes (Wilson, *ANET* 378 n. 18). It is to be noted that in this context Israel and Kharu are both personified, which may bear further on how differently the Egyptian scribes understood the two names.
   The understanding of Israel's location hinges on how the final section of the text is arranged. In his discussion of the various proposals for the ring structure, Iskander ("The Reign of Merneptah," 308) regards none to be definitive; see also the survey of H. Engel, "Die Siegesstele des Merenptah. Kritischer Überblick über die verschiedenen Versuche historischer Auswertung des Schlussabschnitts," *Biblica* 60 (1979) 373–99, esp. 388–89. Some scholars claim that Israel is parallel to Kharu, a general term for Syria-Palestine (see the discussion of Hoffmeier, *COS* 1.41). In this case, Israel would seem to be a people (assuming the correct use of the determinative) located in Syria-Palestine. Other scholars claim that the text's ring-structure provides considerable historical significance for understanding earliest Israel based. Anson F. Rainey takes the first line ("The Great Ones are prostrate saying 'Peace'") as the heading for the overall chiasm or ring-structure of the hymn that follows; this would mean that Kharu corresponds to Canaan, which would be suitable from a geographical perspective (see Anson F. Rainey and R. Steven Notley, *The Sacred Bridge* [Jerusalem: Carta, 2006] 99), suggesting that Israel is not paired with another term (such as Canaan; see below), but follows the other place-names of Canaan, Ashkelon, Gezer and Yenoam. In contrast to this proposal, others scholars take the first two lines (including the initial line that Rainey and Notley take to be outside of the ring-structure) as corresponding to the final two lines; see Gerhard Fecht, "Die Israelstele, Gestalt und Aussage," in: *Fontes atque Pontes: Eine Festgabe für Hellmut Brunner* (ed. M. Görg; Ägypten und Altes Testament 5; Wiesbaden: Harrassowitz, 1983) 106–38; and Gösta W. Ahlström and Diana Edelman, "Merneptah's Israel," *JNES* 44 (1985) 59–61. Neither the first two lines nor the last two lines in the ring-structure contain any specific place-names while the lines in-between them do. Niccacci ("La stele d'Israël," 88) observes that "the Nine Bows" of the second line would seem to parallel "all lands" of the penultimate line and not the specific places of Thehenu and Khatti, as set out by Rainey and Notley. If so, then Thehenu and Khatti correspond to Kharu, and then Canaan and Israel would correspond as the terms outside of the three places, Ashkelon, Gezer and Yenoam. This reading also conforms to the layout of lines suggested by John Wilson (*ANET* 378), with Ashkelon and Gezer in a single line parallel to the line mentioning Yenoam (see also the observations of Niccacci, "La stele d'Israël," 89); the lengths of the two lines containing these three place-names would suit this view. If correct, it would militate in favor of the correspondence of Israel with the mention of Canaan. This correspondence would leave open a location for Israel as a group in Canaan, either in Cisjordan or Transjordan. For Cisjordan, see Ahlström and Edelman (cited above); Niccacci, "La stele d'Israël," 102; and André Lemaire, in various publications: "Asriel, ŠR'L, Israel et l'origine de la

an intermediate or transitional period marked by fragmentation of international structures. Israel emerged in a world governed more by contiguous, political relations and less by international structures.[34] Its subsequent demise and communal history was deeply shaped by the emergence of a later international age dominated by Mesopotamian powers. In-between these two great international periods, Israel's own form of translatability functioned in the context of the regional structures that obtained in the Iron Age Levant.[35]

Several biblical texts show a regional form of translatability. All but one of the examples discussed below derive from Judges and Kings.[36] They are

---

confederation Israelite," *VT* 23 (1973) 239–43; "Aux origins d'Israël: la montagne d'Ephraïm et le territoire de Manassé," in: *La protohistoire d'Israël. De l'exode à la monarchie* (ed. E.M. Laperrousaz; Paris: Cerf, 1990) 183–292; and *The Birth of Monotheism*, 30–31. For Transjordan, Rainey, "Amarna and Later: Aspects of Social History," 180–84. Rainey sees Yenoam as in Transjordan, further favoring his view; see also Nadav Na'aman, *Canaan in the Second Millennium B.C.E.: Collected Essays. Volume 2* (Winona Lake, IN: Eisenbrauns, 2005) 195–203. Rainey and Na'aman reason that since Yenoam is in Transjordan, Israel in the Merneptah stele was as well.

[34] For the larger context of the transition, see two collections of essays: *The Crisis Years: The 12th Century B.C. from beyond the Danube to the Tigris* (ed. William A. Ward and Martha S. Joukowsky; Dubuque, Iowa: Kendall/Hnut, 1992); and *Mediterranean Peoples in Transition: Thirteenth Century to the Early Tenth Centuries BCE* (ed. Seymour Gitin, Ami Mazar and Ephraim Stern; Jerusalem: Israel Exploration Society, 1998). Note also Susan Sherratt, "The Mediterranean Economy: 'Globalization' at the End of the Second Millennium B.C.E.," in: *Symbiosis, Symbolism, and the Power of the Past: Canaan, Ancient Israel, and Their Neighbors – From the Late Bronze Age through Roman Palaestina* (ed. William G. Dever and Seymour Gitin; the AIAR Anniversary Volume; Winona Lake, IN: Eisenbrauns, 2003) 37–62.

[35] The following discussion draws on the important article by Simon B. Parker, although his characterization of the religious worldview differs in a number of respects. See Parker, "The Beginning of the Reign of God. Psalm 82 as Myth and Liturgy," *RB* 102 (1995) 532–59. Note also Eric Voegelin's interesting discussion of some of these passages, in: *The Collected Works of Eric Voegelin: Volume 14. Order and History* (ed. Maurice P. Hogan; Columbia, MI: University of Missouri, 2000) 266–67.

[36] On the characterization of these works as "deuteronomistic," see the helpful surveys by Thomas Römer and Albert de Pury, "Deuteronomistic Historiography (DH): History of Research and Debated Issues," in: *Israel Constructs its History: Deuteronomistic Historiography in Recent Research* (ed. Albert de Pury, Thomas Römer and Jean-Daniel Macchi; JSOTSup 306; Sheffield: Sheffield, 2000) 24–141; and Gary Knoppers, "Is There a Future for the Deuteronomistic History?" in: *The Future of the Deuteronomistic History* (ed. Thomas Römer; Bibliotheca ephemeridum theologicarum lovaniensium 147; Leuven: University/Uitgeverij Peeters, 2000) 119–34. Already in light of older critiques, yet more forcefully since the treatment of Ernst Würthwein, it seems no longer possible to accept Martin Noth's notion of a single editorial project for Joshua-Judges-Samuel-Kings, though it may still be argued that these books have received various editorial handling influenced by the book of Deuteronomy or at least the tradition in which it stands. See Würthwein, *Studien zum deuteronomistischen Geschichtswerk* (BZAW 227; Berlin: de Gruyter, 1994) esp. 1–11. The books of Judges and Kings, in contrast to the books of Samuel, appear more marked by deuteronomistic influence, as commentators have long

anachronistic in many cases, reflecting the conditions of the monarchic period and later. It is to be noted that the examples treated in this section are marked only somewhat by language considered to be either deuterono-mistic or late Biblical Hebrew. These matters are considered in some detail in passing. These texts (or least some core of the passages) may be reason-ably situated largely in the monarchic period. While some of the examples surveyed in this section could have been composed or redacted later (some argue multiple times),[37] it would seem that their tradition, if not their basic composition, dates to the period of the monarchy. Moreover, despite in-stances of later rewriting or additions, the information about translatability in these texts suits a pre-exilic milieu.

The passages contain literary representations of cultural realities, and the cultural knowledge embedded in these stories includes translatability both in the more specific equation of deities and the broader political "ecumenism" involving gods and their divine capabilities. To be clear, the representation of divinity in ancient Israel in the passages surveyed below does not depend on the historicity of specific details in the stories; instead, the texts are being analyzed for the cultural attitudes of the writers and their audiences towards translatability of divinity. Since the nineteenth century scholars have identified in one or another of these texts what Assmann calls translatability. One passage clearly conforms to his narrow sort of translat-ability in explicitly equating named deities, one Israelite and one non-Isra-elite (Judges 11:24). Others show his broader categories of translatability (or international political ecumenism), in the form of Israelite recognition of non-Israelite deities. The non-Israelite god in question is sometimes named explicitly (Genesis 31; 2 Kings 1), while at other times the non-Israelite god is implicit (2 Kings 3). Still other passages represent foreigners as translat-ing the Israelite god at work (Judges 7; 1 Kings 20), without confessional formulas (unlike some passages, such as Exodus 18:11; Joshua 2:11; cf. 2 Kings 5:17).[38] Taken together, the texts surveyed in this section indicate that contrary to Assmann's "Mosaic distinction," ancient Israel did construct cross-cultural translatability of divinity. For the sake of convenience, we review examples in their order of appearance in the Hebrew Bible.

---

noted. At the same time, some commentators are coming to dispute the entire notion of such influence (see the surveys cited above).

[37] Remarks concerning the various issues for these passages are offered in passing below.

[38] These are addressed in the following section.

Genesis 31: Cross-Cultural Ecumenism of Personal Gods

We begin our survey of translatability with Genesis 31:43–53. At first glance, this case does not appear to present a particularly strong example of translatability, as it involves two figures belonging to the same clan.[39] Moreover, it has been thought from a literary and compositional perspective to be a rather difficult chapter.[40] At the same time, the story deserves our attention, as it contains several features that appear in other biblical representations of translatability. Indeed, even though family members are involved here, there is a certain cross-cultural representation being made in this chapter between an Israelite and an Aramean. In his oath to the covenant that Jacob and his Aramean uncle Laban are making, the latter figure closes his words with a standard formula (verse 53): "May the god of Abraham and the god of Nahor adjudicate (**špt*) between us."[41] Then the verse relates how "Jacob swore by the Fear of his father, Isaac."

---

[39] As noted by Paul Kalluveettil, *Declaration and Covenant: A Comprehensive Review of Covenant Formulae from the Old Testament and the Ancient Near East* (Analecta Biblica 88; Rome: Pontifical Biblical Institute, 1982) 8, 90 n. 351. There are other examples according to him: Jacob-Esau, Moses-Jethro and David-Jonathan. In the case of Jacob and Esau, the treaty is designed to restore relations between brothers; and in the case of Moses and Jethro as well as David and Jonathan, it is designed to create further or more direct relations between in-laws of different groups. The covenants between family members are hardly superfluous; indeed, they are designed to acknowledge and establish closer bonds than had been enjoyed previously between two specific members within the family and not the family in general.

[40] For the considerable textual issues in this section, see José Loza Vera, "Le berît entre Laban et Jacob (Gn. 31,43–54)," in: *The World of the Arameans I: Studies in Language and Literature in Honour of Paul-Eugène Dion* (ed. P. M. Michèle Daviau, John W. Wevers and Michael Weigl; JSOTSup 324; Sheffield: Sheffield, 2001) 60–62. For early tradition behind this account, see Erhard Blum, *Die Komposition der Vätergeschichte* (Wissenschaftliche Untersuchungen zum Alten und Neuen Testament 57; Neukirchen-Vluyn: Neukirchener, 1984) 132–38; see also David M. Carr, *Reading the Fractures of Genesis: Historical and Literary Approaches* (Louisville, KY: Westminster John Knox, 1996) 270. A treatment of Genesis 31:43–54 focusing on its later composition and redaction can be found in· Christoph Levin, *Der Jahwist* (FRLANT 157; Göttingen: Vandenhoeck & Ruprecht, 1993) 241–44. In defense of Levin's approach, it is to be noted that the application of such cross-cultural relations to relations within the family unit, along with its literary representation of different languages, would make sense as literary reworking. The tradition of the story evokes the Iron II period, specifically the context of Israelite-Aramean relations. (Might the term *gal'ed* perhaps also evoke Gilead, mentioned in verse 25, as the geographically contested area? See the Gileadites and *'ed* in Joshua 22:34; cf. their conflict with the Ammonites in Judges 11.) In contrast to Levin's exilic dating for the "J" source, a pre-exilic dating for this putative source in Genesis 31:43–53 has been maintained based on two rather general grammatical features by Richard M. Wright. See Wright, *Linguistic Evidence for the Pre-Exilic Date of the Yahwistic Source* (Library of Hebrew Bible/Old Testament Studies 419; London/New York: T & T Clark International, 2005) 106, 128. Resolution of these issues is not required for the argument here.

[41] Levin (*Der Jahwist*, 242, 244) assigns verse 53 to "Nachendredaktionelle Ergänzungen." At the same time, it is to be noted that this sort of practice in verse 53a is quite

Like the treaties surveyed in Chapter One, this biblical passage invokes the deities of the two parties as guarantors of their pact.[42] In this case, Laban mentions the god of each party. From the narrative's apparent reference to what many scholars have taken as Isaac's deity or as his title ("The Fear"),[43] it would appear that the patron or family god is what is meant by "the god of Abraham," and that a corresponding ancestral divinity is assumed for Laban as well. To highlight the fact that two deities are involved here, we may contrast the pact made between the Reubenites and the Gadites in Joshua 22:34, where to signal the pact they name the altar: "It is a witness between us and them that Yahweh is our god" (cf. Judges 11:10). This instance of a "witness" mentions only one god, specifically the god shared by the two parties. In contrast, in Genesis 31:53 different deities are called as witnesses to the pact.

Verses 48 and 52 seem to suggest that the "heap" (of stones) is to be the "witness," but implicitly it is the gods of the parties who are reminded by the "heap" to serve as the proper witnesses to the covenant.[44] Accordingly,

---

ancient. See the ending of a Late Bronze Age letter from Hazor, lines 20–22: "The gods have decided between me and them/*judged* (*špt*) *me*". For this letter, see Wayne Horowitz and Takayoshi Oshima with Seth Sanders, *Cuneiform in Canaan: Cuneiform Sources from the Land of Israel in Ancient Times* (Jerusalem: Israel Exploration Society/The Hebrew University of Jerusalem, 2006) 81. It is possible that older tradition lies behind the putatively reworked material, as argued by Levin.

[42] See Cross, *Canaanite Myth and Hebrew Epic*, 269; Joel S. Burnett, *A Reassessment of Biblical Elohim* (SBLDS 183; Atlanta: Society of Biblical Literature, 2001) 64–65; Theodore J. Lewis, "Covenant and Blood Rituals: Understanding Exodus 24:3–8 in Its Ancient Near Eastern Context," in: *Confronting the Past: Archaeological and Historical Essays on Ancient Israel in Honor of William G. Dever* (ed. S. Gitin, J. E. Wright and J. P. Dessel; Winona Lake, IN: Eisenbrauns, 2006) 341–50, esp. 342. The covenant in this case is regarded as a pact of "mutual non-aggression" by Kalluveettil, *Declaration and Covenant*, 34; so also Loza Vera, ""Le berît," 57, 66. See also Kalluveettil's comments on p. 170 n. 187 concerning *ʻbr* in verse 52, which suggest geographical parameters for their mutually recognized realms of operation (cf. the oath concerning boundaries, taken by Assyrian and Kassite kings in the Synchronistic Chronicle, lines 1–7, in: A. K. Grayson, *Assyrian and Babylonian Chronicles* [Winona Lake, IN: Eisenbrauns, 2000] 108–9).

[43] For this understanding of the term, see Albrecht Alt, "The God of the Fathers," in his collection, *Essays on Old Testament History and Religion* (trans. R. A. Wilson; Garden City, NY: Anchor Books, Doubleday, 1968) 3–100, esp. 32–33. See also Cross, *Canaanite Myth and Hebrew Epic*, 4, 269; Emile Puech, "Fear of Isaac," *ABD* 2. 779–80; and Karel van der Toorn, *Family Religion in Babylonia, Syria and Israel: Continuity and Change in the Forms of Religious Life* (Studies in the History and Culture of the Ancient Near East VII; Leiden/New York/Köln: Brill, 1996) 256–57. Note the proper cautionary remarks made by Matthias Köckert, "Fear of Isaac," *DDD* 329–31.

[44] So Kalluveettil, *Declaration and Covenant*, 103. Following older scholars such as Albright and Cross (see *Canaanite Myth and Hebrew Epic*, 269), he further entertains the proposal that *galʻed* should be read **gal-ʻad* (literally, "heap of pact"; cf. Aramaic *ʻdy'/ʻdn*, Akkadian *ade*) in order to match Biblical Hebrew *berit*, "covenant." This interpretation, while quite fitting for the general context of treaty, works against the interpretation provided by the text in verses 48 and 52. Kalluveettil appeals to a theory of later redaction

the gods of the two parties are invoked in verse 53 to "judge between us." The meal that transpires in verse 54 may be designed to bring together the gods of the parties involved as much as the parties themselves.[45] In some of the international treaties discussed in Chapter One, the deities of different treaty partners come together in an international divine meeting to mark the treaty. In this respect, the agreement between Jacob and Laban is represented as an international agreement.[46] In this context, it is relevant to mention Raymond Westbrook's comparison of the oath and meal of Jacob and Laban with the allusion to the meal shared by treaty partners, Aziru of Amurru and the ruler of Qidsha, in EA 162.[47] The oath and meal shared by Jacob and Laban place their relationship squarely in treaty terms, much as one finds broadly in the Amarna letters discussed in Chapter One.

In concept, this case is little different from the examples of Late Bronze Age treaties seen in Chapter One, but in application there is a contrast to be noted. On one level, this translatability is presented as operative within perceived branches of the same family; thus the picture represented is not entirely cross-cultural. On another level, we may say that translatability is in effect here, as this meeting between Laban and Jacob involves translation across the languages of Hebrew and Aramaic.[48] Laban calls the site accordingly Aramaic *yegar-sahaduta,* while Jacob names it with the Hebrew, *gal'ed* (Genesis 31:47).[49] To contextualize the use of Aramaic in this case, we may note the Sefire inscription,[50] with its invocation of the deities of

---

to account for the semantic discrepancy. For another reading along these lines for these verses, see Levin, *Der Jahwist,* 240–42.

[45] Cf. Kalluveettil, *Declaration and Covenant,* 11, 13.

[46] As emphasized by Burnett, *A Reassessment of Biblical Elohim,* 71–72.

[47] Westbrook, "International Law in the Amarna Age," in: *Amarna Diplomacy: The Beginnings of International Relations* (ed. Raymond Cohen and Raymond Westbrook; Baltimore/London: Johns Hopkins University, 2000) 38. See also the discussion of Theodore J. Lewis, "Covenant and Blood Rituals: Understanding Exodus 24:3–8 in Its Ancient Near Eastern Context," in: *Confronting the Past: Archaeological and Historical Essays on Ancient Israel in Honor of William G. Dever* (ed. S. Gitin, J.E. Wright and J.P. Dessel; Winona Lake, IN: Eisenbrauns, 2006) 342; and p. 58 above.

[48] For the representation of the bilingualism here, see Werner Weinberg, *Essays on Hebrew* (ed. Paul Citrin; South Florida Studies in the History of Judaism 46; Atlanta: Scholars, 1993) 54; and Avi Hurvitz, "Hebrew and Aramaic in the Biblical Period: The Problem of 'Aramaisms' in Linguistic Research on the Hebrew Bible," in: *Biblical Hebrew: Studies in Chronology and Typology* (ed. Ian Young; JSOTSup 369; London/New York: T & T Clark International, 2003) 25. Hurvitz comments on the anachronistic character of the account from a linguistic perspective.

[49] Levin (*Der Jahwist,* 244) regards this as a later gloss. At the same time, a literary effort to render Laban's speech in Aramaic need not be late.

[50] For a thoughtful consideration of the cultural background of this treaty, see William S. Morrow, "The Sefire Treaty Stipulations and the Mesopotamian Treaty Tradition," in: *The World of the Arameans III: Studies in Language and Literature in Honour of Paul-*

the two parties.[51] Like the Jacob-Laban pact, it involves Aramaic as one of the languages of the pact. We also see the invocation of Aramean and Assyrian deities in the well-known treaties of Ashur-Nirari V with Mati'-ilu of Arpad and of Esarhaddon with Baal of Tyre.[52] The story of Jacob and Laban may be designed to presage Israelite-Aramean relations.[53] In sum, the literary representation of the Jacob-Laban pact draws on some conventional features of intercultural political relations in the Levant during this period.

Judges 3: Cross-Cultural Sharing of Divinity

The book of Judges provides better examples of cross-cultural translatability in a broad sense, and we will address these in order of appearance in the book. The first, in Judges 3:20, involves a humorous and anachronistic representation[54] of a communication between Ehud and his Moabite overlord, King Eglon.[55] Ehud presents tribute on behalf of the Israelites to Eglon (verse 17), and after doing so, he requests a private meeting with the king (verse 18). Ehud informs the king that he has a secret message for him (verse 19),[56] at which point the monarch dismisses his court. Ehud reiterates to Eglon (verse 20), literally rendered, "I have a divine word (or matter)/word of God for you" (*debar-'elohim li 'eleka*). At this point, with his left hand Ehud pulls out his hidden dagger and plunges it into Eglon's

---

Eugène Dion (ed. P. M. Michèle Daviau, John W. Wevers and Michael Weigl; JSOTSup 326; Sheffield: Sheffield, 2001) 83–99.

[51] See Sefire I, face A, lines 6–14 (KAI 222), in: Joseph Fitzmyer, *The Aramaic Inscription of Sefire* (Biblica et Orientalia 19; Rome: Pontifical Biblical Institute, 1967) 12–13; face B, in: Fitzmyer, *The Aramaic Inscription*, 16–17, etc. Sefire lies about 16 miles (25.7 km.) southeast of Aleppo.

[52] For handy reference, see Simo Parpola and Kazuko Watanabe, *Neo-Assyrian Treaties and Loyalty Oaths* (SAA II; Helsinki: Helsinki University, 1988) 13 and 27 respectively.

[53] So Burnett, *A Reassessment of Biblical Elohim*, 71–72.

[54] For the literary dimensions of the passage, see the rather different discussions of Baruch Halpern, *The First Historians: The Hebrew Bible and History* (San Francisco: Harper & Row, 1988) 39–75; Marc Zvi Brettler, "The Ehud Story as Satire," in: *The Creation of History in Ancient Israel* (London/New York: Routledge, 1995) 79–90; Yairah Amit, *The Book of Judges: The Art of Editing* (Biblical Interpretation Series 38; Leiden/Boston: Brill, 1999) 171–98, esp. 184–85; and Philippe Guillaume, *Waiting for Josiah: The Judges* (JSOTSup 385; London/New York: T & T Clark International, 2004) 27–29. Note also the "meta-comments" on the story in: Jacobus Marais, *Representation in Old Testament Narrative Texts* (Biblical Interpretation Series 38; Leiden/Boston/Köln: Brill, 1998) 92–96; and the interesting survey of readings of the story by David M. Gunn, *Judges* (Blackwell Bible Commentaries; Malden, MA/Oxford/ Carlton, Australia: Blackwell, 2005) 34–52. See Rainey and Notley, *The Sacred Bridge*, 137, for a useful discussion and map detailing locations named in the narrative.

[55] For the vassalage context, see Kalluveettil, *Declaration and Covenant*, 66.

[56] Sometimes verse 19a has been considered a possible doublet of verse 20. See Nowack, *Richter-Ruth*, 27. This is not a necessary reading, and the repetition arguably serves to build the suspense in setting up a private audience between Eglon and Ehud.

fat belly (verse 21). The narrative emphasis falls on the physical attribute of Eglon's size, in particular how his stomach swallows up the dagger (verse 22). The narrative also plays on the phrase "word (or matter) of God" (or perhaps, "divine word/matter").[57] Perhaps a commonplace for this context, the expression serves to conceal Ehud's true intent.[58]

The narrative represents a Moabite and an Israelite preparing to discuss a matter in the context of overlord-vassal relations. The communication is expressed within the situation of an expected delivery of tribute from the vassal party. Whether one translates *'elohim* as "God" or "divine" in 3:20, the word suggests that the term of divinity shared by the Israelites' representative and their Moabite overlord was operative in the worldview of the author(s) during the monarchy.[59] In this case, we do not see literal translation of two deities. Indeed, it involved a matter of communication from a divinity that the two figures could share. In this context, J. Clinton McCann comments: "Since Eglon would have known that Ehud had crossed the Jordan to deliver the tribute, Eglon may even have been expecting from Ehud a favorable word from Eglon's own god, Chemosh."[60] While this possible scenario is rather speculative, it highlights the assumption of shared discourse about divinity between overlord and vassal despite the context's relatively minor expression about divinity as such. This situation presupposes the broader notion of international political ecumenism that we discussed in Chapter One. As we saw with treaties, it is in this sort of vassal-overlord relations where we find a general expression of translation of divinity across cultures. For a passage that contains a more extensive representation of translation, we turn to Judges 7.

---

[57] Kalluveettil (*Declaration and Covenant*, 57) takes *debar* as a term for treaty stipulations. In context this is a matter of a vassal who is giving the word (cf. Kalluveettil, *Declaration and Covenant*, 143–44), which would not suggest *debar* as stipulation but communication as a vassal. Still perhaps some wordplay could be involved here. In terms of context, a "secret message," perhaps compares with *rgm//hwt* in *KTU* 1.3 III 20–22, IV 13–14, which to my mind also reflects the world of communication of treaty partners, transposed to the world of divinities. Some commentators have regarded *debar* as an oracle. See Gottlieb Ludwig Studer, *Das Buch der Richter grammatisch und historisch erklärt* (Bern/Chur/Leipzig: J.F.J. Dalp, 1835) 86. For speculations about what Eglon could have thought this word might concern, see Victor H. Matthews, *Judges and Ruth* (New Cambridge Bible Commentary; Cambridge, UK/New York: Cambridge University, 2004) 61–62.

[58] For its literary function, see the remarks of Robert H. O'Connell, *The Rhetoric of the Book of Judges* (VTSup 63; Leiden/Boston/Köln: Brill, 1996) 91–92 n. 52.

[59] For this use of *'elohim*, see especially Burnett, *A Reassessment of Biblical Elohim*, 70–72. The Israelite-Moabite relations represented in this chapter suit an audience during the monarchy. See Marc Zvi Brettler, *The Book of Judges* (Old Testament Readings; London/New York: Routledge, 2002) 32–33.

[60] McCann, *Judges* (Interpretation; Louisville, KY: Westminster John Knox, 2002) 44.

Judges 7: Cross-Cultural Interpretation of the Israelite God

Another example of translatability is represented in the story of military conflict between Gideon and his forces against Midian (verse 1, named along with the Amalek and the Qedemites in verse 12). In a night reconnaissance mission, Gideon is presented as overhearing one man in the enemy camp telling another about a dream that he had.[61] The former is said to report how in the dream a loaf or cake[62] leveled the Midianite camp (verse 13). His fellow soldier responds to the dream by informing him that this can only mean, "God has delivered Midian and all the camp into his power" (verse 14). Gideon takes the enemy's dream and his compatriot's interpretation[63] as a sign of divine favor, and Gideon proceeds to win the battle (verse 15).

This passage represents an Israelite view that a non-Israelite could have an authentic dream involving the Israelite deity, and that a second non-Israelite could properly interpret the dream as such. Moreover, the term for divinity *'elohim*[64] is represented as being used by the foreigner in verse 14 and understood by Gideon, thus showing a shared discourse about divinity. Gideon in verse 15 translates this shared term for divinity into his own culturally specific expression for divinity, namely his own

---

[61] For discussion of this passage, see Wolfgang Bluedorn, *Yahweh Versus Baalism: A Theological Reading of the Gideon-Abimilech Narrative* (JSOTSup 329; Sheffield: Sheffield, 2001) 132–38. Bluedorn compares other dreams and their interpretation in Genesis 37 and 40 as well as Daniel 2–4, but in contrast the enemy interpretation of the dream in Judges 7:14 is cross-cultural in nature.

[62] The word *ṣelul* (Ketib)/*ṣelil* (Qere), attested only here in BH, is uncertain; LXX *magis*, "cake." On this word C. F. Burney, *The Book of Judges: with Introduction and Notes* (London: Rivingtons, 1918) 213, comments how "the context demands a flat circular cake or a round loaf." Frants Buhl connected this word with Ethiopic *ṣalata, ṣallata*, "bake bread," and thus took the biblical phrase as "ein Kuchen Gerstenbrotes." See Frants Buhl, *Wilhelm Gesenius' Hebräisches und Aramäisches Handwörterbuch über das Alte Testament* (17th ed.; Leipzig: F. C. W. Vogel, 1921) 683, noted by Wolf Leslau, *Comparative Dictionary of Ge'ez (Classical Ethiopic)* (Wiesbaden: Harrassowitz, 1987) 556. Robert G. Boling interprets the word as "stale" or "moldy," based on Arabic *salla*, "become dry or cracked, became putrid, stank, had gone bad." See Boling, *Judges* (AB 6A; New York: Doubleday, 1975) 146. See further discussion in: Bluedorn, *Yahweh Versus Baalism*, 134 n. 231.

[63] The meaning of **šeber* as "interpretation" is widely accepted. The etymology from **šbr*, "to break," is likewise accepted, though this would be the only passage where this semantic application would be attested. Michael Fishbane views the word instead as a loan (reinterpreted) from Akkadian *šubrû* (the causative stem of *barû*, "to look, observe, inspect'), which is used for the revelation of a dream or vision (*CAD B:*119, #5b); see Fishbane, *Biblical Interpretation in Ancient Israel* (Oxford: Clarendon, 1985) 456–57. Note also Shaul Bar, *A Letter That Has not Been Heard: Dreams in the Hebrew Bible* (trans. Lenn J. Schramm; Monographs of the Hebrew Union College 25; Cincinnati: Hebrew Union College, 2001) 79–80. At the same time, Fishbane notes that his proposal entails a significant etymological difficulty.

[64] LXX B *theos;* cf. LXX A and Lucianic *kurios* and Targum Jonathan *ywy*.

god, Yahweh.[65] In short, the Israelite author credits non-Israelites with an ability to translate for themselves a revelation from the Israelite divinity based on their own experience. This passage involves engagement between Israelites and its neighbors, as does the next example of translatability from the book of Judges.

Judges 11: Cross-Cultural Equation of National Gods

A recognition of the god of others is represented in Judges 11:24. The context involves a verbal negotiation between Jephthah and the Ammonite king who wishes to have land restored to him from the Israelites (verse 12–13). The passage thus involves a territorial dispute between neighbors. The Israelite messenger tells the Ammonite king how Israelites did not take Moabite or Ammonite land during their travels (verses 14–19), only that the Israelite god gave to the Israelites the land of Sihon the Amorite, the king of Heshbon, in battle (verses 19–22). Then the message poses the point (verses 23–24): "And so Yahweh the god of Israel dispossessed the Amorites before His people Israel and it is you who should possess it? Do you not possess what Chemosh your god made you possess? So we will possess what Yahweh our god has caused us to possess."[66]

Like the preceding passage, this one names[67] the alleged deity of each party in a local negotiation between neighbors. According to Robert O'Connell, the narrative draws on the milieu of what he calls "royal covenant disputation," found in many ancient Near Eastern treaties and letters.[68] The story reflects the wider setting of inter-cultural political discourse that we saw for the Late Bronze Age in Chapter One. In this context, the names of the

---

[65] See Barry G. Webb, *The Book of Judges: An Integrated Reading* (JSOTSup 46; Sheffield: Sheffield, 1987) 231–32 n. 13. Webb comments on the narrative function of this switch of terms for divinity. J. Paul Tanner comments how "the irony is stunning: hearing the promise directly for the Lord did not convince Gideon, but hearing it from the Midianite soldier did." Tanner, "The Gideon Narrative as the Focal Point of Judges," *Bibliotheca Sacra* 149 (1992) 159, cited by McCann, *Judges,* 67.

[66] For a defense of the MT, see O'Connell, *The Rhetoric of the Book of Judges,* 470.

[67] Boling (*Judges,* 203, 205) imputes a certain "risk" to Jephthah's comparison of the two gods, since for Boling, Jephthah is giving too much credence to Chemosh, but this seems to be reading into the text. Burnett treats this verse as a good example of *'elohim* for national gods (*A Reassessment of Biblical Elohim,* 65), while in connection with other texts he notes the international use of *'elohim* (*A Reassessment of Biblical Elohim,* 70–76); Judges 11:24 involves both. For a reverse case, note 1 Samuel 4:8, which describes the Philistines discussing Israel's divinity as "these mighty gods … they are the gods who struck Egyptians with a blow in the wilderness." For discussion of this passage, see Burnett, *A Reassessment of Biblical Elohim,* 82–105. For foreigners referring to divinity in the plural, compare 1 Kings 19:2. In these instances, the Israelite authors of such passages imagine the foreigners as polytheists compared to them.

[68] O'Connell, *The Rhetoric of the Book of Judges,* 193–94.

two gods of the parties are explicitly mentioned. It should be noted parenthetically that the passage has been thought to involve a case of mistaken
divine identity: Chemosh is the chief god of the Moabites (as in KAI 181,
Numbers 21:29, Jeremiah 48:46, 1 Kings 11:7 and 2 Kings 23:13[69]); and it is
Milkom who is the chief deity of the Ammonites (as indicated by 1 Kings
11:5 and 2 Kings 23:13 and arguably punned on in Amos 1:15 = Jeremiah
49:3, vocalized as *malkam*, "their king").[70] Whatever the reason for the representation of divine names in Judges 11:24,[71] this passage lies in the realm
of international relations. Here we may be reminded of the Amarna letters
discussed in Chapter One, especially correspondence that mention deities
of the two parties. In this case from Judges 11 the two gods are identified
as divinities that provide military victory to their peoples. Thus we have
a representation of the explicit recognition of deities of the parties across
cultures.[72] In addition, we have the implicit equation of the two deities based
on their comparable roles as national warrior-gods.[73]

This representation has been long recognized by commentators, for
example by Gottlieb Ludwig Studer in his 1835 commentary on Judges.[74]
In 1913, C.F. Burney commented on the picture of the two gods in this
way:

The speaker assumes just as real an *existence* for Chemosh as for Yahweh. He is no
monotheist in the proper sense of the term, i.e. he does not hold the doctrine that
Yahweh is the one and only god of the whole earth, and that the existence of the
other gods is a delusion. Yahweh is for him, doubtless, the sole object of Yahweh's
allegiance and worship; the holding of this faith (monolatry) does not hinder him
from believing that Chemosh really stands in the same kind of relationship to Moab
as Yahweh does to his own nation; i.e. he thinks of Yahweh as the *national God* of
Israel, not as the god of the whole earth.[75]

---

[69] H.P. Müller, "Chemosh," *DDD* 187–88.

[70] See E. Puech, "Milkom," *DDD* 576. Puech also discusses the meager Ammonite
evidence for *mlkm*.

[71] For an effort to explain the problem as a matter of perspective within the book of
Judges, see O'Connell, *The Rhetoric of the Book of Judges*, 196–97. One might also pursue
a historical explanation: might the apparent confusion indicate historical developments in
the status of Heshbon? As Frank M. Cross observes, the biblical data that place Heshbon
in both Moab and Ammon may reflect political changes. See Cross, *Leaves from an
Epigrapher's Notebook: Collected Papers in Hebrew and West Semitic Palaeography and
Epigraphy* (HSS 51; Winona Lake, IN: Eisenbrauns, 2003) 93.

[72] See Parker, "The Beginning of the Reign of God," 551 and below.

[73] See the comments by Gerald Mattingly, "Moabite Religion," in: *Studies in the Mesha
Inscription and Moab* (ed. Andrew Dearman; American Schools of Oriental Research/The
Society of Biblical Literature Archaeology and Biblical Studies 2; Atlanta: Scholars, 1989)
214–25, esp. 218–19.

[74] Studer, *Das Buch der Richter grammatisch und historisch erklärt*, 289.

[75] Burney, *The Book of Judges*, 314–15. Burney's italics.

In more recent years, the dissonance between the expression in Judges 11:24 and later expressions of monotheism has been noted. Yairah Amit comments: "One still finds in this book representation of a pagan entity engaged in confrontation with the God of Israel and having power in its own right".[76] Critics have further noted the ideological difference between the worldview expressed in this verse and deuteronomistic material. Robert O'Connell comments: "Jephthah's legitimation of Chemosh as peer of YHWH is hardly in line with deuteronomistic theology."[77] Manfred Görg likewise comments: "Die Feststellung wirft ein interessantes Licht auf die ideologische Konzeption des Redeautors, der den Adressaten immerhin eine den Ansprüchen Israels analoge religiöse Legitimation zugesteht."[78] J. Clinton McCann compares Deuteronomy 32:8–9,[79] a text that we will examine below. Like Judges 11:24, this passage reflects a recognition that other peoples and their own gods express proper claims to their lands. Interestingly, Studer commented that it is this representation of the two gods that might suggest "ein höheres Alterthum" for the passage.[80]

In representing a correspondence of divine roles between Yahweh and Chemosh, Judges 11:24 shows the sort of typologies evident in some of the Bronze Age treaties and correspondence discussed in Chapter One. What we see at work in this passage is the Iron Age religious worldview that for purposes of international relations recognizes the chief deity of the nations around Israel. It is, of course, possible that the author hardly approved of such a correspondence (perhaps the speech was intended to be heard in a negative manner, perhaps even as sarcastic), and later reception of this text would brand the reference to Chemosh here as idolatry (e. g., the addition of "your idol" in Targum Jonathan). The author is surely a representative of his culture, for in verse 27, it is only Yahweh, and not Yahweh and Chemosh together, who is invoked as judge between the Israelites and Ammonites.[81] However, the significant fact is that the author represents the correspondence of gods at all. It indicates that this sort of representation encodes part of the known interactions between Israel and its neighbors involving Israel's god and the chief gods of its neighbors. We will return to this point following our consideration of two more passages found in the books of Kings.

---

[76] Amit, *The Book of Judges,* 379.

[77] O'Connell, *The Rhetoric of the Book of Judges,* 198 n. 280.

[78] Görg, *Richter,* 66.

[79] McCann, *Judges,* 80.

[80] Studer, *Das Buch der Richter,* 289. To be clear, Studer believes that on the whole the passage is quite late.

[81] See above the discussion above of Genesis 31:53, pp. 104–6.

1 Kings 20: Cross-Cultural Knowledge of the Warrior-Mountain God of Israel

This chapter recalls a series of conflicts between Ahab and Ben-hadad.[82] In preparation for a second engagement following an initial Israelite victory, the Aramean king is presented as deciding to conduct battle on the plain, based on advice given to him: "The servants of the king of Aram said to him: 'Their gods are gods of the mountains. That is why they defeated us. But if we fight them on level ground, we shall be sure to defeat them'" (verse 23). Accordingly, the Arameans plan their next engagement with the Israelites in battle. In order to demonstrate Yahweh's might, this deity sends a man of God to the king of Israel and tells him: "Yahweh says, 'Because Aram has said Yahweh is a god of mountains, not a god of plains, I will deliver up to you all this large army, that you may know that I am Yahweh" (verse 28).[83] As a result, the Israelites win the second military engagement.

These verses show that an Israelite author could represent Arameans recognizing the Israelite god in his capacity as a divine warrior. I. Benzinger comments: "Die Syrer erklären ihre Niederlage damit, dass Israels Götter Berggötter seien, die nur in den Bergen Macht haben."[84] James A. Montgomery viewed this expression as part and parcel of the monarchic age: "The polytheistic expression has true colour, even as it is put into the mouth of the Philistines (I Sam 4$_8$), of Goliath (ib 17$_{43}$), of Jezebel (I Kgs 19$_2$)."[85] Here the Arameans are represented as thinking that this divine warrior has a preferred topographical zone for his military activity. In other words, the Israelite author can represent Arameans as recognizing Yahweh the warrior in terms familiar to the Israelites. Like the Jacob-Laban story, this

---

[82] For the historical problems, see Wayne T. Pitard, *Ancient Damascus: A Historical Study of the Syrian City-State from Earliest Times until its Fall to the Assyrians in 732 B.C.E.* (Winona Lake, IN: Eisenbrauns, 1987) 114–25; and Edward Lipiński, *The Arameans: Their Ancient History, Culture, Religion* (OLA 100; Leuven/Paris/Sterling, VA: Uitgeverij Peeters/Departement Oosterse Studies, 2000) 397–400. See also the comments of Mordechai Cogan, *I Kings* (AB 10; New York: Doubleday, 2000) 471–74; Bruce Routledge, *Moab in the Iron Age: Hegemony, Polity, Archaeology* (Philadelphia: University of Pennsylvania, 2001) 150; and Rainey and Notley, *The Sacred Bridge*, 199.

[83] The last line appears to belong to a later hand. See Volkmar Fritz, *1 & 2 Kings: A Continental Commentary* (trans. Anselm Hagedorn; Minneapolis: Fortress, 2003) 208. It has been claimed that verses 22–25 likewise reflect a later redactor (see Fritz, *1 & 2 Kings,* 207), but the content associated with Yahweh as the god of the highlands hardly constitutes a standard trope for later redactors in Kings.

[84] I. Benzinger, *Die Bücher der Könige erklärt* (Kurzer Hand-Commentar zum Alten Testament IX; Freiburg/Leipzig/Tübingen: J. C. B. Mohr [Paul Siebeck, 1899] 120. See also A. Šanda, *Die Bücher der Könige* (two vols.; Exegetisches Handbuch zum Alten Testament 9; Münster: Aschendorffsche Verlagsbuchhandlung, 1911) 1.480.

[85] Montgomery, *A Critical and Exegetical Commentary on the Books of Kings* (ed. Henry Snyder Gehman; ICC; Edinburgh: T. & T. Clark, 1951) 323–24.

case of cross-cultural recognition of deities involves an Israelite-Aramean encounter.

2 Kings 1: Cross-Cultural Discussion of Gods of Divination

This passage relates an injury suffered by Ahaziah, the king of Israel, and the divine recourse that he takes as a result. The monarch instructs his messengers to make inquiry of Baal-zebub, called "the god of Ekron" (verse 2), in order to find out whether he would recover from his injury. On the way, they are met and reproved by the prophet Elijah for seeking inquiry of the Philistine god: "Is there no god in Israel such that you go to inquire of Baal-zebub, the god of Ekron?" (verse 6). The dialogue between these messengers and Elijah presupposes that inquiry of a deity can be addressed to both Yahweh and this Philistine god (verses 3, 6 and 16).[86] The particular appeal of the god of Ekron for Ahaziah cannot be determined from the context or from the divinity named[87]; commentators surmise that this deity had a noteworthy or least sufficient reputation for providing divine help (see verse 16).[88]

In the larger context, the dispute could be read in conformity with deuteronomistic norms and thus serve their larger interests, and indeed one may read the story as a relatively late exaltation of the prophet.[89] At the

---

[86] See Dany Nocquet, *Le 'livret noir de Baal': La polémique contre le dieu Baal dans la Bible hébraïque et l'ancien Israël* (Actes et Recherches; Geneva: Labor et Fides, 2004) 167, 173.

[87] For the various views, see the surveys of Day, *Yahweh,* 77–81; Wolfgang Herrmann, "Baal Zebub," *DDD* 154–56; Theodore J. Lewis, "Beelzebul," *ABD* 1:638–40; and Benjamin Uffenheimer, *Early Prophecy in Israel* (trans. David Louvish; Jerusalem: Magnes, 2000) 344–45 n. 45. In view of the textual evidence as well as the attestations to Beelzebul in the New Testament synoptic gospels (Matthew 10:25, 12:24, 27; Mark 3:22; Luke 11:15, 18–19), the emendation to Baal Zebul favored by many critics seems warranted; if so, the deity may be "Prince Baal" as known from the Ugaritic texts (e. g., *CAT* 1.2 I 38, 43; 1.2 IV 8; 1.9.17; see also his longer title, "Prince Baal/Lord of the Earth," in 1.5 VI 10; 1.6 I 42, III 3, 9, 21, IV 5, 16). In this case, this deity belongs to the indigenous West Semitic pantheon, like Dagon who is attested as a god among the Philistines (Judges 16:23; 1 Samuel 5:1–7; 1 Maccabees 10:83–84; see John F. Healey, "Dagon," *DDD* 216–19). If the identity of Baal Zebub/Zebul as the West Semitic storm-god is correct, then Elijah is represented as opposing the same sort of god here that he is portrayed as combating on Mount Carmel in 1 Kings 18.

[88] For example, Ernst Würthwein, *Die Bücher der Könige: 1. Kön. 17 – 2. Kön. 25* (Das Alte Testament Deutsch 11,2; Göttingen: Vandenhoeck & Ruprecht, 1984) 267.

[89] Commentators such as James A. Montgomery have noted arguments for earlier and later levels of the text. In most assessments, the initial speech concerning the two deities (in verses 3 and 6; cf. verse 16) is assigned to an earlier stratum. See Montgomery, *A Critical and Exegetical Commentary on the Books of Kings,* 348–49. Robert R. Wilson notes the lack of deuteronomistic editing in the text of the story. See Wilson, *Prophecy and Society in Ancient Israel* (Philadelphia: Fortress, 1980) 200–1. Following C. F. Burney, Alexander Rofé regards the story as late, based in part on linguistic features that Gary A. Rendsburg

same time, the dialogue in itself seems to presuppose that both deities, one Israelite and one Philistine, are capable and reliable gods in matters of divine consultation.[90] And at least the notion of cross-cultural recognition of the god and his capabilities seems to enjoy an older cultural history in Israel, as suggested by the reverse case of 2 Kings 8:7–10.[91] In 2 Kings 1 (verses 3, 6, and 16), Elijah does not deny the existence or power of the other god; nor does he discredit the information that may be potentially received from this deity. He prefers Israel's own god for the task. In this passage, Israelites are represented as discussing the relative merits of the Philistine and Israelite

---

would take as signs of northern Hebrew and thus not late, but as rather authentic. See Burney, *Notes on the Hebrew Text of the Books of Kings* (Oxford: Clarendon, 1903) 214; Rofé, *The Prophetical Stories: The Narratives about the Prophets in the Hebrew Bible. Their Literary Types and History* (Jerusalem: Magnes, 1988) 33–40; and the critical response by Rendsburg, *Israelian Hebrew and the Book of Kings* (Occasional Publications of the Department of Near Eastern Studies and the Program of Jewish Studies Cornell University 5; Bethesda, MD: CDL, 2002) 80–81; see also his remarks in "Hurvitz Redux: On the Continued Scholarly Inattention to a Simple Principle of Hebrew Principle of Hebrew Philology," in: *Biblical Hebrew: Studies in Chronology and Typology* (ed. Ian Young; London/New York: T & T Clark International, 2003) 117. It is interesting that Rofé and Rendsburg draw on some of the same features for their widely varying views for the date of the passage's linguistic milieu. For a critique of Rendsburg's claim for *meh* as one of three northernisms in this chapter (verse 7), see William Schniedewind and Daniel Sivan, "The Elijah-Elisha Narratives: A Test Case for the Northern Dialect of Hebrew," *JQR* 87 (1997) 316. In view of the minimal number of northernisms claimed by Rendsburg, the view of Burney and Rofé might gain in credibility, but the number of clearly late features that conform to the methodology for distinguishing pre-exilic and post-exilic Hebrew is no less lacking, especially for the material pertaining to the two deities under discussion. For recent discussions of this method and criticism, see Ian Young, ed., *Biblical Hebrew: Studies in Chronology and Typology* (London/New York: T & T Clark International, 2003); and the essays of the "Symposium: Can Biblical Texts be Dated Linguistically?" in: *Hebrew Studies* 46 (2005) 321–76. For another critique of Rofé's analysis and conclusions, see Nocquet, *Le 'livret noir de Baal'*, 159–87, esp. 181–82. Nocquet surveys other views as well, and despite claims to the contrary, his close anaysis of the language and themes in the passage suggest to him only very limited deuteronomistic material in this passage. He concludes that the basic story is pre-deuteronomistic. It is evident from the diversity of views that the date of this passage, at least for the material concerning the two deities, cannot be easily determined. Based on the arguments presented, the passage does not seem particularly late. If this particular material were late (perhaps post-deuteronomistic?), it is perhaps surprising that the condemnation of the god of Ekron is not more categorical. For further discussion, see note 91.

[90] Note the observation of the story's "original local colour," by Montgomery, *A Critical and Exegetical Commentary on the Books of Kings,* 349.

[91] The parallel use of material in 2 Kings 8:9//1:2 suggests that the notion of cross-cultural consultation is traditional, but in turn this observation may suggest the possibility that 2 Kings 8 may have served as a (literary?) model for the description of Ahaziah's interest in consulting the god of Ekron in 2 Kings 1 (see also the predictions in 2 Kings 1:4, 6 and 16 versus 8:10; and for the idiom "to make inquiry of (a deity)," note the relatively unusual **drš b-* in 2 Kings 1:2 versus *drš 't* in 2 Kings 8:9). See note 89. Thus one might be inclined to see the account in 2 Kings 1 as secondary, but it is unclear how late it is.

gods for providing a divine word. Here translatability is an implicit assumption made by both parties in their dispute. The discussion presupposes that Israelites recognize the capability of the god of Ekron; they arguably differ over his merits relative to their own Israelite god.[92]

2 Kings 3: Implicit Israelite Recognition of the Moabite National God

Our final text of Israelite translatability is also an implicit case, and that is 2 Kings 3:27. This passage relates a battle by an alliance of the Israelites, Judeans and Edomites against the Moabites.[93] They muster their shared resources (verse 7)[94] after they receive a positive oracle from the prophet Elisha. The battle is going badly for the Moabites (verses 24–26). In order to avoid defeat, it is attributed to the Moabite king that he "took his son the first-born who was to rule as his successor and he offered him up as an *'ola*-offering on the wall, and a great wrath came upon Israel, and they journeyed from him and returned to the land" (verse 27).[95]

As with the preceding passages, the context involves international relations, but in this case the narrative relates the failure to resolve conflict. Instead, the king of Moab in a last, final act of desperation offers his son as

---

[92] One might hazard a further speculation based on the proposed identification of Baal Zebub/Zebul as "Prince Baal" (noted above): consultation to Yahweh for a divine answer was considered direct, as it was with El, as reflected in the story of Kirta (*CAT* 1.14 I–III, in *UNP* 12–18; cf. Hannah in 1 Samuel 1–2), while consultation to Baal represented an intermediary step of intercession taken toward getting a word to and from El, as dramatized in the narrative of Aqhat (*CAT* 1.17 I–II, in: *UNP* 51–57). For an insightful discussion of this divine function in these passages, see C. L. Seow, *Myth, Drama, and the Politics of David's Dance* (HSM 44; Atlanta: Scholars, 1989) 11–69, esp. 25–36. If this speculation were correct, it might indicate the basis for the discussion between the prophet and the king's messengers, but this would exceed the evidence in the text.

[93] For the international treaty context, see the remarks of Kalluveettil, *Declaration and Covenant*, 34, 75, 173. For the geographical context of the campaign, see Pierre Bordreuil, "A propos de l'inscription de Mesha': deux notes," in: *The World of the Aramaeans III: Studies in Language and Literature in Honour of Paul-Eugène Dion* (ed. P. M. Michèle Daviau, John W. Wevers and Michael Weigl; JSOTSup 326; Sheffield: Sheffield, 2001) 162–65; and Rainey and Notley, *The Sacred Bridge*, 205. For the general context of 2 Kings 3, see Jesse C. Long, Jr., and Mark Sneed, " 'Yahweh Has Given These Three Kings into the Hand of Moab': A Socio-Literary Reading of 2 Kings 3," in: *Inspired Speech: Prophecy in the Ancient Near East: Essays in Honor of Herbert B. Huffmon* (ed. John Kaltner and Louis Stulman; JSOTSup 378; London/New York: T&T Clark, 2004) 253–75.

[94] For the expression of shared resources, see also 1 Kings 22:4 (cf. Ruth 1:16–17). For discussion of these passages and the underlying conceptualization, see my essay, " 'Your People Shall be My People': Family and Covenant in Ruth 1:16–17," *CBQ* 69 (2007) 233–49; and the discussion in Chapter One.

[95] For the use of **'ly* for child sacrifice in Phoenician and Punic, see *'lt* cited by Cross, *Leaves*, 233–34. As elsewhere for sacrifice, the application of this root indicates a whole burnt offering.

an offering, and a great wrath results. What is remarkable about this passage is its recognition of the efficacy of child sacrifice by a non-Israelite, represented in the setting of warfare.[96] The narrative does not state explicitly the names of the gods behind the success of the offering. The passage leaves it to its Israelite audience to infer the ritual practice here, namely an offering made to Chemosh, the god of the Moabites.[97] The audience would have assumed that since Mesha made the offering, the sacrifice's efficacy as represented would have been due to his god, not to the god of Israel,[98] and no less, by means of a practice regarded as illegitimate, in at least some Israelite circles.[99] It is possible that the Israelite audience might have assumed

---

[96] There has been some doubt as to whether this act of child sacrifice or child sacrifice in Israel in general is historically accurate. For the purposes of this analysis, which focuses on the cultural attitudes of the writer(s), such an issue is not crucial. However, there is no reason why it could not be so. This is not the sort of outcome that a later writer would have composed. The practice of child sacrifice is attested in other sources, and it would be particularly fitting in the context of warfare. For a brief discussion, see Cross, *Leaves*, 231–37, esp. 233, 237, with earlier references to studies of the Phoenician and Punic material as well as classical literature. For further bibliography, see Smith, *The Early History of God*, 176–77.

[97] So commentators such as Carl Friedrich Keil, *Die Bücher der Könige* (second ed.; Biblischer Commentar über das Alte Testament II/3; Leipzig: Dörffling und Franke, 1876) 255; Benzinger, *Die Bücher der Könige erklärt*, 135; Rudolph Kittel, *Die Bücher der Könige übersetzt und erklärt* (Handkommentar zum Alten Testament I/5; Göttingen: Vandenhoeck & Ruprecht, 1900) 196.

[98] So many commentators, e.g., Otto Thenius, *Die Bücher der Könige* (Kurzgefasstes exegetisches Handbuch zum Alten Testament 9; Leipzig: Weidmannsche Buchhandlung, 1849) 277; Burney, *Notes on the Hebrew Text of the Books of Kings*, 272; and Montgomery, *A Critical and Exegetical Commentary on the Books of Kings*, 363–64. In contrast, Rainey and Notley (*The Sacred Bridge*, 205) suggest that in the battle of verse 26, Mesha managed to capture the son and heir of the Edomite king whom Mesha then sacrificed. This is an old view, reflected in medieval commentators (David Kimchi cited by Rainey and Notley), and in nineteenth century debates, for example, in: W. Pakenham Walsh, *The Moabite Stone* (sixth edition; Dublin: G. Herbert; London: Hamilton and Co./J. Nisbet and Co., 1873) 63–65. Walsh took "fury" (*qeṣep*) in 2 Kings 3:27 as the Moabites' own fury following in the wake of Mesha's offering of his son. The solution of Rainey and Notley assumes considerable information behind the text, and it is arguable that it does not read particularly well with it. For example, verse 26a in the Hebrew more readily reads in context: "He [Mesha] took his son." Walsh noted his own objection to this view: "The offering up of the son of his enemy would not be deemed so likely to propitiate Chemosh as the sacrifice of his own child".

[99] See Jeremiah 7:31, 32:35; Ezekiel 20:25–26. For related issues involving the divine word "which I did not command them," see the various formulations in Deuteronomy 17:3, 18:20; Jeremiah 14:14, 23:32, 29:23 (see Mark S. Smith, *The Memoirs of God: History, Memory, and the Experience of God in Ancient Israel* [Minneapolis: Fortress, 2004] 107–10, 151–52). The date of these texts suggest a seventh-sixth strategy used to clarify the interpretation of older texts that may (and arguably should) be read as allowing the practices mentioned. Thus the passages about child sacrifice seem to be addressing what their authors evidently thought as the wrong understanding of Exodus 22:28b or the like.

that power of Chemosh here was allowed by the god of Israel,[100] but it is particularly interesting that the text does not speak to the issue as such and does not show an effort to resolve any perceived problem. Commentators have long compared the representation of Chemosh in the Moabite stele (KAI 181) and its declaration of Moabite victory over the Israelites,[101] with the further suggestion that the account in 2 Kings 3 reflects an awareness of this Moabite victory.[102] Whatever the precise case, the passage attributes to the Moabite side a victory generated through a religious act on the part of the Moabites themselves. In short, the passage implicitly recognizes divine power apart from the Israelite national god.[103] Given the Bible's rejection of other gods, this passage with its implicit act of cross-cultural recognition would appear to stand out. However, if such a passage is contextualized in its Iron Age setting when such a view of national gods was more common, the passage seems less remarkable.[104]

It is to be noted that in proposing Levites as a substitute for first-born Israelites, Numbers 8:17–18 shows that the commandment was taken to apply to first-born humans. The passages in Deuteronomy, Jeremiah and Ezekiel are the earliest instances that deliberately raise the problem of such laws. On the question of interpretation more broadly, see Scott Walker Hahn and John Seitze Bergsma, "What Laws Were 'Not Good'? A Canonical Approach to the Theological Problem of Ezekiel 20:25–26," *JBL* 123 (2004) 201–18. For a survey of the textual relations among the passages involved, see John van Seters, "From Child Sacrifice to Paschal Lamb: A Remarkable Transformation in Israelite Religion," *Old Testament Essays* 16/2 (2003) 453–63.

[100] Thenius, *Die Bücher der Könige,* 272: "*als wäre Jahwe selbst voll grosser Erbitterung auf Israel*" (Thenius's italics).

[101] Walsh, *The Moabite Stone,* 63–65; Šanda, *Die Bücher der Könige,* 2.23; Burney, *Notes on the Hebrew Text of the Books of Kings,* 272; and Montgomery, *A Critical and Exegetical Commentary on the Books of Kings,* 363–64. Burney and Montgomery compare the *qeṣep* to the report in the Mesha stele (KAI 181:5), how "Chemosh was angry" (*y'np*).

[102] See the comments of Keil, *Die Bücher der Könige,* 255–56 n. 1.

[103] Kittel, *Die Bücher der Könige,* 196: "Nach semitischem Glauben, an dem auch das alte Israel teilweise festhält, herrscht im Machtbereich des Kemos nicht Jahve, sondern Kemos; vgl. Jdc 11₂₄ I Sam 26₁₉." See also Šanda, *Die Bücher der Könige,* 2.24.

[104] For this reason, it seems unlikely that the passage was composed by a deuteronomistic redactor, as claimed by Fritz, *1 & 2 Kings,* 245, following Ernst Würthwein. Indeed, the passage is remarkably non-deuteronomistic in both language and worldview. Moshe Weinfeld notes the explicit difference between 2 Kings 3:19 and Deuteronomy 20:19–20, with respect to the treatment of trees. See Weinfeld, *Deuteronomy and the Deuteronomic School* (Oxford: Oxford University, 1972; repr., Winona Lake, IN: Eisenbrauns, 1992) 239. Weinfeld (p. 16) also notes how the prophetic word about the violent death of the king in this passage (verses 16–19) contrasts with the deuteronomic word that portends the fate of the royal house.

3. Translatability and National Gods

Taken as a whole, the passages surveyed in the preceding section reflect various forms of translatability largely involving the recognition of the class of national, military gods across cultural boundaries. With this class we have one clear instance of the sort of typology of divinity that we saw in Chapter One in many different texts. What these biblical passages represent is a form of translatability, specifically a component in a monarchic period worldview that sees the various chief gods of the nations who stand more or less on par with one another. These deities have been called national gods,[105] and they figure in an international religious worldview (or, what might perhaps be called a "world theology").[106]

We might think that such cross-cultural recognition would work only in contexts of negotiations or alliances. However, contexts of conflict also reflect the presupposition of translatability. Sometimes this worldview is reflected in polemic against national gods belonging to non-Israelites. Thus in its "woe" oracle against Moab, Numbers 21:29 calls it "the people of Chemosh" (cf. Jeremiah 48:46), just as Israel is called "the people of Yahweh" in Judges 5:11 (see also Numbers 11:29; 1 Samuel 2:24 and 2 Samuel 1:12).[107] Here the national patron god of a neighbor people is emblematic of

---

[105] See F. M. Cross, *From Epic to Canon: History and Literature in Ancient Israel* (Baltimore/London: Johns Hopkins University, 1998) 49; see also Keel and Uehlinger, *Gods*, 138. McCarter characterizes the national god in Iron Age Levantine religions as "almost the sole object of worship" ("The Religious Reforms," p. 73) and as "the divine" perceived as "an essential singularity" (p. 74). These assertions are based in no small measure on an argument from silence; yet even the available evidence is inconsistent with these characterizations. The claim made by André Lemaire that the religion of the national god was monolatrous (worship of only one deity) might apply at national sanctuaries, but this, too, is probably not the case if the available evidence about other deities is to be taken seriously (cf. Ezekiel 8–10). See Lemaire, *Naissance du monothéisme: Point de vue d'un historian* (Paris: Bayard, 2003) 59–63. It seems more consistent with the known evidence that the cult of the national god regards him as without divine peer, hardly a formula for monolatry as such. The polytheistic context of national religion is seen by Day, *Yahweh;* Hendel, "Israelite Religion," *ER* 7:4742–43; and Smith, *The Early History of God.*

[106] Parker, "The Beginning of the Reign of God," 551–52; Smith, *The Memoirs of God,* 54–56, 110; cf. Norman Gottwald, "Proto-Globalization and Proto-Secularization in Ancient Israel," in: *Confronting the Past: Archaeological and Historical Essays on Ancient Israel in Honor of William G. Dever* (ed. S. Gitin, J. E. Wright and J. P. Dessel; Winona Lake, IN: Eisenbrauns, 2006) 207–14, esp. 209. I am using "theology" here in its literal sense as "god-discourse" and not so much as in its usage as "second-order discourse," although such statements arguably assume a second-order level of reflection. (First-order discourse is discourse expressed in and of religious experience, such as prayer; second-order discourse involves discourse representing intellectual reflection about the content of that experience, as in theology or philosophy of religion or history of religion or comparative religion.) To avoid confusion possibly created by the use of the word "theology," I often use the term "worldview" in this context.

[107] Cross, *From Epic to Canon,* 12 and 49.

its status. This worldview was operative not only in Israel, but also in Moab. The Moabite stele (KAI 181) relates the victory of Mesha over the Israelites. The king brags: "And I took from there the [ves]sels (*[k]ly*)/altar-hearths (*'r['ly*) of Yahweh and I hauled them before Chemosh" (lines 17–18).[108] However one is to resolve the epigraphic difficulties at the end of line 17, this royal boast works on the assumption that Yahweh and Chemosh are the chief gods of their respective peoples.[109] The stele offers a Moabite mirror image of the Israelite religious worldview of national gods.

National Gods in Deuteronomistic Historiography

The worldview in ancient Israel that I have laid out can be gleaned further from some other narrative texts in the Bible. Behind these passages stands a prior understanding of national gods, more specifically a notion that each territory or nation had its own chief god, who rules over that polity. A number of narrative contexts illustrate this understanding. We begin with 1 Samuel 26. In Israel, Yahweh is the proprietary god of Israel, as represented by the words of David. In the context, verses 18–20, David is said to ask Saul why he seeks to kill him:

"But why does my lord continue to pursue his servant? What have I done, and what wrong am I guilty of? Now let my lord the king hear his servant out. If Yahweh has incited you against me, let Him be appeased by an offering; but if it is men, let them be accursed of Yahweh! For they have driven me out today so that I cannot have a share in *the inheritance of Yahweh,* but am told, 'Go and *worship other gods.*' Oh, let my blood not fall to the ground, away from the presence of Yahweh! For the king of Israel has come out to seek a single flea – as if he were hunting a partridge in the hills." (my italics)

Yahweh is the god of the nation; to worship other gods in this context here means to leave Israel, which is "the inheritance of Yahweh" (as stated in Deuteronomy 32:9, discussed below; cf. Psalm 82). A number of scholars

---

[108] See Kent Jackson and J. Andrew Dearman, "The Text of the Mesha' Inscription," in: *Studies in the Mesha Inscription and Moab* (ed. Andrew Dearman; Atlanta: Scholars, 1989) 94, 98, 116. The translation used here also draws on Bruce Routledge, *Moab in the Iron Age: Hegemony, Polity, Archaeology* (Philadelphia: University of Pennsylvania, 2004) 136; note also his comments on the context of the inscription on pp. 133–53, esp. 149–50; and Rainey and Notley, *The Sacred Bridge,* 204. The second option for the end of line 17 derives from André Lemaire, "Le ḥérem dans le monde nord-ouest sémitique," in: *Guerre et conquête dans le Proche-Orient ancien: Actes de la table ronde du 14 novembre 1998* (ed. Laïla Nehmé; Antiquités sémitiques 4; Paris: J. Maisonneuve, 1999) 79–92, esp. 83–85, with a discussion of the reading. See also Nocquet, *Le 'livret noir de Baal',* 320–21.

[109] See also the reconstruction of lines 8–9 by P. K. McCarter, Jr. (*Ancient Inscriptions: Voices from the Biblical World* [Washington, DC: Biblical Archaeology Society, 1996] 91–92): "and 'Yahweh' resided there during his days and the days of his sons – 40 years! But Chemosh resided there in my days."

get the point right that it is the national god here who is being described.[110] In the words of Shimon Bar-Efrat, David's speech reflects "the popular belief that each nation has its own god, who rules over that nation's territory."[111] This does not mean that David is suggesting that there are no other deities known in Israel, only that there is only one god who really matters. In the context of the text, this refers to the national god of Israel, Yahweh.[112] The other divinities in Israel by comparison are lesser figures in this worldview.

The polemic of Elijah against the prophets of Baal on Mount Carmel in 1 Kings 18 would seem to reflect a rejection of translatability. Indeed, the story has sometimes been read as an expression of biblical monotheism,[113] in particular in verse 39, literally, "Yahweh is the god."[114] It has also been argued that the narrative contains some deuteronomistic elements.[115] At the same

---

[110] For example, P. K. McCarter, Jr., *1 Samuel* (AB 8; New York: Doubleday, 1980) 408. Hans Wilhelm Hertzberg regards this notion as an "ancient idea" that predates the notion that the God of Israel exerts power beyond such national boundaries; see Hertzberg, *I & II Samuel: A Commentary* (trans. J. S. Bowden; OTL; Philadelphia: Westminster, 1964) 210. Cf. the legendary story of the Asiatic (Hyksos) king Apophis (ca. 1615–1575) in Papyrus Sallier I, which relates how "King Apophis – life, prosperity, health! – made him Seth as lord, and he would not serve any god who was in the land [except] Seth" (*ANET* 231; Redford, *Egypt, Canaan, and Israel in Ancient Times,* 233). To extrapolate, one might regard the worship of the national god in royal sanctuaries as the context for expressions in 1 Samuel 26:19 and elsewhere, perhaps Exodus 22:19: "Whoever sacrifices to a god other than Yahweh alone shall be proscribed."

[111] Quoted from the exegetical note to this verse by Bar-Efrat, "First Samuel," in: *The Jewish Study Bible* (ed. Adele Berlin and Marc Zvi Brettler; Oxford/New York: Oxford University, 2004) 620.

[112] 1 Kings 4:4 likewise uses "other gods" to refer to the patron (and/or most famous) deities associated with the peoples named in verse 5.

[113] So NJPS for this verse: "The Lord alone is God" (see also Judges 8:23). See also this view in: Alexander Rofé, *The Prophetical Stories: The Narratives about the Prophets in the Hebrew Bible. Their Literary Types and History* (Jerusalem: Magnes, 1988) 192; Fritz, *1 & 2 Kings,* 193. It is arguable that the statement in 1 Kings 18:39 means more literally "Yahweh is THE god" for the speaker, and not the other god in this context, specifically Baal, as correctly noted by Lemaire (*The Birth of Monotheism,* 52–53; see also Nocquet, *Le 'livret noir de Baal',* 108–9). Writer(s) would have no difficulty expressing "Yahweh alone" (cf. 1 Kings 19:10: "and I alone am left," with *lebaddi* explicitly marking Elijah-alone; see also Exodus 22:19 and Judges 3:20), as noted by Stephen A. Geller ("The God of the Covenant," in: *One God or Many? Concepts of Divinity in the Ancient World* (ed. Barbara Nevling Porter; Transactions of the Casco Bay Assyriological Institute, vol. 1; np: np, 2000] 291). Nor would the deuteronomistic writer later in the book of Kings have had any trouble adding this qualification in speaking of God (2 Kings 19:15). In contrast, no such grammatical qualification marks the declaration of 1 Kings 18:39, contrary to its translation by NJPS (cf. NJPS to 2 Samuel 24:17, which instead might be better translated, "I am the one who sinned …").

[114] It is possible to render the pronoun as a copula or to take the initial term as a casus pendens: "as for Yahweh, he is the god."

[115] For example, the warning against foreign worship in verses 18 and 21 (see Weinfeld, *Deuteronomy and the Deuteronomic School,* 320, 332). See, however, the following note.

time, it is not a wholesale deuteronomistic composition.[116] It is preferable to view the passage as evidencing a non-deuteronomistic (or, perhaps better, a pre-deuteronomistic[117]) worldview,[118] involving an older form of competition between major gods, which has been filtered through a later deuteronomistic redaction with its sense of Yahweh as the only god. Peter Machinist has put the point well: "… in the course of transmission through the exilic redaction of the Deuteronomistic History, this context came to be seen more explicitly as a justification of Yahweh's unique qualification as deity."[119]

So what does the conflict entail? The passage does not contain a specific expression of monotheism. The narrative instead presents a conflict between two gods represented by their religious personnel.[120] More specifically, the

---

[116] Nocquet (*Le 'livret noir de Baal'*, 231 n. 1) lists the following verses in 1 Kings 18 as dtr or later: 18b, 19 (only the mention of the 450 prophets of Asherah), 22, 31, 32b, and 36b.

[117] For the argument that 1 Kings 18:21–40 is post-deuteronomistic, see Juha Pakkala, "The Monotheism of the Deuteronomistic History," *Scandinavian Journal of the Old Testament* (in press). Pakkala argues: "That the Mt. Carmel scene in 1 Kgs 18:21–40 was added in a post-nomistic phase is also suggested by the fact that the author of the text did not consider it problematic to sacrifice outside Jerusalem (see Deut 12)." On the contrary, sacrifice outside of Jerusalem would have been considered problematic by a later user of Deuteronomy, such as the nomistic editor that Pakkala credits with this passage. In fact, Pakkala's argument here supports the case for pre-deuteronomistic tradition. Pakkala notes that other commentators argue for a pre-deuteronomistic layer in the passage, e. g., Ernst Würthwein, *Die Bücher der Könige 1. Kön. 17 – 2. Kön. 25*, 207–20; see also a critique of the approach taken by Pakkala in Nocquet, *Le 'livret noir de Baal'*, 243. My argument here does not rule out possible secondary additions or redaction of an earlier version of the account in verses 21–40. For linguistic and literary arguments for an older story involved here, see the following note.

[118] The basic story reads like a scribal, court-elaborated composition as opposed to prophetic legenda with a popular, oral background, according to Rofé, *The Prophetical Stories*, 186–96. Rofé would locate the story in the reign of Manasseh, but the episode shows a northern background, with features such as "sons of Jacob" in 18:31 instead of the standard "sons of Israel" (Schniedewind and Sivan,"The Elijah-Elisha Narratives," 325–26); *kad* in 18:34 (Schniedewind and Sivan,"The Elijah-Elisha Narratives," 327); and perhaps "Abraham, Isaac and Israel" in 18:36 instead of "Abraham, Isaac and Jacob." Based on these features, a northern background appears to be indicated, and not a composition in the south during the reign of Manasseh, unless one were to assume that a southern author is making an effort to imitate northern dialect. The anti-Baal critique of the story would fit the court of Jehu and his anti-Omride polemic. For this view, see Marsha White, *The Elijah Legends and Jehu's Coup* (Brown Judaic Studies 311; Atlanta: Scholars, 1997) 24–43; and Nocquet, *Le 'livret noir de Baal'*, 264–84.

[119] Machinist, "Mesopotamian Imperialism and Israelite Religion: A Case Study from the Second Isaiah," in: *Symbiosis, Symbolism, and the Power of the Past: Canaan, Ancient Israel, and Their Neighbors – From the Late Bronze Age through Roman Palaestina* (ed. William G. Dever and Seymour Gitin; the AIAR Anniversary Volume; Winona Lake, IN: Eisenbrauns, 2003) 243 n. 13.

[120] Cf. the characterization of the conflict by Arthur Darby Nock as a "*Gottesurteil* (with a competitive nuance)," in his *Essays on Religion and the Ancient World* (vol. 1; ed. Zeph Stewart; Cambridge, MA: Harvard University, 1972) 328.

story explores the issue of the proper place of Baal in Israelite religion. Is Baal simply an outsider, as Elijah would maintain (verse 18), or does he represent a god acceptable to Israelites, as they are represented (verse 21)? The story's critique of Baal indicates, even as it rejects, a cross-cultural acceptance of Phoenician Baal, championed by his prophets,[121] alongside Yahweh.[122] It may also point to a further, inner-cultural acceptance of Baal on the part of some Israelites. Several scholars, including André Lemaire[123] and Peter Machinist,[124] have viewed the passage in terms of a geographical or local contest of power between Yahweh and Baal. To explore this approach further, we might take a broader view of the geographical distribution of the deities involved in the larger cultural context.

We may begin with the figures of Elijah and Elisha: a great deal of their prophetic activity is placed in the eastern side of the highlands and in Transjordan.[125] David V. Santis has studied the geographical significance of the religious traditions of the Transjordan.[126] Santis highlights Elijah's home in Transjordan (specifically from Gilead), with its strong El traditions.[127] On the other hand, the storm-god Baal seems to enjoy particular devotion in the coastal region. As largely a coastal god, Baal might not have enjoyed the same level of cult in the Transjordan. The dialogue in 2 Kings 1 and the competition in 1 Kings 18 may represent a larger competition for the zone lying in-between, namely the highlands between the coast and Transjordan.

---

[121] The prophetic self-laceration mentioned in verse 28 finds a suitable parallel in the description of the prophet in the Middle Babylonian text from Ugarit sometimes called "the Righteous Sufferer.' As noted by Martti Nissinen, the text mentions several kinds of divination comparing people to prophets who "bathe in their blood." See Nissinen, "The Dubious Image of Prophecy," in: *Prophets, Prophecy and Prophetic Texts in Second Temple Judaism* (ed. Michael H. Floyd and Robert D. Haak; Library of Hebrew Bible/Old Testament Studies 427; London/New York: T & T Clark, 2006) 37. This discussion also relates the prophetic polemic in Zechariah 13. For the text, see Nissinen, *Prophets and Prophecy in the Ancient Near East* (SBLWAW 12; Atlanta: Society of Biblical Literature, 2003) 184.

[122] For the religious context, see Day, *Yahweh,* 70–77; Keel and Uehlinger, *Gods,* 259–62; Lemaire, *The Birth of Monotheism,* 49–55; Smith, *The Early History of God,* 65–72.

[123] Lemaire, *The Birth of Monotheism,* 52. Lemaire constructs the geographical issue in terms of coastal Tyrian Baal versus Yahweh at home in Israel. In view of the people's devotion to Baal, the religious situation in Israel at the time may be more complex. See below.

[124] Machinist, "Mesopotamian Imperialism," 243 n. 13.

[125] For a handy visual, see Rainey and Notley, *The Sacred Bridge,* 213.

[126] Santis, "The Land of Transjordan Israel in the Iron Age and its Religious Traditions" (Ph.D. dissertation, New York University, 2004). See the discussion of Mark S. Smith, Review Article of *The Religions of Ancient Israel: A Synthesis of Parallactic Approaches* (Ziony Zevit), *Maarav* 11/2 (2004) 176–77.

[127] On this point, Santis is following his mentor Baruch Levine. See Levine, *Numbers 21–36,* 229; and Chalmers, "Who is the Real El?" 611–30. See also the discussion above about El.

To be sure, the highlands by this time were thought to belong to Yahweh (1 Kings 20:23, 28 discussed above; and perhaps the Khirbet beit Lei inscription[128]; cf. 1 Maccabees 10:70; Judith 7:11). Yet this need not preclude devotion also to Baal, who may also have become traditional to the highlands. In short, Elijah's position represents a minority voice (verse 22); the majority is seen as supporting Baal and Yahweh. The support for Baal may even be cross-cultural if Israelites are identifying the Phoenician Baal with a Baal traditionally known in Israel prior to the Omrides.[129] Whether issues of translatability between Baal and Yahweh are involved as such is unclear from the story; it is possible.[130] In sum, although the narrative was readily amenable to later monotheistic reception within Israel, it is hardly monotheistic, but reflects the conflict between two national gods. We are closer to the world of Mesha's exaltation of his national god, Chemosh, over Yahweh (KAI 181) than to the monotheism of considerably later generations.

2 Kings 5 perhaps offers another representation of the concept of the national god.[131] The Aramean general Naaman, following his healing through the help of Elisha and his god, proclaims his new allegiance to this Israelite deity. Naaman makes the following promise (verse 17): "Your servant will never again offer up burnt offering or sacrifice to any god, except Yahweh." However, he also adds the condition that when he is with the king of Aram in the temple of Rimmon, he will have to honor this god (verse 19): "When my master enters the temple of Rimmon to bow low to worship there, and he is leaning on my arm so that I must bow down low in the temple of Rimmon – when I bow low in the temple of Rimmon, may Yahweh pardon your servant in this." To this request Elisha responds to Naaman, "Go in peace." Here we see the two national gods represented as the options that count. Commentators sometimes regard verse 17 as an expression of monotheism (the belief in only one deity).[132] In fact, there is no statement of monotheism; it seems to be a pledge to Israel's national god, without addressing the question of lesser deities. Moreover, room is left for the special situation that Naaman finds himself in, namely an occasion of reverence to Rimmon. This is hardly the "monotheism" of later biblical tradition (although one can understand how later interpreters would come to this view of this passage). Instead, we see an exchange of one national god for another, with exceptions permitted as necessity would require of Naaman.

---

[128] For translation and discussion of this possible reading, see *COS* 2.180.

[129] For this possibility, see Smith, *The Early History of God*, 66, 71.

[130] For the possibility, see Smith, *The Early History of God*, 73.

[131] See the discussion of Rofé, *The Prophetical Stories*, 126–31.

[132] For example, Rofé, *The Prophetical Stories*, 127; and Ziony Zevit, "First Kings," in: *The Jewish Study Bible*, 736.

2 Kings 17:26 represents Yahweh as "the god of the land" who has rules unknown to the peoples transplanted there. The passage goes on to criticize these peoples in verse 29: "For each nation continued to make its own gods and to set them up in the cult places which had been made by the people of Samaria." At first glance, this statement would seem to indicate only that different peoples had different deities. However, the next verse goes on to name one god per people for the first three peoples in the list: "The Babylonians made Succoth-benoth, and the men of Cuth made Nergal, and the men of Hamath made Ashima." Afterwards the verses name more than one deity per group for the other two peoples. As a whole, the verse in this polemical context would suggest that one or two main gods were associated with each nation.[133] In short, these passages illustrate the Israelite notion that each nation had a main god, in most if not all cases, a national god.

In addition to these narratives, there is evidence for this worldview in biblical polemics. One may point to the deuteronomistic rejection of the worldview as evidence for it, since in expressing such rejection, it is acknowledged at the same time. Above we noted the names of Chemosh and Milkom in 1 Kings 11:5 and 7 as well as 2 Kings 23:13. These texts condemn by name the national deities of Israel's neighbors. As deuteronomistic texts, they indicate a prior date for the worldview that they are condemning. Moreover, the worldview dates to pre-deuteronomistic tradition during the monarchic period. Thus as we saw with Judges 11:24 and 2 Kings 3:27, we have further evidence of the worldview operative in the period of the monarchy.

Before we pass on to other texts, we should note the additional information afforded by 1 Kings 11:7. The verse itself is rather critical of Solomon's support (it is apparently the basis for the highly negative, deuteronomistic commentary of 1 Kings 11:4). 1 Kings 11:7 may be historically accurate in reporting Solomon's hospitality to shrines for the gods of his wives (or, perhaps to some of them). If so, it may be an indication of a cultic praxis of translatability, to the degree that Solomon offers a cultic support for other deities in the larger area of the cult of the Israelite national god in Jerusalem. Marriage to non-Israelites in this case involves an intercultural engagement on the religious level, and as with the two examples of the praxis of translatability that we discussed in Chapter One (the statue of Shauska in the Egyptian court in El-Amarna letter 23, and Serabit el-Khadem 345), translatability might play out not only in the rhetoric of international encounter, but also in the cultic realities that issue from such relations. Cases of cultic translatability are relatively rare, and perhaps they indicate that translatability could become an acute issue when it came to cultic praxis.

---

[133] See Burnett, *A Reassessment of Biblical Elohim,* 66.

In other words, the problem involved in 1 Kings 11:4–7 may not have been simply an issue of foreigners worshiping their own deities within Israel. Instead, it may have been the potential religious dissonance posed by cultic translatability that induced some circles in ancient Israel to draw a line against foreign deities.

Other biblical polemics point to translatability at work in ancient Israel. The deuteronomistic editor of Judges works with a representation of translatability, in the form of a picture of Baalim and Ashtarot/Asherot as the gods of the nations (e. g., Judges 2:11, 13; 3:7[134]). The gender typology for divinities is unsurprising, as we noted for the Late Bronze Age material. In addition, the moralizing deuteronomistic editor performs a sort of analysis of the deities through an exegesis of the stories that he inherited. More specifically, the editor, having picked up the name of Baal-berit as the beginning of the old story in Judges 9:4, re-uses the divine name of Baal-berit in his moralizing introduction in 8:33 to exemplify the negative effects of the Baalim. Thus, the moralizing scribe apparently exegeted the divine name and title as one of the Baalim.[135]

Translatability and Biblical Foreigners

As we have noted, a number of biblical passages sometimes read as polemics against translatability may at the same time presuppose it. Some of these cases involve the representation of foreigners proclaiming the greatness of the Israelite god.[136] Even though these statements are readily heard as acclamations of Yahweh and essentially regarded as expressions of non-translatability (and were thus preserved), these passages perhaps provide implicit evidence for translatability. Before explaining exactly what I mean, let us briefly review two passages. Jethro, the Midianite father-in-law of Moses, is presented as proclaiming in Exodus 18:11: "Now I know that Yahweh is greater than all the gods." It may be relatively easy to hear this statement as a claim to monotheism or non-translatability, but this declaration does not seem to speak to either issue. Instead, it addresses the matter of Yahweh's power relative to other deities. Thus William H. C. Propp comments: "It is unclear whether the author conceives Jethro to be a monotheist, or a

---

[134] Cf. Judges 10:6, with the Hebrew particle, waw before "the gods of Aram" perhaps as appositional or specifying, to be translated "namely" and not "and." Cf. Micah 4:5.

[135] Interestingly, the editorial interpretation of the title Baal-berit as one of the Baalim runs counter to the view of most scholars, who see the title as belonging to El (see El-berit in 9:46). See Theodore J. Lewis, "The Identity and Function of El/Baal Berith," *JBL* 115 (1996) 401–23; Smith, *The Origins of Biblical Monotheism,* 140.

[136] On this theme more broadly, see Frank Spina, *The Faith of the Outsider: Exclusion and Inclusion in the Biblical Story* (Grand Rapids, MI: Eerdmans, 2005).

polytheist who confesses Yahweh's unique greatness."[137] A second example comes from Joshua 2. On the eve of Israel's initial conquest in the land, an inhabitant of Jericho, Rahab, is represented as making two claims about the god of the Israelites. In verse 10a she is presented as recognizing the divine victory at the Sea of Reeds. In verse 11b she is shown making the additional claim: "for Yahweh your god is THE god in heaven above and on the earth below" (Joshua 2:11; my capitalization).

The statement from Exodus 18:11 constitutes the foreigner's recognition of the power of Yahweh. By comparison, the second from Joshua 2:11, considered a deuteronomistic addition to the story,[138] goes further in its declaration about the god of Israel. As such, it has been thought that this deuteronomistic declaration in verse 11b is monotheistic (hence NJPS: "the only God").[139] This claim sounds like the sort of expression put into the mouths of foreign figures that proclaim Yahweh as the only deity in the world (e.g., Naaman in 2 Kings 5:15). In contrast, Rahab's declaration in verse 10a, as part of the older tradition of the story,[140] may be characterized as a foreigner's recognition of the power of another god manifest in a time of military conflict.

We might well imagine comparable expressions made by Israelites about their neighbors' deities in times of their military successes, but the biblical authors do not provide such expressions in their representations of Israel-

---

[137] Propp, *Exodus 1–18: A New Translation with Introduction and Commentary* (AB 2; New York: Doubleday, 1998) 630.

[138] So following Martin Noth, *Das Buch Josua* (third ed.; Handbuch zum Alten Testament I/7; Tübingen: Mohr Siebeck, 1971) 30, which compares Deuteronomy 4:39; Volkmar Fritz, *Das Buch Josua* (Handbuch zum Alten Testament I/7; Tübingen: Mohr Siebeck, 1994) 40; William L. Moran, *The Most Magic Word* (ed. Ronald S. Hendel; CBQMS 35; Washington, DC: The Catholic Biblical Association of America, 2002) 168; Richard D. Nelson, *Joshua: A Commentary* (OTL; Louisville, KY: Westminster John Knox, 1997) 41. See also Weinfeld, *Deuteronomy and the Deuteronomic School,* 331.

[139] In adding the word "alone," the NJPS translation puts considerable weight on the definite article attached to the word, "god" (see also Weinfeld, *Deuteronomy and the Deuteronomic School,* 331). See the critique above in n. 113. The translation here represents an attempt to stay closer to the Hebrew and render the definite article more literally, with a certain superlative quality that in English may be expressed by the definite article. (Perhaps it is like the usage in American English, "she/he is THE one" or even "she/he is the only one for me," which hardly suggests that there are no other persons in the world, only for the person who expresses such a sentiment.) While one might not preclude the possibility that this addition is intended to express a monotheistic cosmology, it is to be noted that one of the closest parallels to 2:11b, in Deuteronomy 4:39, adds *'en 'od.*

[140] For the purposes of this discussion, it matters little whether the composition is entirely deuteronomistic, as long as it represents reworking of an older known tradition. However, since the narrative reads reasonably well without the more explicitly deuteronomistic material, one need not believe that the story was created whole cloth by a later deuteronomistic editor.

ites.[141] In any case, the biblical passages need not indicate conversion, as is sometimes claimed.[142] In fact, it might be suggested that the proclamations of Yahweh by foreigners indicate the success of translatability in times of cross-cultural encounter and conflict. Such non-Israelites do not deny the existence of other gods, nor do their declarations speak to the question of whether such gods might be powerful on another military occasion (such as Mesha's victory over Israel that he proclaims on his stele, noted in the preceding section of this chapter). Thus what might appear at first glance to constitute cases against translatability arguably point to it being operative on occasions of cross-cultural contact.

To summarize the picture for ancient Israel, our survey of translatability points to its use in intercultural contacts, in particular in contexts involving relations between Israel and its neighbors. A good deal of the discourse is reminiscent of the Late Bronze Age treaties and letters that we surveyed in Chapter One. To be sure, translatability is not as pervasive in the Iron Age context. Compared to our available sources for the Late Bronze Age, the Iron Age sources do not show examples of translatability as such in cult.[143] Moreover, the range of deities in the Late Bronze Age is considerably more diverse; the Iron Age situation offers examples largely revolving around national gods. Thus translatability did not flourish to the same degree in

---

[141] Cf. Jeremiah 44, where the Queen of Heaven and not Yahweh alone is recognized by Judeans as the source of their wellbeing. This passage, however, involves an inner-Judean discussion.

[142] Commenting on the stories of Rahab and Na'aman, Tikva Frymer-Kensky remarks: "This literary use may have its origins in a rite of passage, a kind of proto-conversion that may have been practiced in ancient Israel. See Frymer-Kensky, "Reading Rahab," in: *Studies in Bible and Feminist Criticism* (JPS Scholars of Distinction series; Philadelphia: The Jewish Publication Society, 2006) 213–14. See also the remarks of Moran, *The Most Magic Word,* 168–69.

[143] There are of course possible examples of borrowings into cult, such as the imagery in Psalm 29 and Sapon in Psalm 48:3. Psalm 29 has often been viewed as a Canaanite or Phoenician text modified for Israelite usage since the 1938 study of H. L. Ginsberg, "A Phoenician Hymn in the Psalter," in: *Atti XIX Congresso internazionale degli Orientalisti* (Rome: Tipografia del Senato, 1938) 472–76. Following Ginsberg's approach, Aloysius Fitzgerald, F.S.C., brilliantly noted that substituting the name of Baal for Yahweh in the extant text of Psalm 29 dramatically increases its alliteration; Fitzgerald, "A Note on Psalm 29," *BASOR* 214 (1974) 61–63. Fitzgerald saw in this feature some confirmation of Ginsberg's view. In contrast, Dennis Pardee has recently argued that Psalm 29 is an Israelite composition that lays claim to the "Canaanite" diction to Baal's powers for Yahweh. See Pardee, "On Psalm 29: Structure and Meaning," in: *The Book of Psalms: Composition and Reception* (ed. Peter W. Flint and Patrick D. Miller, Jr., with the assistance of Aaron Brunell and Ryan Roberts; VTSup XCIX; Leiden/Boston: Brill, 2005) 153–83, esp. 168–70 and 178 n. 65. In either case, Psalm 29 shows signs of borrowing, yet by Assmann's definition, such a borrowing does not constitute translatability, as two deities are not brought together in the text. The same basic point applies to Psalm 48:3, on which see Day, *Yahweh,* 107–16; Koch, *Der Gott Israels und die Götter des Orients,* 119–70, esp. 121–24; and Smith, *The Early History of God,* 88–90.

ancient Israel that it did in the Late Bronze Age settings that we examined in Chapter One.

In closing this chapter, I would like to return briefly to the figure of Balaam with whom we began this chapter. It was his oracle in Numbers 23:9 that sets the stage for Hendel's claim for non-translatability in ancient Israel. Thus far in this discussion of foreigners' proclamations of Yahweh, we have seen that these are not nearly as monotheistic as they have been interpreted. Instead, they reflect translatability, recognition of the power of another god. Balaam's oracle about Israel might be viewed similarly. On the occasion of Balaam's cross-cultural encounter with Israel, this non-Israelite clearly notes the power of Israel's god. Although he is a non-Israelite, he is recognized in the Bible as a prophet (Numbers 23:4–5, 16; 24:2, 4; cf. Joshua 24:10). Numbers 24:4 characterizes Balaam with the classic prophetic term, "visionary" (*ḥzh*): "word of the one who hears the words of El, who envisions the visions of Shadday." Balaam himself was recognizaed cross-culturally by Israel, as seen in Numbers 22–24, and by non-Israelites, as indicated by the extra-biblical Deir 'Alla inscription that bear his words.[144] The "written record" (*spr*) of the Balaam inscription, as it is called in the first line, relates the oracles of "Balaam, son of Beor," the very title for this figure in Numbers 24:3 and 15, and in Micah 6:5. The inscription also calls him "a seer of the gods" (*ḥzh 'lhn*), the same word applied to him in Numbers 24:4. A prophet who crosses cultural and religious boundaries, Balaam is a quin-tessential figure of translatability. Interestingly enough, the god particularly prominent in both the biblical and non-biblical texts quoting his words is El, the very source of his divine inspiration (see Numbers 23:22–23; 24:4, 8). In the biblical account of Balaam, this El is readily identified as Yahweh (Numbers 23:8), but outside the Bible in the Deir 'Alla inscription, this El operates without any reference to the Israelite god. Thus El could function

---

[144] The inscription is conveniently edited with text, translation and notes, by Jo Ann Hackett, *The Balaam Text from Deir 'Allā* (HSM 31; Chico, CA: Scholars, 1980). See also Baruch A. Levine in: *COS* 2.140–45 (with further bibliography). For discussions of the biblical and inscriptional material, see the summary of Jo Ann Hackett, "Religious Tradition in Israelite Transjordan," in: *Ancient Israelite Religion: Essays in Honor of Frank Moore Cross* (ed. Patrick D. Miller, Jr., Paul D. Hanson, and S. Dean McBride; Philadelphia: Fortress, 1987) 125–36; and the detailed treatment by Levine, *Numbers 21–36* (AB 4A; New York: Doubleday, 2000) 137–275. Note also the remarks by André Lemaire, "Oracles, politique et literature dans le royaume araméens et transjordaniens," in: *Oracles et prophéties dans l'Antiquité: Actes du Colloque de Strasbourg 15–17 juin 1995* (ed. Jean-Georges Heintz; Université des sciences humaines de Strasbourg. Travaux du centre de recherche sur le proche-orient et la grèce antiques; Paris: De Boccard, 1997) 188–93. For the archaeological context of the inscription, see Henk Franken, "Balaam at Deir 'Alla and the Cult of Baal," in: *Archaeology, History and Culture in Palestine and the Near East: Essays in Memory of Albert E. Glock* (ed. Tomis Kapitan; American Schools of Oriental Research Books 3; Atlanta: Scholars, 1999) 183–202.

inside Israel and outside of it as the god behind Balaam's prophetic activity. Balaam and his god El both stand as figures of translatability.

With time, Israel's translatability met a number of difficulties. The rise of the Neo-Assyrian empire in particular undermined the context for Israel's regional translatability, both in theoretical terms and in more practical ways. The impact of Mesopotamian power would forever alter the mental and physical landscape of Israel. The story of this influence, and in particular its impact on translatability in Israel, is offered in Chapter Three.

Chapter Three

The Rejection of Translatability in Israel
and the Impact of Mesopotamian Empires on Divinity

To whom can you liken God?
Isaiah 40:18

1. Rejecting Translatability in Ancient Israel

The preceding chapter discusses cases of Israelite translatability and the worldview that gave expression to it. In this worldview, each nation had a national god who operated more or less on par with one another. In addition to the texts surveyed in Chapter Two, there are important cases that dramatize this form of translatability at the same time that they explicitly reject it. This may sound contradictory, but it is common for polemical texts to discuss the very idea that they condemn.[1] In embodying the older worldview of translatability and the newer one that rejects it, these texts are particularly helpful for illustrating the shift in the circles that produced these texts. Three particularly relevant cases are Psalm 82, Deuteronomy 32:8–9,[2] and Deuteronomy 6:4 (the Shema), which we may now address in turn.

Psalm 82

This psalm presents a scene of the gods meeting together in divine council.[3] In order to provide a better sense of this picture in Psalm 82, I would like to provide a basic translation (with some headings added in italics):

---

[1] On this dimension of religious polemics, see the essays in: *Religious Polemics in Context: Papers presented to the Second International Conference of the Leiden Institute for the Study of Religions (LISOR), held at Leiden 27–28 April 2000* (ed. T. L. Hettema and A. van der Kooij; Leuven: Peeters, 2004). See in particular "the Introduction," xi–xv, by T. L. Hettema and A. van der Kooij, as well as the several essays devoted to polemic in the Hebrew Bible.

[2] These two texts are addressed by Simon B. Parker ("The Beginning of the Reign of God. Psalm 82 as Myth and Liturgy," *RB* 102 [1995] 548–53) as cases of what he calls "universal monolatry."

[3] Older treatments of Psalm 82 include Henrik S. Nyberg, *Studien zum Hoseabuche: Zugleich ein Beitrag zur Klärung des Problems der alttestamentlichen Textkritik* (Uppsala Universitets Årsskrift 1935:6; Uppsala: Almqvist & Wiksells, 1935) 122–25; and Otto

Prose Label (superscription)
A Psalm of Asaph

Psalm proper (in poetic lines, mostly couplets)
Narrative Statement about God (Elohim) in the Divine Assembly Headed by El/Elyon
1   Elohim stands (sg.) in the council of El
   Among the elohim he pronounces judgment:

God's Indictment of the Other Gods in the Assembly
2   "How long will you judge perversely,
   Show favor to the wicked?
3   Judge the wretched and the orphan,
   Vindicate the lowly and the poor,
4   Rescue the wretched and the needy,
   Save them from the hand of the wicked."
5   They neither know nor understand,
   They go about in darkness,
   All the foundations of the world totter.
6   "I had taken you for gods,
   sons of *Elyon*, all of you;
7   However, you shall die like a human,
   Fall like one of the princes."

Command addressed to God
8   Arise, O Elohim (sg.), judge the earth,
   For You *inherit* all the nations.

Eissfeldt, "Neue Götter im Alten Testament," in: *Atti del XIX Congresso Internazionale degli Orientalisti. Roma, 23–29 Settembre 1935 – XIII* (Rome: Tipografia del Senato, 1938) 479. The best treatment remains Simon B. Parker, "The Beginning of the Reign of God. Psalm 82 as Myth and Liturgy," *RB* 102 (1995) 532–59. See also J. F. A. Sawyer, "Biblical Alternatives to Monotheism," *Theology* 87 (1984) 172–80; Manfried Dietrich and Oswald Loretz, *"Jahwe und seine Aschera": Anthropomorphes Kultbild in Mesopotamien, Ugarit und Israel. Das biblische Bilderverbot* (Ugaritisch-biblische Literatur 9; Münster: Ugarit, 1992) 134–57; Heinz-Dieter Neef, *Gottes himmlischer Thronrat: Hintergrund und Bedeutung von sôd JHWH im Alten Testament* (Arbeiten zur Theologie 79; Stuttgart: Calwer, 1994) 13–17; Adrian Schenker, "Le monothéisme israélite: un dieu qui transcende le monde et les dieux," *Biblica* 78 (1997) 442–44; Oswald Loretz, "Rechtfertigung aus der Perspektive altorientalischer und alttestamentlicher juristischer Terminologie," *Teologinen Aikakauskirja* 105 (2000) 75–88, esp. 80–81; and Konrad Schmid, "Gibt es 'Reste hebräischen Heidentums' im Alten Testament? Methodische Überlegungen anhand von Dtn 32,8f und Ps 82," in: *Primäre und sekundäre Religion als Kategorie der Religionsgeschichte des Alten Testaments* (ed. Andreas Wagner; BZAW 364; Berlin/New York: de Gruyter, 2006) 105–120, esp. 116–18. Among the commentaries, see Klaus Seybold, *Die Psalmen* (Handbuch zum Alten Testament I/15; Tübingen: Mohr Siebeck, 1996) 324–26. See also remarks in: Peter Machinist, "Mesopotamian Imperialism and Israelite Religion: A Case Study from the Second Isaiah," in: *Symbiosis, Symbolism, and the Power of the Past: Canaan, Ancient Israel, and Their Neighbors – From the Late Bronze Age through Roman Palaestina* (ed. William G. Dever and Seymour Gitin; the AIAR Anniversary Volume; Winona Lake, IN: Eisenbrauns, 2003) 243 n. 13.

In this context, Elohim (here representing the god of Israel, Yahweh) is one member of this larger divine assembly of the gods. In the first half of verse 1, Elohim literally "sets himself" and thus "stands," or perhaps "takes his place,"[4] in the divine council. This may be understood literally as "the

---

[4] The verb *niṣṣab*, is often understood as taking a stand, to assume the body posture for addressing the divine council (so *BDB* 662, #1a, "takes his stand to plead"; cf. NAB, "rises"). This view of Elohim "taking his place" (see NRSV) suits the context of Psalm 82:1 as well as a number of other biblical passages with the root (see Exodus 7:15). The verb may mean, "God stands" (NJPS) or "God stood" (cf. LXX *este*, "he stood"). 1 Samuel 22:9 uses the singular in a group setting: "Doeg the Edomite, while he was standing (*niṣṣab*), among (*'al*) the servants of Saul, spoke up." More grammatically proximate cases, with **nṣb*, in the niphal with the preposition *b-* as in Psalm 82:1, include Numbers 22:23 and 31, which use the verb-preposition combination for "the angel of Yhwh standing in the way" (see Numbers 22:25, in the hithpael of the related root **yṣb*; note also Exodus 19:17, 1 Samuel 10:23, 2 Samuel 23:12 //1 Chronicles 11:14, and Jeremiah 46:4, all in the hithpael of *yṣb*; 2 Samuel 21:5, with the hithpael infinitive; cf. *niṣṣab*, *b-* applied to the divine word in heaven, in Psalm 119:89). In 1 Samuel 12:7, Samuel tells the people to stand (hithpael of *yṣb*) so that he can give judgment (**špṭ*). In this case, Samuel defends himself against negative judgment, the opposite of the situation in Psalm 82. In Deuteronomy 31:14, Moses and Joshua are to take their stand or their place in the tent of meeting (*mo'ed*), reflecting the language of assembly as in Psalm 82:1. NJPS translates the use of **yṣb*, (hithpael) plus *b-* in Deuteronomy 31:14 as "present themselves" (cf. Deuteronomy 29:9). Isaiah 3:13 uses *niṣṣab* for Yahweh standing to deliver the divine *rîb*.

Attention has been devoted to other passages where the root is used in the context of divine and human collectives. Parker ("The Beginning of the Reign of God," 537–38) cites the root in Job 1:6 and 2:1 for divine attendants, as well as Genesis 45:1 and 2 Samuel 13:31, which use the root for royal attendants (cf. *niṣṣabim*, in 1 Kings 4:5 as a term for officials). In the Joban passages, the divine children "came to present themselves" (so NJPS for **yṣb*, here in hithpael) before Yhwh. To these cases may be added the Deir 'Alla inscription, in combination I, lines 5–6: "the gods gather together, and the *šdyn*-gods take their stand (*nṣbw*) , in/as a council (*mw'd*)." For discussion, including comparison with Psalm 82:1, see Hackett, *The Balaam Text from Deir 'Allā*, 29, 40; J. Hoftijzer and K. Jongeling, *Dictionary of North-west Semitic Inscriptions: Part Two. M–T* (Handbuch der Orientalistik I/21; Leiden/New York/Köln: Brill, 1995) 750; and Jonas C. Greenfield, *'Al Kanfei Yonah: Collected Studies of Jonas C. Greenfield on Semitic Philology* (ed. Shalom M. Paul, Michael E. Stone and Avital Pinnick; two vols.; Leiden/Boston/Köln: Brill; Jerusalem: Magnes, 2001) 2.809. The context of the verb in the Deir 'Alla inscription seems to indicate not that the gods literally stand up, but that they form an assembly (thus the preceding verb, "join together"). Joel S. Burnett (*A Reassessment of Biblical Elohim* [SBLDS 183; Atlanta: Society of Biblical Literature, 2001] 37–38) suggests that in other respects the Deir 'Alla inscription and its biblical parallels reflect a shared literary tradition; if so, the opening line of Psalm 82:1 and its parallel in the Deir 'Alla inscription would reflect a shared concept of the deity in the divine council. Both use a standard expression for the divine assembly.

One might think that the Israelite adaptation of the expression, applied to a singular deity, might incur a concomitant shift in the verb's semantics. Seeing only a single major god represented in Psalm 82 might suggest the possibility that *niṣṣab* might mean, "to convene" or the like (I thank Peter Machinist for drawing my attention to this theoretical possibility.) Cf. the G-stem of the root in Ugaritic and Phoenician, with transitive meaning, "to erect (a stele)" (*CAT/KTU* 1.17 I 26 and parallels; *DNWSI* 2.749–50), and in Phoenician and Aramaic, "to plant (trees)." However, Psalm 82:1 combines the N-stem verb (and not G-stem) with the preposition *b-*, "in," which together would seem to

council of El."[5] The figure Elohim (God) indicts[6] as mere mortals the other gods (*'elohim,* verses 1b and 6), whom he had thought were all sons of Elyon (verse 6). As the indictment indicates, the denounced figures were considered to be gods, all divine children of Elyon, but now they are to be viewed not as gods but as dead like humans (verse 7). The psalm concludes (verse 8) with the human speaker calling on Elohim to "judge, rule" (less likely, to "prevail"[7]) and to assume all the nations as his "inheritance." This call represents a move for Yahweh to extend his dominion beyond Israel,

point to the verb's meaning, "to stand in" (for a literal usage, cf. Exodus 15:8). Western peripheral Akkadian likewise uses **naṣābu* in an intransitive middle voice. Most relevant for Psalm 82:1 is EA 148:42, with its description of the king of Hazor: he "has abandoned his house and *has aligned himself* with the 'Apiru." See William L. Moran, *The Amarna Letters* (Baltimore/London: Johns Hopkins University, 1992) 235; cf. *CAD N/II:*33 (for comparable expressions in the Amarna correspondence, see Moran, "Join the 'Apiru or Become One?" in: *"Working with No Data": Semitic and Egyptian Studies Presented to Thomas O. Lambdin* [ed. David M. Golomb; Winona Lake, IN: Eisenbrauns, 1987] 209–12, esp. 211). Anson Rainey understands the verb similarly (perhaps more literally): "The king of Hazor has abandoned his house and has taken up a position with the *'apiru*" (Rainey's italics); Rainey, *Canaanite in the Amarna Tablets: A Linguistic Analysis of the Mixed Dialect used by the Scribes from Canaan* (4 vols.; Leiden: New York/Köln: Brill, 1996) 2.94. It is also to be noted that EA 148:42 is describing one party joining a pre-existing collective. Likewise instructive for Psalm 82:1 is the contrast between the intransitive G-stem of Akkadian **paḫāru,* as used for the gathering of the divine council (see *CAD P:* 26–27; cf. the intransitive cases in the *Gtn*-stem in *CAD P:* 28), as opposed to its transitive D-stem forms predicated of deities (see *CAD P:* 30; cf. the intransitive D-stem of *kamāsu,* "to gather, collect," used of deities for residing in a temple, *CAD K:* 117). The biblical and extra-biblical texts using **nṣb/*yṣb* suggest that in the context of Psalm 82:1, Elohim literally "sets himself" and thus "stands" or "takes his place." In Psalm 82 Elohim is present in the divine assembly; the verb does not represent this divinity as its convener.

[5] Some scholars regard BH *'el* here to be a name for Yahweh in this context; see Cross, *Canaanite Myth and Hebrew Epic,* 44, 186; Burnett, *A Reassessment of Biblical Elohim,* 78 n. 209. Cross (*Canaanite Myth and Hebrew Epic,* 72) also describes Psalm 82 as "the court of El." Cross (*Canaanite Myth and Hebrew Epic,* 179 n. 142) also calls *'adat 'el* in this context identical to the Ugaritic *'[d]t 'ilm,* "co[un]cil of El" in Ugaritic, specifically, *KTU/CAT* 1.15 II 11. It is clear that Cross recognizes the broader background of the type-scene, yet views the divine names and titles as references to Yahweh (cf. the view cited in the preceding note). As Cross' discussion indicates, the references to El and Elyon are vestiges of the old type-scene, but perhaps without the author explicitly making the identifications as Cross would claim. One may be disinclined to follow the implicit presupposition of this argument that the picture in Psalm 82 should be conformed to the depictions of other divine council scenes that show Yahweh as its head (e. g., 1 Kings 22:19; Isaiah 6; Job 1–2). See further below.

[6] The verb **špṭ* in this psalm does not refer to ruling the divine council itself. In verse 1 it characterizes the divine indictment of the other deities, while in verses 2–3 and 6 it denotes proper rule or adjudication within a god's divine realm.

[7] Note this interpretation of **qwm* for Psalm 1:5 by Shalom Paul in light of the semantic usage for Akkadian *uzzuzu,* "to stand," in its sense of "prevailing over an adversary in a lawsuit." See Paul, *Divrei Shalom: Collected Studies of Shalom M. Paul on the Bible and the Ancient Near East 1967–2005* (CHANE 23; Leiden/Boston: Brill, 2005) 105–6.

the traditional "inheritance" of this deity, as we noted in 1 Samuel 25:19 and as we will see shortly in Deuteronomy 32:9. Israel as the "inheritance" of Yahweh is a widespread image in the Bible (1 Samuel 10:1; 1 Kings 8:53; 2 Kings 21:14; Isaiah 19:25; Micah 7:18; Psalms 33:12, 68:10, 106:5; cf. 2 Samuel 20:19, 21:3). Psalm 82:6 plays on this traditional notion in expressing its vision of God's dominion over the world.

Scholars have generally noted biblical references to El Elyon (e. g., Genesis 14:19–22) and compared the Ugaritic background of this type-scene of the divine council headed by the god El especially in *KTU/CAT* 1.2 I.[8] This type-scene includes the idea of the gods as the sons of the god El, which is also well known from other texts. Many commentators have viewed Psalm 82 in light of this traditional usage. Accordingly, El in verse 1 and Elyon in verse 6 seem to be vestiges of the older notion of the god El as the head of the divine assembly, as many commentators have noted. To be sure, this figure in the assembly remains in the background, as the text is focused on the victory of Elohim over the other elohim. In recent years, it has been questioned more recently whether or not Psalm 82 represents Elohim and El/Elyon as two different figures.[9] The psalm is not explicit on the question, and the presentation in Deuteronomy 32:8–9 (to be discussed shortly), with its similarities to Psalm 82, might seem to favor the identification.

At the same time, the marks of the language of El/Elyon are particularly pronounced in Psalm 82 compared with any other divine council scene represented in the Hebrew Bible. Moreover, reading El/Elyon and Elohim as the same figure creates interpretational problems.[10] First, this view requires that the other divine elohim are Yahweh-El's children (verse 6), which would be unusual. One could get around this objection by taking "sons" in the sense of those belonging to a general class, which is attested in biblical Hebrew (cf. *ben-ḥayil*, "a son of strength," for a warrior). However, this would mean interpreting *'elyon* in verse 6 not as a divine title, but as a sort of generic term (those belonging to the class of "high" or "exalted"), arguably

---

[8] In addition to the parallels noted by Parker ("The Reign of God"), see the survey of Robert P. Gordon, "Standing in the Council: When Prophets Encounter God," in: *The God of Israel* (ed. Robert P. Gordon; University of Cambridge Oriental Publications 64; Cambridge: Cambridge University, 2007) 190–204.

[9] See Michael S. Heiser, "Are Yahweh and El Distinct Deities in Deut. 32:8–9 and Psalm 82?" *HIPHIL* 3 (2006); online journal, http://www.seej.net/Default.aspx?tabid=77 (posted October 3, 2006); Gordon, "Standing in the Council," 200. See also Neef, *Gottes himmlischer Thronrat*, 13–17. Neef renders the El terminology here as a common noun (*'adat 'el* as "Gottesversammlung" and *bene 'elyon* as "Söhne des Höchsten") with no acknowledgement of the older usage associated with the god El. Neef's reading arguably mirrors how ancient readers of Psalm 82 could have read the poem without recognizing its vestigial El imagery and language.

[10] I am grateful to Peter Machinist for our discussions of the interpretation of Psalm 82, which have helped me to clarify my reading.

an exceptional tack. Such a view of "sons of Elyon" would also ignore the well-known trope of the gods as the children of El. Second, if the elohim were put in such a class, then it is unclear that their status would be in any respect less than the rank of Elohim. Third, one may ask (as Klaus Koch has) why the poem would use El and Elohim for the same individual deity.[11] Fourth and finally, the picture presupposing the identification of Elohim and El/Elyon would issue in a less dramatic contest between Elohim and the other gods. It would suggest that Elohim-El Elyon is in effect the ruler from the outset of the text who takes divinity away from his own children. This approach in identifying Elohim and El/Elyon issues in a less forceful contest between Elohim and the other elohim. Instead, it seems equally plausible that the author used the old type-scene and focused on the Israelite god as the divine figure who denounces the other gods. As a result, the old element of the presiding god El Elyon was implicitly retained, even if the author discusses only a single god.[12] Unlike other examples of divine council scenes in the biblical corpus, Psalm 82 shows particularly strong marks of its West Semitic background. For these reasons, one might not be inclined to dismiss the literary representation of El/Elyon in this context and conflate it with the figure of Elohim.

In any case, whether one views El/Elyon and Elohim as one or two figures, it does not affect the older translatability or its rejection, as represented in this text. This representation of non-translatability can be explicated further, thanks to a remarkable text from Mari,[13] which J.J.M. Roberts

---

[11] Koch, *Der Gott Israels und die Götter des Orients,* 182 n. 62.

[12] This situation might be compared to juxtapositions of older and newer views of divinity produced by the same author in the Greco-Roman context, what H. S. Versnel has called "concealed inconsistency." See Versnel, "Thrice One: Three Greek Experiments in Oneness," in: *One God or Many? Concepts of Divinity in the Ancient World* (ed. Barbara Nevling Porter; Transactions of the Casco Bay Assyriological Institute, vol. 1; np: np, 2000) 93–94.

[13] For text edition and discussion, see Jean-Marie Durand, *Archives épistolaires de Mari I/1* (ARM 26/1; Paris: Éditions Recherche sur les civilisations, 1988) 385. For translation and notes, see Wolfgang Heimpel, *Letters to the King of Mari: A New Translation, with Historical Introduction, Notes, and Commentary* (Winona Lake, IN: Eisenbrauns, 2003) 250–51; Martti Nissinen, *Prophets and Prophecy in the Ancient Near East* (SBLWAW 12; Atlanta: Society of Biblical Literature, 2003) 26–27; and J.J.M. Roberts, *The Bible and the Ancient Near East: Collected Essays* (Winona Lake, IN: Eisenbrauns, 2002) 218–219. For further discussion of this letter, see Martti Nissinen, "Prophets and the Divine Council," in: *Kein Land für sich allein: Studien zum Kulturkontakt in Kanaan, Israel/Palästina und Ebirnâri für Manfred Weippert zum 65. Geburtstag* (ed. Ulrich Hübner and Ernst Axel Knauf; OBO 186; Fribourg: Universitätsverlag; Göttingen: Vandenhoeck & Ruprecht, 2002) 8–9; Christoph Uehlinger, "Audienz in der Götterwelt. Anthropomorphismus und Soziomorphismus in der Ikonographie eines altsyrischen Zylindersiegels," *UF* 24 (1992) 339–59, esp. 352; and Karel van der Toorn, "A Prophetic Role-Play Mistaken for an Apocalyptic Vision (ARM 26 no. 196)," *Nouvelles Assyriologiques Bréves et Utilitaires* 1998/1:3–4. See also the brief comments of Jean-Marie Durand, "Les prophéties des textes

insightfully connected with Psalm 82.[14] A letter, ARM 26 196 (A.3719), was sent to the king of Mari, Zimri-lim, by his servant, Shamash-Nasir.[15] The letter begins by citing Zimri-lim's earlier demand for a report from "the city of the god," specifically for information about prophetic activity "in the house of the god."[16] It would appear that Shamash-Nasir follows the king's instructions, because following a break, the city god Dagan is reported as passing judgment on another god, Tishpak: "... you have ruled the land. Now your day has passed. You will confront your day like Ekallatum."[17] Wolfgang Heimpel comments on the difficult word, *ú-ut-ka* ("your day"): "ud in Sumerian may denote specifically the last day, or the day of death."[18] The derivation of the word is difficult, and although commentators agree on its meaning, it is less clear that it bears the specific freight given to it by Heimpel. For interpretive purposes, not too much weight is to be placed on the word. The letter continues to relate another prophecy and then a matter regarding grain brought from the province of Terqa. According to Dominique Charpin,[19] the letter is not about the removal of Tishpak's power over Eshnunna or eastern Mesopotamia. Instead, Dagan denies Tishpak and Eshnunna the right to rule the middle Euphrates, the area associated with Dagan. During the reign of Shamshi-Adad, who had begun his rule from

---

de Mari," in: *Oracles et prophéties dans l'Antiquité: Actes du Colloque de Strasbourg 15–17 juin 1995* (ed. Jean-Georges Heinz; Paris: De Boccard, 1997) 131–32. I wish to thank Martti Nissinen for some of these secondary references, and Daniel Fleming for his helpful comments and references reflected in the following comments and footnotes.

[14] Roberts, *The Bible and the Ancient Near East: Collected Essays* (Winona Lake, IN: Eisenbrauns, 2002) 218–219 (reference courtesy of Peter Machinist). Both this Mari text and Psalm 82 are mentioned in two other publications on the topic, though not in relation to one another. See Oswald Loretz, "Rechtfertigung aus der Perspektive altorientalischer und alttestamentlicher juristischer Terminologie," *Teologinen Aikakauskirja* 105 (2000) 75–88, esp. 80–81; and Robert P. Gordon, "Standing in the Council: When Prophets Encounter God," in: *The God of Israel* (ed. Robert P. Gordon; University of Cambridge Oriental Publications 64; Cambridge, UK: Cambridge University, 2007) 191.

[15] Shamash-nasir is the *abu bitim* or assistant administrator of the Terqa district. For this role and the identification of this figure in this capacity, see Brigitte Lion, "Les gouverneurs provinciaux du royaume de Mari à l'époque de Zimrî-Lîm," *Amurru* 2 (2001) 147, 195–96 (information and reference courtesy of Daniel Fleming).

[16] Heimpel, *Letters to the King of Mari*, 250. The term for "oracle" in this section is partially broken: *e-g[e-e]r-ru-u₂-um*. Daniel Fleming informs me that part of every sign is visible. For discussion of the broader context of the "oracle" here, see Beate Pongratz-Leisten, *Herrschaftenwissen in Mesopotamien: Formen der Kommunikation zwischen Gott und König im 2. und 1. Jahrtausend v. Chr.* (SAA X; Helsinki: Helsinki University, 1999) 66, 70–71.

[17] Nissinen, *Prophets*, 27.

[18] Heimpel, *Letters to the King of Mari*, 250. Heimpel (*Letters to the King of Mari*, 260) and Nissinen (*Prophets*, 27) compare the expression, "his days are near, he will not live," in ARM 26 212 = ARM 10 6 = A.3217 (line 8').

[19] Dominique Charpin, "Prophètes et rois dans le Proche-Orient amorrite: nouvelles données, nouvelles perspectives," *Florilegium marianum* VI (2002) 29.

Ekallatum (cited in the prophecy), the middle Euphrates had been governed by an eastern king, but this was no longer the case.[20] In this context of ARM 26 196, Dagan denies Eshnunna the right of incursion.

This Mari letter offers help for interpreting Psalm 82 on several fronts. We may begin with the broad similarities of the texts. Both represent divine conflict in the context of multiple divinities. Psalm 82 is a divine council scene, as is ARM 26 196.[21] Both texts specifically present a prophetic judgment of one god against another. Indeed, the same West Semitic root, "to judge, rule" (*špṭ) is involved in both pronouncements (see Psalm 82:8). Both texts involve a denial of the right of other divinity to rule. In the case of the Mari letter, this might be conveyed additionally through the expression, "your day," while Psalm 82 strengthens the point by saying that the gods "die like humans" (verse 7). On the matter of the larger context of Psalm 82, ARM 26 196 may also make a contribution. It is possible that for the immediate context, both texts may involve prophetic activity located, to cite the terms used by ARM 26 196, in "the city of the god," specifically in his "house."[22] In the Mari letter, this is the temple of Dagan in Terqa, while the Jerusalem temple would be a candidate in the case of Psalm 82. Furthermore, the divine judgments expressed in the texts may reflect contentious political situations.

The significant differences between the two texts are equally important for understanding Psalm 82. ARM 26 196 is a letter that contains prophetic material; in others words its prophecy is brought into the world of royal correspondence and politics. Psalm 82 is presently labeled as a song (*mizmor*, verse 1) and thus prophecy brought into the realm of liturgy (this does not preclude a political dimension, but there is no overt sign of human, political power standing behind this prophecy). The prophetic material in ARM 26 196 is explicitly named as prophecy, while this feature is not explicitly marked in Psalm 82, but it is presupposed in verse 8 (cf. Isaiah 14:21). Furthermore, Dagan is a regional or territorial god associated with Terqa and Tuttul, on the western edge of the kingdom of Mari. He is not a national god. In contrast, Yahweh begins in Psalm 82 as the national god and ends up proclaimed as the god of the world. Another significant difference for our discussion is that the condemnation of Psalm 82 attacks all of the (other) "sons of Elyon," not just one other god as in ARM 26 196. ARM 26 126 speaks to the passing of the power of one god, while Psalm 82

---

[20] Nissinen (*Prophets*, 27) reads the situation differently: "The point is that the 'judgment' of Dagan, the principal god of Mari, over Tišpak, the god of Eshnunna, corresponds to Zimri-Lim's hoped-for victory over Ibalpiel II of Ešnunna."

[21] On this point, see Nissinen, "Prophets and the Divine Council," 9; Uehlinger, "Audienz in der Götterwelt," 352; and Gordon, "Standing in the Council," 191. Nissinen emphasizes the presence of the deities Hanat and Ikrub-El in this divine council scene.

[22] See the temple context of Isaiah 6 as opposed to the prophetic narrative in 1 Kings 22, which is set in the threshing floor located at the city gate of Samaria (verse 10).

applies this notion to all other deities of the international divine family. The difference between the regional and international expressions involved with Dagan and Yahweh in these two texts is very strong.

These comparisons help to sharpen the understanding of Psalm 82. The operating assumption in Psalm 82 is that the other gods had been the gods of all the nations, but now in its final prophetic call, Elohim the god of Israel is to assume divine authority over all the nations. In short, Psalm 82 calls for an end to translatability. It is evident that Psalm 82 presupposes, even as it disputes, an older worldview of the nations each headed by its own national god. The translatability expressed in the worldview is acknowledged at the same time that it is being rejected.

Deuteronomy 32

The second text that shows the older religious worldview even as it rejects it is Deuteronomy 32:8–9. I will discuss this passage at some length in Chapter Four as one of two main cases of biblical censorship.[23] At this point, I turn to this text to show how it modifies the old worldview of translatability. The poem of Deuteronomy 32 begins by recounting how Israel became associated with Yahweh. Verses 8–9 first specify how (El) Elyon divided the world into nations as the inherited portion for the various gods. Then the passage says how Jacob (i.e., Israel) became Yahweh's allotment. In some textual versions, namely the Septuagint (LXX) and the Hebrew Dead Sea Scrolls (DSS, in manuscript j of the book of Deuteronomy from Cave Four), there is an older reading of this verse that the divine allotment was made according to the number of the "sons of God," but in the Masoretic Text (MT), it is according to the number of "the children of Israel" (literally, "the sons of Israel"). It may be easier to see this basic difference by laying out these manuscript versions in the context of a translation for verses 8–9[24]:

---

[23] A recent discussion of these verses is by Konrad Schmid, "Gibt es 'Reste hebräischen Heidentums' im Alten Testament? Methodische Überlegungen anhand von Dtn 32,8f und Ps 82," in: *Primäre und sekundäre Religion als Kategorie der Religionsgeschichte des Alten Testaments* (ed. Andreas Wagner; BZAW 364; Berlin/New York: de Gruyter, 2006) 105–120. See also the important reflections of Adrian Schenker, "Le monothéisme israélite: un dieu qui transcende le monde et les dieux," *Biblica* 78 (1997) 442–44; and Tigay, *Deuteronomy*, 514–15. For these points in the context of the development of Israelite notions of divinity, see the discussions in: Mark S. Smith, *The Origins of Biblical Monotheism: Israel's Polytheistic Background and the Ugaritic Texts* (Oxford/New York: Oxford University, 2001) 48–49, 143–44, 156–57; and *The Memoirs of God: History, Memory, and the Experience of God in Ancient Israel* (Minneapolis: Fortress, 2004) 107–10, 151–52. See also the works cited in the following footnotes.

[24] For the textual witnesses, see Julie A. Duncan, in: *Qumran Cave 4. IX: Deuteronomy, Joshua, Judges, Kings* (ed. E. Ulrich and F. M. Cross; DJD XIV; Oxford: Clarendon, 1995) 90. See also *BHS* to Deuteronomy 32:8 note d; Emanuel Tov, *Textual Criticism of the Hebrew Bible* (Minneapolis: Fortress; Assen/Maastricht: Van Gorcum, 1992) 269;

(8) When the Most High (Elyon) gave the nations their
    inheritance,
and divided humanity (literally, "the sons of a human being"),
He [Elyon] established the boundaries of peoples,
[according] to the number of
   (1) the sons of Israel – *bene yiśra'el* (MT, SP, Targum, Peshitta,
       Vulgate)
   (2) the sons of God – *bene 'elohim* (DSS 4QDeut^j)
   (3) the sons of God – *huion theou* (LXX 848, 106c)[25]
   (4) the angels of God – *aggelon theou* (LXX most
       manuscripts).
(9) For the portion of Yahweh is his people,
Jacob, his inherited measure.

Depending on the two major options in the manuscript evidence, the number of divine sons is said in verse 8 to be according to the number of the children of Israel (option #1 in the translation), or according to the number of divine children (options #2 and #3), or according to the number of the angels of God (option #4). Verse 9 then describes how among these many nations, the nation belonging to Yahweh is his people, explicitly named in the following line as Jacob.[26] I save the textual discussion and the larger in-

---

Michael Fishbane, *Biblical Interpretation in Ancient Israel* (Oxford: Clarendon, 1985) 69; Julio Trebolle Barrera, *The Jewish Bible and the Christian Bible: An Introduction to the History of the Bible* (trans. Wilfred G. E. Watson; Leiden/New York/Köln: Brill; Grand Rapids, MI/Cambridge, UK: Eerdmans, 1998) 377; Adrian Schenker, "Le monothéisme israélite: un dieu qui transcende le monde et les dieux," *Biblica* 78 (1997) 438, and "Gott als Stifter der Religionen der Welt. Unerwartete Früchte textgeschichtlicher Forschung," in: *La double transmission du texte biblique: Etudes d'histoire du texte offertes en hommages à Adrian Schenker* (ed. Yohanan Goldman and Christoph Uehlinger; OBO 179; Fribourg: Editions Universitaires; Göttingen: Vandehoeck & Ruprecht, 2001) 99–102; Schmid, "Gibt es 'Reste hebräischen Heidentums' im Alten Testament?," 108–9. For a different view of the manuscript witnesses here as different traditions, see I. Himbaza, "Dt 32, 8, une correction tardive des scribes: Essai d'interpretation et de datation," *Biblica* 83 (2002) 527–48. Even a choice of different traditions may functionally result in censorship of other traditions. See also Michael Heiser, "Deuteronomy 32·8 and the Sons of God," *Bibliotheca Sacra* (January-March 2001) 52–74.
[25] For the LXX manuscripts, see Tov, *Textual Criticism,* 269.
[26] It lies beyond the scope of this discussion to establish the background of Deuteronomy 32. For the issues and options, see Paul Sanders, *The Provenance of Deuteronomy 32* (Oudstestamentische Studiën 37; Leiden/New York/Köln: Brill, 1996). Some scholars favor a rather early date, based on putatively archaic features. Certainly there are elements that reflect older tradition, yet even these have been reworked (see on verses 5–6, Greenfield, *'Al Kanfei Yonah,* 2.795–96). At the same time, eighth century (and later) features are equally recognized (for example, see the balanced treatment of Tigay, *Deuteronomy,* 512–13). It is the later ones that serve as the basis for dating, possibly except for sections if they are lacking such later elements. A date in the eighth, possibly the seventh, century is plausible. See Andreas Reichert, "The Song of Moses (Dt. 32) and the Quest for Early Deuteronomic Psalmody," in: *Proceedings of the Ninth World Congress of Jewish Studies: Division A. The Period of the Bible* (Jerusalem: World Union of Jewish Studies, 1986)

terpretation of the poem for Chapter Four, but what I want to note specifically here is the national worldview presupposed by the older reading of the verses and the rejection of its implied polytheism in the larger context of the poem. Conversely, it is clear that that the poem as a whole rejects translatability. This is evident from the poem in verse 39: "there is no god (along) with me."[27] It is also implicit in verses 17 and 21, which characterize other gods as "no-gods." On the other hand, it is also clear that the scribe who produced option #1 felt the force of polytheism in verse 8 and altered it.

The vast majority of scholars who have addressed verses 8–9 view option #1 as a deliberate alteration to avoid the picture of polytheism. Emanuel Tov comments: "the scribe of an early text … did not feel at ease with the possible polytheistic picture and replaced … 'sons of El' with …"sons of Israel'."[28] In this picture, El Elyon is the head god who oversees the division of the world into nations given to the various gods of the world, and in this scenario, Yahweh is one of the gods who receives his inheritance from El

---

53–60. The reference to Jacob here may suggest a northern provenience, as may the mention of Bashan in verse 14. Sanders (*The Provenance,* 232) has also made a point of the cliché in verse 36, *ʿaṣur weʿazub* as a northernism (see the contexts of 1 Kings 14:10, 21:21 and 2 Kings 9:8). A northern (or Transjordanian) setting would also fit with the use of *šedim* in verse 17, which has often been compared with the *šdyn*-gods in the Deir ʿAlla inscription (see Hackett, *The Balaam Text from Deir ʿAllā,* 85–89; Paul V. Mankowski, S.J., *Akkadian Loanwords in Biblical Hebrew* [HSS 47; Winona Lake, IN: Eisenbrauns, 2000] 138–40). The morphology might suggest a northern provenance (but on *'azlat* in verse 36, see Baruch Halpern, "Dialect Distribution in Canaan and the Deir Alla Inscriptions," in: *"Working with No Data": Semitic and Egyptian Studies Presented to Thomas O. Lambdin* [ed. David M. Golomb, with the assistance of Susan T. Hollis; Winona Lake, IN: Eisenbrauns, 1987] 127; Sanders, *The Provenance,* 231; David Talshir, "The Habitat and History of Hebrew during the Second Temple Period," in: *Biblical Hebrew: Studies in Chronology and Typology* [ed. Ian Young; JSOTSup 369; London/New York: T & T Clark, 2003] 272). Some of the vocabulary does not inspire confidence in a date earlier than the eighth century (although such a line of argument inevitably involves an argument from silence). For example, see **hablehem* in verse 21 applied to other deities. For this usage of the word and its distribution, see Paul, *Divrei Shalom,* 438. From these diverse data, the occasion for the poem may be a military defeat (mentioned in verses 21–25) in the northern kingdom (specifically in Transjordan?). Thus it is unsurprising that Greenfield finds parallels to verse 20 in treaty-curses of this period (*ʿAl Kanfei Yonah,* 1.270). It is also to be noted that the origins story of verses 10–14 lacks reference to either the exodus from Egypt or Sinai as the site of the divine mountain or the place associated with either Moses or an original teaching. This would compare with the foundational narrative in Hosea 2. Again this comparison points in the direction of a northern tradition. Whatever the correct provenance for the poem, it does not affect the matter of this discussion.

[27] The expressions in this poem are not explicitly or unambiguously monotheistic, compared with their counterparts in Second Isaiah (Isaiah 43:10–11, 44:6, 8, 45:5–7, 14, 18, 21 and 46:9) and elsewhere (see Deuteronomy 4:35, 39; 1 Samuel 2:2; 2 Kings 19:15, 19 = Isaiah 37:16, 20; Jeremiah 16:19, 20; Nehemiah 8:6; Psalm 86:10, 96:5 = 1 Chronicles 16:26). It is suggested below that non-translatability is presupposed by later statements of monotheism.

[28] Tov, *Textual Criticism,* 269.

Elyon; in Yahweh's case, the people Jacob is his portion. It is evident that the picture in verses 8–9 drew on an older polytheistic worldview, as scholars have long noted. In this worldview, the old god El and his consort Asherah had seventy divine children, as found in the Ugaritic texts (*KTU/CAT* 1.4 VI 44–46).[29] Othmar Keel and Christoph Uehlinger[30] compare a speech in the story of Wenamun with Deuteronomy 32:8–9: "For Amun makes thunder in the sky ever since he placed Seth beside him! Indeed Amun has founded all the lands. He founded them after having founded the land of Egypt from which you have come."[31] This theme survived in later Levantine tradition, well down into the Greco-Roman period as witnessed in Philo of Byblos's work, *The Phoenician History*. According to Philo, the god Kronos, who is identified explicitly with El, went about the world assigning different lands to various gods (PE 1.10.32, 38).[32] Thus Deuteronomy 32:8–9 reflects an old version of the divine founding of the world known in broader West Semitic tradition, one that is otherwise eclipsed in the biblical record by Israel's specific foundational traditions.

Even though the older polytheistic worldview showed through Deuteronomy 32:8–9 enough to bother the scribe of option #1, the composer of Deuteronomy 32 had implicitly effaced this polytheistic notion that had been inherited from Israel's old literary heritage by combining it with clear monolatrous statements later in his poem. Despite possible appearances to the contrary (at least for the scribe of option #1), the composer did not intend any picture of polytheism with his rendering of verses 8–9. In fact, he likely thought of El and Elyon simply as two of Yahweh's titles (as they are elsewhere in the Bible[33]) and not as a separate god, El. The implied reference to the multiple divine sons likely did not bother the composer of the

---

[29] For text and translation, see Mark S. Smith, "The Baal Cycle," in: *UNP* 134. For discussion, see Smith, *The Origins of Biblical Monotheism*, 45, 55, 157.

[30] Keel and Uehlinger, *Gods, Goddesses, and Images of God in Ancient Israel* (trans. Thomas H. Trapp; Minneapolis: Fortress, 1998) 116.

[31] Miriam Lichtheim, *Ancient Egyptian Literature. Volume II: The New Kingdom* (Berkeley/Los Angeles/London: University of California, 1976) 227 and *COS* 1.91. The speech goes on: "Thus craftsmanship came from it in order to reach the place where I am! Thus learning came from it in order to reach the places where I am!" The larger context involves a Syrian accommodation to (or inversion of) the Egyptian worldview that sees Amun over all. Lichtheim (*Ancient Egyptian Literature*, 230 n. 13, and *COS* 1.91 n. 13) comments: "The gist of the prince's speech is that, although Egypt was created by Amun before all other lands and is thus the motherland of all the arts, the civilization of Syria is now fully grown and no longer dependent on Egypt." See pp. 71–72 for further discussion.

[32] For text and translation, see H. W. Attridge and R. A. Oden, Jr., *Philo of Byblos. The Phoenician History: Introduction, Critical Text, Translation, Notes* (CBQMS 9; Washington, DC: The Catholic Biblical Association, 1981) 56–57, 58–59. See also the discussion in Chapter Five, pp. 266–67.

[33] See Genesis 14:19–22, and the extensive discussion of this passage on pp. 212–14.

poem. In the wake of the identification of Elyon as a title of Yahweh, the "divine sons" are only implied in the text at best. It was probably easy for the composer to pay little or no attention to this matter, as this was a standard trope of divinity that the composer had inherited.[34] Indeed, as Adrian Schenker has emphasized, the old worldview shining through the text of Deuteronomy 32:8–9 construes God as the establisher of the religions of the world, "Gott als Stifter der Religionen der Welt," and the basis for the national religion through Yahweh, "die *Gründung der Nationalreligionen durch JHWH.*"[35] Thus the passage shows something of the older worldview of translatability of the national gods even as it ultimately rejects it.

Deuteronomy 6:4

For many readers, Deuteronomy 6:4 is a monotheistic[36] text that opposes any translatability: "Hear, O Israel! Yahweh our god, Yahweh is one (*'eḥad*)." Working on the assumption that the verse constitutes an expression of monotheism, NJPS translates *'eḥad* as "alone." However, the word arguably does not mean "alone." Indeed, many commentators do not take the verse as a monotheistic declaration as such. Before engaging in any further interpretation of the verse, it is to be noted that Deuteronomy 6 provides what may be a later interpretive context for the reception of this expression.[37] Working along these lines, Norbert Lohfink understands Deuteronomy 6 as a sort of commentary with respect to 6:4–5: "Ist Dtn 6 ein 'Kommentar', dann gehört der kurze alte Kulttext 6, 4 b. 5 eher zum Kommentierten als zum Kommentierenden! Während in 6, 12–16 durch midrashartige Umrankung kommmentiert wird, geschieht hier die Kommentierung einfach durch Einsetzung des Textes in das anders gestimmte

---

[34] For similar juxtapositions of older and newer views of divinity produced by the same author, see the interesting reflections on "concealed inconsistency" by Versnel, "Thrice One: Three Greek Experiments in Oneness," 93–94.

[35] Schenker, "Gott als Stifter der Religionen der Welt," 99, 101 (Schenker's italics).

[36] So S. R. Driver, *A Critical and Exegetical Commentary on Deuteronomy* (ICC; third edition; Edinburgh: T. & T. Clark, 1986) 90.

[37] Norbert Lohfink, *Das Hauptgebot: Eine Untersuchung literarischer Einleitungsfragen zu Dtn 5–11* (Analecta Biblica 20; Romae: Pontificio Instituto Biblico, 1963) 164. See also Juha Pakkala, *Intolerant Monolatry in the Deuteronomistic History* (Publications of the Finnish Exegetical Society 76; Helsinki: The Finnish Exegetical Society; Göttingen: Vandenhoeck & Ruprecht, 1999) 73–84. Tigay's discussion (*Deuteronomy*, 76, 439–40) contains several critical comments. At the same time, it in effect reads the Shema in light of later interpretation (despite his recognition of the problems with this view), which does not address the possibility of an earlier context. For a theological approach, see R. W. L. Moberly, "Toward an Interpretation of the Shema," in: *Theological Exegesis: Essays in Conversation with Brevard S. Childs* (ed. Christopher Seitz and Kathryn Greene-Mc-Creight; Grand Rapids, MI: Eerdmans, 1999) 124–44.

Gesamtgefüge."[38] If the verse's context represents a secondary interpretive environment, then the expression's original setting may be lost.[39] Without access to the context of the verse's coinage, its interpretation at least in light of its original context may be unavailable.

Bearing in mind this difficulty, it remains to address the interpretation of its semantic content. Since the syntax of Deuteronomy 6:4 as such is not the issue for this discussion, one may prescind from an analysis of this matter,[40] but focus on the immediate problem at hand, namely the application of *'eḥad* to Yahweh.[41] The major proposals[42] for the word *'eḥad* converge reasonably well with the worldview of Yahweh as king over Israel. First, the word has been thought to express the single nature of the god despite his worship in multiple locations in Israel.[43] In this view, Deuteronomy 6:4 expresses the point that Yahweh is not the Yahweh of a particular place (e. g., Yahweh of Teman or Yahweh of Samaria),[44] but of Israel as whole. He is the national god. Second, Ugaritic *'aḥdy* as predicated of Baal (*KTU/CAT* 1.4 VII 49–52) has been compared by Oswald Loretz: "I am the one who rules over gods/indeed, fattens gods and men/who sat[es] the masses of the earth."[45] For Loretz, Yahweh's role is qualified compared to this declara-

---

[38] Lohfink, *Das Hauptgebot,* 164. See also the reflections of S. Dean McBride, "The Essence of Orthodoxy: Deuteronomy 5:6–10 and Exodus 20:2–6," *Interpretation* 60 (2006) 133–50.

[39] Pakkala, *Intolerant Monolatry,* 74.

[40] For discussion of the syntax, see R. W. L. Moberly, " 'YHWH is One': The Translation of the Shema," in: *Studies in the Pentateuch* (ed. John A. Emerton; VTSup XLI; Leiden: Brill, 1990) 209–15; and the response of Timo Veijola, "Höre Israel! Der Sinn und Hintergrund von Deteronomium VI 4–9," *VT* 42 (1992) 528–41, esp. p. 331. See the response and further discussion of Moberly, "Toward an Interpretation of the Shema," 124–44, esp. 125–26 n. 3.

[41] However, see Pakkala, *Intolerant Monolatry,* 75–77.

[42] The discussion of these proposals in general follows Tigay, *Deuteronomy,* 438–40 and 531.

[43] See P. Kyle McCarter, "The Religious Reforms of Hezekiah and Josiah," in: *Aspects of Monotheism: How God is One* (ed. Hershel Shanks and Jack Meinhardt; Washington, DC: Biblical Archaeological Society, 1997) 65. For discussion and critique of this approach, see Tigay, *Deuteronomy,* 439–40; and Pakkala, *Intolerant Monolatry,* 77.

[44] Both expressions appear in the Kuntillet 'Ajrud inscriptions. For handy reference, see F. W. Dobbs-Allsopp, J. J. M. Roberts, C. L. Seow and R. E. Whitaker, *Hebrew Inscriptions: Texts from the Biblical Period of the Monarchy with Concordance* (New Haven/London: Yale University, 2005) 285, 290–92, 296.

[45] Loretz, *Des Gottes Einzigkeit: Ein altorientalisches Argumentationsmodell zum "Schma Jisrael"* (Darmstadt: Wissenschaftliche Buchgesellschaft, 1997) 57; and "Die Einzigkeit eines Gottes im Polytheismus von Ugarit: Zur Levante als Ursprungsort des biblischen Monotheismus," in: *Polytheismus und Monotheismus in den Religionen des Vorderen Orients* (ed. Manfred Krebernik and Jürgen van Oorschot; AOAT 298; Münster: Ugarit, 2002) 71–89, esp. 83. See in the same volume, Jürgen van Oorschot, " 'Höre Israel …' (Dtn 6,4 f.) – der eine und einzige Gott Israels im Widerstreit," 113–35, esp. 125–26. For further discussions, see N. Lohfink and J. Bergman, " *'echadh,*" in: *Theological*

tion by Baal. Yahweh is the only god with respect to Israel, the addressee of the statement in Deuteronomy 6:4. Third, the word *'eḥad* here may be compared with Akkadian *išten*, literally "one," in its application to deities and kings in the sense, "unique, outstanding."[46] For example, there is "one god," *ilu išten* in Atrahasis I 173 (Late Assyrian) and *ilam išten* in I 208 (Old Babylonian).[47] The phrase is applied to the god who is the head or leader of a group of divinities.[48] With no other deities in view, the statement in Deuteronomy 6:4 is unique or incomparable. All three of these interpretations would point to Yahweh as the one main god for Israel.[49] It is to be noted that, even if Deuteronomy 6:4 would appear *prima facie* not to address the matter of translatability, it may express, in Juha Pakkala's words, "monolatry and intolerance,"[50] in other words non-translatability. Deuteronomy 6:4 may further presuppose the treaty/covenant worldview of Yahweh as Israel's king. It may belong to the larger effort of Deuteronomy to express its reaction against neo-Assyrian empire "one-god" worldviews. The expression may literally mean that Yahweh (and thus not Assyria, its ruler and its god) is for Israel the one god deserving and requiring Israel's convenantal obedience and allegiance, what Eckart Otto calls "ungeteilte Loyalität."[51]

In closing this discussion of Deuteronomy 6:4, we may consider how its oneness was understood later within Israel. Like some modern critics, ancient readers viewed it as an expression of monotheism, for example, in Zechariah 14:9.[52] This verse identifies one god and one name as the single divinity: "And Yahweh will be king over all the earth; on that day, Yahweh

---

Dictionary of the Old Testament: Volume 1 (revised ed.; ed. G. Johannes Botterweck and Helmer Ringgren; trans. John T. Willis; Grand Rapids, MI: William B. Eerdmans, 1974) 196. See also the remarks of Jeffrey H. Tigay, *The JPS Torah Commentary: Deuteronomy* (Philadelphia/Jerusalem: The Jewish Publication Society, 1996) 76–77. 193–201, esp. 195–96; Eckart Otto, *Das Deuteronomium: Politische Theologie und Rechtsreform in Juda und Assyrien* (BZAW 284; Berlin/New York: de Gruyter, 1999) 360–62; Smith, *The Origins of Biblical Monotheism*, 153.

[46] *CAD I/J*: 278. This view is noted by Tigay, *Deuteronomy*, 439 and 531 n. 4.

[47] Wilfred G. Lambert and Alan R. Millard, *Atra-ḫasīs: The Babylonian Story of the Flood* (with the Sumerian Flood Story by M. Civil) (Oxford: Clarendon, 1969) 52 and 58.

[48] See William L. Moran, *The Most Magic Word* (ed. Ronald S. Hendel; CBQMS 35; Washington, DC: The Catholic Biblical Association of America, 2002) 80–81.

[49] I am essentially following Lohfink and Bergman, "*'echadh*," 193. See further below.

[50] Pakkala, *Intolerant Monolatry*, 82.

[51] Otto, *Das Deuteronomium*, 362. Otto's view is based on his comparison of neo-Assyrian formulary with various passages in Deuteronomy, an approach to the book that has been quite accepted in the last two decades. For example, see Norbert Lohfink and Jan Bergman, "*'echadh*," See also below for the discussion of the work of Otto as well as others, including Paul Dion and Bernard Levinson.

[52] See Driver, *A Critical and Exegetical Commentary on Deuteronomy*, 90; Tigay, *Deuteronomy*, 76; and Carol L. Meyers and Eric M. Meyers, *Zechariah 9–14* (AB 25C; New York: Doubleday, 1993) 440.

will be one and his name will be one." Given that the monotheism of Deuteronomy 6:4 was a secondary reading of the verse, it may be asked what impact such a reading generated in terms of the verse's meaning. If "oneness" becomes an essential feature of the deity, what might this mean in comparative terms? Egypt's deities are described by John Baines as "fluid."[53] For Baines, Egyptian deities shift and combine different manifestations or constitute entities exceeding the variability of the normal human person. Divine personality by comparison is dictated not by some general sense of a deity's name, identity and functions. Instead, given the range of possibilities that are available to a worshipper, divine personality depends as much on the situation of the worshipper or the deity. There was often a matter of local versus national gods, but further complications in divinity sometimes undermine what might be regarded in a monotheistic system as clear or stable identity for Egyptian deities. Indeed, deities could be combined into yet a third expression of divinity. In a developed polytheistic situation, divinity may not simply be a matter of a number of well-defined individual deities. Indeed, such an approach applies a monotheistic model to polytheism, which may further involve overlaps and convergences with respect to divine personality, function, and spheres of activity or cosmic realms. Citing Baines' discussion, Barbara Nevling Porter picks up this issue in her discussion of Mesopotamian deities and contrasts what she calls "the more familiar God of the Hebrew Bible."[54]

If this way of looking at polytheism is correct, the end of translatability in biblical texts ultimately generated a radical shift in divine identity in Israel. The change does not involve simply Yahweh as the only deity, nor does it concern only a change in the understanding of divinity as one "stable" reality or order of reality. The change involved the combination or identification of these two features of reality in tandem, *both* Yahweh as the only deity *and* deity (in terms of name, personality and images, roles and functions, and realms of operation) stabilized and made one (or at least ontologically participating singly) in the figure of Yahweh.[55] As we will see below, this

---

[53] Baines, "Egyptian Deities in Context: Multiplicity, Unity, and the Problem of Change," in: *One God or Many? Concepts of Divinity in the Ancient World* (ed. Barbara Nevling Porter; Transactions of the Casco Bay Assyriological Institute, vol. 1; np: np, 2000) 27–29, 31–35

[54] Porter, "The Anxiety of Multiplicity: Concepts of Divinity as One and Many in Ancient Assyria," in: *One God or Many? Concepts of Divinity in the Ancient World* (ed. Barbara Nevling Porter; Transactions of the Casco Bay Assyriological Institute, vol. 1; np: np, 2000) 248.

[55] Here I am influenced by the discussion of Beate Pongratz-Leisten, "When the Gods are Speaking: Toward Defining the Interface between Polytheism and Monotheism," in: *Propheten in Mari, Assyrien und Israel* (ed. Matthias Köckert and Martti Nissinen; FRLANT 201; Göttingen: Vandenhoeck & Ruprecht, 2003) 162–68. This question remains a significant matter for research on divinity in the ancient Near East. In part, it

development obtained in a context of non-translatability in Judah, which was deeply impacted by Mesopotamian culture, possibly including its own religious non-translatability. We will take up this comparative matter toward the end of this chapter.

Looking over the passages addressed in this section, it is evident in these cases that ancient Israel developed a rejection of translatability, as Assman and Hendel have argued. At the same time, it is equally clear from the passages surveyed in Chapter Two that the rejection of translatability was not a fundamental, original feature of Israel. We see this not only in the examples discussed in the preceding chapter, but even within Psalm 82 and Deuteronomy 32:8–9. It is evident that the old worldview was rather well developed within Israel during the monarchy. Non-translatability appeared toward the end of the monarchic period, into the exile and beyond. It is possible that the idea of non-translatability in Israel may predate its explicit expressions of monotheism and contributed to Israelite formulations of monotheism.[56] Monotheism is not simply a claim to non-translatability, but a further denial of any other deities, whether foreign or indigenous.[57]

In order to better understand the rejection of translatability within ancient Israel, I would like to return briefly to the distinction that I made earlier between geographical or horizontal translatability (as we note in sources in both the Late Bronze and Hellenistic period), versus temporal or vertical translatability (as we will see in Chapter Five regarding Philo of Byblos). During the period of the kingdoms of Israel and Judah, translatability was operative as a matter of horizontal translatability (expressions across geography). At the same time, Israel was transmitting, interpreting and thus translating its traditions about its divinity through time (vertical translatability). However, toward the end of the Judean monarchy in many quarters horizontal translatability receded. In the wake of this development, vertical translatability came dramatically to the fore. The questions are why and how.

---

depends on the notion of deities as persons and powers (see further below), and thus on ancient Near Eastern notions of human personhood and their cultural contexts. For this question, see Robert A. Di Vito, "Old Testament Anthropology and the Construction of Personal Identity," *CBQ* 61 (1999) 217–38.

[56] To illustrate this distinction, we may point to the rereading of Deuteronomy 32:8–9 in Deuteronomy 4, which includes an interpretation of this passage in verse 19 as well as explicit expressions of monotheism in verse 35 and 39. For discussion of this re-reading, see Chapter Four, especially pp. 203–8.

[57] See Baruch Halpern, "Late Israelite Astronomies and the Early Greeks," in: *Symbiosis, Symbolism, and the Power of the Past: Canaan, Ancient Israel, and Their Neighbors – From the Late Bronze Age through Roman Palaestina* (ed. William G. Dever and Seymour Gitin; the AIAR Anniversary Volume; Winona Lake, IN: Eisenbrauns, 2003) 343–44.

The Waning of Horizontal Translatability
and Israel's Aetiology of Idolatry

It would not be difficult to lean on some biblical passages to see an early rejection of political translatability. For example, as we noted in Chapter Two, the Elijah story of 1 Kings 18 was read and received as a narrative illustrating the problem of translatability. The potential perceived threat of displacement of Yahweh as the national god of Israel by the Phoenician Baal arguably could have led to a rejection of translatability on the part of some non-royal segment of the population.[58] We also noted above other passages that explicitly raise the problem of translatability. Thus it is plausible to suggest that translatability became a matter of debate within Israel during the monarchy.

The waning of translatability can be correlated with other changes in Israel's religious landscape. Most fundamentally, El and Yahweh were identified as a single divine figure. As noted above, some scholars have argued that Yahweh was originally a title (or part of a title) of El,[59] but many scholars do not share this view, given the difference in the character of the two gods in Israel's so-called early poetry.[60] In these texts, Yahweh is a warrior god, a profile on the whole quite lacking for El. If this original difference is correct, then the two deities were eventually identified, a process reflected at different levels of Israelite tradition, ranging from early parallelism (the Balaam poems noted above), to implicit identification (Deuteronomy 32:8–9, as discussed above) and explicit identification (Exodus 6:2–3), to later scribal alteration (as in the addition of the name Yahweh to Genesis 14:22).[61] In any case, in time these two figures were understood as a single god, and the tradition in turn championed only one chief god in early Israel, and understood that early Israel had had only one god. As a corollary, the various titles of El were understood to be titles for Yahweh, and *'el/'elohim* (in its various

---

[58] See the discussion above; and Smith, *The Memoirs of God*, 113.

[59] Cross, *Canaanite Myth and Hebrew Epic*, 15–75; Day, *Yahweh*, 13–17; Meindert Dijkstra, "El, Yhwh and their Asherah: On Continuity and Discontinuity in Canaanite and Ancient Israelite Religion," in: *Ugarit: Ein ostmediterranes Kulturzentrum im Alten Orient. Ergebnisse und Perspektiven der Forschung. Band I: Ugarit und seine altorientalische Umwelt* (ed. Manfried Dietrich and Oswald Loretz; Abhandlungen zur Literatur Alt-Syrien-Palästinas 7; Münster: Ugarit, 1995) 43–73; Koch, *Der Gott Israels und die Götter des Orients,* 13–20, 171–209; and Lemaire, *The Birth of Monotheism,* 19–28.

[60] See Day, *Yahweh*, 13–17, who traces the view to F. K. Movers and cites Otto Eissfeldt and T. N. D. Mettinger. See also Klaus Koch, *Der Gott Israels und die Götter des Orients,* 13–20, 171–209; and Mark S. Smith, *The Early History of God,* 32–33, and *The Origins of Biblical Monotheism: Israel's Polytheistic Background and the Ugaritic Texts* (Oxford/New York: Oxford University, 2001) 143–46.

[61] See the discussion of Genesis 14:22 in Chapter Four. Cf. the comments of Nahum Sarna, *The JPS Torah Commentary. Genesis* (Philadelphia/New York/Jerusalem: The Jewish Publication Society, 1989) 381–82.

forms) was understood to be common nouns for "god," as represented by the story of Judges 3 (discussed above). As a result, these terms, denuded of any particular association with El as such, served more readily as general terms for divinity.

In the wake of this development, the tradition generated a foundational myth that early Israel only had a single deity and thus other deities were "new gods" or "other gods." This myth is found in Deuteronomy 32:17.[62] In the poem of Deuteronomy 32, we see the identification of Elyon with Yahweh, the claim to a single god and the further claim that other gods were new gods whom Israel had not known. This view in turn may have influenced other accounts of early Israel. For example, one line in Judges 5:8 as rendered by the traditional Hebrew text (MT), that "it chose new gods," may reflect the influence of the worldview of Deuteronomy 32:17. It is clear that this translation of Judges 5:8 does not comport well with its context, which is concerned with leadership. Accordingly, Frank M. Cross chooses to read in Judges 5:8, "they chose new chiefs," and to see the reading of "new gods" as a secondary interpretation facilitated by the similar spellings in Hebrew for "chiefs, rams" (*'lym/'ylm*) and "gods" (*'lym*).[63] In this scenario, the older composition, Judges 5:8, was secondarily reread under the historiographical influence of the later composition, Deuteronomy 32:17. Whether this particular reconstruction of Judges 5:8 is correct, the characterization of "new gods" in Deuteronomy 32:17 represents a strong claim about Israel's early career in divinity and signals a major shift in its historiography about divinity.

2. *"One-God" Worldviews in Mesopotamia and Israel and Their Lack of Translatability*

The data about divinity in Israel during the eighth to the sixth centuries involve important political and cultural developments within Mesopotamia and their influence on Israel. It is thought that the Neo-Assyrian empire had a strong cultural impact on ancient Israel and Judah in a variety of areas,[64]

---

[62] For discussion of the verse and in particular the term *šedim*, see Paul V. Mankowski, S.J., *Akkadian Loanwords in Biblical Hebrew* (HSS 47; Winona Lake, IN: Eisenbrauns, 2000) 138–40.

[63] Cross, *Canaanite Myth and Hebrew Epic*, 122–23 n. 34.

[64] For a helpful contextualization of the Neo-Assyrian impact on the Levant, see Simo Parpola, "Assyria's Expansion in the 8th and 7th Centuries and Its Long-Term Repercussions in the West," in: *Symbiosis, Symbolism, and the Power of the Past: Canaan, Ancient Israel, and Their Neighbors – From the Late Bronze Age through Roman Palaestina* (ed. William G. Dever and Seymour Gitin; the AIAR Anniversary Volume; Winona Lake, IN: Eisenbrauns, 2003) 99–111. For the Neo-Babylonian context, see in the same volume,

including aspects of material culture,[65] loanwords from Assyrian into Hebrew,[66] political and literary expressions,[67] scribal techniques[68] as well as a

---

Machinist, "Mesopotamian Imperialism and Israelite Religion," 237–64. For further discussion of Neo-Assyrian cultural impact and exchange, see Bernard Levinson, "The Neo-Assyrian Origins of the Canon Formula in Deuteronomy 13:1," (forthcoming in the Festschrift for Michael Fishbane; graciously made available to me by the author). For some more specifics, see the discussion below and the works cited therein.

[65] For archaeological evidence for the neo-Assyrian impact on Judah, see Ephraim Stern, *Archaeology of the Land of the Bible: Volume II. The Assyrian, Babylonian, and Persian Periods (732–332 B. C. E.)* (ABRL; New York: Doubleday, 2001) 168, 177, 187–88, 212–15. For Assyrian influence in Judah, Stern cites a colored wall painting imitating Assyrian style as well as seal carving, pottery production, and Assyrian influenced stone incense altars. William S. Morrow mentions Assyrian "palace style" pottery at sites such as Ramat Rahel as well as Assyrian goods are often cited in this regard. See Morrow, "Cuneiform Literacy and Deuteronomic Composition," *Bibliotheca Orientalis* 62 (2005) 209. Stern's volume also provides evidence for the broader archaeological context among Judah's neighbors. For the larger political and economic picture involved, see Seymour Gitin, "The Neo-Assyrian Empire and its Western Periphery," in: *Assyria 1995: Proceedings of the 10th Anniversary Symposium of the Neo-Assyrian Text Corpus Project. Helsinki, September 7–11, 1995* (ed. S. Parpola and R. M. Whiting; Helsinki: The Neo-Assyrian Text Corpus Project, 1997) 77–103.

[66] For loanwords from Assyrian (as opposed to Babylonian) into Hebrew, see the synoptic charts in: Paul V. Mankowski, S. J., *Akkadian Loanwords in Biblical Hebrew* (HSS 47; Winona Lake, IN: Eisenbrauns, 2000) 167–70 and 173–75. The vast majority of such loans isolated by Mankowski involve neo-Assyrian terms for political and military authority, with the highest number of loans found in the major prophets and the Psalms.

[67] Moran (*The Most Magic Word*, 177) noted what he called "one of the most striking parallels the writer knows between cuneiform and biblical literature," namely Deuteronomy 29:23 f. and the following from the annals of Assurbanipal that references the curses in his treaty with Arubu (as rendered by Moran): "The people of Arubu asked one and other again and again, 'Why has such an evil thing as this overtaken Arubu?' (and) they say, 'Because we have not kept the mighty oaths of the god Assur, we have sinned against the favor shown us by Assurbanipal, the king beloved of Enlil." Also well known is the comparison of a curse in the vassal treaties of Esarhaddon (*ANET* 539, para. 64) and Deuteronomy 28:23; see Jeffrey H. Tigay, "Excursus 27: The Literary Background of Deuteronomy 28," in his *The JPS Torah Commentary: Deuteronomy* (Philadelphia/Jerusalem: The Jewish Publication Society, 1996) 496. For neo-Assyrian impact on the book of Deuteronomy more broadly, see Karel van der Toorn, *Scribal Culture and the Making of the Hebrew Bible* (Cambridge, MA/London: Harvard University, 2007) 154–55. For other parallels, see Peter Machinist, "Assyria and Its Image in the First Isaiah," *JAOS* 103 (1983) 719–37; and "Mesopotamian Imperialism and Israelite Religion: A Case Study from the Second Isaiah," in: *Symbiosis, Symbolism, and the Power of the Past. Canaan, Ancient Israel, and Their Neighbors: Proceedings of the Centennial Symposium W. F. Albright Institute of Archaeological Research and American Schools of Oriental Research, May 29–31, 2000* (ed. William G. Dever and Seymour Gitin; Winona Lake, IN: Eisenbrauns, 2003) 237–64; and Smith, *The Origins of Biblical Monotheism*, 179–93. See below for the discussion of Genesis 1–11 and its Mesopotamian congeners.

[68] In addition to some of the secondary literature cited below, see William S. Morrow, "Mesopotamian Scribal Techniques and Deuteronomic Composition: Notes on Deuteronomy and the Hermeneutics of Legal Innovation," *Zeitschrift für Altorientalische und Biblische Rechtsgeschichte* 6 (2000) 302–13.

number of genres,[69] astral science and symbolism,[70] and religious iconography.[71] The Neo-Assyrian texts that have been discovered at sites in ancient Israel (including Gezer) would comport with this scenario.[72] All in all, this evidence has been taken as evidence of cross-cultural exchange between Assyria and its vassal, Judah. Political imposition was clearly key to the Assyrian project. As we will see shortly, the echoing of the Vassal Treaties of Esarhaddon (VTE)[73] in the book of Deuteronomy reflects a familiarity with Assyrian terms of vassalage. In view of this evidence, the context of cultural exchange involved a vast economic network dominated by Assyrian political control as well as diplomatic activity between the Assyrian center and the Judean periphery. Assyria also projected its royal image through the empire through the practice of erecting steles. To judge from the vestiges of this interaction in the Bible, this larger political framework helped to issue in local conditions that advanced mechanisms of intellectual exchange, specifically a Judean scribal and diplomatic elite informed about Assyrian imperial propaganda and worldview and arguably conversant to some degree with Akkadian language idiom, including political and cultural expressions. Peter Machinist detects specific instances of Assyrian borrowings in biblical works

---

[69] Usually cited for loan genres are the law-code and treaty/covenant. For the matter of treaties and the book of Deuteronomy, see below. For the possibility of Israelite borrowing of the royal chronicle from Mesopotamia, see Mark S. Smith, "Biblical Narrative between Ugaritic and Akkadian Literature· Part II: Mesopotamian Impact on Biblical Narrative," *RB* 114 (2007) 189–207, esp. 198–201.

[70] For an effort to connect Mesopotamian astral science and ancient Israel, see the iconographic material assembled by Keel and Uehlinger, *Gods,* 327–429. See also Baruch Halpern, "Late Israelite Astronomies and the Early Greeks," in: *Symbiosis, Symbolism, and the Power of the Past: Canaan, Ancient Israel, and Their Neighbors – From the Late Bronze Age through Roman Palaestina* (ed. William G. Dever and Seymour Gitin; the AIAR Anniversary Volume; Winona Lake, IN: Eisenbrauns, 2003) 323–52, esp. 323–34, 345–47.

[71] For the impact as reflected in the iconographic record, see Keel and Uehlinger, *Gods,* 283–372. The influence of Ishtar in the region is known also through iconography. See Keel and Uehlinger, *Gods,* 336–41; and Tallay Ornan, "Ištar as Depicted on Finds from Israel," in: *Studies in the Archaeology of the Iron Age in Israel and Jordan* (ed. Amihai Mazar, with the assistance of Ginny Mathias; JSOTSup 331; Sheffield: Sheffield, 2001) 235–56. See also below for the discussion below regarding whether diminished anthropomorphism in iconography of deities reflects Mesopotamian influence in this period.

[72] For a convenient collection, see Wayne Horowitz and Takayoshi Oshima, with Seth Sanders, *Cuneiform in Canaan: Cuneiform Sources from the Land of Israel in Ancient Times* (Jerusalem: Israel Exploration Society/The Hebrew University of Jerusalem, 2006) 19–22. See further Morrow, "Cuneiform Literacy and Deuteronomic Composition," 207. The datable stele material dates to the reigns of Sargon II and Esarhaddon.

[73] For a handy edition and translation, see D. J. Wiseman, "The Vassal-Treaties of Esarhaddon," *Iraq* 20 (1958) 1–99 plus pls., reprinted as a monograph by Wiseman, *The Vassal-Treaties of Esarhaddon* (London: British School of Archaeology in Iraq, 1958). For another translation, see *ANET* 534–41.

including First Isaiah (especially 10:5–15) and Nahum, and he emphasizes that the Judean response in such cases involves a "fundamental inversion" of the Assyrian royal inscriptional tradition.[74] Indeed, it is from such biblical vestiges that two stages are evidenced in this cultural impact: reception of cultural and political materials; and in some instances, reformulations as deliberate acts of literary inversion and religious resistance.[75] Or, in the terms suggested by Beate Pongratz-Leisten, these two stages involved "*Wirkungsgeschichte,*" what she calls "impacts and dependencies," and "*Rezeptionsgeschichte,*" the "free decision between what a respective user wants to select and adapt to his own cultural system and what he does not, and understands reception as a creative and productive process."[76]

The network of scribal exchange may have been more complex, with Judeans receiving some scribal training in Assyrian language and culture not only at home, but also in Mesopotamian centers.[77] We may have echoes of this practice in the figure of Daniel especially in chapters 1–6 in the biblical book named after him. One might wish to speculate further based on the figure of Ahiqar, a West Semitic scribe who is now known to have worked in the courts of Sennacherib and Esarhaddon under an Akkadian name, Aba-enlil-dari: "Aba'Enlidari who is called by the Ahlamu (i.e., the Arameans) Ahuqar was the *ummanu.*"[78] This Akkadian word denotes a

---

[74] Machinist, "Assyria and Its Image in the First Isaiah," 723–36; and his "Final Response: On the Study of the Ancients, Language Writing, and the State," in: *Margins of Writing, Origins of Cultures: New Approaches to Writing and Reading in the Ancient Near East. Papers from the Symposium Held February 25–26, 2005 (Oriental Seminars)* (ed. Seth Sanders; Chicago: Oriental Institute, 2006) 296–98. See also Baruch A. Levine, " 'Ah, Assyria! Rod of My Rage' (Isa 10:15): Biblical Monotheism as Seen in International Perspective," *Eretz Israel* 27 (2003) 138–39 (Heb.). For a balanced review, see Morrow, "Cuneiform Literacy and Deuteronomic Composition," 204–13, esp. 208–10.

[75] Machinist, "Final Response," 296–98.

[76] Beate Pongratz-Leisten, " 'Lying King' and 'False Prophet': the Intercultural Transfer of a Rhetorical Device within ancient Near Eastern Ideologies," in: *Melammu Symposia III* (ed. Antonio Panaino and Giovanni Pettinato; Milan: Università di Bologna & Istituto Italiano per l'Africa e l'Oriente (IsIAO), 2002) 216–17.

[77] For this possibility, see Halpern, "Late Israelite Astronomies and the Early Greeks," 346–47.

[78] For this material, see Jonas C. Greenfield, "Aqihar in the Book of Tobit," in: *De la Torah au Messie: Études offertes à Henri Cazelles pour ses années d'enseignement à l'Institut Catholique de Paris (Octobre 1979)* (ed. M. Carrez, J. Dore, and P. Grelot (Paris: Desclé, 1981) 330–31, reprinted in: *'Al Kanfei Yonah: Collected Studies of Jonas C. Greenfield on Semitic Philology* (ed. S. M. Paul, M. E. Stone and A. Pinnick; Leiden/Boston/Köln: Brill; Jerusalem: Magnes, 2001) 1.197–98; and James C. VanderKam, "Ahikar/Ahiqar," *ABD* 1.113–15. The tablet in question, which dates from the Seleucid period, was published by J. van Dijk, "Die Inschriftenfunde," in: *XVIII. vorlaüfiger Bericht über die von dem Deutschen Archäologischen Institut und der Deutschen Orient-Gesellschaft aus Mitteln der Deutschen Forschungsgemeinschaft unternommenen Ausgrabungen in Uruk-Warka* (ed. Heinrich Jakob Lensen; Berlin: Gebr. Mann, 1962) 44–52. For further information, see Paul-Alain Beaulieu, "Official and Vernacular Languages: The Shifting

"sage" who served as author and royal advisor.[79] Stories about Ahiqar in the Mesopotamian court and proverbs attributed to him are known in a wide range of ancient sources including Aramaic.[80] Figures such as Ahiqar are indicative of West Semitic scribes working in Mesopotamian centers. With West Semitic scribes receiving training both in Assyria and at home, it might be surmised that not only diplomatic matters but scribal learning as well may have trafficked between Levantine vassals and the Assyrian center.[81] A reconstruction proposed by Baruch Halpern entertains Judean scribes working in the Assyrian center and at home working at advanced levels of the neo-Assyrian scribal curriculum, including astronomical scholarship.[82] Perhaps one of the stronger claims made for a high level of Akkadian language knowledge has been the argument by Martin Arneth that Psalm 72 reflects a Neo-Assyrian *Vorlage*.[83]

Some of these claims exceed the presently available evidence and several matters in this discussion remain unclear. The degree of knowledge about Akkadian language and literature in Judah is disputed. It is also argued how much this cultural familiarity was filtered through Aramaic, which had become a major language in Mesopotamia and the Levant.[84] Some scholars have suggested seeing an Assyro-Aramean symbiosis as the larger

---

Sands of Imperial and Cultural Identities in First Millennium B.C. Mesopotamia," in: *Margins of Writing, Origins of Cultures: New Approaches to Writing and Reading in the Ancient Near East. Papers from the Symposium Held February 25–26, 2005 (Oriental Seminars)* (ed. Seth Sanders; Chicago: Oriental Institute, 2006) 190–91.

[79] Van der Toorn, *Scribal Culture,* 57 comments: "the line between 'scribe' (*tupšarru*) and 'scholar' (*ummânu*) if often difficult to draw, since the scribes were the academics of their time; the scribe is by definition an expert (*mūdû,* literally "one who knows") according to a Babylonian gloss." For the background of Aramaic scribes in the Assyrian court, see Paul Garelli, "Importance et rôle des araméens dans l'administration de l'empire assyriens," in: *Mesopotamien und seine Nachbarn: Politische und Kulturelle Wechselbeziehungen im alten Vorderasien vom 4. bis 1. Jahrtausend v. Chr. XXVᵉ Rencontre Assyriologique Internationale, Berlin, 3.–7. Juli 1978* (ed. H. Kühne, H. Nissen and J. Renger; Berliner Beiträge zum Vorderen Orient 1; Berlin: D. Reimer, 1982) 434–47.

[80] For a convenient summary, see James C. VanderKam, "Ahiqar, Book of," *ABD* 1.119–20.

[81] For cultural exchange among elites of empires in the first millennium, see Pongratz-Leisten, " 'Lying King' and 'False Prophet,' " 215. She also holds to this general sort of exchange between elites in the Assyrian empire center and its Judean vassal (personal communication).

[82] For this possibility, see Halpern, "Late Israelite Astronomies and the Early Greeks," 346–47. For a summary of the curriculum in this period, see van der Toorn, *Scribal Culture,* 56–58. Astrology was one of the advanced specialities.

[83] Martin Arneth, *"Sonne der Gerechtigkeit": Studien zur Solarisierung der Jahwe-Religion im Lichte von Psalm 72* (Beihefte zur Zeitschrift für Altorientalische und Biblische Rechtsgeschichte 1; Wiesbaden: Harrassowitz, 2000).

[84] See J.N. Postgate, "Ancient Assyria – Multi-racial State," *Aram* 1 (1989) 1–10; and Hayim Tadmor, "On the Role of Aramaic in the Assyrian Empire," in: *Near Eastern Studies Dedicated to H. I. H. Prince Takahito Mikasa on the Occasion of His Seventy-Fifth*

cultural context for Mesopotamian influence on Iron II Judah.[85] Accordingly, one might consider Akkadian-Aramaic bilingual texts as an indicator of the mechanism of scribal translation. Here the curse formulas of the Tell Fekheriyeh inscription appear potentially instructive.[86] This inscription is suggestive of the Assyro-Aramean scribal symbiosis, known already in Mesopotamia and emblemized by figures such as Daniel and Ahiqar. Neo-Assyrian wall painting, for example from Tel Barsip, shows a cuneiform scribe working alongside an Aramaic writing scribe.[87] In this connection, we may also note Neo-Babylonian *sepiru*, "scribe writing alphabetic script (mostly on skin)."[88] Closer to ancient Israel, the ancient site of Hama yielded texts in Akkadian and Aramaic during excavations conducted in the 1930s. The Akkadian texts includes two letters, one dating to the ninth and the other to ninth-eighth centuries, as well as "about 20 … cuneiform tablets, mainly of medical, magical and astrological contexts" from a building that appears to have been destroyed in an Assyrian attack in 720 B.C.E.[89] The Aramaic inscriptions from the site appear on objects. Many are personal names scratched on the surface of slabs sometimes with petitionary formulas; there are also a few seal impressions and ostraca with names.[90] The disposition of the presently available material suggests that Akkadian

---

Birthday (ed. M. Mori, H. Ogawa, and M. Yoshikawa; Bulletin of the Middle Eastern Culture Center in Japan 5; Wiesbaden: Harrassowitz, 1991) 419–26.

[85] See Cogan, *Imperialism and Religion*, 113.

[86] For the *editio princeps*, see A. Abou Assaf, Pierre Bordreuil and Alan R. Millard, *La statue de Tel Fekherye et son inscription bilingue assyro-araméenne* (Etudes assyriologiques; Cahiers 10; Paris: Editions Recherche sur les civilisations, 1982).

[87] See *ANEP* 235.

[88] *CAD S*:225. Note also the verb *sepēru*, "to write in Alphabetic script (on skin)" (*CAD S*:225). Both words are labeled by *CAD* as Aramaic loanwords into Akkadian (I thank Karel van der Toorn for bringing this matter to my attention). For further discussion, see Beaulieu, "Official and Vernacular Languages," 188; and Laurie E. Pearce, "Sepiru and LU2.A.BA: Scribes of the Late First Millennium," in: *Language and Cultures in Contact: At the Crossroads of Civilizations in the Syro-Mesopotamian Realm. Proceedings of the 42th Rencontre Assyriologique Internationale* (ed. K. van Kerberghe and G. Voet; OLA 96; Leuven: Peeters, 1999) 355–367, 362 (reference courtesy of Beate Pongratz-Leisten).

[89] The two letters were published by Simo Parpola, "Letter from Marduk-Apla-Usur to Rudamu, King of Hamath," in: *Hama: Fouilles et Recherches de la Foundation Carlsberg 1931–1938 II 2. Les objets de la période dite Syro-Hittite (Âge du Fer)* (ed. P.J. Riis and M.-L. Buhl; Nationalmuseets Skifter Storre Beretningen XII; Copenhagen: Nationalmuseet, 1990) 257–65. The quoted information comes from Parpola (p. 257). I am grateful to Peter Machinist for drawing this material to my attention and for discussing it with me.

[90] These were published by B. Otzen, "The Aramaic Inscriptions," in: *Hama: Fouilles et Recherches de la Foundation Carlsberg 1931–1938 II 2. Les objets de la période dite Syro-Hittite (Âge du Fer)* (ed. P.J. Riis and M.-L. Buhl; Nationalmuseets Skifter Storre Beretninger XII; Copenhagen: Nationalmuseet, 1990) 266–318.

continued to be used for professional purposes while Aramaic served for identification and other personal use.

It is unclear how representative the evidence from Hama is for the wider Levantine context in the Iron Age, especially in the southern Levant. Some scholars, most recently Paul-Alain Beaulieu, have suggested that Akkadian may be in some retreat from the Levant in the first millennium in favor of Aramaic.[91] As Beaulieu notes, this deduction would fit the situation in Judah, if the story of the Rab-shaqeh in 2 Kings 18/Isaiah 36 is a proper indication. According to 2 Kings 18:26//Isaiah 36:11, he is asked to give his speech not in "Judean", but in Aramaic. It is to be noted that if Akkadian were the lingua franca, then the Rab-shaqeh would have been asked to give his speech instead in Akkadian. In short, Akkadian as a lingua franca could be in retreat in the southern Levant, even as Aramaic is becoming an important language medium even within the Mesopotamian heartland.[92] Given its rising importance at that time, Aramaic as a means of mediation of Assyrian texts seems plausible, for at least some biblical material. Still, this is difficult to confirm. Indeed, there are not so many Aramaic loan-words into Hebrew for this period (perhaps *bar* in Psalm 2:12[93] suiting a monarchic-period context), which one might expect if Aramaic had been a mediating language. Instead, what little Aramaic there is in Genesis-2 Kings (e. g., Genesis 31:47) could derive from the proximity of Aramean territory and ancient Israel (cf. 2 Kings 5:20, 8:28–29; the Tel Dan inscription)[94]. In short, the idea of Aramaic displacing Akkadian in the southern Levant seems to be a limited solution for explaining the broad Mesopotamian impact on biblical works.

There is also a considerable discussion regarding Judean knowledge of Assyrian national cult. There is some evidence for local adoption and adaptations in the spheres of cult and deity, which was perhaps a matter of cultural prestige for local elites in vassal states.[95] (Within this context, it is disputed

---

[91] Beaulieu, "Official and Vernacular Languages," 181–211. See also the comments of Parpola, "Assyria's Expansion," 100–1. According to Parpola, Tiglath-Pileser III introduced Aramaic as the lingua franca for purposes of imperial control.

[92] If so, the loss of Aramaic versions of texts might be explained as a question of the medium used for Aramaic texts in the Mesopotamian context. The palace of Assurbanipal has records of texts that came into his library, many of which were written on writing boards subsequently lost, and the relief from Tel Barsip mentioned above shows the Aramaic writing scribe working with skin. Both materials are highly perishable.

[93] Both *bar* and *ben* (see *beni* in verse 7) are evidently known to the author of Psalm 2; so it may be asked why *ben* was not used in both instances. Perhaps the word *bar* was used in verse 12 for its resonance with *beyir'a* and *bir'ada* in the preceding verse. Thus known Aramaic forms could serve poetic purposes and perhaps others as well.

[94] See the discussion of Genesis 31 in Chapter Two, pp. 104–7.

[95] See Cogan, *Imperialism and Religion*, 47; McKay, *Religion in Judah*, 68; and Mark S. Smith, "When the Heavens Darkened: Yahweh, El, and the Divine Astral Family in Iron

whether the Assyrian imperium extended to cultic imposition of its deity.[96])
In any event, the Judean elite may have been conversant with a good deal of
Assyrian political and religious forms.[97] Beyond what the evidence shows,
it is disputed how much more the Judean elite would have been informed
about the Assyrian religious worldview. It is quite possible that the Judean
scribal and royal elite knew considerably more than what evidence shows
at present. Indeed, it is possible to entertain scenarios of intense exchange
in political, religious and cultural information. At the same time, it may be
expected that an asymmetry would exist between Assyria and her vassals
with regard to knowledge about its ritual and politics.[98] Some of this may
have been exposed to Judean vassals perhaps through diplomatic contact
with the Assyrian court, but its full import would not have been accessible.
In any event, the basic structure of Assyrian claims about divinity seems to
have been understood in Judah all too well, and this issued in a number of
literary and religious reactions preserved in the Bible.

Age II Judah," in: *Symbiosis, Symbolism, and the Power of the Past: Canaan, Ancient Israel, and Their Neighbors – From the Late Bronze Age through Roman Palaestina* (ed. W. G. Dever and S. Gitin; the AIAR Anniversary Volume; Winona Lake, IN: Eisenbrauns, 2003) 273.

[96] Assyrian political imposition of the cult of its national god on its vassals has been debated. The idea was rejected by John William McKay, *Religion in Judah under the Assyrians, 732–609 BC* (London, SCM, 1973); and Mordecai Cogan, *Imperialism and Religion: Assyria, Judah, and Israel in the Eighth and Seventh Centuries B. C. E.* (SBLMS 19; Missoula, MT: Society of Biblical Literature, distributed by Scholars, 1974). In contrast, the view was defended in the valuable work of Hermann Spieckermann, *Juda unter Assur in der Sargonidenzeit* (Göttingen: Vandenhoeck & Ruprecht, 1982). For a critique, see Cogan, "Judah under Assyrian Hegemony: A Reexamination of *Imperialism and Religion,*" *JBL* 112 (1993) 403–14. For a balanced discussion of the issue, see the superb book by Steven W. Holloway, *Aššur is King! Aššur is King! Religion in the Exercise of Power in the Neo-Assyrian Empire* (CHANE 10; Leiden/Boston/Köln: Brill, 2002) 163–64, 198–99, 211–16, and 423. Cogan revisited the question in "Discussions," in: *Symbiosis, Symbolism, and the Power of the Past: Canaan, Ancient Israel, and Their Neighbors – From the Late Bronze Age through Roman Palaestina* (ed. W. G. Dever and S. Gitin; the AIAR Anniversary Volume; Winona Lake, IN: Eisenbrauns, 2003) 548–550. Against Cogan, Simo Parpola cites inscriptional evidence that he believes supports Spieckermann's view; see Parpola, "Assyria's Expansion," 100–1 n. 4 and 104 n. 13. According to Parpola, the Vassal Treaties of Esarhaddon (henceforth VTE), sections 33–34 (= lines 377–396), require vassals to swear to accept the god Assur as their god (for VTE, see further below). Parpola also revisits references to steles bearing images of Assyrian gods being set up in vassal states.

[97] So Parpola, "Assyria's Expansion," 104.

[98] This last phrase is used on purpose to evoke the sorts of contents of Assyrian political ceremony and theological speculations discussed by Barbara Nevling Porter, "Interactions of Ritual and Politics in Mesopotamia," in: *Ritual and Politics in Ancient Mesopotamia* (ed. Barbara Nevling Porter; AOS 88; New Haven, CT: American Oriental Society, 2005) 1–6. Note also Simo Parpola on Assyrian royal ideology and religious speculation (cited in n. 115 below).

As a result, it has also been thought that biblical expressions of monotheism entailed an Assyrian impact.[99] The following discussion takes up this matter as it informs our discussion of translatability in Mesopotamia and Judah. Modern scholarship on this topic is complicated by the various terms that scholars use for divinity, including monotheism. Accordingly, the discussion in this section begins with a general consideration of Israelite and Mesopotamian divinity in roughly the eighth through the sixth centuries, then addresses the matter of modern terms used for "one-god" theism in Mesopotamia (monotheism, henotheism, and summodeism), and finally presents textual examples of "one-god" theism in Mesopotamia and Israel and their significance for contextualizing non-translatability in this period.

The Larger Context for Israel and Mesopotamia

"One-god" theism in Mesopotamia and Israel developed with the rise of the neo-Assyrian empire, followed by the impact of the Neo-Babylonian and Persian empires. While translatability worked among the great powers in the Late Bronze Age local and in the Iron Age Levantine context in Israel and its immediate neighbors, conditions changed dramatically with the extension of the Neo-Assyrian empire to the Levant. These empires were overwhelming to the relatively tiny states of Israel and Judah. In short, the reality of empire engulfed regional translatability. Parity no longer worked conceptually, and Israel retreated in its worldview of translatability of national gods. The emergent "monotheistic" model in Israel in part responded to the lack of parity of national gods decimated by the Mesopotamian empire power.

At this time, Mesopotamia was developing its constructions of non-translatability, in the form of "one-god" presentations of the empire-god, in particular Assur in Assyria[100] and Marduk in Babylon.[101] Within the wider

---

[99] For example, see Halpern, "Late Israelite Astronomies and the Early Greeks," 345–47; and Baruch Levine, "Assyrian Ideology and Biblical Monotheism," *Iraq* 67 (2005) 411–27.

[100] For this god, see G. van Driel, *The Cult of Aššur* (Assen: van Gorcum, 1969); W.G. Lambert, "The God Aššur," *Iraq* 45 (1983) 82–86; A. Livingstone, "Assur," *DDD* 108–9; and Grant Frame, "The God Aššur in Babylonia," in: *Assyria 1995: Proceedings of the 10th Anniversary Symposium of the Neo-Assyrian Text Corpus Project. Helsinki, September 7–11, 1995* (ed. S. Parpola and R.M. Whiting; Helsinki: The Neo-Assyrian Text Corpus Project, 1997) 55–64. See also Holloway, *Aššur is King!* 160–77. Holloway (pp. 1–79, esp. 35, 43, 47, 51 and pp. 427–44, esp. 434) also provides a useful summary of the early history of research, which includes claims about comparable forms of monotheism in Israel and Mesopotamia.

[101] For this god, see Walter Sommerfeld, *Der Aufstieg Marduks. Die Stellung Marduks in der babylonischen Religion des zweiten Jahrtausends v. Chr.* (AOAT 213; Neukirchen-Vluyn: Neukirchener, 1982); Tzvi Abusch, "Marduk," *DDD* 543–49; and Barbara Nevling Porter, "What the Assyrians Thought the Babylonians Thought about the Relative Status of Nabû and Marduk in the Late Assyrian Period," in: *Assyria 1995: Proceedings of the 10th*

context of its traditional polytheistic forms, the empire's scribal culture and royal cult especially in Babylon developed "mono-modes" of discourse revolving around Marduk (as well as other deities). We should be clear that such expressions of "one-god" theism do not displace traditional expressions of polytheism. In this vein, Thorkild Jacobsen comments: "we should have to assume that they reflect the idiosyncrasies of a very few individuals, for nowhere else is there any indication that the gods identified here with aspects of Marduk or parts of Ninurta's body ceased to be depicted, described, addressed or worshiped as anything other than themselves."[102] Though rare compared with the contemporary Mesopotamian representations and symbolizations of multiple deities, these "one-god" constructions emerge in this period as a particular trope within the political context of Mesopotamia.[103] These "one-god" models entail a single god at the top who in some sense underlies the reality of other deities and is ultimately not translatable into any of them.[104] In these texts, the construction of theism does not pursue

---

Anniversary Symposium of the Neo-Assyrian Text Corpus Project. Helsinki, September 7–11, 1995 (ed. S. Parpola and R. M. Whiting; Helsinki: The Neo-Assyrian Text Corpus Project, 1997) 253–60.

[102] Jacobsen, *Treasures of Darkness: A History of Mesopotamian Religion* (New Haven/London: Yale University, 1976) 235–36. In contrast, Simo Parpola believes that the complex of ideas including this "one-god" notion (monotheism, for Parpola) was widespread in Assyria. See Parpola, "Monotheism in Ancient Assyria," *One God or Many? Concepts of Divinity in the Ancient World* (ed. Barbara Nevling Porter; Transactions of the Casco Bay Assyriological Institute, vol. 1; np: np, 2000) 166–67.

[103] Examples and further discussion are provided in the following sections. The Mesopotamian material is quite complex, and a full exposition is beyond the scope of this study. It is discussed here insofar as its representation of theism seems to leave little space for translatability.

[104] Within Mesopotamia, the reality could be more complex. In this connection, one may note the Assyrian recognition of Babylonian divinity, for example expressed in one of Esarhaddon's inscriptions; see Riekele Borger, *Die Inschriften Asarhaddons, Königs von Assyrien* (Graz: E. Weidner, 1956) 88, text 57 lines 9–24 (I thank Beate Pongratz-Leisten for this information). At the same time, Babylon's cultural prestige and its religious standing represented an exceptional situation for Assyria. See Peter Machinist, "The Assyrians and Their Babylonian Problem: Some Reflections," *Jahrbuch* (*Wissenschaftskolleg zu Berlin;* 1984/85) 353–64. In this connection, we may note the Assyrian borrowing of Enuma Elish (see further below) with the god Anshar (Assur) cast as the hero instead of Marduk. On one level, this case might be regarded as a literary case of translatability, where the national hero-god fits the appropriate slot in the text. At the same time, the literary appropriation arrogates the prestige of the Babylonian text to Assyria and its national deity; no real translatability appears intended. For the Assyrian version, see Wilfred G. Lambert, "The Assyrian Recension of Enuma Eliš," in: *Assyrien im Wandel der Zeiten. XXXIXᵉ Rencontre Assyriologique Internationale, Heidelberg, 6.–10. Juli 1992* (ed. H. Waetzoldt and H. Hauptmann; Heidelberger Studien zum Alten Orient 6; Heidelberg: Heidelberger Orientverlag, 1997) 77–79. See also the reflections of Piotr Michalowski, "Presence at the Creation," in: *Lingering Over Words: Studies in Ancient Near Eastern Literature in Honor of William L. Moran* (ed. Tzvi Abusch, John Huehnergard, and Piotr Steinkeller; HSS 37; Atlanta: Scholars, 1990) 389–90. Note also the citations of Enuma Elish in the

cross-cultural translatability with deities outside of Mesopotamia.[105] At the same time, in order to be clear, these expressions do not preclude other cultural expressions allowing for polytheism[106] as well as translatability.[107] In fact, expressions of such "one-god" theism remain firmly rooted in Mesopotamian polytheistic discourse.

It was in this period that Israel's own "one-god" expressions took the form of monotheistic declarations and representations of reality.[108] Israel constructed its own monotheistic "one-god" formulations perhaps under the larger atmosphere of Mesopotamian "one-god" expressions. At the same time, the form of Israel's "one-god" theism involved a separation of its deity from the polytheistic worldview of Israel. In other words, Israel's "one-god" formulations are tied to a rejection of Israel's polytheism, standing in significant contrast both with its own Israelite polytheistic heritage and the polytheism of its local neighbors and its Assyrian overlords. Rather thoughtful essays by Peter Machinist and Edward Greenstein address bibli-

---

Assyrian versions of the Marduk Ordeal (KAR 143, lines 34 and 54; and K6333+, lines 28 and 44), provided in Alisdair Livingstone, *Court Poetry and Literary Miscellanea* (SAA III; Helsinki: Helsinki University, 1989) 82–91. In this case, the Assyrian co-opting of Babylonian tradition entailed an implicit claim to non-translatability, compounded by an implicit denial of Marduk.

[105] In her book, *The Triumph of the Symbol, Pictorial Representation of Deities in Mesopotamia and the Biblical Image Ban* (OBO 213; Fribourg: Academic; Göttingen: Vandenhoeck & Ruprecht, 2005), Ornan has argued from the iconographic record that Mesopotamia and Israel show a distinctive reduction in anthropomorphism. Might such a reduction of anthropomorphism be correlated in some manner with the emergence of "one-god" theisms that with their representation of non-translatability displace other deities? It is to be noted additionally that "one-god" theisms bear the potential for generating a stability in the correspondence of divine name, meaning, functions and representations, which otherwise may vary among different deities. Cf. Keel and Uehlinger, *Gods*, 105–6.

[106] For example, "one-god" theism hardly precluded hymns and iconography devoted to the chief divine couple, such as Assur and Ninlil/Mulissu. See Tallay Ornan, *The Triumph of the Symbol*, 81–82, 85, 101.

[107] For translatability in this period of the sort that we saw in Chapter One, see the Standard Babylonian version of Anzu, tablet III, lines 131 f.: "In Elam they gave (you) your name Hurabtil, In Susa they speak of you as Inshushinak ...". Benjamin R. Foster, *Before the Muses: An Anthology of Akkadian Literature* (third ed.; Bethesda, MD: CDL, 2005) 576. Compare also the Neo-Assyrian hymn to Nanaya, presented in: Erica Reiner, "A Sumero-Akkadian Hymn of Nanâ," *JNES* 33 (1974) 221–36; and Brigitte Groneberg, "Aspekte der 'Göttlichkeit' in Mesopotamien: Zur Klassifizierung von Göttern und Zwischenwesen," in: *Götterbilder – Gottesbilder – Weltbilder. Band I: Ägypten, Mesopotamien, Persien, Kleinasien, Syrien, Palästina* (ed. Reinhard G. Kratz and Hermann Spieckermann; FAT 2/17; Tübingen: Mohr Siebeck, 2006) 140–41.

[108] For a summary, see Smith, *The Origins of Biblical Monotheism*, 149–94. See also the detailed work of Sven Petry, "Die Entgrenzung Jhwhs: Monolatrie, Bilderverbot und Monotheismus im Deuteronomium, in Deuterojesaja und im Ezechielbuch" (doctoral dissertation, Georg-August-Universität Göttingen = FAT 2/27; Tübingen: Mohr Siebeck, 2007).

cal claims about "others" as expressions of Israel's cultural sense of difference.[109] Machinist focuses on Israel itself vis-à-vis the nations, while Greenstein concentrates on the God of Israel as opposed to the gods of Canaan. It
is this sort of claim that removes monotheism from its polytheistic context,
while the lack of such claims in Mesopotamia reflect the polytheistic setting
of its "one-god" theism.

Mesopotamian influence on Israel has been detected in its construction
of "one-god" theism. It has been argued that Israel's non-translatability of
divinity represented a reaction against neo-Assyrian and later neo-Babylonian power. If the core of Deuteronomy is any indication,[110] it may be said
that Judean monotheism also served as an expression of religious resistance
against this empire power. Deuteronomy 13, in particular, with its evident
dependence of Neo-Assyrian treaty materials, suggests a form of literary
resistance to Assyria.[111] Simo Parpola has nicely captured the point in his

---

[109] Machinist, "The Question of Distinctiveness in Ancient Israel," 196–212; and
Greenstein, "The God of Israel and the Gods of Canaan: How Different Were They," in:
*Proceedings of the Twelfth World Congress of Jewish Studies. Jerusalem, July 29 – August 5,
1997: Division A. The Bible and Its World* (ed. Ron Margolin; Jerusalem: World Union of
Jewish Studies, 1999) 47*–58*.

[110] Comparisons of Deuteronomy and Assyrian treaties have generally suggested a late
Judean date for the core of Deuteronomy. See Rintje Frankena, "The Vassal Treaties of Esarhaddon and the Dating of Deuteronomy," *Oudtestamentische Studiën* 14 (1965) 122–54;
and Moshe Weinfeld, "Traces of Assyrian Treaty Formulae in Deuteronomy," *Biblica* 46
(1965) 417–27, and *Deuteronomy and the Deuteronomic School* (Oxford: Clarendon, 1972;
repr., Winona Lake, IN: Eisenbrauns, 1992) 59–157, with references to earlier literature.
Likewise, Robert R. Wilson thinks that the deuteronomic plan of centralization in Deuteronomy 12 suits the reign of Hezekiah or Josiah rather than the exile or later. See Wilson,
"Deuteronomy, Ethnicity, and Reform: Reflections on the Social Setting of the Book of
Deuteronomy," in: *Constituting the Community: Studies on the Polity of Ancient Israel
in Honor of S. Dean McBride Jr.* (ed. John T. Strong and Steven S. Tuell; Winona Lake:
Eisenbrauns, 2005) 107–23. Karel van der Toorn similarly dates the core of Deuteronomy
to the reign of Josiah, with subsequent revisions through the sixth century; van der Toorn,
Scribal Culture and the Making of the Hebrew Bible, 143–73, esp. 149. See the following
note as well. The issues lie beyond the scope of this investigation. In contrast, it has been
generally accepted that the book's frame is later. For Deuteronomy 4:1–40 and 30 as exilic
or post-exilic compositions, see Georg Braulik, "Literarkritik und die Einrahmung von
Gemälden: Zur literarkritischen und redaktionsgeschichtlichen Analyse von Dtn 4,1–6,3
und 29,2–30,10 durch D. Knapp," *RB* 96 (1989) 266–86; A.D.H. Mayes, "Deuteronomy
4 and the Literary Criticism of Deuteronomy," *JBL* 100 (1981) 23–51; Pakkala, *Intolerant
Monolatry*, 85–93; and Sven Petry, *Die Entgrenzung Jhwhs*, 70–100. See Chapter Four for
further discussion.

[111] The comparison of Deuteronomy 13 and Esarhaddon's vassal treaties (VTE), para.
10, has generated considerable discussion in the secondary literature, especially since
Weinfeld (see the preceding note): Paul E. Dion, "Deuteronomy 13: The Suppression
of Alien Religious Propaganda in Israel during the Late Monarchical Era," in: *Law and
Ideology in Monarchic Israel* (ed. Baruch Halpern and Deborah W. Hobson; JSOTSup
124; Sheffield: Sheffield, 1991) 147–206; Bernard M. Levinson, " 'But You Shall Surely
Kill Him!' The Text-Critical and Neo-Assyrian Evidence for MT Deuteronomy 13:10,"

2. "One-God" Worldviews in Mesopotamia and Israel

comments: *"in the mind of the writer of Deuteronomy 13, the God of Israel has taken the place previously occupied in the collective mind of the nation by the feared, almighty king of Assyria* ... The conclusion seems inescapable that the Deuteronomic concept of God, which according to current scholarly consensus evolved in the late 7th or early 6th century B.C.E. and is basic to all later Judaism, is heavily indebted to Assyrian religion and royal ideology."[112]

in: *Bundesdokument und Gesetz: Studien zum Deuteronomium* (ed. Georg Braulik; Freiburg: Herder, 1995) 37–63, esp. 54–61, "Textual Criticism, Assyriology, and the History of Interpretation: Deuteronomy 13:7a as a Test Case in Method," *JBL* 120 (2001) 211–43, esp. 236–41; and Eckart Otto, "Treueid und Gesetz: Die Ursprünge des Deuteronomiums im Horizont neuassyrischen Vertragsrechts," *Zeitschrift für Altorientalische und Biblische Rechtsgeschichte* 2 (1996) 1–52. See also Otto, "Political Theology in Judah and Assyria," *Svensk Exegetisk Årsbok* 65 (2000) 62–65, and his book, *Das Deuteronomium*. For a substantial response to Otto's particular proposals, see Morrow, "Cuneiform Literacy and Deuteronomic Composition," 210–13. See also Parpola, "Assyria's Expansion," 104. These scholars generally take the late Judean monarchy as the setting for the Judean assimilation of neo-Assyrian material. Timo Veijola challenged this approach and preferred a postexilic dating; Veijola, "Wahrheit und Intoleranz nach Deuteronomium 13," *ZThK* 92 (1995) 287–314. For a response to this approach, see Levinson, "'But You Shall Surely Kill Him!'," 236 n. 73. In his discussion of the issue of literary dependence, Pakkala (*Intolerant Monolatry*, 43) disputes direct dependence of Deuteronomy 13 on VTE 10, and sees instead a broader dependence of the chapter on vassal treaties. He also suggests the exilic period or later for its setting. See Pakkala, *Intolerant Monolatry*, 20–50; and "Der literar- und religionsgeschichtliche Ort von Deuteronomium 13," in: *Die deuteronomistischen Geschichtswerke: Redaktions- und religionsgeschichtliche Perspektiven zur "Deuteronomismus"-Diskussion in Tora und Vorderen Propheten* (ed. Markus Witte et al.; BZAW 365; Berlin: de Gruyter, 2006) 125–37 (reference courtesy of Bernard Levinson). For a critique of Pakkala's approach, see Levinson, "The Neo-Assyrian Origins of the Canon Formula in Deuteronomy 13:1," (forthcoming in the Festschrift for Michael Fishbane; graciously made available to me by the author), with further literature and discussion. Part of the force of Levinson's critique is the specificity of the parallels between VTE 10 and Deuteronomy 13 that Pakkala's study does not sufficiently address. Despite noting critical problems, Pakkala's discussion acknowledges the ultimate debt of Deuteronomy 13 to neo-Assyrian vassal treaties. It is reasonable to suppose that this would have taken place during the late Judean monarchy, probably prior to the impact of the Neo-Babylonian expansion to the west. Pakkala (*Intolerant Monolatry*, 44) would assume instead that neo-Babylonian rulers continued the neo-Assyrian treaty forms, but this approach based on silence is *ad hoc* and arguably unpersuasive, as noted by Levinson (*Deuteronomy*, 123 n. n. 65). Martti Nissinen has recently revisited this discussion (with further bibliography). See Nissinen, "The Dubious Image of Prophecy," in: *Prophets, Prophecy and Prophetic Texts in Second Temple Judaism* (ed. Michael H. Floyd and Robert D. Haak; Library of Hebrew Bible/Old Testament Studies 427; London/New York: T & T Clark, 2006) 26–41, esp. 27–30. Nissinen endorses the literary dependence (though not necessarily a direct one), and argues that Deuteronomy 13:2–6 is not a translation of any paragraph from VTE. Whatever the precise nature of the dependence of Deuteronomy 13 on VTE, the late Judean context remains more convincing for the setting of the chapter than the exilic or post-exilic period.

[112] Parpola, "Assyria's Expansion," 105. Parpola's italics. See also Mark W. Hamilton, "The Past as Destiny: Historical Vision in Sam'al and Judah under Assyrian Hegemony," *HTR* 91 (1998) 228–47; and Eckart Otto, "Die besiegten Sieger. Von der Macht und

In both religious practices[113] and literary characterization,[114] Judean resistance to Mesopotamian culture may be reflected through the end of the mon-

Unmacht der Ideen in der Geschichte am Beispiel der neuassyrischen Großreichpolitik," *BZ* 43 (1999) 180–203 (references courtesy of Robert D. Miller II, S. F. O.). For reflections on Assyrian royal ideology, see Hayim Tadmor, "Propaganda, Literature, Historiography: Cracking the Code of the Assyrian Royal Inscriptions," in: *Assyria 1995: Proceedings of the 10ᵗʰ Anniversary Symposium of the Neo-Assyrian Text Corpus Project. Helsinki, September 7–11, 1995* (ed. S. Parpola and R. M. Whiting; Helsinki: The Neo-Assyrian Text Corpus Project, 1997) 325–38. For considerations of this matter from an iconographic perspective, see in the same volume the essay by Irene Winter, "Art *in* Empire: The Royal Image and the Visual Dimensions of Assyrian Ideology," 359–81.

[113] Local reaction against Mesopotamian religious practice might be seen in Jeremiah 7:18 and 44:17–25. For a critical appraisal of the latter chapter, see Bob Becking, "Jeremiah 44: A Dispute on History and Religion," in: *Religious Polemics in Context: Papers presented to the Second International Conference of the Leiden Institute for the Study of Religions (LISOR), held at Leiden 27–28 April 2000* (ed. T. L. Hettema and A. van der Kooij; Leuven: Peeters, 2004) 255–64. The prophet's interlocutors show an acceptance of the Queen of Heaven with her cakes, called *kawwanim* (Jeremiah 7:18, 44:19), which is recognized as an Akkadian loanword into Hebrew. See Moshe Held, "Studies in Biblical Lexicography in Light of Akkadian," *Eretz Israel* 16 (1982) 76–85; and Mankowski, *Akkadian Loanwords,* 61–62. The prophets' interlocutors make *kawwanim* dedicated to the unnamed "queen of heaven," reflecting the figure of Ishtar. See the summaries of Keel and Uehlinger, *Gods,* 336–41; Cornelis Houtman, "Queen of Heaven," *DDD* 678–80; André Lemaire, *The Birth of Monotheism: The Rise and Disappearance of Yahwism* (Washington, DC: Biblical Archaeology Society, 2007) 97–98. The influence of Ishtar in the region is known also through iconography. See Keel and Uehlinger, *Gods,* 336–41; and Tallay Ornan, "Ištar as Depicted on Finds from Israel," in: *Studies in the Archaeology of the Iron Age in Israel and Jordan* (ed. Amihai Mazar, with the assistance of Ginny Mathias; JSOTSup 331; Sheffield: Sheffield, 2001) 235–56. The prophet rejects the goddess and her cult, perhaps with the knowledge of its foreign origins, as reflected in the use of the loanword; had the cult of the goddess been entirely indigenous, it is arguable that no loanword would have been employed. It is additionally possible that the Judean acceptance of this goddess presupposed an equation of the Mesopotamian goddess with a regional West Semitic goddess, such as Astarte (see Saul M. Olyan, "Some Observations Concerning the Identity of the Queen of Heaven," *UF* 19 [1987] 161–74; Smith, *The Early History of God,* 127; cf. Keel and Uehlinger, *Gods,* 338–39). In this connection, the cake-moulds in the form of the goddess in Cyprus may be noted; see V. Karageorghis, "Another Mould for Cakes from Cyprus A. The Mould and Its Interpretation," *Rivista di Studi Fenici* 28 (2000) 3–5; and L. E. Stager, "[Another Mould for Cakes from Cyprus] B. In the Queen's Image," *Rivista di Studi Fenici* 28 (2000) 6–11. Keel and Uehlinger (*Gods,* 340) point to possibly related evidence from Ramat Rahel in the form of a clay stamp. In any case, a Judean translation may be involved between the Mesopotamian goddess and her local Judean counterpart, issuing in what Keel and Uehlinger (*Gods,* 340) call a "local *interpretatio judaica.*" If translation was involved, then its rejection by the prophet may mark resistance to it. Insofar as the goddess was perceived to be also a divine patron of Assyrian power, the response of Jeremiah may reflect a Judean response against Assyrian religion, in short an act of prophetic resistance. One might view other critical biblical references to Assyrian deities in this manner (cf. Mesopotamian astral gods, Sakkut and Kaiwan, named in Amos 5:26 (see M. Stol, "Sakkuth," *DDD* 722–23; see further Mankowski, *Akkadian Loanwords,* 63–65) or Bel (aka

archy. Unlike the context of Mesopotamian "one-god" expressions, Israelite monotheistic non-translatability emerged as an important cultural self-expression for Israel, one that was eventually considered so significant that it became a particular religious marker for the Judean people in the post-exilic period. That non-translatability has been considered the general, normative view of the Bible by its traditional readers might be regarded as a testament to its success.

Modern Terms of Discussion

In this period, monotheism has been viewed as the form of theism being expressed for both Yahweh and Marduk. A number of scholars, most notably Simo Parpola,[115] would situate biblical monotheism within these Mesopotamian expressions for Marduk. Both Israel and Mesopotamia, Parpola argues, expressed monotheism.[116] Perhaps from the distance of the modern

---

Marduk) and Nebo (Nabu) in Isaiah 46:1–2 (see Machinist, "Mesopotamian Imperialism and Israelite Religion," 251–52).

[114] For various aspects of Genesis 1–11 as a form of literary resistance to Mesopotamian culture and religion, see Ronald S. Hendel, "Genesis 1–11 and its Mesopotamian Problem," in: *Cultural Borrowings and Ethnic Appropriations in Antiquity. Oriens et Occidens* (ed. Erich S. Gruen; Studien zu antiken Kulturkontakten und ihrem Nachleben 8; Stuttgart: F. Steiner, 2005) 23–36.

[115] Parpola, "Monotheism in Ancient Assyria," 165–209. See also his article, "The Assyrian Tree of Life: Tracing the Origins of Jewish Monotheism and Greek Philosophy," *JNES* 52 (1993) 161–208, and the introduction to his book, *Assyrian Prophecies* (SAA IX; Helsinki: Helsinki University, 1997) xv–xliv. Parpola's particular interest lies in comparing the structures of neo-Assyrian state theology and forms of Kabbalistic speculation, and his discussion includes Jewish and Christian monotheism more broadly. Parpola's efforts to take seriously religious language and representations of religious experience are admirable. His ideas comparing Assyrian divinity and Kabbalistic thought have been severely criticized by some Assyriologists, in particular Jerrold Cooper, "Assyrian Prophecies, the Assyrian Tree, and the Mesopotamian Origins of Jewish Monotheism, Greek Philosophy, Christian Theology, Gnosticism, and Much More," *JAOS* 120 (2000) 430–43; cf. the more appreciative responses by Barbara Nevling Porter of Parpola's *Assyrian Prophecies,* in: *Bibliotheca Orientalis* 61 (1999) 685–90; and Ithamar Gruenwald, " 'How Much Qabbalah in Ancient Assyria?' – Methodological Reflections on the Study of a Cross-Cultural Phenomenon," in: *Assyria 1995: Proceedings of the 10ᵗʰ Anniversary Symposium of the Neo-Assyrian Text Corpus Project. Helsinki, September 7–11, 1995* (ed. S. Parpola and R. M. Whiting; Helsinki: The Neo-Assyrian Text Corpus Project, 1997) 115–27. Despite criticisms, Parpola's observations challenge the field to give deeper thought to Assyrian religious expression and its possible value for exploring other ancient, religious systems of thought. Even if the relations tend toward the more heuristic than the genetic, it remains valuable, as a comparison with the recent work of Rebecca Lesses shows. See her fine essay, "Speaking with Angels: Jewish and Greco-Egyptian Revelatory Adjurations," *HTR* 89 (1996) esp. 47–48. I return to this question in Chapter Six.

[116] Parpola, "Monotheism in Ancient Assyria," 165–209. See also Wilfred G. Lambert's characteristerization of CT 24 50 (discussed below) as "pushing toward a monotheistic conception of Marduk." See Lambert, "Götterlisten," in: *Reallexikon der Assyriologie* 3 (1971) 478. Note also the characterization of exaltation theologies of Marduk "as a type

vantage point, the two may look more similar than other ancient expressions of divinity.[117] However, there are difficulties in equating these Mesopotamian "one-god" representations with biblical expressions of monotheism, by any standard definition of monotheism (as opposed to highly qualified definitions sometimes used by scholars). The general understanding of the term, monotheism, is "the doctrine or belief that there is only one God."[118]

of monotheism," by Karel van der Toorn, "Theology, Priests, and Worship in Canaan and Ancient Israel," *CANE* 3.2056. Cf. McCarter, "The Religious Reforms of Hezekiah and Josiah," 67–72, esp. p. 68. Peter Machinist considers narrower and broader terminological definitions in his essay, "The Question of Distinctiveness in Ancient Israel: An Essay," in: *Ah, Assyria …: Studies in Assyrian History and Ancient Near Eastern Historiography Presented to Hayim Tadmor* (ed. M. Cogan and I. Eph'al; Scripta Hierosolymitana 33; Jerusalem: Magnes, 1991) 198. This approach is not to be confused with the notion that monotheism underlies polytheism, see Theodore M. Ludwig ("Monotheism," *ER* 9.6156), who writes of the "streams of the monotheistic vision" running "through the fertile valleys of archaic agricultural religions with their pluralistic experience of the forces of nature centered on Mother Earth." Whatever one thinks of the content of such speculation, it essentially eviscerates monotheism and polytheism of any intellectual contrast and the terms that ancient cultures express of their own religious experience (cf. Ludwig's discussion at p. 6158). For thinking in this general vein, see also Dennis Baly, "Geography of Monotheism," in: *Translating and Understanding the Old Testament: Essays in Honor of Herbert Gordon May* (ed. H. T. Frank and W. Reed; Nashville: Abingdon, 1970) 253–78; and Norbert Lohfink, "Gott und die Götter im Alten Testament," *Theologische Akademie* 6 (1969) 50–71. In his survey of scholarship on the topic, Gnuse (*No Other Gods*, 62–128) alludes to a number of authors who distinguish the development of "true monotheism" in Israel. A term such as this arguably masks claims of monotheism lying within forms of polytheism (as suggested by its implied opposite, "false monotheism").

[117] As Parpola notes, several of these Mesopotamian visions of divine reality were produced and sometimes mediated by the figure of the king. I would also highlight the role of the king in this sort of expression. Chapter One of this study cites cases in the Amarna letters where the reality of major deities was also mediated via the figure of the king. There it was observed that the king served as a means for figuring translatability within the larger context of empire. Parpola ("Assyria's Expansion," 105) places importance on the Neo-Assyrian period for the image of "the Deuteronomic God" as a "person." For the other side of the equation, namely the larger Mesopotamian context for kingship cast in terms of divinity, see Peter Machinist, "Kingship and Divinity in Imperial Assyria," in: *Text, Artifact, and Image: Revealing Ancient Israelite Religion* (ed. Gary Beckman and Theodore J. Lewis; Brown Judaic Studies 346; Providence, RI: Brown Judaic Studies, 2006) 152–88.

[118] So *The Compact Edition of the Oxford English Dictionary: Complete Text Produced Micrographically. Volume I: A–O* (Glasgow: Oxford University, 1971) under letter M, p. 627, traced back to Henry More in 1660. This definition is a better representation of what the Bible sometimes represents, but the definition itself arguably derives from a reading of biblical statements on the matter, and thus merely restates the biblical view (hence my discussion in: *The Origins of Biblical Monotheism*, 151–54). Some scholars of comparative religion prefer a broader definition of monotheism as a theism focused on one deity, in part driven by a comparative framework that would allow for ready comparison; see Ludwig, "Monotheism," in: *ER* 9.6157. Like the biblical view of monotheism, this notion too is driven by a certain agenda, in this case comparative in nature. Even if one were to allow for this sort of wider definition, the question of understanding the contrast in the ancient sources remains.

Monotheism leaves little room for other deities, while Mesopotamian expression do. In fact, these Mesopotamian cases are tied to the polytheistic milieu, while Israelite monotheism works precisely because of its effort to make a sharp divide from other deities, Israelite or otherwise.

To obviate the terminological difficulty, the similarity of "one-god" theism in Israel and Mesopotamia is sometimes posed in terms of different types of monotheisms. For example, Israel's "exclusive monotheism"[119] contrasts with Mesopotamian "inclusive monotheism" or "emanational mystical monotheism."[120] Mesopotamian monotheism is said to be represented in some texts by the figure of Marduk, in that he embodies or expresses by name and function the other gods in different ways. By comparison, Yahweh in Israelite monotheistic expressions excludes all other deities and would thus represent an "exclusive monotheism." Some scholars see a terminological weakness in using the contrast of "exclusive monotheism" and "inclusive monotheism." Lester L. Grabbe has remarked: "the devotion exclusively to Yhwh is not itself monotheism if it does not deny that other gods exist. The issue has been clouded by the use of terms such as 'inclusive monotheism' and 'exclusive monotheism'."[121] The former might suggest that the other gods still exist, and in fact they receive offerings, a functional sign of their perceived reality. In short, monotheism, even with various qualifiers, may not represent the most helpful term for capturing the similarity. While ancient Israel evidently constructed its expressions of

---

[119] The term is rather standard. For an example from the field of religion, see Theodore M. Ludwig, "Monotheism," in: *ER* 9.6157. For this usage applied to the area of ancient Near Eastern religion, see Jan Assmann, "Theology, Theodicy, Philosophy: Introduction," in: *Religions of the Ancient World: A Guide* (ed. Sarah Iles Johnston; Cambridge, MA/London: Belknap, 2004) 531–32; Klaus Koch, "Der hebräische Gott und die Gotteserfahrungen der Nachbarvölker: Inklusiver und exklusiver Monotheismus im Alten Testament," in: Koch, *Der Gott Israels und die Götter des Orients,* 9–41. See also the presentations in: Robert Karl Gnuse, *No Other Gods: Emergent Monotheism in Israel* (JSOTSup 241; Sheffield: Sheffield, 1997) 93; and Nili Fox, "Concepts of God in Israel and the Question of Monotheism," in: *Text, Artifact, and Image: Revealing Ancient Israelite Religion* (ed. Gary Beckman and Theodore J. Lewis; Brown Judaic Studies 346; Providence, RI: Brown Judaic Studies, 2006) 326 n. 1. The characterization of monotheism as "inclusive" and "exclusive" monotheism also appears in New Testament studies, e. g., William Horbury, *Herodian Judaism and New Testament Study* (WUNT 193; Tübingen: Mohr Siebeck, 2006) 3, 9–10, 12; and Larry W. Hurtado, *Lord Jesus Christ: Devotion to Jesus in Earliest Christianity* (Grand Rapids, MI/Cambridge, UK: Eerdmans, 2003) 49–50. The view goes back at least to the second of Friedrich Delitzsch's famous series of lectures delivered in 1902, entitled "Babel and Bible." For discussion, see Mogens Trolle Larsen, "The 'Babel/Bible' Controversy and Its Aftermath," *CANE* 1.101.

[120] Ludwig, "Monotheism," *ER* 9.6160.

[121] Grabbe, *A History of Jews and Judaism in the Second Temple Period, Volume 1. Yehud: A History of the Persian Period of Judah* (Library of Second Temple Studies 47; London/New York: T & T Clark International, 2004) 240.

monotheism in response to the larger discourse of divinity taking place in the ancient Near East in this period, the result is as notable for its difference as it is for its similarity. As we will see shortly, Israelite monotheistic expressions seem to construct an inverse view of reality, compared with Mesopotamian one-god expressions. Furthermore, monotheism in the Bible constitutes a local or regional inner-cultural feature that did not develop in the rest of the ancient Near East. In time, it became culturally normative for Israel, while in Mesopotamia it did not.

What we see in Israel and Mesopotamia at this time may be called "one-god" theism. This seems to be a fair representation of the underlying similarity. The terminological and theoretical question is how to express the difference in "one-god" theism in Israel and Mesopotamia. This requires careful consideration. Another term has been used to capture the difference, namely "henotheism" (devotion to "one god").[122] This term in scholarly discussions of religion was deployed first by the nineteenth century scholar of Sanskrit texts and historian of religion, F. Max Müller (1823–1900), who derived it from Friedrich Schelling (1775–1854).[123] Müller used the word to capture the idea of belief in single gods considered supreme in some sense without denying the existence of other deities, which he saw in a number of Vedic texts,[124] as opposed to monotheism, which involves the belief in only one God.[125] Müller cited Rigveda V.3.1 as an example of henotheism: "Thou at thy birth, O Agni, art Varuna; when kindled thou become Mitra; in thee, O Son of Might, all gods are centered; thou art Indra to the worshipper."[126] He also cited Atharva-veda XIII.3.13: "In the evening Agni becomes Varuna; he becomes Mitra when rising in the morning; having become Savitri

---

[122] See Versnel, "Thrice One: Three Greek Experiments in Oneness," in: *One God or Many? Concepts of Divinity in the Ancient World* (ed. Barbara Nevling Porter; Transactions of the Casco Bay Assyriological Institute, vol. 1; np: np, 2000) 87, 130–31, noting Erik Hornung, *Der Eine und die Vielen: Ägyptische Göttervorstellungen* (Darmstadt: Wissenschaftliche Buchgesellschaft, 1971) 233. The book was translated as *Conceptions of God in Ancient Egypt* (trans. John Baines; Ithaca, NY: Corenell University, 1982) 236–37. For a somewhat similar definition of henotheism, see Theodore M. Ludwig, "Monotheism," *ER* 9.6158. For the modern history of the term, see Michiko Yusa, "Henotheism," *ER* 6.3913–14.

[123] For citations and discussion, see Yusa, "Henotheism," *ER* 6.3913. For a sketch of Müller, see Jon R. Stone, "Müller, F, Max," *ER* 9:6234–37. I wish to thank Professor David Carpenter for his help in this discussion.

[124] Müller, *Lectures on the Origin and Growth of Religion as Illustrated by the Religions of India* (New York: Ch. Scribner's, 1891) 285. See also the eighth of his 1888–1892 Gifford lectures published as *Physical Religion* (New York: AMS, [1975]). The two texts cited below are quoted and discussed in this lecture.

[125] So Yusa, "Henotheism," *ER* 6.3913. In this discussion, Müller is also credited with the term "kathenotheism."

[126] A. A. Macdonnell, *A History of Sanskrit Literature* (New York: D. Appleton and Company, 1900) 70.

he passes through the sky; having become Indra he warms the heaven in the centre." Subsequent scholars of Hinduism echoed Müller's usage of the term. For Arthur A. Macdonnell, it refers to " 'the belief in individual gods alternately regarded as the highest,'" with an individual "god addressed as if he were an absolutely independent and supreme deity."[127] Critics have noted that Müller's use of the term henotheism carried a certain intellectual baggage, as it represented a stage in his developmental scheme in the history of religion.[128]

"Henotheism" could well be used for the sort of representation noted in Chapter One for some Late Bronze Age Egyptian hymns.[129] This kind of theism might also characterize Mesopotamia "one-god" constructions that we will see shortly below, and we will again encounter this sort of construction of divinity in a massive, cross-cultural way in the Greco-Roman context in Chapter Five.[130] This henotheism, whether in the Rigveda, the Late Bronze Egyptian hymns, Mesopotamian "one-god" representations, or the Greco-Roman world, involves textual constructions of one deity as the sum of the reality of other deities.[131] It is expressed sometimes as one deity as the realization of functions or aspects of divinity traditionally asso-

---

[127] Macdonnell, *A History of Sanskrit Literature,* 71. See also Walter H. Maurer, *Pinnacles of India's Past: Selections from the Ṛgveda* (University of Pennsylvania Studies on South Asia Volume 2; Amsterdam/Philadelphia: J. Benjamins, 1986) 7.

[128] For this point, see Yusa, "Henotheism," 3913. For the broader context of Müller's thought, see the discussion in: Andrew Von Hendy, *The Modern Construction of Myth* (Bloomington/Indianapolis: Indiana University, 2002) 79–83. The problem is complicated by the modern situation: the definition of theism in Hindu texts given by western Indologists was influenced by the baggage of western monotheism, and in turn, there have been many Hindu attempts to accommodate monotheism in Hindu thought. For these matters, see the discussion of R. C. Zaehner, *Hinduism* (Oxford/New York: Oxford University, 1966) 147–69. Further consideration of the complexity of Hindu theism lies beyond the scope of this discussion.

[129] For example, the Hymn to Amun (Papyrus Leiden I 350), chapter 300: "All the gods are three: Amun, the Sun and Ptah, without their seconds. His (the supreme god?) identity is hidden in Amun, his is the Sun as face, his body as Ptah" (*COS* 1.25). Note also Papyrus Chester Beatty IV recto x 2 (cited in *ANET* 372). See James P. Allen, "Monotheism in Ancient Egypt," in: *Text, Artifact, and Image: Revealing Ancient Israelite Religion* (ed. Gary Beckman and Theodore J. Lewis; Brown Judaic Studies 346; Providence, RI: Brown Judaic Studies, 2006) 320–25; Jan Assmann, *The Search for God in Ancient Egypt* (trans. David Lorton; Ithaca, NY/London: Cornell University, 2001) 10–13; and his book, *Of God and Gods: Egypt, Israel, and the Rise of Monotheism* (Madison, WI: University of Wisconsin, 2008) 64–65; and John Baines, "Egyptian Deities in Context," in: *One God or Many? Concepts of Divinity in the Ancient World* (ed. Barbara Nevling Porter; Transactions of the Casco Bay Assyriological Institute, Volume 1; np: np, 2000) 56–62.

[130] See also for classical sources the essay of Versnel, "Thrice One: Three Greek Experiments in Oneness," 79–163. Some of the cases that he regards as henotheistic involve what is here called "summodeism."

[131] Cf. Parpola, *Assyrian Prophecies,* xxi and lxxxii–lxxxiii n. 30.

ciated with the other deities. At other times the one deity is the embodiment of other deities, as we will see in examples presented below. Thus the term henotheism might be used for what we see in Mesopotamian "one-god" constructions.

At the same time, the intellectual baggage associated with henotheism does not recommend this term for the Mesopotamian material.[132] Moreover, there is a quality in the ancient Near Eastern material lacking in Vedic expressions of henotheism, and that is the clear hierarchical character of the god praised. In the Vedic material cited above, the "one-god" does not occupy the peak of a "pyramid" of gods, the highest point in a hierarchy. It involves the sum or totality of divinity, but not its summit; in the Vedic material it does not express political hierarchy. Indeed, there does not seem to be a political metaphor operating here, and certainly empire is not the operative context, as it is in a good deal of the ancient Near Eastern material.[133] Instead of henotheism, it would be preferable to deploy a term that captures the idea of one deity as the sum and summit of other deities who remain deities in their own right.

For this form of theism, the term "summodeism" may be considered. The term was introduced by the historian and political philosopher, Eric Voegelin (1901–1985), in order to characterize "worship of a supreme god as head of a polytheistic pantheon."[134] This expression, I think, works better for the ancient Near Eastern material under discussion. I am led in the direction of Voegelin's coinage by a penetrating essay of Henk S. Versnel, entitled "Thrice One: Three Greek Experiments in Oneness."[135] Versnel himself uses henotheism as the paradigm of divinity to describe the Greco-Roman situation. Henotheism for Versnel is "the privileged devotion to one god, who is regarded as uniquely superior, while other gods are neither depreciated nor rejected and continue receiving the cultic observance whenever this

---

[132] Writers also sometimes complain about the varied ways in which the word is used. For an example, see Porter, "The Anxiety of Multiplicity," 254 n. 69.

[133] I owe these observations about the Vedic material to David Carpenter. For the political setting of "absolute monarchy" in the Mesopotamian expressions discussed below, see Thorkild Jacobsen, *Treasures of Darkness: A History of Mesopotamian Religion* (New Haven/London: Yale University, 1976) 236.

[134] Eric Voegelin, *The Collected Works: Volume 14. Order and History* (ed. Maurice P. Hogan; Columbia, MI: University of Missouri, 2000) 46–47, 73–74, 267. On p. 267, Voegelin used the term for the highest gods in a pantheon, specifically for the national gods, as described in Chapter Two. Voegelin was followed in this usage by Jan Assmann, *Akhanyati's Theology of Light and Time* (The Israel Academy of Sciences and Humanities Proceedings, vol. VII No. 4; Jerusalem, 1992) 146 [4] n. 15. See also Assmann, "Monotheism and Polytheism," in: *Religions of the Ancient World: A Guide* (ed. Sarah Iles Johnston; Cambridge, MA/London: Belknap, 2004) 18.

[135] See Versnel, "Thrice One," 79–163.

is ritually required."[136] Henotheism works for the Greco-Roman context, as the political sense of divine hierarchy expressed in the devotion to a given deity recedes. In some of these instances of henotheism found in the Greco-Roman context,[137] the Latin *summus* is used.[138] In view of its etymological roots, the term "summodeism" may be used to convey the notion of one deity as the sum and summit of the reality of other deities. Understood in this way, "summodeism" conveys a theism in which the deities are regarded as aspects or functions of a chief god, with political power often key to its expression. Before proceeding to a discussion of Mesopotamian "summodeism," I hasten to add that I use these labels only as a short hand way to press closer to various representations of deities. In this discussion, none of these forms of theism is represented or regarded as superior to the others, nor does this study offer or presuppose a developmental scheme leading from one form of theism to another.[139] Indeed, these theoretical terms and the distinctions that they represent would probably have been largely unclear to the ancient authors or their audiences.[140] The purpose in using them is to gain some clarity for analysis and discussion.

---

[136] Versnel, "Thrice One," 87.

[137] See Chapter Six for discussion.

[138] See Arthur Darby Nock, *Essays on Religion and the Ancient World* (vol. 1; ed. Zeph Stewart; Cambridge, MA: Harvard University, 1972) 426, esp. n. 76: "*summus* had a wide use in Latin from early times: it is in no sense specific, though it could be adapted to the henotheistic trend."

[139] Contrast Joseph Cardinal Ratzinger, *Truth and Tolerance: Christian Belief and World Religions* (trans. Henry Taylor; San Francisco: Ignatius, 2004) 224. Ratzinger identifies what he calls "three stages." The first, polytheism, precedes and is subject eventually to a second state of a critique or enlightenment, which can lead to its collapse. At this point, monotheism appears as the third stage. According to Ratzinger, "monotheism offers a reconciliation between enlightenment and religion: the Divinity toward which reason is moving is the same as the Divinity who shows himself in revelation. Revelation and reason correspond to one another. There is the 'true religion'; the question concerning truth and the question of God have been reconciled." One might wonder if Ratzinger would concede the truth of monotheisms apart from Judaism or Christianity, for example the monotheism attributed to Akhenaten or the clear monotheism of Islam. Apart from this matter, one may rightly wonder how well this description captures the situation of monotheism in ancient Israel.

[140] As suggested above, the users who would have been quite deliberate about making distinctions would be monotheistic biblical authors in their polemics against other deities. Making such a distinction is fundamental to their project. On this matter, see Peter Machinist, "The Question of Distinctiveness in Ancient Israel: An Essay," in: *Ah, Assyria …: Studies in Assyrian History and Ancient Near Eastern Historiography Presented to Hayim Tadmor* (ed. M. Cogan and I. Eph'al; Scripta Hierosolymitana 33; Jerusalem: Magnes, 1991) 196–212, reprinted in *Essential Papers on Israel and the Ancient Near East* (ed. Frederick E. Greenspahn; New York/London: New York University, 1991) 420–42. See also the discussion above, where relative conceptual proximity to a polytheistic worldview is raised as a possible difference between Israelite monotheism and Mesopotamian summodeism. Pongratz-Leisten ("When the Gods are Speaking," 168) rightly notes the lack of antagonism between polytheism and monotheism in Mesopotamia, but it is just

Mesopotamian Summodeism

The term summodeism reasonably characterizes the representation of Marduk and Ninurta in a number of texts. The following discussion is not a comprehensive survey of the texts, yet it is sufficient to indicate Mesopotamian texts containing expressions of "one-god" theism that would appear to set aside translatability.[141] Thorkild Jacobsen observes that the first millennium marks a new expression in the consolidation of divine power in a single deity.[142] The most famous example may be the neo-Babylonian version of Enuma Elish,[143] the narrative hymn in praise of this god.[144] Accord-

---

this antagonism in Judah that competed with other Judean worldviews lacking such an antagonism. In other words, from a comparative perspective Israelite monotheism might be viewed as a separation of summodeism from its polytheistic context.

[141] For more extensive discussions, particularly recommended is Barbara Nevling Porter, "The Anxiety of Multiplicity: Concepts of Divinity as One and Many in Ancient Assyria," in: *One God or Many? Concepts of Divinity in the Ancient World* (ed. Barbara Nevling Porter; Transactions of the Casco Bay Assyriological Institute, vol. 1; np: np, 2000) 211–71. Of immense value, especially for its attention to the matter of definitions as well as the role of goddesses in Assyrian cosmology and divinity, is the essay of Beate Pongratz-Leisten, "When the Gods are Speaking: Toward Defining the Interface between Polytheism and Monotheism," in: *Propheten in Mari, Assyrien und Israel* (ed. Matthias Köckert and Martti Nissinen; FRLANT 201; Göttingen: Vandenhoeck & Ruprecht, 2003) 132–68.

[142] Jacobsen, *Treasures of Darkness*, 234–35.

[143] Modern scholars sometimes call this work "the Epic of Creation," for example, Dalley, *Myths from Mesopotamia*, 228–77; and Foster, *Before the Muses*, 436–86. Critics such as Michalowski ("Presence at the Creation," 383–84) have noted that creation is only one dimension of the text, and the contents would favor a different title, perhaps "the Epic of Marduk," "the Exaltation of Marduk" (as suggested by Moran, *The Most Magic Word*, 198), or "the Song of Marduk." Michalowski ("Presence at the Creation," 384) cites F. M. Cornford's suggestion that Enuma Elish be regarded as a hymn, a proposal based on general considerations of content: "This document is a hymn to Marduk, recounting his exploits in creating and ordering the world of gods and men." If an English title is to be used, an alternative based on the text might be "the Song of Marduk," since the closing section of the narrative poem, in tablet VII, refers to the text as "the song of Marduk, How he defeated Tiamat and took kingship." See Foster, *Before the Muses*, 485. See also the following note. For the Babylonian context, see Beate Pongratz-Leisten, "Prozession(sstrasse). A," *Reallexikon der Assyriologie* 11 (2006) 101–2.

[144] Cf. the end of Atrahasis (III viii 18–19): "I have sung of the flood to all peoples: Listen!" (Foster, *Before the Muses*, 253). Lambert and Millard (*Atra-Ḫasīs*, 7–8, 105, 165) favor seeing court singers as the backdrop to this quote, and also for the end of the so-called Erra Epic (Foster, *Before the Muses*, 911; see also Michalowski, "Presence at the Creation," 395). For another example of a mythic hymn, see the Ugaritic text often called "Nikkal wa-Ib," *KTU/CAT* 1.24 (*UNP* 215–18). In connection with the idea that these "myths" are narrative hymns or songs, it is worth noting the reflections of Thorkild Jacobsen: "The strictly literary Sumerian works can be defined generally as works of praise. The praise can be for something extant and enjoyed, a temple, a deity, or a human king. It can take narrative form as myth or epic, or descriptive form as hymn." Jacobsen, *The Harps That Once ...: Sumerian Poetry in Translation* (New Haven/London: Yale University, 1987) xiii.

ing to Enuma Elish, Marduk defeats the cosmic enemy, Tiamat, and then he receives acclamation of divine kingship from all the deities and builds the universe out of her carcass, with Babylon and his temple the Esagila at the center. In addition, the other gods are given their places in the universe that he has created. The final portion of the narrative, which takes more than an entire tablet out of a total of seven tablets, presents the names of the other gods as his. He is thus the sum of divinity relative to them.[145] We will return to this text shortly, but for the moment, we may say that this text narrates the reality of the whole world in terms of Marduk.

The text known from its first line as Ludlul bel nemeqi ("I will praise the lord of wisdom") shows Marduk's "super-god" status in a different manner. In this case, the passage in question puts the point in a way appropriate to a text concerned with human theodicy. The "one-god" vision is expressed here largely in terms of mind and thoughts:

> The lord divines the gods' innermost thoughts,
> (but) no [god] understands his behavior.
> Marduk divines the gods' innermost thoughts,
> Which god understands his mind?[146]

The mind of Marduk penetrates those of the other deities, but like humans, they cannot grasp even the external manifestation of his behavior. Marduk is far beyond any deities, much less humans.

There are more theoretical expressions of summodeism for Marduk.[147] A well-known text construes other gods as Marduk in various roles or qualities:

Urash (is)	Marduk of planting
Lugalidda (is)	Marduk of the abyss
Ninurta (is)	Marduk of the pickaxe
Nergal (is)	Marduk of battle
Zababa (is)	Marduk of warfare

---

[145] See the further discussion of Enuma Elish below.

[146] Benjamin R. Foster in: COS 1.487.

[147] Biblical scholars have taken note of these texts. See B. Hartmann, "Monotheismus in Mesopotamien?" in: *Monotheismus im Alten Israel und seiner Umwelt* (ed. Othmar Keel; Biblische Beiträge 14; Fribourg: Schweizerisches Katholisches Bibelwerk, 1980) 64; Hendel, "Aniconism and Anthropomorphism in Ancient Israel," 208–10; P. Kyle McCarter, "The Religious Reforms of Hezekiah and Josiah," in: *Aspects of Monotheism: How God is One* (ed. H. Shanks and J. Meinhardt; Washington, DC: Biblical Archaeology Society, 1997) 67–69; and Smith, *The Origins of Biblical Monotheism*, 87–88, 245 nn. 27–30 (from which much of the following discussion draws). The most comprehensive and recent survey of the pertinent texts appears in important article by Barbara Nevling Porter, "The Anxiety of Multiplicity: Concepts of Divinity as One and Many in Ancient Assyria," in: *One God or Many? Concepts of Divinity in the Ancient World* (ed. Barbara Nevling Porter; Transactions of the Casco Bay Assyriological Institute, vol. 1; np: np, 2000) 211–71.

Enlil (is)	Marduk of lordship and consultations
Nabu (is)	Marduk of accounting
Sin (is)	Marduk who lights up the night
Shamash (is)	Marduk of justice
Adad (is)	Marduk of rain
Tishpak (is)	Marduk of troops
Great Anu (is)	Marduk …
Shuqamuna (is)	Marduk of the container.
[ ] (is)	Marduk of everything.[148]

This text marks "the recognition of a high level of integration of divine power,"[149] by connecting the deities to the figure of Marduk through their functions. All divinity is ultimately operative through Marduk. In the cosmos, he is the "first cause."

Wilfred G. Lambert notes a prayer that explains various deities as aspects of Marduk:

Sin is your divinity, Anu your sovereignty,
Dagan is your lordship, Enlil your kingship,
Adad is your might, wise Ea your perception,
Nabu, the holder of the tablet stylus, is your skill,
Your leadership (in battle) is Ninurta, your might, Nergal,
Your counsel is Nus[ku], your superb [minister],
Your judgeship is radiant Shamash, who arouses [no] dispute,
Your eminent name is Marduk, sage of the gods.[150]

Barbara Nevling Porter draws particular attention to the context of this expression. It is found on a tablet belonging to a prayer collection. She comments: "The prayer's initial lines identify it as an incantation to Marduk, and its conclusion gives instructions for its use in ritual, indicating that it probably was not simply a literary effort, but meant for use in worship."[151]

---

[148] L. W. King, *Cuneiform Texts from Babylonian Tablets of the British Museum* 24 (London British Museum, 1908), plate 50 (BM 47406), with the translation taken from Wilfred G. Lambert, "The Historical Development of the Mesopotamian Pantheon: A Study in Sophisticated Polytheism," in: *Unity and Diversity* (ed. Hans Goedicke and J. J. M. Roberts; Baltimore/London: Johns Hopkins University, 1975) 198. See also Jacobsen, *Treasures of Darkness,* 235; and Peter Machinist, "On Self-Consciousness in Mesopotamia," in: *The Origins and Diversity of Axial Age Civilizations* (ed. S. N. Eisenstadt; SUNY Series in Near Eastern Studies; Albany, NY: State University of New York, 1986) 197–98. Machinist locates this text in the context of the older *Listenwissenschaft* involving deities discussed in Chapter One.

[149] Machinist, "On Self-Consciousness in Mesopotamia," 198.

[150] KAR 25 II 3–24, with translation in: Foster, *Before the Muses,* 692. For this text, see also the discussions in: Wilfred G. Lambert, "The Reign of Nebuchadnezzar I: A Turning Point in the History of Ancient Mesopotamian Religion," in: *The Seed of Wisdom: Essays in Honour of T. J. Meek* (ed. W. S. McCullough; Toronto: University of Toronto, 1964) 5; and Porter, "The Anxiety of Multiplicity," 252–54.

[151] Porter, "The Anxiety of Multiplicity," 253.

This sort of prayer addressed to Marduk is not exceptional. Lambert notes another liturgical text, a hymn that identifies a particular aspect of Marduk with Adad, Nannar, Shamash and Ninurta.[152]

In other first millennium texts, the body serves as a conceptual vehicle for conveying "one-god" theism.[153] In these texts, parts of bodies of supreme deities (such as Marduk, or Ninurta or Ishtar) are identified with other deities; these supreme deities literally "embody" the others.[154] One hymn to the warrior Ninurta renders him in such terms:

> O lord, your face is the sun god, your hair Aya,
> Your eyes, O lord, are Enlil and Ninlil.
> The pupils of your eyes are Gula and Belet-ili,
> The irises of your eyes are the twins, Sin and Shamash,
> The lashes of your eyes are the rays of the sun that …
> The appearance of your mouth, o lord, is Ishtar of the stars
> Anu and Antum are your lips, your command …
> Your tongue (?) is Pabilsag of the above …
> The roof of your mouth, o lord, is the vault
> Of heaven and earth, your divine abode,
> Your teeth are the seven gods who lay low the evil ones.[155]

Alisdair Livingstone explains the approach that this text takes to Ninurta's divinity: "Not only are the parts of Ninurta's body equated with other gods, but the particular characteristic of the god in question which is being

---

[152] KAR 304 and 337, discussed and presented in Lambert, "The Reign of Nebuchadnezzar I," 5, 11–13.

[153] Ronald S. Hendel has nicely captured the cases cast in terms of the divine body with his expression, "transcendent anthropomorphism." See Hendel, "Aniconism and Anthropomorphism in Ancient Israel," in: *The Image and the Book: Iconic Cults, Aniconism, and the Rise of Book Religion in Israel and the Ancient Near East* (ed. Karel van der Toorn; Leuven: Peeters, 1997) 206–8 and further below.

[154] See Jacobsen, *Treasures of Darkness*, 234–36; Livingstone, *Mystical and Mythological Explanatory Works*, 101–2, 233, and *Court Poetry and Literary Miscellanea* (SSA III; Helsinki: Helsinki University, 1989) 99; Lambert, "The Historical Development of the Mesopotamian Pantheon: A Study in Sophisticated Polytheism," 191–200, and "Syncretism and Religious Controversy in Babylonia," *Altorientalische Forschungen* 24 (1997) 158–62. This sort of comparison is reminiscent of incantations invoking divine help by identifying parts of the body with various deities. For an example, see Thorkild Jacobsen, "Mesopotamia," in: Henri Frankfort et al., *The Intellectual Adventure of Ancient Man: An Essay on Speculative Thought in the Ancient East* (Chicago/London: University of Chicago, 1946) 133. One might see this bodily sort of representation of Marduk as informed by medical practice. In this connection, one might also mention the question of how the human body was understood and reflected in descriptions of divine bodies. See note 55. Divine personhood remains an important matter for research.

[155] KAR 102, lines 10–19, quoted in: Jacobsen, *Treasures of Darkness*, 235; note also Foster, *Before the Muses*, 713. See also Livingstone, *Mystical and Mythological Explanatory Works*, 101; and Porter, "The Anxiety of Multiplicity," 248–51.

attributed to Ninurta is explained."[156] Porter locates this section of the text within its larger context.[157] She notes how the second part, quoted above, fits in the text. The first section describes Ninurta as praised by other gods and as one who gathers their powers to himself, while the second with its images of the other gods as various parts of Ninurta's head is continued in the third part that describes yet other deities as other parts of his body. In her rich analysis of this text's divine imagery, Porter's main point is that it focuses all divinity on Ninurta in his various aspects (as divine person, as astral phenomenon, and as an embodiment of all important earthly activities and powers). At the same time, it does not truly assert "Ninurta's absorption of everything represented by each of the other *ilu*s into himself."[158] In this hymn, the universe is represented as parts of a single body. The parts continue to belong to other deities, thus making up a whole body that is Ninurta's.[159] This god, in a sense, comprises the cosmos and the divinity that it manifests. For Porter, the other deities are hardly erased from the conceptual canvas.

As in this case, Mesopotamian "one-god" theism remains integrally tied to its larger polytheistic textual and cultural context, and the scribal culture that was producing it. It might be said that this form of theism derives its power in part by drawing on the imagery of other deities. To a great extent, its force as religious or hymnic poetry flows from the power of tradition about other deities operative at the time. It is also to be noted these Mesopotamian texts hardly constitute a distinct genre. Indeed, some are some literary while others are liturgical. What they share is an effort to describe particular divine figures in terms of other deities and what they represent as deities. In Enuma Elish this is a matter of narrating the world's origins. In Ludlul bel nemeqi, the "mind" and thought are key terms of the relationship between the god and the other deities. The "one-deity" expressions in prayers and hymns interpret the other deities as aspects or functions of the one god or as parts of that deity's body. One additional way of expressing this idea involves the divine name.

---

[156] Livingstone, *Mystical and Mythological Explanatory Works*, 101.

[157] Porter, "The Anxiety of Multiplicity," 250–51.

[158] Porter, "The Anxiety of Multiplicity," 251.

[159] Livingstone (*Mystical and Explanatory Works*, 266 n. 7) compares the description of Rigveda X.90.12–13, which explains how the various castes and deities originated as different parts of the cosmic giant, Purusa, the primeval male who is the victim in a sacrifice. For a handy translation and notes for this text, see Wendy Doniger O'Flaherty, *The Rig Veda: An Anthology* (New York: Penguin, 1981) 29–32.

Divine Names in Enuma Elish and the Hebrew Bible

The empire discourses about Assur and Marduk noted above and the roughly contemporary representations of Yahweh in the Hebrew Bible are inner-cultural expressions of divinity. These do not involve an effort at cross-cultural translatability or inter-cultural discourse about divinity, but internal expressions about the singular place of one's deity in the universe relative to other deities. Marduk was the chief god of the Neo-Babylonian empire, the very expression of its "empire-thinking." Marduk's character corresponds to the place that the empire saw for itself in the world. To dramatize the contrast between Marduk and Yahweh, I would like to juxtapose Enuma Elish and a biblical text. Of particular interest for this discussion is the ending of Enuma Elish, which lists fifty divine names and relates them to the figure of Marduk. Names 1–9 belong to Marduk to the sixth tablet,[160] while names 10–50 are grouped largely around other names presented in praise of Marduk in the seventh tablet. Prior to the listing of the fifty names, the text closes the preceding section about the assignment of all the gods to their homes with this proclamation about Marduk (VI, lines 119–120):

> Let the people of this land be divided as to gods,
> (But) by whatever name we call him, let him be our god.[161]

Benjamin R. Foster comments on the second line: "Marduk is to be the one god of all the gods, no matter how many gods humankind may serve."[162] There is a feature of the second line relevant to the question of non-translatability, namely that all the names of other deities ultimately translate into Marduk. Even the names of the three great gods are made subordinate to the reality of Marduk. Anu-Enlil-Ea is presented as a single name of Marduk (VI, line 64; cf. VII, lines 136, 140).[163] Divine names, even those belonging to the traditional great gods, are ultimately reflections of his reality.[164] The empire-god has no comparable corresponding figure on the divine level and

---

[160] Foster, *Before the Muses,* 473.

[161] Foster, *Before the Muses,* 473. For the second line, compare the translation of Dalley (*Myths from Mesopotamia,* 265): "And as for us, no matter by which name we call him, he shall be our god."

[162] Foster, *Before the Muses,* 473 n. 2.

[163] Foster, *Before the Muses,* 471 n. 3.

[164] The iconographic record for Marduk points to his "appropriation" of other deities such as Adad, parallel to his listing as the forty-seventh name of Marduk in Enuma Elish (Foster, *Before the Muses,* 482–83). For an iconographic example, see Ornan, *The Triumph of the Symbol,* 67.

is therefore the untranslatable one and only. For this text other gods have their reality expressed as a function of the god Marduk and his name.[165]

As noted above, translatability in Israel was severely reduced in this period, yet it operated differently compared to what we see in Enuma Elish. The end of the Judean monarchy witnessed a religious and political struggle over gods other than Yahweh. In some quarters, such deities were viewed as foreign.[166] Accordingly, Judean expressions of non-translatability come out differently from what we see in Enuma Elish. For example, in Jeremiah 16:21, divine revelation to the nations is to issue in their recognition of the god who is lord of not only Israel, but also the entire cosmos:

> Therefore, I am about to make them know (*yd^c),
> This time I will make them know (*yd^c)
> My power (literally, my hand) and my strength,
> And they will know (*yd^c) that my name[167] is Yahweh.

And, arguably by implication, God is not known (*yd^c) by any other name. According to Enuma Elish when the people of Babylon invoke other names, they are considered to be calling on Marduk. In Jeremiah 16:21, all people, whether in Israel or elsewhere in the world, will know Yahweh by name (Exodus 9:16; Psalm 97:7–8, cf. 29:1–2; 99:3) and they do not access Yahweh by other names. While Marduk has all other names as his own, Jeremiah 16:21 presents the name of Yahweh as demarcated from all other names.[168] A somewhat similar declaration is made in the post-exilic context of Isaiah 26:13: "O Lord, our god, lords other than you possessed us, but you alone, your name do we call upon."[169] While the figure of Marduk em-

---

[165] In this connection, Porter and Parpola discuss personal names such as Aššur-gabbu-ilani, "Aššur-is-all-the-gods," and gabbu-adad, "All-is-Adad." See "Discussions and Conclusions," in: *One God or Many?* 332.

[166] See the debate represented in Jeremiah 7 and 44, discussed above, in the preceding section.

[167] A few Hebrew manuscripts read "I" instead of "my name." According to William L. Holladay, this "alternative reading seems to be an accommodation to the repeated phraseology of Ezekiel (Ezekiel 6:7 and often)." See Holladay, *Jeremiah 1* (ed. Paul D. Hanson; Hermaneia; Philadelphia: Fortress, 1986) 480. According to Holladay (*Jeremiah 1*, 481), there "are no internal clues by which one might determine a date or historical context for the passage." For interesting speculations as to an exilic setting for verse 21, see Robert P. Carroll, *Jeremiah* (OTL; Philadelphia: Westminster, 1986) 347–48.

[168] See also the discussion above of Zechariah 14:9 in connection with Deuteronomy 6:4. Christoph Levin has pointed out to me the precedent represented by Amos 4:13 and 9:6 in the emphasis placed on the divine name of Yahweh.

[169] For the appositional construction of "your name" following "you," compare 1 Kings 21:19; cf. apposition of the independent pronoun and the divine name in Jeremiah 12:3, 15:15, and Exodus 6:3, discussed by W. Randall Garr, "The Grammar of Exodus 6:3," *JBL* 111 (1992) 389–96. Note also *KTU/CAT* 1.2 IV 11–12 and 19, discussed in: M. S. Smith, *The Ugaritic Baal Cycle: Volume 1. Introduction with Text, Translation and Commentary of KTU 1.1–1.2* (VTSup 55; Leiden: Brill, 1994) 342.

braces the power and importance associated with the divinity of the other names, for Yahweh there are no other powers, and no other deity has any importance.

The contrast between Marduk and Yahweh is explicitly made from an Israelite perspective in the work known as "Second Isaiah" (Isaiah 40–55).[170] This composition poses the question of comparison with Yahweh in two chapters. Isaiah 40:18 and 25 formulate the matter as a rhetorical question: to whom can one liken God?[171] The answer intended is clear from the polemical description of the manufacture of Babylonian images in verses 19–20 contrasting with the exalted description of God in verses 21–24: no other god compares with God. In verse 26, which follows the reiteration of the question in verse 25, it is this one God who calls the other deities by name, which would include even Marduk. The same question appears in Isaiah 46:5 shortly following the sarcastic description of Bel (Marduk), in tandem with Nebo (Nabu), in Isaiah 46:1.[172] Scholars have suggested that this passage pokes fun at the cultic procession of Marduk and Nabu in Babylon[173] in the *zagmukku/akitu* (New Year) festival.[174] Whatever the precise setting of

---

[170] For context, see Machinist, "Mesopotamian Imperialism and Israelite Religion," 237–64; and Smith, *The Origins of Biblical Monotheism,* 179–93, esp. 192–93. For the comparison of Second Isaiah's polemics against making images and the Mesopotamian *mis pi* ritual, see Michael B. Dick, "Prophetic Parodies of Making the Cult Image," in: *Born in Heaven, Made on Earth: The Making of the Cult Image in the Ancient Near East* (ed. M.B. Dick; Winona Lake, IN: Eisenbrauns, 1999) 1–53; Angelika Berlejung, *Die Theologie der Bilder: Herstellung und Einweihung von Kultbildern in Mesopotamien und die alttestamentliche Bilderpolemik* (OBO 162; Fribourg: Universitätsverlag; Göttingen: Vandenhoeck & Ruprecht, 1998); and Smith, *The Origins of Biblical Monotheism,* 184–88 for discussion and 299–300 n. 23 for further bibliography. For the text of the *mis pi,* see Christopher Walker and Michael Dick, *The Induction of the Cult Image in Ancient Mesopotamia: The Mesopotamian Mīs Pî Ritual. Transliteration, Translation, and Commentary* (SAA Literary Texts 1; Helsinki: The Neo-Assyrian Text Corpus Project, 2001). For the technology reflected in Isaiah 40, see Aloysius Fitzgerald, F.S.C., "The Technology of Isaiah 40:19–20 + 41:6–7," *CBQ* 51 (1989) 426–446.

[171] In addition to Isaiah 40:18, 25 and 46:5, compare Psalm 40:6c, which perhaps is to be rendered, "none can equal You" (NJPS 1460 note a). See Klaus Koch, "Ugaritic Polytheism and Hebrew Monotheism," in: *The God of Israel* (ed. Robert P. Gordon; University of Cambridge Oriental Publications 64; Cambridge: Cambridge University, 2007) 221.

[172] Chris Franke regards verses 1–2 as an introduction to verses 3–13. See Franke, *Isaiah 46, 47, and 48: A New Literary-Critical Reading* (Biblical and Judaic Studies 3; Winona Lake, IN: Eisenbrauns, 1994) 82.

[173] See the insightful consideration of the two gods by Barbara Nevling Porter, "What the Assyrians Thought the Babylonians Thought about the Relative Status of Nabû and Marduk in the Late Assyrian Period," in: *Assyria 1995: Proceedings of the 10th Anniversary Symposium of the Neo-Assyrian Text Corpus Project. Helsinki, September 7–11, 1995* (ed. S. Parpola and R.M. Whiting; Helsinki: The Neo-Assyrian Text Corpus Project, 1997) 253–60.

[174] For this view as well as an alternative, with a critical evaluation of both, see Machinist, "Mesopotamian Imperialism and Israelite Religion," 251–52. For the background of the

this polemic, the passage signals the critical argument about any comparison with Marduk or any other competing figures. These passages are particularly interesting for the indigenous vocabulary for translatability (**dmh* as well as **ʿrk* and **šwy*) that they provide.[175] In doing so, these texts affirm the impossibility of comparison with the Israelite deity. Indeed, unlike hymnic passages with these verbs (see **ʿrk* and **dmh* in Psalm 89:7), these passages in Second Isaiah are deliberately aimed against Mesopotamian deities. In this discussion, it is interesting that Second Isaiah does not place much importance on the name of Yahweh itself. The work shows a preference instead for the common word *ʾel,* arguably to generate a pun between the Israelite God and what the Mesopotamian craftsmen may think is a god (e.g., Isaiah 44:17).[176] However, as we move into the post-exilic period and beyond, the very name of Yahweh came to assume a particular religious importance. Compared to all other names, the name of Yahweh comes to be viewed as distinctive, even ineffable,[177] and the practices associated with the writing and speaking of the name come to reflect the unique regard for it.[178] With the one and only name, divinity ends generally in non-translatability in ancient Israel.[179]

We might contextualize this difference regarding the divine name in Israel and Mesopotamia with the general political context of the period. At the time, Israel's situation stands in inverse relationship to Mesopotamian empire. Israel lived under the shadow and threat of empire just as it was expressing its most explicit monotheistic formulations,[180] and it was doing so in accordance with its own experience and traditions that at this point

---

akitu, see Beate Pongratz-Leisten, "The Interplay of Military Strategy and Cultic Practice in Assyrian Politics," in: *Assyria 1995: Proceedings of the 10ᵗʰ Anniversary Symposium of the Neo-Assyrian Text Corpus Project. Helsinki, September 7–11, 1995* (ed. S. Parpola and R. M. Whiting; Helsinki: The Neo-Assyrian Text Corpus Project, 1997) 245–52.

[175] For **dmh* in these passages, see Franke, *Isaiah 46, 47, and 48,* 41; and Jan L. Koole, *Isaiah III: Volume I. Isaiah 40–48* (Historical Commentary on the Old Testament; Kampen: Kok Pharos, 1997) 100. See also H.D. Preuss, "*dāmāh; dᵉmûth,*" *TDOT* 3.250–60, esp. 255–56. For the same group of verbs together, see Lamentations 2:13.

[176] Smith, *The Origins of Biblical Monotheism,* 189, #8.

[177] The personified name is represented as capable of acting as a divine warrior in its own right (Isaiah 30:27). NJPS translates *šem-yhwh* as "the Lord Himself" (NJPS also provides in a footnote the literal rendering, "the name of the Lord"). For a helpful survey with relevant works cited, see Herbert B. Huffman, "Name," in *DDD* 610–12. For the West Semitic evidence for the name (*KTU/CAT* 1.16 VI 56; *KAI* 14:8; personal names of the type with "name of DN") as well as an attempt to provide an account for this anthropomorphic presentation of the name, see Smith, *The Origins of Biblical Monotheism,* 74–76.

[178] See the discussion of the Jewish divine names in Chapter Six.

[179] Cf. the sixth century Khirbet beit Lei inscription, rendered by P. Kyle McCarter as: "Yahweh is the god of the whole earth" (*COS* 2.180).

[180] This point for Israel is developed in my book, *The Origins of Biblical Monotheism,* 149–66, esp. 165, with older literature addressing this approach.

in its history distinguished it from its neighbors.[181] Israel's monotheism emerged in the context of its lack of power in the face of empires, perhaps

---

[181] I take this to be one of the fundamental points made by Stephen A. Geller, "The God of the Covenant," in: *One God or Many? Concepts of Divinity in the Ancient World* (ed. Barbara Nevling Porter; Transactions of the Casco Bay Assyriological Institute, vol. 1; np: np, 2000) 273–319. Geller's argument that the Israelite god develops a highly anthropomorphic personality compared with deities elsewhere is a highly intriguing suggestion, especially as he lines this view up in a trajectory with the Christian view of Jesus as the literal anthropomorphic embodiment of God. Note also the comment of S. David Sperling, "God: God in the Hebrew Scriptures," *ER* 5.3543: "Paradoxically, Yahveh is at once the most transcendent god of the ancient Near East and the most human." Giorgio Buccellati ("Ethics and Piety in the Ancient Near East," *CANE* 3.1694) comments in a related manner (Exodus 33 notwithstanding): "While the gods are windows onto the absolute, the God of Israel is perceived as the absolute who of his own volition opens himself to direct access – who is, as it were, his own window." Cf. my own less expansive efforts in this vein in: Smith, *The Early History of God*, 207.

It is a question whether divine anthropomorphism in the Bible in contrast to Mesopotamian descriptions of other deities (for example, in a text such as Atrahasis) can be generalized along the lines suggested by Geller and Sperling. Very poignant representations of deities appear in the former, for example in Atrahasis compared with its biblical congeners, as beautifully conveyed by Moran, in his essay, "A Mesopotamian Myth and its Biblical Transformation," in: *The Most Magic Word,* 59–74. Neither paradoxical representations of deities nor deeply moving portraits of deities constitute a unique feature of the biblical deity as such (for example, the figure of Marduk in Ludlul bel nemeqi; again, see Moran, "The Babylonian Job," in: *The Most Magic Word,* 182–200; for translation, see Foster in: *COS* 1.487–92). It might be argued that the biblical shift relative to the ancient Near Eastern context on this score involved the *combination* of transcendence and absolute status in the universe with no less a capacity for a deeply affective anthropomorphism. However, this may be overstating the case. It may be better to view ancient Israel, like Mesopotamia and other parts of the ancient Near East, as engaged in a broad search to understand divinity through a variety of emerging strategies, with summodeism and monotheism being one area of discussion and various forms of anthropomorphism being another. In matters of divine anthropomorphism and transcendence, the relative nuances found among the various ancient cultures hardly militate for a general claim for Israel's distinctiveness in divinity compared with its larger context. Or, one might say, that all areas of the ancient Near East are to be studied for their respective cultural distinctiveness, which would include the realm of their deities.

In this connection, it is particularly important to note the contribution of feminist scholarship in this area (among other matters). See, for example, the important works on divinity by Tikva Frymer-Kensky, *In the Wake of the Goddesses: Women, Culture, and the Biblical Transformation of Pagan Myth* (New York: Free, 1992); and in the title essay of Mayer I. Gruber, *The Motherhood of God and Other Studies* (South Florida Studies in the History of Judaism 57; Atlanta: Scholars, 1992) 3–15. The studies of Frymer-Kensky and Gruber point to important female representations of deities in both Mesopotamian and biblical material. In light of Geller's remark about anthropomorphism and Christianity, it may not be inapt to note that in view of the studies of Frymer-Kensky and Gruber, the textual trajectory of female language for the divinity in Christian texts is arguably not so much the canonical New Testament as later Christian works that invoke God as mother (such as the third century CE/AD work known as the Acts of the Holy Apostle Thomas; for translation of the passages involved, see David R. Cartlidge and David L. Dungan, ed., *Documents for the Study of the Gospels* (revised and enlarged edition; Minneapolis: Fortress, 1994] 33 and 35). See the issues of sexuality thought to be underlying Trinitarian

as a form of resistance to them.[182] This is not the whole picture (nor hardly a novel suggestion). The contrasting situations, nonetheless, show a comparable result in the area of translatability. While earlier ancient Near Eastern empires produced various forms of translatability of deities, seventh-sixth century Mesopotamia and Israel both stand out by comparison for developing non-translatability of divinity. Let me emphasize this contrast: the contemporary "great powers" of the Late Bronze Age produced an intense intercultural discussion that included translatability, while the successive empires of the Iron Age did not generate such a sustained discourse of this sort. Thus in these different situations of imperium, the very form of empire informs the degree and nature of translatability. In Mesopotamian summodeism, Marduk and Assur (as empire gods reign supreme over all other gods) as well as Ninurta are the very expression of other deities. In the perspective of these Mesopotamian empires, there is no equation or identification or parity of the empire gods. In turn, the imperial situation perhaps affected Israel. Translatability has no place in Israelite expressions of monotheism. Yahweh is the only god, regardless of whether other deities are foreign or belong to Israel's old religious heritage.[183] In the new picture for Israel, all other deities are ultimately alien to Israel's reality with Yahweh; in this view, they in fact have no reality. None can compare to God (cf. Isaiah 40:18a, 25a; 46:5). Thus, in the inverse expressions of Mesopotamian summodeism and Israelite monotheism, other deities are ultimately of little importance. At the end of the Iron Age, both contexts issue in expressions of non-translatability.

3. Ugarit and Israel: Case Studies of Local Responses to Empires

To understand further the situation of Israel vis-à-vis Mesopotamia, it may be instructive to contrast how Ugarit and Israel handled Mesopotamian hegemony in their respective situations. Ugarit's situation vis-à-vis Mesopotamian cultural hegemony was discussed in Chapter One, and it is evident that Israel exhibits an important cultural similarity with Ugarit. Under the looming shadow of a dominant Mesopotamian scribal culture, both produced their own literature in their vernaculars, a point brilliantly

---

formulations, discussed in the work of Virginia Burrus, *"Begotten Not Made": Conceiving Manhood in Late Antiquity* (Stanford, CA: Stanford University, 2000) 185–93.

[182] See above. This represents significant evidence against the claim that monotheism is a political ideology inherently linked to violence, discussed by Theodore M. Ludwig, "Monotheism," *ER* 9.6160; and discussed in the Introduction above.

[183] For this view of Israel's older West Semitic deities, see Smith, *The Early History of God*, esp. 19–159.

noted by Seth Sanders.[184] As Sanders observes, it was in the context of the larger international hegemony of the Akkadian language in general and of the Mesopotamian scribal culture in particular, that both Ugarit and Israel generated literary works in their own languages. There is in addition a great and important difference to be noted within this similarity. The first aspect of this contrast involves the literary situation, and the second the literary representation of divinity.

Ugarit and Israel: The Literary Contrast

Ugarit developed its literature in its own language, while the classics of Mesopotamia were produced at Ugarit in their native language of Akkadian. As we saw in Chapter One, Ugarit attests to the traditions of Atrahasis, Gilgamesh and other compositions of the Mesopotamian scribal tradition.[185]

---

[184] Sanders, "What Was the Alphabet For? The Rise of Written Vernaculars and the Making of Israelite National Literature," *Maarav* 11/1 (2004) 25–56. See also the comments by William S. Morrow, "Cuneiform Literacy and Deuteronomic Composition," *Bibliotheca Orientalis* 62 (2005) 207–8; and Carole Roche, "Introduction à la civilization d'Ougarit" in: *La Bible et l'héritage d'Ougarit* (ed. Jean-Marc Michaud; Proche-Orient et Littérature Ougaritique; Sherbrooke, Canada: Editions GGC, 2005) 39–40. Morrow notes in particular the independence of the Ugaritic versions of Mesopotamian omen literature, medical texts and lexical lists.

[185] The Atrahasis text at Ras Shamra, RS 22.421, was published in: J. Nougayrol et al., *Ugaritica V* (Mission de Ras Shamra XVI; Paris: Imprimerie Nationale/Librairie Orientaliste Paul Geuthner, 1968) # 167, 300–4. See also Lambert and Millard, *Atra-ḫasīs*, 131–33; Moran, *The Most Magic Word,* 53 n. 23, 72. For a convenient survey of flood traditions with secondary literature, see B. B. Schmidt, "Flood Narratives of Ancient Western Asia," *CANE* 4.2337–2351. For reference to Gilgamesh, Huwawa and Enkidu reconstructed in the so-called "Poem of Early Rulers," RS 25.130, *Ugaritica V,* #164 (p. 293), see Andrew R. George, *The Babylonian Gilgamesh Epic: Introduction, Critical Edition and Cuneiform Texts* (Volume I; Oxford: Oxford University, 1999) 99. The names of these figures are reconstructed in this text on the basis of the Daniel Arnaud, *Recherches au pays d'Aštata: Emar VI/4* (Mission archéologique de Meskéné-emar; 'Synthèse' n° 28; Paris: Editions Recherche sur les Civilisations, 1987), #767, lines 13–15, p. 360 (in part reconstructed on the basis of CT 44 18 ii' 5'–7'). For the spelling of the name ᵈbìl.ga.mes in the Weidner god list from Ras Shamra, see George, *The Babylonian Gilgamesh Epic,* 76, 121 n. 125. Some tradition of Gilgamesh has been thought to be reflected in RS 22.219 + 22.398 in: *Ugaritica V,* #168 (pp. 304–10), but this was disputed by W. von Soden, "Bemerkungen zu einigen literatischen Texten in akkadischer Sprache aus Ugarit," *UF* 1 (1969) 189–95. The Gilgamesh material from the 1994 excavations in the House of Urtenu at Ugarit was published by Daniel Arnaud, *Corpus des Textes de Bibliothèque de Ras Shamra-Ougarit (1936–2000) en Sumerien babylonien et et assyrien* (Aula Orientales Supplementa 23; Barcelona: Editorial AUSA, 2007) 130–38. For Gilgamesh at Middle Bronze Megiddo, see George, *The Babylonian Gilgamesh Epic,* 24, 339, 340–47, 351; Horowitz and Oshima, *Cuneiform in Canaan,* 102–5. Nougayrol believed that RS 25.460 (*Ugaritica V,* #162, pp. 265–73) is related to Ludlul Bel Nemeqi. For discussion of these texts as well as other Mesopotamian compositions at Ras Shamra, see Loren R. Mack-Fisher, "A Survey and Reading Guide to the Didactic Literature of Ugarit: Prolegomenon to a Study on the Sage," in: *The Sage in Israel and the Ancient Near East* (ed. John G. Gammie and Leo

Despite the presence of these Akkadian classics at Ugarit, there was a *development* of a vernacular at Ugarit without the *translation* of Mesopotamian literature into Ugaritic vernacular literature.[186] In sharp contrast, the Bible shows not only the *development* of an indigenous literary corpus in the local language of Hebrew, but also *translatability* of literary works or motifs into this vernacular. The Bible's authors fashioned whatever they may have inherited of the Mesopotamian literary tradition on their own terms.

To illustrate this argument for the Bible, let me briefly mention the case of Genesis 1–11. It is commonly accepted that parts of Genesis 1–11 show literary dependence, either directly or indirectly, on Mesopotamian literary tradition.[187] The best test case would be the flood story in Genesis 6–9.[188] In contrast, Genesis 2–3 may combine a general sensibility of Mesopotamian tradition with West Semitic motifs[189]; it is hard to say for certain. In either case, the lack of verbal agreement with parallel Akkadian texts, as opposed to motifs and the relative paucity of loaned vocabulary in literature, militates against a theory of direct literary dependence. With Genesis 1–11 we seem to be working more with shared motifs and basic plotlines that originated in Mesopotamia rather than with actually known texts directed borrowed into Israel.[190]

G. Perdue; Winona Lake, IN: Eisenbrauns, 1990) 67–80. For cuneiform literature in Late Bronze Levant, see Karel van der Toorn, "Cuneiform Documents from Syria-Palestine. Texts, Scribes and Schools," *ZDPV* 116 (2000) 97–103; and Horowitz and Oshima, *Cuneiform in Canaan,* esp. 15–18. Literary influence also moved from west to east in the second millennium; see W. G. Lambert, "Interchange of Ideas between Southern Mesopotamia and Syria-Palestine as Seen in Literature," in: *Mesopotamien und seine Nachbarn* (ed. H. J. Nissen and J. Renger; CRAI 25; Berlin: D. Reimer, 1982) 311–16.

[186] The translatability that we noted in Chapter One concerned a Hurrian case (Nikkal wa-Ib, *KTU/CAT* 1.24) and an indirect Egyptian instance (the name of Ptah's home, Memphis, used for Kothar wa-Hasis, in *KTU/CAT* 1.3 VI and 1.17 V). Thus the cases are not technically speaking Mesopotamian.

[187] For a sophisticated consideration of these chapters, see Hendel, "Genesis 1–11 and its Mesopotamian Problem," 23–36.

[188] According to Hendel ("Genesis 1–11 and its Mesopotamian Problem," 26), the biblical flood story minimizes its Mesopotamian origins in order to express an Israelite cultural perspective, specifically the covenant with Noah.

[189] For a maximal argument for Mesopotamian influence, see Bernard F. Batto, *Slaying the Dragon: Mythmaking in the Biblical Tradition* (Louisville: Westminster John Knox, 1992) 41–72; and "The Institution of Marriage in Genesis 2 and in Atrahasis," *CBQ* 62 (2000) 621–31. For West Semitic elements in Genesis 2–3, see Howard Wallace, *The Eden Narrative* (HSM 32; Atlanta: Scholars, 1985); and Torje Stordalen, *Echoes of Eden: Genesis 2–3 and Symbolism of the Eden Garden in Biblical Hebrew Literature* (Contributions to Biblical Exegesis and Theology 25; Leuven: Peeters, 2000).

[190] Stephanie Dalley, *Myths from Mesopotamia: Creation, the Flood, Gilgamesh, and Others* (Oxford/New York: Oxford University, 1991) 7–8.

Ugarit and Israel: The Contrast in the Literary Representation of Divinity

The literary difference may be correlated further with the way that deities and types or categories of divinity were handled across cultures. Ugarit correlated foreign deities with their own local deities in both god-lists and treaties, but only rarely in its vernacular literature. As we saw in Chapter One, in the ancient Near East correlation of deities in treaties and other forms was common practice at Ugarit in Akkadian texts; it was rare in its vernacular literature (though somewhat evident in ritual). In contrast, Israelite literature as enshrined in the Bible, while translating Mesopotamian literary material into its vernacular, did not posit translatability of deity. Instead, biblical literature, even where it shows the operation of translating Mesopotamian classical tradition (or series of operations), renders divinity on its terms.[191]

For this argument regarding the Bible, Genesis 1–11 may again serve as an illustration. For ancient Israel there is a translation of literature, but it does not show translatability of divinity. Instead, there is absorption of divinity (Yahweh as the repository of all positive divine character) as well as counter-construction (Yahweh powerful beyond the empire gods who are in fact powerless). In any case, there is no translation of deity in this literature. The eventual Israelite rejection of translatability in this context is arguably a form of inverse hegemony, whereby the dominant culture of Mesopotamia, its literary contribution and its understandings of divinity are reduced and subordinated to Israelite visions of reality. In short, the Bible uses the traditions of the empire ruling over Israel and Judah and establishes Israelite identity over and against it. In the biblical texts where this literary reaction is evident (such as Deuteronomy and Second Isaiah), it was evidently the product of elite writers. Other figures, perhaps prophets and priests, would further propagate this viewpoint, yet it would take centuries to work out the theoretical meanings and applications of monotheism and non-translatability. The ongoing construction of the Bible over the course of the post-exilic period and into the Second Temple context signals a literary and religious victory opposite to Israel's political realities.

The Aftermath

As we move through the Persian and Greco-Roman periods, the conditions of translatability shift.[192] The Persian empire arguably provided fertile ground for the further development of the Israelite "one-god" worldview,

---

[191] For an interesting discussion involving the well-known biblical transformation of the Mesopotamian flood tradition, see Moran, *The Most Magic Word,* 59–74.

[192] Other important factors are considered in: Smith, *The Origins of Biblical Monotheism,* 149–66. Prior discussions in this vein are also cited there.

especially if some influence is to be seen coming from the Persian worldview of Ahura-Mazda as universal god, as is sometimes claimed.[193] In Chapters Five and Six we will see the factor of empire again at work, this time in the Greco-Roman context,[194] with its several expressions of multiple major deities as "one." Taking a long-range view stretching from the Late Bronze Age through the Roman period, it appears that the contrast between divine conceptualization correlating summodeism sponsored by various ancient empire powers versus Israel's monotheism and its domination by empire seems to be a compelling way to view the overall situation. Over the course of the post-exilic period, Israel engaged in several practices that helped it to maintain and develop its non-translatability. Externally, Judeans would be engaged in negotiating its general non-translatability in the wider world.

---

[193] It is under these conditions that Persian influence on Judean monotheism might be expected. For arguments in this direction, see Mary Boyce, *History of Zoroastrianism* (two vols.; Leiden: Brill, 1975/1982) 2.4; Morton Smith, "II Isaiah and the Persians," *JAOS* 83 (1963) 415–421; Koch, *Der Gott Israels und die Götter des Orients,* 29–30, 317–18; and Parpola, "Assyria's Expansion," 105. Note also the brief comments on possible Zoroastrian influence on Second Isaiah by Erik Aurelius, " 'Ich bin der Herr, dein Gott': Israel und sein Gott zwischen Katastrophe und Neuanfang," in: *Götterbilder – Gottesbilder – Weltbilder. Band I: Ägypten, Mesopotamien, Persien, Kleinasien, Syrien, Palästina* (ed. Reinhard G. Kratz and Hermann Spieckermann; FAT 2/17; Tübingen: Mohr Siebeck, 2006) 335. The evidence in support of Persian influence on the Judean view of Yahweh has been judged to be circumstantial at best. See the critical assessments of Lester L. Grabbe, "The Question of Persian Influence on Jewish Religion and Thought," in: *A History of the Jews and Judaism in the Second Temple Period, Volume 1: Yehud: A History of the Persian Province of Judah* (Library of Second Temple Studies 47; London/New York: T & T Clark International, 2004) 361–64; and Simon J. Sherwin, "Old Testament Monotheism and Zoroastrian Influence," in: *The God of Israel* (ed. Robert P. Gordon; University of Cambridge Oriental Publications 64; Cambridge: Cambridge University, 2007) 113–24. See also the survey of views in: Edwin M. Yamauchi, *Persia and the Bible* (Grand Rapids, MI: Baker, 1990) 458–66.

[194] Persian influence has been seen in this later context. It has been claimed that the Qumran teaching of the universe divided into good and evil spirits found for example in 1QS 3:13–4:26, was influenced by Iranian dualism. See the differing discussions in Shaul Shaked, "Qumran and Iran," in: *Christianity, Judaism and Other Greco-Roman Cults* (ed. Jacob Neusner; Leiden: Brill, 1975) 433–46; and David Winston, "The Iranian Component in the Bible, Apocrypha, and Qumran: A Review of the Evidence," *History of Religions* 5 (1966) 183–216. For a detailed discussion with a survey of views, see P.J. Kobelski, *Melchizedek and Melchireša‘* (CBQMS 10; Washington, DC: The Catholic Biblical Association of America, 1981) 84–98. For a brief assessment for limited Iranian influence on Judaism in this period, see Arnoldo Momigliano, *Essays on Ancient and Modern Judaism* (ed. Silvia Berti; trans. Maura Masella-Gayley; Chicago: The University of Chicago, 1994) 12–13. On the matter of Iranian dualism, see also François de Blois, "Dualism in Iranian and Christian Traditions," *Journal of the Royal Asiatic Society,* series 3, 10/1 (2000) 1–19, esp. 2–7; and Philip G. Kreyenbroek, "Theological Questions in an Oral Tradition: the Case of Zoroastrianism," in: *Götterbilder – Gottesbilder – Weltbilder,* 199–222. For a recent discussion of the intellectual challenges facing comparisons with New Testament material, see Bryan Rennie, "Zoroastrianism: The Iranian Roots of Christianity?" *Bulletin: The Council of Societies for the Study of Religion* 36/1 (February 2007) 3–7.

Internally, they would be engaged in the process of interpreting the meanings of monotheism and non-translatability in religious terms. One result of the internal communal process involved the development of a corpus of sacred texts that chartered their religious and social identity. The process of developing this corpus affected the treatment of some biblical passages that do not maintain the appearance of non-translatability. In the next chapter, we will examine reinterpretation of some older biblical texts, specifically in the form of censorship resulting from the diminution of translatability in Israel. As we will see, textual censorship pertaining to divinity served as the "protection of God." In other words, it offered a defense against translatability expressed in earlier biblical passages. At this point we turn to the Persian period and Greco-Roman context for the Judean "protection of God."

Chapter Four

"Protecting God" Against Translatability: Biblical Censorship in Post-Exilic Israel

Culture hides much more than it reveals,
and strangely enough what it hides,
it hides most effectively from its own participants.
Edward T. Hall, *The Silent Language*[1]

1. Censorship Now and Then

The notion that there is censorship in the Bible should seem unwarranted, given that the Bible is considered by most traditional readers to be monotheistic. Why would there by any need to censor the Bible? Despite possible expectations to the contrary, we do find some evidence of censorship involving the deity. Indeed, it is important for understanding "biblical censorship" to note that there was a vast range of deities in ancient Israel and the Bible and the monotheism of the Bible is an outcome of a long historical and textual process, not simply the perspective that guided all of its authors.[2] Many biblical scholars have traced various developments of divinity in ancient Israel, including Israel's expression of belief in a single deity, what has generally been labeled as "monotheism." In doing so, they have followed a longstanding scholarly tradition of noting the differing deities as well as viewpoints about divinity in the Bible. This effort to trace biblical profiles in divinity and their development has not been an easy task, as we lack a great deal of information. In the end, it is clear that we work with the remains of the day, and those remains include textual and archaeological vestiges of the processes lying behind religious developments in ancient Israel; we are told little about the processes themselves.[3]

---

[1] Edward T. Hall, *The Silent Language* (Garden City, NY Doubleday, 1959) 53.

[2] It is for this very reason that the field of biblical studies now has a whole "dictionary" of almost a thousand pages in the *Dictionary of Deities and Demons in the Bible,* abbreviated in this book as *DDD.*

[3] In addition to the entries for these deities in the *DDD,* important books on these subjects include the following collections of essays: *Ein Gott allein? JHWH-Verehrung und biblischer Monotheismus im Kontext der israelitischen und altorientalischen Religionsgeschichte* (ed. Walter Dietrich and Martin A. Klopfenstein; OBO 139; Fribourg: Universitätsverlag; Göttingen: Vandenhoeck & Ruprecht, 1994); Bob Becking et al., *Only One*

Once details about these various deities in the Bible and in the archaeo-logical record are recognized, it is apparent that they played a role in the long process (or series of processes) that eventuated in the picture of monotheism that many readers assume for the Bible. This situation leaves an important yet simple question. If the Bible really is "monotheistic," then why does it contain various sorts of information about divinity? And in turn, how is it that adherents to the Jewish and Christian traditions readily read the Bible's referents to various forms of divinity as simple object les-sons against "idolatry"? How did the Bible achieve this effect? Particularly important for this chapter, the disparity between the various remains of divinity in the Bible versus its overarching monotheistic purpose is a basic feature of the Bible that calls for exploration. Historians of religion who work on divinity in the Bible have highlighted the range of divinity in it, but their research has not provided a sufficient account of how the Bible preserved the various expressions of divinity and managed to produce what the traditions that formed, received and transmitted it regarded as a proc-

God? Monotheism in Ancient Israel and the Veneration of the Goddess Asherah (The Biblical Seminar 77; London/New York: Sheffield, 2001); *The Crisis of Israelite Religion: Transformation of Religious Tradition in Exilic and Post-Exilic Times* (ed. Bob Becking and Marjo C. A. Korpel; Leiden/Boston: Brill, 1999); *Polytheismus und Monotheismus in den Religionen des Vorderen Orients* (ed. Manfred Krebernik and Jürgen van Oorschot; AOAT 298; Münster: Ugarit, 2002); *Der eine Gott und die Götter: Polytheismus und Monotheismus im antiken Israel* (ed. Manfred Oeming and Konrad Schmid; Zürich: The-ologischer Verlag, 2003); *Yahwism After the Exile: Perspectives on Israelite Religion after the Exile* (ed. Rainer Albertz and Bob Becking; Studies in Theology and Religion (STAR) 5; Assen: Van Gorcum, 2003).

Single-author volumes that address the matter of deities in Israel include: the worth-while collection of essays of Manfred Weippert conveniently collected as *Jahwe und die anderen Götter* (FAT 18; Tübingen: Mohr Siebeck, 1997); the fine summary by John Day, *Yahweh and the Gods and Goddesses of Canaan* (JSOTSup 265; Sheffield: Shef-field, 2003); the popular historical overview produced by André Lemaire, *Naissance du monothéisme: Point de vue d'un historian* (Paris: Bayard, 2003), translated as *The Birth of Monotheism: The Rise and Disappearance of Yahwism* (Washington, DC: Biblical Archaeological Society, 2007); and my books, *The Early History of God: Yahweh and the Other Deities in Ancient Israel* (San Francisco/New York: Harper & Row, 1990, second, paperback edition, The Biblical Resource Series, Grand Rapids, MI/Cambridge, UK: Eerdmans; Dearborn, MI: Dove, 2002); and *The Origins of Biblical Monotheism: Israel's Polytheistic Background and the Ugaritic Texts* (Oxford/New York: Oxford University, 2001). A streamlined discussion of these matters appears in my work, *The Memoirs of God: History, Memory, and the Experience of God in Ancient Israel* (Minneapolis: For-tress, 2004), especially Chapter Three. See also the study of Herbert Niehr, *Der höchste Gott: Alttestamentlicher JHWH-Glaube im Kontext syrisch-kanaanäischer Religion des 1. Jahrtausends v. Chr.* (BZAW 190; Berlin/New York: de Gruyter, 1990); and Meindert Dijkstra, "El, Yhwh and their Asherah: On Continuity and Discontinuity in Canaanite and Ancient Israelite Religion," in: *Ugarit: Ein ostmediterranes Kulturzentrum im Alten Orient. Ergebnisse und Perspektiven der Forschung. Band I: Ugarit und seine altorienta-lische Umwelt* (ed. Manfried Dietrich and Oswald Loretz; Abhandlungen zur Literatur Alt-Syrien-Palästinas 7; Münster: Ugarit, 1995) 43–73.

lamation of their monotheism. As one element in this matter, what may fall under the rubric of "biblical censorship" has yet to receive an adequate account.[4] The larger question of how the biblical tradition handled such polytheistic expressions and conformed them to its monotheistic lens, in other words "biblical censorship," has not been sufficiently addressed.

In contrast to the situation in biblical studies, censorship in modern societies and its larger social role has been the subject of considerable scholarly attention in recent years. This effort includes a number of works focused chiefly on modern Europe: Dominic Boyer on the former East Germany (German Democratic Republic, abbreviated as GDR)[5]; a collection of essays edited by Marianna Tax Choldin and Maurice Friedberg on the former Union of Soviet Socialist Republics (USSR)[6]; and a study by Richard Darnton comparing France ca. 1789 and East Germany ca. 1989.[7] We also have more general considerations of censorship authored by Sue Curry Jansen.[8] An essay by Michael Holquist, entitled "Corrupt Originals: The Paradox of Censorship," serves as the introduction to the initial number of the 1994 issue of the *PMLA* on the topic of literature and censorship.[9] Several of these works look at the culture of censors within their social and political contexts. They attempt to go beyond the stereotype of the censor as simply a bad or immoral puppet of the political system, a lesser mind in service to the party line. Moreover, some of these studies have been attentive to censorship beyond politically repressive regimes. Indeed, at this particular time in the history of the United States, various forms of censorship and self-censorship have been noted in the allegedly open American press. And contrary to popular belief in university circles, censorship has been observed within the world of academic publication.[10]

---

[4] This critique includes my books, which never really raised the question except for the brief treatment in: *The Memoirs of God,* 151–58.

[5] Boyer, "Censorship as a Vocation: The Institutions, Practices, and Cultural Logic of Media Control in the German Democratic Republic," *Comparative Studies in History and Society* 45/3 (2003) 511–45. See also Boyer's book, *Spirit and System: Media, Intellectuals, and the Dialectic in Modern German Culture* (Chicago/London: University of Chicago, 2005) 114–16, 132–147. I am indebted to Boyer's study for introducing me to the studies of the following authors.

[6] Choldin and Friedberg, ed., *The Red Pencil: Artists, Scholars and Censors in the USSR* (Boston: Unwin Hyman, 1989).

[7] Darnton, "Censorship, a Comparative View: France, 1789 – East Germany, 1989," *Representations* 49 (Winter, 1995) 40–60.

[8] Jansen, *Censorship: The Knot that Binds Power and Knowledge* (Oxford: Oxford University, 1988). Note also the work of J. M. Coetzee, *Giving Offense: Essays on Censorship* (Chicago: University of Chicago, 1996).

[9] Holquist, "Corrupt Originals: The Paradox of Censorship," *PMLA* 109/1 (January 1994) 14–25.

[10] See Edward Shils, "The University World Turned Upside Down: Does Confidentiality of Assessment by Peers Guarantee the Quality of Academic Appointment?" *Minerva*

In order to understand how the work of censors fits into the larger intellectual activity of the societies involved, these scholars probe the larger contexts of censorship from the inside of the political and intellectual culture in which censors operate. Of these writers, particularly helpful is Dominic Boyer on the former East German republic (German Democratic Republic, or GDR).[11] In this chapter, I will attempt to generate a picture of the larger context for biblical censorship by entering into dialogue with Boyer's study of the GDR. What is valuable about Boyer's work is how it explores stereotypical notions of censorship and then how he debunks them, specifically by showing how censorship belonged to a set of cultural practices situated within a larger context of the production of media and knowledge in the GDR. Let us begin by comparing Boyer's stereotypical censor and the depiction of censorship in ancient Israel by some biblical scholars. Boyer paints his stereotypical scenario: a man sitting at a table has before him a jar filled with blue pencils, a coffee cup, a phone for obsequious consultation with higher-ups, perhaps an ideological reference manual or sheaf of instructions for the job.[12] In the minds of many readers, censorship evokes an air of conscious choice, a petty one "far beneath the work of the truly gifted and intelligent."[13] This intellectual practice involves a "negation of self." We are in the world of "an absence of morality and ethics, the inversion of standards and norms."[14] This censor is inferior talent, ideologically informed and driven to replicate the party line and its ideology, or at least required to do so, sometimes perhaps against his own will.

At first glance, this sort of picture may look a good deal like what some biblical scholars have to say on the subject of the Bible and censorship. Let me provide a sample from three highly respected scholars who have produced important works on Israelite religion (I have placed the operative terms about censorship quoted from their work in italics). Morton Smith commented explicitly on censorship in his well-known book, *Palestinian Parties and Politics:* "names originally compounded with those of other deities ... are also common in the preserved records of the early period and were probably more common in the records which have now been lost by *censorship*."[15] Karel van der Toorn addressed the selection process underlying the Bible: "it is mainly due to *theological bias* of the editors of

---

28/3 (1990) 324–34. This concern is also a running theme in the article of Boyer, "Censorship as a Vocation."

[11] Boyer, "Censorship as a Vocation: The Institutions, Practices, and Cultural Logic of Media Control in the German Democratic Republic," *Society for Comparative Study of Society and History* 2003:511–545.

[12] Boyer, "Censorship as a Vocation," 511.

[13] Boyer, "Censorship as a Vocation," 512.

[14] Boyer, "Censorship as a Vocation," 512.

[15] Morton Smith, *Palestinian Parties and Politics That Shaped the Old Testament*

the Hebrew Bible – those who *selected* the texts, and those who *corrected* them if need be – that many goddesses have been condemned to oblivion"[16] More recently, William Dever has offered a similar picture: "Yahwistic monotheism was the *ideal* of most of the orthodox, nationalist parties who *wrote and edited* the Hebrew Bible, but for the majority it had not been the *reality* throughout most of ancient Israel's history."[17] According to Dever, the biblical writers "are openly partisan, championing the cause of extreme nationalism and orthodox Yahwism, that is, the *Truth* as *they* see it. They had no tolerance for divergent views."[18]

The three descriptions focus on writing as the locus of control. To judge from their broader descriptions of the situation, all three scholars evidently would identify the institution of priestly scribes[19] as a major social location for this activity. At the same time, the three scholarly descriptions differ somewhat over the operative practices. For scribal practice, Morton Smith uses the term censorship; van der Toorn specifies selection and correction; and Dever focuses on writing and editing. For the cultural process behind the scribal practice, Smith focuses on lost works; for him, the processes of transmission preserved some works, but it "lost" others. Van der Toorn mentions two sides of the process: selection, specifically retention of theologically acceptable material; and correction, namely material changes made

---

(second corrected ed.; London: SCM, 1987; first edition published in 1971) 15; see also pp. 12 and 14.

[16] Van der Toorn, "God (I)," *DDD* 363. I hasten to add that this is a comment made in a context that seems not allow the author to develop his points. In fact, van der Toorn's understanding of these and related matters is sophisticated, as is clear from his recent book, *Scribal Culture and the Making of the Hebrew Bible* (Cambridge, MA/London: Harvard University, 2007).

[17] William G. Dever, *Did God Have a Wife?* (Grand Rapids, MI: Eerdmans, 2004) 252 (Dever's italics). For further comments in this vein, see Dever, *Did God Have a Wife?* 286, 295–96, 299.

[18] Dever, *Did God Have a Wife?* 71 (Dever's italics).

[19] For the sake of convenience, the text below sometimes uses the male personal pronoun for a scribe, since scribes in ancient Israel were male as far as we know. Of course, it was not impossible that there were female scribes; just as women might serve in other elite capacities (cf. the biblical representations of Deborah, Miriam, perhaps Huldah), theoretically they might have served in this one as well (cf. 1 Kings 21:8–9 where Jezebel is said to write letters but this passage probably means that she arranged to have scribes write these letters). In Israel, scribal training was conducted among males, organized within family lines at least during the post-exilic period (e.g., the families of scribes named in 1 Chronicles 2:55), if not earlier (cf. J. R. Lundbom, "Baruch," *ABD* 1:617: "as far back as the Old Babylonian period, ... scribes were known to cluster in families"). In contrast to the situation in Israel, some sources in Syro-Mesopotamia attest to female scribes, although the norm is male scribal transmission often passed on from father to son. See Laurie Pearce, "The Scribe and Scholars of Ancient Mesopotamia," *CANE* 4.2265–78, esp. 2266 and 2277–78 (bibliography on the subject); and Andrew R. George, *The Babylonian Gilgamesh Epic: Introduction, Critical Edition and Cuneiform Texts. Volume I* (Oxford/New York: Oxford University, 2003) 37–38, 483 n. 129. See further below.

to the otherwise acceptable texts. In speaking of writing, Dever may have in mind something along the lines of van der Toorn's selection, and his notion of editing seems to echo van der Toorn's notion of correction. Overall, the differences among these authors are not great; put together, a three-part process underlies what Smith calls censorship: production of material that includes what is later seen as orthodox and unorthodox; the selection out of unorthodox material; and editing, specifically correction of unorthodox material. In sum, all three scholars seem to agree on the basic features of censorship: it is scribal, and it involves an inversion of older standards and norms. And, to judge from the tone of Dever's remarks, it is "bad."

While there is much that is correct in the remarks quoted above, it may be asked how well this sort of description captures the activity and context of biblical censorship. I pose this question not so much to dispute the general approach as to raise a question about the complexities that inform this picture. One may ask if these assessments best reflect the information that did remain in the Bible. For a work that is regarded by Dever as "largely a late theological construct,"[20] the Bible retained a tremendous amount of information about divinity in ancient Israel that one might think its transmitters would have opposed.[21] In fact, it is largely thanks to the biblical remains of the day that scholars have been able to venture histories of divinity in ancient Israel. To be sure, this area of research is aided greatly by material provided by archaeological discoveries, most especially the inscriptions from the sites of Kuntillet Ajrud and Khirbet el Qom in the south and Samaria in the north. However, despite Dever's strongly expressed emphasis to the contrary, the archaeological data do not measure up to the Bible's own *range* of witness to various forms of worship apart from and addition to God. It is arguable that more is known about the *range* of Israelite polytheism from the Bible than from the record of Iron Age archaeology.

In their writings, Morton Smith, Karel van der Toorn and William Dever operate with the notion that the cause of censorship was a theological bias of a certain elite exercising control over the scribal production of texts, especially from the exile onwards. So they have an idea of the institutional locus of such work, namely the priestly elite(s) operating from the late monarchy through the Greco-Roman period. To my mind, all three authors are largely right, especially about the priestly nature of the elite involved. Both van der Toorn and I regard this activity as largely Levitical or Aaronid in nature.[22]

---

[20] Dever, *Did God Have a Wife?* 286.

[21] Fishbane (*Biblical Interpretation in Ancient Israel* [Oxford: Clarendon, 1985] 71) rightly refers to the "non-systematic nature" of theological scribal activity.

[22] See van der Toorn, *Scribal Culture,* 89–96. I sketched out my view of the priestly-Levitical role in the production of scriptural texts in: "The Priestly Lines and the Production of Exodus," which appeared in my book, *Pilgrimage Pattern in Exodus,* with contribu-

This priestly side is reflected on one side by works, such as the priestly portions of the Pentateuch and in the book of Ezekiel, and on the other side the Levitical role is arguably represented by works such as the collection of the book of Psalms as well as Jeremiah and Deuteronomy.

Whatever the precise social history lying behind the production of biblical texts, they show signs of textual harmonization and alterations. These include some examples of textual censorship. As a matter of procedure, it is important to ground the process of censorship by addressing specific textual cases. We will begin with a detailed analysis of two cases of censorship, Deuteronomy 32:8–9 and Genesis 14:22. Following the examination of these passages, comments are offered on the larger context of censorship in the post-exilic period in the spirit of Boyer's work. At this point, we may turn to two case studies of biblical censorship designed to "protect God."

2. Censorship in and for Israel: The Cases of Deuteronomy 32:8–9 and Genesis 14:22

For instances of biblical censorship, we turn to textual evidence, specifically differences among the various manuscripts of scriptural passages found in Hebrew and in the variety of other ancient languages into which the biblical works were translated, in particular, Greek and Latin, Aramaic and Syriac.

---

tions by Elizabeth M. Bloch-Smith (JSOTSup 239; Sheffield: Sheffield Academic, 1997) 257–61. It is evident that some Levites were scribes (e.g., possibly Deuteronomy 17:18, 1 Chronicles 24:6, 2 Chronicles 34:13; see Smith, *The Pilgrimage Pattern in Exodus*, 261; van der Toorn, *Scribal Culture*, 89–96, 102, 105) and priests (Deuteronomy 17:18; cf. Deuteronomy 33:8–11). On this matter, see further the discussion below. Ezra is perhaps emblematic of the post-exilic priest-scribe: he is said to be "the priest, the scribe, scribe (or, "scholar," so NJPS) of the words of Yahweh's commandments and his statutes to Israel" (Ezra 7:11; for the information in the latter part of this quote, cf. verses 6 and 10; Nehemiah 8:1, 4, 9, 13; 12:26, 36). For the scribe Baruch, see Jeremiah 36:26, 32; 45:1. See also the reflections on the scribe also in Ben Sira 38–39. A maximal case for priestly-Levitical production of scriptural works has been made by John W. Miller, *The Origins of the Bible: Rethinking Canon History* (New York: Paulist, 1994). The priesthood in the Persian and Hellenistic periods has received considerable attention in recent years. See Risto Nurmela, *The Levites: Their Emergence as a Second-class Priesthood* (South Florida Studies in the History of Judaism 198; Atlanta: Scholars, 1998); Joachim Schaper, *Priester und Leviten im achämenidischen Juda: Studien zur Kult- und Sozialgeschichte Israels in persischer Zeit* (FAT 31; Tübingen: Mohr Siebeck, 2000); and Alice Hunt, *Missing Priests: The Zadokites in Tradition and History* (London: T & T Clark International, 2006). Related works include recent books on the high priesthood: Deborah W. Rooke, *Zadok's Heirs: The Role and Development of the High Priesthood in Ancient Israel* (Oxford Theological Monographs; Oxford/New York: Oxford University, 2000); James C. VanderKam, *From Joshua to Caiaphas: High Priests after the Exile* (Minneapolis: Fortress; Assen: Van Gorcum, 2004); and Maria Brutti, *The Development of the High Priesthood during the Pre-Hasmonean Period: History, Ideology, Theology* (JSJSup 108; Leiden/Boston: Brill, 2006).

The main versions that often show differences helpful for our study of biblical censorship are: the Hebrew Masoretic Text (MT), the traditional text used for the reading of the Bible in synagogues; the Hebrew text of the Pentateuch used by the Samaritans (SP); the main Greek translations of the Bible, in particular the Septuagint (LXX), the Aramaic Targum; the Syriac Peshitta; and the Latin Vulgate. For this text-critical study, we are aided further by the Dead Sea Scrolls, which contains the oldest copies of biblical manuscripts.[23]

The witnesses of the scrolls in conjunction with other manuscript evidence of biblical works provide test cases of what we may justifiably label "biblical censorship." In other words, where the versions differ in matters of religious content, we may identify what Emanuel Tov calls "editorial intervention."[24] Among such instances, we can see "censorship" specifically in the differences among biblical manuscripts preserved among the Dead Sea Scrolls and the other manuscript witnesses to the text of the Bible. In many instances, the manuscripts from the Dead Sea Scrolls agree with one or another of these witnesses against others; occasionally it contains a reading of its own. Some of these cases involve theological matters, including censorship of deities other than Yahweh. We may now take a look at two cases in detail.[25]

---

[23] See Emanuel Tov, *Scribal Practices and Approaches Reflected in the Judean Desert* (STDJ 54; Leiden/Boston: Brill, 2004) 1. Tov's works cites a broader discussion of ancient scribal practices by J. Ashton, "The Persistence, Diffusion and Interchangeability of Scribal Habits in the Ancient Near East before the Codex" (Ph. D. diss, University of Sydney, 1999). This work is unavailable to me.

[24] Tov, *Scribal Practices and Approaches Reflected in the Judean Desert*, 253: "The various witnesses of the Torah (MT, SP, Qumran scrolls, and the *Vorlage* of the LXX) reflect the same degree of editorial intervention as the other books of the Hebrew Scriptures."

[25] I pass over some other theological changes made by editors. For example, Julio Trebolle Barrera (*The Jewish Bible and the Christian Bible: An Introduction to the History of the Bible* [trans. W. G. E. Watson; Leiden/New York/Köln: Brill; Grand Rapids, MI/Cambridge, UK: Eerdmans, 1998] 376) cites the case of 2 Samuel 24:1 ("Yahweh incited David to count the Israelites"), corrected in the parallel text of 1 Chronicles 21:2, with the name Yahweh replaced by Satan. It might be argued that the theological reformulation involving Satan here and the satan in the prologue to Job (Job 1:6, etc.) might involve some level of Persian influence (perhaps the dualistic model of Ahura Mazda versus Angra-Mainyu) and thus some transfer of Persian religious ideas to Yehud (see the critical discussion of Victor Hamilton, "Satan," *ABD* 5: 988). However, such influence, if understood correctly, is more convincing for later Second Temple texts where the figure is more clearly evil or demonic in character. For an argument instead for Greek influence, see Daniel E. Gershenson, "The Name Satan," *ZAW* 114 (2002) 443–45. For (the) satan in the Hebrew Bible, see Cilliers Breytenbach and Peggy L. Day, "Satan," *DDD* 726–32 (with bibliography); Hans Strauss, "השטן in den Traditionen des hebräisches Kanons," *ZAW* 111 (1999) 256–58; and T. J. Wray and Gregory Mobley, *The Birth of Satan: Tracing the Devil's Biblical Roots* (New York: Palgrave Macmillan, 2005). For the satan's later career, see Henry A. Kelly, *Satan: A Biography* (Cambridge/New York: Cambridge University, 2006). Whatever the correct dating for these texts, the case of the satan/Satan does not

Deuteronomy 32:8–9

Biblical scholars have long detected evidence of theological alteration in the differences among the manuscripts of Deuteronomy 32:8.[26] The poem of Deuteronomy 32 recounts how Israel became associated with Yahweh. The initial verse introduces the voice of the speaker (verses 1–2), who turns to the topic of Israel's relationship with Yahweh (verses 3–7). Then the poem (verses 8–9) opens the story of this relationship by recalling how Elyon (usually translated "Most High") divided the world into nations and then how Jacob (i. e., Israel) became Yahweh's allotment. The poem goes on to explain how Yahweh found Israel in the wilderness and brought Israel to a good land that supplied it with its needs without any other deity (verses 10–12). As a result of this divine care, Israel "grew fat" and abandoned its god, and instead turned to gods that the text variously calls "demons," "gods they had not known," and "new gods" (verses 13–18). As a result, Yahweh became angry at Israel (verses 19–25), and would have destroyed it but for the thought that its enemies might have claimed credit for destroying Israel (verses 26–35). The poem then moves to appeal to Israel, by emphasizing that Yahweh is their god ("there is no god with me," verse 39), and that it is this God who can save it from its enemies (verses 36–43).

The case of censorship has been detected in verse 8. In order to highlight the theological alteration in question, the following translation of verses 8–9 additionally supplies for the final clause in verse 8 the variations for the textual witnesses: the Hebrew Masoretic text (MT); the Hebrew Samaritan Pentateuch (SP), one Hebrew manuscript of the book of Deuteronomy among the Dead Sea Scrolls from Cave Four at Qumran; the Aramaic Targum and Syriac Peshitta; readings in manuscripts of the Septuagint (LXX); and the Latin Vulgate:

---

comport with Assmann's understanding of translatability with two deities named or brought together in a text (see Chapter One). For other theologically motivated changes, see Fishbane, *Biblical Interpretation*, 69–72; and Emanuel Tov, *Textual Criticism of the Hebrew Bible* (Minneapolis: Fortress; Assen/Maastricht: Van Gorcum, 1992) 267–69.

[26] The following discussion is based on Julie A. Duncan, *Qumran Cave 4. IX: Deuteronomy, Joshua, Judges, Kings* (ed. E. Ulrich and F. M. Cross; DJD XIV; Oxford: Clarendon, 1995) 90. See also *BHS* to Deuteronomy 32:8 note d DJD XIV, 90; Tov, *Textual Criticism of the Hebrew Bible*, 269. See also Fishbane, *Biblical Interpretation*, 69; Trebolle Barrera, *The Jewish Bible and the Christian Bible*, 377; and Adrian Schenker, "Le monothéisme israélite: un dieu qui transcende le monde et les dieux," *Biblica* 78 (1997) 438; idem, "Gott als Stifter der Religionen der Welt. Unerwartete Früchte textgeschichtlicher Forschung," in: *La double transmission du texte biblique: Etudes d'histoire du texte offertes en hommage à Adrian Schenker* (ed. Yohanan Goldman and Christoph Uehlinger; OBO 179; Fribourg: Editions Universitaires; Göttingen: Vandenhoeck & Ruprecht, 2001) 99–102; Smith, *The Origins of Biblical Monotheism*, 48–49, 78, 100, 143–44, 156–57, 165, 223 n. 64.

(8) When the Most High (El Elyon) gave the nations their inheritance,
   and divided humanity (literally, "the sons of a human being"),
He [El Elyon] established the boundaries of peoples,
[according] to the number of
   (1) the sons of Israel – *yiśra'el* (MT, SP, Targum, Peshitta, Vulgate)
   (2) the sons of God – *bene 'elohim* (DSS 4QDeut^j)
   (3) the sons of God – *huion theou* (LXX 848, 106c)
   (4) the angels of God – *aggelon theou* (LXX most manuscripts).
(9) For the portion of Yahweh is his people,
   Jacob, his inherited measure.[27]

In these two verses, there is a description of how Elyon divided the world into various nations. The number is said to be according to the number of the children of Israel (option #1), or according to the number of divine children (options #2 and #3), or according to the number of the angels of God (option #4). Then the next verse describes how among these many nations, the nation belonging to Yahweh is his people, named in the following line as Jacob.

Within the clause marked off with the four options, there are two specific differences to be noted among these. The first difference involves "Israel" in the MT, the Samaritan Pentateuch, Targum, Peshitta, and Vulgate (option #1) versus Elohim/God in the other witnesses (options #2 and #3). Many scholars view option #1 as a deliberate alteration to avoid the picture of polytheism. As Tov writes, "the scribe of an early text … did not feel at ease with the possible polytheistic picture and replaced … 'sons of El' with … "sons of Israel'."[28] In this picture, El Elyon is the head god who oversees the division of the world into nations given to the various gods of the world. In this scenario, Yahweh is one of the gods who receives his inheritance from El Elyon; in Yahweh's case, the people Jacob is his portion. (It would be difficult to explain a motivation for the opposite direction of influence, namely why an early scribe would change Israel to God.) The second shift is reflected in option #4, LXX (in most manuscripts), which reads "angels of God" for "sons of God." The shift is arguably theological, one that explains

---

[27] For more details, see the discussion of this passage in Chapter Three.
[28] Tov, *Textual Criticism,* 269; Smith, *The Origins of Biblical Monotheism,* 48–49, 78, 100, 143–44, 156–57, 165, 223 n. 64. Tov (*Textual Criticism,* 269 n. 44) believes no theological alteration was involved. While he does not give his reason for this view, one might think it is because "sons of Elohim" is used without difficulty in some biblical books elsewhere, as noted above, e.g., *bene ha'elohim* in Job 1:6, 2:1. It is not clear that Elohim would not also represent a deliberate theologically motivated alteration. Indeed, the difference between Elohim and Israel would still represent a significant shift and apparently one with theological motivation. For a view of the manuscript witnesses here as a matter of different traditions, see I. Himbaza, "Dt 32, 8, une correction tardive des scribes: Essai d'interpretation et de datation," *Biblica* 83 (2002) 527–48. For a speculative yet brilliant reconstruction behind option #1, see Jan Joosten, "A Note on the Text of Deuteronomy xxxii 8," *VT* 57 (2007) 548–55. If correct, Joosten's proposal would provide a text-critical reading behind option #1.

or at least conforms the expression, the "divine sons" (in options #2 and #3) to the later notion of "angels."

This difference is extremely important, as it highlights different attitudes or strategies about the text in question. Before commenting further, it is important to note that despite the differences, all of the textual witnesses understood the poem to be monotheistic, even the witnesses that make no alteration. This point is clear from the poem in verse 39 but also implicitly in verses 17 and 21 (characterizing other gods as "no-gods"). At the same time, it is evident that the picture in verses 8–9 drew on an older polytheistic tradition, as scholars have long noted. In this tradition, the old god El and his consort Asherah had seventy divine children, as known from the Ugaritic texts (*KTU/CAT* 1.4 VI 44–46).[29] Generally speaking, this sort of theme was a rather broad one in the ancient world. To the east of Ugarit and Israel, we may point to the Mesopotamian account of Atrahasis (Old Babylonian, Tablet I, lines 11–16) with its description of the gods dividing up the world for themselves by lot. To the west, the theme appears in the Iliad, book XV, lines 187–193.[30] However, the composer of Deuteronomy 32 had implicitly effaced this polytheistic notion that had been inherited from Israel's old literary heritage, by combining it with statements that expresses divinity in more exclusive terms ("no-gods" in verses 17 and 21 as well as verse 39). The question for the textual traditions of verses 8–9 was not monotheism or not, but how to understand this monotheistic text with its apparent polytheistic representation. After we examine three different strategies evidenced in the different manuscript versions, we will address the question of how the original composer of the poem understood the situation in verses 8–9.

Strategy #1: The Censor at Work

The first strategy that we may note among the versions involves option #1, the editorial alteration in reading "Israel" (MT, SP, Targum, Peshitta, Vulgate). With this change, we have two stereotypical features of censorship, textual or editorial alteration and the "party line" informing such a change. Yet the change to Israel is not simply a matter of an easy switch motivated by crude religious prejudice, evocative of the picture of our stereotypical censor mentioned at the outset of this discussion. Instead, in the worldview of post-

---

[29] For text and translation, see M. S. Smith, "The Baal Cycle," in: *UNP* 134. For discussion, see Smith, *The Origins of Biblical Monotheism*, 45, 55, 157. Note also the sixty-six sons and daughters of the mother goddess Aruru in a short second millennium Akkadian myth; see Benjamin R. Foster, *Before the Muses: An Anthology of Akkadian Literature* (third ed.; Bethesda, MD: CDL, 2005) 579.

[30] For this information, I have drawn from Stephanie Dalley, *Myths from Mesopotamia: Creation, the Flood, Gilgamesh, and Others* (Oxford/New York: Oxford University, 1991) 36 n. 4.

exilic Yehudian scribes, the story of the passage, when it was recognized as polytheistic, probably did not make sense to the scribal tradent responsible for the change. This monotheistic concern is also evident in the MT at verse 43 where it apparently substitutes the word "servants," compared with the divine "sons" found in LXX and 4QDeuteronomy j.[31] Monotheism was the norm for the later priestly-scribal tradition of the text. (This is represented already in Ezra 9: note the Levites mentioned in verse 5 and the theme of monotheism sounded at the outset of the speech in verse 6.)

We may make an educated guess at the intellectual means deployed to make sense of the text of Deuteronomy 32:8–9. Again, the means taken seems hardly arbitrary or capricious. We may speculate that the change involved a correlation between the immediate context of Deuteronomy 32:8–9 and a second context available from what was regarded in this period as Scripture. The scribe, operating in the Greco-Roman period, could have been drawn from a passage in "the Law of the Most High," "prophecies," and other scriptural texts, as suggested in Ben Sira 38:34, 39:1–3. These were understood to be "the Law, the prophets and the other writings" in the Prologue of Ben Sira, penned by the grandson (cf. Torah, prophets and Psalms mentioned in Luke 24:44).[32] The intellectual fuel accessible to this scribe is a manual of sorts; it is the Bible, or more accurately, the works called "holy

---

[31] So Trebolle Barrera, *The Jewish Bible and the Christian Bible*, 377–78. See further Alexander Rofé, "The End of the Song of Moses (Deuteronomy 32:43)," in: *Liebe und Gebot: Studien zum Deuteronomium. Festschrift zum 70. Geburtstag von Lothar Perlitt* (ed. Reinhard G. Kratz and Hermann Spieckermann; FRLANT 190; Göttingen: Vandenhoeck & Ruprecht, 2000) 164–72.

[32] This matter is complex and widely discussed; see Julio Trebolle Barrera, "Origins of a Tripartite Old Testament Canon," in: *The Canon Debate* (ed. Lee Martin McDonald and James A. Sanders; Peabody, MA: Hendrickson, 2002) 128–145; Jonathan G. Campbell, "4QMMT(d) and the Tripartite Canon," *Journal of Jewish Studies* 51 (2000) 181–190; Timothy H. Lim, "The Alleged Reference to the Tripartite Division of the Hebrew Bible," *RdQ* 20 (2001) 23–37; Eugene Ulrich, "The Non-attestation of a Tripartite Canon in 4QMMT," *CBQ* 65 (2003) 202–214. (A number of these references come courtesy of Moshe Bernstein.) For an optimistic view of a relatively early tripartite canon (especially compared to the discussions of Eugene Ulrich), see Stephen Dempster, "From Many Texts to One: The Formation of the Hebrew Bible," in: *The World of the Aramaeans I: Studies in Language and Literature in Honour of Paul-Eugène Dion* (ed. P. M. Michèle Daviau, John W. Wevers and Michael Weigl; JSOTSup 324; Sheffield: Sheffield, 2001) 19–56. The range on related issues is likewise immense. For example, different approaches to quotations of scripture in the Qumran texts have lead to different impressions. Moshe J. Bernstein notes that the Dead Sea Scrolls contain relatively few citations of non-scriptural works, and comments on the possible implications: "Such citations might once again raise the question of the extent of the Qumran 'canon'." See Bernstein, "Scripture: Quotation and Use," in: *Encyclopedia of the Dead Sea Scrolls* (ed. Lawrence H. Schiffman and James C. VanderKam; two vols.; Oxford/New York: Oxford University, 2000) 2.840. For a contrary view, that such quotations (as well as allusions) suggest that no part of the later canon was closed at this time, see Armin Lange, "Pre-Maccabean Literature from the Qumran Library and the Hebrew Bible," *Dead Sea Discoveries* 13 (2006) 277–305.

writings" or "scriptures" at the time[33] and perhaps other texts sanctioned by the traditions that show this reading. To be clear on this matter, scriptural reading was not canonical with a fixed list of works as in later canons,[34]

---

[33] Using "holy writings" or "scriptures" (rather than the later term, Bible) is supported by the following expressions attested in the Greco-Roman period, well before the term for canon is used in Jewish or Christian circles:

"the law, the prophets, and the later authors"; and "the law, the prophets, and the rest of the books of our ancestors": Ben Sira prologue

"in the writings," *basseparim:* Daniel 9:2

"the holy works," *ta biblia ta hagia:* 1 Maccabees 12:9

"holy writings," *graphais hagiais:* Romans 1:2

"writing," *graphon:* Romans 15:4; "writings," *graphas,* 1 Corinthians 15:3, 4

"holy writings," *hiera grammata:* 2 Timothy 3:15

"For what does the writing say?" *ti gar he graphe legei,* Romans 4:3, in citation of Genesis 15:6; cf. Romans 9:17, 10:11, 11:2; Galatians 3:8, 22; 4:30

"the writing," *ten graphen,* John 20:9; "(it says) in the writing," *en graphe,* 1 Peter 2:6, "there is no prophecy of scripture," *graphes,* 2 Peter 1:20

"scripture (is inspired by God)," *graphe,* and "the holy writings," *hiera grammata* in 2 Timothy 3:15–16

"the holy writings," *hai hierai graphai:* Josephus, *Contra Apionem,* 2.4 para. 45 (see also "our *biblia*" in 1.38–40); Philo, *De Abrahamo,* 61; *De congressu eruditionis gratia,* 34, 90.

In contrast, the term Bible is usually understood (though it would not need to do so with the proper qualifications) as a fixed group of books of Scripture, in other words a canon that is closed and is not to be added to. A closed canon (or, one should say, canons as these varied among Jews and Christians) did not develop until later, in the early church and synagogue. Thus a closed canon did not yet exist as such at the time under discussion, namely the second century BCE/BC through the first century CE/AD. Thus John J. Collins argues against Louis Hartman and Alexander A. DiLella that Daniel 9:2 does not refer to "canonized Sacred Writings," as Hartman and Di Lella would have it. See Collins, *Daniel: A Commentary on the Book of Daniel* (Hermaneia; Minneapolis: Fortress, 1993) 348; Hartman and Di Lella, *The Book of Daniel* (AB 23; Garden City, NY: Doubleday, 1978) 241. It is unclear that Daniel 9:2 is limited to prophetic books, as Collins opines. See further in the following note.

[34] For this matter, see Eugene Ulrich, *The Dead Sea Scrolls and the Origins of the Bible* (Studies in the Dead Sea Scrolls and Related Literature; Grand Rapids, MI/Cambridge, UK: Eerdmans; Leiden: Brill, 1999). See also David M. Carr, *Writing on the Tablet of the Heart: Origins of Scripture and Literature* (Oxford/New York: Oxford University, 2005) 290; and van der Toorn, *Scribal Culture,* 256, 260, 262; cf. the comments of Robert Hanhart, "Introduction: Problems in the History of the LXX Text from Its Beginnings to Origen," in: *The Septuagint as Christian Scripture* (ed. Martin Hengel, with the assistance of Roland Deines; trans. Mark E. Biddle; Old Testament Studies; Edinburgh/New York: T & T Clark, 2002) 2–4. The recognized writings or scriptures are "holy writings" or "scriptures," in other words authoritative, religious works, without constituting a delimited, fixed corpus, in other words the canon of the Bible. They were instead a core group of texts consisting at least of the Torah or Pentateuch, most if not all of the prophets (note the varying position of Daniel in later canons) and probably the Psalms (see Luke 24:44 and the numerous copies of Psalms among the Dead Sea Scrolls); these would have been accepted generally in this period by Jews and Jewish-Christians. On this point, see Carr, *Writing on the Tablet of the Heart,* 260–67. At the same time, this group of authoritative religious works was not yet a closed corpus, as various Jewish groups considered

but it was a matter of reading works in tandem. Reading across works as if they represent a coordinated divine plan is what scriptures constitute at this point. This form of coordinated reading is reflected in identifications of Torah as wisdom[35] and in the idea of Torah as inspired like the prophets.[36]

From the context of Deuteronomy 32:8–9, the scribe of option #1 read the name of Jacob (elsewhere known as Israel) as well as a number of nations. This scriptural information was evidently the touchstone used to make sense of the passage. Given that the number of nations elsewhere in the biblical tradition was known to be seventy (for example, in the so-called Table of Nations in Genesis 10), we may speculate that the scribe knew the notion that the number of peoples in the world was seventy. At the same time, sensing the polytheism in this representation, the scribe of option #1 knowing also that the number of Israel was likewise seventy when it left Egypt (Genesis 46:27; Exodus 1:5) drew the conclusion that the number of nations was "according to the number of the children of Israel," as noted by Arie van der Kooij.[37] The Aramaic Targum Pseudo-Jonathan explicitly

---

additional works as Scripture, and opinion on this matter varied. (This variation can be seen in the books of Scripture, e.g, Ben Sira; 1 and 2 Maccabees, etc., that did not make their way into the later Jewish and Protestant canons, but did make it into the later canon of the Roman Catholic Church as well as the canons of a number of important, eastern churches.) See the preceding note.

[35] For identification of Wisdom with Jewish teaching (Torah, often translated "law") in this period, see Baruch 4:1, where personified wisdom is identified as "the book of the precepts of God, the law that endures forever"; and Ben Sira 24:22, "All this is true of the book of the Most High's covenant, the law which Moses commanded us, as an inheritance for the community of Jacob. It overflows like the Pishon with wisdom." In this worldview, "all wisdom comes from the Lord" and "if you desire wisdom, keep the commandments" (Ben Sira 1:1, 23). The Dead Sea Scrolls also relate Wisdom and Torah. They are associated in Psalm 154 in 11Q5 = 11QPsᵃ, column XVIII, line 14: "the right-eous" who hear the voice of Wisdom have "their *śiḥ* (often translated as "meditation" or the like) on the Torah of Elyon." 4Q525 (Beatitudes), fragment 2, column II, lines 3–4 likewise relates the two: "Blessed is the one who attains wisdom *vacat* and betakes himself in the Torah of Elyon". For discussion, see Shannon Burkes, " 'Life' Redefined: Wisdom and Law in Fourth Ezra and *Second Baruch,*" *CBQ* 63 (2001) 55–71; John Cook, "Law and Wisdom in the Dead Sea Scrolls with Reference to Hellenistic Judaism," in: *Wisdom and Apocalypticism in the Dead Sea Scrolls and in the Biblical Tradition* (ed. F. García Martínez; Bibliotheca Ephemeridum Theologicarum Lovaniensium CLXVIII; Leuven: University; Leuven/Paris/Dudley, MA: Uitgeverij Peeters, 2003) 323–42; and Peter Schäfer, *Mirror of His Beauty: Feminine Images of God from the Bible to the Early Kabbalah* (Princeton/Oxford: Princeton University, 2002) 29–38.

[36] For a recent discussion, with secondary literature, see Martti Nissinen, "What Is Prophecy? An Ancient Near Eastern Perspective," in: *Inspired Speech: Prophecy in the Ancient Near East: Essays in Honor of Herbert B. Huffmon* (ed. John Kaltner and Louis Stulman; JSOTSup 378; London/New York: T & T Clark, 2004) 30.

[37] Van der Kooij, "Ancient Emendations in MT," in: *L'Ecrit et L'Espirit: Etudes d'histoire du texte et de théologie biblique en hommage à Adrian Schenker* (ed. Dieter

makes this connection with the number of Genesis 46:27 and Exodus 1:5, even as it witnesses at the same time to the notion that the *'elohim* are angels (as in most LXX manuscripts discussed below): "He [God] cast lots with the seventy angels, princes of the nations, with whom He revealed himself to see the city [where the Tower of Babel was being built], and at the same time He established the boundaries of the nations equal to the number of the seventy Israelite persons who went down to Egypt."[38] Evidently the scribe connected his reading of Deuteronomy 32:8–9 with Exodus 1:5. According to van der Kooij, the scribal change is to be dated to the second century BCE/BC and stemmed from official priestly circles responsible for the transmission of scriptural texts. This is a plausible scenario, and it highlights a salient feature of the so-called censor: this scribal tradent is learned and deploys relatively sophisticated chains of textual logic and interpretation to make sense of the textual world that he is involved in transmitting.

Strategy #2: Interpretation at Work without Censorship

The second sort of change is found in the witness of option #4, the LXX in most manuscripts, which reads "angels of God." This version indicates another perspective on the story being told in Deuteronomy 32:8–9. In this case, there is a different interpretative strategy at work. The witness to "angels of God" provided an avenue for conforming the picture in this text to the boundaries of the tradition. It shows how the tradition has moved the line in its understanding or interpretation of *'elohim,* construed here to refer more narrowly to "angels" and not "divine beings" more generally.[39] As with the change to "Israel," the change to "angels" involves a sort of censorship that is also in effect a matter of interpretation. The notion that the "ruler" of each nation is an angel (and not a god as such) is clear in Daniel 10 ("Michael, your prince," in verse 21).[40] The notion of seventy angels corresponding to the number of nations, met in later Jewish tradition (e. g., 1 Enoch 89:59, 90:22–25; bT. Shabbat 88b, Sukkah 55b),[41] was probably driven by the sort of interpretation found in Deuteronomy 32:8–9.

Böhler, Innocent Himbaza, and Philippe Hugo; OBO 214; Fribourg: Academic; Göttingen: Vandenhoeck & Ruprecht, 2005) 152–59. See also Schenker, "Gott als Stifter der Religionen der Welt," 100. Cf. seventy-five in LXX Genesis 46:27 and Acts 7:14.

[38] J. H. Tigay, *The JPS Torah Commentary: Deuteronomy* (Philadelphia/Jerusalem: The Jewish Publication Society, 1996) 513. Tigay, like many scholars, notes this witness of the Targum. He does not discuss the exegetical logic underlying its usage.

[39] Cf. the discussion of *'elohim* in the Introduction above, pp. 11–15.

[40] Cited in connection to Ben Sira 17:17 by Patrick W. Skehan and Alexander A. Di Lella, *The Wisdom of Ben Sira: A New Translation with Notes* (AB 39; New Work: Doubleday, 1987) 283; and Tigay, *Deuteronomy,* 514.

[41] See Tigay, *Deuteronomy,* 514–15; Smith, *The Origins of Biblical Monotheism,* 55.

The interpretation involved with this LXX group of textual witnesses to Deuteronomy 32:8 was not the product of a chain of textual deduction like the change to "Israel" in option #1. Instead, option #4 seems to have resulted from applying the norm of monotheism as understood at the time.[42] The interpretive process apparently seeks to provide theological clarification for the text, compared with the reading that the scribe(s) had received. The motif of the seventy nations with seventy patron-gods has a prehistory predating the Bible (as we noted with El, Asherah and their seventy children in the Ugaritic texts), and it is this divine worldview that informs the presentation in Deuteronomy 32:8–9. It is understandable that the polytheism embedded in the motif might be perceived by later scribes, who sought to redress the perceived mistake or offence through specification or clarification. To echo the main title of an article by Michael Holquist,[43] the tradents had before them what could be viewed as "corrupt originals" in need of modification. As Holquist's subtitle suggests, this textual move captures "the paradox of censorship": what was really the "original"? How did the ancients know? What was the interpretation that accompanied the original?

Strategy #3: The Understanding of the Original Composer

The witnesses in the Dead Sea Scrolls and some LXX texts that manifest no change, namely options #2 and #3, may provide a clue to answering these questions. This group of textual witnesses is helpful for this matter because they point to scribes who did not resort to censorship. These retained "sons of *'elohim/theos.*" In view of the changes made by other scribes as noted above, why were these reading retained? As we consider this question, it is important to bear in mind that this reading is considered to be original; we may regard its polytheism as vestigial[44] from the perspective of the textual tradition. That this polytheism survives in the poem is confirmed from the textual variants in verse 43: where the MT addresses "the nations," 4QDeuteronomy, manuscript q invokes "heavens" and "all the gods," while LXX preserves both of these sets of addressees.[45] Thus MT avoids any polythe-

---

[42] For a survey of monotheism in the Persian period, see Erik Aurelius, " 'Ich bin der Herr, dein Gott': Israel und sein Gott zwischen Katastrophe und Neuanfang," in: *Götterbilder – Gottesbilder – Weltbilder. Band I: Ägypten, Mesopotamien, Persien, Kleinasien, Syrien, Palästina* (ed. Reinhard G. Kratz and Hermann Spieckermann; FAT 2/17; Tübingen: Mohr Siebeck, 2006) 325–45.

[43] Holquist, "Corrupt Originals: The Paradox of Censorship," *PMLA* 109 (January, 1994) 14–25; cited by Boyer, "Censorship as a Vocation," 512 n. 2, 528, 542.

[44] Smith, *The Origins of Biblical Monotheism,* 78.

[45] So Tigay, *Deuteronomy,* 516, in his convenient presentation of the textual witnesses. For 4QDeuteronomy manuscript q in comparison with the MT, see Patrick W. Skehan and Eugene Ulrich, "4QDeut^q," in: *Qumran Cave 4. IX: Deuteronomy, Joshua, and Kings* (DJD XIV; Oxford: Clarendon, 1995) 139–42.

istic representation not only in verses 8–9 but also in verse 43. The fact that no alteration was made in the other witnesses suggests a reading tradition that did not read this text in a polytheistic way, or at least not in a manner that the scribal tradition found objectionable. In other words, the scribal witnesses probably embodied an interpretive tradition that permitted it to read the passage according to its monotheistic norms. More specifically, the original composer understood El Elyon as a title of Yahweh. Despite drawing on the old polytheistic type-element, the author intended no polytheism and perhaps knew none in this case.[46]

This is no mere guess or supposition, based simply on attestations of El Elyon as a title of Yahweh (as in Genesis 14:19–22, to be discussed shortly). There is specific evidence within the biblical corpus for this equation or identification of El Elyon with Yahweh in Deuteronomy 8–9. We can identify this interpretive tradition already by the early post-exilic period within the biblical corpus itself. Before proceeding, I would highlight the importance of examining later manuscript evidence in tandem with inner-biblical echoes of the same verses that stand between the older composition of Deuteronomy 32:8–9 and later scribal changes in the manuscript record. Usually, textual criticism on a biblical passage is performed without little consideration of echoes of the same passage found in its later biblical and extra-biblical reuses. Such reuses may predate the alterations in the manuscript evidence that took place in the Greco-Roman context and may provide a witness to the reading strategy (or, to the range of strategies) that was available to the scribes who transmitted the passage in the various manuscript traditions. Thus these reuses may illuminate the possible range of interpretations available to later scribes who transmitted – and in some cases altered – a given passage. This appears to be the situation with reuses of Deuteronomy 32:8–9 within the biblical period. We may review some of these in order to gauge the reading of the verse in the Persian and Greco-Roman contexts.

We find old witnesses to this monotheistic interpretation of the verse[47] in two prose passages within Deuteronomy, in 4:19 and 29:25.[48] (The rel-

---

[46] For similar juxtapositions of older and newer views of divinity produced by the same author, see the interesting reflections on "concealed inconsistency" by H. S. Versnel, "Thrice One: Three Greek Experiments in Oneness," in: *One God or Many? Concepts of Divinity in the Ancient World* (ed. Barbara Nevling Porter; Transactions of the Casco Bay Assyriological Institute, vol. 1; np: np, 2000) 93–94.

[47] See also Jeremiah 10:16 = 51:19 and Zechariah 2:16.

[48] See Patrick W. Skehan, *Studies in Israelite Poetry and Wisdom* (CBQMS 1; Washington, DC: The Catholic Biblical Association of America, 1971) 68–69; Moshe Weinfeld, *Deuteronomy and the Deuteronomic School* (Oxford: Oxford University, 1972; repr., Winona Lake, IN: Eisenbrauns, 1992) 294, 320. See also Weinfeld, *Deuteronomy 1–11* (AB 5; New York: Doubleday, 1991) 206; see also pp. 227 and 361, with comparison with

evant echoes in these texts are put in italics.) The first verse warns against
idolatry: "… lest you look up to the heavens and you behold the sun and
the moon and the stars, all the host of heaven, you must not be compelled
into bowing down to them and serving them, because *Yahweh your God
apportioned them to all the peoples* under all the heavens." The second verse
likewise condemns the service of "other gods … gods which they had not
known nor *had been apportioned to them.*" The final clauses of both 4:19
and 29:25 (in italics) show dependence on Deuteronomy 32:8–9 even as
they modify the wording of the passage. It is clear that these passages see a
division in religious devotion, Yahweh for the Israelites and the other gods
for the other nations. (In the case of 4:19, it is evident that the tradition that
joined 4:1–31 to 4:32–40 did not put any stock in these other gods, as is clear
from the larger context of Deuteronomy 4:1–40, especially verses 35 and 39:
"there is no other apart from Him/there is no other."[49]) The composer of
4:19 here re-uses the language of Deuteronomy 32:8, in particular the root
*ḥlq, "to apportion," to describe the divine plan of the world. While later
sensibilities may be struck by the apparent resulting picture that God in
effect made idols for the other nations for which they are then condemned,
the interpretational context for Deuteronomy 4:19 is more complex. The
composer of Deuteronomy 4:19 was appropriating the old religious worldview or "world theology" in his monotheistic picture.[50] Patrick W. Skehan
and Jeffrey H. Tigay note that 4:19 reverses the picture in 32:8: whereas the
poetic line of 32:8 assigns all the nations to the various divine beings, the
prose re-appropriation in 4:19 assigns these gods to the peoples.[51] In short,

---

Jeremiah 10:2. As Weinfeld notes (*Deuteronomy and the Deuteronomic School*, 324), the
element in 29:25, "gods whom they did not know," is also grounded in Deuteronomy 32,
specifically in verse 17. See also William Horbury, *Herodian Judaism and New Testament
Study* (WUNT 193; Tübingen: Mohr Siebeck, 2006) 21–23, 26–27 (especially for Deuteronomy 4:19 in later sources); and Schmid, "Gibt es 'Reste hebräischen Heidentums' im
Alten Testament?" 113.

[49] See the comment of Christoph Dohmen, *Das Bilderverbot: Seine Entstehung und seine
Entwicklung im Alten Testament* (second ed.; BBB 62; Frankfurt am Main: Athenäum,
1987) 206: "Für V. 19b ist folglich keine Vorstellung besonderer Toleranz anzunehmen,
sondern eine Kontrastierung von Israel und den übrigen Völkern." See also Petry, *Die
Entgrenzung Jhwhs*, 80–81. See below for further discussion of Deuteronomy 4:19.

[50] See Hermann Spieckermann, *Juda unter Assur in der Sargonidzeit* (FRLANT 129;
Göttingen: Vandenhoeck & Ruprecht, 1982) 258–59; Dohmen, *Das Bilderverbot*, 206–7;
Smith, *The Memoirs of God*, 54–56; Petry, *Die Entgrenzung Jhwhs*, 80–81. This religious
worldview or "world-theology" is discussed in Chapter Two.

[51] Skehan, *Studies*, 68; Tigay, *Deuteronomy*, 50. The echo of 32:8–9 in 4:19 would
seem to undermine Georg Braulik's claim that "there are no signs that the song of Moses
influenced the doctrine of God in Deuteronomy, even less that this doctrine is dependent
on the Song of Moses." See Braulik, "Deuteronomy and the Birth of Monotheism," in:
The Theology of Deuteronomy: Collected Essays of Georg Braulik, O. S. B. (trans. Ulrika
Lindblad; Bibal Collected Essays 2; N. Richland Hills, TX: Bibal, 1994) 117; originally
published as "Das Deuteronomium und die Geburt des Monotheismus," in: *Gott, der*

4:19 presupposes the identification of El Elyon as the god of Israel in 32:8. If Deuteronomy 1:1–4:40 + 4:41–43 does represent additions prefixed to Deuteronomy 4:44 and following (note the new introduction of this verse)[52] and assuming that 1:1–4:40 (or at least 4:1–40[53]) may be dated to the post-exilic period (as suggested by the reference to exile among the nations in 4:27),[54] then Deuteronomy 4:19's echo of Deuteronomy 32:8–9 may date to the post-exilic period.[55] The same dating and worldview may be suggested for 29:25. Monotheism is already the norm for this tradition, yet the tradition at this point is still dealing with material about the gods of the other nations, specifically national gods from the worldview of the monarchy.[56]

What is the view in Deuteronomy 4:19 and 29:25 regarding the status of the "sun, moon and the heavenly host"? For Skehan, the beings in 4:19 are to be regarded as angels, while according to Tigay, the gods are creations of the god of Israel.[57] The text does not bear out either conclusion, at least explicitly. Georg Braulik O.S.B. suggests that Deuteronomy 4:19 avoids using the term "gods," and thus they are "reduced to purely 'secular' sta-

---

einzige: Zur Entstehung des Monotheismus in Israel (ed. Ernest Haag; Quaestiones Disputatae 104; Freiburg: Herder, 1985) 119, reprinted in: Braulik, *Studien zur Theologie des Deuteronomiums* (Stuttgarter biblische Aufsatzbände 2; Stuttgart: Katholisches Bibelwerk, 1988) 300.

[52] See the comments made by Gerhard von Rad in his *Deuteronomy: A Commentary* (trans. Dorothea Barton; OTL; London: SCM, 1966) 55.

[53] On Deuteronomy 4:1–40 as a unit, see Rad, *Deuteronomy,* 48; Georg Braulik, "Literarkritik und archäologische Stratigraphie: Zu S. Mittmanns Analyse von Deuteronomium 1,1–40," *Biblica* 59 (1978) 351–83; and "Literarkritik und die Einrahmung von Gemälden: Zur literarkritischen und redaktionsgeschichtlichen Analyse von Dtn 4,1–6,3 und 29,2–30.20 durch D. Knapp," *RB* 96 (1989) 266–86; A.D.H. Mayes, "Deuteronomy 4 and the Literary Criticism of Deuteronomy," *JBL* 100 (1981) 23–51; and Sven Petry, *Die Entgrenzung Jhwhs: Monolatrie, Bilderverbot und Monotheismus im Deuteronomium, in Deuterojesaja und im Ezechielbuch* (doctoral dissertation, Georg-August-Universität Göttingen, = FAT 2/27; Tübingen: Mohr Siebeck, 2007) 70–100. Several scholars do not view Deuteronomy 4:1–40 as a unity. For discussion, see Juha Pakkala, *Intolerant Monolatry in the Deuteronomistic History* (Publications of the Finnish Exegetical Society 76; Helsinki: The Finnish Exegetical Society; Göttingen: Vandenhoeck & Ruprecht, 1999) 85–93. Drawing on earlier analyses, Pakkala regards 4:19 as a late nomistic piece and verses 32–40 as a post-nomistic addition. These specific attributions have little bearing on the specifics of the argument here

[54] See von Rad, *Deuteronomy,* 55. Note also Weinfeld, *Deuteronomy 1–11,* 228–29, 234–35. See in particular the list of theological features in Deuteronomy 1:1–4:40 on pp. 234–25 that Weinfeld would situate in the exile, yet he also notes (p. 223) that 4:25–31 is "about Exile and restoration," which might imply composition in the post-exilic period. Finally, Weinfeld (*Deuteronomy 1–11,* 226) observes an echo of Deuteronomy 32:9 in Jeremiah 10:16 that parallels Deuteronomy 4:19.

[55] The view is common, e.g., van der Toorn, *Scribal Culture,* 162–66, 226, 350 n. 76. See further below. For a discussion of national gods, see Chapter Two.

[56] Smith, *The Memoirs of God,* 54–56. For a recent survey of Judean monotheism in this period, see Petry, *Die Entgrenzung Jhwhs.*

[57] Skehan, *Studies,* 68; Tigay, *Deuteronomy,* 50.

tus."[58] It appears that Braulik thinks that "the sun, the moon and the stars, all the hosts of heaven" in verse 19 are not represented as gods but simply as natural phenomena previously – and wrongly – thought to be gods. Braulik may well be right here, in what is ostensibly an argument from silence. And yet the silence is palpable, when Deuteronomy 4:19 is compared with 17:3,[59] a text arguably known to the author of 4:19 (if it is not a later secondary addition). Deuteronomy 17:3 puts "the sun, moon and the heavenly host" under the rubric of "other gods" (cf. Jeremiah 19:13). In contrast to 17:3, 4:19 does not include "other gods" in its description of the sun, moon and the heavenly host, and so it seems to be making a different statement. Indeed, this language in Deuteronomy 4:19 does not explicitly address the ontological implications of the heavenly hosts.

It has been thought that Deuteronomy 4:19 expresses a sort of "natural religion." Braulik remarks in this vein:

In addition, YHWH himself is said to have given them to the other nations as objects of worship (cf. 29:25). This (only apparently) liberal acceptance of a kind of "natural religion" serves to bridge the gulf between YHWH's universal power and uniqueness on the one hand and the plain fact that other nations do not worship him on the other.[60]

To be sure, 4:19 does not go as far as the post-exilic parallel, Nehemiah 9:6, which identifies all the heavenly hosts as Yahweh's creations. The explicit expression found in Nehemiah 9:6 is not present in Deuteronomy 4:19, and readers may wonder whether or not the author sought to express by implicit means what the author of Nehemiah 9:6 expressed explicitly (as Tigay and Braulik essentially would resolve the issue). It is possible, and in certain respects this solution suits the context, but it is difficult to know. At the same time, 4:19 by its omission of "gods" seems to indicate that its author does not view the astral bodies as deities. The verse recognizes that they may be

---

[58] Braulik, "Deuteronomy and the Birth of Monotheism," in: *The Theology of Deuteronomy: Collected Essays of Georg Braulik, O. S. B.* (trans. Ulrika Lindblad; Bibal Collected Essays 2; N. Richland Hills, TX: Bibal, 1994) 117; originally published as "Das Deuteronomium und die Geburt des Monotheismus," in: *Gott, der einzige: Zur Entstehung des Monotheismus in Israel* (ed. Ernst Haag; Quaestiones disputatae 104; Freiburg: Herder, 1985) 115–19, and reprinted in: *Studien zur Theologie des Deuteronomiums* (Stuttgarter biblische Aufsatzbände 2; Stuttgart: Katholisches Bibelwerk, 1988) 257–300.

[59] See Weinfeld, *Deuteronomy and the Deuteronomic School,* 321. See also Petry, *Die Entgrenzung Jhwhs,* 80–81.

[60] Braulik, "Deuteronomy and the Birth of Monotheism," 117. Cf. the observation of Daniel Dubuisson, *The Western Construction of Religion: Myth, Knowledge, and Ideology* (trans. William Sayers; Baltimore/London: Johns Hopkins University, 2003) 29: The history of religions "has preferred, as a good daughter of the West, to grant a religion to each people and culture, and this despite the anachronisms, absurdities, and paradoxes to which this ethnocentrism led it."

treated as such by other nations, but this is not the same as claiming that the author of the passage thought that they are deities in reality.[61] Instead, 4:19 seems to address only the situation among the other nations.[62] However one is to resolve the interpretation of the other nations and their astral worship in Deuteronomy 4:19, the verse shows an assumption of Yahweh as the god

---

[61] Because of this problem, monotheism would not be seen in Deuteronomy 4:19 by Nathan MacDonald, *Deuteronomy and the Meaning of 'Monotheism'* (FAT 2/1; Tübingen: Mohr Siebeck, 2003), or by Adrian Schenker, "L'Institution des dieux et des religions. L'unicité du Dieu de la Bible," in: *Bible et sciences des religions: Judaïsme, christianisme, islam* (ed. Françoise Mies; Brussels/Lessius/Namur: Presses universitaires de Namur, 2005) 17–40. MacDonald would see 4:19 as an expression of "henotheism" and accordingly re-interpret monotheistic passages as henotheistic. Schenker develops a view of the "unicity" of God, based on this and other passages (1 Samuel 5; Psalm 82), which represents God as the sole authority over all deities who may be worshipped by other peoples (his is what I regard as the older world theology; as the examples above indicate, this notion earlier was translatable, and the difficulty comes when it is no longer considered to be so). MacDonald and Schenker are making an important point about Deuteronomy 4:19. However, to generalize from this one "henotheistic" expression in 4:19 to the expressions of monotheism elsewhere and to claim that these are not monotheistic but "henotheistic" or the like is to conform the interpretation of the vast majority of texts to the one apparent exception. For criticism of MacDonald's view with defense of the more traditional approach to this matter, see the comments by Petry, *Die Entgrenzung Jhwhs*, 91, as well as the review of MacDonald's book by Yairah Amit in: *Review of Biblical Literature* 07/2005 (http://www.bookreviews.org/pdf/4297_4272.pdf); and Eckart Otto, "Monotheismus im Deuteronomium. Wieviel Aufklärung es in der Alttestamentlichen Wissenschaft geben soll: Zu einem Buch von Nathan McDonald [sic]," *Zeitschrift für Altorientalische und Biblische Rechtsgeschichte* 9 (2003) 251–57.

[62] Deuteronomy 4 arguably involves a crafting of "compromise language" both modifying the older worldview and adding newer monotheistic expressions. Deuteronomy 4:19 is not simply reducible to the monotheistic expressions in 4:35 and 39. The presentation in 4:19 has an earlier history, as reflected in its echoing Deuteronomy 32:8–9. In its larger redactional context, it stands in an important relationship to the statements in 4:35 and 4:39. One question is how the ancient redactors would have related 4:19 to 4:35 and 39. To address this problem, the passage may be recognized as containing a "concealed inconsistency," as outlined by Versnel, "Thrice One: Three Greek Experiments in Oneness," 93–94. In other words, Deuteronomy 4 juxtaposes the older worldview in 4:19 with the monotheistic statements in 4:35 and 39. The larger redactional context of Deuteronomy 4 is clearly monotheistic (as reflected in verses 35 and 39), which has incorporated the older "henotheistic" expression of verse 19. Thus the context locates the older worldview of verse 19 in the larger context of the discourse that includes the newer expressions of explicit monotheism in 4:35 and 39, not the other way around. For this reason, 4:19 with its expression of the older way of thinking about God and the gods is read in context through the monotheistic expressions of 4:35 and 39. From a diachronic view, perhaps 4:32–40, with its two monotheistic statements in verses 35 and 39, is to be read as a sort of "inner-biblical" commentary on the preceding material, including verse 19. For discussion, see Georg Braulik, "Monotheismus im Deuteronomium: Zu Syntax, Redeform und Gotteserkenntnis in 4,32–40," *Zeitschrift für Altorientalische und Biblische Rechtsgeschichte* 10 (2004) 169–94; and Juha Pakkala, "The Monotheism of the Deuteronomistic History," *Scandinavian Journal of the Old Testament* (in press; pre-publication copy of this essay generously made available courtesy of its author).

fully in control over the divine arrangement, with little credence given to the astral bodies.

Deuteronomy 29:25 might appear to represent a greater impediment to this conclusion, since it does use the phrase, "other gods."[63] *A priori,* one might deduce that the figures in this case are not simply phenomena mistakenly taken to be gods, but given what is known of the rest of Deuteronomy, this view seems incorrect. In its larger context, the verse does not regard "other gods" as ontologically divine, but function wrongly as "other gods" to those whom the authors would regard as idolaters. What we see is an older tradition of formulation being brought into line with the larger monotheistic understanding of reality. In conclusion, the author(s) of Deuteronomy 4:19 and 29:25 could live with the "concealed inconsistency" in their formulations, since the texts show little concern for addressing the logical issue in an explicit manner.[64] In sum, these echoes of Deuteronomy 32:8–9 in the book of Deuteronomy show a monotheistic reading that identifies Yahweh as El Elyon.

Like Deuteronomy 4:19 and 29:25, a number of Greco-Roman period texts draw on Deuteronomy 32:8–9. Two instances dependent on this passage come from the book of Ben Sira (also called Sirach and Ecclesiasticus), which was composed originally in Hebrew and is attested in Hebrew in several fragments manuscripts from Masada, the Dead Sea Scrolls and the Cairo Geniza. The book in its Greek translation, as we learn from the Prologue to Ben Sira, was produced in Alexandria by the grandson of the author of the Hebrew text.[65] The passages in Ben Sira pertinent to our topic operate with an interpretive strategy attested in the textual witnesses to Deuteronomy 32:8–9 that understand El Elyon in the initial line as Yahweh. One echo of this passage occurs in Ben Sira 17:17: "Over every nation he [the Lord] places a ruler, but the Lord's *own portion is Israel.*"[66] Ben Sira 44:1–2 contains another echoing: "I will now praise those godly people, our ancestors, each in his own time – The *Most High's portion,* great in glory, reserved

---

[63] For the literary-critical context, see Pakkala, *Intolerant Monolatry in the Deuteronomistic History,* 99–103.

[64] One may wonder whether the inconsistency "concealed" was not apparent to the author himself. See Hall, *The Silent Language,* 53.

[65] Such prefatory information about translation from vernaculars into Greek can be noted as well in the later work, Philo of Byblos' *The Phoenician History (PE* 1.9.20; see H. W. Attridge and R. A. Oden, Jr., *Philo of Byblos The Phoenician History: Introduction, Critical Text, Translation, Notes* [CBQMS 9; Washington, DC: The Catholic Biblical Association of America, 1981] 18, 19).

[66] Smith, *The Early History of God* (second ed.), 32 n. 43. The translation comes from Skehan and Di Lella, *The Wisdom of Ben Sira,* 277; see their discussion on pp. 280, 283; and Skehan, *Studies,* 69. See also Tigay, *Deuteronomy,* 514.

to himself from ancient days."[67] Both verses read Deuteronomy 32:8–9 as saying that El Elyon – implicitly Yahweh – divided the world up according to the number of his sons – implicitly his angels (as in Job 1:6 and 2:1); and according to the second verse, Yahweh chose to keep Jacob for himself. It may be added that since Greek Ben Sira was produced in Alexandria (as mentioned by the Prologue to Ben Sira), its echoes of Deuteronomy 32:8–9 indicate that the monotheistic interpretation of this passage was operative in the larger community of Alexandria. Here we may make an observation about the shared cultural context of translating both older religious works and generating translation of newer works: the later literary echoes of Deuteronomy 32:8–9 in Ben Sira were known in the same Alexandrian Jewish milieu that produced the Greek textual witness to Deuteronomy 32:8–9. The Alexandrian cultural context of transmitting and translating old religious texts (in this case Deuteronomy 32:8–9) was the same context for transmitting newer works (in this case, Ben Sira 17:17 and 44:1–2) based on the same older text (Deuteronomy 32:8–9). The two passages in Ben Sira indicate a monotheistic witness to Yahweh as El Elyon and "the sons of God" as angels in their interpretation of Deuteronomy 32:8–9 within Alexandria around the time of the Septuagint's translation of these verses.

Further echoes of Deuteronomy 32:8–9 appear in the Dead Sea Scrolls, and as we shall see, they may point to the connection between literary echoing of the scriptural text and its textual production in various forms specifically in manuscript versions. 4Q418, fragments 81 + 81a (= 4Q423 fragment 8?), line 3, reads: "and He [God] is your *portion* and your *inheritance* among humanity (literally, the sons of human), [and over] his in[he]ritance he has given them ruler."[68] In echoing Deuteronomy 32:8–9 (only to omit some of its more salient theological context), this text presupposes the conflation of El Elyon (Most High) with the god of Israel. This conflation of divinity appears again in the double-echo of Deuteronomy 32:8–9 in the War Scroll column 10 (1QM X, 9 and 14–15) as well as Jubilees 15:31–32 (cf. 22:11). It is important to see these echoes at work in the Dead Sea Scrolls and Second

---

[67] Smith, *The Origins of Biblical Monotheism,* 223 n. 65. The translation comes from Skehan and Di Lella, *The Wisdom of Ben Sira,* 497; see their discussion on p. 498. See also P. W. Skehan, "Staves, Nails, and Scribal Slips (Ben Sira 44:2–5)," *BASOR* 200 (1970) 66–71. Cf. E. D. Reymond, *Innovations in Hebrew Poetry: Parallelism and the Poems of Sirach* (Studies in Biblical Literature 9; Atlanta: Society of Biblical Literature, 2004) 79 n. 153, who parses *ḥlq* in Ben Sira 44:2 ms. B understandably as a verb following the Greek and Syriac versions; his view could be further supported by an appeal to the verbal form used in the echo of Deuteronomy 32:8 in Deuteronomy 4:19 (discussed above).

[68] The apparently third person plural suffix on the final verb here is difficult. Cf. Geza Vermes, *The Complete Dead Sea Scrolls in English* (fourth edition; New York: Penguin, 1997) 410, which translates it as second person. For another possible echo, see 1QM 10:15.

Temple literature more broadly. It indicates that this sort of use of Deuteronomy 32:8–9 was operative in the very context that also produced a textual
witness to the biblical passage that did *not* alter the text. The transmission of
Hebrew textual tradition of Deuteronomy 32:8–9 at Qumran was also the
cultural context for the production of new texts echoing this passage. Just as
the Alexandrian context attests to both the translation of the base text and
its echoes in Ben Sira, so also the Qumran texts show how the one and same
cultural context both transmitted textual traditions in the form of biblical
manuscripts and drew on these traditions for new community works. We
may observe then that the same locus for tradition processes at Qumran
generated *both* biblical manuscripts at Qumran *and* new texts that reuse
the same biblical material, as seen in the Qumran community literature such
as the War Scroll. In the echoes of Deuteronomy 32:8–9, we may detect
the interpretive shifts that underlie both the manuscripts' handling of the
passage and the production of newer texts that deliberately echo them.[69] In
closing this overview of the re-use of Deuteronomy 32:8–9, we may observe
that this text seems to have achieved the status of a standard or charter text
for the topic of the deities of the other nations. That this would continue
to be the case is suggested by the evident echo of the verses in Acts of the
Apostles 14:16.[70]

At this point let us return to Deuteronomy 32:8–9. The original composer
of the text drew on an old polytheistic picture. This polytheistic picture did
not belong simply to some pre-biblical culture, but in fact was at home in
early Israel. As we noted in Chapter Three, Deuteronomy 32:8–9 shows a
number of thematic links with Psalm 82, and many scholars have related the
two texts, especially as they both mention Elyon. Where the Deuteronomy
passage might have appeared ambiguous about the ontological status of
these *'elohim* for some later readers (as we have see above with options #1
and #4 among the textual witnesses), Psalm 82 weighs in clearly on their
ontological status. According to this psalm, they had been thought to be
gods, but in fact were mere mortals. In this poem, God (the god of Israel)
takes his stand in the divine council (literally, "council of El") and indicts as
mere mortals the other gods (*'elohim,* verses 1 and 6), whom he had thought
were all sons of (El) Elyon (verse 6). The final verse calls on Yahweh to assume all the nations as his own inheritance; compare Deuteronomy 32:8–9
where only Jacob/Israel is the *inheritance* of God. We do not know the date
of Psalm 82, nor do we really know whether it was an echo of Deuteronomy

---

[69] The passage and its apparent witness to Israelite polytheism were used by the later
polemic of Julian (331/32–363) in his *Against the Galilaeans.* See John Granger Cook,
The Interpretation of the Old Testament in Greco-Roman Paganism (Studien und Texte
zu Antike und Christentum 23; Tübingen: Mohr Siebeck, 2004) 312–14.

[70] See Chapter Six for discussion, pp. 306–8.

32:8–9. Therefore, we should perhaps be circumspect in making claims about any direct relationship between these two texts. Still Psalm 82 contributes to our understanding of the larger hermeneutical shift that informs the textual censorship operative in Deuteronomy 32:8–9, and in Genesis 14:22 as well, as we will see shortly.

In view of the larger context of Deuteronomy 32 (especially verses 12, 17, 21, 31, and 39), it is evident that the composer presupposed the monotheistic identification of Yahweh in verse 9 with Elyon in verse 8.[71] This reading leaves open the question of how the composer then regarded the ontological status of these beings. These might have been regarded as similar to the figures in the somewhat later passages in Job 1:6, 2:1, the "sons of Elohim," who come and go in the heavenly court and report to God as to the doings in the world. Whether or not these should be reduced precisely to "angels" of later tradition (as in option #4),[72] they clearly hold no status remotely close to that of Yahweh. What we perhaps have in Deuteronomy 32:8–9 is a notion of minor divinities, who serve the absolute divine King; these are, relatively speaking, so powerless compared to Yahweh that for the composer, they do not truly constitute gods like Yahweh. They are perhaps like the 'elim of the Qumran Songs of the Sabbbath Sacrifices, minor "divinities," actually angels, but hardly gods in the modern, conventional sense.

In the end, it would seem that the uncensored version of Deuteronomy 32:8–9, in options #2 and #3, likely preserves an older, perhaps even "original," reading strategy for this passage. We may then ask: why was the reading then not left by all texts and read monotheistically? Why did some scribes see polytheism in the text while others did not? The answer lies in part in perception of the text's foreground versus its background: some scribes saw the foreground of the text, namely the composer's own monotheism which attempted to reduce and harmonize the old polytheism, while other scribes felt the potential polytheistic sensibility of the motif. We might say that these latter scribes were perceptive in sensing the old polytheism pushing through the monotheistic veneer of the author's formulation. Perhaps something in the cultural contexts of the relevant textual witnesses informed this difference, but we do not have access to this information. In the end, to echo the title of Michael Holquist's essay, "Corrupt Originals," the author's "original" composition may have been incomplete in erasing Israel's old polytheism, but it was not necessarily "corrupt." It was in fact correct after all. Both the older and newer presentations of Yahweh in relation to other gods had been embedded in the textual tradition, and they

---

[71] Smith, *The Memoirs of God*, 152.

[72] Echoing the later tradition, Tigay (*Deuteronomy*, 514) calls them "angel-like beings."

required subsequent textual mediation, by contextualizing and harmonizing the old idea within the context of the new. If such a reading of the composer's strategy seems misplaced, we need only look to our second example of censorship in Genesis 14:22, generated in this case not through alteration, but by means of addition.

Genesis 14:22

Compared with Deuteronomy 32:8–9, this passage is not as well-known a case of censorship. Tov does include it in his discussion of interpolations (exegetical additions).[73] Genesis 14 relates Abram's victory over a coalition of kings (verses 1–16). The text then introduces the kings of Sodom and Salem (verse 17), who apparently wish to make peace with him. The name of the king of Salem is given in verse 18 as Melchizedek, who is said to also be a priest of El Elyon ("God the Most High," in many translations). In verses 19–20, Melchizedek offers a blessing for Abram in the name of "El Elyon, creator of heaven and earth."[74] In turn, Abram offers Melchizedek a tenth of his take from the battle. In verse 21, the king of Sodom proposes that Abram give him the people taken captive in battle, but that Abram keep the possessions for himself. In verses 22–23, Abram swears by the deity that he will not take anything. The crucial item of interest for our discussion involves Abram's mention of the deity in his oath. Tov lays out three variations in the textual witnesses:

1. Yahweh, El Elyon, creator of heaven and earth (MT, Targums, Vulgate)
2. El Elyon, creator of heaven and earth (LXX, Peshitta;
    cf. 1QapGen, ar, col. XXII, line 21)
3. God (*ha'elohim*), El Elyon, creator of heaven and earth (SP)

Commentators who note the textual difference take the name of Yahweh as an interpolation or editorial gloss.[75] Tov suggests that the original form of the divine name in verse is simply El Elyon, as found not only among the list of textual witnesses (under #2 above), but also in Melchizedek's words in verse 19.[76]

---

[73] Tov, *Textual Criticism*, 282.

[74] The title of El Elyon here, "creator of the earth," stems from a long tradition that goes back to El in the Late Bronze Age. See the discussion in Chapter One. El's title passed into Israelite tradition and also into Phoenician-Punic tradition. For references and discussion, see Patrick D. Miller, Jr., "El, the Creator of the Earth," *BASOR* 239 (1980) 43–46; and Wolfgang Röllig, "El-Creator-of-the-Earth," *DDD* 280–81. Note also the older work by M. Fantar, *Le dieu de la mer chez les pheniciens et les puniques* (Studi semitici 48; Rome: Consiglio nazionale delle recherché, 1977) 97–103.

[75] Tov, *Textual Criticism*, 282. Astour ("Melchizedek," *ABD* 4:685) comments: "it should be considered a late editorial gloss."

[76] Tov, *Textual Criticism*, 282.

We may ask about the purpose of adding Yahweh to the verse. It may be that the scribal tradition was concerned with the appearance of Abram's orthodoxy as a follower of Yahweh. In adding Yahweh, the text ensures that Abram would be recalled as faithful to the covenant that he had made with Yahweh in Genesis 17. Another way of reading the addition is that it serves also to assert the status of Yahweh as the supreme god, as El Elyon. In other words, it is the status of Yahweh at stake and not simply Abram's as his follower. In adding the divine name here, the scribe implicitly demotes El Elyon from a separate main god and turns him into a title for his own deity, the god of Israel.[77] In any case, the identification of Yahweh as El Elyon is hardly restricted to this case. We have already seen it in the text of Deuteronomy 32:8, not only in some of textual versions or later literary echoes, but quite probably in the original composition, which used the old language of El Elyon in its picture of Yahweh. We also noted such interpretation at work in Psalm 82, where God (the god of Israel) takes his stand in the council and indicts as mere mortals the other gods (*'elohim,* verses 1, 6), whom he had thought were all sons of (El) Elyon (verse 6). In these texts, we seem to have a thematic constellation informed by an innovative hermeneutical shift: El Elyon, originally a separate figure known to be the father of the divine children, is either secondarily identified with Yahweh (Deuteronomy 32:8–9; Genesis 14:22), or relegated to the background and essentially ignored (Psalm 82).

This thematic constellation also appears in a text in the Dead Sea Scrolls that cites Psalm 82 in connection with the figure of Melchizedek. This text, 11QMelchizedek (11Q13, column II),[78] draws on a number of scriptural texts to explain the eschatological judgments to be executed; these include the condemnation of wicked spirits, which the text explicates by citing Psalm 82:1–2. For 11QMelchizedek, the *'elohim* of Psalm 82:1 are nothing more than "Belial and the spirits of his lot."[79] This passage shows a second shift with respect to *'elohim:* Melchizedek himself is represented no longer

---

[77] See Baruch A. Levine, *Numbers 21–36: A New Translation with Introduction and Commentary* (AB 4A; New York: Doubleday, 2000) 229: "we may conclude that Deuteronomy 32 … must surely have been composed after El was synthesized with YHWH. The Balaam poems [in Numbers 23–24], in contrast, were composed before this synthesis took place, so that they portray El, Elyon and Shadday as independent beings." I would note further that the religious situation described by Levine stands in Israelite texts, and suggest that there may be vestiges of translatability of El and Yahweh in verses where the two gods stand in parallelism (e. g., 23:8). For discussion, see Chapter Two.

[78] For this text, see Paul J. Kobelski, *Melchizedek and Melchireša'* (CBQMS 10; Washington, DC: The Catholic Biblical Association of America, 1981) 3–23, 49–74. See further Joseph A. Fitzmyer, "Melchizedek in the MT, LXX, and the NT," *Biblica* 81 (2000) 63–69; and Martin McNamara, "Melchizedek: Gen 14,17–20 in the Targums, in Rabbinic and Early Christian Literature," *Biblica* 81 (2000) 1–31.

[79] For convenient presentations of the text and translation, see Donald W. Parry and

as a non-Israelite king of Israel's past, but as a major divine force[80] serving with "all the gods (*'ly*) [of justice?]" in the eschatological plan of God (column II, line 14). The figure of Melchizedek is also characterized in the Songs of the Sabbath Sacrifice at Qumran as "priest in the [divine] assem[bly]" (4Q401, fragment 11, line 3),[81] a characterization that perhaps echoes the council of God in Psalm 82:1 and shows another reconfiguration of this thematic constellation. In these cases, the indeterminacy of the word *'elohim* (God, god, gods) was both tool and an issue for the tradition: in many cases, it permitted identification with Yahweh through a monotheistic rereading of such figures, but in other cases, it might seem ambiguous and problematic.

To return to Genesis 14:22, the textual addition of Yahweh censors the past. For the ancients, addition was a form of censorship, an inversion of deletion that we might otherwise think of as characteristic of the censor's work. In fact, in the ancient Near East, addition was easily as normative as deletion in the scribe's work; many scholars would in fact argue that prior to the Greco-Roman period, addition or expansion was more the scribal norm.[82] What were the consequences of the addition in our particular case? As we shall see, if El Elyon is simply a title for Yahweh, then it means there really were no old gods who belonged to Israel's ancestors before their relationship with Yahweh.

Emanuel Tov, *The Dead Sea Scrolls Reader: Part 2. Exegetical Texts* (Leiden/Boston: Brill, 2004) 24–29; and *DSSSE* 2:1206–7.

[80] Might this view of Melchizedek ("king of righteousness") be due in part to an implicit, secondary interpretation of his name as *mal(')ak-ṣedeq*, "angel of righteousness" (with the loss of medial 'aleph being quite common in MT and DSS; for the former, Tov, *Textual Criticism*, 255)? For evidence for this possibility, see Kobelski, *Melchizedek and Melchireša'*, 52, 79–80.

[81] For convenient presentations of the text and translation, see Donald W. Parry and Emanuel Tov, ed., *The Dead Sea Scrolls Reader: Part 5. Poetical and Liturgical Texts* (Leiden/Boston: Brill, 2005) 364–65; and *DSSSE* 2.810–11. The first half of the name of the figure Melchizedek in this context is partially reconstructed.

[82] This can be seen in a number of biblical examples of composition, based on massive differences in textual witnesses. Emanuel Tov as well as Eugene Ulrich and Julio Trebolla Barrera have noted multiple editions of individual biblical books. See Tov, *Textual Criticism*, 313–49; Ulrich, *The Dead Sea Scrolls and the Origins of the Bible* (Studies in the Dead Sea Scrolls and Related Literature; Grand Rapids, MI/Cambridge, UK: Eerdmans; Leiden: Brill, 1999); Trebolle Barrera, *The Jewish Bible and the Christian Bible*, 390–404. Scribal addition is explicitly mentioned in Jeremiah 36:32b: "Jeremiah took another scroll and gave it to Baruch son of Neriah the scribe and he [Baruch] wrote in it from the mouth of [*mippi*] Jeremiah all the words of the scroll that Jehoiakim king of Judah had burned in fire, and besides, many words like these were added to them." Although expansion is common in textual traditions, some examples of textual compression can be found, however (e.g., the Akkadian text of the Descent of Ishtar to the Underworld compared with its Sumerian prototype, The Descent of Inanna; see Dalley, *Myths*, 154).

The Foundational Myth of "New Gods"

The interpretation of Yahweh as El Elyon that we see in these passages permitted a reading of Israel's past that serves to reinforce the monotheistic interpretation of divinity when and where it appears positively in the record of Israel's past that was transmitted. This interpretive process represents a concomitant development of textual production, as its first clear witness emerges in texts that identify Yahweh and El Elyon. As we noted earlier, Deuteronomy 32, in telling the story of Israel's relationship with its God, begins with a single divine head, Yahweh El Elyon. For the author, there was no differentiation in Israel's past between the figure of El and the figure of Yahweh (verse 8). They are identified as one, and in effect they always were one and the same in this understanding of the past (see also Exodus 6:2–3 for a parallel interpretive move). If there was only one god for Israel in the beginning, then by default, the other gods belong only to the other nations (verse 9). Thus Israel's association with any other gods is interpreted for Israel as "gods they had not known" (i. e., never had a covenant with); these then are "new gods" (verse 17). As we noted in Chapter Three, Israel's "aetiology of idolatry" did not simply deny other gods, but additionally interpreted any god other than Yahweh as a "new god."

The new foundational story of other gods as "new gods," generated in part by the identification of Yahweh and El Elyon, helped to issue in a new monotheistic picture for Israel that would serve as the norm for all time. Thus divine description of the past is divine prescription for the present and future. With the picture of Yahweh and El Elyon in the past reconfigured, the story of Israel with respect to other gods was in turn reconfigured. The potential "hermeneutical power" of this correlation in divinity was considerable. The ultimate goal in the new foundational narrative of divinity was the harmonization of scribal, intellectual labors within post-exilic Yehud/ Judea with the hermeneutics of social life calibrated within the priestly elite. (Here I deliberately echo Boyer: "The ultimate goal of the exercise of hermeneutical power was the harmonization of all individual intellectual labors in the GDR with the hermeneutics of social life calibrated within the party elite."[83]) The new monotheistic foundational narrative may have been, in effect, the strongest element of censorship that we have considered thus far, as it allowed Israel's tradition to divide divinity more neatly into a contrast between Yahweh and his minor, divine helpers (*'elohim*) and other gods (*'elohim 'aḥerim*), who are ultimately mere idols belonging to the other nations. As a result (or perhaps as a concomitant development), the rather complicated divine world of early Israel (evoked by the list of *'elohim* in the Introduction) was tidied up. This was made possible in part

---

[83] Boyer, "Censorship as a Vocation," 522.

by the identification of the major divine figures of Yahweh and El, provided by the Levitical scribal operation functioning under the larger aegis of the Levitical-Aaronid leadership of the post-exilic period. And yet the rather different treatments of *'elohim* in Deuteronomy 32:8–9 seen across the textual witnesses and literary echoes indicate that the sense of both Israel's newer monotheism and its older texts were not so neat. The reality as they saw it was perhaps a relative monotheism, Yahweh and his *'elohim,* but the norm they were attempting to generate was an absolute one, Yahweh alone and his angels. The textual battle of an absolute monotheism subjugating not simply polytheism but even a relative monotheism in the memory of Israel's past would be an ongoing process under the Persian empire, continuing well into Israel's textual and interpretive tradition down through the turn of the era. The completion of the monotheistic victory over Israel's past would have to a wait acts of stronger, interpretive leverage well beyond the establishment of the sacred writings into the Bible.

3. The Cultural Context of Biblical Censorship in the Post-Exilic Period

Having examined two cases of biblical censorship, we may turn to Boyer's model of censorship as it applies to the Germany Democratic Republic (GDR), better known in North America as (the former) East Germany. The application is somewhat incongruous, given the religious setting of censorship in ancient Israel versus the governmental context in the GDR. However, at many crucial points Boyer's article uses religious language to characterize the situation of censorship in the GDR despite the fact that the censorship that he is discussing is not located in a religious institution as such. Boyer deploys a number of religious expressions to characterize the situation within the bodies of censorship in the GDR. I highlight the following instances by putting the explicitly religious terms used in italics.

The first religious usage appears in Boyer's stereotypical picture of the censor where he quotes the historian Robert Darnton: "The trouble with the history of censorship is that it looks so simple: it *pits the children of light against the children of darkness.*"[84] The religious language continues in Boyer's own formulations. The use of Marxism-Leninism is said, "to *sacralize* their judgments."[85] GDR professional intellectuals are said to serve as "to quote Stalin, 'engineers of the *soul*'."[86] "The General Secretary's determina-

---

[84] Boyer, "Censorship as a Vocation," 512.
[85] Boyer, "Censorship as a Vocation," 522.
[86] Boyer, "Censorship as a Vocation," 522.

tions of interpretive order were held *sacrosanct.*[87] "That even Honecker's spelling errors and factual inaccuracies were *taboo* underscores his *sanctified position ... Ordained* the most expert among expert intellectuals ...".[88] We also meet the expression, "the absolute *sanctity* of the party line."[89] State-control media meetings were remembered as "a *ritualized genuflection* to the power of the party-line."[90] And "media language was perceived to be capable of *mystically coupling the sanctified* hermeneutics of party discourse with the *Meinungen* (opinions) of each of its citizens".[91]

One poignant expression of this sort, one hardly so remote from the scenario that we will shortly entertain for our ancient context, comes from the GDR censors themselves, according to Boyer's account:

Any sign of discord with the *Parteilinie* in the lower hierarchical ranks was greeted with immediate public censure, part disciplinary actions, and in the worst cases, also with being '*sent into the desert*' (*in die Wüste geschickt*) as party parlance described as being cast out of the fertile cultural Eden of the SED.[92]

This sort of religious language deployed by both Boyer and his subjects functions analogously and not literally. We are not really talking about religious officials or churches as such. At the same time, we may note that the structures involved were very much structures of belief and authority capable of enforcing such beliefs and adherence to such belief. The threat to the state-media intellectuals was no mere analogy, but rather quite concrete in the GDR. Despite the ostensible non-religious nature of the GDR, its officials use religious language for a reason. In its capacity to usurp the authority of the church and other institutions in the life of the country, the state takes on the apparatus of authority and belief-structure.[93] While religious language was embedded in the GDR governmental worldview, political structures internal to the Persian period Yehud were informed by the priestly apparatus and its worldview. Thus in both situations the religious and political were linked in important ways.

The overlap of the religious and the political in the two contexts invite the probing of some comparisons between the political apparatus of the GDR and the religious circumstances within ancient Yehud/Judea, despite their radical differences (which are explored further below). The language of the "the children of light against the children of darkness" cited above from the historian Robert Darnton echoes the Dead Sea Scrolls (e.g., the Rule of

---

[87] Boyer, "Censorship as a Vocation," 524.
[88] Boyer, "Censorship as a Vocation," 526.
[89] Boyer, "Censorship as a Vocation," 527.
[90] Boyer, "Censorship as a Vocation," 527.
[91] Boyer, "Censorship as a Vocation," 535.
[92] Boyer, "Censorship as a Vocation," 524–25.
[93] In his personal communications with me, Boyer accepts this observation.

the Community, 1QS 1:9–10; War Scroll, 1QM). To draw on the last quote above, it was precisely the self-perception of the Dead Sea community that had indeed required its relocation, in the desert, *"in die Wüste"* (1QS 8:14 citing Isaiah 40:3). The circumstances in both the GDR and ancient Yehud involved conflict over the proper political control of "priestly" authority and its various media. The two stories that Boyer and I tell are thus not entirely different. Both involve highly political and religious answers to terrible stress in the social fabric. In view of the religious use of language by Boyer and his informants, we might go further and even say that religious censorship as imagined by later western historians constitutes the implicit paradigm generally for studies of censorship, whether religious, political or otherwise. And if so, the Bible arguably represents the ancient roots for understanding later paradigms of censorship.

Having made this general point, I hasten to add that this religious connection is rather broad and general. It might seem inapt to suggest analogies between the GDR and ancient Israel, and indeed I think it is important to state at the outset that I do not regard the two situations as analogous as such. The situation in Germany in the nineteenth and twentieth centuries involves various forms of a modern nation-state entirely removed from the type of religious situation that obtained in ancient Israel during the period of the monarchy, and later under the provincial unit of Yehud, succeeded by a series of Hellenistic polities under the name of Judea in Jewish sources in the Greco-Roman world (including the New Testament). In fact, Germany of the nineteenth century constitutes in several ways, politically, religiously and textually, an inverse situation from what we see in Yehud. Germany was emerging as a major modern nation-state. In contrast, Yehud faced the loss of its independence and lived as a unit within the Persian empire, and then experienced great political fragmentation and social stress over the course of the Hellenistic period. Thus the situations are opposite in terms of political power and attitudes toward religion. Moreover, the situations are inverse insofar as Greco-Roman Judea was in the process of generating Scriptures as the central textual focus of its religiously identity, while Germany of the nineteenth and twentieth centuries is spawning ever-increasing bodies of literature of various sorts, in some cases in opposition to its forms of its own traditional Christianity, not to mention against Judaism and Jews more specifically. Thus politically, religiously and textually the situations are arguably quite opposite. Surely many other sorts of differences, by way of worldview, economy and social structure for example, could be noted as well.

Given these differences, there are limitations at several points (perhaps at every point) in the discussion that follows. As I enter into the spirit of Boyer's intellectual project, I consider my efforts heuristic and provisional, as a way to think about our cases of censorship in the Bible. To anticipate the discussion below, there are some cultural comparisons that may be of value for sharpening our probing of the ancient situation in Persian period Yehud and Greco-Roman Judea. We may note both some significant interesting contours of similarity and major differences. Thus, the project here is largely heuristic in using Boyer's considerations of censorship in the GDR and its historical roots as an aid to better understand censorship in the biblical text and the religious roots of the production of the biblical text. With these concerns noted, we may explore aspects of the situation in ancient Yehud/Judea over the course of the Persian and Hellenistic periods[94] in relation to modern Germany in the nineteenth and twentieth centuries.

In our discussion above of Deuteronomy 32 and Genesis 14, we see that the context of censorship involved exegetical activity, combined with varying interpretive strategies. This interpretive operation was embedded in a larger context of textual activity and knowledge. This sort of context is evoked in Nehemiah 8:8, with its description of Levites presenting the text to the people. This verse uses three expressions bearing on textual activity: *meporaš*, which has been rendered variously as "translating" (NJPS), "interpreting" (NAB), "reading carefully" (so Michael Fishbane), or "explaining/giving exposition" (also Fishbane)[95]; *wesom śekel*, "and giving sense" (to the text); and *wayyabinu bammiqra'*, "and they expounded the text" (cf. verse 9). These operations seem part and parcel of the Levitical scribal role attested elsewhere. It may be noted further that some of the vocabulary for interpretation here seems to derive from older divinatory language.[96]

---

[94] For descriptions of Yehud in this period, see Jon L. Berquist, *Judah in Persia's Shadow: A Social and Historical Approach* (Minneapolis: Fortress, 1995); and Charles E. Carter, *The Emergence of Yehud in the Persian Period: A Social and Demographic Study* (JSOTSup 294; Sheffield: Sheffield, 1999). Berquist's study is largely textual in its evidence, while Carter's draws extensively on archaeological materials. In different ways, these studies help to break out of some of the older stereotypes about the religious nature of Yehud.

[95] Fishbane characterizes *meporaš* as both reading and as explanation or exposition (*Biblical Interpretation in Ancient Israel*, 109, 245). For Fishbane, the root in Numbers 15:34 means to be "decided" and thus in Nehemiah 8:8 to fix or to be read precisely. He is also suggesting that the usage in Nehemiah 8:8 mean to explain text. See also van der Toorn, *Scribal Culture*, 79. Explication may also be involved in Nehemiah 8:8. Cf. interpretation and explication in the Letter of Aristeas 15 and 305 (*OTPs* 2.13, 33); and see the discussion by Jed Wyrick, *The Ascension of Authorship: Attribution and Canon Formation in Jewish, Hellenistic, and Christian Traditions* (Harvard Studies in Comparative Literature Founded by William Henry Schofield 49; Cambridge, MA/London: Harvard University, 2004) 260–72.

[96] The notion that divination provides the semantics for textual interpretation finds support in Hebrew *pešer*/Aramaic *pišra'*, attested in Ecclesiastes 8:1 and Daniel 4:3, 5:15, 26, 7:16. The Pesharim texts of the Dead Sea Scrolls provide written examples of inter-

Accordingly, interpretation of this sort seeks to divine in the traditional text understandings applicable to the current context of the interpreters and their audience. Thus reading may be viewed as a sort of "textual divination" or perhaps "textual prophecy."[97] In sum, the Bible offers a picture of Levites who write, read and interpret.

We might further characterize this complex of textual activity as "scripturalizing." By this, I mean that texts regarded as holy or inspired were coming to be read and interpreted together; that words or complexes of terms shared by different religious texts not only could be read in context but should be read together across the boundaries of their original contexts, beyond the limits of an individual passage or document. (I try to avoid using the word, "book," since this word is anachronistic in this period; and as noted above, I use scripture or religious writing to match the terms used in this period – there was not yet a canon of biblical works and thus not a Bible

---

pretation of the written text as "the revealed" (*nglh*) that contains mysteries (*rzym*) or "the hidden" (*hnstrwt*) that can only be divined (as it were) by approved textual masters (1QS V:9, 11–12, VIII:1, 15–16; IX:13, 18–19; see also see 1QpHab VII and XI). Note also the "interpreting scribe" (*spr prš'*) in 4Q203 8,4; 4Q206 2,2; and 4Q530 2ii+6–12,14. Hebrew *pešer*/Aramaic *pišra'* is related to Akkadian *pišru*, "interpretation, explanation," used in astrological reports (*CAD P*:42; so van der Toorn, *Scribal Culture,* 103; and Martti Nissinen, "Pesharim as Divination: Qumran Exegesis, Omen Interpretation and Literary Prophecy," in: *On Prophecy in the Dead Sea Scrolls and in the Hebrew Bible* (ed. Kristin De Troyer and Armin Lange, with assistance of Lucas L. Schulte; Contributions to Biblical Exegesis and Theology; Louvain: Peeters, in press). For the word's etymological complexities, see S. David Sperling, "Studies in Late Hebrew Lexicography in Light of Akkadian" (Ph. D. dissertation, Columbia University, 1973) 67–92; Douglas Leonard Penney, "Towards a Prehistory of Biblical Hebrew Roots: Phoneme Constraint and Polymorphism (Ph.D. dissertation, University of Chicago, 1993) 127–28; and Shaul Bar, *A Letter That Has Not Been Read: Dreams in the Hebrew Bible* (trans. Lenn J. Schramm; Monographs of the Hebrew Union College 25; Cincinnati: Hebrew Union College Press, 2001) 78–81. Other discussions relate this term to divination by dreams (oneiromancy). For the secondary literature, see Maren Niehoff, "A Dream which is not Interpreted is like a Letter which is not Read," *Journal of Jewish Studies* 43 (1992) 58–84.

Another biblical term for textual interpretation might also have a divinatory background. Penney ("Towards a Prehistory," 128) relates *meporaš* in Nehemiah 8:8 to *ⁿpšr* via early metathesis, and Fishbane (*Biblical Interpretation in Ancient Israel,* 109 n. 11) would compare Akkadian *pirsu*. As a possible alternative, the term *meporaš* in Nehemiah 8:8 (see above) might be related to Akkadian *parāšu*, which with the noun *warkatu* can refer to investigating a case or to determine by divination (*CAD P:* 173–74, esp. c). At the same time, the Akkadian contexts are mostly legal and administrative, and not generally divinatory in nature. For the notion that the scriptural reading was considered comparable to non-Jewish divinatory practice, one might note 1 Maccabees 3:48 (NAB): "They unrolled the scroll of the law, to learn about the things for which the Gentiles consulted the images of their idols." NAB (p. 557, note) suggests that the verse refers to "favorable omens for the coming battle. The meaning of the verse is disputed, however. See Jonathan A. Goldstein, *1 Maccabees* (AB 41; Garden City, NY: Doubleday, 1976) 261–62.

[97] For a prophetic understanding of this sort of textual activity, see the discussion in: Carter, *The Emergence of Yehud in the Persian Period,* 286–87.

as such.[98]) Writing the writings and collecting them in turned reinforced collecting their interpretations and cross-referencing them. All in all, these various functions were part of the scribal vocation; censorship in the narrow sense was one element in this operation, and as with these other functions, it is one that aimed at a harmony of worldview. With this sense of the textual complexity informing our two cases of biblical censorship, we may now turn to Boyer's exploration of the larger cultural practices of censorship in order to help sketch a cultural history of censorship in ancient Israel.

As we noted earlier, Boyer begins his discussion with the popular, negative stereotype of the evil censor, precisely in order to question it. He proposes in its place,

> the somewhat counter-intuitive argument that, as a kind of operation upon public language and upon public knowledge, censorship is a productive, intellectual practice not unlike other professional intellectual labors … under certain social and historical conditions, censorship may even be regarded as an intellectual vocation.[99]

The censorship that Boyer discusses is often less a matter of omissions, and more a matter of correctly formulated language. Boyer rarely mentions censorship in the sense of crossing out text in a document, as in our stereotypical picture of the evil censor. Instead, the activity largely involved the authorities getting "the party line" correct in the minds of their media specialists.[100] The work was less concerned with censoring textual materials than the "proper" self-censorship on the part of the media personnel, what many former East German journalists are said to have described as *Schere im Kopf,* "scissors in the head."[101] This additional factor noted by Boyer will aid in our probing later into the scribal culture of censorship for Israel.

Yehud (Israel) in the Persian Period and Germany in the Nineteenth Century

In his story of censorship in the GDR, Boyer backs up to the nineteenth century to explore how "a politicized faction of intellectuals sought monopoly control over state power to realize a social agenda first articulated among the nineteenth-century German cultural bourgeoisie – the world-historical transcendence of the particularities and contradictions of capitalism and the cultivation of a new modern *Volk* (people, nation) held together by means

---

[98] As discussed above. This point has been emphasized recently also by van der Toorn, *Scribal Culture,* 9–26; the problem is particularly captured by the title of his chapter, "books that are not books."

[99] Boyer, "Censorship as a Vocation," 512.

[100] Cf. the title of Gunter Holzweissung's book, *Zensur ohne Zensor* ("Censorship without a Censor"), cited by Boyer, "Censorship as a Vocation," 527.

[101] Boyer, "Censorship as a Vocation," 530; see also p. 529.

of a non-extractive (that is, homogeneous and state-directed) economy of cultural production."[102] One may locate the roots of biblical censorship in the milieu of religious cultural production in the sixth to fourth centuries down into the early Greco-Roman period, in particular with the cultivation of a notion of "people-ness" that stood in relation to, but was no longer identical with, the polities of the pre-exilic "nations" of Judah and Israel, nor co-equal with the people living in the land of Yehud. It itself was not the territorial successor even to the southern kingdom of Judah, but a considerably reduced area centered on Jerusalem.

In the pre-exilic period, especially through the eighth century, the bundle of identity-features of people, land, polity and deity, were not disembedded with respect to one another. However, subsequent political circumstances somewhat disentangled this web of identity-relations. Inherent in these general features of identity both before and after the exile were specific markers of "religion." Scholars of antiquity at this juncture might hasten to add that religion does not represent a category of identity distinguished in indigenous language terms; it is rarely separate from other aspects of identity. (To support this point, they sometimes note that there is no ancient Hebrew word for "religion" in the modern sense.) Still, already in the Persian period we may identify efforts in ancient Yehud's internal agenda to modify its tradition's notion of the "world-historical transcendence" (to echo Boyer) concerning the particularities and contradictions of its own historical experience, specifically the loss of monarchy and the resulting questioning of its national patron deity. In its notion of a world-god, not simply an empire-god, and in additionally denying the gods of the empires as gods, ancient Yehud continued the "one-god" monotheistic conceptualization of its deity emergent already in the period of the Neo-Assyrian and Neo-Babylonian empires.[103] Thus ancient Yehud continued the shift from national-god to empire-god to world-god, in apparent contradiction to the historical particularities of its people's experience.

This effort included Yehudians applying to their own god divine titles used for various chief gods in the Levant during the Persian period. These included the epithets, "god of heaven,"[104] and "lord of heaven."[105] Employ-

---

[102] Boyer, "Censorship as a Vocation," 515.

[103] See Chapter Three for discussion. The impact of the Persian empire and its religion arguably reinforced this shift for ancient Yehud in the Persian period and perhaps issued in some further influences, for example in the form of angelic dualism (as mentioned above) on p. 184 n. 194, p. 194 n. 25.

[104] The title is well attested in Yehudian sources (including representations of official documents): AP 27:15, 30:2, 27–28, and 31:2, 26–27; Ezra 1:2, Nehemiah 1:4, 5; 2:4, 20 (Hebrew); Daniel 2:18, 19, 37, 44; Ezra 5:11, 12, 6:9, 10 and 7:12, 21 and 23 (Aramaic); Tobit 10:11; Judith 5:8, 6:19. See Bezalel Porten, *Archives from Elephantine: The Life of an Ancient Jewish Military Colony* (Berkeley/Los Angeles: University of California,

ing these sorts of cross-culturally known titles drew Yehudians into what André Lemaire calls a "dialogue of the religions."[106] Thus Yehudians engaged the terms of divinity current in the period. At the same time, drawing on the larger religious terms of the Levant, Yehudians asserted their own notion of deity as an expression of its "world-historical transcendence." Its divine oneness helped to communicate the oneness of people, itself under threat of fragmentation both within Yehud and beyond. Indeed, it may be argued that the textual capital inherited by the post-exilic center of cultural production was marshaled in order to express a further "transhistorical" claim, in this case about its own identity: the Israel of its ancient texts was essentially the same not only within its various pre-exilic manifestations, despite the different uses of "Israel" (both geographically and politically during this period); it also represented the same reality in the post-exilic context, despite the fact that Israel as such no longer existed (with people from this area known as Judeans).[107]

1968) 108 n. 12, 109; Niehr, *Der höchste Gott*, 45, 49; Lemaire, *The Birth of Monotheism*, 111–13; and James K. Aitken, "The God of the pre-Maccabees: Designation of the Divine in the Early Hellenistic Period," in: *The God of Israel* (ed. Robert P. Gordon; University of Cambridge Oriental Publications 64; Cambridge, UK: Cambridge University, 2007) 259–64.

[105] For non-Judean sources, the evidence is rich; for Judean sources, it is considerably less so. For the latter, see AP 30:15, Daniel 4:34, 5:23, and Tobit 10:12. See Porten, *Archives from Elephantine*, 108 n. 12; Niehr, *Der höchste Gott*, 45, 49; and Lemaire, *The Birth of Monotheism*, 113. An allusion to this title is seen in the Aramaic proverbs of Ahiqar (#13) from Elephantine; see James M. Lindenberger, "The Gods of Ahiqar," *UF* 14 (1982) 114–16; and *The Aramaic Proverbs of Ahiqar* (The Johns Hopkins Near Eastern Studies; Baltimore/London: Johns Hopkins University, 1983) 69; and Wolfgang Röllig, "Baal-Shamem," *DDD* 149–51. Moshe Bernstein has pointed out to me attestations of "lord of heaven" in the Genesis Apocryphon: 7:7 (7:19?), 11:12–[13], 11:15, 12:17; cf. 22:16, 21); curiously, the Apocryphon contains no cases of "god of heaven," which in Judean sources is otherwise more common (see preceding note).

[106] Lemaire, *The Birth of Monotheism*, 113. See Carter, *The Emergence of Yehud in the Persian Period*, 256–59, concerning extra-provincial contact.

[107] Smith, *The Memoirs of God*, 46: "the very definition of 'Israel' went through several transformations, thanks to the many transformations taking place in Israel's different political, social, and religious landscapes." These transformations took place, even as the textual tradents of "Israelite-ness" maintained the appearance of the tradition's essential continuity. "Judean" remains the term of identity through the second century BCE. Like other West Semitic groups living in Mesopotamia in the Persian period, Judeans lived in enclaves named for their geographical home. For "Judah-town" in Persian period cuneiform sources, see F. Joannès and A. Lemaire, "Trois tablettes cunéiformes à onomastique ouest-sémitique (collection Sh. Moussaïeff)," *Transeuphratène* 17 (1999) 17–34; and Laurie E. Pearce, "New Evidence for Judeans in Babylonia," in: *Judah and Judeans in the Persian Period* (ed. Oded Lipschits and Manfred Oeming; Winona Lake, IN: Eisenbrauns, 2006) 399–411. See also Ran Zadok, *The Earliest Diaspora: Israelites and Judeans in Pre-Hellenistic Mesopotamia* (Publications of the Diaspora Research Institute 151; Tel Aviv: The Diaspora Research Institute, Tel Aviv University, 2002) 33–35, 61; and Lemaire, *The Birth of Monotheism*, 100–1. At Elephantine the operative terms are *yhdy* (e. g., AP 10:3) and

To echo Boyer's point about the production of "German-ness,"[108] "Isra-elite-ness" was a work in progress, in part generated by Judean and Yehu-dian "knowledge specialists, actively crafted to produce a vision of collec-tive culture consonant with intellectuals' own phenomenological intuition about the nature of social and religious relations." While "German-ness" served purposes of an emergent nation-state, in contrast "Israelite-ness" functioned as a claim to identity in a period of political shrinkage. The claim about "Israelite-ness" further influenced its "transhistorical" claim about the god of Israel (what I have called "vertical translatability" in Chapter Three). The notion of its national deity was generalized not only geographi-cally as the god of the universe,[109] as noted above; it was correspondingly generalized across time, as the god, the only god of this Israel's history. Uni-versality and singularity of divinity was asserted across both space and time. Thus the "key signifiers of imagined, collective"[110] "Israelite-ness" included not only monotheism in time and space and the single deity's relationship to the people. It was further expressed in the religious teaching (Torah) reserved for and by this people, that not only asserted these claims about this one deity and this one people, but also conveyed its reality as the one authoritative collection emblemized in the one authoritative figure of Moses as remembered in it.[111] Various aspects of this worldview had enjoyed a long history that reached well back into the pre-exilic period, and in fact it was this considerable history that lent prestige to them in the post-exilic context (again, as part of Israel's "vertical translatability"). The particular highlighting and interweaving of these aspects largely represented a post-exilic innovation. It was an innovation cloaked in the august robes of hoary antiquity, precisely the hallmark of the religious traditioning process.

The constellation of notions about divinity, people and text was in large measure generated, again to cite Boyer's terms, "by means of a non-extrac-tive (that is, homogeneous and state-directed) economy of cultural produc-tion." Here we may identify the cultural segments that in Boyer's terms, "defined their social identity primarily through the distinction of *Bildung*

---

yhwdy' (e. g., AP 31:26; see also AP 22, col. 1:2). Shaye J. D. Cohen has noted that Judean, the ethnic-geographical and religious designation, represents the standard term well into the second century BCE; *Ioudaios,* he asserts, never means "Jew" (as a primarily religious-ethnic designation) until the end of the second century BCE. See Cohen, *The Beginning of Jewishness: Boundaries, Varieties, Uncertainties* (Berkeley/Los Angeles/London: Uni-versity of California, 1999) 82–83.

[108] Boyer, "Censorship as a Vocation," 516.

[109] For "universalism" of the Judean deity in this period, see Lemaire, *The Birth of Monotheism,* 105–16.

[110] Boyer, "Censorship as a Vocation," 516.

[111] For Moses in tradition, see the recent summation by Eckart Otto, *Mose: Geschichte und Legende* (München: C. H. Beck, 2006).

(education, moral formation)."[112] Cultural production, prior to the exile, largely flowed from the needs of monarchy in its many religious themes and claims, yet it also included both voices that it sponsored in the form of its own central priesthood as well as alternative voices (for example echoed in the book of Deuteronomy, especially in chapters 12–25); these militated for different religious and political claims. (Already in this time, family religion and its claims, for example in its specific notions of the family god, had been receding or co-opted in the face of centralized priestly and royal power from the eighth century onwards.[113]) Following the exile, monarchy no longer was the dominant source and voice of cultural production. The post-exilic period witnesses to the emergence of old social-religious forces, both those formerly sponsored by the monarchy (its central priesthood) as well as others involved in cultural production. It is evident that however one understands the history of the priesthood, it emerged as the dominant force of cultural production in the post-exilic context, and in doing it used the emergent expression of monotheism as one of the most important markers for expressing cultural identity: as the priestly presentation of God in the Pentateuch represents Israel's god, this deity, only this deity, this deity alone who was known among and via this people was the only god in the world. This was arguably a form of notional imperialism on the part of a people with no claim or capacity to imperialism of its own. The ultimate textual expression of the priestly god was the priestly text of Genesis 1:1–2:3, which closes with a deity ceasing from labor.[114]

In its political circumstances, this expression of "world-transcendence" as a people was not state-directed, in any conventional sense. As a small province within the Persian satrapy known as "Beyond the River" (Ezra 4:20), Yehud did not constitute an independent polity. If its cultural production was designed to assert identity over and against other political claims (such as Yehud's subjugation to the Persian empire), then these were authoritative claims made within their territory, in the fabric of their very political reality. The standard against which they rhetorically fought was not the capitalist economy next door with its apparent success (the situation of GDR with

---

[112] Boyer, "Censorship as a Vocation," 516.

[113] For discussion, see Smith, *The Memoirs of God*, 133–34, 137.

[114] See among innumerable commentators essays by Edwin Firmage, "Genesis 1 and the Priestly Agenda," *JSOT* 82 (1999) 97–114; and S. Dean McBride, "Divine Protocol: Genesis 1:1–2:3 as Prologue to the Pentateuch," in: *God Who Creates: Essays in Honor of W. Sibley Towner* (ed. W. P. Brown and S. Dean McBride Jr.; Grand Rapids, MI/Cambridge, UK: Eerdmans, 2000) 3–41. Firmage prefers the assignment of this chapter to H rather than P. I prescind from this issue here, as both H and P are priestly. For the issue, see Israel Knohl, *The Sanctuary of Silence: the Priestly Torah and the Holiness School* (Minneapolis: Fortress, 1995); and Jacob Milgrom, *Leviticus 1–16* (AB 3; New York: Doubleday, 1991) 13–42. See further below, in n. 118.

West Germany, as discussed by Boyer); the standard was represented in the political realities at home. Cultural production within Yehud was arguably not homogeneous, despite the picture sometimes sketched by historians of ancient Israel. On the contrary, conflict both within the mechanisms of priestly cultural production and its opponents outside this milieu seem to constitute one of the longstanding problems in this period. This debate would include defining the proper boundaries of religious life, its internal religious dynamics and the worldview that would integrate both. The shifting nature of this process hardly indicates a homogeneous economy of cultural production. A relatively basic reading of post-exilic institutions sees the priesthood in Jerusalem as the central locus of cultural production (note the representation of society as "the people of Israel, priests and Levites," in Ezra 9:1; cf. 1 Chronicles 9:1–16). Still after a rather substantial period of transition of authority from monarchy, we can identify the eventual dominant position of priesthood over other potential sources of authority; the latter would include the remnants of monarchic aspirations, represented literarily by the figure of Zerubbabel in Zechariah 4 and perhaps emblemized in the person of Qohelet as wise king in Jerusalem. (The work may better represent the voice of broader wisdom circles in the late Persian period.[115] The spirit of the book signals a rather jaundiced view of what God has given to humans.) Otherwise, the priestly-Levitical generation of holy writings during the Persian period,[116] with its emergent interconnected reading praxis, perhaps served in the sort of role that Boyer imagines for the Germany in the nineteenth century: the text was "treated as a mystic source of interconnectedness."[117] We may take a brief look at both the internal and external pressures operative with the priesthood at the time.

Internally, we may detect strains behind the gradual coalescence of a hierarchy of priestly authority. This hierarchy eventuated in a partial differentiation of identity and labor: in this period priests and Levites were distinguished (Ezra 8:30, 9:1). The Aaronid priesthood maintained and

---

[115] Many scholars place Ecclesiastes (Qohelet) in the Hellenistic period, largely based on their sense of the ideas in the book. See Martin Hengel, "Judaism and Hellenism Revisited," in: *Hellenism in the Land of Israel* (ed. John J. Collins and Gregory E. Sterling; Christianity and Judaism in Antiquity Series 13; South Bend, in: University of Notre Dame, 2001) 20–21. Questions with this Hellenistic dating have been raised; I mention two: Hellenistic-type ideas may have been present in Yehud during the late Persian period; the book lacks the sorts of grammatical features associated with the Hellenistic period (e. g., Greek loanwords) but contains features associated with the Persian period (e. g., a Persian loanword, in the word, *pardesim*, in 2:5). Still some scholars would dispute or ignore such criteria. For further discussion, see note 141 below.

[116] See the discussion of "Scripture citing Scripture" in Ezra, Nehemiah and 1–2 Chronicles by H. G. M. Williamson, *Studies in Persian Period History and Historiography* (FAT 38; Tübingen: Mohr Siebeck, 2004) 232–43.

[117] Boyer, "Censorship as a Vocation," 517.

generated sacrificial practice in a temple re-established in the late sixth century.[118] As a concomitant feature of this practice, scribes – either Aaronids and/or Levites working under their authority – continued a tradition of production of priestly texts for their use and maintenance, in particular in the so-called priestly prescriptive material in the Pentateuch. Initially, such cultural production was designed for internal priestly consumption. At the same time, it is clear that the Aaronids accepted the survival of their internal competitors, in the form of the book of Ezekiel (produced by the more specific inner-priestly Aaronid line known as the Zadokites). When and under what circumstances the Aaronids started to produce their own narrative literature (e. g., Genesis 1:1–2:3 and other so-called "P" or Holiness school narrative texts in the Pentateuch) is unclear. The motivation for putting these works in the public domain later lay perhaps in a textual assertion of the primacy of the worldview of the Aaronids/Holiness "schools" (as they are sometimes called).

By comparison, non-Aaronid Levites seemed to have become regarded as second-class personnel, no longer sacrificial priests as such. Formerly priests responsible for sacrificial cult and teaching (Deuteronomy 33:8–11), these Levites saw their role in sacrificial cult usurped by the Aaronids (whether or not the Aaronids originated as a separate priestly group or emerged from out of the Levites themselves). In the post-exilic context, Levites served in the Jerusalem temple in a number of capacities, such as musical personnel, officials, gatekeepers, and scribes, according to 2 Chronicles 34:13. Above

---

[118] For the sake of convenience here, I am including under this rubric both Aaronid priests and the priests behind the Holiness Code of Leviticus 17–26 as well as the so-called Holiness redaction detected in the Pentateuch. On the Holiness Code of Leviticus 17–26 in recent discussion, see in particular Baruch Schwartz, *The Holiness Legislation: Studies in the Priestly Code* (Jerusalem: Magnes, 1999) (Heb.). Recent discussion on the Holiness redaction and its relationship to other priestly corpora has taken a new turn, thanks to the work by Israel Knohl, *The Sanctuary of Silence: The Priestly Torah and the Holiness School* (trans. J. Feldman and P. Rodman; Minneapolis: Fortress, 1996). For a constructive response to Knohl, see Saul Olyan, *Rites and Rank: Hierarchy in Biblical Representations of Cult* (Princeton: Princeton University, 2000); and his study, "Exodus 31:12–17: The Sabbath According to H or the Sabbath According to P and H?" *JBL* 124 (2005) 201–9. See also Alan Cooper and Bernard Goldstein ("Exodus and *Maṣṣôt* in History and Tradition," in: *Maarav* 8/2 [1992] = *Let Your Colleagues Praise You: Studies in Memory of Stanley Gevirtz* [ed. Robert Ratner et al.; two vols.; Rolling Hill Estates, CA: Western, 1992], 2.15–37, esp. 25 n. 35), who also regard H as a redaction post-dating P. On the relationship between the Holiness Code and P, see further Hans-Wienfried Jüngling, "Das Buch Levitikus in der Forschung seit Karl Elligers Kommentar aus dem Jahr 1966," in: *Levitikus als Buch* (ed. Heinz-Joseph Fabry and H.-W. Jüngling; BBB 119; Berlin/Bodenheim: Philo, 1999) 1–45. A fine discussion and critique of various positions has been laid out more recently by Jeffrey R. Stackert, *Rewriting the Torah: Literary Revision and the Holiness Legislation* (FAT 52; Tübingen: Mohr Siebeck, 2007).

we mentioned their role as scribes (e.g., possibly Deuteronomy 17:18, 1 Chronicles 24:6), in conjunction with their roles as readers of sacred texts with an accompanying capacity for exposition (Nehemiah 8:8). Their role as religious teachers as known from the pre-exilic context of Deuteronomy 33:8–11 (if no later additions are involved here) seems to continue in this period, and those of their ranks involved in scribal activity also exercised roles as teachers and musicians. It is for this reason that Levitical authorship or at least transmission has been ascribed to widely different works, such as Deuteronomy, Jeremiah, Malachi and Psalms.[119] The Levites may have operated as the scribal arm of the Jerusalem establishment more broadly.

Externally, the priesthood also evidences considerable strains. Josephus (*Antiquities,* Book 11, lines 297–303) records fourth century intermarriage between the leading priestly families in Jerusalem and Samaria. Conflict over the marriage contributed to a split in relations between the two priestly establishments, with some defection from the Judean priestly ranks to Samaria.[120] From this brief rehearsal, it might be suggested that the apparatus of media control was dominated generally by this priesthood, which itself sometimes varied internally in its views. From the outside, the "party line" may have looked quite set, but internally there seems to have been a range of perspectives on some issues, and in fact some scribal activity later was specifically designed to address differences over such matters (such as cultic prescriptions) in the face of ongoing post-exilic circumstances.[121] Rather than solidifying further in the subsequent period, the priestly apparatus of media control would splinter.

The Greco-Roman Context of Biblical Censorship and the GDR

In ancient Yehud, we do not see an emergent nation-state as with late nineteenth century Germany, but a province. In the Greco-Roman context of

---

[119] For a summary, see Smith, *Pilgrimage Pattern in Exodus,* 257–61. For a maximalist case for the priestly authorship of biblical works, see John W. Miller, *The Origins of the Bible: Rethinking Canon History* (New York/Mahwah, NJ: Paulist, 1994). Caution is warranted in some of these cases. Cf. the more nuanced view of Karel van der Toorn, *Scribal Culture and the Making of the Hebrew Bible* (Cambridge, MA/London: Harvard University, 2007) 89–96, 102, 107, 145–47, 158–60. See the critical discussion of Hosea along these lines by Stephen L. Cook, "The Lineage Roots of Hosea's Yahwism," *Semeia* 87 (1999) = *The Social World of the Hebrew Bible: Twenty-Five Years of the Social Sciences in the Academy* (ed. Ronald A. Simkins and Stephen L. Cook) 145–61. For the post-exilic context, see Cook, *Prophecy & Apocalyticism: The Postexilic Social Setting* (Minneapolis: Fortress, 1995). For discussion of the Levites as scribes, see above.

[120] For a convenient resource on this matter, see Lawrence Schiffman, *Texts and Traditions: A Source Reader for the Study of Second Temple and Rabbinic Judaism* (Hoboken, NJ: KTAV, 1998) 92–93.

[121] See Fishbane, *Biblical Interpretation,* 114–23; cf. Williamson, *Studies in Persian Period History and Historiography,* 234–39.

Judea, we are even further removed from the German situation. Whereas Germany was in the process of unifying, Judea in the Greco-Roman period was a contested territory between two of the successors of Alexander's empire, the Ptolemies based in Egypt and the Seleucids in Syria.[122] From the end of the fourth century and through the third century, Judea was gradually wrested from the grip of the Ptolemies by the Seleucids. The cultural context in the late fourth and third centuries is difficult to gauge, in view of the meager sources at our disposal, but the sources show the ongoing importance of the priesthood in the life of Judea. The book of Ben Sira (also known as Sirach or Ecclesiasticus), produced in the first quarter of the second century BCE in Judea, gives a view of the Judean high priest held by its scribal elite. The author, a contemporary of the high priest Simon, evokes a scene of the Jerusalem temple with this figure at its center, "the greatest among his brethren, the glory of his people" (Ben Sira 50:1, Hebrew ms. B) as glorious as any star, shining moon, sun or rainbow (see verses 50:6–7; Hebrew ms. B). There his appearance would be met by a sound of the blast by "the sons of Aaron" (50:16 Hebrew ms. B). The scene is generally thought to evoke the liturgy for the Day of Atonement (or, perhaps the daily sin-offering).[123] Behind this glowing picture, divisions in the priesthood lurk in the background. We have already heard of the split in the priestly families in Samaria and Jerusalem in the Persian period, and we will hear shortly of a similar split issuing in the founding of the Qumran community; we may surmise that in the intervening years, the Jerusalem priesthood, despite the inspiring picture in Ben Sira was subject to considerable external and internal strains.

It is in this larger context that we may locate our two examples of biblical censorship. As noted above, Arie van der Kooij has placed the case of censorship that we saw with Deuteronomy 32:8 specifically within the context of the second century BCE/BC and suggests that the change stemmed from priestly circles responsible for transmitting scriptural texts.[124] The second of our cases, Genesis 14:22, apparently points to the continuing concern for "protecting God," as the evidence of 1QapGen, ar, col. XXII, line 21 (without the addition) seems to point to a later date for this change in this verse. Thus scribal attention for the presentation of God in the biblical text seems to have continued to be a concern through the second century. Insofar as the priestly character of the community at Qumran can be discerned through

---

[122] For the outlines of the cultural situation of Jewish institutions and practices during this period, see the helpful discussion of Seth Schwartz, *Imperialism and Jewish Society, 200 B. C. E. to 640 C. E.* (Princeton/Oxford: Princeton University, 2001) 25–31.

[123] See the discussion of Skehan and Di Lella, *The Wisdom of Ben Sira*, 550–51.

[124] Van der Kooij, "Ancient Emendations in MT," 152–59. See below pp. 241, 283–88.

the lens of the Dead Sea Scrolls, it would appear that the priestly concern for the understanding of God was an ongoing matter.

The Priestly Community at Qumran

From the Maccabean revolt of ca. 167 onward, the political situation became further charged. This political crisis translated into a crisis of authority within the Jerusalem priesthood thanks to the Maccabean arrogation of the high priesthood. The resulting priestly split, around 150,[125] eventuated in the establishment of priestly led community at Qumran[126] and perhaps the wider Essene movement. Indeed, the communal establishment at Qumran may be viewed as part of a larger group or movement[127] of Essenes known to have operated at a number of locations, but perhaps established particularly at Qumran.

An analogy with the late nineteenth-early twentieth century German situation might be applied to the Judean political situation in the Maccabean period. Many in the priestly ranks saw the fruits of their advocacy

---

[125] This date has become something of a general view. See Lawrence H. Schiffman, *Reclaiming the Dead Sea Scrolls: Their True Meaning for Judaism and Christianity* (ABRL; New York: Doubleday, 1994) 83–95; and James C. VanderKam, *The Dead Sea Scrolls Today* (Grand Rapids, MI: Eerdmans, 1994) 100–4. Frank Moore Cross considers a range of dates, with the upper limit "suitably drawn about 150 BC" and the lower limit "no earlier than the reign of Simon (142–134 BC)"; see Cross, *The Ancient Library of Qumran* (third ed.; The Biblical Seminar; Sheffield: Sheffield, 1995) 97.

[126] According to the survey of the archaeological evidence by Jodi Magness, there is no evidence for the communal settlement at Qumran before 100 B.C.E.; see Jodi Magness, *The Archaeology of Qumran and the Dead Sea Scrolls* (Grand Rapids, MI/Cambridge, UK: Eerdmans, 2002) 66. For the priestly identity of the community, see Schiffman, *Reclaiming the Dead Sea Scrolls,* 113–21; and "Utopia and Reality: Political Leadership and Organization in the Dead Sea Scrolls Community," in: *Emanuel: Studies in Hebrew Bible, Septuagint and the Dead Sea Scrolls in Honor of Emanuel Tov* (ed. Shalom M. Paul, Robert A. Kraft, Lawrence H. Schiffman and Weston W. Fields; Leiden/Boston: Brill, 2003) 413–27, esp. 416–20. See also Schiffman's consideration of the matter in: "Pre-Maccabean Halakhah in the Dead Sea Scrolls," *Dead Sea Discoveries* 13/3 (2006) 348–61; "Holiness and Sanctity in the Dead Sea Scrolls," in: *A Holy People: Jewish and Christian Perspectives on Religious Communal Identity* (ed. Marcel Poorthuis and Joshua Schwartz; Leiden/Boston: Brill, 2006) 53–67, esp. 54–55. See further below.

[127] I tend to avoid using the word "sect" for the Qumran community not simply for its modern, negative connotations, but also for its historical inaccuracy, as recently emphasized by John Collins in its analysis of Qumran community terms in different documents, e.g., 1QS 6:1b–8, and references to "camps" notably with married people in CD ms A, VII, line 6 = CD ms. B, XIX, line 2, versus the Qumran community where relatively speaking marriage seems hardly the norm). See John J. Collins, "The *Yaḥad* and 'the Qumran Community',," in: *Biblical Traditions in Transmission: Essays in Honour of Michael A. Knibb* (ed. C. Hempel and J. Lieu; Leiden: Brill, 2005) 81–96. See also Torleif Elgvin, "The *Yaḥad* is More than Qumran," in: *Enoch and Qumran Origins: New Light on a Forgotten Connection* (ed. Gabriele Boccaccini; Grand Rapids, MI/Cambridge, UK: Eerdmans, 2005) 273–79.

for religious systematicity increasingly co-opted in the name of political expediency.[128] With the high priesthood usurped by the Maccabeans themselves and in turn bought and sold, the people's religious character became an opportune medium for rationalizing variant political patterns (including as well accommodations to intervening and influential foreign powers). To paraphrase Boyer, it was the explosion of discourse around national political identity from within the priestly elite and the resulting polysemy that were at the root of this cultural elite's anxiety about the religious order slipping away.[129] It was from within this context of intellectual-cultural anxiety and the political, social and religious instability of the mid-second century,[130] that the imagination of apocalyptic visions fully emerged not in the sort of new political order as Boyer sees for Germany in the 1920s, but in a polity afflicted by increasing Roman deformation[131] and deterioration of local political authority. The emergence of the priestly-led Qumran "camps" (as well as Qumran community) and other movements alienated from the Jerusalem priesthood represents, again to echo Boyer (with my brackets added for comparative purposes), "parallel political and religious responses to the climate of anxiety and pessimism about national-cultural decline that became widespread in German [read, Judean] intellectual culture in the late nineteenth century [read, Maccabean period] and reached its crescendo in the Weimar period [read, Roman imperium from 63 BCE on, through the Jewish revolt against Rome in 66 and the subsequent Roman conquest]."[132] This phase witnessed "scribed acrimonious and sometimes cryptic responses to them,"[133] for example in the Dead Sea Scrolls, in particular, the Pesharim.

In its own way, the Qumran community continued its version of the traditional priestly hierarchy of priests and Levites (e.g., 1QS 1:21–22, 2:11, 19–20; cf. 1QS 5:9, "the sons of Zadok"), with the Levites still reputed for their production of texts (Jubilees 45:15 and 47:9; 4QTQahat, fragment 1, lines 11–12, cf. 4QAmram^c, fragment 1, lines 1–2). Still, to mark boundaries, the Qumran community (and the larger movement in which it arguably participated) generated its own textual production and categories of replacement. Removed from the Jerusalem priestly establishment, the Qumran leadership created new boundaries for its religious expression, one lodged in Temple categories without the physical reality

[128] Cf. Boyer ("Censorship as a Vocation," 518): "In this new arrangements of powers within the German societal elite, intellectuals saw the fruits of their advocacy for national systematicity increasingly co-opted in the name of political expediency."
[129] Boyer, "Censorship as a Vocation," 518.
[130] Boyer, "Censorship as a Vocation," 519.
[131] Boyer, "Censorship as a Vocation," 519.
[132] Boyer, "Censorship as a Vocation," 520.
[133] Boyer, "Censorship as a Vocation," 525.

of the Temple or its sacrificial praxis (see the Songs of the Shabbat Sacrifice). It remained priestly at heart, not simply for those themselves from priestly ranks but also for the community as a whole. From their own displaced position at Qumran, the priestly leadership likely mimicked their Jerusalem counterparts: both were "invested with the privilege and responsibility of generating epistemic order from the orthographic to the hermeneutic."[134] The power of the community to compile a list of "taboos and rationales" required likewise rings true; the Scrolls abound with the sort of interdictions cited of the GDR by Boyer.[135] The difference perhaps was that rationales were not required; still, Qumran texts often provide them anyway. Indeed, for the media apparatus of both the GDR and the Qumran community, "manipulating referential determination became a goal second only to control over the circulation of signs."[136] The Qumran community's "production of collective consciousness"[137] might bear further comparison with Boyer's discussion of the exercise of media power in the GDR. Indeed, the role of authoritative texts played a role in both settings, and a certain belief in the worldview advocated is met in both contexts. Both believed in their "higher collective purpose."[138]

The Limits of Our Analogy and the Role of Scripture in Judea

At this point we again reach the limits of our analogy, in particular with the role of religious experience – even mystical experience – that the Qumran texts express (and arguably with some of the religious uses to which such texts were put at least). On this score, the GDR has little analogue with the Qumran community (at least, in Boyer's account). From what we can tell from such a great historical distance, we might surmise from the Qumran corpus that the community was apparently in less need of self-convincing as to its "vision." We reach a similar impasse with our analogy with the nature of texts themselves. To be sure, textual production was crucial to both situations. Whether in Jerusalem or Qumran, textual life remained at the heart of religious identity. Land or political order also provided an important sense of identity in Judea,[139] and like textual production, these became increasingly contested features of identity. The ongoing production of holy texts arguably provided a source of refuge. However, the arrange-

---

[134] Boyer, "Censorship as a Vocation," 526.
[135] Boyer, "Censorship as a Vocation," 527–28.
[136] Boyer, "Censorship as a Vocation," 528.
[137] Boyer, "Censorship as a Vocation," 521.
[138] Boyer, "Censorship as a Vocation," 530.
[139] I reiterate Cohen's argument that "Judean" remained an ethnic-geographical-religious term well into the second century. See above, p. 224 n. 107.

ment of texts, in particular the specific relation of approved Scriptural texts to one another, does not play as great a role in Boyer's scenario as it does in the ancient context.

In the time of Ben Sira, we see a number of religious works, "Law of the Most High," "prophecies," et cetera (Ben Sira 38:34, 39:1–3). In the Maccabean period (and as well into the Hasmonean period), we see a coordinated collection effort of the Law and the prophets and also their coordinated representation as authorities (1QS 1:3, 8:15–16; CD 5:21–6:1). This was true not only at home, but already in the Alexandria of Ben Sira's grandson (ca. 132), in his characterization of the holy writing as "the Law, the prophets and the other writings" in his Prologue. Elsewhere we see the sacred Teaching (torah) identified in various ways with or as wisdom (Ben Sira 24; Baruch 3:9–4:4, especially 4:1; "Psalm 154" in Cave 11 Psalms Scroll, column 18; 4Q525, also called 4QBeatitudes, fragment 2, column II, lines 3–4), an association intimated already in the book of Deuteronomy.[140] The collection process as well as the attendant understanding of the collection process can be glimpsed in the figure of David who emblemizes the combination of prophecy, wisdom and psalms in the Cave 11 Psalms Scroll (11QPsᵃ = 11Q5, column 27, lines 2–11).[141] This was not only to appeal

---

[140] Deuteronomy 4:6 in particular characterizes the divine teaching as *ḥokma,* "wisdom," as noted by Weinfeld, *Deuteronomy and the Deuteronomic School,* 264–65. For a broader consideration of wisdom in Deuteronomy, see Weinfeld, *Deuteronomy and the Deuteronomic School,* 260–74; and Karin Finsterbusch, *Weisung für Israel: Studien zu religiösem Lehren und Lernen im Deuteronomium und in seinem Umfeld* (FAT 44; Tübingen: Mohr Siebeck, 2005) 117–316. Van der Toorn (*Scribal Culture,* 162–66, 226, 350 n. 76) sees in Deuteronomy 4 and 30 signs of a specific wisdom edition of the book that views Torah as a source of divine wisdom. For the identification of Wisdom with Jewish teaching (Torah, often translated "law") in this period, see above p. 200 n. 35.

[141] One might see in this development an effort at fostering a certain piety, which may perhaps be gauged by a comparison with Ecclesiastes (Qohelet). Seth Schwartz (*Imperialism and Jewish Society,* 29; see also p. 83) regards Ecclesiastes as coming "closer than any other ancient writer in Hebrew to produce a Greek-style philosophical treatise." This approach has been defended in a thoughtful piece by Peter Machinist, "Fate, *miqreh,* and Reason: Some Reflections on Qohelet and Biblical Thought," in: *Solving Riddles and Untying Knots: Biblical, Epigraphic, and Semitic Studies Presented to Jonas C. Greenfield* (ed. Z. Zevit, S. Gitin and M. Sokoloff; Winona Lake, IN: Eisenbrauns, 1995) 159–75. As indicated by Machinist's remarks (pp. 174–75), any philosophical proximity between Ecclesiastes and Greek philosophical tradition hardly precludes a dating of the former in the late Persian period (for discussion, see above n. 115). Indeed, putative Greek influence may date to the fifth or fourth century. Whatever its precise date, Jewish wisdom circles in the Greco-Roman period partake of the sort of piety sanctioned in the wisdom works of Ben Sira and Wisdom of Solomon, which was relatively lacking in Hellenistic thought, as noted by Schwartz (*Imperialism and Jewish Society,* 31). Both of these works also take recourse in a recitation of the past, unlike Ecclesiastes. The Jewish piety associated with these wisdom works perhaps shows a tendency in this period to rein in "outliers" or the attitude of relative "outliers," perhaps represented by the likes of an Ecclesiastes.

to the importance of having one's own indigenous source of wisdom in a world dominated by the standard of Hellenistic wisdom[142]; this may have developed in part due to what may be called "scripturalizing" reading, by which various forms of sanctioned writings came to be read in conjunction with one another (as discussed above). The textual process shows a kind of integration that may be said to stand in contradistinction to the contemporary political and social conditions in Judea at the time.

The Role of Hebrew Language

Boyer also notes the important role that the German language played in generating political identity. Here we may note his comment that "the naturalness' of linguistic coherence is also ideological."[143] In this context, the use of Hebrew at home asserted a religious value of continuity for some groups, in the face of Hellenistic influence. (As an example, we may note the nationalist purposes of Hebrew in the later Bar Kochba rebellion of 132 CE.) Despite the stereotype that Greek was relatively minor in Jewish life in Judea at this time, it is clear that it was a considerable force in Judean culture.[144] Even Qumran preserves Greek texts, and even Greek translations of sacred writings.[145] Despite the substantial use of Greek in Judea – or perhaps because of it, Hebrew would continue its special role in religious life in the Temple and in the production of sacred texts, in particular Torah literature. Seth Schwartz has suggested that with the Temple and Torah assuming greater importance as markers of Jewish identity,[146] scribal and Temple elites used Hebrew both to distinguish themselves from the rest of the population, which generally spoke Aramaic, and to evoke Jewish distinctiveness from its neighbors, who spoke various dialects of Aramaic and other languages.[147] Thus, for Jewish elites, Hebrew served to

---

[142] See below pp. 270–72.

[143] Boyer, "Censorship as a Vocation," 533.

[144] Momigliano, *Essays on Ancient and Modern Judaism*, 21–22. See also the critical reevaluation of the epigraphic evidence by P. W. Van der Horst, "Greek in Jewish Palestine," in: *Hellenism in the Land of Israel* (ed. John J. Collins and Gregory E. Sterling; Christianity and Judaism in Antiquity Series 13; South Bend, in: University of Notre Dame, 2001) 154–74.

[145] James VanderKam, "Greek at Qumran," in: *Hellenism in the Land of Israel* (ed. John J. Collins and Gregory E. Sterling; Christianity and Judaism in Antiquity Series 13; South Bend, in: University of Notre Dame, 2001) 175–81.

[146] Schwartz, *Imperialism and Jewish Society*, 52–66.

[147] Schwartz, "Hebrew and Imperialism in Jewish Palestine," in: *Ancient Judaism in its Hellenistic Context* (ed. Carol Bakhos; JSJSup 95; Leiden/Boston: Brill, 2005) 53–84, esp. 55 and 61–81. Schwartz's view of Aramaic as the general spoken language among the wider populace receives general support (though with some nuances) from the older survey by Joseph A. Fitzmyer, S.J., "The Languages of Palestine in the First Century A.D.," *CBQ*

address Jewish identity both for an insider context and an outsider context. Hebrew language marked Judean religious "interconnectedness" not just to the Jewish past as it was recalled, but also to other Jews who shared this traditional sensibility.[148]

The Qumran community participated in this language ethos and developed it in its own ways. In the literature we meet phrases such as "the revealed tongue" (Jubilees 12:25–27) and "the holy tongue" (4Q464, fragment 3 i, lines 8–9).[149] (The expression was perhaps derived by the community perhaps from Zechariah 3:9 which mentions the "pure speech," which all peoples will use in order to call on the name of Yahweh.) Qumran perhaps did go farther than the priestly establishment from which its originators detached themselves, in using Hebrew to designate and design its parallel yet alternative universe. William Schniedewind has emphasized the special role of Hebrew for the Qumran community, not just its apparent aversion to Greek loanwords in its Hebrew texts,[150] but also as a creator and sustainer of community resistant to the larger world that does not share this religious "dialect."[151] Beyond employing Hebrew in such a

---

32 (1970) 501–31, reprinted in: Fitzmyer, *A Wandering Aramean: Collected Aramaic Essays* (SBLMS 25; Chico, CA: Scholars, 1979) 29–56. According to Fitzmyer, there is very little colloquial Hebrew attested in Palestine in the first century outside of the Qumran texts. Within the scrolls literature, 4QMMT approximates the colloquial verbal system, in contrast with other major texts from Qumran; see Smith, *The Origins and Development of the Waw-Consecutive: Northwest Semitic Evidence from Ugarit to Qumran* (HSS 39; Atlanta, GA: Scholars, 1991), 35–63, and "Grammatically Speaking: The Participle as a Main Verb of Clauses (Predicative Participle) in Direct Discourse and Narrative in Pre-Mishnaic Hebrew," in: *Sirach, Scrolls and Sages: Proceedings of a Second International Symposium on the Hebrew of the Dead Sea Scrolls, Ben Sira and the Mishnah, held at Leiden University, 15–17 December 1997* (ed. T. Muraoka and J. F. Elwolde; Studies in the Texts of the Judean Desert 33; Leiden/Boston: Brill, 1999) 278–332, esp. 313–18. 4QMMT may represent a good test-case for Schwartz's elite spoken Hebrew. In this connection, one may note the use of the predicative participle not only in 4QMMT, but also in the liturgical Songs of the Sabbath Sacrifice. In Schwartz's model, Aramaic texts such as the Genesis Apocryphon, Enoch and the Targum of Job, might be explained as efforts by the elite to make Genesis and Job more widely accessible according to the norms of their authors. However, this sort of explanation would not indicate why literary texts such as the New Jerusalem, the Testament of Levi or Tobit, were produced in Aramaic. Additional factors may be involved.

[148] Cf. Boyer, "Censorship as a Vocation," 517.

[149] This information is drawn from VanderKam, "Greek at Qumran,"175–81, esp. 176. VanderKam cites the more detailed treatment of the 4Q464 passage by E. Eshel and M. Stone, "The Holy Language at the End of Days Found in Light of a New Fragment Found at Qumran," *Tarbiz* 62 (1993) 169–77 (Hebrew).

[150] VanderKam, "Greek at Qumran," 176–79.

[151] Schniedewind, "Qumran Hebrew as an Antilanguage," *JBL* 118 (1999) 235–52. See also Steve Weitzman, "Why did the Qumran Community Write in Hebrew?" *JAOS* 119 (1999) 35–45; George Brooke, "Between Authority and Canon: The Significance of Reworking the Bible for Understanding the Canonical Process," in: *Reworking the*

linguistically dominant manner, the Qumran community generated its own system of self-referential language drawn exegetically (or perhaps eisegetically, depending on one's perspective) from biblical terms (e. g., leadership terms such as "the Teacher of Righteousness," cf. Hosea 10:12, Joel 2:23; note also *doreš, mebaqqer, maśkil* and *paqid,* all biblical terms),[152] and from emblematic biblical figures (not only famous figures claimed more broadly, especially Moses and David,[153] but also other biblical figures such as Enoch and Melchiṣedeq).

The classicizing tendencies of Qumran Hebrew point to a related effort to claim the biblical past as continuous with its present: the Qumran community as the Israel of old.[154] James VanderKam has suggested that this biblical reclamation included the picture of the Qumran community as the Israel journeying in the wilderness and receiving the Torah at Mount Sinai.[155] VanderKam believes that the community's very name for itself, *yḥd (literally, "unity") derives from the Sinai covenant as described in

---

Bible: Apocryphal and Related Texts at Qumran: Proceedings of a Joint Symposium by the Orion Center for the Study of the Dead Sea Scrolls and Associated Literature and the Hebrew University Institute for Advanced Studies Research Group on Qumran, 15–17 January, 2002 (ed. Esther G. Chazon, Devorah Dimant and Ruth A. Clements; STDJ LVIII; Leiden/Boston: Brill, 2005) 91–94; and David M. Carr, *Writing on the Tablet of the Heart: Origins of Scripture and Literature* (Oxford/New York: Oxford University, 2005) 253–60.

[152] Note also the polemical "movers of the boundaries" in CD 6:2–11, 19:15–16, 4Q266 1a–b 4, 4Q280 3 2, borrowed evidently from Hosea 5:10 (see Schiffman, *Reclaiming the Dead Sea Scrolls,* 249). See also "seekers of flattery" in 1QH^a 10:32, 4Q163 23 ii 10, 4Q169 3–4 I 2 and 7, 4 ii 2–7 taken from Daniel 11:32 (so Cross, *The Ancient Library of Qumran,* 97 n. 2)

[153] The claims laid to biblical figures were hardly indiscriminant. For example, there are no biblical wisdom figures such as Solomon serving emblematically in the Qumran literature (the name of Solomon occurs only 7 times in only 5 different texts: twice for locations in 3Q15 V, 6, 8; once for some sort of chronology in 4Q247, fragment 1, line 3; the other passages are unclear). In contrast, David is mentioned 31 times in 15 different texts, including one that glorifies David's wisdom (11QPs^a 27:2), with the number of his compositions put at 4,050 (11QPs^a 27:10), apparently said quite deliberately to exceed those of Solomon put at 4,005 in MT 1 Kings 5:12. Even the reference to Solomon in 11QPsAp^a has been seen to glorify David; so Pablo A. Torijano, *Solomon the Esoteric King: From King to Magus, Development of a Tradition* (JSJ Supplements 73; Leiden/Boston/Köln: Brill, 2002) 46–50. Might this lack of appeal to Solomon represent some sort of reaction at Qumran against wisdom as a particular category of religious expression or against some forms of it? In Qumran literature, the words, "wise one" (*ḥkm*) and "wisdom" (*ḥkmh*), take on a rather general cast, often situated within the constellation of terms for religious understanding and piety. In the case of 11QPs^a 27:2–11, David as *ḥkm* is an element within a larger construal of wisdom as part and parcel of piety and prophecy.

[154] Schniedewind, "Qumran Hebrew as an Antilanguage," 244–47; Brooke, "Between Authority and Canon," 99.

[155] James C. VanderKam, "Sinai Revisited," in: *Biblical Interpretation at Qumran* (ed. Matthias Henze; Grand Rapids, MI/Cambridge, UK: Eerdmans, 2005) 44–60.

Exodus 19:7: "The people all answered together [*yḥdw*]: 'Everything that Yahweh has spoken we will do.'" John Collins proposes a similar biblical basis for the community name, "the union (*yaḥad*) of the tribes of Israel" in Deuteronomy 33:5.[156] These biblical passages provide the sort of Hebrew expression that the Qumran movement used for itself,[157] perhaps as a Jewish translation responding to, perhaps even reacting against, the sort of organization known in Greek terms as a *koinon,* "association, union."[158] In any case, the Qumran use of biblical language creates the movement in the image of biblical Israel. A precise calibration of Israel past and Israel present made in Qumran texts, accessed through the community's use of scripture, aimed for the ideal picture, a self-model of and for the community. In Boyer's terms, "such labors were believed to channel the productivity of language toward an ontohistorically determined and perfected mode of representation, not … to simply restrict creative and political possibilities."[159] To deploy a true language for ontological reality was arguably the supreme act of creative, textual possibility for the community.

Protecting God: The Role of Censorship in the Greco-Roman Context

To return to the cases of censorship, they may be located in this larger context of linguistic coherence, textual production and cultural capital developed for the benefit of the religious tradition and the perceived well-being of the people. Linguistic coherence seems to be a major goal: "mass media language had to maximally rid itself of polyvalent meanings and imprecise significations."[160] This factor may well be part of the ancient story. Perhaps the ancient tradents viewed the two passages that they corrected as in need

---

[156] Collins, "The *Yaḥad* and 'the Qumran Community'."

[157] For the biblical use of the word for covenantal contexts, see further Paul Kalluveettil, *Declaration and Covenant: A Comprehensive Review of Covenant Formulae from the Old Testament and the Ancient Near East* (Analecta Biblica 88; Rome: Pontifical Biblical Institute, 1982) 53.

[158] So Bruno W. Dombrowski, "היחד in 1QS and *to koinon:* An Instance of Early Greek and Jewish Synthesis," *HTR* 59 (1966) 293–307 (reference courtesy of John Collins). Perhaps striking for Dombrowski's view is the attestation in this period of *to koinon* on a Greek inscription accompanying a Phoenician inscription concerning the Sidonian community (*gw;* KAI 60:2, 5, 7, 8). For the Phoenician usage, see Charles Krahmalkov, *Phoenician-Punic Dictionary* (OLA 90; Studia Phoenicia XV; Leuven: Peeters/Department of Oriental Studies, 2000) 137–38. The attestation of the word in KAI 164:3 is not mentioned by Krahmalkov, and it is listed as an uncertain reading in *DNWSI* 1.215. See also the important monograph by Moshe Weinfeld, *The Organizational Pattern and Penal Code of the Qumran Sect: A Comparison with Guilds and Religious Associations of the Hellenistic-Roman World* (Fribourg: Editions Universitaires; Göttingen: Vandenhoeck & Ruprecht, 1986).

[159] Boyer, "Censorship as a Vocation," 537.

[160] Boyer, "Censorship as a Vocation," 533.

of such clarification. Yet, one may ask about their goal, since they did not think of themselves as censors (note Boyer, "there was no ministry of media control in the GDR, there were even no 'official' censors"[161]). Moreover, this textual production was used against the perceived cultural pressures of Hellenistic learning and prestige (read for the GDR situation, "the West German state, which had simply given in to the default 'stomach-society' of international capitalism" for the GDR situation[162]).

The two cases of textual censorship are particularly striking for their emphasis on the singularity of the deity. While monotheism had been important within the Jewish people from the exile onwards, it does not entirely preclude Judean translatability in host countries. Thus we meet in a Persian period letter from Egypt addressed by one Judean to another with the blessing: "I bless you by Yaho and Khn[ub]."[163] Whatever the correct reconstruction, it is evident, as H. L. Ginsberg notes, that "the writer in any case invokes another deity besides Yaho."[164] Blessings of "the gods" ('*lhy*', governing the plural verb *yš'lw*, "may they seek") are requested in other Judean texts from Elephantine.[165] Some instances are clear (AP 39:2; 56:1 + 34:1), while others are reconstructed, at least in part (AP 21:2; 37:1–2, showing the plural form of the verb). Similar expressions of "the gods" appear in the proverbs of Ahiqar #37 (lines 123b–124a) and #39 (line 126).[166] Accordingly, this usage may be viewed as part and parcel of the larger context of the Elephantine Judean community. Perhaps not so much weight should be put on this sort of expression, as it may be little more than "a fossilized formula."[167] At the same time, sometimes Judeans use the name of their god in the same blessing formula when they address fellow Judeans.[168] So perhaps the usage is an indicator of religious sensibility. Taken together, the evidence from Elephantine points to at least a limited or general translatability on the

---

[161] Boyer, "Censorship as a Vocation," 524. See futher below pp. 270–72.

[162] Boyer, "Censorship as a Vocation," 531.

[163] *ANET* 491. In connection with the question of translatability at Elephantine, it is to be added that in view of the scholarly disagreements, this study will not enter into the knotty problems surrounding the figures of Eshembethel, Anatbethel and Herembethel in the Elephantine material. This is an old problem; see Emil G. Kraeling, *The Brooklyn Museum Aramaic Papyri: New Documents of the Fifth Century B. C. from the Jewish Colony at Elephantine* (New Haven: Yale University; London: Geoffrey Cumberlege, Oxford University, 1953) 87–91; and Porten, *Archives from Elephantine,* 151–86.

[164] *ANET* 491 n. 11. See also Kraeling, *The Brooklyn Museum Aramaic Papyri,* 86.

[165] See Kraeling, *The Brooklyn Museum Aramaic Papyri,* 84.

[166] Lindenberger, "The Gods of Ahiqar," *UF* 14 (1982) 107–8.

[167] So Ginsberg, *ANET* 491 n. 3, with reference only to the so-called "Passover Payrus," AP 21.

[168] For example, Clermont-Ganneau 186, lines 1–2 (ca. 475 BCE), edited in more recent years by James M. Lindenberger, *Ancient Aramaic and Hebrew Letters* (ed. Kent Harold Richards; SBLWAW 4; Atlanta: Scholars, 1994) 49.

part of Judeans in Egypt. Translatability within the land was also possible in the Persian period. A possible case of iconography involving translatability has been thought to obtain in the case of a famous fourth century BCE coin marked with the name of the Persian province, Yehud (*yhd*) and portraying a bearded, enthroned figure that reminds some commentators of Zeus; he presumably is to be identified with the Jewish god, in view of the place-name on the coin.[169] Over the course of the Persian period, Judean translatability was hardly exceptional. How far it went is another matter.

With Chapters Five and Six we move into the Greco-Roman context. In this context Judean engagement within the wider world seems to intensify from both sides. Judean monotheism contributed to the palatability of Jewish identity in the wider context of the Hellenistic world, where philosophy had been becoming increasingly "monotheistic" as well.[170] Indeed, monotheism was asserted as a prestigious element of Jewish identity (Letter of Aristeas, 131–141), considered compatible with Platonic thought (Philo of Alexandria, *De opificio mundi*, 170–172).[171] The potential reverse danger for Jewish monotheism in this context involves what we have been calling in this study "translatability" of divinity, namely the claim sometimes expressed by Judeans outside the land that the Jewish god could be identified with Greek gods. In Chapter Six, we will look at cases of Jewish translatability from the Letter of Aristeas and the Jewish historian, Aristobulus.

The two cases of textual censorship that we saw correlate with the lack of textual cases of translatability of divinity within Judea. To be sure, embrace

---

[169] For a drawing of the coin with discussion of various views, see Ya'akov Meshorer, *Ancient Jewish Coinage: Volume I: Persian Period through Hasmonaeans* (Dix Hills, NY: Amphora, 1982) 21–26; see also Lester L. Grabbe, *A History of Jews and Judaism in the Second Temple Period, Volume 1. Yehud: A History of the Persian Period of Judah* (Library of Second Temple Studies 47; London/New York: T & T Clark International, 2004) 66–67. For this figure, compare Samarian coinage with the name and image of Zeus as well as the seated male thought to be Yahweh. For the former, see Ya'akov Meshorer and Shraga Qedar, *Samarian Coinage* (Publications of the Israel Numismatic Society, Numismatic Studies and Researches IX; Jerusalem: The Israel Numismatic Society, 1999) 29 and 90, coin #40; for the latter, see Meshorer and Qedar, *Samarian Coinage,* 37, 85, 99 and 106, coins #13, 84, 100, 124. Both are bearded male figures.
[170] See John J. Collins, *Between Athens and Jerusalem: Jewish Identity in the Hellenistic Diaspora* (second ed.; The Biblical Resources Series; Grand Rapids, MI/Cambridge, UK: Eerdmans; Livonia, MI: Dove, 2000) 158–59.
[171] See J. M. G. Barclay, *Jews in the Mediterranean Diaspora: From Alexander to Trajan (323 BCE – 117 CE)* (Berkeley/Los Angeles/London: University of California, 1996) 145, 164–65, 429–32; Collins, *Between Athens and Jerusalem,* 158. For the latter passage, see F. H. Colson and G. H. Whitaker, *Philo I* (LCL; Cambridge: Harvard University; London: W. Heinemann, 1956) 134–35.

of so-called Hellenistic culture was evident.[172] In John Collins' terms, Judeans embraced Hellenistic culture prior to the Maccabean revolt (including the institutions of the gymnasium). However, Judeans seem to have deployed considerably less intellectual energy to demonstrate philosophical compatability, compared with their compatriots in the Alexandrian context (see the didactic poem of Pseudo-Phocylides[173]); we have no philosophical works in Judea in contrast to the Alexandrian context. Instead, a major concern for many Jews in Judea was to assert their traditional religious practices against Hellenistic cult backed by the ruling powers (such as the Herodians). It may be supposed that such notions of translatability could be entertained by various thinkers,[174] but as John Collins and Steven Fine suggest,[175] the actual practice of cult represented a general dividing line. Even sacrifice performed for the emperor represented a Jewish strategy that acknowledged the larger political situation without abdicating traditional sacrificial or religious norms. This cultic line of division perhaps included the conceptual centerpiece of its cultic practice, its monotheism, as expressed in concrete, ritual practice. If this understanding of the situation within Judea is correct, then the story about translatability and its lack in Judea would bring us back to the original question about biblical censorship: the concern about the relativity of divinity in the Greco-Roman context potentially seen in expressions of translatability may lie at the root of the cases of biblical censorship that also appear in this period.

From this discussion, it may be surmised that protection of this precious cultural commodity of scriptural text and deity within the land might have played a role in the two cases of censorship that we examined in this chapter. These textual traditions, too, derive from the land (MT, Targums, Vulgate). Possible perceptions of polytheism in their own textual traditions might have made Judeans seem to themselves too much like the Greek polytheism of the pre-Alexandrian era, or perhaps even more threatening, too akin to the philosophical monotheism expressed in the Greco-Roman

---

[172] See the surveys of Momigliano, *Essays on Ancient and Modern Judaism,* 19–24; Hengel, "Judaism and Hellenism Revisited," 6–37; and Collins, "Cult and Culture: The Limits of Hellenization," in: *Hellenism in the Land of Israel* (ed. John J. Collins and Gregory E. Sterling; Christianity and Judaism in Antiquity Series 13; South Bend, in: University of Notre Dame, 2001) 38–61.
[173] See Barclay, *Jews in the Mediterranean Diaspora,* 337–41.
[174] This subject is taken up in Chapter Six.
[175] Collins, "Cult and Culture," 38–61; Steven Fine, *Art and Judaism in the Greco-Roman World: Toward a New Jewish Archaeology* (Cambridge: Cambridge University, 2005) 70–73. Fine places particular weight on the Maccabean revolt as a point of transition when aniconism (what he would prefer to understand as a stricture against idolatrous imagery or "anti-idolatry") increased in status as a marker of Jewish identity. See also the remarks of Martin Goodman, "Trajan and the Origins of Roman Hostility to the Jews," *Past and Present* 182 (2004) 11–12.

world. Small textual changes may represent a reaction against expressions of translatability between the Jewish god and non-Jewish gods (discussed in Chapter Six). As the Seleucids with their efforts to alter the Temple to their liking[176] impinged on the Jewish people in Judea, it perhaps ventured into own past in order to prevent what it regarded as false intimations of its own ancient idolatry and to salvage its own cultural identity. In some instances, it overwrote possible biblical antecedents for negotiating between the Jewish god and other gods; in others, it simply overlooked them or read them monotheistically. This general operation clearly adhered to the larger guidelines about other gods present in the Bible and seconded by tradition. Thus biblical censorship perhaps played a role, perhaps a relatively minor one, not only in "saving" Jewish monotheism from appearances of polytheism (Genesis 14:22), but also from the appearance of translatability between the Jewish god and its apparently nearest non-Jewish comparands (Deuteronomy 32:8–9). There would be exceptions, as Jews and Jewish texts engaged the wider Greco-Roman world.

Finally, we may relate this discussion about censorship here to a basic insight about culture from Edward T. Hall's book, *The Silent Language*. In his work, Hall suggests: "Culture hides much more than it reveals, and strangely enough what it hides, it hides most effectively from its own participants."[177] For the GDR as for ancient Judea, Hall's pithy formulation (used as the epigraph for this chapter) perhaps expresses the first motivation and final aim of textual censorship: censors perform explicitly what cultures do implicitly, so that what they think at a given point in time or tradition is represented as if it had always been so and should be and hopefully would be in the future. And in expressing their belief that their socialist state was superior to the competitive world of West Germany (as they understood it), GDR censors could hope to hide from themselves what they would or did not face. Perhaps Israel and its textual tradents, in expressing its belief that there were no other deities apart from Yahweh, could hide signs of its own polytheistic past. Perhaps they did so unconsciously; it was a past hidden even from them.

In the next chapter, we turn to the Greco-Roman world, when the question of translatability emerges as an intense topic throughout the Mediterranean. The international context of the Greco-Roman world altered the relationship between summodeism and translatability, compared with what we noted in Chapter Three for seventh-sixth century Mesopotamia and Israel. For, as we will see in Chapter Five, the international context of the

---

[176] See Chapter Six, in particular pp. 283–88 for Seleucid efforts at effecting translatability with the Jewish god with their changes to the Temple.

[177] Hall, *The Silent Language,* 53. See also Holquist, "Corrupt Originals," 15.

Greco-Roman world generated forms of summodeism that were hardly the end of translatability. Rather, this period witnessed an explosion in the cross-cultural understanding of divinity. It is to this new era of translatability that we now turn.

Chapter Five

"The Beautiful Essence of All the Gods": Translatability in the Greco-Roman World

One Zeus, one Hades,
one Helios, one Dionysius,
One god in all.
Orphic Fragment 239[1]

1. Jan Assmann on Translatability in the Greco-Roman Period

As we enter the Greco-Roman period, we meet an explosion in translatability across the Mediterranean. Compared with either the Late Bronze Age context or Iron Age Israel, the Greco-Roman period represents a dramatic increase in cases of translatability as well as the range of its genres and social settings. Jan Assmann mentions "well-known cases" of the "*interpretatio Latina* of Greek divinities and the *interpretatio Graeca* of Egyptian ones."[2] Pliny the Elder (*Natural History*, Book II, v 15) puts the general point in a pithy formulation for deities in the world, that they are a matter of "different names to different peoples" (*nomina alia aliis gentibus*).[3]

Assmann cites some very striking examples of the same divinity said to be underlying the names of various deities in different lands. He notes a particularly good case in the eleventh book of the *Metamorphoses* (also

---

[1] This text is discussed by Assmann, *Moses the Egyptian: The Memory of Egypt in Western Monotheism* (Cambridge, MA: Harvard University, 1997) 51, 228 n. 71. The citation derives from Pseudo-Justin, *Cohortatio ad Graecos*, 15 (Carl R. Holladay, *Fragments from Hellenistic Jewish Authors. Volume IV: Orphica* [SBLTT 40, Pseudepigrapha series 14; Atlanta: Scholars Press, 1996] 107) = *Orphicorum Fragmenta*, 239 (Otto Kern, *Ophicorum Fragmenta* [Berlin: Weidmann, 1922; repr., 1963] 251–52). The first part is quoted also in Macrobius, *The Saturnalia*, 1.18.17. For a handy translation of the passage in Macrobius, see Percival Vaughan Davies, *Macrobius. The Saturnalia* (New York/London: Columbia University, 1969) 131. Kern treats the variants.

[2] Assmann, *Moses the Egyptian*, 45. See also *Interpretatio Romana*, in: Alain Cadotte, *La romanisation des dieux: l'interpretatio romana en Afrique du Nord sous le Haut-Empire* (Religions in the Graeco-Roman World 158; Leiden: Brill, 2006).

[3] H. Rackham, *Pliny. Natural History I. Praefatio. Libri I, II* (LCL; Cambridge, MA: Harvard University; London: W. Heinemann, 1938) 178–79: "different races have different names."

known as *The Golden Ass*), written by Apuleius of Madaurus in the second century CE. The "Queen of Heaven," invoked by the figure of Lucius toward the opening of this book (11.2), goes by different names among different peoples:

My divinity is one, worshipped by all the world under different forms, with various rites, and by manifold names. In one place, the Phrygians, first-born of men, call me Pessinuntine Mother of the Gods [Cybele], in another the autochthonous people of Attica call me Cecropian Minerva [Athene], in another the sea-washed Cyprians call me Paphian Venus [probably West Semitic Astarte]; to the arrow-bearing Cretans I am Dictynna Diana, to the trilingual Sicilians Ortygian Proserpina, to the ancient people of Eleusis Attic Ceres; some call me Juno, some Bellona, others Hecate, and still others Rhamnusia [Nemesis].[4]

In her response to Lucius, the goddess reveals her "true name" (*Metamorphoses*, XI, 5): "the Egyptians who excel by having the original doctrine honor me with my distinctive rites and give me my true name of Queen Isis."[5] This sort of identification of a deity by different names was neither unique nor novel. Interpretation of many deities as deriving from one deity (and not merely subordinate) was a relatively common feature of Greco-Roman philosophical literature.[6]

---

[4] See J. Arthur Hanson, *Apuleius. Metamorphoses II* (LCL; Cambridge, MA/London: Harvard University, 1989) 299, 301. I have added in square brackets the commonly accepted identifications of some of these figures, almost all of which are provided by Hanson. For further information, see J. Gwen Griffiths, *The Isis-Book (Metamorphoses XI): Apuleius of Madauros* (EPRO 39; Leiden: Brill, 1975).

[5] This is the translation in: Assmann, *Moses the Egyptian*, 48–49; cf. Hanson, *Apuleius. Metamorphoses II*, 301. See also the discussion of Fritz Graf, "What is Ancient Mediterranean Religion," in: *Religions of the Ancient World: A Guide* (ed. Sarah Iles Johnston; Cambridge, MA/London: Belknap, 2004) 3; and Theodore M. Ludwig, "Monotheism," in: *ER* 9.6156. Isis was attributed divine names in the Isis aretalogies that relate this goddess to deities of other lands; see, for example, the Kyme aretalogy presented in: Ross Shepard Kraemer, ed., *Women's Religions in the Greco-Roman World: A Sourcebook* (Oxford/New York: Oxford University, 2004) 456–58. For the aretalogies more generally, see Sharon Kelly Heyob, *The Cult of Isis among Women in the Greco-Roman World* (EPRO 51; Leiden: Brill, 1975) 45–47; Garth Fowden, *The Egyptian Hermes. A Historical Approach to the Pagan Mind* (Princeton, NJ: Princeton University, 1986) 45–52; and Henk S. Versnel, "Thrice One: Three Greek Experiments in Oneness," in: *One God or Many? Concepts of Divinity in the Ancient World* (ed. Barbara Nevling Porter; Transactions of the Casco Bay Assyriological Institute, vol. 1; np: np, 2000) 132–38. Compare Isis in Plutarch; see J.G. Griffiths, *Plutarch's De Iside et Osiride* (Cambridge: Cambridge University, 1970) esp. 502–3; Daniel S. Richter, "Plutarch on Isis and Osiris: Text, Cult and Cultural Appreciation," *Transactions of the American Philological Association* 131 (2001) 191–216; *PDMT* 285 n. 6; and for a convenient translation, see Kraemer, ed., *Women's Religions*, 433–38. For Isis generally, see also the interesting study of H.S. Versnel, *Inconsistencies in Greek and Roman Religion I: Ter Unus. Isis, Dionysius, Hermes: Three Studies in Henotheism* (second ed.; Studies in Greek and Roman Religion, vol. 6, I; Leiden/New York/Köln: Brill, 1998) 39–95.

[6] See Michael Frede, "Monotheism and Pagan Philosophy in Later Antiquity," in:

Assmann locates this one-deity notion within a long lineage going back to the Late Bronze Age. For the one-deity notion in this period, Assmann[7] cites the case of the Hymn to Amun (Papyrus Leiden I 350), chapter 300: "All the gods are three: Amun, the Sun and Ptah, without their seconds. His (the supreme god?) identity is hidden in Amun, his is the Sun as face, his body as Ptah."[8] Assmann also notes Papyrus Chester Beatty IV recto x 2.[9] Alfonso Archi[10] compares Isis as universal goddess (cited above) with the Late Bronze Age prayer of Pudu-hepa to the Sun-goddess of Arinna, whom she sees behind the goddess Hebat: "O Sun-goddess of Arinna, queen of all countries! In the Hatti country you bear the name of the Sun-goddess of Arinna; but in the land which you made the cedar land you bear the name Hebat."[11] This representation may evoke the description of Isis as "the beautiful essence of all the gods" (*theon hapanton to kalon zoon*) in a text from the Oxyrhynchus papyri (11.1380, lines 126–127, used for the title of this chapter).[12] So in particular texts, it might be suggested that there was a notion of a "universal" god or "universal" goddess. For an example from the Iron Age, we might look to the figure of Marduk in Enuma Elish, and in particular the god's fifty names discussed in Chapter Three. Marduk is considered the god no matter what name is used; a number of his names are West Semitic and not originally Mesopotamian (such as Adad). Like Mar-

---

Pagan Monotheism in Late Antiquity (ed. Polymnia Athanassiadi and Michael Frede; Oxford: Clarendon; New York: Oxford University, 1999) 41–67, esp. 51–55. In addition to the material cited, note Zeus as the focus of monotheistic or near-monotheistic expression in Stoic circles, for example in Cleanthes' *Hymn to Zeus*. See the discussion in: Johan C. Thom, *Cleanthes' Hymn to Zeus* (Studien und Texte zu Antike und Christentum 33; Tübingen: Mohr Siebeck, 2005) 45, 47, 48 n. 33. For further discussion, see Polymnia Athanassiadi and Michael Frede, "Introduction," in: *Pagan Monotheism in Late Antiquity* (ed. Polymnia Athanassiadi and Michael Frede; Oxford: Clarendon; New York: Oxford University, 1999) 8; and William Horbury, *Herodian Judaism and New Testament Study* (WUNT 193; Tübingen: Mohr Siebeck, 2006) 2–33.

    [7] Assmann, *The Search for God in Ancient Egypt* (trans. David Lorton; Ithaca, NY/ London: Cornell University, 2001) 10–13. See above p. 55 n. 81.

    [8] *COS* 1.25.

    [9] See *ANET* 372.

    [10] Alfonso Archi includes this prayer as well as the deities cited in treaties (discussed in Chapter One) with a number of Greco-Roman cases discussed in this chapter (in particular, Herodotus, *History*, Book 2, 50–58). See Archi, "Hurrian Gods and the Festivals of the Hattian-Hittite Layer," in: *The Life and Times of Ḫattušili III and Tutḫaliya IV: Proceedings of a Symposium in Honour of J. De Roos, 12–13 December, 20003, Leiden* (ed. Theo P. J. van den Hout, with the assistance of C. H. van Zoest (Leiden: Nederlands Instituut voor het Nabije Oosten, 2006) 147–48.

    [11] *ANET* 393. See the discussion above and in Chapter One, pp. 88–89 above.

    [12] As noted by Assmann, *Moses the Egyptian,* 50, 228 n. 67, cited from Bernard P. Grenfell and Arthur S. Hunt, *The Oxyrhynchus Papyri: Part 11* (London: Egypt Exploration Fund, 1915) 197–98. For a convenient translation, see Kraemer, ed., *Women's Religions,* 454–56.

duk, Isis is her "true name." Like Marduk, Isis in some contexts is regarded in a sense as the sum of divinity, as a form of what I called "summodeism," in Chapter Three.

At the same time, there are important differences in the summodeism of Amun and Marduk compared with Isis. The "one-god" discourse in both the Bronze Age and Iron Age contexts, whether for Amun, or for Marduk and Assur or Yahweh, was not cross-cultural; it was rather an inner-cultural discourse. There is no consistent matching of Marduk's alternative names with the peoples of other nations, as there is for Isis. In contrast, Greco-Roman "one-god" discourse is often cross-cultural. It is thus a new form of summodeism, certainly a new development compared to what appeared with Marduk, Assur and Yahweh toward the end of the Iron Age. The "one-god" discourse of Marduk (and arguably for Amun) was not a matter of translatability, but an expression of political power. The imperialist expressions of the gods Assur and Marduk as the one god are particularly notable in this regard.

Compared with either the Bronze or Iron Ages, the Greco-Roman context is particularly marked by this one-god discourse. Compared with earlier periods, this one is remarkable in this regard. The recognition of the same super-deity underlying the chief deity of various peoples was broader than the case of Isis. Assmann's examples include what he calls the idea of a "Supreme Being" (Greek *hupsistos,* "the Highest One").[13] The examples noted by Assmann involve three or four gods regarded as manifestations of this one super-god, such as the Orphic Fragment 239 used as the epigraph for this chapter: "One Zeus, one Hades, one Helios, one Dionysius, One god in all." This sort of super-deity is one important type of divine translatability that Assmann observes in this period. In addition to the various Greco-Roman instances discussed by Assmann, we may note different genres exhibiting cases of translatability.

---

[13] The following discussion and examples draw from Assmann, *Moses the Egyptian,* 51. For this title, see also the older, fine study by Arthur Darby Nock, with C. Roberts and T. C. Skeat, "The Gild of Zeus Hypsistos," in his *Essays on Religion and the Ancient World* (vol. 1; ed. Zeph Stewart; Cambridge, MA: Harvard University, 1972) 414–43; and the recent observations of James K. Aitken, "The God of the pre-Maccabees: Designation of the Divine in the Early Hellenistic Period," in: *The God of Israel* (ed. Robert P. Gordon; University of Cambridge Oriental Publications 64; Cambridge, UK: Cambridge University, 2007) 264–65.

2. Genres of Greco-Roman Translatability

This discussion surveys Greco-Roman genres of translatability as known in earlier periods and then other types of texts particularly notable in the Greco-Roman context. We start with multilingual texts and treaties, then move into blessings and curses (particularly in magic), and finally turn to histories and philosophical discourse. The goal of this discussion is not an overall survey, but in keeping with a work focused on the "biblical world," the bulk of the cases addressed hail from the eastern Mediterranean.

Multi-lingual Texts and Treaties

Multi-lingual texts in the Greco-Roman period reflect a long tradition of translatability continued from earlier periods. The site of Pyrgi (modern Santa Severa), one of the port-towns serving the Etruscan town of Caere (modern Cerveteri) about 30 miles west-northwest of Rome, yielded a Phoenician-Etruscan bilingual from the Persian period.[14] The text (KAI 277), dated ca. 500, identifies Astarte with Uni-Juno.[15] This sort of translatability was part and parcel of an Etruscan translatability that took over Greek gods such as Apollo.[16] It would become more widespread in the Roman appropriation of Greek gods, their iconography and their stories.[17] Translatability of Greek deities is also well known further east in the Greco-Roman period.

We have a number of multilingual inscriptions from Cyprus that illustrate the practice. A well-known bilingual Phoenician-Greek dedicatory inscription from Lapethos dated to the late fourth century (KAI 42:1) identifies Anat and Athena. Edward Lipiński notes an earlier temple of Athena as well as some inscriptional evidence for this goddess at Idalion.[18] Based on this evidence, Lipiński suggests that the identification of Athena with Anat in this region could go back at least to the sixth century. If

---

[14] See Joseph A. Fitzmyer, "The Phoenician Inscription from Pyrgi," *JAOS* 86 (1966) 285. For the dialect (Phoenician and not Punic), see Philip C. Schmitz, "The Phoenician Text from the Etruscan Sanctuary at Pyrgi," *JAOS* 115 (1995) 559–75, with extensive bibliography.

[15] Robert Turcan, *The Cults of the Roman Empire* (trans. Antonia Nevill; Oxford/Malden, MA: Blackwell, 1996) 4. For further discussion of context and date, see Fitzmyer, "The Phoenician Inscription from Pyrgi," 288–89.

[16] Cf. what has been called *Interpretatio Etrusca;* see L. B. van der Meer, *Interpretatio Etrusca: Greek Myths on Etruscan Mirrors* (Leiden: Brill, 1995).

[17] In this vein, see Fritz Graf, "Myth," in: *Religions of the Ancient World: A Guide* (ed. Sarah Iles Johnston; Cambridge, MA/London: Belknap, 2004) 56.

[18] Lipiński, *Dieux et déesses de l'univers phénicien et punique* (OLA 64; Studia Phoenicia XIV; Leuven: Peeters and Departement Oosterse Studies, 1995) 309–13, esp. 312.

correct, this particular example of translatability enjoyed a considerably long history in this part of Cyprus. The island offers other examples of translatability. Texts from the island identified male deities, just as they do for goddesses. In an inscription from Tomassos (KAI 41) dated ca. 363, the Semitic deity Resheph (generally reconstructed *[rš]p* in line 3 of the broken portion of the Phoenician) corresponds to the god Apollo in the Greek (line 4, spelled *apeiloni* in the Greek and *a-pe-i-lo-ni* in the Cyprian). The same identification appears in the Phoenician-Cypriot bilingual from Idalion (KAI 39:3, ca. 389).[19] This figure is not Resheph in general, but a specific Resheph known by the title *(h)mkl* (KAI 38:2, 39:3, 40:5).[20] This epithet derives from the name of a sanctuary of Apollo in the Peloponnesus, according to Lipiński. Thus in this case, Resheph was known by a particular Greek identification. As with Athena and Anat, there was a substantial tradition for the correspondence between the Greek god and his local Phoenician counterpart.

A similar sort of identification in Greek and Punic appears in multilingual contexts further west in the Mediterranean.[21] In texts from Algeria, the votive formula that begins in Punic with "the lord Baal Ḥmn and the lady Tnt, Face of Baal" (e.g., KAI 164:1), opens in the Greek translations of the same formulary with "Kronos (and) Thenneith, face of Baal" (e.g., KAI 176:1–3).[22] Thus Baal Ḥmn is represented in the Greek versions as Kronos. We could review more cases in the Mediterranean west (such as the second century Phoenician-Greek text from Malta, KAI 47). Whether in the west or the east, these multilingual texts are somewhat reminiscent of the Ugaritic

---

[19] See William J. Fulco, S.J., *The Canaanite God Rešep* (AOS Essays 8; New Haven, CT: American Oriental Society, 1976) 51–52.

[20] For evidence and discussion, see Lipiński, "Resheph Amyklos," in: *Phoenicia and the Eastern Mediterranean in the First Millennium B. C.* (ed. E. Lipiński; OLA 22; Leuven: Peeters and Departement Oosterse Studies, 1987) 87–99. See also Lipiński, *Dieux et déesses de l'univers phénicien et punique,* 188.

[21] The following examples derive from Levantine colonization of North Africa. For the broader question in the Roman period, see Alain Cadotte, ed., *La romanisation des dieux: l'interpretatio romana en Afrique du Nord sous le Haut-Empire* (Religions in the Graeco-Roman World 158; Leiden: Brill, 2006).

[22] For further discussion, see Karel Jongeling and Robert M. Kerr, ed., *Late Punic Epigraphy* (Tübingen: Mohr Siebeck, 2005) 79–80, which regards the Greek form as a calque of the Punic (see p. 84 for further Punic attestations of Baal Ḥmn). For discussion of the name in Punic, Greek and Latin sources, see Maurice Sznycer, *Les passages puniques en transcription Latine dans le 'Poenulus' de Plaute* (Études et commentaries LXV; Paris: Librairie C. Klincksieck, 1967) 50–51. For the identification of Baal Ḥmn as "Lord of the Amanus," see Frank M. Cross, *Canaanite Myth and Hebrew Epic: Essays in the History of the Religion of Israel* (Cambridge, MA/London: Harvard University, 1973) 25–26, 35–36; and the critique of this identification in: Albert I. Baumgarten, *The Phoenician History of Philo of Byblos: A Commentary* (EPRO 89; Leiden: Brill, 1981) 154–55.

multi-columned polyglot with divine names (discussed in Chapter One), insofar as they show parallel divine names in texts where cultures meet. These situations around the Mediterranean basin involve identifications of Semitic and non-Semitic deities.

Bilingual treaties in this period cite the deities of the human parties involved as witnesses, as we find in the Late Bronze Age context. For example, we see the traditional listing of deities in the treaty of Philip V of Macedonia and Hannibal of Carthage concluded in 215 BCE/BC.[23] Such instances are not so far removed from the practices of the Bronze Age context that we examined earlier in Chapter One. As an instructive contrast, we may illustrate literary expressions of international relations used *without* any list of deities. For example, 1 Maccabees 12:19–23 contains the following expression:

This is a copy of the letter that was sent to Onias:
"Arius king of the Spartans sends greetings to Onias the high priest.
A document has been found stating that the Spartans and the Jews are brothers; both nations descended from Abraham. Now that we have learned this, kindly write to us about your welfare. We, on our part, are informing you that *your cattle and your possessions are ours, and ours are yours* (*ta ktene humon kai he huparxis humon hemin estin kai ta hemon humin estin*). We have, therefore, given orders that you should be told of this." (NAB)

Apart from showing the old notion of shared resources that we saw in Chapter One, this instance claims a putatively shared ancestry in the figure of Abraham.[24] The question of divinity is not raised here.

The same point applies to the expression of oneness of identity attested in a literary context, the portrait of Galba drawn by the Roman historian Suetonius (*The Twelve Caesars*, Book VII, paragraph 20). His account of the death of the emperor Galba (seven months after his accession in 68–69) relates how this former general was met by soldiers sent on a mission to assassinate him. As he realized their intent, he "is said to have shouted out: 'What is all this, comrades? I am yours, you are mine! (*ego vester sum et vos mei*)'."[25] Like the cases from the Late Bronze Ages discussed in Chapter

---

[23] This treaty is extant only in a tenth or eleventh century CE/AD Byzantine manuscript now in the Vatican, which is thought to go back to a Roman copy based on the third-century BCE/BC original. For discussion, see Michael L. Barré, *The God-List in the Treaty between Hannibal and Philip V of Macedonia: A Study in Light of the Ancient Near East Treaty Tradition* (The Johns Hopkins Near Eastern Studies; Baltimore/London: Johns Hopkins University, 1983) 94.

[24] 1 Maccabees 9:23–32 is not discussed in this connection, as it seems to present only the stipulations and not the basis for the treaty relations.

[25] See J. C. Rolfe, *Suetonius, with an English Translation* (two vols.; LCL; Cambridge, MA: Harvard University; London: W. Heinemann, 1914) 2.222. The translation is taken

One, these Greco-Roman instances show the concepts of shared resources and oneness. However, they lack any translatability of divinity.

Unlike the political documents of the Bronze Age, translating divinity in the Greco-Roman context was hardly restricted to the scribal apparatus or treaties of political powers. Rather, it was a broader discourse influenced by literature and philosophy and appeared as well in general wishes of blessing and cursing.

Blessings and Curses

As a social courtesy of greeting, blessings offer a ready occasion for cross-cultural translatability. The opening blessing of a Phoenician letter discovered at Saqqara (KAI 50) not unexpectedly combines a Phoenician deity with those in Tahpanhes (in Egypt): "I bless you by Baal-Saphon and all the gods of Tahpanhes."[26] Compared with blessings, curse formulas are perhaps more indicative of the larger cultural context of translatability. As we saw in Chapter One, an important feature in Late Bronze treaties involves deities in their curse formularies. The deities of multi-national parties engaged in treaties of this era are called as witnesses and then as guarantors of the treaty conditions. If and when these stipulations are not met, the deities of the parties are to serve as enforcers of the curses to befall the party that fails to live up to the treaty. As we move into the Greco-Roman context, this tradition of multi-national deities invoked in treaty curses appears also in magical spells.[27] John G. Gager, Fritz Graf and Christopher A. Faraone have noted the continuity of the curses and spells from the Late Bronze Age down into this period in examples of magical curses.[28] The cases from this period com-

---

from Gaius Suetonius Tranquillus, *The Twelves Caesars* (trans. Robert Graves; rev. with introduction by Michael Grant; London: Penguin, 2003) 259.

[26] See James M. Lindenberger, *Ancient Aramaic and Hebrew Letters* (ed. Kent Harold Richards; SBLWAW 4; Atlanta: Scholars, 1994) 120, lines 1–2.

[27] The literature on the subject of magic in this period is vast. See the surveys of primary sources and secondary literature noted by Fritz Graf, *Magic in the Ancient World* (trans. Franklin Philip; Revealing Antiquity vol. 10; Cambridge, MA/London: Harvard University 1997) 1–19; and Scott Noegel, Joel Walker, and Brannon Wheeler, "Introduction," in: *Prayer, Magic, and the Stars in the Ancient and Late Antique World* (ed. Scott Noegel, Joel Walker, and Brannon Wheeler; University Park, PA: Pennsylvania State University, 2003) 2–7. See also the further discussion in Chapter Six.

[28] Gager, *Curse Tablets and Binding Spells from the Ancient World* (New York/Oxford: Oxford University, 1992) 26–27; Graf, *Magic in the Ancient World*, 169–74; and Faraone, *Ancient Greek Love Magic* (Cambridge, MA/London: Harvard University, 1999) 31, 78, 101–5. For a readily accessible example, see the mention of the Sumerian goddess Ereshkigal in the Leiden Papyrus, recto, column VII, line 26 in: F. L. Griffith and Herbert Thompson, *The Leyden Papyrus: An Egyptian Magical Book* (New York: Dover, 1974) 60–61. See also *PGM* LXX.4–25 in: *PGMT* 297. For possible Canaanite forerunners in magical formulary, see C. A. Faraone, B. Garnand, and C. López-Ruiz, "Micah's Mother (Judg. 17:1–4) and a Curse from Carthage (KAI 89): Canaanite Precedents for Greek and

bine deities from around the Mediterranean world in their curse formulas. To take one example, a lead tablet found on the Via Appia in Rome invokes an interesting mélange of divinities, including Egyptian divine names, angels and archangels, the Phrygian goddess, the Nymph goddess, Eidonea (perhaps Adonai, the God of the Bible, as the same formula reads in other texts) and spirits.[29] There are, in fact, many instances of non-Jewish magic using the name of the Jewish god. A number of these cases are presented at the outset of Chapter Six.

At this point, we may make an observation concerning the expansion in the social location of magical texts compared with the curses found in treaty texts. In the Late Bronze Age, the curse formulas that invoked deities across cultural boundaries were often generated by court specialists, and were used in particular by royal scribes for the purposes of treaty formulary, as we saw in Chapter One. In contrast, magical curses in the Greco-Roman world were issued by specialists, often unattached to a particular political ruler.[30] As noted by Christopher Faraone, their clientele consisted of all sorts of people who wanted help for different aspects of life, including gambling, professional competition, love, sexual relations and marriage.

World and Local Histories

Translatability took place in another sphere of Greco-Roman textual production, and that involved the historical works of the period. The classical tradition of historiography shows a number of translations of divine names.[31] According to the famous Greek historian, Herodotus, Aphrodite is "called Mylitta by the Assyrians, Alilat by the Arabians, and Mitra by

---

Latin Curses Against Thieves?" *JNES* 64 (2005) 161–86. The authors interpret the literary parallels as further evidence of Walter Burkert's case for an east-to-west migration of "religious technology." See Burkert, *The Orientalizing Revolution: Near Eastern Influence on Greek Culture in the Early Archaic Age* (trans. M. E. Pinder and W. Burkert; Cambridge, MA: Harvard University, 1990) 14–87. For historical and archaeological perspective on this westward migration, see Hans G. Niemeyer, "Trade Before the Flag? On the Principles of Phoenician Expansion in the Mediterranean," in: *Biblical Archaeology Today 1990: Proceedings of the Second International Congress on Biblical Archaeology, Jerusalem, June-July 1990* (ed. Avraham Biran and Joseph Aviram; [Jerusalem]: Israel Exploration Society/Israel Academy of Sciences and Humanities, 1993) 335–44.

[29] Gager, *Curse Tablets,* 70–71. This is not to say that some could not look rather monotheistic, for example, the 4th–5th Hebrew/Aramaic amulet originally from Aleppo now housed in the Church of the Flagellation in Jerusalem. For text edition, translation and notes (including older bibliography), see *Inscriptiones Judaicae Orientis: III. Syria and Cyprus* (ed. David Noy and Hanswulf Bloedhorn; TSAJ 12; Tübingen: Mohr Siebeck, 2004) 121–26. However, this case is significantly later.

[30] See the interesting taxonomy for Greek love magic in: Faraone, *Ancient Greek Love Magic,* 28.

[31] See Richard Lattimore, "Herodotus and the Names of Egyptian Gods," *Classical Philology* 34 (1939) 357–65.

the Persians" (*Histories*, 1.131). Similarly, Herodotus offers identifications of Egyptian Horus with Greek Apollo, and Egyptian Osiris with Greek Dionysius (*Histories*, 2.144).[32] Herodotus also expresses a general principle regarding the *interpretatio Graeca* of Egyptian gods (*Histories*, 2.50): "The names of almost all the gods also came to Greece from Egypt."[33] Herodotus notes a number of exceptions to this basic view, but the examples cited are indicative of the larger trend toward identifying deities cross-culturally. World-history thus locates divinity across the known world.

A rather comparable sort of discussion appears in local histories produced by figures such as Berossos of Babylonia and Philo of Byblos. Born in the second half of the fourth century, Berossos wrote his *History of Babylonia* ca. 290 CBE/BC. Berossos is attributed the use of Greek names for his local gods, for example, Kronos for Enki in the retelling of the Mesopotamian flood-story[34] or equations of Zeus and Mesopotamian Bel, Herakles and Cilician (?) Sandes, Aphrodite and Persian Anaitis (Avestan Anahita).[35] Clear examples of substitutions and equations of divine names come from *The Phoenician History* of Philo of Byblos. According to the primary source of information regarding Philo (the medieval lexicon known as the Suda), Philo was a grammarian (*grammatikos*) born in the time of Nero (54–68 CE/AD).[36] Writing in the lingua franca of the day, Philo rewrote stories said to derive from a Phoenician source, the so-called Sanchuniaton (himself said to be from Beirut or Tyre).[37] In his comments on deities, Philo generally uses Greek names known in the classical and late classical periods, but sometimes he uses indigenous terms. Occasionally he uses both, with

---

[32] See also 2.52, discussed by I. M. Linforth, "Greek and Egyptian Gods (Herodotus II 50 and 52)," *Classical Philology* 35 (1940) 300–1. For Egyptian-Greek cases, see also Fowden, *The Egyptian Hermes*, 18–19.

[33] Robin Waterfield, *Herodotus, The Histories: A New Translation* (Oxford/New York: Oxford University, 1998) 116. See the discussion of this passage by Archi, "Hurrian Gods and the Festivals of the Hattian-Hittite Layer," 147–48.

[34] See Gerald P. Verbrugghe and John M. Wickersham, *Berossos and Manetho, Introduced and Translated: Native Traditions in Ancient Mesopotamia and Egypt* (Ann Arbor, MI: University of Michigan, 1996) 49 n. 17. It is possible that the substitution comes from the later tradent Syncellus.

[35] Verbrugghe and Wickersham, *Berossos and Manetho*, 62–63.

[36] See Baumgarten, *The Phoenician History of Philo of Byblos*, 31–40. Baumgarten (p. 34) suggests that Philo was perhaps born after Nero's reign, ca. 70 AD, with his *floruit* falling at the end of Trajan's reign or early in Hadrian's. For the text of the Suda with translation, see H. W. Attridge and R. A. Oden, Jr., *Philo of Byblos. The Phoenician History: Introduction, Critical Text, Translation, Notes* (CBQMS 9; Washington, DC: The Catholic Biblical Association, 1981) 16–17; for their discussion of the Suda for Philo's dates, see p. 22 nn. 1–2.

[37] For an insightful consideration of Philo and his source(s), see Baumgarten, *The Phoenician History of Philo of Byblos*, esp. 261–68.

an explicit translation of divinity. The five examples provided here illustrate different aspects of translatability expressed by Philo:

1. "… they called him Beelsamem, which is 'Lord of Heaven' in Phoenician, Zeus in Greek" (*PE* 1.10.7)[38]

2. "Chousor practiced verbal arts including spells and prophecies. He is, in fact, Hephaistos" (*PE* 1.10.11)[39]

3. "Kronos whom the Phoenicians call El" (*PE* 1.10.44 = 4.16.11; also in 1.10.29)[40]

4. "The Phoenicians say that Astarte is Aphrodite" (*PE* 1.10.32)[41]

5. "The Egyptians call him Thouth and the Alexandrians Thoth and the Greeks translated his name as Hermes." (*PE* 1.9.24)[42]

The first case is notable for mentioning the two languages used for the names of the two gods. Philo of Byblos further explains this identification with his comment (*PE* 1.10.31) that Zeus is "called both Demarous and Adodos,"[43] two titles that are known in Ugaritic for the god, Baal. The second case is interesting for mentioning some features of Chousor that he does not share with Hephaistos. The two are identified, however, because they are both divine craftsmen. The third case, the equation of Kronos and El, is quite common in this material. In this instance, the Greek name is given as the basic name for the god. The fourth case relates the practice of Phoenicians in the matter of a divine name. The fifth and final case involves the common equation of Thoth and Hermes, found in authors such as Cicero (*De Natura Deorum*, 3.22.56).[44] This example is of further interest, as it is the only one of the five from Philo that does not involve a god originally from

---

[38] The text and translation are found in Attridge and Oden, *Philo of Byblos*, 40–41.

[39] Attridge and Oden, *Philo of Byblos*, 44–45.

[40] Attridge and Oden, *Philo of Byblos*, 62–63 and 54–55.

[41] Attridge and Oden, *Philo of Byblos*, 54–55. Cf. *De Dea Syria*, paragraph 4, which identifies Astarte and Selene. For text and translation, see H. W. Attridge and R. A. Oden, *The Syrian Goddess (De Dea Syria) Attributed to Lucian* (SBLTT 9, Graeco-Roman Religion series 1; Missoula, MT: Scholars, 1976) 12–13.

[42] Baumgarten, *The Phoenician History of Philo of Byblos*, 64, 68–72, 120; Attridge and Oden, *Philo of Byblos*, 28–29. Note also 1.10.14, Attridge and Oden, *Philo of Byblos*, 46–47. For further discussion, see Fowden, *The Egyptian Hermes*, 22–32 and 162, 216–17; and G. Mussies, "The Interpretatio Judaica of Thot-Hermes," in: *Studies in Egyptian Religion Dedicated to Professor Jan Zandee* (ed. M. Heerman van Voss et al.; Leiden: Brill, 1982) 89–120. The figure of "Taautos" lies beyond the scope of this discussion.

[43] Attridge and Oden, *Philo of Byblos*, 54–55. The Ugaritic titles are *dmrn* and *hd*, respectively; they occur together in 1.4 VIII 38–39 (*UNP* 137), where Baal addresses his enemies: "O Enemies of Hadd" (*hd*), why do you quake? Why quake, O Weapon-wielders of the Warrior (*dmrn*)?"

[44] H. Rackham, *Cicero. De Natura Deorum. Academica* (LCL; Cambridge, MA: Harvard University; London: W. Heinemann, 1933) 340–41. Theuth is given in this context as one of several names for Hermes.

his region. With these five cases, we get rather different formulations for divine translatability, and other cases from Philo of Byblos could be added. Implicit to these equations is a theory of divinity based on the perceived function or character.

Occasionally in Philo of Byblos, translatability works in a more complex manner. Let me return to the second example above, regarding Chousor and Hephaistos, who are identified thanks to the fact that both were recognized craftsman-gods. As a Phoenician god,[45] Chousor is provided with a second identification as Zeus Meilichios (gentle Zeus).[46] With this second identification with Zeus, we have a second type of translatability applied to Phoenician Chousor. Then there is a third interpretive step taken. Chousor is said to have brothers, which has been understood as a way to interpret the second element of his double name as known from the Ugaritic texts, namely Kothar wa-Hasis. Thus the interpretation of Chousor's identity requires three acts of translation. Out of these three, two involve identifications with two different Greek deities.

This case of translatability shows an additional dimension to this religious phenomenon, specifically its long cultural backdrop known from earlier sources. Thanks to the discovery of the Ugaritic texts in the early twentieth century, the equation of Chousor and Ptah is seen by scholars as going back to the Late Bronze Age. Chousor is accepted as a Phoenician form of the name of Kothar, the Ugaritic craftsman-god.[47] As we noted in Chapter One, one of Kothar's homes is said to be Hikuptah, namely Memphis, literally "the house of the soul (*ka*) of Ptah" (*CAT* 1.3 VI 15–16; cf. 1. 17 V 20–21); Memphis was so named as Ptah was the chief god of the city. The identification of Kothar with Ptah was based also on some similarity of

---

[45] In addition to the witness of Philo, Chousor is known as a Phoenician-Punic deity, based on the theophoric element in Phoenician and Punic proper names; see Dennis Pardee, "Koshar," *DDD* 490. The later tradition found in Pseudo-Melito that Kothar was the king of the Phoenicians likewise points to Kothar at least as theophoric in a Phoenician personal name. For this tradition, see William Cureton, *Spicilegium Syriacum: Containing Remains of Bardesan, Meliton, Ambrose and Mara Bar Serapion* (London: F. and J. Rivington, 1885) 44; Johannes Quasten, *Patrology* (vol. 1; Westminster, MD: Newman, 1951) 247; William F. Albright, *Yahweh and the Gods of Canaan,* 147–48; Robert A. Oden, *Studies in Lucian's De Dea Syria* (HSM 15; Missoula, MT: Scholars, 1977) 127–28. For this divinity in this and other later sources, see the summary in: Smith, "Kothar wa-Hasis, The Ugaritic Craftsman God," 12–14, 75–77.

[46] *PE* 1.10.11, cited in: Attridge and Oden, *Philo of Byblos,* 44–45. For the classical references as well as the information that follows, see Attridge and Oden, *Philo of Byblos,* 84 n. 68.

[47] For this god, see Pardee, "Koshar," *DDD* 490–91; and the older work of Mark S. Smith, "Kothar wa-Hasis, the Ugaritic Craftsman God" (Ph.D. dissertation, Yale University, 1985).

divine functions: like Kothar, Ptah was associated with arts and crafts.[48] If correct, then the implicit identification shows that the older Levantine or West Semitic translatability enjoyed an ongoing tradition down into the Greco-Roman period. Translatability, at least in specific instances, itself endured from earlier periods to later ones.[49] Thus translatability was built into local traditions and not made simply anew in the Greco-Roman period. In such cases the translatability passed down in local traditions constituted a component of what may be termed diachronic or "vertical" translatability, a matter that we will address at the end of this chapter.

Philosophical Discourse and Translatability

Compared with the situation of translatability in the Bronze and Iron Ages, there are some rather telling features in the Greco-Roman context. Philosophical discourse was a common medium used to contextualize and render one's own culture in the Mediterranean world, and this sort of discourse about divinity and its translation served to advance one's case within this larger setting.[50] Whereas translatability in the earlier periods was often a correlate and expression of political relations and power, in the Greco-Roman context translatability of divinity was a topic within the international philosophical-religious *ecumene*. The discussion here focuses on the local reception of such philosophical discourse, in particular in Philo of Byblos.

A central feature of philosophical translatability involves the role of interpretation in discourse about deities. We met typologies of divinity in the Bronze Age material, and it is evident that implicit interpretation of deities is a hallmark of the earlier periods. The Greco-Roman context, by contrast, shows explicit interpretation as well as additional methods of interpretation deployed in its typologies of divinities.[51] For example, interpreters of

---

[48] See Jacobus van Dijk, "Ptah," in: *OEAE*, 3.74–76, with relevant studies. (Perhaps the Ugaritic equation further reflected local recognition of the impact that Egyptian craftsmanship made on the Levantine coastal cities under Egyptian influence. Cf. Wenamun: "craftsmanship came from it [Egypt] in order to reach the place where I am [Byblos]." Miriam Lichtheim, *Ancient Egyptian Literature. Volume II: The New Kingdom* (Berkeley/Los Angeles/London: University of California, 1976) 227 and *COS* 1.91.

[49] For another case, note the figure of Baal-Seth that apparently survives in the form of the Greco-Roman name of Bolchoseth, found on amulets as well as curse tablets and binding spells normally inscribed on thin metal sheets (*defixiones*) in late classical magical texts. For Baal-Seth and his iconography, see Othmar Keel and Christoph Uehlinger, *Gods, Goddesses, and Images of God in Ancient Israel* (trans. Thomas Trapp; Minneapolis: Fortress, 1998) 76–78, 88, 146 n. 16, 169. For Greco-Roman evidence, see Gager, *Curse Tablets*, 266.

[50] For the context, see the remarks of Turcan, *The Cults of the Roman Empire*, 1–27.

[51] The contrast appears to be as much a matter of the development of genres as much as anything else. By this contrast, there is no intention to imply that earlier Near Eastern

divinities such as Philo of Byblos aimed at correlating older, indigenous information about deities in terms of newer methods of interpretation. While Philo's treatment shows typologies of deities as found in our earlier treaty material (discussed in Chapter One), his presentation manifests methods of rationalist interpretation applied to divinity in his day. Particularly well known at the time was the theory of euhemerism (associated with the name of the fourth-century figure Euhemerus of Messene), which viewed deities of traditional mythology as humans beings accorded divine honor after their deaths because of their achievements or benefactions to humanity.[52] This view finds an extended expression in Philo of Byblos (*PE* 1.9.22)[53]:

It is necessary to make a preliminary clarification for the sake of subsequent clarity and for the analysis of particular questions. The most ancient of the barbarians, and especially Phoenicians and Egyptians, from whom the rest of mankind received their traditions, considered as greatest gods those men who had made discoveries valuable for life's necessities for those who had in some way benefited their nations. Since they considered these men as benefactors and sources of many blessings, they worshiped them as gods even as they had passed on. They built temples and also consecrated steles and staves in their name.[54]

Following this discussion, Philo indulges in classic euhemeristic interpretation of the gods as deified humans[55] in a number of stories (*PE* 1.9.29–1.10.6).[56] As Martha Himmelfarb has observed, Philo does not make the deities just into humans; he makes them into Phoenicians.[57]

---

thinking was not capable of theorizing or abstract thought. For this point, see the important considerations of Peter Machinist, "On Self-Consciousness in Mesopotamia," in: *The Origins and Diversity of Axial Age Civilizations* (ed. S. N. Eisenstadt; SUNY Series in Near Eastern Studies; Albany, NY: State University of New York, 1986) 183–202, 511–18.

[52] Only slightly modified from Attridge and Oden, *Philo of Byblos,* 7.

[53] See Kees W. Bolle, "Euhemerus and Euhemerism," *ER* 5.2882–84. For a handy presentation of Euhemerus on the gods (preserved by Diodorus Siculus), see Michel Austin, *The Hellenistic World from Alexander to the Roman Conquest: A Selection of Ancient Sources in Translation* (second ed.; Cambridge: Cambridge University, 2006) 96–97. For discussions of Euhemerism as it bears on Philo of Byblos, see Attridge and Oden, *Philo of Byblos,* 7; and Baumgarten, *The Phoenician History of Philo of Byblos,* 76–77.

[54] Attridge and Oden, *Philo of Byblos,* 32–33.

[55] See the view among the classical authors of Saturn as a man, for example those cited by Tertullian, *Apologeticus* 10, in fragment 3, in: C. R. Holladay, *Fragments from Hellenistic Jewish Authors: Volume I: Historians* (SBLTT 20, Pseudepigrapha Series 10; Chico, CA: Scholars, 1983) 358–59.

[56] Attridge and Oden, *Philo of Byblos,* 32–35. According to Baumgarten (*The Phoenician History of Philo of Byblos,* 76–77), it is the sort of physiological and allegorical interpretations found in Plutarch's *De Iside et Osiride* that Philo of Byblos is attacking with his deployment of euhemerist interpretation.

[57] Himmelfarb, "The Torah between Athens and Jerusalem: Jewish Difference in Antiquity," in: *Ancient Judaism in its Hellenistic Context* (ed. Carol Bakhos; JSJSup 95; Leiden/Boston: Brill, 2005) 125.

Greco-Roman interpretation of deities as astral bodies was also absorbed by Philo (*PE* 1.9.29): "Among things of nature they acknowledged as gods only the sun, the moon, the other planets, the elements and their combinations."[58] This approach comports with the older, Near Eastern view that deities could be identified with various astral bodies.[59] However, there was an important difference in the Greco-Roman context. In this period, this approach also *explained* deities as stars. In earlier periods, the stars represent the abodes or manifestation of deities, but in the Greco-Roman period, deities were interpreted in terms of forces of nature or its elements, an approach that goes back to the sixth century pre-Socratic philosophers.[60] A good example of this approach appears in Philo's account of the creation of the world (*PE* 1.9.30–1.10.2). At the outset of his cosmogony, he initially draws primarily on the elements of Greek cosmology, with little reference to Phoenician tradition and its deities (*PE* 1.9.30–1.10.1):

He [Sanchuniathon] presents the Phoenician theology roughly as follows: He posits as the source of the universe a dark and windy gas, or a stream of dark gas, and turbid, gloomy chaos. These things were unbounded and for ages were without limit.[61]

Following this introduction, the cosmogony is based largely on natural elements (e. g., wind, mud, watery mixture),[62] yet some of its elements depart from a purely "natural" understanding. Some elements are rendered in anthropomorphic terms: "wind lusted after its own sources and a mixture came into being, that combination was called Desire."[63] We also see in Philo

---

[58] Attridge and Oden, *Philo of Byblos,* 32–33.

[59] For this view as embedded in the Ugaritic texts and then later in Israelite material, see Mark S. Smith, *The Origins of Biblical Monotheism: Israel's Polytheistic Background and the Ugaritic Texts* (Oxford/New York: Oxford University, 2001) 61–66. At the same time, this is not the exclusive understanding of deities in the older material, by any means.

[60] Baumgarten, *The Phoenician History of Philo of Byblos,* 121–22.

[61] Attridge and Oden, *Philo of Byblos,* 36–37.

[62] Richard J. Clifford emphasizes the borrowing from Egyptian cosmogonies as well, in particular "those of Heliopolis and Hermapolis, which form part of the Egyptian legacy of Phoenicia." See Clifford, *Creation Accounts in the Ancient Near East and in the Bible* (CBQMS 26; Washington, DC: The Catholic Biblical Association of America, 1994) 129. For Clifford, Philo's elements of air, and moisture would reflect the divine couple, Shu and Tefnut, in the Heliopolis cosmogony, while the water and darkness may echo the emergence of Ptah from Nun, the primeval ocean, and embodying himself in darkness, as found in the Hermapolis cosmogony.

[63] See Klaus Koch, "Wind und Zeit als Konstituenten des Kosmos in phönikischer Mythologie und spätalttestamentlichen Texten" in: *Mesopotamia – Ugaritica – Biblica: Festschrift für Kurt Bergerhof zur Vollendung seines 70. Lebensjahres am 7. Mai 1992* (ed. Manfred Dietrich and Oswald Loretz; AOAT 232; Kevelaer: Butzon & Bercker; Neukirchen-Vluyn: Neukirchener, 1993) 59–91; reprinted in: Koch, *Der Gott Israels und die Götter des Orients: Religionsgeschichtliche Studien II. Zum 80. Geburtstag von Klaus Koch* (ed. Friedhelm Hartenstein and Martin Rösel; FRLANT 216; Göttingen: Vandenhoeck & Ruprecht, 2007) 86–118; and Hans-Peter Müller, "Der Welt- und

the addition of what may be mythological beings, such as Zophesemin, perhaps the heavenly watchers as known also from 1 Enoch 1:5, 10:9 and 12:2,[64] and perhaps Mot known in Ugaritic as the god of Death.[65] If these are such mythological figures, then what we see here is Philo's working of such older figures into his essentially "natural" cosmogony.[66]

Philo's euhemerism, his interpretation of the deities as planetary bodies and his naturalist interpretation of cosmogony are part and parcel of the interpretation of deities in this period. Earlier in this chapter, we saw the reference to the god Chousor within a cosmogony according to a figure named Mochos.[67] Compared to Philo's cosmogony, Mochos' offers a less thinly veiled traditional West Semitic cosmogony, with the names of many divinities, yet it is concerned with the identification of "first principles." These two examples of Phoenician cosmogony compare with the sort of Stoic interpretation found in Plutarch, *De Iside et Osiride,* the so-called book of Hermes, which is said to view the names of the gods as natural powers: "the power placed in charge of the sun's course is Horus, and the Greeks call it Apollo; while the power in charge of the wind is called Osiris, by others Sarapis." This representation Garth Fowden characterizes as "theological Hermetica, which described the gods in a Stoic manner, in terms of the powers inherent in physical creation, and discussed the names variously assigned them by the Egyptians and the Greeks."[68] At the base of these authors' constructions is the notion that deities are anthropomorphic means to describe natural powers. In short, the natural powers that had formerly been understood to be the terrestrial manifestation of deities were basically evacuated of their independent divine identity. In this connection, we might look additionally at the role of allegory in interpretation in this period. Suffice it to say, allegory generally played a major role in reinvesting traditional narratives with the current philosophical understandings of reality, and this included deities.

These forms of interpretation of divinities downplay translation between specific deities of various peoples. There is a translation of divinity, but of a different sort: divinity is being translated into, or at least correlated with, natural categories of non-divinity. In these ancient "naturalist" strategies of

---

Kulturentstehungsmythos von Philo Byblios und die biblische Urgeschichte," *ZAW* 112 (2000) 161–79. The force of these studies is to suggest a shared West Semitic cosmogonic tradition in later periods.

[64] Attridge and Oden, *Philo of Byblos,* 77 n. 33; Baumgarten, *The Phoenician History of Philo of Byblos,* 114–15, 120; Clifford, *Creation Accounts in the Ancient Near East and in the Bible,* 130.

[65] Attridge and Oden, *Philo of Byblos,* 76–77 n. 29.

[66] Clifford (*Creation Accounts in the Ancient Near East and in the Bible,* 129) refers to Philo's "antitheological bias."

[67] See above, and Attridge and Oden, *Philo of Byblos,* 102–3.

[68] Fowden, *The Egyptian Hermes,* 138.

interpretation of deities, we have what Baumgarten calls "critical" interpretations of divinity.[69] In his closing words about Philo of Byblos, Baumgarten points to a number of features relevant to this investigation:

> Philo could not accept the naïve religion of popular piety ... His Euhemerism provided a "critical" account of the origins of religion which prevented him from finding popular practice and belief intellectually satisfying. Many of his contemporaries (e. g. Pausanias' Sidonian, and Plutarch) were finding new meaning in the ancient traditions through allegorical and physiological interpretations, but Philo believed these interpretations to be distortions. Philo's *History* is thus an intensely felt product of his age, and testimony to one man's interpretation of his native tradition in the light of contemporary thought.[70]

In this comment, Baumgarten mentions several crucial issues about ancient and modern interpretation. Before proceeding with our discussion of ancient interpretation of divinity, it is worth pausing to reflect on a major point raised by Baumgarten's remarks. Critical theory is as much a function of one's period as it is about penetrating into the truth of the matter. Second-order discourse takes in the evidence as fully as possible and with as much critical energy as can be mustered. According to the accounts attesting to Philo and his contemporaries, their efforts were literally voluminous.[71] Their critical energies, clearly driven by some of the philosophical trends of the times, are no less evident.

Baumgarten's picture provides an analogue to modern theories about the origins of religion, insofar as modern historians of religion pursue an analysis that undertakes an understanding of traditions in light of contemporary critical theories. It is arguable that Philo is in this respect little different than many modern historians of religion. For example, J. Samuel Preus, in his important book, *Explaining Religion,* rehearses the work of famous names informing modern critical theory, including among others, Giambattista Vico, David Hume, August Comte, Emile Durkheim, and Sigmund Freud.[72] Most every field in the humanities and social sciences operates with its own list of great figures central to their sense of critical analysis.[73] Philo similarly

---

[69] Baumgarten, *The Phoenician History of Philo of Byblos,* 77, 268.

[70] Baumgarten, *The Phoenician History of Philo of Byblos,* 268, referring to Pausanias, *Description of Greece,* 7.23.7–8; see W. H. S. Jones, *Pausanias, Description of Greece: III. Books VI–VIII (I–XXI)* (LCL; London: W. Heinemann; Cambridge, MA: Harvard University, 1918) 308–9.

[71] See, for example, the "eight books" or "the nine books," variously attributed to Philo of Byblos. See Attridge and Oden, *Philo of Byblos,* 16–17, 28–29, 72 n. 3.

[72] Preus, *Explaining Religion: Criticism and Theory from Bodin to Freud* (New Haven/London: Yale University, 1987).

[73] To cite only one example, an interesting look at such a list for the field of anthropology is provided by the thoughtful work of Clifford Geertz, *Works and Lives: The Anthropologist as Author* (Stanford, CA: Stanford University, 1988).

operated with the "critical" theory of his day. In both ancient and modern interpretations, the overall trend in "critical" discussions of religion is toward accounting for it entirely by natural causes. Finally, Philo's philosophical discussion correlates the past that he inherited with the thinking current in his day. Interpretation functions in part to mediate between the older, national forms of discourse centered on divinity and newer, more international and prestige forms of discourse drawing on philosophy.

3. The Cultural Contours of Greco-Roman Translatability

Jan Assmann's discussion of translatability in this period is important, as it was a crucial feature of ancient religion. Assmann's is not intended to be a comprehensive treatment, and in fact his presentation of translatability belongs to his larger discussion that essentially pits ancient notions of translatability against the biblical "Mosaic distinction," which in his thinking precluded translatability.[74] The following discussion of the contours of translatability is essentially an extension of Assmann's treatment. At the same time, in order to appreciate more fully what divine translatability involves in this period, it is necessary to address some matters. There are shifts in translatability and attendant cultural factors in this period, which differ from the conditions in earlier periods. We have already noted the dramatic increase in magical texts as a locus for international discourse of divine translatability. I also have in mind the wider range of religious-philosophical discourse in this period, not to mention the personnel who are making divine translations in such texts and the sorts of theoretical interests that they are expressing. There are also observations to be made about how translatability works as a result of this difference in personnel. Its explicitly philosophical character is particularly notable.

   As these cultural factors are noted, it is worth observing continuity as well as differences in the contours of divine translation from earlier periods. Assmann points to the general line of continuity with earlier cases. In his discussion of the Bronze Age situation, he comments: "this concept of religion as the common background of cultural diversity and the principle of cultural translatability eventually led to the late Hellenistic mentality for which the names of the gods mattered little in view of the overwhelming natural evidence of their existence."[75] There are more specific points of comparison lying at hand. Finally, we will take note of how the categories of

---

[74] This question is addressed in Chapters Two and Three, and it is relevant to the discussion in Chapter Six.

[75] Assmann, *Moses the Egyptian,* 47.

translatability correspond to modern assessments by historians of religion. To take only one basic item, we can trace features of divine translatability from our Bronze Age examples through our Iron Age and Greco-Roman contexts down through modern comparative religion. For example, it is a rather consistent that the gender of the deities in translation remained distinctive. In the examples cited by Assmann, translations rarely cross gender lines, apart from the final summary about Isis that she is "the beautiful essence of all the gods." Gender for divinities largely remained a male-female construction, just as it tends to be in modern construction of categories in comparative religion. We will note other conceptual categories implicit in the Greco-Roman material. Assmann touches briefly on some of these matters, yet in order to appreciate his insights, it is necessary to elaborate on these factors. Thus laying out more of the lines of continuity as well as the differences will serve to indicate more about the nature of divine translatability in this period. To situate various features of translatability within a broader historical and cultural context, the discussion begins with a word about the personnel involved.

Human and Divine Mobility

Compared with their Bronze and Iron Age predecessors, intellectual personnel of the Greco-Roman period differed somewhat in their roles and in their mobility. While scribes and other personnel circulated through different royal courts in the Late Bronze Age,[76] mobility in the Greco-Roman world was considerably broader, involving various sorts of religious and philosophical figures.[77] According to Jonathan Z. Smith, the mobility of religious intelligentsia was a hallmark of this period.[78] It was fueled in part by the creation of new libraries and the hiring of scholarly staffs, especially

---

[76] A helpful sense of international communication in this context may be gleaned from the survey by Gary H. Oller, "Messengers and Ambassadors in Ancient Western Asia," in: *CANE* 3.1465–73 (with bibliography). This Late Bronze interconnectedness between royal courts is also reflected by discussions about the exchange of personnel, for example, a physician in EA 49 and a diviner in EA 35. See Carlo Zaccagnini, "The Interdependence of the Great Powers," in: *Amarna Diplomacy: The Beginnings of International Relations* (ed. Raymond Cohen and Raymond Westbrook; Baltimore/London: Johns Hopkins University, 2000) 146. See above p. 43.

[77] For this point, see Frede, "Monotheism and Pagan Philosophy in Later Antiquity," 41–67.

[78] Smith, "Here, There, and Anywhere," in: *Prayer, Magic, and the Stars in the Ancient and Late Antique World* (ed. Scott Noegel, Joel Walker, and Brannon Wheeler; University Park, PA: Pennsylvania State University, 2003) 21–36; see esp. Smith's formulations on pp. 23 and 35. In the same volume ("Hebrew, Hebrew Everywhere? Notes on the Interpretation of *Vox Magicae*," 74), Gideon Bohak has also commented on the international character of magic in late antiquity. On mobility in the ancient world, see Lionel Casson, *Travel in the Ancient World* (Baltimore/London: Johns Hopkins University, 1994).

at centers, such as Alexandria and Pergamum, sponsored by the Ptolemaic and Attalid dynasties, respectively. At first glance, the situation seems parallel to what we saw for the Late Bronze Age: while kings sponsored royal archives and scholars for purposes of statecraft in the earlier period, in the Greco-Roman context monarchs sponsored the creation of libraries for the new prestige activity of education. Similarly, Akkadian and Greek both functioned as languages of education in their respective heydays. While the situations may be viewed in analogous terms, the differences involved in the Greco-Roman period cannot be underestimated.

First of all, in scope and concept libraries in the Greco-Roman context are distinctly Hellenistic and not Near Eastern. The newer model has been traced to Peripatos of Athens (the school associated with Aristotle),[79] rather than the temple and palace libraries of the Near East.[80] Under the patronage of Hellenistic rulers, the ambitious collection of works became a hallmark of this institution.[81] To collect was a major goal, in addition to the production of the scribal curriculum and administration as generally seen in ancient Near Eastern contexts. The scale of libraries likewise expanded well beyond the cuneiform scribal education of the Late Bronze Age.[82] The Greco-Roman practice might seem to have an analogue in Neo-Assyrian libraries,[83] for example, Ashurbanipal's great library at Nineveh, with its

---

[79] So the summary on "Libraries," in: *The Oxford Dictionary of the Classical World* (ed. John Roberts; Oxford/New York: Oxford University, 2005) 418–20. Every major Greek town had an archive or library, according to Jenö Platthy, *Sources of the Earliest Greek Libraries with the Testimonia* (Amsterdam: Adolf M. Hakkert, 1968) 2. For the library associated with Judas Maccabeus, see 2 Maccabees 2:15–17. See David M. Carr, *Writing on the Tablet of the Heart: Origins of Scripture and Literature* (Oxford/New York: Oxford University, 2005) 263.

[80] See the remarks of Carr, *Writing on the Tablet of the Heart*, 186; van der Toorn, *Scribal Culture*, 51, 63–64, 236–44.

[81] For this theme, see the case of The Letter of Aristeas 9–10 (*OTPs* 2.12).

[82] Late Bronze Age site such as Ugarit show a number of private houses containing tablets and other inscribed objects, for example, the several hundred tablets discovered in the house of Urtenu (Marguerite Yon, *The City of Ugarit at Tell Ras Shamra* [Winona Lake, IN: Eisenbrauns, 2006] 20, 87–88); the house of a priest with texts in Akkadian, Hurrian and Ugaritic (Yon, *The City of Ugarit,* 100); and the texts found in the house (of the so-called high priest) located between two temples (Yon, *The City of Ugarit,* 106, 111), which included the main known literary texts (the Baal Cycle, 1.1–1.6; Kirta, 1.14–1.16; and Aqhat, 1.17–1.19; the Rituals and Myths of the Goodly Gods, 1.23; and Nikkal wa-Ib, 1.24; see Chapter One for further discussion. To these one might compare and contrast individual libraries in the classical and Greco-Roman periods; see Platthy, *Sources of the Earliest Greek Libraries with the Testimonia,* 121–33.

[83] This policy of collection is expressed in a letter (BM 45642 lines 11–12) sent to Ashurbanipal from the scribal establishment at Borsipppa: "Regarding the instruction that our lord the king wrote as follows (saying) 'Write out all the scribal learning in the property of Nabû and send it to me. Execute the instruction! … Now, we will not neglect the king's command. We will strain and toil day and night to execute the instruction for our lord the king. We will write on boards of *musukkannu*-wood …". For this transla-

policy of collection.[84] Estimates for the library's tablets have been put at about 5,000.[85] However, this number for this greatest of Neo-Assyrian libraries hardly compares with the scale of the major libraries of Alexandria and Pergamum. Based on information provided by later sources, estimates for the scrolls in the great library of Alexandria have been put in the range of 500,000–700,000.[86] The library at Pergamum has been estimated at

---

tion see A.R. George, "Assyria and the Western World," in: *Assyria 1995: Proceedings of the 10th Anniversary Symposium of the Neo-Assyrian Text Corpus Project. Helsinki, September 7–11, 1995* (ed. S. Parpola and R.M. Whiting; Helsinki: The Neo-Assyrian Text Corpus Project, 1997) 71–72, with the text given on p. 75 n. 9. For the library of Ashurbanipal, see D.T. Potts, "Before Alexandria: Libraries in the Ancient Near East," in: *The Library of Alexandria: Centre of Learning in the Ancient World* (ed. Roy MacLeod; London/New York: I.B. Tauris, 2000) 19–33; and the useful summary in: Benjamin R. Foster, *Before the Muses: An Anthology of Akkadian Literature* (third ed.; Bethesda, MD: CDL, 2005) 8–10. Generally for archives in Mesopotamia, see Olof Pedersén, *Archives and Libraries in the Ancient Near East, 1500–300 B.C.* (Bethesda, MD: CDL, 1998); and the essays in: *Cuneiform Archives and Libraries: Papers Read at the 30e Rencontre assyriologique internationale, Leiden 4–8 July 1983* (ed. Klaas R. Veenhof; Uitgaven van het Nederlands Historisch-Archaeologisch Instituut te Istanbul; [Istanbul]: Nederlands Historisch-Archaeologisch Instituut te Istanbul, 1986). For some texts relating to the nature of the library, see Alisdair Livingstone, *Court Poetry and Literary Miscellanea* (SAA III; Helsinki: Helsinki University, 1989) xviii.

[84] For a helpful discussion of the issues involved in understanding this collection, see Simo Parpola, "Assyrian Library Records," *JNES* 42 (1983) 1–29, as well as the material collected in his book, *Letters from Assyrian and Babylonian Scholars* (State Archives of Assyria X; Helsinki: Helsinki University, 1993); and Stephen J. Lieberman, "Canonical and Official Cuneiform Texts: Towards an Understanding of Assurbanipal's Personal Tablet Collection," in: *Lingering Over Words: Studies in Ancient Near Eastern Literature in Honor of William L. Moran* (ed. Tzvi Abusch, John Huehnergard, and Piotr Steinkeller; HSS 37; Atlanta: Scholars, 1990) 305–36.

[85] This estimate goes back to Ernst Weidner, "Die Bibliothek Tiglatpilesers I," *Archiv für Orientforschung* 16 (1952/3) 197–98, and it has received some recent confirmation; see Potts, "Before Alexandria," 23. A lower figure of 1,500 was given by A. Leo Oppenheim, *Ancient Mesopotamia: Portrait of a Dead Civilization* (rev. ed.; ed. Erica Reiner; Chicago: University of Chicago, 1977) 16–17. See also Foster, *Before the Muses*, 8 n. 3.

[86] The lower figure derives from information provided by John Tzetzes (a Byzantine scholar who lived ca. 1110–1180 AD/CE), who refers to "400,000 mixed books and 90,000 single, unmixed books" in "the internal library of the court and palace," not counting the "42,800 books" of "the external library" (for the passage in question, see Rudolph Blum, *Kallimachos, The Alexandrian Library and the Origins of Bibliography* [trans. H.W. Wellisch; Madison, WI: University of Wisconsin, 1991] 110–13). Blum (*Kallimachos,* 110–13) puts the holdings of the two libraries at Alexandria at a total of 532,800 scrolls. The higher figure derives from the second century CE/AD literary scholar Aulus Gellus. For discussion, see Robert Barnes, "Cloistered Bookworms in the Chicken-Coop of the Muses: The Ancient Library of Alexandria," in: *The Library of Alexandria: Centre of Learning in the Ancient World* (ed. Roy MacLeod; London/New York: I.B. Tauris, 2000) 64–65. This higher figure is followed by Samuel N.C. Lieu, "Scholars and Students in the Roman East," in: *The Library of Alexandria: Centre of Learning in the Ancient World* (ed. Roy MacLeod; London/New York: I.B. Tauris, 2000) 128. Note also the two figures of over 200,000 and the stated goal of 500,000 given in the imagined dialogue in The Letter of Aristeas 10 (*OTPs* 2.12).

200,000 volumes.[87] In short, there is no comparison in scale between Neo-Assyrian and Greco-Roman royal libraries. The same is true with regard to the range of works. The Sumero-Akkadian curriculum consisted of traditional works in a variety of genres, including sign-lists, vocabularies, letters, legal contracts, royal hymns, proverb collections, literary texts and mathematics.[88] As we noted in Chapter One, the Sumero-Akkadian scribal curriculum spread to western Asia and was adapted in various kingdoms, ranging from Hatti in the north to Egypt in the south.[89] By comparison, the Greco-Roman textual process was revolutionary. The new breed of historical, philosophical and scientific learning generated works aimed at including the learning of "other" peoples.[90] In sum, the scale of this collection and production in the Greco-Roman context was massive by comparison with earlier periods.

The distinctive character of the new institution of the library extended to personnel. Like "book exports,"[91] scholarly experts moved around the Mediterranean to accept posts in royal courts and libraries. While Late Bronze Age scribes served their royal patrons in communication and administration and Neo-Assyrian and Neo-Babylonian scribes additionally developed long and intricate literary texts (often replete with political messages),[92] Greco-Roman scholars served as tutors to various Hellenistic rulers and as staff to the libraries.[93] Ben Sira 39:4 (LXX) portrays the scribe's

---

[87] Lieu, "Scholars and Students in the Roman East," 127.

[88] For the Old Babylonian scribal school and curriculum, see Laurie E. Pearce, "The Scribe and Scholars of Ancient Mesopotamia," *CANE* 4.2270–71. For a useful discussion for the neo-Assyrian period, see Francesa Rochberg-Halton, "Canonicity in Cuneiform Texts," *Journal of Cuneiform Studies* 36 (1984) 127–44.

[89] See the discussion in Chapter One.

[90] In this vein, Barnes ("Cloistered Bookworms in the Chicken-Coop of the Muses," 67) cites various authors who mention works from various countries in the library.

[91] The expression comes from Martin Hengel, *The Septuagint as Christian Scripture* (with the assistance of Roland Deines; trans. Mark E. Biddle; Old Testament Studies; Edinburgh/New York: T & T Clark, 2002) 81.

[92] See Piotr Michalowski, "Presence at the Creation," in. *Lingering Over Words: Studies in ancient Near Eastern Literature in Honor of William L. Moran* (ed. Tzvi Abusch, John Huehnergard, and Piotr Steinkeller; HSS 37; Atlanta: Scholars, 1990) 381–96, esp. 393–95. See further below; and note the discussion in Chapter Three.

[93] See the older study of Edward Alexander Parsons, *The Alexandrian Library. Glory of the Hellenic World: Its Rise, Antiquities, and Destructions* (New York: American Elsevier, 1952). More recent and useful is Rudolf Blum, *Kallimachos, the Alexandrian Library and the Origins of Bibliography* (trans. Hans H. Wellisch; Madison, WI: University of Wisconsin, 1991). See also the volume of essays entitled *The Library of Alexandria: Centre of Learning in the Ancient World* (ed. Roy MacLeod; London/New York: I. B. Tauris, 2000); some are cited below. Note also the entertaining, novelistic retelling of the story of the library of Alexandria by Luciano Canfora, *The Vanished Library: A Wonder of the Ancient World* (trans. Martin Ryle; Berkeley/Los Angeles: University of California, 1990). For the librarian Demetrius of Phalerum, see Nina L. Collins, *The Library in Alexandria and the*

travels: "He is in attendance and has entrance to the ruler; he travels among the people of foreign lands to test what is good and evil among people."[94] Scholarship was part and parcel of the education of the scribal elite, forming a constitutive element of royal establishments.

In the Greco-Roman context, not only were the personnel more mobile; so were people more generally. While the Late Bronze and Iron Ages witnessed migrations of groups,[95] movement of people was more extensive in the Greco-Roman period.[96] According to Jonathan Z. Smith, this increase in general mobility generated what he calls the religion of "anywhere," namely small groups that could replicate its religious constitution regardless of specific location (in part by applying to themselves family language of traditional religions).[97] For the Roman period, Robert Turcan's 1996 *The Cults of the Roman Empire* is a veritable catalogue of Smith's religions of "anywhere." Within such practice the individual often plays an important role.[98] In terms of personal identity, national boundaries were considerably

---

Bible in Greek (VTSup 82; Leiden/Boston: Brill, 2000) 82–114. For the political context of "Alexandrian scholarship," see the summary by Günther Hölbl, *A History of the Ptolemaic Empire* (trans. Tina Saavedra; London/New York: Routledge, 2001) 63–65.

[94] NAB translation. See also Patrick W. Skehan and Alexander A. Di Lella, O. F. M., *The Wisdom of Ben Sira* (AB 39; New York: Doubleday, 1987) 446, 452. The passage came to my attention thanks to van der Toorn, *Scribal Culture*, 53.

[95] For case studies, see the essays in: *Immigration and Emigration within the Ancient Near East: Festschrift E. Lipiński* (ed. K. Van Lerberghe and A. Schoors; OLA 65; Leuven: Peeters/Departement Oriëntalistiek, 1995).

[96] For specific cases and aspects of travel in the ancient Mediterranean world, see the essays in: *Travel, Geography and Culture in Ancient Greece and the Near East* (ed. Colin Adams and Jim Roy; Oxford: Oxbow, 2007).

[97] Although Smith does not say so, such groups would include presumably the cults of Mithras in Greece, Italy and elsewhere in the west, and the early Christian house churches in Syria, Asia Minor and Greece. Synagogues could likewise provide such a function. The Italian port-town of Ostia Antica is a particularly interesting representative of these religious practices. See Lily Ross Taylor, *The Cults of Ostia: Greek and Roman Gods, Imperial Cult, Oriental Gods* (Baltimore, 1913; repr. Chicago: Ares, 1976, 1985); Maria Floriani Squarciapino, *I culti orientali ad Ostia* (Leiden: Brill, 1962); Samuel Laeuchli, *Mithraism in Ostia: Mystery Religion and Christianity in the Ancient Port of Rome* (Garrett Theological Studies 1; [Evanston, IL]: Northwestern University, 1967); and Birger Olsson, Dieter Mittermacht and Olof Brandt, ed., *The Synagogue of Ancient Ostia and the Jews of Rome: Interdisciplinary Studies* (Skrifter utgivna av Svenska institutet i Rom.4o; Jonsered, Sweden: P. Aströms, 2001). See also Jan Theo Bakker, *Living and Working with the Gods: Studies of Evidence for Private Religion and its Material Environment in the City of Ostia (100–500 AD)* (Dutch Monographs on Ancient History and Archaeology, 12; Amsterdam: J. C. Gieben, 1994).

[98] For example, Arthur Darby Nock comments: "We are here in the sphere of individualistic religion." He makes this remark in the context of the personal identification of the speaker with the deity Hermes in *PGM* XIII 795: "fore thou art I and I am thou. Thy name is mine, my name is thine, for I am thy image." See Nock, *Essays on Religion and the Ancient World* (vol. 1; ed. Zeph Stewart; Cambridge, MA: Harvard University, 1972) 192. Cases of such individual piety could be easily multiplied.

less important in this period compared to earlier periods. To put the point into perspective, one might say, following Jan Bremmer, that the cultures of the ancient Mediterranean and Near Eastern from the Late Bronze Age and into the Iron Age and Persian period showed some "permeability,"[99] yet traditional boundaries in the Greco-Roman period were more broadly permeable. By comparison, this feature seems to a particular hallmark of the Greco-Roman situation.

Mobility in this period did not entail only human institutions and personnel. Mobility affected descriptions of divinity. Classical writers such as Apollodorus include stories of divine travel. In one section of *The Library* (1.4.1),[100] he details Hera's pursuit of Latona over the entire earth, Apollo's travel to Delphi, and Poseidon's going to Chio to woo Merope. Divine mobility is a feature also of Levantine authors of this period. Philo of Byblos discusses how Kronos, explicitly identified with El in other contexts of *The Phoenician History*,[101] went about the world assigning different lands to various deities:

Also when Kronos was traveling around the world, he gave the kingdom of Attica to his own daughter Athena … in addition, Kronos gave the city Byblos to the goddess Baaltis, who is also Dione, and the city Beirut to Poseidon … When he went to the southern land, Kronos transferred all of Egypt to the god Taautos, so that it might become his kingdom.[102]

Whereas Levantine antecedents, such as the Ugaritic Baal Cycle, represent El as the head of the seventy children who rule the world, it does not show the god traveling in order to parcel out the lands to the various deities. This applies as well to Wenamun's account of Amun-Re founding the lands of the world (discussed in Chapter One).[103] The same is true of the type-scene evoked in Deuteronomy 32:8–9 (as we saw in Chapter Three).

By comparison, the accounts in Apollodorus and Philo of Byblos seem to point to the construal of divine mobility as an innovation in the Greco-Roman context. This period also witnesses to the notion of divine travel applied to Yahweh's surrogate, the figure of Wisdom personified. In Ben

---

[99] Bremmer, "Ritual," in: *Religions of the Ancient World*, 33. Bremmer's remark concerns the cross-cultural migration of ritual in particular.

[100] Sir James George Frazer, *Apollodorus. The Library I* (LCL; Cambridge, MA: Harvard University; London: W. Heinemann, 1921) 25–29.

[101] *PE* 1.10.44. For text and translation, see Attridge and Oden, *Philo of Byblos*, 62–63. This case is discussed in the preceding section of this chapter.

[102] *PE* 1.10.32, 35, 38; Attridge and Oden, *Philo of Byblos*, 56–57, 58–59. See below about Taautos.

[103] For translation, see Miriam Lichtheim, *COS* 1.91. For discussion of this passage in Wenamun, see Chapter One; and for discussion of its conceptual relationship with Deuteronomy 32:8–9, see Chapter Three.

Sira (also called Sirach or Ecclesiasticus) 24:6–8, Wisdom describes her search for a resting place over all the lands, peoples and nations, but it is finally in Jacob//Israel that she makes her dwelling.[104] The language of inheritance and the order of Jacob//Israel suggests here a conscious echoing and modification of Deuteronomy 32:8–9. Yet this antecedent text shows no notion of divine mobility. 1 Enoch 42:1–3 takes the motif further in its description of Wisdom's mobility: she is unable to find a home among humans, so she returns to the heavens and dwells with the angels.[105] The motif of divine mobility in these passages goes back in part to the older West Semitic *topos* of the divine division of the world into nations allotted to the gods. However, unlike their immediate predecessor texts, Philo of Byblos, Ben Sira and 1 Enoch reconfigure the motif with the feature of divine travel, which would have made particularly good sense in a world of considerable religious mobility. The inverse motif of the human journey to the heavens and back, also quite popular during the Greco-Roman era, may likewise reflect the development of mobility in this period.[106]

There is a further feature of conceptual mobility evident in the Greco-Roman period, one that is central to the general topic of divine translatability. When we look at cases of divine translatability in either the Late Bronze Age (Chapter One) or in the Iron Age (Chapter Two), it appears in discourse between two parties from different cultures, and it informs their cross-cultural discourse. We might also say that for scribes especially in the Late Bronze Age context, this sort of discourse represents a theoretical operation that enhances their capacity to link their respective societies, achieved in part through a series of recognized, shared ideas about deities. This sort of cross-cultural conceptualization constitutes a reflective sort of discourse, one not born of religious experience, but of political reflection and context. In other words, translatability in the earlier periods is mostly a matter of second-order discourse; only rarely do we see it in an expression of religious experience. (Even the case represented by the prayer of Puduhepa resulted from the treaty-relationship that the Hittites

---

[104] For a discussion of this passage, see Randall A. Argall, *1 Enoch and Sirach: A Comparative Literary and Conceptual Analysis of the Themes of Revelation, Creation and Judgment* (Society of Biblical Literature Early Judaism and Its Literature 8; Atlanta: Scholars, 1995) 53–57. See also John 1:10–14.

[105] *OTPs* 1.33.

[106] See Martha Himmelfarb, *Ascent to Heaven in Jewish and Christian Apocalypses* (Oxford: Oxford University, 1993); J. Edward Wright, *The Early History of Heaven* (Oxford/New York: Oxford University, 2000) esp. 98–116 and 139–84; and Leif Carlsson, *Round Trips to Heaven: Otherworldly Travelers in Early Judaism and Christianity* (Lund Studies in History of Religions 19; Stockholm: Almqvist & Wiksell, 2004). For the development of heavenly journeys in this period, Wright stresses the importance in the change of astronomical ideas, in particular the heavenly spheres.

had concluded with their vassals in Syria.) In contrast, the Greco-Roman material shows considerably more cases of first-order prayers, curses, magical charms and other religious expressions where translatability is conceptually constitutive. As we have seen in this chapter, translatability marks a wide range of first-order religious discourse. In other words, translatability, which was a second-order discourse in the earlier periods, strongly informed first-order religious expression in the Greco-Roman period.

Local Works as Acts of Resistance to "Universal Works"

The divine identifications made by figures like Philo of Byblos were not merely a scribal practice on the part of local professionals. There was considerably more to the intellectual project involved. What we see in *The Phoenician History* of Philo of Byblos as opposed to another historical work, *The Library of History* of Didorus Siculus, may serve to exemplify some of the larger currents running through the intellectual project found across the Mediterranean world during this period. Let us begin with the latter work. Diodorus Siculus is representative of the larger literature of Greco-Roman "general history" that surveyed the known world. Diodorus Siculus opens his work with praise for those writers who compose *koinas historias*, "universal histories" (1.1.1).[107] As he recognized (1.4.3), such a project was a function of the supremacy of Rome. Hand-in-hand with such a universalizing project were compilations of information about peoples and their various customs, including their deities, which in turn provided opportunity for comparisons between them.[108]

In contrast, *The Phoenician History* of Philo of Byblos is representative of local traditions that asserted themselves against – yet also fit into – the larger intellectual project of Greco-Roman history. Following his description of his local source, Sanchuniaton who is said to have drawn his information from Phoenician shrines, Philo of Byblos (*PE* 1.9.26–27) takes issue with "the Greek authors":

From that time the practice of mysteries arose, which had not yet reached the Greeks ... These discoveries were made by us, who have earnestly desired to understand Phoenician culture and who have investigated much material apart from that in

---

[107] C. H. Oldfather, *Diodorus Siculus I. Books I–II, 1–34* (LCL; Cambridge, MA: Harvard University; London: W. Heinemann, 1933) 4–5; and for 1.4.3, see pp. 18–19.
[108] The same sort of universal project specifically focused on deities appears in Cicero's *De Natura Deorum*. For text and translation, see H. Rackham, *Cicero. De Natura Deorum. Academica* (LCL; Cambridge, MA: Harvard University; London: W. Heinemann, 1933).

Greek authors, for this is inconsistent and composed by some people more for the sake of disputation than for truth.[109]

Philo of Byblos claims a place for his work over and against what he perceives as the inadequacies and errors of "the Greek authors."[110]

Later in his work, Philo of Byblos comments in a similar vein, yet adds a further claim (*PE* 1.10.40–41):

The Greeks, who surpass all men in their natural cleverness, first appropriated most of these tales. They then dramatized them in various ways with additional literary ornaments, and intending to beguile with the delights of myths, they embellished them in all sorts of ways. Thence Hesiod and the highly touted cyclic poets fabricated their own versions and made excerpts of Theogonies and Giants' Battles and Titans' Battles, which they carried about and with which they defeated the truth. Our ears have for ages become habituated to and predisposed by their fictions. We preserve the received mythology as a sacred trust, as I said also at the beginning. Assisted by the force of time, it has rendered its hold inescapable, so that the truth is regarded as drivel and the bastard tale as truth.[111]

Here Philo is clear on the historical origins of "most of these tales": they were originally Phoenician. Parenthetically, it may be noted that his historical claim prefigures historical research, with modern studies[112] indicating that a good deal of his local tradition goes back to Bronze Age material.[113]

The heart of Philo's comments in this passage is concerned with the displacing effects of Hellenistic culture, how "our ears have for ages become habituated to and predisposed by their fictions." Here Philo enters into his rhetoric of resistance to Greek culture, especially in its effects of effacing his own tradition even to the point of its being regarded as "drivel," rather than "the sacred trust" he believed it to be. In this sensibility, Philo was hardly

---

[109] Attridge and Oden, *Philo of Byblos,* 30–31.

[110] See Baumgarten, *The Phoenician History of Philo of Byblos,* 230–31, 267–68. Baumgarten compares the critical attitude of the Sidonian whom Pausanias met at the shrine of Asklepios in Achaia (Pausanias, *Description of Greece,* 7.23.7–8; W. H. S. Jones, *Pausanias, Description of Greece: III. Books VI–VIII (I–XXI)* (LCL; Cambridge, MA: Harvard University; London: W. Heinemann; 1918) 308–9.

[111] Attridge and Oden, *Philo of Byblos,* 60–61.

[112] This point is made abundantly clear by the notes on such comparisons found in the works of Baumgarten, *The Phoenician History of Philo of Byblos,* and Attridge and Oden, *Philo of Byblos.* The issues involving the pathways of transmission as well as the additions made at various points in transmission are complex, however. For a particularly interesting case, see Baumgarten, *The Phoenician History of Philo of Byblos,* 235–43, on the "kingship in heaven" theme found in Philo and Hesiod. Baumgarten (p. 242) arrives at the conclusion that Philo "knew a more or less contemporary Byblian version of the 'Kingship in Heaven' theme."

[113] This point remains true, even bearing in mind the important caveats expressed by James Barr, "Philo of Byblos and his 'Phoenician History'," *Bulletin of the John Rylands Library* 57 (1974) 17–68.

alone. This sort of local resistance was felt elsewhere around the eastern Mediterranean basin.[114] Despite his counter-stance, it is also clear that Philo of Byblos operates in much the same manner as the "universal histories," as indicated by his parroting of the identification of Thoth and Hermes noted above. Even as Philo resists the intellectual project's purpose, he employs its intellectual methods and horizons, for example, Hellenistic euhemerism (discussed above).[115] Not only does Philo deploy comparable strategies, he has analogous purposes in mind. Albert I. Baumgarten has compared Philo of Byblos' efforts at bringing harmony to the diverse local traditions that he had inherited with what Hesiod and Homer attempted for local Greek traditions.[116]

A similar effort may be at work in Judea in the production of scriptural works (contained in what later emerges as the Hebrew Bible). This may represent a local project to generate "a national literature,"[117] as a counterpoint to Hellenistic philosophy and literature. Perhaps ironically, this project did so by drawing from Greco-Roman forms. In the case of the "Torah and the prophets," David M. Carr notes that their presentation and understanding

---

[114] On the situation in Egyptian religious-intellectual circles, see Fowden, *The Egyptian Hermes*, 15–16, 37, 53. For the sense of trauma in Egyptian sources of the period, see Fowden, *The Egyptian Hermes*, 42–44. Cf. the awareness of Jewish history represented in non-Jewish sources in 2 Maccabees 2:23, which relates how the five volumes by Jason of Cyrene setting forth the Jewish history of the Maccabean period serves as the basis for the narrative of 2 Maccabees; and note 2:28: "we leave the responsibility for exact details to the original author." Note further the reflection on what constitutes "professional history": "To enter into questions and examine them thoroughly from all sides is the task of the professional historian" (verse 30).

[115] Baumgarten, *The Phoenician History of Philo of Byblos*, 262–63.

[116] Baumgarten, *The Phoenician History of Philo of Byblos*, 267.

[117] The point for biblical works and the expression used here derive from van der Toorn, *Scribal Culture*, 259. David M. Carr (*Writing on the Tablet of the Heart*, 253–72) views the Hebrew Bible as an effort on the part of the Hasmonean royal priesthood to develop curriculum (or more specifically what he calls "text-supported education-enculturation"), with a "pro-Jewish, anti-Greek ideology" (p. 267) aimed to serve a Jewish alternative to Greco-Roman philosophy and literature: "Such 'Hebrew Scripture' formed a counterpoint to Greek textuality in a monarchy that cultivated a pro-Torah, anti-Hellenistic image – however fictional" (p. 269). In support of the idea of the local tradition of works, Carr cites 2 Maccabees 2:13–14 and 15:9. Jewish works from Judea do exalt the Torah observance as a bulwark against non-Jewish practice, e. g., Jubilees 1:7–11 (*OTPs* 2.52–53). There is an approximation of the idea of Torah as counter-curriculum in: The Letter of Aristeas 31 (*OTPs* 2.15); note also 121 (*OTPs* 2.21). Indeed, the letter, at least to some degree, represents an effort to defend the place of Jewish Torah and prophets alongside Greco-Roman learning. Ben Sira 39:1–11 praises the student of Torah, including his travels "to learn what is good and evil among men" (verse 5, NAB). I am not aware of any Jewish texts of this period from Judea that explicitly contrast the "Law and the Prophets" with Greek works. However, Carr would not necessarily understand the formation of "Law and prophets" as a conscious counter-curriculum as such. See below for Carr's clarification on this point as well as his further reflections since the publication of his book.

"represented a hyperversion of the Greek forms of textuality it opposed."[118] Carr thinks of the emergent Torah-Prophets "Hebrew Bible" on analogy with hybrid native literatures such as the rich tradition of Indian novels in English or emergent post-colonial African literature in French, English and native languages.[119] On the one hand, such literature is a flowering of native culture and writing in the wake of imperial rule. Though only some authors explicitly reflect on this, the timing of the literature and its character has suggested to many that such literature is, to varying degrees, postcolonial in push. On the other hand, such literature is intimately and intricately shaped by the cultural influence of the former imperial power. The genre of "novel," for example, is not native to India (though there are analogies, they are quite different). The language is different as well. In sum, such native literatures – whether written in native languages or not – represent a form of postcolonial cultural nationalism even as they also reflect influence from the culture which they are rebounding against. (Carr uses the word "rebound," because it reflects a fuller range of possible reactions to the former culture than something like "cultural resistance" or "anti-Greek/English/etc.")

For Carr, this has been the key analogy in his effort to explain a range of cultural phenomena in the Hasmonean period, such as Hebrew linguistic nationalism reflected in both Maccabees (and probably indirectly at Qumran), and paleo-Hebrew on (Greek-style) Hasmonean coins. For him, these point to the emergence of a more Greek-style educational system in Hebrew texts, and the probable emergence during the Hasmonean period of a more clearly defined Hebrew (Torah-Prophets) collection that is both a contrast to and yet approximation of the relatively clearly defined Hellenistic-period Greek educational collection seen especially in Greek diaspora contexts such as Egypt. These cultural phenomena both resemble and contrast with Greek counterparts. Despite the proud references to discourses in the "native tongue" in Maccabees, none explicitly promotes Hebrew as anti-Greek, nor use of paleo-Hebrew on Greek coins, let alone the emergence of more Greek-style education and a semi-Greek style, defined educational "canon." These cultural phenomena are not so much anti-Greek in impetus, as pro-Hebrew culture in the wake of and in cultural competition with Greek cultural dominance. And like their much later, postcolonial hybrid counterparts in India, Africa, etc., one may not assume that the promoters of

---

[118] Carr, *Writing on the Tablet of the Heart*, 270. To be clear, Carr is referring to features such as paragraph markers and Hellenistic categorizations of the Torah as "ancestral laws" and not to the forms of the Torah and prophets as specific works that predate this period; instead Carr is focusing on their collection and use.

[119] This further description of Carr's view is a direct excerpt of his e-mail response (11 July 2007) to a query of mine concerning these points in his book. I am grateful for his gracious permission to use this summary in this context.

these various cultural phenomena (Hebrew, paleo-Hebrew script, etc.) were even conscious of, let alone explicit about, the mix of cultural impetuses involved in their cultural productions. Carr's reading of the formation of the Torah and prophets in the Hasmonean context locates these works within a larger effort on the part of local literary projects responding to the larger Greco-Roman environment.

To summarize, the situation around the Mediterranean generated large textual projects out of the centers of cultural power (and sometimes political power), which in turn inspired local histories to stake their counterclaims even as they were beholden to the operating assumptions of universal philosophy and history. It is evident that these projects, whether from the center or the periphery, flourished in the aftermath of earlier Hellenistic kingdoms, and again in the wake of later Roman imperialism. (It was an intellectual effort affected less directly by the larger political context, as we saw in Chapter One with the Bronze Age expressions about translatability, with the situation with monarchic Israel standing somewhere in-between, as seen in Chapter Two.) At the same time, translatability on the part of local writers drew heavily on their regional traditions in order to defend their identity within the larger Greco-Roman discourse emerging out of Hellenistic philosophical and literary centers. As we have seen, local writers made identifications between their own older deities and Greco-Roman deities in order to maintain their local religious identity against the general Greco-Roman practice of identifying deities across the Mediterranean basin. Local writers reached back in time to the traditions that they inherited as support. We may now turn to this local strategy of interpreting deities.

Temporal or "Vertical" Translatability

One last feature in the Greco-Roman context deserving of attention is the local interest in translatability down through time. In general, the vast majority of our cases of translatability discussed up this point, whether in the Late Bronze Age or Greco-Roman contexts, involve translation across contemporaneous cultures. This translatability operated across geographical regions and thus in character it is spatial, or we might say, horizontal. There is also translatability though time, whereby an local author wishes to translate terms of older deities of his culture into deities prevalent in the times of the larger culture in which he finds himself. A parade example of such a writer is Philo of Byblos. Above are noted the following equations: "they called him Beelsamem, which is 'Lord of Heaven' in Phoenician, Zeus in Greek"; "Chousor practiced verbal arts including spells and prophecies. He is, in fact, Hephaistos"; "Kronos whom the Phoenicians call El"; and "The Phoenicians say that Astarte is Aprodite." These figures go back to an earlier period. Baalshamem was a leading Phoenician god. Chousor has been traced back to Ugaritic Kothar wa-Hasis, and El was the well-known head of the Ugaritic pantheon. Astarte (Athtart) is well known in Ugaritic and Phoenician sources. All of these figures are translated into Greek. This act of translatability is temporal, in moving from the older Phoenician source to the Greco-Roman context, or we might say, vertical. This vertical dimension is important for understanding Philo's project. It is part of his purpose to appeal to the antiquity of local tradition, as Harold Attridge and Robert Oden comment, "a *topos* among 'barbarian' apologists in the Hellenistic and Roman era."[120] Thus vertical translatability, linked to horizontal translatability, functions in this period to help regional writers stake their local claims over and against the larger enterprise of Hellenistic learning. Compared to what we saw for the Bronze and Iron Ages, vertical translatability is added to the project of horizontal translatability. Vertical translatability is likewise an issue in Jewish and Jewish-Christian accounts of its deity. Or stated differently, vertical translatability in Jewish and Jewish-Christian writings in the Greco-Roman period plays a significant role in their expressions of horizontal translatability. These authors, and their efforts in translatability, are the topic of Chapter Six.

---

[120] Attridge and Oden, *Philo of Byblos,* 8.

The Biblical God in the World:
Jewish and Christian Translatability and Its Limits

For "In him we live and move and have our being,"
as even some of your own poets have said,
"For we too are his offspring."
Acts 17:28 (RNAB)

1. Translations of God from Jewish to Non-Jewish Sources

The preceding chapter surveyed a variety of non-Jewish texts involving translatability of divinity. Within this web of translation were a number of different conceptual representations of divinity, ranging from straightforward equations or identifications of deities to more complex cross-cultural expressions of divine oneness. Within non-Jewish contexts, the Jewish god took a place among the other deities. Many non-Jewish authors were familiar with the Jewish divine name Iao and at times discussed it, as we see in the following remarks of Philo of Byblos:

There has been and is much disagreement among theologians about the god honored among the Hebrews ... the Roman Varro says, in discussing him, that among the Chaldaeans in their mysteries he is called Iao, which stands for "intelligible light" in the Phoenician language, as Herennius says.[1]

The Jewish god was discussed by other classical writers. Around the turn of the era, Strabo of Amaseia recounted the origins of Jewish religion, in particular the teaching of Moses, which included Jewish aniconism, "for according to him, God is this one thing alone that encompasses us all and encompasses land and sea."[2] In discussions by classical authors such

---

[1] As preserved in: Lydus, *De mensibus*, 4.53, text and translation in: Menachem Stern, ed., *Greek and Latin Authors on Jews and Judaism* (three vols.; Jerusalem: Israel Academy of Sciences and Humanities, 1976–84) 2.211–12; and H. W. Attridge and R. A. Oden, Jr., *Philo of Byblos. The Phoenician History: Introduction, Critical Text, Translation, Notes* (CBQMS 9; Washington, DC: The Catholic Biblical Association of America, 1981) 70–71.

[2] Strabo, *Geography*, 16.2.35. See Horace Leonard Jones, *The Geography of Strabo VII: Books XV–XVI* (LCL; Cambridge, MA: Harvard University; London: W. Heineman, 1930) 282–83; and Stern, *Greek and Latin Authors on the Jews and Judaism*, 1.294, 299–300. This passage is discussed in the context of Jewish aniconism during this period

as Tacitus,[3] Jewish monotheism was known, as was the Jewish god more generally.[4] Moreover, the Jewish god figured in cases of non-Jewish translatability, with Dionysius[5] or Zeus[6] or Jupiter.[7] In the Greco-Roman context, these instances occasion little surprise. Before reviewing some of the more interesting cases, we should take note of the warning offered by John Gager, who advises against seeing in every instance of Iao an attestation of the Jewish divine name.[8] In accordance with this cautionary note, we will limit our discussion to what seem to be clear uses of the Jewish divine name in contexts involving translatability.

---

by Steven Fine, *Art and Judaism in the Greco-Roman World: Toward a New Jewish Archaeology* (Cambridge: Cambridge University, 2005) 70. Fine sees Jewish opposition to images as a matter not against any representation in general, but specifically against non-Jewish religious iconography; for this reason he prefers the label, "anti-idolic," to "aniconic."

[3] Tacitus, *Historiae* 5.5, cited in: Stern, *Greek and Latin Authors on Jews and Judaism,* 2.19 and 26.

[4] For example, Diodorus Siculus, *Bibliotheca Historica* 1.92.2, cited in: Stern, *Greek and Latin Authors on Jews and Judaism,* 2.171–72. See also Antonius Julianus, as represented by Minucius Felix in his *Octavius* 33.2–4, cited in: Stern, *Greek and Latin Authors on Jews and Judaism,* 1.460; Juvenal, *Saturae* 14.97, in: Stern, *Greek and Latin Authors on Jews and Judaism,* 2.102; Celsus, in: Origen, *Contra Celsus* 1.22–23, in: Stern, *Greek and Latin Authors on Jews and Judaism,* 2.233, 265; Cassius Dio, *Historia Romana* 37.17.2, in: Stern, *Greek and Latin Authors on Jews and Judaism,* 2.349, 351.

[5] Plutarch, *Quaestiones Convivales* 6.2, cited in: Stern, *Greek and Latin Authors on Jews and Judaism,* 1.553. In this connection one may note an inscription from Iasos in Asia Minor that records the donation of Niketas, the son of Jason from Jerusalem, for the feast of Dionysius (*Corpus Inscriptiorum Judaicorum* 749). For discussion, see Arnoldo Momigliano, *Essays on Ancient and Modern Judaism* (ed. Silvia Berti; trans. Maura Masella-Gayley; Chicago: University of Chicago, 1994) 21.

[6] For an accessible case, see the prayer to Helios in a ritual context in *PGM* III 212, conveniently presented by John Dillon and E. N. O'Neil in *PGMT* 24.

[7] Varro, cited in: Augustine, *De Consensu Evangelistarum* 1.22.30, 31 and 1.27.42 cited in: Stern, *Greek and Latin Authors on Jews and Judaism,* 1.210–11; and discussed by Schäfer, *Judeophobia,* 37–38. This example as well as others drawn above from classical sources are discussed in: Marcel Simon, "Jupiter-Yahvé: sur un essai de théologie paganojuive," *Numen* 23 (1976) 40–66; Gideon Bohak, "The Impact of Jewish Monotheism on the Greco-Roman World," *Jewish Studies Quarterly* 7 (2000) 11–13; and Lester L. Grabbe, *Judaic Religion in the Second Temple Period: Belief and Practice from the Exile to Yavneh* (London/New York: Routledge 2000) 218. In addition, the identification of the Jewish god as Jupiter Sabazius appears in a number of classical authors, for example Valerius Maximus (see Stern, *Greek and Latin Authors on Jews and Judaism,* 1.358, with discussion on p. 359; and Schäfer, *Judeophobia,* 51). The older authors cited by Stern view the identification as arising from the misconception of the Phrygian god Sabazius as the god of the Sabbath or from the identification of the Jewish god with Dionysius. For Sabazius in Roman Asia Minor, see Philip A. Harland, *Associations, Synagogues, and Congregations: Claiming a Place in Ancient Mediterranean Society* (Minneapolis, MN: Fortress, 2003) 44–45. Schäfer sees Jupiter Sabazius either as a corruption of Iao Sabaoth in a Latin source (the one used by either Valerius Maximus or by Iulius Paris or by his medieval copyists) or as a non-Jewish effort to identify the Jewish god with Jupiter.

[8] Gager, *Curse Tablets,* 144 n. 94.

Greco-Roman "One-God" Formulations with Iao

In some rather complex instances of translatability, Iao is construed as the highest god or supreme god of gods. For example, Jan Assmann[9] cites an elaborate instance in *The Saturnalia* by Macrobius.[10] Writing his imaginary dialogue on the eve of the Christian Roman empire. Macrobius (1.18.18) prefaces his reference to Iao with a citation of the Orphic verse: "one Zeus, one Hades, one Sun, one Dionysius, one god in all."[11] Macrobius goes on to claim warrant for the identification of this one god as Iao, based on the oracle of Apollo of Claros (1.18.18–20):

For when Apollo of Claros was asked who among the gods was to be regarded as the god called Iao, he replied: "Those who have learned the mysteries should hide the unsearchable secrets, but, if the understanding is small and the mind weak, then ponder this: that Iao is the supreme god of all gods; in winter, Hades, at spring's beginning, Zeus, the Sun in summer; and in autumn, the splendid Iao.

Macrobius then concludes the discussion of Iao with his comment (1.18.21): "For the meaning of this oracle and for the explanation, of the deity and his name, which identifies Iao with Liber Pater and the sun, our authority is Cornelius Labeo in his book entitled *On the Oracle of Apollo of Claros*." Here Macrobius does not show any particular understanding of the Jewish background of this deity, who had made his way into the Greco-Roman world. Nonetheless, this is a cross-cultural, universal god, with Iao given for its name. With this sort of text, Assmann locates the Jewish God within the Greco-Roman "quest for the sole and supreme divine principle beyond the innumerable multitude of specific deities."[12]

Another of Assmann's examples, a magical consecration text (*PGM* XII 263–266), represents a speaker who addresses the supreme god Iao with the "names of the nations":

I invoke you as do the Egyptians: "Phno eai Iabok,"
As do the Jews: Adonaie Sabaoth,
As do the Greek, king, ruling as monarch over all,
As do the high priests, hidden one, invisible one, who looks upon all,
As do the Parthians, OYERTO [the great one of earth] almighty.[13]

---

[9] Assmann, *Moses the Egyptian,* 50–51.

[10] Assmann, *Moses the Egyptian,* 50–51.

[11] The translation comes from Percival Vaughan Davies, *Macrobius. The Saturnalia* (New York/London: Columbia University, 1969) 131. See also Stern, *Greek and Latin Authors on Jews and Judaism,* 2.411–12; and the discussion of Schäfer, *Judeophobia,* 52–53. Nicely illustrating general translatability of this period surveyed in Chapter Five, this quote serves as the epigraph to that chapter.

[12] Assmann, *Moses the Egyptian,* 51.

[13] This is Assmann's translation, with the bracketed translation of the title drawn from Robert K. Ritner's correlation of it with an Egyptian title in *PGMT* 163 n. 79. See also the translation by Morton Smith in *PGMT* 163.

These cases point to the role that the Jewish divine name played in the wider international discourse of Greco-Roman magical texts.

Many magical texts, both Greek and Demotic, deploy a translatability involving Iao, as Assmann's examples exemplify. Yet we are not speaking only of translatability in the narrow sense. This period also shows the Jewish divine name playing a magical role alongside other deities and their names. In this way, the Jewish god joins an international congress of deities recognized for their power. It is the quality of power that is recognized as the basis for deities and their names functioning either together or individually within magical texts. Among spells in late antiquity, several invoke the Jewish god in two forms, often in the more common Greek Iao (cf. 4QpapLXXLeviticus[b] to Leviticus 2–5, at 3:12 and 4:27),[14] but sometimes with the rarer Demotic Iaho (which stands closer to the Hebrew short forms of the name, Yahu/Yah).[15] In addition to these forms of the divine name, we see the title Adonai.[16]

Occasionally the Jewish divine name serves as part of a larger concept of divinity. For example, a spell (*PGM* CV.1–10) contains the following prayer:

The one having appeared [before] the universe in [accordance with your] eternal nature, the untiring one, the one who ... I call upon you, lord [Almighty], the unknown one, the pure soul, I, the one ... having been sanctified. Be merciful to me, O Zeus-Iao-Zen-Helios ...[17]

---

[14] See Patrick W. Skehan et al., *Qumran Cave, IV: Palaeo-Hebrew and Greek Biblical Manuscripts* (DJD 9; Oxford: Clarendon, 1992) 168; and Emanuel Tov, *Scribal Practices and Approaches Reflected in the Texts Found in the Judean Desert* (STDJ 54; Leiden/Boston: Brill, 2004) 220–21. See also André Lemaire, *Naissance du monothéisme: Point de vue d'un historien* (Paris: Bayard, 2003) 164.

[15] For examples of the Jewish divine name Iao in magical texts (many of which are relatively late for our study), see among others, *PGM* III 146 = *PGMT* 22, *PGM* III 212 = *PGMT* 24. For discussion, see *PGMT* 335 with citation of further literature; and the listing of occurrences of Iao in the *PGMT* with discussion, by Morton Smith, "The Jewish Elements in the Magical Papyri," *SBL 1986 Seminar Papers* (ed. Kent Harold Richards; SBL Seminar Papers series 26; Atlanta: Scholars, 1986) 455–62, reprinted in a revised form in: Smith, *Studies in the Cult of Yahweh* (Religions of the Graeco-Roman World 130; two vols.; Leiden: Brill, 1996) 2.242–56. Other cases of Iao appear in the material treated by John G. Gager, ed., *Curse Tablets and Binding Spells from the Ancient World* (New York/Oxford: Oxford University, 1992) 63, 64, 67, 70 n. 95, 94, 100, 101, 104, 136, 137, 144, 216, 226. See also Fritz Graf, *Magic in the Ancient World* (trans. Franklin Philip; Revealing Antiquity vol. 10; Cambridge, MA/London: Harvard University, 1997) 201–2. For the name Iaho see below.

[16] For examples of Adonai in the magical texts, see *PGM* I 310 = *PGMT* 11; *PGM* III 147 = *PGMT* 22; *PGM* III 221 = *PGMT* 24, etc.; and the discussion at *PGMT* 331; see Iao Adoneai in: *PGM* XII 63 = *PGMT* 155.

[17] Roy Kotansky, in: *PGMT* 310.

In this instance, Iao is part of a long combination (or "fusion") name consisting of important deities, thus issuing in a single super-deity. Another example comes from a love spell attested in the great papyrus in the Paris Bibliothèque Nationale (*PGM* IV, 296–466).[18] The ritual is designed to bind the object of the speaker's desire to himself. In one component of the ritual, the names of various deities are to be written on different parts of a magical female figurine. As Fritz Graf suggests, this procedure reflects a correlation in hierarchy between deities and body-parts, with Iao assigned the head, Ammon the face, Thoth the heart and "derivatives of the Semitic *melech*, 'king'," the arms and hands. In this vision of the divine body, Iao is accorded the highest rank.[19] These two magical texts exhibit different sides of magical praxis using the name of Iao in tandem with different major deities: the invocation of a long combination-name and a magical figurine. These magical usages are not distant from some models of divinity known from earlier periods in the ancient Near East, such as various gods construed as the different body-parts of Marduk (as we saw in Chapter Three) or the combination Amun-Re in the Late Bronze Age.[20] There are, of course, differences. The earlier usages largely derive from national religion and politics, while the context for these two Greco-Roman texts is individual and personal. What is particularly distinctive for this investigation is that the deities in Greco-Roman combinations of deities may come from different regions of the Mediterranean. It is cross-cultural in character, in contrast with the "one-god" representations of Amun-Re in the Late Bronze Age, or Marduk and Assur or Yahweh in the Iron Age that we met in Chapter Three.

From this magical text, we may make a further cultural observation. This document, with its particular combination of Egyptian gods with the Jewish Iao, seems to point to Alexandrian Judaism as one conduit through which the name of the Jewish deity passed into broader Greco-Roman

---

[18] Graf, *Magic in the Ancient World*, 137–44. For the text, see *PGM* IV 296–466; for translation, see E. N. O'Neal in: *PGMT* 44–47. The text is thought to represent a fifth-century CE/AD handbook of magic from Egypt (see Faraone, *Ancient Greek Love Magic*, 14, with secondary literature).

[19] Graf, *Magic in the Ancient World*, 143–44. The DN *mlk* is known. See George C. Heider, "Molech," *DDD* 582–83; Mark S. Smith, *The Early History of God: Yahweh and the Other Deities in Ancient Israel* (second ed.; The Biblical Resource Series; Grand Rapids, MI/Cambridge, UK: Eerdmans; Dearborn, MI: Dove, 2002) 178–80. The relationship of this figure to biblical "Molech" is disputed.

[20] For this deity, see Jan Assmann, *Re und Amun: Die Krise des polytheistischen Weltbilds im Ägypten der 18.–20. Dynastie* (OBO 51; Fribourg: Universitätsverlag; Göttingen: Vandenhoeck & Ruprecht, 1983). This work appeared in English as *Egyptian Solar Religion in the New Kingdom: Re, Amun and the Crisis of Polytheism* (trans. Anthony Alcock; London/New York: Kegan Paul, 1995).

magical discourse.[21] This view would comport with evidence known from a third century CE/AD Egyptian magical text from Egypt known as the Leiden Papyrus.[22] This Demotic magical book contains numerous spells with the Jewish god under his name, Yaho (*y'h-'o*).[23] This form of the divine name stands closer to its original Hebrew form than Greek Iao. At the same time, this text shows signs of Greek influence on the Jewish elements that can be identified in it. For example, there is the form of the divine name Iao, *y'-'o*, in the same papyrus, which reflects the influence of Greek Iao.[24] In addition, one magical text in this papyrus uses the Greek form of the name of Moses (*mwses*),[25] in calling on a series of figures, and makes the following request: "reveal yourself to me here today in the fashion of the revelation to Moses which you made upon the mountain, before whom you yourself created darkness and light."[26]

The Jewish elements in these Egyptian magical texts may point to Alexandria as their source, a context reflected also in the Letter of Aristeas.[27] This document was designed to explain the origins of the Septuagint translation in Alexandria. In line 140 of this text, the speaker attributes to Egyptian priests recognition of Jews as "men of God," a designation that in Erich Gruen's words, was "accorded only to those who worship the true God."[28] From a Jewish center such as Alexandria, we might expect further dispersal

---

[21] Garth Fowden likewise attributes the absorption of Jewish ideas by Hermetic writers to the large Jewish population in Alexandria. See Fowden, *The Egyptian Hermes: A Historical Approach to the Pagan Mind* (Princeton: Princeton University, 1986) 36.

[22] For convenience, see F. L. Griffith and Herbert Thompson, *The Leyden Papyrus: An Egyptian Magical Book* (New York: Dover, 1974); this volume was originally published in 1904 under the name, *The Demotic Magical Papyrus of London and Leiden*.

[23] Griffith and Thompson, *The Leyden Papyrus*, 198–99, verso, column XXVII, lines 6–7: "Iaho is my name, Iaho is my true name" (see also recto, column VII, line 33, and VIII, line 3, pp. 62–63; column XIII, line 27, pp. 98–99; column XIX, line 18, pp. 124–25, and line 39, pp. 128–29; column XXI, line 6, pp. 134–35; column XXI, line 7, pp. 164–65; verso, column XII, line 7, pp. 184–85). Note also Adonai and Sabaoth in this papyrus in verso, column XV, line 6 (pp. 188–189) and in verso, column XXII, line 9 (pp. 194–195), respectively. The form Iaho appears in Jerome's *Commentarius ad Psalmos* VIII, 2, as noted by Lemaire, *Naissance du monotheisme, 1//.

[24] Griffith and Thompson, *The Leyden Papyrus*, 110–11, recto, column XVI, line 5. See Bohak, "The Impact of Jewish Monotheism on the Greco-Roman World," 4–5. See the rendering Iao by Janet Johnson in: *PGMT* 221.

[25] So Griffith and Thompson, *The Leyden Papyrus*, 46, note to line 14. See John Gager, *Moses in Greco-Roman Paganism* (SBLMS 16; Nashville: Abingdon, 1972).

[26] Griffith and Thompson, *The Leyden Papyrus*, 46–47, recto, column V, lines 13–14; *PGMT* 202.

[27] For a convenient translation of the passage in question, see R. J. H. Shutt, "Letter of Aristeas," in: *OTPs* 2.22. The Letter of Aristeas is discussed below.

[28] Gruen, *Heritage and Hellenism: The Reinvention of Jewish Tradition* (Berkeley/Los Angeles/London: University of California, 1998) 217. For the emphasis on God in the Letter of Aristeas, see John G. Gammie, "The Hellenization of Jewish Wisdom in the Letter of Aristeas," in: *Proceedings of the Ninth World Congress of Jewish Studies: Divi-*

of the Jewish divine name.[29] At the same time, while Alexandria served as a major contact point between Jews and non-Jews, we should be careful not to necessarily imply a single point of contact. In the Egyptian context in this period,[30] we may also note the sort of translatability involving the name of the Jewish god found in the unusual text of Papyrus Amherst 63, which was written in Aramaic language but in Demotic script.[31] This text includes a version of the biblical Psalm 20 in Aramaic written in Demotic, with the name of Horus substituting for the Jewish divine name.[32] Such substitutions

---

sion A. The Period of the Bible (Jerusalem: World Union of Jewish Studies, 1986) 207–14, esp. 210.

[29] In this connection, we may note a later case, a third century CE/AD text from North Africa that cites only the Jewish god, accompanied by some biblical echoes. See Gager, *Curse Tablets,* 112–15. For other Jewish elements in magical formulary (in addition to citations above), see Gideon Bohak, "Hebrew, Hebrew Everywhere? Notes on the Interpretation of *Voces Magicae,*" in: *Prayer, Magic, and the Stars in the Ancient and Late Antique World* (ed. Scott Noegel, Joel Walker, and Brannon Wheeler; University Park, PA: Pennsylvania State University, 2003) 69–82.

[30] One might add to this discussion material from Elephantine insofar as it reflects deities imported from the Levant. This subject lies beyond the scope of this discussion, and its place within the context of translatability remains controversial. Compare the discussions (in order of date) of Bezalel Porten, *Archives from Elephantine: The Life of an Ancient Jewish Military Colony* (Berkeley/Los Angeles: University of California, 1968) 154–56, 165–70, 178–79, 317; Robert du Mesnil du Buisson, *Études sur les dieux phéniciens hérités par l'empire romain* (EPRO 14; Leiden: Brill, 1970) 117–28; P. Kyle McCarter, Jr., "Aspects of the Religion of the Israelite Monarchy: Biblical and Epigraphic Data," in: *Ancient Israelite Religion: Essays in Honor of Frank Moore Cross* (ed. Patrick D. Miller, Jr., Paul D. Hanson, and S. Dean McBride; Philadelphia: Fortress, 1987) 147–48; Karel van der Toorn, "Anat-Yahu, Some Other Deities, and the Jews of Elephantine," *Numen* 39 (1992) 80–101; and Smith, *The Early History of God,* 101–3.

[31] For this text, see Richard C. Steiner, "The Aramaic Text in Demotic Script: The Liturgy of a New Year's Festival Imported from Bethel to Syene by Exiles from Rash," *JAOS* 111 (1991) 362–63; Richard C. Steiner and Charles F. Nims, "You Can't Offer Your Sacrifice and Eat It Too: A Polemical Poem from the Aramaic Text in Demotic Script," *JNES* 43 (1984) 89–114; "Ashurbanipal and Shamash-shum-ukin: A Tale of Two Brothers from the Aramaic Text in Demotic Script," *RB* 92 (1985) 60–81; Steiner, "Papyrus Amherst 63: A New Source for the Language, Literature, Religion, and History of the Arameans," in: *Studia Aramaica: New Sources and New Approaches* (ed. M. J. Geller, J. C. Greenfield, and M. P. Weitzman; Oxford: Oxford University, 1995) 199–207. For a translation with some notes, see Steiner, "The Aramaic Text in Demotic Script," in: *COS* 1.309–327. See also S. P. Vleeming and J. W. Wesselius, *Studies in Papyrus Amherst 63: Essays on the Aramaic Text in Aramaic/demotic Papyrus Amherst 63. Volume I* (Amsterdam: Juda Palache Instituut, 1985); and *Studies in Papyrus Amherst 63: Essays on the Aramaic Text in Aramaic/Demotic Papyrus Amherst 63. Volume II* (Amsterdam: Juda Palache Instituut, 1990). A critical edition of the full text has yet to appear.

[32] It is unknown whether the substitution was made in the Hellenistic period by Jews in Egypt (perhaps in Edfu) or by non-Jews who may have adapted the text for their use. For discussion, see Charles F. Nims and Richard C. Steiner, "A Paganized Version of Ps 20:2–6 from the Aramaic Text in Demotic Script," *JAOS* 103 (1983) 261–74, and especially p. 272. See also the studies of K. A. D. Smelik, "The Origins of Psalm 20," *Journal for the Society of the Old Testament* 31 (1985) 75–81; Moshe Weinfeld, "The Pagan Version of

were rather common in this period, and in this practice the name of the Jewish god was hardly exceptional. This text has often been placed considerably south of Alexandria at Edfu. It may not be a coincidence that two later Jewish inscriptions found at the temple of the god Pan at Edfu thank him and address him as "the god" (*ho theos*).[33]

The translation of the Jewish divine name into magical discourse was hardly a uniform process. A handful of Greek and Demotic texts with Iao show some further Jewish content or sensibility. In contrast, most uses of the Jewish divine name in Demotic and Greek magical texts reflect little or no understanding of Jewish material. Thus one might be inclined to follow Gideon Bohak in highlighting the basic disjunction between Jewish religious culture and Greco-Roman magic.[34] Bohak offers an important caution when he suggests that on the whole the penetration of Hebrew and Aramaic into non-Jewish magic was "a relatively rare occurrence."[35] Still these uses of the Jewish divine name in its various forms point to the Jewish contribution to the larger religious culture in this period. Like philosophy, magic was a widespread international discourse in this period, and Jewish elements slipped into place. Jewish divinity was thus incorporated into international discourse of divinity outside of Jewish circles.[36] In sum, Jewish divinity could be used in the broader Greco-Roman milieu in a variety of discourses, philosophical, religious and magical.

In contrast to non-Jewish recognition of the Jewish god, Assmann's "Mosaic distinction"[37] would seem to preclude translatability working in the opposite direction, with Jewish writers attempting some form of translatability of specific non-Jewish deities with their own. Assmann is quite correct to note the relative lack of translatability for many Jewish and Christian authors, for while Jewish authors regularly appropriated non-Jewish ideas about divinity and occasionally expressed translatability of

---

Psalm 20,2–6: Vicissitudes of a Psalmodic Creation in Israel and Its Neighbors, *Eretz-Israel* 18 (1985) 130–40; and Ziony Zevit, "The Common Origin of the Aramaicized Prayer to Horus and of Psalm 20," *JAOS* 11 (1990) 213–28 (Zevit's reconstruction of this relationship is more complex and worthy of consideration). I wish to thank Ron Hendel for suggesting inclusion of this case.

[33] For this information, see Pieter W. van der Horst, "The Unknown God (Acts 17:23)," in: *Knowledge of God in the Graeco-Roman World* (ed. R. van den Broek, T. Baarda, and J. Mansfield; EPRO 112; Leiden: Brill, 1988) 36.

[34] Bohak, "Hebrew, Hebrew Everywhere!" 77. For his argument and evidence, see Bohak, "Hebrew, Hebrew Everywhere!" 69–82.

[35] Bohak, "Hebrew, Hebrew Everywhere!" 77. There are at best few counter-indications, sometimes from other genres. One might point to a considerably later text, a second century CE/AD inscription from Chalcis attests to a non-Jew drawing on the Septuagint. See Gager, *Curse Tablets*, 184–85.

[36] Gager, *Curse Tablets*, 170 n. 74.

[37] See the discussion in the opening section of Chapter Two.

divinity, the level of cross-cultural translation of deities by Jewish authors was hardly comparable with what we meet among non-Jewish authors in this period.[38] Thus Martin Goodman notes: "Jews and Christians were unique in the Roman world in their belief that their God would be jealous of cult to other gods."[39] Similarly, John J. Collins and Steven Fine have argued that Jews in Judea drew the line at cultic and religious practice.[40] This line against translatability was already a relative standard one, drawn already in some circles in pre-exilic Israel[41] and maintained within the post-exilic scribal-priestly establishment in Jerusalem in matters of both cult and textual production.[42] Thus at a certain point, non-Jewish translatability would encounter Jewish non-translatability in this period. As we will see, there seems to be some difference on this score between the Jewish diaspora and Judaism within Judea.

Translatability in the Jerusalem Temple?

One flash point of conflict between non-Jewish translatability and Jewish non-translatability in Judea was apparently set off by cultic changes made to the Jerusalem Temple sponsored by the Seleucid ruler, Antiochus IV Epiphanes.[43] 2 Maccabees 6:2 identifies the change as some form of cultic devotion to Zeus Olympius, and commentators have noted the identification of this form of Zeus with Syrian Baal Shamem,[44] an example of translatability

---

[38] Generally see the classic work of Martin Hengel, *Judaism and Hellenism: Studies in their Encounter in Palestine during the Early Hellenistic Period* (second one-volume ed.; Minneapolis: Fortress, 1991). See also his retrospective essay, "Judaism and Hellenism Revisited," in: *Hellenism in the Land of Israel* (ed. John J. Collins and Gregory E. Sterling; Christianity and Judaism in Antiquity Series 13; South Bend, in: University of Notre Dame, 2001) 6–37. For the early centuries CE, note also the seminal work of Saul Lieberman, *Greek in Jewish Palestine Hellenism in Jewish Palestine* (with a new introduction by Dov Zlotnick; New York: Jewish Theological Seminary of America, 1994).

[39] Goodman, "Trajan and the Origins of Roman Hostility to the Jews," *Past and Present* 182 (2004) 11–12.

[40] Collins, "Cult and Culture," 38–61; and Fine, *Art and Judaism in the Greco-Roman World,* 70–73. Fine places particular weight on the Maccabean revolt as a point of transition when aniconism (what he would prefer to understand as a stricture against idolatrous imagery or "anti-idolism") increased in status as a marker of Jewish identity.

[41] See the discussion of 1 Kings 11:4–7 in Chapter Two, pp. 125–26.

[42] See Chapter Four.

[43] This is an immense topic with a considerable range of views surveyed by Lester L. Grabbe, *Judaism from Cyrus to Hadrian. Volume One. The Persian and Greek Periods* (Minneapolis: Fortress, 1992) 246–59.

[44] For example, Louis F. Hartman and Alexander A. Di Lella, *Daniel* (AB 23; Garden City, NY: Doubleday, 1978) 299; Klaus-Dietrich Schunck, *I. Makkabäerbuch* (Jüdische Schriften aus hellenistisch-römischer Zeit I; Gütersloh: Mohn, 1980) 302 note b to verse 54; John Kampen, "Olympian Zeus, Temple of," *ABD* 5:15; John J. Collins, *Daniel: A Commentary on the Book of Daniel* (Hermeneia; Minneapolis: Fortress, 1993) 357.

of deities made also by Philo of Byblos (noted in Chapter Five).[45] However, the worship intended may not have been only a Syrian-Greek one. There may have been a second level of translatability attempted here. The alteration in the Temple has been viewed as a further effort on the part of its Seleucid sponsors at some form of translatability with the Jewish god,[46] apparently supported to some extent by the Jewish population, including some local Jewish leaders (see 1 Maccabees 1:11–15, 43, 52; 3:15; cf. 2 Maccabees 5:15).[47] Morton Smith notes that before the Maccabean revolt Yahweh was identified in Jerusalem with Zeus and Dionysius.[48] Building on the work of E. J. Bickerman and V. A. Tcherikover, Klaus Bringmann has suggested that the cultic situation under the Seleucids may have included an effort at adding the Jewish god to the larger equation of Greek Zeus Olympius and Syrian Baal Shamem.[49] Lawrence H. Schiffman comments similarly: "The Jewish Hellenizers, Menelaus and his party, saw these gods as equivalent to the God of Israel, and thus in their view this was not really foreign worship."[50]

---

[45] Collins (*Daniel*, 357 n. 102), too, notes the correspondence of Zeus with Baal Shamem in Philo of Byblos (*PE* 1.10.7), and cites H. W. Attridge and R. A. Oden, Jr., *Philo of Byblos The Phoenician History: Introduction, Critical Text, Translation, Notes* (CBQMS 9; Washington, DC: The Catholic Biblical Association of America, 1981) 40.

[46] See the range of views discussed by Kampen, "Olympian Zeus, Temple of," 15. Kampen is critical of this view of translatability as one of the Seleucid aims.

[47] Particular emphasis on the political aspects of the issue has been made by Klaus Bringmann, *Hellenistische Reform und Religionsverfolgung in Judäa: eine Untersuchung zur jüdisch-hellenistischen Geschichte (175–163 v. Chr.)* (Abhandlungen der Akademie der Wissenschaften in Göttingen, Philologisch-Historische Klasse 3/132; Göttingen: Vandenhoeck & Ruprecht, 1983). For critical remarks on this emphasis (to the virtual exclusion of religious considerations), see Hengel, "Judaism and Hellenism Revisited," 17. Seth Schwartz also discusses the role of Jason in this regard. See Schwartz, *Imperialism and Jewish Society, 200 B. C. E. to 640 C. E.* (Princeton/Oxford: Princeton University, 2001) 32.

[48] Morton Smith, *The Cult of Yahweh,* 1.231–32.

[49] Bringmann, *Hellenistische Reform und Religionsverfolgung in Judäa,* 120–140. See the appraisals by Herbert Niehr, "God of Heaven," *DDD* 371; and by Grabbe, *Judaism from Cyrus to Hadrian,* 253–55. Grabbe (*Judaism from Cyrus to Hadrian,* 257–58) compares this situation at the Jerusalem Temple with the Samaritan temple at Shechem dedicated to Zeus Xenios, which shows no indication of new Hellenistic changes: "Rather, the Samaritans apparently continued to operate a cult very similar to that which had been banned in Jerusalem, but under a Greek label." See also Graf, "Zeus," *DDD* 939. In this connection, one may also note the inscription of the name of Zeus on one Samaritan coin, viewed as a Greek equivalent for Yahweh at Samaria by Ephraim Stern, *Archaeology of the Land of the Bible. Volume II: The Assyrian, Babylonian, and Persian Periods (732–332 B. C. E.)* (ABRL; New York: Doubleday, 2001) 570. Bringmann focuses on the military settlers established by Antiochus in Jerusalem as the source of the worship of Baal Shamem; at the same time, the cultic innovation is laid at the feet of Antiochus.

[50] Schiffman, *From Text to Tradition: A History of Second Temple and Rabbinic Judaism* (Hoboken, NJ: Ktav, 1991) 76. Schiffman comments further that Jewish Hellenizers "regarded the ancestral God of Israel as simply another manifestation of the supreme deity known in Syria as Baal Shamin (Master of Heaven) and in the Greek world as

The precise nature of the cultic change involved is unclear.[51] According to 1 Maccabees 1:54, it was a "sacrilege on the altar of burnt offering." 2 Maccabees 6:5 says that "the altar was covered by abominable offerings." The object involved might seem to be something placed or built upon (and in proximity to) an altar that could take the offerings deemed idolatrous. Daniel 9:27 places the idolatry "at the corner of" (*'al kanap*), which might suit a pre-existing altar.[52] A significant number of commentators, including Klaus-Dietrich Schunck and John J. Collins, view the innovation as a new altar.[53] Other scholars propose to see some sort of additional religious symbol. Klaus Koch suggests "ein astrales Symbol über dem Hauptaltar im Vorhof,"[54] while Jonathan Goldstein suggests three meteorite cult-stones representing the God of the Jews, his female consort, the Queen of Heaven and his divine son, Dionysius.[55] Collins characterizes Goldstein's view as

---

Zeus Olympius. In this way they rationalized their behavior." It is unclear which form of translatability this represented in their minds. Perhaps the sort of high view of Iao in Macrobius (cited above) is what they thought they were championing even if their Seleucid patron did not share this view. Perhaps they genuinely believed in it and it was no mere rationalization.

[51] Seleucid oversight of sanctuaries was evidently an administrative matter. See the description of administrative appointment in 2 Maccabees 6:1–2, which includes the temples in Jerusalem and Gerizim. Cf. the unpublished Greek stele dated to 178, which describes Seleucus IV's appointment of the senior Greek clerk Olympiodorus to oversee sanctuaries in Israel and surrounding areas, described in http://www.haaretz.com/hasen/spages/856802.html.

[52] Cf. the addition in NJPS: "at the corner [of the altar]." James A. Montgomery likewise took the Hebrew here seriously despite the Greek witnesses to "on the temple." See Montgomery, *A Critical and Exegetical Commentary on the Book of Daniel* (ICC; Edinburgh: T & T Clark, 1927) 388; for a critique, see Collins, *Daniel*, 358. One might argue that the Hebrew represents the more difficult reading here. For an older proposal to see **b'l* behind *'l*, see Otto Eissfeldt, *Kleine Schriften: Zweiter Band* (ed. Rudolph Sellheim and Fritz Maass; Tübingen: Mohr Siebeck, 1963) 431–34; discussed by Otto Plöger, *Das Buch Daniel* (Kommentar zum Alten Testament 18; Gütersloh: Mohn, 1965) 135; and Hengel, "Judaism and Hellenism Revisited," 18–19.

[53] For this view, Schunck (*I. Makkabäerbuch*, 302, note b to verse 54) and Collins (*Daniel*, 357–58) cite Josephus, *Antiquities* 12.5.4, which Collins notes is based on 2 Maccabees 6:5. See also Fritz Graf, "Zeus," *DDD* 938. However, Collins observes that 2 Maccabees 6:5 does not speak to the issue of the addition of a new altar as such.

[54] Koch, *Der Gott Israels und die Götter des Orient*, 32.

[55] Goldstein, *I Maccabees* (AB 41; Garden City, NY: Doubleday, 1976) 143–57, 224. See also his article, "The Persecution of the Jews by Antiochus IV," in: *Proceedings of the Sixth World Congress of Jewish Studies: Volume I* (ed. Avigdor Shinan; Jerusalem: World Union of Jewish Studies, 1977) 135–47. See further along these lines JoAnn Scurlock, "167 BCE: Hellenism or Reform?" *JSJ* 31 (2000) 125–61. Note the reference to Dionysius in 2 Maccabees 6:7. As Greek and Roman authors identified Dionysios and Yahweh (Plutarch, *Quaest. Conv.* 4,6; Tacitus, *Hist.* 5, 5), "it seems a learned way to classify Jewish religion according to the rules of *interpretatio Graeca*" (Fritz Graf, "Dionysus," *DDD* 257).

"very speculative."[56] The entire matter remains quite unclear,[57] and it is even possible that multiple alterations underlie the various witnesses. In any case, it would have involved one or more features that suited the worldview of its Seleucid sponsor as well as his Jewish supporters.

Whatever the nature of the cultic change(s), the Seleucid innovation may be viewed as an effort to fit the Jewish monotheism, as it was understood by the Seleucids, within a broader translation of the Jewish god with Zeus Olympius and Baal Shamem. This might not have appeared monotheistic to many Jews by traditional standards,[58] especially when it is viewed in light of the lack of cultic translatability in the Iron Age Israelite texts that we saw in Chapter Three and the Persian period texts mentioned in Chapter Four. It was instead a Greco-Roman form of oneness of divinity of the sort that we saw in Chapter Five that Antiochus and his Jewish supporters sought to accommodate with Jewish monotheism. The idea was perhaps a relative simple notion of translation or perhaps an effort to represent divinity as "one Zeus, one Baal Shamem, one Iao, one Dionysius, one god in all" (to echo Orphic Fragment 239, cited at the outset of Chapter Five), quite similar to the formulation of Macrobius (quoted toward the beginning of this chapter). With this cultic alteration, perhaps the Jewish constituents for this change were to view Iao as the divine reality or god underlying the translatability. Thus the Seleucids, with their Greco-Roman worldview of translatability of the major Syrian god with the major god of Greco-Roman culture, arguably believed that its addition of the Jewish god to this equation would not be problematic for their Jewish supporters, much less for the broader Jewish populace, especially if its god retained supremacy within Jerusalem and Judea. Whatever the precise religious logic of the translation and its cultic realization in the Temple, it is important to note that the change would hardly have been politically neutral in character: translatability here likely served the purposes of foreign, royal power.

The Syrian attempt at translation, however, was hardly successful among some segments of the Jewish populace. Indeed, it was represented as one of the central factors precipitating the Maccabean revolt against the Seleucids (1 Maccabees 1; 2 Maccabees 6). Dramatically negative responses to the Seleucid makeover of the Temple can be identified in two different works of this period. The Seleucid alteration is labeled "an abomination that desolates," expressed in three variations in Daniel 9:27, 11:31, and 12:11 (*šiqquṣim mešomem / haššiqquṣ mešomem / šiqquṣim šomem*). In 1 Maccabees 1:54 it is called "the abomination of desolation" (*bdelugma*

---

[56] Collins, *Daniel*, 358 n. 105.

[57] Other sources are even more vague, e.g., Jubilees 23:21 (*OTPs* 2.101).

[58] Goldstein, *I Maccabees*, 145: "It was not monotheistic."

eremoseos).[59] Over a century ago Eberhard Nestle identified in the Hebrew phrase in Daniel a deliberately critical wordplay on the name of the Seleucid Baal Shamem, and this proposal has enjoyed wide acceptance.[60] Nestle's approach was taken a step further by scholars who understood the phrase in its various forms as reflecting two biblical strategies for handling foreign deities. As James Montgomery noted,[61] the phrase's first word *šiqquṣim* in Daniel 9:27, or *šiqquṣ* in 11:31 and 12:11, echoes the same word applied to foreign deities in the books of Kings, such as Milcom in 1 Kings 11:5, 7; Chemosh in 1 Kings 11:5 and 2 Kings 23:13; and Ashtoreth in 1 Kings 11:5 and 7 (see also Deuteronomy 29:16).[62] Following Montgomery's lead, it may be noted that the second term *mešomem/šomem* recalls earlier biblical polemical re-labellings such as the name Ishbosheth, literally "man of shame" (2 Samuel 2:8) for Ishbaal, "man of Baal" (1 Chronicles 8:33, 9:39) and Mepiboshet (2 Samuel 4:4 and 21:8) for Meribaal (1 Chronicles 8:34, 9:40) as well as the name of Jezebel (*'îzebel*, 1 Kings 16:31, 18:4, etc.) for **'i-zbl*, "where is the Prince," the latter element known in the Ugaritic texts as a title of Baal (CAT 1.2 I 38, 43; 1.2 IV 8; 1.3 I 3–4, etc.; cf. *'izbl b'l*, "where is Prince Baal," in 1.6 IV 5; cf. 1.5 IV 6–7).[63] The unusual and compact Hebrew phrase in Daniel 9:27, 11:31 and 12:11 thus bears the freight of older biblical usages likewise aimed at idolatry. Viewed in this light, the phrase redeploys traditional scriptural terms and strategies in an effort at evoking biblical sanction against the Seleucid makeover of the Temple.

---

[59] The phrase, in its three Hebrew variants, is difficult. The first word appears both with the definite article (11:31) and without it (9:27 and 12:11); it also varies in number between the singular form (11:31 and 12:11) and plural (9:27). The form of the second word also varies slightly; it seems to be a participle, qal in the case of 12:11 and poal in 9:27 and 11:31 (see *BDB* 1030–31). Goldstein objects to the grammar of the Hebrew phrases and would revocalize the second word as the preposition *min* plus a noun (so Goldstein, *I Maccabees*, 143 n. 240, with text-critical support taken from Theodotion to 9:27, *apo aphanismou*); this "solution," though perhaps not impossible, seems a bit stilted for Hebrew grammar. Following the attestation of the singular rather than the plural in 11:31, the easier revocalization for the phrase in 9:27 would take the final mem of the first word as a dittography. For this approach, see Mayer I. Gruber, "Abomination," *DDD* 2–3. This solution also better suits the evident pun on the name of Baal Shamem. See also Daniel 8:13.

[60] Nestle, "Zu Daniel," *ZAW* 4 (1884) 247–48. See Collins, *Daniel*, 357; Goldstein, *I Maccabees*, 147; Hengel, "Judaism and Hellenism Revisited," 18; and Martin Mulder, "God of the Fortresses," *DDD* 369.

[61] Montgomery, *Daniel*, 388.

[62] Gruber, "Abomination," 2. See above pp. 111 and 125.

[63] It should be noted that this long-held view of these names has been challenged in recent years. Gordon J. Hamilton has suggested seeing a legitimate and positive title behind these uses of BH *bošet*, based on Akkadian *baštu*, "protective spirit." See Hamilton, "New Evidence for the Authenticity of *bšt* in Hebrew Personal Names and for Its Use as a Divine epithet in Biblical Texts," *CBQ* 60 (1998) 228–50; for a more jaundiced view of this proposal, see H. D. Galter, "Bashtu," *DDD* 164. The old meaning as posited by Hamilton would not have been at issue in the second century.

1 Maccabees and Daniel represent different backgrounds, and the proximity of their labels suggests a Jewish currency for this wordplay broader than the circles that produced these two works. With the pun, we see a reversal of divinity, a negative sort of "translation" aimed against the effort at translatability. It is one characterized not as divinity, but as disgusting idolatry. The wordplay may constitute an act of verbal resistance to the Seleucid change in Temple cult. As events unfolded, Seleucid translatability in the Temple cult was problematic in Judea in this period. At the same time, it cannot be assumed that the negative reaction was uniformly shared by the local Jewish population or even among all its leaders. It is the view that eventually wins the day, but it is hardly clear that this was the case at the time.

Competing "One-God" Theisms: Jewish Non-Translatability
versus Greco-Roman Translatability

Overall the larger contexts of 1 Maccabees and Daniel speak against translatability of divinity. 1 Maccabees reflects a nationalist agenda looking back on the revolt as the foundational moment in rejecting empire and its aspirations to imperial translatability. Such nationalist literature was opposed to the invasion of foreigners and deities whom they might seek to equate. This sort of national literature burns conceptual bridges to the deities of others. A few passages in 1 Maccabees may further illustrate the point. The speech of Judas Maccabee in 1 Maccabees 4:9–11 reflects what has been called above "vertical translatability," specifically translation between divinity in the past with divinity of the present within the same tradition. Judas' speech calls to mind the victory of the Jewish god over the Egyptians at Red Sea in the hope that the same divine help may now provide aid, which will result in the same knowledge of the divinity: "All the Gentiles shall know that there is One who redeems and delivers Israel" (NAB; cf. Exodus 14:18). Other expressions focusing on the singular character of the Jewish God (e.g., 1 Maccabees 2:24–29; 2 Maccabees 3:24) might also be viewed as precluding horizontal translatability. Consistent with this view, the prosecution of other deities' cult is represented as an element of the Maccabean program (1 Maccabees 10:84). As Mattathias is said to put the point in 1 Maccabees 2:22b, "we will not depart from our religion in the slightest degree" (cf. NAB; more literally, not "to transgress our worship,[64] to the right or to the left," *parelthein ten latreian hemon dechian earisteran*).[65]

---

[64] That is, service to the deity. For *latreian,* see Frederick William Danker, ed., *A Greek-English Lexicon of the New Testament and Other Christian Literature* (third ed.; Chicago/London: University of Chicago, 2000) 587. For a possible biblical model, see Deuteronomy 5:29.

A similar concern informs the book of Daniel.⁶⁶ It, too, represents the Seleucid imposition as a defining moment in history. This turn in time will induce a divine intervention that is to overturn the course of empires and their idolatry. The beasts corresponding to the empires in Daniel 7 represent the divine monstrous opponents of the patron god. These shall be destroyed by "the Most High" (verses 26–27), a title of God known from early works in the Hebrew Bible, as opposed to Baal Shamem, "Most High Lord."⁶⁷ Daniel 9 presents in summary form the plan of history after a long supplication on Daniel's part. Echoing the older theology of the book of Deuteronomy (see especially in verse 11), the prayer attributes the subjugation by empire to divine judgment on Israel's sin. An angel then appears in order to answer Daniel's prayer. The angelic interpretation is structured by reference to

---

⁶⁵ This is not to comment on the general Maccabean political response, which was considerably flexible, according to Steven Weitzman, *Cultural Persistence in Jewish Antiquity* (Cambridge, MA/London: Harvard University, 2005) 34–54. Weitzman (p. 53) characterizes the Maccabean political strategy as "opportunistic" in "the treacherous world of Hellenistic politics," which commonly involved "side-switching and double-dealing." For another jaundiced view of Maccabean motivations, see Schwartz, *Imperialism and Jewish Society*, 33–34. Note also Schwartz's claim that subsequent "Hasmonean imperialism was a small-scale version of Roman imperialism" (*Imperialism and Jewish Society*, 40 n. 55).

⁶⁶ Apart from references to the "wise" (*maśkilim*) in Daniel 11:33–35 and 12:3, the social setting of the author(s) of Daniel is difficult to ferret out. For discussion, see Collins, *Daniel*, 61–70. See also the remarks of George W. Nickelsburg, "Social Aspects of Palestinian Jewish Apocalypticism," in: *Apocalypticism in the Mediterranean World and the Near East: Proceedings of the International Colloquium on Apocalypticism Uppsala, August 12–17, 1979* (ed. David Hellholm; second ed.; Tübingen: Mohr Siebeck, 1989) 645–46.

⁶⁷ For the title *theos hupsistos,* see Arthur Darby Nock, with C. Roberts and T.C. Skeat, "The Gild of Zeus Hypsistos," in his *Essays on Religion and the Ancient World* (vol. 1; ed. Zeph Stewart; Cambridge, MA: Harvard University, 1972) 414–43. They remark: the title is "a term in use, vague enough to suit any god treated as the supreme being … It fitted Jahwe perfectly, and Jewish and Christian writers put it in the mouths of non-Israelites who recognized their god; but would it suggest him to anyone except a Jew or Christian?" (p. 425). For more recent discussions of the title in Acts 7:48 and 16:17, see C. Breytenbach, "Hypsistos," in *DDD* 439–43; and Stephen Mitchell, "The Cult of Theos Hypsistos between Pagans, Jews, and Christians," in: *Pagan Monotheism in Late Antiquity* (ed. Polymnia Athanassiadi and Michael Frede; Oxford: Clarendon; New York: Oxford University, 1999) 81–148. For the West Semitic usage of the title, "Most High," see Herbert Niehr, *Der höchste Gott: Alttestamentlicher JHWH-Glaube im Kontext syrisch-kanaanäischer Religion des 1. Jahrtausends v. Chr.* (BZAW 190; Berlin/New York: de Gruyter, 1990); E. E. Elnes and P. D. Miller, "Elyon," *DDD* 293–99; and the discussion in Chapters Three and Four. (These are discussed in Chapter Four in the discussion of Genesis 14:18–22 and its use of Elyon.) As noted by Elnes and Miller, the Greek word *hupsistos* is taken up in particularly in Luke (1:32, 35, 76; 6:35; 8:28) and Acts (7:48; 16:17). Otherwise, it is rare in the New Testament (Mark 5:7; Hebrew 7:1). The case of Hebrew 7:1 arguably shows the Greek term most strongly echoing traditional use of "Most High" as a term for God since this usage appears in a citation of Genesis 14:18, part of a *locus classicus* for the divine title Elyon.

"seventy weeks" mentioned in Jeremiah 25 and 29. With the allusions to Deuteronomy and Jeremiah, the composer of Daniel 9 constructs a creative interpretation of vertical translatability[68] applied to his time, which is to issue in divine intervention.[69] Yet such intervention can be postponed by the divine representatives of empires, as the next chapter informs its audience; in 10:13, this is "the prince of the kingdom of Persia" (see also 10:20), succeeded in 10:20 by "the prince of Greece." Such opposing divine figures represent the cosmic power of empires, but still a greater angel (10:21; 12:1) will eventually prevail.

The empires and their cosmic counterparts stand in opposition to the will of the patron god who is presented as the god of the universe. Viewed from the composer's perspective, translatability was ruled out by definition. The apocalypse was a genre often directed against empires and, by implication, against their deities. A particularly favorite among local writers around the eastern Mediterranean from Egypt (e. g., the Demotic Chronicle) to Turkey (e. g., the New Testament book of Revelation),[70] the genre of apocalyptic in its very structure is the quintessential expression of local opposition to the Greek kingdoms and the Roman empire.[71] It might be said that without such powers, there would not have been apocalypses.[72] In these works,

---

[68] The book's pseudonymous authorship relates the name of Daniel to prior biblical tradition (Ezekiel 14:14, 20); in other words, pseudonymous authorship serves to help connect the work to the larger biblical tradition, arguably as a construction further enhancing vertical translatability. In this respect Jewish apocalypses show a particular concern for locating themselves within the larger framework of what they perceive as biblical and Jewish tradition. As Collins (*Daniel*, 56) remarks: "All the Jewish apocalypses are pseudonymous."

[69] On apocalyptic as essentially an exegetical literature, see the comments of Wayne Meeks, "Social Functions of Apocalyptic Languages," in: *Apocalypticism in the Mediterranean World and the Near East: Proceedings of the International Colloquium on Apocalypticism Uppsala, August 12–17, 1979* (ed. David Hellhom; second ed.; Tübingen: Mohr Siebeck, 1989) 697–98.

[70] See the essays in: *Apocalypse: The Morphology of a Genre* (ed. John J. Collins) = *Semeia* 14 (1979).

[71] See generally the essays in the landmark volume, *Apocalypticism in the Mediterranean World and the Near East: Proceedings of the International Colloquium on Apocalypticisim Uppsala, August 12–17, 1979* (ed. David Hellhom; Tübingen: Mohr Siebeck, 1979; second ed., 1989). For a recent survey of Jewish apocalyptic, see Lawrence H. Schiffman, "War in Jewish Apocalyptic Thought," in: *War and Peace in the Jewish Tradition* (ed. Lawrence Schiffman and Joel B. Wolowelsky; The Orthodox Forum; New York: Yeshiva University, 2007) 477–95. A proper survey of works that could be included in this discussion lies beyond the scope of the treatment here.

[72] See the comment by Collins (*Daniel*, 71): "The development of apocalypticism, then, cannot be plotted on a straight line but must be understood as a weaving together of old traditions in light of the new circumstances of the Hellenistic age." Note also the remark regarding "the Pharisaic expectation of individual resurrection" made by Hengel ("Judaism and Hellenism Revisited," 27): "This apocalyptic hope is also a fruit the 'Hellenistic

it was the god favored by the local writers who could end the power of a world empire. In short, the apocalypse served as a genre of local resistance and non-translatability aimed at the imperium of foreign powers.[73]

Expressions against translatability are prevalent in Jewish literature of this period. When we examine the Dead Sea Scrolls on the matter of divinity, we do not find translatability. To be sure, there is considerable language of "gods," but it is also clear that these are angelic figures who serve God, who is called "God of gods" (*'l 'lym*, 4Q510 = Songs of the Sage, fragment 1, line 2; see also 4Q403, fragment 1, line 26), just as the deity is in Daniel 2:47 and 11:36 (see also *PGM* XXIIb, line 20 = *PGMT* 261).[74] Generally the scrolls show the continuation of Jewish tradition, a sort of Jewish "vertical translatability" of the god of Israel's past as preserved in the Scriptures with the god of Judeans. Indeed, it might be argued that compared with what we saw in Chapter Five with non-Jewish sources of this period such as Philo of Byblos, Jewish circles in this period particularly use their sense of tradition to construct a vertical translatability that conformed older scriptural representations to their understandings of the deity. There is no real horizontal translatability in the Dead Sea Scrolls, which is to be expected for a movement arguably seeking greater observance and adherence to tradition, compared with other Jewish movements of the time (such as the Pharisees, and later the Christian "Way").[75]

This impression applies more widely to Jewish literature in the wider Mediterranean world, as surveyed by John M. G. Barclay.[76] He notes the range of Jewish views on the deity, and while these sometimes struggle with the terms of engagement in the wider Greco-Roman context, the overall

---

Zeitgeist' in a typical Jewish Palestinian garb." For the social setting of the older, related biblical material, see the important book by Stephen L. Cook, *Prophecy & Apocalypticism: The Post-Exilic Social Setting* (Minneapolis: Fortress, 1995).

[73] See Weitzman's discussion (*Surviving Sacrilege,* 122–37) about Jewish reliance on the supernatural in defiance to worldly empire in this period, as expressed in the War Scroll among other works. Note also the discussion of apocalyptic in: Schwartz, *Imperialism and Jewish Society,* 74–87. Schwartz's helpful corrective in this discussion involves his noting the shifting congruence between apocalyptic myth and Torah. It is particularly salutary that apocalyptic and Torah not be viewed either in sharp contrast to one another or in isolation from one another.

[74] See Martin Rösel and Uwe Glessmer, "God," in: *Encyclopedia of the Dead Sea Scrolls* (ed. Lawrence H. Schiffman and James C. VanderKam; two vols.; Oxford/New York: Oxford University, 2000) 1.317–21, esp. 318–19.

[75] For a sketch of the movements of the Pharisees, Sadducees and Essenes (sometimes called "sects"), see Schwartz, *Imperialism and Jewish Society,* 91–98.

[76] Barclay, *Jews in the Mediterranean Diaspora: From Alexander to Trajan (323 BCE – 117 CE)* (Berkeley/Los Angeles/London: University of California, 1996) esp. 429–34.

impression is a rather traditional picture of Jewish monotheism.[77] (We will examine the situation in more detail in the following section.) If we step back and look at the larger situation, the difference in Jewish and Christian monotheisms versus the Greco-Roman discourse might be viewed in broad terms as a contrast between monotheism and "summodeism" of a particular sort that we noted in Chapter Three, namely the idea of one deity as the sum and total of other deities who nonetheless remain deities in their own right. Henk S. Versnel discusses henotheism as an important paradigm of divinity in the Greco-Roman world.[78] Henotheism according to Versnel is "the privileged devotion to one god, who is regarded as uniquely superior, while other gods are neither depreciated nor rejected and continue to receiving the cultic observance whenever this is ritually required."[79] His essay highlights what he considers to be a form of henotheism, namely the notion that one god is the sum of the others in some sense (what I have called in "summodeism" in Chapter Three).[80] As we see in a number of our cases cited at the outset of this chapter, this model for divinity was applied cross-culturally to Iao in Greco-Roman discourse. At the turn of the era, this model is rarely monotheistic according to Versnel,[81] and as such it never was established in Jewish or Christian circles in any discernible manner, except to address the wider Greco-Roman world where it enjoyed considerable currency.[82] In

---

[77] For this view, see also Larry W. Hurtado, *Lord Jesus Christ: Devotion to Jesus in Earliest Christianity* (Grand Rapids, MI/Cambridge, UK: Eerdmans, 2003) 29–53.

[78] Versnel, "Thrice One: Three Greek Experiments in Oneness," in: *One God or Many? Concepts of Divinity in the Ancient World* (ed. Barbara Nevling Porter; Transactions of the Casco Bay Assyriological Institute, vol. 1; np: np, 2000) 79–163. See also Theodore M. Ludwig, "Monotheism," *ER* 9.6158. For the modern history of the term, see Michiko Yusa, "Henotheism," *ER* 6.3913–14; according to this account, the term was coined by Friedrich Schelling (1775–1854) and first used extensively in the academic study of religion by F. Max Müller (1823–1900). See above pp. 166–67.

[79] Versnel, "Thrice One: Three Greek Experiments in Oneness," 87.

[80] See above pp. 166–69. The term, "theocrasy," is used by Schäfer (*Judeophobia*, 50) for "the 'blending' of various gods in one 'highest' god."

[81] To be clear, my remarks here do not address developments in Christian theology of the second or third centuries where the situation differs.

[82] See Chapter Three for the discussions of the Babylonian texts that interpret the other deities as various aspects of Marduk. For a convenient source for the text citations and bibliography involved, see Barbara N. Porter, "The Anxiety of Multiplicity: Concepts of Divinity as One and Many in Ancient Assyria," in: *One God or Many? Concepts of Divinity in the Ancient World* (ed. Barbara Nevling Porter; Transactions of the Casco Bay Assyriological Institute, vol. 1; np: np, 2000) 211–71. Biblical scholars have taken note of these texts; for a convenient listing of bibliography with discussion, see Smith, *The Origins of Biblical Monotheism*, 87–88, 245 nn. 27–30. For a rather different sort of state mystical henotheism in Mesopotamia, see the case of Simo Parpola, "Monotheism in Ancient Assyria," in: *One God or Many? Concepts of Divinity in the Ancient World* (ed. Barbara Nevling Porter; Transactions of the Casco Bay Assyriological Institute, vol. 1; np: np, 2000) 165–209. As noted in Chapters One and Three, the category of henotheism would also work for a number of important Egyptian compositions; see John Baines,

turn, monotheism of the sort that we see in the Bible was never established in the ancient Near East or Greco-Roman context.[83] Posed in comparative terms, Jewish monotheism might be viewed as a Jewish separation of summodeism from its larger Greco-Roman polytheistic context.

At the same time, the situation surrounding these forms of divinity is in reality quite complex. Forms of monotheism and polytheism can sometimes look rather similar, and they seem to resemble one another in more ambiguous contexts so much so that scholars working in a comparative paradigm group these together.[84] To illustrate the issue, let me briefly mention some pertinent cases. First, we may mention Philo of Alexandria in his *Questions on Genesis* (2.62). In this context, he refers to the *logos* as "the second God": "nothing mortal can be made in the likeness of the most High One and father of the universe, but only in that of the second God (*ton deuteron theon*), who is His logos."[85] This representation of divinity might seem little different structurally from Christian notions of the status of Jesus as *logos* (John 1). There is, of course, a major difference in content. As John J. Collins notes, Philo's is an effort to reconcile Stoic thought on the *logos* with Jewish belief about the deity. In fact, Jewish efforts at identifying the *logos* or wisdom with Jewish notions of divinity or Jewish torah (teaching) may serve as bulwarks against translatability.[86] Such a move may serve to

---

"Egyptian Deities in Context: Multiplicity, Unity, and the Problem of Change," in: *One God or Many? Concepts of Divinity in the Ancient World* (ed. Barbara Nevling Porter; Transactions of the Casco Bay Assyriological Institute, vol. 1; np: np, 2000) 56–62.

[83] In this connection, see P. Athanassiadi and Michael Frede, ed., *Pagan Monotheism in Late Antiquity* (Oxford: Clarendon; New York: Oxford University, 1999).

[84] See Simo Parpola, "Monotheism in Ancient Assyria," 209.

[85] Cited from Collins, "Jewish Monotheism and Christian Theology," in: *Aspects of Monotheism: How God is One* (ed. Hershel Shanks and Jack Meinhardt; Washington, DC: Biblical Archaeology Society, 1997) 92.

[86] For the identification of Wisdom with Jewish teaching (Torah, often translated "law") in this period, see Baruch 4:1, where personified wisdom is identified as "the book of the precepts of God, the law that endures forever"; and Ben Sira 24:22, "All this is true of the book of the Most High's covenant, the law which Moses commanded us, as an inheritance for the community of Jacob. It overflows like the Pishon with wisdom." In this worldview, "all wisdom comes from the Lord" and "if you desire wisdom, keep the commandments" (Ben Sira 1:1, 23). The Dead Sea Scrolls also relate Wisdom and Torah. They are associated in Psalm 154 in 11Q5 = 11QPs[a], column XVIII, line 14: "the righteous who hear the voice of Wisdom have their *śiaḥ* (often translated as "meditation" or the like) on the Torah of Elyon." 4Q525 (Beatitudes), fragment 2, column II, lines 3–4 likewise relates the two: "Blessed is the one who attains wisdom *vacat* and betakes himself in the Torah of Elyon". For more recent discussions, see Shannon Burkes, " 'Life' Redefined: Wisdom and Law in Fourth Ezra and *Second Baruch*," *CBQ* 63 (2001) 55–71; and John Cook, "Law and Wisdom in the Dead Sea Scrolls with Reference to Hellenistic Judaism," in: *Wisdom and Apocalypticism in the Dead Sea Scrolls and in the Biblical Tradition* (ed. F. García Martínez; Bibliotheca Ephemeridum Theologicarum Lovaniensium CLXVIII; Leuven: University; Leuven/Paris/Dudley, MA: Uitgeverij Peeters, 2003) 323–42.

bolster "vertical translatability," by conveying the notion that the fullness of divinity resides in the Jewish god. The appropriation of the *logos* in Jewish authors (Philo) and Christian circles (John 1) arguably functions in analogous manner.[87] What seems from a later perspective as sitting on the fringe in one system (Philo's philosophical Judaism) stands at the heart of several forms of another (Christianity). Both would have been regarded by their proponents[88] as standing within their understanding of monotheism.[89] This complex of notions about divinity leads our discussion to the thornier matter of Jewish expressions of multiplicity of divinity.

Jewish Theistic Multiplicities

At home in the Jewish milieu, at least in Judea, are various expressions of divine multiplicity involving angelic powers. Apocalyptic literature shows a proliferation of heavenly figures[90] standing ultimately under the power of a supreme god. This form of divinity can appear structurally quite similar to some examples of Greco-Roman summodeism. It can sometimes seem that the world of divinities in Jewish apocalyptic and in Greco-Roman magical texts hardly differs in structure and powers; they seem to differ in the name of theism only, monotheism versus polytheism. There seems to be little doubt that the authors of Daniel 7–12 thought themselves to believe in a single god. As we have seen for the Dead Scrolls, there seems to be no question as to the monotheistic worldview even in a text such as the Songs

---

[87] On the question of the *logos,* see Collins, "Jewish Monotheism and Christian Theology," 92, 101. In developing the notion of the *logos,* John 1 appropriates prior Jewish notions of wisdom. See Thomas H. Tobin, "The Prologue of John and Hellenistic Wisdom Speculation," *CBQ* 52 (1990) 252–69. For wide-ranging discussions of the Jewish background of the *logos* in John 1, see Daniel Boyarin, *Border Lines: The Partition of Judaeo-Christianity* (Philadelphia: University of Pennsylvania, 2004) 113–16, 128–47 and 296 n. 6; and Eliot R. Wolfson, "Inscribed in the Book of the Living: *Gospel of Truth* and Jewish Christology," *JSJ* 38 (2007) 234–71. It may be noted that Christian appropriation of wisdom in the Johannine prologue as well as Philippians 2:6–11 and Colossians 1:15–20 may well represent a form of "vertical translatability" (I thank Paul Aspan for driving home this point to me).

[88] For this view, see Hurtado, *Lord Jesus Christ,* 29–53, esp. 36. In contrast to Collins, Hurtado distinguishes the question of Jewish monotheism from various concepts and formulations of divinity that do not seem terribly monotheistic as first glance.

[89] So also among classical authors, for example, in Tacitus' *Histories* (5.1, 2) on the Jews that *nec quidquam prius imbuuntur quam contemnere deos,* "the earliest lesson they learn is to despise the gods" (so Stern, *Greek and Latin Authors on Jews and Judaism,* 2.19 and 26).

[90] Cf. Frank Moore Cross, quoted in: "Contrasting Insights of Biblical Giants: BAR Interviews Elie Wiesel and Frank Moore Cross," *Biblical Archaeology Review* 30/4 (July/August 2004) 32: "With the Hebrew Bible, you're living in an austere world. When you come to the New Testament you can't even swing a cat without hitting three demons and two spirits."

of Sabbath Sacrifice. At a first glance, a reading of the Songs of the Sabbath Sacrifice with its language of *'lym*, "gods," might interpret it as a form of polytheism. Yet it is arguable that this view would be misplaced. Despite difficulties, there is an important standard for distinguishing the basic form or structure of divinity in texts such as Daniel and the Song of the Sabbath Sacrifice, from the perspective of their writers and audiences: does the structure of divinity stand or fall if the one, major god is removed from the picture? In the case of various forms of Jewish monotheism, the answer is affirmative: clearly if the Most High God is removed from the picture in these texts, the various angels and *'lym* would as well. It is not clear that the same can be said for expressions of summodeism. If one god, even a central one, is removed from the formulations of summodeism presented earlier in this chapter, the formulation can still stand with the names of other deities in its place; or another expression could be substituted. Put differently, if Yahweh were removed from Jewish worship or from its worldview, the entire system would collapse; the same cannot be claimed for a particular deity in the larger Greco-Roman context.

Despite this standard, later Jewish angelologies sound rather non-mono-theistic, at least by modern judgments. Although these texts exceed the scope of this study, a brief discussion of them is in order, as several authors, including Alan Segal, Eliot Wolfson and Daniel Boyarin, have included them in their discussions of Jewish divinity in the Greco-Roman context. In general terms, Rebecca Lesses comments on theistic similarities between Greco-Roman literature and later Hekhalot literature and magical texts:

The polytheistic vision of the hekhalot literature resembles the profusion of dei-ties and angels that are addressed in the Greco-Egyptian adjurations … Some of the Greco-Egyptian adjurations, on the other had, approach a kind of monotheistic or henotheistic vision, in which one deity assumes the names and attributes of several others or subordinates all others to his or her power.[91]

For Lesses, it is difficult to draw the line between these forms of monothe-ism and polytheism. Within the complex of Jewish medieval mysticism, a number of scholars going back to Gershom Scholem have noted a par-ticularly telling case involving the angel Metatron in Sefer Hekhalot, also known as 3 Enoch.[92] Thought to date to the fifth or sixth century CE/AD

---

[91] Lesses, "Speaking with Angels: Jewish and Greco-Egyptian Revelatory Adjura-tions," *HTR* 89 (1996) 47–48. See also the remarks of Peter Schäfer, "Geschichte und Gedächtnisgeschichte: Jan Assmanns 'Mosaische Unterscheidung'," in: *Memoria – Wege jüdischen Erinnerns: Festschrift für Michael Brocke zum 65. Geburtstag* (ed. Birgit E. Klein and Christiane E. Müller; Berlin: Metropol, 2005) 23–24.

[92] For a discussion of the text with translation and notes, see P. Alexander, "3 (Hebrew Apocalypse of) Enoch," *OTPs* 1.223–302. The scholars include those cited in the follow-ing discussion. See also the critical discussion of Lawrence H. Schiffman, "3 Enoch and the

(but perhaps considerably later), this work refers to the angel Metatron as "the lesser Yahweh," literally, "Yahweh, the little one," *yhwh ḥqṭwn* (3 Enoch 12:5).[93] The characterization of Metatron stands in contrast to "the greater Yahweh" (48B:1, name 44). As noted by scholars, Gnostic texts (e. g., Pistis Sophia, chapter 7, dating to the third century CE/AD) mention "the lesser Yao," which would seem to point to an early tradition of the double-form of Yhwh.[94] The representation of "two powers in heaven" in the Talmudic account of Elisha ben Abuyah (called Aher) in Hagigah 15a,[95] repeated in 3 Enoch 16, serves as the basis for Alan Segal's dating of this "bimorphic" view of divinity to at least the third century CE/AD, and perhaps even to the second century CE/AD.[96] Segal considers 3 Enoch 12:5 in connection with Philo's view of the *logos* as "the second God" (noted above) as well as his use of "two gods" (*De Somniis* 1.227–229).[97] While the formulations of "angel" and "word" may seem quite distinctive, for Philo these were already related for him in part by his scriptural interpretation, as Segal has observed.[98]

Following the work of Elliot Wolfson and his student Daniel Abrams,[99] Daniel Boyarin characterizes the usages in Philo and 3 Enoch as "Jewish binitarianism,"[100] which he believes to have been quite widespread and even

---

Enoch Tradition," in: *Enoch and Qumran Origins: New Light on a Forgotten Connection* (ed. Gabriele Boccaccini; Grand Rapids, MI/Cambridge, UK: Eerdmans, 2005) 152–61.

[93] For this characterization of Metatron, see Alan Segal, *Two Powers in Heaven: Early Rabbinic Reports about Christianity and Gnosticism* (Studies in Judaism in Late Antiquity 25; Leiden: Brill, 1977) 65–66; Andrei A. Orlov, *The Enoch-Metatron Tradition* (TSAJ 107; Tübingen: Mohr Siebeck, 2005) 136–43. For a useful effort to locate Metatron as the name of the deity in a larger history of religion context, see Saul M. Olyan, *A Thousand Thousands Served Him* (TSAJ 36; Tübingen: Mohr Siebeck, 1993) 17 n. 16, 88, 90 n. 5, 106–7. Olyan notes instances in older West Semitic literature where one deity is called the "name" of another.

[94] As Segal (*Two Powers in Heaven,* 197) notes; so too Orlov (*The Enoch-Metatron Tradition,* 140 n. 251), following Gershom Scholem.

[95] For the presentation of Elisha ben Abuyah in bT. Hagigah 15a, see Jeffrey L. Rubinstein, *Talmudic Stories: Narrative Art, Composition, and Culture* (Baltimore/London: Johns Hopkins University, 1999) 64–104.

[96] Segal, *Two Powers in Heaven,* 66.

[97] Segal, *Two Powers in Heaven,* 159–81. See also Collins, "Jewish Monotheism and Christian Theology," in: *Aspects of Monotheism: How God is One* (ed. Hershel Shanks and Jack Meinhardt; Washington, DC: Biblical Archaeology Society, 1997) 92.

[98] Segal, *Two Powers in Heaven,* 169–71, with citations on 169 n. 24.

[99] Wolfson, *Through a Speculum That Shines: Vision and Imagination in Medieval Jewish Literature* (Princeton: Princeton University, 1994) 256–60; Abrams, "The Boundaries of Divine Ontology: The Inclusion and Exclusion of Meṭaṭron in the Godhead," *HTR* 87 (1994) 291–321.

[100] Boyarin, "The Gospel of the Memra: Jewish Binitarianism and the Prologue to John," *HTR* 94 (2001) 243–84; "Two Powers in Heaven; or, The Making of a Heresy," in: *The Idea of Biblical Interpretation: Essays in Honor of James L. Kugel* (Leiden: Brill, 2003) 331–70; and *Border Lines,* 120–27, 131, 137–38. Boyarin ("Two Powers in Heaven," 334)

normative in Judaism in the Second Temple period prior to the rabbis.[101] This conclusion is highly controversial. The date of 3 Enoch concerning

would go as far as to claim that many, if not most, Jews held to a binitarian view of the deity. This claim exceeds the available evidence. Segal's more circumscribed approach hews more closely to the known data. Writing on Philo's expression of the logos as a "second god," Segal (*Two Powers in Heaven,* 261) comments: "It is impossible to speculate on how the Pharisees would have reacted to Philo's system." Boyarin also believes Daniel 7:13 both to preserve an understanding of two powers in heaven ("the ancient of days" and "one like a son of man") as well as its suppression under the interpretation of this verse in Daniel 7:27. Following Margaret Barker, Boyarin also holds that the two gods was a standard feature throughout Israelite religion that did not survive due to its successive suppression (lecture given at the University of Pennsylvania on 12 April 2007). It is difficult to confirm what has been suppressed successfully, but one may point instead to the notion of the human king as the older embodiment of this power and not necessarily a separate young god in Israelite religion. For this discussion, see Paul Mosca, "Ugarit and Daniel 7: A Missing Link," *Biblica* 67 (1986) 496–517; and Mark S. Smith, *The Origins of Biblical Monotheism: Israel's Polytheistic Background and the Ugaritic Texts* (Oxford/New York: Oxford University, 2001) 158–60. Boyarin's view requires further evidence.

[101] Lying beyond the scope of this discussion are Boyarin's claims about Christian "binitarianism" (Father and Son) and New Testament Christologies, but a few comments are offered here. Boyarin is somewhat critical of recent studies that have situated New Testament Christology in the context of angelology; see Peter R. Carrell, *Jesus and the Angels: Angelology and the Christology of the Apocalypse of John* (SNTSMS 95; Cambridge, UK/New York: Cambridge University, 1995); and C. A. Gieschen, *Angelomorphic Christology: Antecedents and Early Evidence* (Leiden/Boston: Brill, 1998). This approach arguably goes a certain distance toward understanding early high Christology, but the evidence is limited. For a critical assessment, see also Loren T. Stuckenbruck, *Angel Veneration and Christology: A Study in Early Judaism and in the Christology of the Apocalypse of John* (WUNT II/70; Tübingen: Mohr Siebeck, 1995); and the various treatments in: C. C. Newman, J. R. Davila and G. S. Lewis, ed., *The Jewish Roots of Christological Monotheism: Papers from the St. Andrews Conference on the Historical Origins of the Worship of Jesus* (JSJSup 63; Leiden: Brill, 1999). For a broader assessment of the situation, see Hurtado, *Lord Jesus Christ.* Boyarin would not accept this "angelomorphic" approach to the matter and instead connects Christian "binitarianism" and trinitarianism with what he regards as Jewish "binitarianism." According to Boyarin ("Two Powers in Heaven," 332), the rabbis construct two powers in heaven as heresy, just at about the time that Christianity declares one power in heaven ("monarchianism," also known as modalism) as heretical. For an older but still useful survey of the Christian controversy, see J. N. D. Kelly, *Early Christian Doctrines* (second edition; New York/Evanston/London: Harper & Row, 1960) 115–23, esp. 117 and 119; and the recent work of Edgar G. Foster, *Angelomorphic Christology and the Exegesis of Psalm 8:5 in Tertullian's Adversus Praxean: An Examination of Tertullian's Reluctance to Attribute Angelic Properties to the Son of God* (Lanham, MD: University Press of America, 2006). As monarchianism's opponents represented it, it claimed that Christianity ran the risk of asserting God the Father and Jesus Christ as two gods. That this was a potential problem may be seen in some Christian formulations, for example, saying #30 in the Coptic Gospel of Thomas: "Jesus said: 'Where there are three gods, they are gods; where there are two or one, I am with him.'" (Thomas O. Lambdin, trans., in: *The Nag Hammadi Library in English* [New York/Hagerstown/Evanston/London: Harper & Row, 1977] 121; see also David R. Cartledge and David L. Dungan, eds., *Documents for the Study of the Gospels* (rev. and enl. ed.; Minneapolis: Fortress, 1994) 22; for another effort in Gnostic Christian circles to define the relationship between the Father and the Son, compare The Tripartite Tractate, in Harold W. Attridge and Dieter

Metatron as the "little Yahweh" is quite late and calls for considerable caution in judging the situation at the turn of the era. Indeed, according to Peter Schäfer,[102] this case is to be seen as a later Jewish response to Christian exaltation of Jesus.

Mystical Jewish literature largely falls outside the scope of this investigation,[103] but it offers further illustration of the conceptual overlap between angels in a monotheistic picture and various divinities in summodeism. Thus structures or forms of divinity may not neatly divide according to the larger label of monotheism versus polytheism. At the same time, it is important to pay attention to the larger Jewish tradition in which these expressions appear. Since ancient Jewish authors understood their tradition as monotheistic, Boyarin's characterization of the *logos* as a "second god" and the mystical presentation of Metatron as "the lesser Yahweh" call for scrutiny. Even if they were to go back to older tradition in the Greco-Roman period, such formulations are hardly indicative of a belief in two gods. Instead, in calling Metatron "the lesser Yahweh," the point may not be an expression of faith in a second god. Instead, this "lesser Yahweh" partakes of the reality of the "greater Yahweh." It is for this reason that the name of Yahweh inheres in both figures. Metatron's ontological reality as "the lesser Yahweh" is based in the reality of the "greater Yahweh." There is no belief in a separate god as such, but in the ontological participation of a lesser figure in the reality

---

Mueller, trans., in: *The Nag Hammmadi Library in English,* 55–97). Still it might be held that these are not efforts to assert multiple distinct gods, but to express within the godhead mediation of transcendent divinity in relation to humanity. Stuckenbruck (*Angel Veneration and Christology,* 272) makes the point: "The exalted status of Christ as an object of worship alongside God was not intended as a breach of monotheism."

In Boyarin's view, Jewish and Christian polarization contributed to their constructing themselves as mirror opposites on this issue of divinity and to claim their respective constructs as one of their defining marks. Christian "binitarianism" was thus a driving force for the Jewish view of monotheism. In turn, in Boyarin's words ("Two Powers in Heaven," 332), "The Rabbis, by defining elements from within their own religious heritage as not Jewish, were, in effect, producing Christianity." Collins ("Powers in Heaven," 28) comments somewhat similarly: "Ultimately such ideas were marginalized in Judaism, perhaps in reaction to the central place of such speculation in Christianity." Stated differently, one might say that Christian views against one power in heaven pushed the rabbis to assert "monotarianism" as the defining view of Jewish monotheism. It would seem that in turn the notion of the Shekinah comes to assume the place left by the second – or perhaps the third – power in heaven. Segal (*Two Powers in Heaven,* 183) sees such Jewish aspects of divinity as a means to combat perceived multiplicity of powers. Thus aspects versus powers became a means to assert a newly clarified "monotarianism" over and against both Christian "binitarianism" and older and ongoing forms of Jewish "binitarianism." Christianity eventually opt outed of both aspects and powers, in using persons (*prosopa*) as the term of choice to express the Trinity.

[102] Schäfer, personal communication. Schäfer informs me that he is working on a book, tentatively entitled *The Origins of Jewish Mysticism,* which argues to this effect.

[103] See the 2005 survey of Orlov, *The Enoch-Metatron Tradition,* 1–19.

of the one god. A comparable point applies to Philo's notion of the *logos* as a "second God." The *logos* serves to mediate "the likeness of the Most High One and father of the universe" to humanity. In other words, the *logos* is hardly a different god, but divine in tandem with the "Most High One."

What is evident from these texts was a negotiation between the general monotheistic rubric given by adherents to Judaism and early Christianity and the various forms or structures that divinity assumes in their texts. As a result, what might pass for monotheism in one context or period might look remarkably like the polytheism in another. This moving line between various forms of Jewish and Christian monotheism and the larger world of discourse about deities was ever developing and subject to religious and cultural renegotiation.[104] Jewish authors used various means to negotiate the religious space between Jewish and non-Jewish discourse about divinity.[105] Some Jewish authors did appeal to notions of a single universal deity that would have made sense in the Greco-Roman world.[106] Moreover, Jewish writers could use basic terms of divinity that were home equally in their tradition and in the Greco-Roman discourse (e. g., "god/God," *theos*,[107] and "Most High," *hupsistos*). As we have seen, broader notions of wisdom or *logos* at home in the Greco-Roman context could also aid in Jewish translation of divinity.[108]

---

[104] It is a question whether the importation of various Greek and Egyptian cults into Palestine in this period may have fostered religious renegotiation along these lines in Jewish circles. For such cults, see Jodi Magness, "The Cults of Isis and Kore at Samaria-Sebaste in the Hellenistic and Roman Periods," *HTR* 94 (2001) 157–77. For local identifications of Greek and Levantine deities in the Hellenistic cities of the southern Levant in this period, see the remarks of Aryeh Kasher, *Jews and Hellenistic Cities in Eretz-Israel* (TSAJ 21; Tübingen: Mohr Siebeck, 1990) 29–48.

[105] See the survey on Jewish divinity in: Peter Schäfer, *Judeophobia: Attitudes toward the Jews in the Ancient World* (Cambridge, MA/London: Harvard University, 1997) 34–65.

[106] For example, Philo, *Legum Allegoria* 3.4–9. See F. H. Colson and G. H. Whitaker, *Philo I* (LCL; Cambridge, MA/London: W. Heinemann, 1929) 302–7; Aristobulus, fragment 4, in: Carl Holladay, *Fragments from Hellenistic Jewish Authors: Volume III. Aristobulus* (SBLTT 39, Pseudepigrapha Series 13; Atlanta, GA: Scholars, 1995) 162–71; and Acts 17:28 discussed below.

[107] The point is nicely stated in the Letter of Aristeas 200–201 (*OTPs* 2.26): "God" is "the basis of their argument ... all power of argument ... has its origins in God." See the discussion of the Letter of Aristeas below.

[108] On these categories, see Collins, "Jewish Monotheism and Christian Theology," 81–105. Collins' piece, which nicely draws out some of the complexities of Jewish monotheism in this period (angels, which he also calls "demigods," exalted human beings and what he calls "the abstract figures of Wisdom and the Word (Logos)," does not take up the question of translatability. For Wisdom speculation in relation to the *logos* in Philo, see Peter Schäfer, *Mirror of His Beauty: Feminine Images of God from the Bible to the Early Kabbalah* (Princeton/Oxford: Princeton University, 2002) 41–46.

These and other notions served as terms of negotiation that Jewish and Christian writers could deploy. If the line between Greco-Roman polytheisms (including its various forms of summodeism) and Jewish or Christian monotheism was a moving reality, it was not, as we noted earlier in this chapter, a generally porous one. These formulations about divinity in Jewish and Christian sources that we have noted above are not examples of translatability according to Assmann's discussion. Instead, they involve structural similarities or ideas between different systems and not translatability of deities as such. Even as many philosophical and religious ideas about divinity were circulating freely, it would remain difficult to square up the vast majority of Jewish forms of monotheism with Greco-Roman summodeism that we meet in this period. Yet this is not the whole story about Jewish translatability of deities. Contrary to Assmann's apparent assumption that monotheistic religion of the Bible *a priori* cannot (or does not) tolerate such intercultural possibilities, we do see more specific instances of translatability of deities in a limited number of Jewish and Christian sources.[109] We turn to these now.

2. Jewish Horizontal Translatability

As we observed at the outset of this chapter, translatability did not work as facilely in Jewish circles as it did in most other segments of Hellenistic intelligentsia. For example, Philo of Byblos seems adept at translating Phoenician and Greco-Roman deities. By contrast, Jewish writers largely desist from this practice, thanks largely to the Bible's standards. In addition, the naturalist methods of interpretation of divinity found in Philo of Byblos are absent from Jewish sources of the period. Still, in the Hellenistic context, some educated Jews sought to defend their deity over and against the larger project of Greco-Roman culture, sometimes even working with the notion that the Jewish god could be identified with Greek gods. There are two notable cases of this sort made by Jewish literati.[110]

---

[109] Assmann, *Moses the Egyptian,* 50.
[110] The following discussion draws from John J. Collins, "Cult and Culture: The Limits of Hellenization," in: *Hellenism in the Land of Israel* (ed. John J. Collins and Gregory E. Sterling; Christianity and Judaism in Antiquity Series 13; South Bend, in: University of Notre Dame, 2001) 40–41. See also Goldstein, *I Maccabees,* 142 n. 237; Sylvie Honigman, *The Septuagint and Homeric Scholarship in Alexandria: A Study in the Narrative of the Letter of Aristeas* (London/New York: Routledge, 2003) 146; and William Horbury, *Herodian Judaism and New Testament Study* (WUNT 193; Tübingen: Mohr Siebeck, 2006) 16–18.

The Letter of Aristeas and the Septuagint

The first case comes from the Letter of Aristeas.[111] We begin with the letter's specific statement of translatability, and then we move to its context within the document. As part of a larger appeal for the release of Jews taken prisoner by the father of Ptolemy II Philadelphus (285–247 BCE), the following claim about divine translatability is put in the mouth of a non-Jewish courtier[112] who speaks before the king (*Letter of Aristeas*, 16): "These people worship God who is overseer and creator of all, whom all worship, but we, O King, address differently as Zeus and Jove."[113] Here we have a claim of divine equation within the Hellenistic *ecumene* in Alexandria.[114] Silvia

---

[111] For the text, see H. St. J. Thackeray, "Appendix: The Letter of Aristeas," in: Henry Barclay Swete, *An Introduction to the Old Testament in Greek* (rev. Richard Rusden Ottley; New York, KTAV, 1968; originally published, 1914; repr., Peabody, MA: Hendrickson, 1989) 551–606. The historical circumstances of the letter are the subject of debate. Nina L. Collins seeks to overturn the recent consensus that the Septuagint translation was undertaken as a Jewish initiative. Instead, she believes the reason given by the text, namely that the translation project was initiated by Ptolemaic authorities for their library in Alexandria. See Collins, *The Library in Alexandria and the Bible in Greek* (VTSup 82; Leiden/Boston: Brill, 2000) 115–44, 164–69. Against this view, Abraham Wasserstein and David J. Wasserstein (*The Legend of the Septuagint: From Classical Antiquity to Today* [New York: Cambridge University, 2006] 15) comment: "the claim made in the *Letter of Aristeas* that the translation owed its origin to royal initiative and patronage is part of Jewish and possibly also Jewish pro-Ptolemaic propaganda but is supported neither by historical evidence nor by any plausible consideration of probability." This issue is not crucial to my discussion here, but it does highlight the difficulty in using this text as a straightforward indicator of translatability, as discussed shortly. For the report of the letter in Josephus, *Antiquities of the Jews* XII, 17–118, see Ralph Marcus, *Josephus. In Nine Volumes: VII. Jewish Antiquities, Books XII–XIV* (LCL; Cambridge, MA: Harvard University; London: W. Heinemann, 1943) 10–59. For the account in the various sources, see Wasserstein and Wasserstein, *The Legend of the Septuagint;* and Luciano Canfora, *Il viaggio di Aristea* (Rome: Editori Laterza, 1996). Note also the remarks in: Giuseppe Veltri, *Eine Tora für den König Talmai: Untersuchungen zum Übersetzungsverständnis in der jüdisch-hellenistischen und rabbinischen Literatur* (TSAJ 41; Tübingen: Mohr Siebeck, 1994) 14–18.

[112] For this representation, see the remarks of Wasserstein and Wasserstein, *The Legend of the Septuagint*, 22, 23: "Aristeas was a Jew ... the whole point of the false authorial self- identification in the *Letter* is that the author wishes to present himself as a non-Jew. Unlike the pseudonymous name of the writer, his fictive *persona* is not chosen completely at random. He is represented as a pagan officer at the court of Ptolemy II Philadelphus, precisely because the work is a piece of Jewish propaganda and a 'pagan' author is presumably thought to be more plausible and persuasive than a Jew." See also Honigman, *The Septuagint and Homeric Scholarship in Alexandria*, 69–71.

[113] The translation here largely follows Barclay, *Jews in the Mediterranean Diaspora*, 143. Cf. *OTPs* 2.13.

[114] See V. Tcherikover, "The Ideology of the Letter of Aristeas," *HTR* 51 (1958) 70; and more recently, Reinhard G. Kratz, " 'Denn dein ist das Reich': Das Judentum in persischer und hellenistisch-römischer Zeit," in: *Götterbilder – Gottesbilder – Weltbilder. Band I: Ägypten, Mesopotamien, Persien, Kleinasien, Syrien, Palästina* (ed. Reinhard G. Kratz and Hermann Spieckermann; FAT 2/17; Tübingen: Mohr Siebeck, 2006) 362–66, esp. 363.

Honigman presents the statement's understanding in these terms: "Greeks and Jews revere the same God under different names. It may be argued that Jews rather than Greeks would have been interested in the religious statements of paragraphs 15–16. However, it may be conceded that the audience targeted by these religious messages is still ambiguous."[115] At the same time, as Barclay emphasizes,[116] the figure of Aristeas is hardly militating for Yahweh simply as a manifestation of Zeus or for the basic equivalence of Greek and Jewish religion. In context, the negotiation of divinity is more complex. It has been suggested that the view espoused in 16 relies not only on an equation of Zeus and the Jewish God, but also on a popular etymology for Zeus (*zen,* "to live"), which would have been suitable for a Hellenistic Jewish audience.[117] At a minimum, the claim made here represents the god of the Jews as palatable, or at least intelligible, to Aristeas' royal patron.

The larger context for the equation shows two concerns. On the one hand, this document notes specific facets of Jewish practice, such as dietary laws (144–171). On the other hand, the text is punctuated by terms of divinity, represented as shared in common by Jewish leaders and their Egyptian royal sponsor. The many questions put by the king to the translators commonly have God at the base of their answers, which he gladly accepts (187–294). Indeed, after the first day of questioning, the king acclaims their answers: "they give appropriate answers, all making God the basis of their argument" (200). In response, the philosopher Menedemus of Eritrea is represented as stating: "it follows that all power and beauty of argument has its origins in God" (201). Thus the Jewish translators, the king and the philosopher of the king's court all share God as a term in common. Even the answer to the question, "what is philosophy?" (256), begins with "a well-reasoned assessment of each occurrence" and ends with the conclusion that "in order to have due care for these things, it is necessary to serve God." Thus God – and a certain traditional attitude of respect towards this God – is a model that is represented as translatable.

This example of translation in the Letter of Aristeas is to be viewed within a larger and more general discourse about God. It is a particular aid to the Jewish side that "God" is a longstanding title for the Jewish God. Similarly, the representation of the king's own expression making "a thank offering to the Most High God" (37) would have made perfect sense to a Jewish audience. Thus we might say that in this sort of discourse, Jewish vertical

---

[115] Honigman, *The Septuagint and Homeric Scholarship in Alexandria,* 28.

[116] Barclay, *Jews in the Mediterranean Diaspora,* 143. Note also Gruen's point about the Letter of Aristeas, that it expresses about Greeks and Egyptians "strong words and powerful sentiments, not to be obscured or suppressed in the warm glow of some alleged universalism." See Gruen, *Heritage and Hellenism,* 216.

[117] Honigman, *The Septuagint and Homeric Scholarship in Alexandria,* 146.

translatability meshes with horizontal translatability within the Alexandrian context. We should perhaps be careful about seeing the Letter of Aristeas as evidence for a general or broad claim for translatability between Jewish and non-Jewish gods, given the relatively minor role that it plays within the document's larger discourse of divinity. We also need to be mindful of the fact that this text offers a Jewish representation of a negotiation in divinity. It may include a notion of how the Jewish god could translate out to the Alexandrian royal court, but the represented context of the document indicates how the general notion of divinity shared in the Greco-Roman milieu could be adapted to fit Jewish sensibilities.

Before we move to the second case of translatability, we may raise the issue of whether the Septuagint itself may contain signs of translatability. After all, the Septuagint is the central concern of the letter of Aristeas, and it is an act (or better, a series of acts) of translation. By its very constitution and setting in Alexandria, the Septuagint might be expected to contain cases of divine translation for its audience in Alexandria. Several scholars have noted one example from the Septuagint, specifically in Exodus 22:27.[118] To illustrate, translations for the Masoretic Hebrew (MT) text of the verse with the Greek Septuagint (LXX) are presented here:

"God/gods[119] (*'elohim*) you shall not revile, nor curse a leader (*naśi'*) among your people." MT

"Gods (*theous*) you shall not revile, nor shall you speak ill of the rulers (*archontas*) of your people." LXX

Compared with the MT, the Greek version addresses the question of "gods" more broadly. In this view, the "gods" and "rulers" in the Septuagint translation arguably speak to how Jews should relate to Egyptian deities and

---

[118] For the most complete discussion, see Pieter W. van der Horst, " 'Thou shalt not Revile the Gods': the LXX Translation of Ex. 22:28 (27), its Background and Influence," *Studia Philonica Annual* 5 (1993) 1–8 (my thanks go to Gregory Sterling for this reference). Note also Barclay, *Jews in the Mediterranean Diaspora,* 431; Gruen, *Heritage and Hellenism,* 67; R. Goldenberg, "The Septuagint Ban on Cursing the Gods," *JSJ* 28 (1997) 381–89; and Bohak, "The Impact," 15. Exodus 22:27 was used later by non-Christian polemicists against Christianity, for example Julian (by Christians nicknamed "the Apostate") in his *Against the Galilaeans.* See John Granger Cook, *The Interpretation of the Old Testament in Greco-Roman Paganism* (Studien und Texte zu Antike und Christentum 23; Tübingen: Mohr Siebeck, 2004) 312–14.

[119] Though usually taken to be a reference to God, one might interpret MT *'elohim* here in its Israelite milieu as promoting respect for family gods more broadly. According to Karel van der Toorn, these would be divinized family ancestors. See van der Toorn, *Family Religion in Babylonia, Syria and Israel: Continuity and Change in the Forms of Religious Life* (Studies in CHANE VII; Leiden/New York/Köln: Brill, 1996) 233–34. This particular religious issue was unlikely still a concern at the time of the LXX translation, however. Yet it may be said that the LXX's witness to Hebrew *'elohim* as a plural is ultimately correct.

rulers in Alexandria. If correct, the LXX renders Hebrew *'elohim* as deities, which would include non-Jewish ones.

The verse in its Greek garb would not simply breath the air of Alexandrian tolerance. For Erich Gruen, the Septuagint translation of Hebrew *'elohim* as *theous* perhaps shows a Jewish concern to offer "a gesture toward Gentiles, perhaps as a defense against Gentile criticism."[120] Indeed, the ancient text of the Jewish people seems to be expressing recognition – even tolerance – of non-Jewish gods in Alexandria. At the same time, it is important to balance this view. Pieter van der Horst suggests a possible Jewish apologetics in defense of Moses in the context of Egyptian culture, not simply "a sincere tolerance toward believers of other religions, or even a tendency toward compromising with paganism."[121] If correct, one might not put too much stock in this passage as evidence of cross-cultural tolerance. Indeed, in contrast with the broad and cross-cultural usage of "God," the divine name itself was viewed in Jewish circles as incomparable, perhaps even untranslatable and unspeakable. Its rendering in various forms in Hebrew and Greek in this period[122] suggests this Jewish understanding of the divine name. Based on the Hodayot and Cave One Isaiah scroll (1QIsaᵃ) from the Dead Sea Scrolls, Patrick W. Skehan suggests that by 100 BCE Adonay (literally, "Lord") served as a name in prayer and as a substitute for religious reading of the divine name in the Scriptures.[123] Recent studies of the divine name in Jewish sources in this period indicate special treatment of the name,[124] which served as an implicit claim against translatability.

---

[120] Gruen, *Heritage and Hellenism,* 67.

[121] Van der Horst, "'Thou shalt not Revile the Gods'," 1–2.

[122] See Skehan, "The Divine Name at Qumran, in the Masada Scroll, and in the Septuagint," *BIOSCS* 13 (1980) 14–44. However, this is clearly not the case in the Persian period Judean texts from Elephantine.

[123] See Skehan, "The Divine Name at Qumran," 6.

[124] See Tov, *Scribal Practices,* 218, 239–43. See also Joseph M. Baumgarten, "A New Qumran Substitute for the Divine Name and Mishnah Sukkah 4.5," *JQR* 83 (1992) 1–5. Regarding reverence for the name, Bohak ("The Impact," 5 n. 13) notes LXX Leviticus 24:16; Philo, *De vita Mosis* 2.114–15; *De somniis,* 1.67; *Legatio ad Gaium* 353; and Josephus, *Antiquities,* 2.275–76. As evidence that such a sensibility was not entirely maintained, Bohak ("The Impact," 4–5) points to the spelling Iaho in a third-century Demotic text (discussed above) as well as a story about the telling of the divine name by Artapanus. These two data are exceptional at best, and the story in Artapanus arguably points to a reverential attitude regarding the power of the divine name, namely that it is only to be whispered.

For the Christian appropriation of this view of the divine name, see Larry W. Hurtado, *The Earliest Christian Artifacts: Manuscripts and Christian Origins* (Grand Rapids, MI/ Cambridge, UK: Eerdmans, 2006) 101–110, esp. 104–5. In this connection, the name of Jesus as "a secret name" (contrasting with "Christ" as "a revealed name") is to be noted in the Gnostic Gospel of Philip. See Wesley W. Isenberg, "The Gospel of Philip," in: *The Nag Hammadi Library in English* (Marvin W. Meyer, managing editor; San Francisco:

The Case of Aristobulus

The second case of Jewish translatability comes from the Jewish author, Aristobulus, as preserved by the church father, Eusebius. Aristobulus emends the divine names Dis and Zeus in passages that he cites from the Greek poets, Orpheus and Aratus. Then he gives his reason for doing so:

> I think it has been demonstrated clearly that the power of God permeates all things. And as was necessary, we have signified this by removing the divine names Dis and Zeus used throughout the verses; for their inherent meaning relates to God, and for this reason we have expressed it this way. We have presented these things therefore in a way not unsuited to the things being discussed. All philosophers agree that it is necessary to hold devout convictions regarding God, something which our school prescribes particularly well.[125]

As with the instance in the Letter of Aristeas, Silvia Honigmann locates this case in the larger Greco-Roman milieu of Alexandria.[126] The equation would have made eminent sense in the Alexandrian context where various chief deities, including Zeus and Isis, had been viewed as the single deities revered by all humanity under different names.[127]

These cases of Jewish translatability are quite limited, which in fact would suggest the relative rarity of divine translatability in Jewish circles in this period. Given the cases that survive, it would seem that Jewish translatability enjoyed relatively little currency especially in Judea. Evidently translatability could be ventured in circumstances where Jewish life was overshadowed in a learned Hellenistic setting such as Alexandria, yet these are few in number. And in these cases, they may involve literary or philosophical translatability, but there are no clear cases of cultic or even literary translatability. The force of the biblical-Jewish tradition with its "vertical" translatability arguably displaced Jewish efforts at "horizontal" translatability. In the following section, we see some efforts at translatabil-

---

Harper & Row, 1977) 134. For a more recent translation, see Cartlidge and Dungan, ed., *Documents for the Study of the Gospels*, 59, #19.

[125] See Carl Holladay, *Fragments from Hellenistic Jewish Authors: Volume III. Aristobulus* (SBLTT 39, Pseudepigrapha Series 13; Atlanta, GA: Scholars, 1995) 172, 173. For another translation, see Adela Collins, *OTPs* 2.841. The fragment comes from Eusebius, *Preparatio Evangelica*, 13.13.3–8. See also the discussion of Aristobulus in John J. Collins, *Between Athens and Jerusalem: Jewish Identity in the Hellenistic Diaspora* (second ed.; The Biblical Resource Series; Grand Rapids, MI/Cambridge, UK: Eerdmans; Livonia, MI: Dove, 2000) 186–90, esp. 189, and of the poem attributed to Orpheus available to Aristobulus, on pp. 219–22; and on the latter, see also Erich S. Gruen, *Heritage and Hellenism: The Reinvention of Jewish Tradition* (Berkeley/Los Angeles/London: University of California, 1998) 248–50. For the text, see Carl Holladay, *Fragments from Hellenistic Jewish Authors: Volume IV. Orphica* (SBLTT 40, Pseudepigrapha 14; Atlanta: Scholars, 1996) 51–54.

[126] Honigman, *The Septuagint and Homeric Scholarship in Alexandria*, 146.

[127] See the discussion in Chapter Five.

ity in Christian encounters in non-Jewish settings. These, too, are largely intercultural in nature.

3. The Christian Message: Lost in Translation?

The early Christian mission, according to New Testament sources, sought to make its case in a variety of settings within the eastern Roman empire. This world involved the Christian movement in an engagement with a variety of philosophical currents and different religious contexts. The most important source for the description of such encounters comes from Acts of the Apostles, and it is for this reason that the following survey of New Testament sources begins with Acts rather than the letters of Paul, which we will examine afterwards. While it can be difficult to square up Luke's Paul in Acts of the Apostles with the Paul of his own letters, Luke's descriptions may be taken as representative of efforts at communicating the gospel made by Christians (Acts 11:26; 26:28 and 1 Peter 4:16,[128] earlier designated "the Way" in Acts 9:2; cf. 18:26, 19:9, 23, 22:4). Before entering into this discussion, it is important to be clear that the issue of translatability in Acts rarely involved an equation of the Christian and non-Christian deities. Instead, the effort at translation involves categories of divinity operative in the idiom of the audiences that Christians used to convey their message. It is also important to be clear that the passages in Acts are not indicative of the historical Paul's actual words and views; rather, they are representations of the author about Paul's ministry and preaching. We will start with Acts 14, 17 and 19, and then we will turn our attention to a number of letters, specifically Galatians 4, 1 Corinthians 8 and 10, Colossians 1–2 and Ephesians 2–3.

Acts of the Apostles (ca. mid-90s CE/AD[129])

Acts 14: Paul and Barnabas at Lystra

In the story of Paul and Barnabas at Lystra (Acts 14:8–21), Paul is credited with healing a cripple. As a result, the crowds react by asserting the following about the two apostles: "The gods have come down to us in human form" (verse 11). The narrative goes on (verse 12): "They called Barnabas 'Zeus' and Paul 'Hermes,' because he was the chief speaker." The priest of Zeus in Lystra honors the two with oxen and garlands (verse 13). Paul and

---

[128] See David G. Horrell, "The Label Χηριστιανος: 1 Peter 4:16 and the Formation of Christian Identity," *JBL* 126 (2007) 361–81.

[129] A date around the mid-90s to about 100 has been argued by Steve Mason, based on the literary relationship that he sees between Josephus and Luke-Acts. See Mason, *Josephus and the New Testament* (Peabody, MA: Hendrickson, 1992) 186–225.

Barnabas respond by informing the people that they are humans and that the real story of divinity involves the living God who made heaven and earth who has left a witness to himself in the form of rains from heaven and fruitful seasons (verses 14–17). In past times God allowed the peoples to go their own ways (verse 16). However, the apostles are unsuccessful in that the crowd could not be restrained from offering them sacrifice (verse 18). The story closes with "some Jews from Antioch and from Iconium" arriving and winning the crowds.[130] Paul is instead stoned and left for dead (verse 19).

The story contains several features pertinent to the general issue of translatability. First, the local populace translates the appearance of Paul and Barnabas into their regional idiom, namely as manifestations of the gods, Hermes and Zeus. Commentators have compared the story of the appearance of Zeus and Hermes as mortals in Ovid, *Metamorphoses,* 8.611–725, which like Acts 14 is set in Asia Minor.[131] Other Greco-Roman texts likewise relate the appearance (*epiphaneia*) of one of the great gods in adult human form.[132] In contrast with the Lycaonians' ability to translate, the two apostles cannot "re-translate" their healing to the local populace into Christian terms. Perhaps even more fundamentally, they cannot even convince their audience that they are not divine. The Lycaonians remain persuaded of their own translation. The very argument that the two apostles use concedes that God allowed different peoples to "go their own ways" (verse 16, NAB). In other words, we seem to have an admission that God permitted different

---

[130] For Jews as Paul's opposition in Acts, see Howard C. Kee, "The Jews in Acts," in: *Diaspora Jews and Judaism: Essays in Honor of, and in Dialogue with, A. Thomas Kraebel* (ed. J. Andrew Overman and Robert S. MacLennan; South Florida Studies in the History of Judaism 41; Atlanta: Scholars, 1992) 183–95, esp. 188–89.

[131] Hans Conzelmann, *Acts of the Apostles* (Hermeneia; trans. James Limburg, A. Thomas Krabel, and Donald H. Juel; Philadelphia: Fortress, 1987) 110; Luke Timothy Johnson, *The Acts of the Apostles* (Sacra Pagina 5; Collegeville, MN: Liturgical, 1992) 248; C. K. Barrett. *A Critical and Exegetical Commentary on the Acts of the Apostles* (ICC; two vols.; Edinburgh: T & T Clark, 1994) 1.676–77 (henceforth, *Acts*). See also L. H. Martin, "Hermes," *DDD* 405–11, esp. 409–10; and Graf, "Zeus," *DDD* 939. To the interpretation of Paul as Hermes in view of the former's speaking role, Conzelmann, Barrett, Johnson and Martin also compare the description of Hermes by Iamblichus, *Mysteries,* 1:1, as "the god who is the leader in speaking" (*theos ho ton logon hegemon*). Hermes generally figured in the larger international discourse about revelation. Cf. the identification of Moses as Hermes by Artapanus; see Carl R. Holladay, *Fragments from Hellenistic Jewish Authors: Volume I: Historians* (SBLTT 20, Pseudepigrapha Series 10; Chico, CA: Scholars, 1983) 210–11. For Hermes more broadly, see H.S. Versnel, *Inconsistencies in Greek and Roman Religion I: Ter Unus. Isis, Dionysius, Hermes: Three Studies in Henotheism* (second ed.; Studies in Greek and Roman Religion, vol. 6, I; Leiden/New York/Köln: Brill, 1998) 213–51. For Zeus in this period, see Graf, "Zeus," *DDD* 934–40.

[132] For a brief discussion of such texts, see Cartlidge and Dungan, *Documents for the Study of the Gospels,* 11–15, with discussion of Acts 14:11–12.

gods to the various nations.[133] In this passage the Lycaonians produce a fine translation of Christian divinity into their own terms,[134] but the translation fails from the perspective of Paul as represented in this passage. Finally, the gospel in this scene is evacuated of any specifics about the figure of Jesus.[135] Instead, verse 17 makes an appeal to a sort of "natural theology," that the divine is manifest through nature.[136] There is nothing specifically Christian represented in Paul's case here. In sum, the attempt to bridge the gap between themselves and their audience in Lystra is unsuccessful from the Christians' side. As C. K. Barrett puts the point, "the reaction of the people of Lystra to Paul and Barnabas has been favorable, though badly misdirected."[137]

Acts 17: Paul at the Areopagus

Acts 17:28 might be regarded as a case of divine translatability made in defense of the Christian view over and against Greek understandings of divinity.[138] The story of Paul in Athens begins with his interactions with Jews in the synagogue and with philosophers in the public area, including some Epicureans and Stoics (Acts 17:16–17).[139] Verse 18 sets the terms of discussion, as Paul is heard as "a preacher of foreign gods." As a result of this engagement, Paul is led to the Areopagus where he is asked about "this new teaching that you speak of" (verse 19). He then makes his case before the Athenians at the Areopagus in verses 22–31. As part of his brief, Paul identifies his god with the local "Unknown God."[140] For his description of this god in verse 28, Paul draws on authors familiar to his audience: "For 'In him we live and move and have our being,' as even some of your poets have

---

[133] Apart from a thematic parallel, the verse (*panta ta ethne*) perhaps echoes LXX Deuteronomy 4:19 (*pasin tois ethnesin*), which would place it within the older interpretive tradition of reading Deuteronomy 32:8–9, as discussed in Chapter Four, pp. 203–10.

[134] Bohak, "The Impact," 10: "The Lyconians clearly had no difficulty incorporating the Jewish god into their own pantheon; in fact, they almost added his messengers as well."

[135] On this point, see the discussion by Barrett, *Acts*, 1.680–81.

[136] Contrast Romans 1:18–32; and see the discussion in: Joseph A. Fitzmyer, *Romans: A New Translation with Introduction and Commentary* (AB 33; New York: Doubleday, 1993) 274–75.

[137] Barrett, *Acts*, 1.683. In contrast, verse 19 relates that the Jewish competition from Antioch and Iconium is said to have "won over the crowds."

[138] This passage came to my attention thanks to the comments of Adela Collins about the text in Aristobulus (discussed in the preceding section) in *OTPs* 2:841, margin.

[139] See the discussion of the broad scene set in the chapter by Barrett, *Acts*, 2.824–31.

[140] The closest Greek parallel is the "altars of gods named Unknown" in Athens mentioned by Pausanias, *Description of Greece,* 1.1.4; W. H. S. Jones, *Pausanias, Description of Greece I* (LCL; London: W. Heinemann, 1918) 7. For this evidence as well as other literary, inscriptional and archaeological evidence, see van der Horst, "The Unknown God (Acts 17:23)," 19–42.

said, 'For we too are his offspring.'" Commentators have traced the first quote to Epimenides of Knossos (sixth century BCE/BC) and the second to Aratus of Soli (a third century BCE/BC poet from Cilicia).[141]

For the better part of his speech, Paul is represented as locating or perhaps universalizing the Jewish god within the cultural horizons of his Athenian audience.[142] Only in verse 31 does the audience hear any particular claims by Paul about the "man" whom God raised from the dead and appointed as judge of the world. (By stressing "the man," the passage is perhaps avoiding the difficulty of appearing to proclaim two gods, arguably reflecting the impact of the Greco-Roman context on the presentation of the gospel.) At the end of the speech, Paul's own claim finally enters, but it is devoid of the gospel's particulars, including the name of Jesus. Hans Conzelmann assesses the representation of Paul's speech here in these terms: "Both the understanding of God and of humanity in this passage are unique in the New Testament. Nevertheless, it should be observed that such statements had enjoyed currency for some time in Hellenistic Judaism as attempts to describe the Jewish idea of God."[143] As a result of the speech, "some did join him and become believers" (verse 34), hardly though a picture of overwhelming success. In Conzelmann's assessment, the author of Acts stands within a tradition of Jewish and Christian engagement with Greco-Roman discourse about divinity. Yet in context it is barely Christian (in any explicit terms), but appeals instead to a rather universal God.

Acts 19: Paul in Ephesus

Paul's encounter in Ephesus is interesting less for how he is heard and more for how he is perceived, for in this story (verses 23–40), the apostle himself does not speak. The story revolves around a debate among the citizens of Ephesus about the Christian movement here called "the Way" (verse 23). It begins with a silversmith named Demetrius who earns his living by making miniature silver shrines for the goddess Artemis (verse 24). Demetrius calls

---

[141] Conzelmann, *Acts of the Apostles,* 144–45; Barrett, *Acts,* 2.846–49; Johnson, *The Acts,* 316. See also Carl R. Holladay, "Acts," in: *Harper's Bible Commentary* (ed. James L. Mays; San Francisco: Harper & Row, 1988) 1103; and also the NAB notes to this verse. For further discussion, with a wider range of primary sources involved, see Conzelmann, *Acts of the Apostles,* 144–45; Barrett, *Acts,* 2.846–49.

[142] However, note the comments of Arthur Darby Nock, *Essays on Religion and the Ancient World* (vol. 2; ed. Zeph Stewart; Cambridge, MA: Harvard University, 1972) 831: "Certainly the Biblical element in the speech is not a veneer; what is unique in it is the pregnant brevity."

[143] Conzelmann, *Acts of the Apostles,* 145, citing Philo, *Legum Allegoria,* 3.4 (Colson and Whitaker, *Philo I,* 302–3); and Aristobulus fragment 4, which cites another context in Aratus (see Holladay, *Fragments from Hellenistic Jewish Authors: Volume III. Aristobulus,* 170–71).

a meeting of the craftsmen of Ephesus (verse 25) to protest Paul's message that "gods made by hands are not gods at all" (verse 26, NAB). The craftsmen react with anger and proclaim the greatness of their divine patron (verse 28): "Great is Artemis of the Ephesians!"[144] As a result, the safety of Paul's traveling companions, Gaius and Aristarchus, is threatened and he himself is cautioned not to get involved (verse 28–31). The assembly is thrown into chaos at this point (verse 32). The story adds here an element of Jewish competition (verses 33–34).

The pertinent part of this story emerges with the response of the civil authority to the situation (verses 35–40). This official, identified as a secretary or clerk (*grammateus*), begins his speech by appealing to the commonly held facts that Ephesus is the guardian[145] of the temple of Artemis and that her image came from the sky (verses 35–36). The clerk goes on to defend Paul and his companions (verse 37): "The men you brought here are not temple robbers, nor have they insulted our goddess." With these words, the clerk narrows the grounds of the claim against Paul by implicitly disassociating his critique of silver miniature shrines from the goddess and her image. As a result, the clerk declares that there is no basis for the actions being taken, and he raises the specter of a potential legal claim against the craftsmen themselves for fomenting a riot (verse 38–40).[146]

This passage presents the issues not by Paul, but by the nameless local clerk about Paul. At the same time, the clerk's speech contains some features that compare with Paul's speeches in Acts 14. In literary terms, the clerk's speech perhaps substitutes for what Paul might have said. First, the clerk appeals in verse 35 to the local religious traditions. Second, he shifts from the local idiom to the issue of intercultural discourse, about how the speech of the outsiders is to be assessed by the insiders. He implicitly includes Paul and his companions as those who do not deny the facts about Artemis (in verse 36), which is true only by omission (there is of course no assent given by them to the facts about Artemis). Here the clerk finds a space for the defense of Paul and his companions ("nor have they insulted our goddess," verse 37). Third, the dispute is given a legal turn (verses 38–40). In religious and legal terms, the clerk's words speak in defense of "the Way."

[144] For this context in Ephesus, see the remarks of Harland, *Associations, Synagogues, and Congregations*, 3–7, 42, 46, 63, 105, 111, and 246.

[145] On the title *neokoros,* "temple warden," as applied to the city, see Steven J. Friesen, *Twice Neokoros: Ephesus, Asia and the Cult of the Flavian Imperial Family* (EPRO 116; Leiden: Brill, 1993); and R. A. Kearsley, "Ephesus: Neokoros of Artemis," in: *New Documents Illustrating Early Christianity: Volume 6: A Review of Greek Inscriptions and Papyri published in 1980–81* (ed. S. R. Llewelyn; np: The Ancient History Documentary Research Centre, Macquarie University, 1992) 203–6.

[146] For the cultural context of this investigation at Ephesus, see the remarks of Harland, *Associations, Synagogues, and Congregations*, 169–70.

These three scenes in Acts represent Christian efforts to render divinity in terms that would seem intelligible and appealing within the larger Greco-Roman philosophical and religious discourse about divinity. At the same time, with two presentations lacking any reference to Jesus and the third referring to him simply as "a man," the Christian presentation is hardly Christian. Here Acts is careful in handling the divine status of Jesus for the Greco-Roman audience in order to avoid giving the impression of proclaiming two gods. At the same time, it is also clear that many, if not most, in Paul's non-Jewish audience do not "get" his religious argument. Despite his missions to the gentiles, Paul's appeals to them, as represented in the book of Acts, fall flat.[147]

There were other means available to aid in these cross-cultural exchanges. None of the passages in Acts refer to the common Greco-Roman idea of the "divine man" (*theios aner/divinus homo*), or any other notion that might have more sense of Jesus' divinity in a Greco-Roman atmosphere.[148] Perhaps the approach in Acts should be chalked up to the fact that the passages in question make their appeals in terms that would have made sense in the specific contexts of Lystra, Athens and Ephesus.[149] Even so, Acts tellingly represents the gulf between the Christology of "the Way" and the notions of divinity in the Greco-Roman paradigm. Early Christians, as represented in Acts, found cross-cultural discourse useful for speaking about God, but they did not deploy it for their case about the person of Jesus. In other words, the representation of Christianity in the book of Acts shows little capacity for theoretical, second-order discourse that would bridge the gap between its own sacred story about Jesus and the various philosophical and religious currents of the time. Acts 14, with its depiction of Paul and Barnabas as "divine men," may signal a Christian sensibility about the dif-

---

[147] Cf. Peter's speech in Acts 15:7, which mentions his divine commission to spread the gospel to the gentiles.

[148] Note the comment of G. W. Bowersock: "The East had grown accustomed to the worship of men and women." Bowersock, *Augustus and the Greek World* (Oxford: Clarendon, 1965; repr. Westport, CT: Greenwood, 1981) 112, which is cited and discussed by T. W. Hillard, "Quasi-divine Honours for a Severe Governor," in: *New Documents Illustrating Early Christianity: Volume 9: A Review of the Greek Inscriptions and Papyri Published in 1986–87* (ed. S. R. Llewelyn; Grand Rapids, MI/Cambridge, UK: Eerdmans, 2002) 16. To be clear, Bowersock makes his comment in the context of his discussion of the imperial cult. For the *theios aner,* see Morton Smith, *The Cult of Yahweh,* 2.3–27 and 28–38; and Helmut Köster, *Introduction to the New Testament: Volume 1. History, Culture, and the Religion of the Hellenistic Age* (second ed.; Berlin/New York: de Gruyter, 1995–2000) 164–65, 280–81. This stands in contrast with the divine man theme that has been claimed for some contexts in the Gospels. See also Carl R. Holladay, *Theios aner in Hellenistic-Judaism: A Critique of the Use of This Category in New Testament Christology* (SBLDS 40; Missoula, MT: Scholars, 1977).

[149] Or, does Acts 14, with its depiction of Paul and Barnabas as "divine men," indicate a perception of a difficulty posed by such category?

ficulty posed by using Greco-Roman notions to present the Christian message. The Christian story would need to be presented on its own, without reference to Greco-Roman concepts of divinity. Indeed, it is just such an emphasis on the Christian sacred story that we find in Paul's own words, to which we now turn.

Pauline Letters

The discourse of divinity in Paul's own letters is emphatically concerned with the figure of Jesus, compared with Luke's Paul in Acts of the Apostles. Perhaps because Paul is communicating with communities that have already accepted Jesus, his divinity receives far greater press than it does in Acts. In any case, some passages in Paul's letters raise the problem of the ontological status of non-Jewish and non-Christian divinity. Yet these issues ultimately are subordinated to the proclamation of the Christian gospel, and the ontological question of such divine powers falls to the side without philosophical resolution. We begin with two passages from 1 Corinthians.

1 Corinthians 8 and 10 (ca. 50 CE/AD)[150]

As with the critique of images in Acts 19, the problem of offerings made to deities raises issues of translatability for Paul. The specific question is taken up first in 1 Corinthians 8:4–6.[151] Verse 4 first affirms basic belief known from Jewish sources ("there is no God but one"). Paul might have continued directly to verse 6, which affirms this divine oneness in Christian terms (even if its term may be indebted ultimately to Stoic language, which identifies the cosmic God with the *logos*). However, the intervening verse 5, even as it serves as a foil to the monotheism of verses 4 and 6, seems to show Paul conceding ground: "Indeed, even though there are so-called gods in heaven and earth (there are, to be sure, many 'gods' and many 'lords') …" (NAB). The RSV and NAB translations put quotation marks around the words "gods" and "lords," in the final clause. These translations point to what would seem to be a difficulty, namely that Paul seems to make some concession to the polytheistic opposition.[152] He might have simply denied

---

[150] The standard chronology for Paul's letters is followed here. For a discussion, critique and a new proposal for this chronology, see Gregory Tatum, O.P., *New Chapters in the Life of Paul: The Relative Chronology of His Career* (CBQMS 41; Washington, DC: Catholic Biblical Association of America, 2006). See especially his proposed relative chronology of letters and events in Paul's adult life on pp. 126–30.

[151] For the context, see Bruce W. Winter, *Seek the Welfare of the City: Christians as Benefactors and Citizens* (First Century Christians in the Graeco-Roman World series; Grand Rapids, MI: Eerdmans; Carlisle, Cumbria: Paternoster, 1994) 131–33.

[152] As noted by Henk S. Versnel, "Thrice One: Three Greek Experiments in Oneness," 86 n. 17 and 130 n. 136.

any reality to such figures, or at least he could have omitted these sorts of considerations. Yet he does not.

One important question is the identity of the "gods" and "lords" mentioned in verse 5. According to Bruce Winter, the "gods on earth" are the deified emperor and members of the imperial family.[153] However, this view would leave open the matter of gods in heaven, as noted by J. C. Hurd as well as David R. Cartlidge and David L. Duncan.[154] One might explain Paul's concession here as a matter of his knowledge of local beliefs in Corinth. Yet even this explanation seems weak, given Paul's statement that "there is no God but one" in verse 4. Perhaps Paul is facing something of the same difficulty expressed also in some passages in the Hebrew Bible, namely the ontological status of the gods of the other nations, a problem that goes back to the Hebrew Scriptures.[155] With 1 Corinthians 8, Paul is beginning to develop a rhetorical argument, providing some initial considerations on the matter of divinities and setting up the further discussion of the topic in 1 Corinthians 10.

Paul develops fuller conclusions on the issue in 1 Corinthians 10:6–22. In verses 6–13, he first sets out a typological relationship between the idolatry of his day with the idolatry in the wilderness, with verse 7 evoking Exodus 32. Then in verses 14–17 he returns to the problem of sacrifices offered to deities.[156] Here Paul adds a further consideration, that such sacrifices constitute a direct attack on the Christian life and the mystical body of Christ. Thus Paul offers a stronger response than what he expresses earlier in 1 Corinthians 8.[157] With verses 18–22, Paul gives a conclusion about such putative deities: such an offering is made "to demons and not to God" (*daimoniois kai ou theo,* verse 20). For his critique here, Paul evidently draws on LXX Deuteronomy 32:17: "to demons and not to God (*daimoniois kai ou theo*).[158] With this language and biblical echo, Paul draws a sharper contrast than he does in chapter 8.

---

[153] Winter, *Seek the Welfare of the City,* 132.

[154] Winter, *Seek the Welfare of the City,* 132 n. 54; Hurd, *The Origins of 1 Corinthians* (London: SPCK, 1965) 125; Cartlidge and Dungan, *Documents for the Study of the Gospels,* 5–9.

[155] Cf. Deuteronomy 32:8–9 (especially as it is interpreted in Deuteronomy 4:19)? See Chapter Four for discussion of these passages, on pp. 203–6.

[156] For the connection between Christian theism and Christians abstaining from sacrifices to Greco-Roman deities ("the central religious rite of antiquity"), see Harland, *Associations, Synagogues, and Congregations,* 245, as well as 214, 240.

[157] The general sense of this passage is conveyed by Fritz Graf, "Myth," in: *Religions of the Ancient World: A Guide* (ed. Sarah Iles Johnston; Cambridge, MA/London: Belknap, 2004) 57: "Confronted with the one living and revealed God, the gods of the gentiles became demons (I Cor. 10.20–21)".

[158] In contrast to the LXX, which takes the two nouns as contrastive, the MT is usually understood as construing "not god" (*lo' 'eloah*) in apposition to *šedim,* as a negative

The main difference between the two chapters involves the mention of table and cup in chapter 10 (verse 21).[159] At this point, Paul evidently turns again to Deuteronomy 32 to make his point. He ends the section by posing the question, "are we provoking the Lord ...?" (*parazeloumen ton kurion*), which may echo the phrase, "they provoked me" (*parezelosan me*) in Deuteronomy 32:21a.[160] The effect is to draw a clear distinction, now using Deuteronomy 32, to continue his evocation of the idolatry in the wilderness. Rather than reaching across to some aspect of the context of the Corinthians, Paul turns in this passage to the Hebrew Bible to bring his rhetorical argument to a conclusion. The "demons" of Deuteronomy 32:17 serve as the interpretive lens for understanding the divinities that receive offerings of meat at Corinth. In other words, Paul translates from the past the view of his traditional texts in order to interpret the present situation. Here for Paul, vertical translatability stands in and arguably precludes horizontal translatability.

In 1 Corinthians 8 and 10, it is interesting to see how Paul draws on different aspects of Deuteronomy 32 for understanding the gods of other peoples. In the first case, he might be using Deuteronomy 32:8–9, which allows for a certain space for foreign gods (at least as it was read in Deuteronomy 4:19; cf. Ben Sira 17:17, 44:1–2). However, such a putative echo is not particularly explicit from Paul's language. In the second context, his use of Deuteronomy 32:17 and 21 for his critique seems more explicit. In short, Paul's discourses about other gods in 1 Corinthians 8 and 10 echo the older issue over translatability (and its lack) in the Hebrew Bible, particularly as it is expressed in Deuteronomy 32. Vertical translatability serves Paul's purposes; little horizontal translatability is expressed.

Galatians 4 (ca. 54 CE/AD)

The issue before Paul in this letter concerns the understanding that members of the Galatian church should have of their Christian character. Paul starts with a general notion that expresses his spiritual kinship with the Galatian church. Before the salvation of Christ, "we were enslaved to the elemental powers of the world" (*ta stoicheia tou kosmou*, verse 3), but with God

---

description of the latter. (Parenthetically, it is to be noted that the LXX rendering takes into account the difference in number between the two nouns.) Cf. MT Psalm 106:37 (LXX Psalm 105:37).

[159] For the archaeological and cultural context, see Jerome Murphy-O'Connor, *St. Paul's Corinth: Texts and Archaeology* (third revised and expanded ed.; Collegeville, MN: Liturgical, 2002) 178–91.

[160] See Elizabeth Schüssler Fiorenza, "1 Corinthians," in: *Harper's Bible Commentary* (ed. James L. Mays; San Francisco: Harper & Row, 1988) 1182.

sending his Son, ransom has been made for their release from enslavement (verses 4–7). The discourse proceeds to exhort the Galatians (verse 8–11):

> At a time when you did not know God, you became slaves to things that by nature are not gods (*theois*); but now that you have come to know God, or rather to be known by God, how can you turn back again to the weak and destitute elemental powers (*stoicheia*)? Do you want to be slaves to them all over again? You are observing days, months, seasons and years. I am afraid on your account that perhaps I have labored in vain.

The speech begins with the situation of the Galatians, prior to their knowing Jesus. Paul chides them for their observance of a ritual calendar (perhaps the Jewish calendar, which would presuppose that Paul faces competition from Jewish opponents in Galatia). What is interesting here is Paul's reference to other powers first as "not being gods" (*me ousin theois*, verse 8) and then as weak and destitute elemental "powers" (*stoichia*, verse 9, echoing verse 3). The context here in Galatians 4:8–9 in effect parallel "powers" with "not gods."[161] The specific nature of the powers in mind is not clear, but the context suggests that they are at least supernatural.[162]

This position seems to approximate or even combine the two rather conflicting views as found in 1 Corinthians 8 and 10. Though "not gods" as in Deuteronomy 32:17, they are recognized as powers (as paralleled also by Deuteronomy 32:8 and 1 Corinthians 8:5). Though viewed as "weak and

---

[161] For a discussion of *stoicheia* here as "elemental powers" versus "elementary principles" or forms of Jewish and Gentile religion, see Danker, *A Greek-English Lexicon,* 946; and the substantial survey of Clinton E. Arnold, *The Colossian Syncretism: The Interface Between Christianity and Folk Belief at Colossae* (WUNT 2/77; Tübingen: Mohr Siebeck, 1995) 158–94, esp. 183–84 for remarks on Galatians 4. See also the summaries of L. J. Alderink, "Stoicheia," *DDD* 815–18 (with recent bibliography); and Stuckenbruck, *Angel Veneration and Christology,* 104–11. Alderink ("Stoicheia," 817) concedes the possibility that these may be some sort of spiritual beings, but prefers to understand them according to "its common meaning in the Greek philosophical tradition," namely as "the basic constituents of the universe in which the soul may be trapped in the elemental disharmony or the soul's misdeeds and from which it can be freed through proper philosophical and religious knowledge." Greek usage of the word sometimes identifies such elements as divinities; see Arnold, *The Colossian Syncretism,* 162–76; and Stuckenbruck, *Angel Veneration and Christology,* 107–8; see further below.

[162] For some possibilities, see in addition to the works cited in the preceding note, Joseph A. Fitzmyer, "The Letter to the Galatians," *NJBC* 787. These would include anthropomorphic versions of the physical elements, sometimes worshipped as deities: "fire, air, water and earth complain to the gods who is over all"; and "heavenly bodies," also "regarded as personal beings and given divine honors." The characterization, "spirit-elements," suggested by Hans Dieter Betz nicely captures the sense; see Betz, *Galatians* (Hermeneia; Philadelphia: Fortress, 1979) 204–5. In contrast, William Baird characterizes these powers broadly as "pagan polytheism"; see Baird, "Galatians," in: *Harper's Bible Commentary* (ed. James L. Mays; San Francisco: Harper & Row, 1988) 1209. The discussion of Arnold (*The Colossian Syncretism,* 169–73, 176–82) indicates how the notion of *stoicheia* had made its way into Judaism and Christianity of the region.

destitute," they are not quite the "demons" of Deuteronomy 32:17 and 1 Corinthians 10:20. At first glance, this presentation may give the impression of conceptual inconsistency. This may be a concession being made to current notions of celestial or astral beings, which are not part of either the Christian gospel or Jewish tradition.[163] However, this assessment may fail to capture the larger conceptual strategy and concern at work. Paul here begins with the Galatians' understanding of the cosmos in order to provide them with an intelligible narrative that is still based on the gospel. In other words, the Christian message of Jesus' salvation builds on the Galatian prior narrative of "elemental powers." Compared with Luke's Paul, Paul in Galatians offers a narrative that partially bridges the conceptual gap between the gospel and the Galatians, not through a particular identification of deities, one Christian and one Galatian, but through a reconfiguring of the Christian narrative that incorporates the Galatians' understanding of the cosmos: the Christian Jesus redeems the Galatians from enslavement to the "elemental powers" of their worldview. Implicitly Paul leaves open the ontological status of such powers; they are weak, but he does not state that they are unreal. Still Paul's point is not philosophical; for him, it is a matter of salvation. In Galatians 4, issues about "powers" are entertained briefly, in the service of conveying the Christian message.

Colossians 1–2 (ca. 70s CE/AD?)

Among the matters of concern to the writer,[164] this letter raises the problem of divine beings in relation to the Christian life. The tone for the issue is set by the citation of what has been understood as an early Christian hymn in 1:15–20.[165] This hymn follows the initial address and prayer for the Colossian community in 1:1–14, which culminates in a declaration of redemption of the Father achieved through the Son. The final statement concerning the Father and the Son in verses 12–14 provides a transition into the hymn,

---

[163] This is not to claim that Jews or Christians knew nothing of such matters. We do not have much access to contemporary evidence on this point, but certainly later Jewish and Christian art in Late Antiquity show considerable familiarity with Roman zodiac art. See Fine, *Art and Judaism in the Greco-Roman World,* 196–205. For example, the Greco-Roman solar god, Helios, plays a role in both Jewish and Christian art. Continuity between the solar motif in this art and earlier, biblical material was studied by Hans Peter Stähli, *Solare Elemente im Jahweglauben des Alten Testaments* (OBO 66; Fribourg: Universitätsverlag; Göttingen: Vandenhoeck & Ruprecht, 1985) 1–12.

[164] Based largely on differences of vocabulary with Paul's other letters, many Pauline scholars do not attribute this letter to Paul but regard it as "deutero-Pauline." See the convenient summary of the question by Maurya P. Horgan, "The Letters to the Colossians," in: *NJBC,* 876–77.

[165] This understanding is common among Pauline scholars. See among others, J. Christian Beker, "Colossians," in: *Harper's Bible Commentary* (ed. James L. Mays; San Francisco: Harper & Row, 1988) 1227.

beginning in verse 15 with its description of the Son as "the image of the invisible god, the first-born of all creation" (echoing the figure of Wisdom, in Proverbs 8:22–31; Wisdom of Solomon 7:22–8:1; Ben Sira, also known as Sirach or Ecclesiasticus, 1:4). The figure is then extolled as the means by which all in heaven and earth were created; these include "thrones or dominions or principalities or powers" (verse 16). In contrast, the Son is "before all things, and in him all things hold together" (verse 17). The hymn then turns to the theme of the Son as head of the church and source of salvation (verses 18–20). For all on earth and in heaven (cf. verse 20), the Son is the crucial, singular divine reality, for "in him all the fullness was pleased to dwell" (verse 19).

The formulations in verses 16 and 19 anticipate later parts in the letter. Following up 1:16, chapter 2 turns to the issue of principalities and powers in verses 10 and 15. Christ is the head of such powers according to verse 10, and their conqueror in verse 15. These themes are more than echoes of the hymn, but reflect a concern in this context evident further in 2:8 and 20, which address the problem of "the elemental powers of the world" (the same phrase that we saw in Galatians 4:3). Clinton E. Arnold and Larry J. Alderink suggest that the phrase, "of the world," points to claims made by a specific philosophical tradition.[166] From this deduction, Alderink would entertain two possible views of *stoicheia* here:

One possible content for the claims would be that the 'elements of kosmos' are the elemental spirits of the universe (1:16; 2:10,15) whom Colossians philosophers, following human thinking (1:18), identified as the powers and rulers who govern society or the angels (2:18) … The identification may equally point to the four basic constituents of the kosmos (2:10) to which Colossian Christians died with Christ: thus demonstrating that living without the world is as possible as living in the world.[167]

---

[166] Arnold, *The Colossian Syncretism*, 185–93; Alderink, "Stoicheia," *DDD* 818.

[167] Alderink, "Stoicheia," *DDD* 818. The nature of these practices and their religious background are disputed. Beker ("Colossians," 1226) comments: "it seems likely that certain Jewish-Hellenistic features formed part of the syncretistic mix, although it is difficult to be precise on this point." For further discussion, see Johannes Lähnemann, *Der Kolosserbrief: Komposition, Situation und Argumentation* (Studien zum Neuen Testament 3; Gütersloh: Mohn, 1971) 82–100; Fred O. Francis, "Humility and Angelic Worship in Col 2:18," in: *Conflict at Colossae: A Problem in the Interpretation of Early Christianity* (ed. Fred O. Francis and Wayne A. Meeks; Sources for Biblical Study 4; Missoula, MT: Society of Biblical Literature, 1973) 163–95; and Horgan, "The Letter to the Colossians," 877 and 881. See also R. A. Kearsley, "Angels in Asia Minor: The Cult of Hosios and Dikaios," in: *New Documents Illustrating Early Christianity: Volume 6: A Review of Greek Inscriptions and Papyri published in 1980–81* (ed. S. R. Llewelyn; np: The Ancient History Documentary Research Centre, Macquarie University, 1992) 206–9. Note the general comments of Collins, "Jewish Monotheism and Christian Theology," 93–94.

The writer regards concern for such powers as inconsistent with life in Christ. Concern with such matters "are shadows of things to come; the reality belongs to Christ" (2:16). On the whole, the author does not deny such powers, but relative to Christ, they are not central. The reason is given in 2:9, "For in him dwells the whole fullness of the deity bodily," which directly echoes 1:19, "For in him all the fullness was pleased to dwell." Colossians 2:10 completes the thought of 2:9, by making the final point in the chain of religious logic that the Colossians participate "in this fullness in him."[168] Thus the theme of divine "fullness" beginning in the hymn informs Paul's foundational "religious logic" that flows from the Father to the Son to the body of Christ, the church. In this argument, the author offers his own pastoral exegesis of the hymn as it applies to the situation of the Colossian church.[169]

While the formulation of Colossians 2:9 sounds like a reasoned understanding of divinity, a philosophical analysis does not seem to be the goal. Indeed, this very context deplores "empty, seductive philosophy" as nothing less than slavery "according to the elemental powers of this world and not according to Christ" (2:8).[170] The author is not presenting a systematic theology of divinity in speaking of the fullness of deity in the figure of Christ Jesus. Deity certainly includes "God, the Father of our Lord Jesus Christ" (1:3; cf. 1:12). Jesus is after all "the beloved Son" (1:13) and "image of the invisible God" (1:15). And clearly the discourse here does not exclude either angels or elemental powers as unreal.[171] In the end, the argument rests on an appeal to religious experience, specifically participation in the Christian church, which is after all is Christ-centered.[172] As such, other powers remain outside of the letter's religious logic; such powers are at best unimportant diversions and at worst highly detrimental to the Christian life.

This letter's representation of principalities and powers ventures no real interest in the issue of translatability of divinities. In a sense, a philosophical reasoning that might engage some sort of effort at translatability would mis-

---

[168] Horgan ("The Letter to the Colossians," 881) compares Romans 15:13: "May the God of hope fill you with all joy and peace in believing, so that you may abound in the hope by the power of the holy spirit."

[169] If the hymn were regarded as Christian scripture in some sense such that Paul cites it here, one might even call his handling of the hymn comparable to "inner-biblical" exegesis or a "parabiblical" composition.

[170] Cf. "wisdom of this age" in 1 Corinthians 2:6; cf. 3:19.

[171] If one were to take a broad, comparative religion or history of religion approach to 2:9, one might say that the view here echoes the representation of divinity in the figure of Marduk who receives the names of the other deities; such acclamation of Marduk does not mean that the other divinities have no reality at all. Rather, they are at once subordinate to him and subsumed in him. See Chapter Three, pp. 170–77, for discussion.

[172] Compare Beker's comment to 2:6–22 ("Colossians," 1227): "The key to the argument can be summarized as 'Christ alone'."

understand reality for Colossians. As we saw in the discussion of 1 Corinthians and Galatians, translatability misses the point. First-order experience in the body of Christ essentially short-circuits theoretical, second-order discourse about divinity. This focus in Colossians on the Christian life is not simply a critique against the excesses of such philosophy, or even a claim about its irrelevance. Here it is more: philosophical second-order discourse generally stands on the same order as "the elemental powers of the world and not according to Christ" (2:8).

Ephesians 2–3 (late first century CE/AD?)[173]

Ephesians 2:1–2 contrasts life in Christ with the "transgressions and sins in which you once lived following the Aeon of this world (*kata ton aiona tou kosmou*), following the ruler of the power of the air (*kata ton archonta tes exousias tou aeros*)."[174] 3:10 relates how the riches of Christ were granted "so that the manifold wisdom of God might now be made known through the church to the principalities and authorities in the heavens (*tais archais kai tais exousias*)."[175] In Ephesians 2–3, the two sets of powers in the cosmos, the "ruler of the power of the air" and "the principalities and authorities in the heavens," are subject to the power of God and its divine manifestation in Christ. The "ruler" is often thought to be the devil,[176] while "the principalities and authorities in the heavens," are consistent with Paul's discussion of the same powers in 1 Corinthians 15:24–25 and Colossians 2:15. In Ephesians 6:12 such powers are clearly inimical.[177] Thus Ephesians

---

[173] This letter is considered like Colossians to be "deutero-Pauline." See Nils Alstrup Dahl, "Ephesians," in: *Harper's Bible Commentary* (ed. James L. Mays; San Francisco: Harper & Row, 1988) 1212–13.

[174] Danker (*A Greek-English Lexicon*, 33) takes Aeon here as "a person" (personified cosmic power). If the two appositional clauses are parallel here, such an interpretation would suit the context. For Aeon here as "an evil power," see Paul Kobelski, "Ephesians," *NJBC*, 887. Dahl ("Ephesians," 1215) stresses the Greco-Roman notion of the "air" as the atmosphere between the earth and the lowest of the celestial spheres, which are the habitats of various powers (stars, subordinate gods, and demons). The notion of the devil then is correlated within this larger cosmology as "the ruler of the power of the air." Cf. Paul "caught up to the third heaven" in 2 Corinthians 12:2, and the three heavens in Testament of Levi 2:7–10, 3:1–4; elsewhere the number of heavens is seven. For Greco-Roman models of the multi-leveled heavens in Paul, see J. Edward Wright, *The Early History of Heaven* (Oxford/New York: Oxford University, 2000) 148–50. For a survey of the usages of "aeon," see Arthur Darby Nock, *Essays on Religion and the Ancient World* (vol. 1; ed. Zeph Stewart; Cambridge, MA: Harvard University, 1972) 377–96.

[175] See Wesley Carr, *Angels and Principalities: The Background, Meaning and Development of the Pauline Phrase hai archai kai hai exousiai* (SNTSMS 42; Cambridge, UK: Cambridge University, 1981).

[176] So Dahl, "Ephesians," 1212; NAB note to 2, 1–10.

[177] Kobelski, "Ephesians," 888.

broaches current notions of hostile cosmic powers within its discourse about Christ.

This survey of New Testament sources provides some general observations about early Christian efforts at communicating the gospel in the larger Greco-Roman world. Acts of the Apostles represents discourse of translatability between the Christian community and various non-Christian audiences. Some of these include local beliefs about divinity, while others show a more philosophical discourse, as at the Areopagus in Athens. The author of Acts does not view translatability as a successful strategy for communicating the gospel (and perhaps not even as particularly desirable). Still the author saw the gospel going out into the large *ecumene* of the Mediterranean and coming into contact with a wide variety of beliefs. These were hardly above being discussed by Christians in their efforts to persuade their audiences of the gospel. At the same time, the efforts at translatability in these cases are represented as generally ineffectual.

The Pauline letters examined in this section look quite different when it comes to the question of translatability. With rare exceptions, theoretical discussions of translatability were basically a dead-end for Christian apology in the first century (in contrast with second and third century Christian apologists). Yet Paul is not entirely above correlating the Christian message with non-Christian beliefs. A number of passages show a larger pattern, namely that whatever powers (other than the Father and the Son) can be identified in the world of the addressees are essentially demonic in reality and lie outside of Christian faith. In Paul, we see a negative application of what I have called "horizontal translatability." In other words, Paul allows horizontal translatability on the level of the supernatural powers opposed to God and to Christ. At the same time, the letters understood the Christian vision of good or positive divinity as ultimately untranslatable to the categories of the larger Greco-Roman world. On the level of positive divine power, Paul regards nothing as comparable to the Father and the Son; there is nothing apart from them in the realm of positive divinity worth comparing with them.

Both Acts and the Pauline letters reflect the core Christian belief in its sacred narrative as well as the religious experience that flowed from and expressed that narrative. Yet between the two sets of texts we see fundamentally different representations of translatability. For Acts, what I have called at various points in our discussion "horizontal translatability" was ventured. At the same time, it was also informed by what I have called at times, "vertical translatability," specifically Christian discourse pertaining to divinity based on traditional Jewish readings of the Hebrew Bible. Acts thus shows some measure of both sorts of translatability. In contrast, for the Pauline letters, "horizontal translatability" is largely beside the point.

All that mattered was "vertical translatability," with Christian discourse drawing on traditional Jewish readings of the Hebrew Bible. Thus the New Testament sources reflect a dynamic tension over the question of horizontal translatability.[178]

With the New Testament, the question of translatability (or not) was only beginning for Christians. Later Christian writers would wrestle with these issues in rather wide-ranging ways. On the one hand, Christian writers would maintain vertical translatability, sometimes literally, for example in new translations of the Bible. In his great Latin translation of the Bible, Jerome would construe *rešep* in Habakkuk 3:5 as *diabolus,* what we often now translate as "devil."[179] In this way, Jerome's translation echoes the strategy of Paul in taking the biblical transformation of the god Resheph (as a member of the retinue of Yahweh) as an evil power. What is interesting here is that Jerome recognized that this figure in Habakkuk 3:5 was a divine power in the first place. On the other hand, early Christian writers would appropriate Greco-Roman discourse for purposes of Christian apologetic. To take only one example, the author Pseudo-Justin (ca. 225–313) could discuss the famous figure of Orpheus and his views of divinity in order to make a case for Christianity. In both his *Cohortatio ad Graecos* and *De Monarchia,*[180] Pseudo-Justin seeks to show that Orpheus began as a great teacher of polytheism who came to monotheism. In the former work, Pseudo-Justin develops this argument by quoting the Orphic verse: "One Zeus, one Hades, one Helios, one Dionysius, One god in all."[181] Thus Pseudo-Justin takes this expression of classic Greco-Roman summodeism and claims that this is ultimately monotheism. With Pseudo-Justin's argument, we come full circle, for he uses the argument about divinity favored in many Greco-Roman authors and fits it into his Christianity. In contrast, we saw at the

---

[178] Cf. Horbury's view regarding a number of the passages in question (Acts 17:28–29; Galatians 4:8; Colossians 2:18) that early Christianity, like Judaism of the era, maintained both "exclusive monotheism" and "inclusive monotheism." See Horbury, *Herodian Judaism and New Testament Study,* 12, 15, 32.

[179] See Robert du Mesnil du Buisson, *Études sur les dieux phéniciens hérités par l'empire romain* (EPRO 14; Leiden: Brill, 1970) xviii.

[180] See Carl R. Holladay, *Fragments from Hellenistic Jewish Authors. Volume IV: Orphica* (SBLTT 40, Pseudepigrapha series 14; Atlanta: Scholars, 1996) 104–13; see also Holladay's discussion of the author on pp. 44, 66 and 72 nn. 4–5. The dates for the author are given on p. 65.

[181] Pseudo-Justin, *Cohortatio ad Graecos,* 15 (Holladay, *Fragments from Hellenistic Jewish Authors. Volume IV: Orphica,* 107). The first part is quoted also in: Macrobius, *The Saturnalia,* 1.18.17. For a handy translation of the passage as it appears in Macrobius, see Percival Vaughan Davies, *Macrobius. The Saturnalia* (New York/London: Columbia University, 1969) 131. My attention was first drawn to this material by Assmann, *Moses the Egyptian,* 51 and 228 n. 71.

outset of this chapter how Greco-Roman authors fit the name of the Jewish god into their theological, philosophical and magical discourses.

What is evident from this study is that the line between biblical, Jewish and Christian forms of monotheism and the larger Greco-Roman discourse about divinity was ever developing and subject to religious and cultural renegotiation. This ongoing reformulation of divinity would remain a hallmark of Jewish and Christian discourse. The issue of later Christian appropriation of Greco-Roman discourse is a considerably longer story, one that lies beyond the scope of our survey. However, there is a final moment for our discussion to consider, if only briefly, and that is our modern context. This is addressed in the Epilogue.

Scholars of God, Then and Now

And the Most High has given Him to His ages,
the interpreters of His beauty,
and the narrators of His glory,
and the confessors of His purpose,
and the preachers of His mind,
and the teachers of His works.
Odes of Solomon 12, line 4[1]

In reaching the end of our survey undertaken in the preceding chapters, it is time to take stock. The discussion calls for a broad assessment on two fronts. We will look first at Jan Assmann's contribution to the topic of translatability, as well as the larger context and contours of translatability in the ancient world and its shifting contours. Then we will turn our attention to some connections between the ancient texts studied in this work and the academic work of modern historians of religion and theologians.

1. Jan Assmann: Contribution and Critique

General Contributions

It is to Assman's credit that he has identified and amplified the importance of translatability of divinity in the ancient world. While he was not the first scholar to note the phenomenon, his discussion elevated it as a topic of scholarly analysis. It is of immense value for understanding discourse about various deities in a wide array of texts spread over more than two millennia. Assmann has successfully observed a wide range of contexts for translatability of divinity, and he has recognized many of its cultural contours. Whatever criticism may be leveled at his discussion of translatability of deities or the role that it plays in his larger construction of ancient religion, Assmann's work remains an important contribution to scholarship on religion in general and specifically on the theory of cultural and religious exchange. If criticism is to be raised, it falls chiefly on the relative brevity devoted to the subject. This is so in part because his interest decidedly lies in

---

[1] James H. Charlesworth, "Odes of Solomon," in: *OTPs* 2.746.

the matter of "the Mosaic distinction," for which translatability of divinity serves as a foil.

Critique, by Chapter

Chapter One highlights the many different genres deploying various sorts of translatability. The spectrum of genres exceeds what Assmann presents. More importantly, these texts show considerable theoretical skill in their constructions of translatability. These range from using various theoretical categories for deities to the incorporation of foreign terms for deities. Translatability thus emerges as a complex phenomenon. For this reason alone, it is deserving of greater attention than Assmann's brief on its behalf. Chapter One also addresses cultural contours omitted by Assmann. While Assmann rightly notes the empire context for translatability in the Late Bronze Age, the conditions of empire are further evident. The situation of competing empires created a network of relations among these empire powers and their vassals, with a corresponding lingua franca and vernaculars that express translatability in a variety of ways, ranging from more literal translation of deities across cultures to equation of deities according to various conceptual categories. Assmann's discussion does not come sufficiently to grip with the different conceptualizations or levels of translatability in this period. One may also contest Assmann's notion that the ancients thought of themselves as worshipping the same god just known by different names. This view is hardly indicated by the textual record. Instead, Assmann comes closer to the mark in understanding international religious discourse shared by ancient royalty and their scribes and their counterparts in other cultures.

Chapter Two focuses on Assmann's case against translatability in ancient Israel, which he claims as a corollary to "the Mosaic distinction." The claim does not stand up to scrutiny in view of biblical texts that clearly point to translatability in monarchic period Israel. The "Mosaic distinction" was hardly a constitutive aspect of ancient Israel. Instead, it is at best an eventual outcome of Israel's religious struggles and political conditions. Chapter Three indicates once again the importance of empires in shaping the discourse aimed against translatability. Indeed, the diminution of translatability discussed in Chapter Three may be located against the backdrop of the Neo-Assyrian and Neo-Babylonian empires and their own forms of empire theism that largely short-circuited translatability. This rather central matter is absent from Assmann's account.

Chapter Four follows up Chapter Three by indicating some of the textual and cultural mechanisms deployed in the Persian and Greco-Roman periods to neutralize monarchic period expressions of translatability. Many of these textual processes are complex matters elided in Assmann's presentation.

In fact, his depiction of the biblical material may be seen as accepting and extending the Bible's hermeneutical camouflaging of translatability. In other words, Assmann's representation of the "Mosaic distinction" conflates the shift to later monotheism from earlier translatability (not to mention Israelite polytheism). Insofar as he fails to recognize this diachronic shift, he uncritically offers a flattened version of the biblical portrait of divinity.

Chapter Five is indebted to Assmann's study of translatability in the Greco-Roman period. The Greco-Roman situation may be broadly characterized as a return to and a massive extension of a wide-ranging sort of translatability that we met in the Late Bronze Age context in Chapter One. In contrast to Assmann's presentation, which tends to note the overall commonalities of translatability in antiquity, the discussion in Chapter Five focuses on several changes in translatability and the corresponding changes in circumstances. While ruling powers remain important as they are for the Late Bronze Age context, the nature of the impact of such powers on the expressions of translatability changed considerably over time. What we see in the Late Bronze Age is simply not the same as what was the case in the Neo-Assyrian and Neo-Babylonian contexts; both differ in some significant ways from the Greco-Roman situation. To mention only one example from this study, the "one-god" discourse in the Late Bronze Age and Iron Age contexts, whether in the forms of Bronze Age Egyptian hymns to Amun[2] or the Iron Age one-god predications for Marduk, Assur or Yahweh,[3] was inner-cultural in character. In contrast, Greco-Roman "one-god" discourse was often cross-cultural.[4] As this difference indicates, the nature of cross-cultural discourse changed rather dramatically with the Greco-Roman context.

Chapter Six indicates the situation of translatability of the Jewish god in non-Jewish translatability and the relative lack of translatability in Jewish and Christian texts. Yet despite "the Mosaic distinction," Jewish and Christian sources are hardly uniform in their rejection of translatability. Even as it seems that no room could be given to it in these traditions, especially given the combined weight of biblical and Jewish tradition, nonetheless some consideration is given to the matter. There is no absolute "Mosaic distinction" in any period.

All in all, Assmann's treatment conflates the diachronic dimensions of the phenomenon that he otherwise so deftly evokes. As a result, his treatment can seem anachronistic or unduly static at points. This issue

---

[2] See Chapter One. These texts have not been discussed in this study at any length, as these are inner-cultural expressions and are not cross-cultural in nature.

[3] See Chapter Two.

[4] See Chapter Five.

applies equally to the larger presentist goal to which he puts the notion of translatability. At the end of the day, he wishes to hold up translatability as a model of religious tolerance in contrast with the religion of "the Mosaic distinction." This is a rather modern political and religious goal on Assmann's part. Everyone can and should affirm the value of religious tolerance, but the ancient correlations that Assmann posits between monotheism and violence, and between translatability of divinity and tolerance, hardly hold up to scrutiny. As noted in the Introduction, violence is hardly the special domain of monotheistic religion in antiquity, and it is not the form of theism that drives violence. On the whole, Assmann's discussion does represent an important advance. At the same time, its own political perspective, particularly in its bias against monotheism, is without basis and therefore is to be jettisoned, as noted in the Introduction. Therefore, it is important to view translatability in context in order to understand it. It is to the shifting conditions of translatability in the ancient context that we now turn.

The Shifting Conditions of Ancient Translatability

In the story of ancient translatability in the biblical world told in the preceding chapters, we see a waxing of translatability in the wider Mediterranean world (Chapters One and Five) and its waning in the more delimited context of Israel from the eighth century onwards, down through the Greco-Roman period (Chapters Three, Four and Six). This story arguably intimates some aspects of modern narratives of textual scholarship, whether in religion or theology. In the contexts of all three periods that we have examined, we have noted several features of translatability of divinity. First of all, it belongs to a larger context of discourse about deities in and across cultures locked in a larger web of relations. Empire is the functioning reality of the Late Bronze and Hellenistic periods. Yet as we saw, translatability of divinity is more directly the tool of political relations in the Late Bronze Age; by comparison, it is less a tool of political powers in the Hellenistic period. In this later era, translatability does not speak directly as the apparatus of empire; rather, it follows in the wake of empire's effects and the prestige of its literary and philosophical discourse.

Second, the social settings for translatability considerably varied over time. In the Bronze Age, the locus for translatability lay in scribal circles of royal courts. In Iron Age Israel and Moab it was largely inspired by the royal worldview; it was reflected further in the tradition of Israelite narrative. In the Hellenistic context the context was greatly expanded by comparison. The philosophical schools of Greece and the libraries of the eastern Mediterranean world with their traditions of learning set the standards for discourse. The discourse in the Hellenistic context in particular involved a series of dialogues between world history and local histories. The latter self-consciously and deliberately reacted against the "Greek writers" on matters pertaining to their own local traditions. Such local historians exercised the freedom to dissent. Yet in doing so, they drew on the categories, ideas and methods used in universal histories. The cultural centers still set the terms of discussion. The comparative project in antiquity was the subject of considerable debate between the dominant cultural centers and the periphery, yet the norms for such debate were set by discourse developed from the imperial centers. Thus translatability did not simply offer a discourse of tolerance and understanding (as Assmann would have it), but ultimately was an extension of empire discourse.

Third, over the eras surveyed in this study translatability moves from its older political context into broader kinds of discourse. In Chapter Five we noted historiographical discourse as well as philosophical and magical texts actively engaging in translatability. In the Greco-Roman world the dominant philosophical trends constitute a shared cultural horizon for the discussion. The philosophical schools that emerged from the Hellenistic center and the academic learning that served to reinforce their broader place in the Mediterranean *ecumene* set the terms of discussion as well as its horizons. This context for translatability entailed explicit interpretation in light of philosophical terms. Thus the Greco-Roman period inherited and used older specific names of deities, as well as older terms of commonality for divinity (such as "god" and "gods," Ugaritic *'il* and *'ilm;* Hebrew *'el* and *'elohim;* Greek *theos* and *theoi*) and divine titles (such as "Most High," *'elyon* and *hupsistos,* and "Lord of Heaven," *b'l šmm*). It also added terms to the discussion, such as *logos,* and deployed them in highly philosophical discourse often without the sort of anthropomorphism associated with older religious discourse. Interpretation in the Greco-Roman context played a major role in the religious categories used. Bronze Age discourse manifested cross-cultural categories of religious typologies, and the Iron Age translatability as attested in monarchic Israel modified the older world view. In the Hellenistic context such typologies further occasioned explicit philosophical interpretation and discussion using various methods (such as euhemerism). Moreover, the Greco-Roman context widened the nature of international discourse. Magic entered into the international *koine* in a way that it never did in either the Late Bronze Age or the Iron Age. Sometimes it loosened deities from their original religious moorings, as we saw for Iao in many Greco-Roman magical charms.

2. Then and Now: Scholarship of God

Cultural Permeability and Scholarship

The ancient contexts, especially in the Greco-Roman period, in some respects anticipate the modern situation. Perhaps the most notable feature of this period that parallels the modern context is its great "permeability."[5] Permeability of identity has developed massively, perhaps as a result of increased mobility in the aftermath of the Second World War. The capacity to travel abroad or to absorb influences from abroad has never been greater than today. The contemporary capacity to modify personal identity by combining "traditional" categories of class, religion, gender or race and to cross these kinds of boundaries seems unprecedented. It is arguable that in this respect no ancient era is more like our own than the Greco-Roman period. Echoing Daniel Boyarin and Amy Richlin in their research on sexuality, the modern period seems to represent "very late antiquity."[6] Mobility and permeability deeply affected identity of all kinds in both the Greco-Roman and modern contexts in very substantial ways.

The analogies hardly end here. The effect of ruling powers on intellectual life is also a marked feature of the Greco-Roman world and our own. Like the philosophical and theological discourse that developed out of varied schools in the Greco-Roman world, the field of theology developed as an intellectual apparatus of the Christian church, in part shaped by empire politics since the time of Constantine. It was also in the wake of modern empires that theology developed over the course of the Reformation, the Counter-Reformation and the Enlightenment. It is not just academic life in the universities that has grown thanks to empires. The very understanding of religion, too, emerged more directly in relation to the functioning of empires. As Ninian Smart and Jonathan Z. Smith have emphasized, the very use of the word "religion" in modern times emerged out of the European encounter with non-European cultures in the so-called New

---

[5] It was in a conversation with Arthur Green that this point first came to my attention, for which I thank him. See also the comment about "permeability," made by Jan Bremmer ("Ritual," in: *Religions of the Ancient World: A Guide* [ed. Sarah Iles Johnston; Cambridge, MA/London: Belknap, 2004] 33) in connection with the cross-cultural migration of ritual in antiquity. For the context of this comment, see Chapter Five.

[6] Boyarin, *Carnal Israel: Reading Sex in Talmudic Culture* (Berkeley: University of California, 1993) ix; and Richlin, "Towards a History of Body History," in: *Inventing Ancient Culture: Historicism, Periodization, and the Ancient World* (ed. Mark Golden and Peter Toohey; London/New York: Routledge, 1997) 27. Richlin in particular has a strong critique of recent scholarly views of ancient sexuality (in particular, Michel Foucault's) and in particular of the interpretation of sexual acts in antiquity. For Richlin, sexuality is not entirely a matter of social construction.

World.[7] The vision of anthropology that moved from the armchair operation of Sir James George Frazer out to the ethnographic researches of Margaret Mead and Bronislaw Malinowski was made possible by the projection
of British power out to the cultures studied by field anthropologists. It is
no accident that Napoleon's expedition to Egypt included scholars who
helped bring home the glories of Egypt. Modern museums of natural history, whether in London, New York or Washington, "brought home" to
the centers of power examples of the cultures that the empire powers had
dominated; empires were key to this capacity.[8]

Academic learning has accompanied expressions of imperial power not
only abroad, but also at home. Consciously or not, academics have worked
in service to the political aspirations of their own nations. Historians of
religion who worked on living religious traditions have likewise translated
the texts that were being recovered, thanks in no small measure to the presence of empires around the world. The academic work of texts and translations, founded on the model of classical studies, was extended to fields
well beyond the traditional arena of Greek and Roman classics, whether in
ancient Egypt, Syria, Mesopotamia or India, or for the more contemporary
cultures of India and East Asia. Parallel to the political powers that worked
with them, the centers of academic power increased in prestige, developing
into even greater centers of learning. Academic aspirations and prestige rose
with imperial achievement. National learning developed in the wake of new
academic achievement. National and university libraries, great schools and
scholarship are as emblematic of our time as they were of the Greco-Roman
world.

Ancient and modern empires did not simply provide an opportunity to
study more remote regions and their religions; it also informed the intellectual vision to universalize. Typology, the very impulse to classify, whether
in Hittite-Egyptian treaties, biblical polemics, Hellenistic universal histories, or in the hands of Mircea Eliade and his intellectual heir, Jonathan
Z. Smith, emerges out of the political and historical experience of empire

---

[7] Smart, *Worldviews: Crosscultural Explorations of Human Beliefs* (third ed.; Upper
Saddle River, NJ: Prentice Hall, 2000) 3; Smith, "Religion, Religions, Religious," in:
Critical Terms for Religious Studies (ed. Mark C. Taylor; Chicago: University of Chicago,
1998) 269–84; reprinted in: Smith, *Relating Religion: Essays in the Study of Religion*
(Chicago/London: University of Chicago, 2004) 179–96.

[8] This point is exemplified by Charles Darwin's comments that close his account of
his famous journey around the world on the HMS Beagle (1831–1836). In the context of
his final reflections on his life as "a young naturalist," Darwin attributes "the march of
improvement" as "consequent on the introduction of Christianity throughout the South
Sea": "these changes have now been effected by the philanthropic spirit of the British
nation … To hoist the British flag, seems to draw with it as a certain consequence, wealth,
prosperity, and civilization." See Darwin, *The Voyage of the Beagle* (paperback ed.; New
York: The Modern Library, 2001) 451–52.

meeting other cultures. In Smith's case in particular, he expresses a near obsession with classification from his childhood experience of biological science.[9] It is an article of academic faith (or idolatry); no academic salvation without classification might serve as the first article of Smith's creed. (This may sound born of personal experience and perspective, something not so far from the basis for theology, in Anselm's terms: "faith seeking understanding," *fides quarens intellectum*.)

At the close of the twentieth century, the dream of empire in both political and intellectual terms faded. In his reflections on the field of anthropology, Clifford Geertz noted the colonial foundations of anthropology and the impact of their demise on the field.[10] The same may be said for the field of religion. In their introduction to their 1996 volume *Myth and Method,* the editors Laurie L. Patton and her teacher, Wendy Doniger of the University of Chicago, eschew the desire to universalize despite the universalizing tradition of the study of religion in which they situate themselves. They note the earlier "hope for an elegant master theory," which they identify with the theorists central to the field of religion over the course of the twentieth century (they name Frazer, Freud, Jung, Lévi-Strauss, and Eliade).[11] They suggest that "now ... no single 'grand unified theory' is vividly present."[12] Doniger argues instead for a cross-cultural approach.[13] Cross-cultural study here works toward intellectual intersection rather than general typology. Cultural particulars are perceived to be more perceptible under such efforts at intersection rather than generalization, which raises anew the basis for intercultural encounter. There is a sense that in the wake of such efforts against universal typology, we may be starting over in many respects, with intersection taking place intellectually by an ever-increasing range of contributors with all their "difference."[14] At the same time, the power of empires past (and perhaps present) continues to exert its influence. Despite the critique of empire thinking, the issue remains alive in the modern context,[15] just as it was in the Greco-Roman

---

[9] Smith, *Relating Religion,* 1–60, esp. 1–2.

[10] Geertz, *Works and Lives: The Anthropologist as Author* (Stanford, CA: Stanford University, 1988) 131–35, 146–47.

[11] Patton and Doniger, "Introduction," to *Myth and Method* (ed. Laurie L. Patton and Wendy Doniger; Studies in Religion and Culture; Charlottesville/London: University of Virginia, 1996) 2.

[12] Patton and Doniger, "Introduction," 3.

[13] Patton and Doniger, "Introduction," 9–10.

[14] Compare the final reflections of Geertz, *Works and Lives,* 146–49. For the meantime, see the problems mentioned in the next section.

[15] To take only two recent authors, see Charles S. Maier, *Among Empires: American Ascendancy and Its Predecessors* (Cambridge, MA: Harvard University, 2006); and Chalmers A. Johnson, *Blowback: The Costs and Consequences of American Empire* (New

world. This can be illustrated by one recent debate between insider and outsider perceptions of major religions.

Out of Empire: Insiders versus Outsiders

In recent years, non-western students of their own religious traditions have engaged in a critique of the way outsiders handle their traditions. In what is perhaps only the most famous case, the representation of various aspects of Hinduism by Wendy Doniger and her student Jeffrey Kripal (now professor at Rice University) has come in for strong criticism by Hindus, such as Rajiv Malhotra, Sankrant Sanu and Gautam Sen.[16] According to reports,[17] in January 1997 controversy erupted in India following the publication of a review of Kripal's *Kali's Child* in the Calcutta daily newspaper, *The Statesman*. In the United States, sharp criticism came in the form of Malhotra's attack on Doniger and her students in 2000.[18] Since Malhotra's salvo, other figures both in the United States and in India have jumped into the discussion, and it has taken on the force of a wholesale critique of "outsider" or "western" Indologists working on Hinduism.[19] Some of the criticism revolves around the quality of the research, but at stake for many "insider" Hindu critics is what they see as negative representations of Hinduism or aspects of Hinduism informed by an application of Freudian sexual analysis to Hindu texts. In the wake of this critique, Doniger has been harassed and threatened (it is reported that an egg was thrown at her during a lecture delivered at the University of London[20]).

This confrontation may become more common with other traditions. At present, there seems to be a fault line deepening between Islam and the critical academics working on it. To be sure, there are several critical Muslim

---

York: Metropolitan Books, 2000). See also his essay, "Republic or Empire: A National Intelligence Estimate on the United States," *Harper's Magazine* 314, No. 1880 (January 2007) 63–69.

[16] For information, see http://en.wikipedia.org/wiki/Wendy_Doniger (with links). For an academic sketch of Doniger and her work, see http://prelec.stanford.edu/lecturers/doniger. For Kripal, see http://en.wikipedia.org/wiki/Jeffrey_Kripal. A full account of this controversy lies beyond the scope of this study; I mention only the outlines of the situation in order to indicate its relevance to the larger topic under discussion here.

[17] So http://en.wikipedia.org/wiki/Jeffrey_Kripal.

[18] See now Rajiv Malhotra, "RISA Lila 1: Wendy Child Syndrome," at http://www.sulekha.com/blogs/blogsisplay.aspx?cid=4489.

[19] See http://www.sulekha.com/blogs/blogsisplay.aspx?cid=4489. For further discussion, see Martin E. Marty, "Scholars of Hinduism Under Attack," www.beliefnet.com/story/128story_12899_1.html; and the response by Sankrant Sanu, "U. S. Hinduism Studies: A Question of Shoddy Scholarship," www.beliefnet.com/story/146/story_14684_1html?rnd=46. Marty's piece includes links to counterviews.

[20] As mentioned by Martin E. Marty, "Scholars of Hinduism Under Attack," www.beliefnet.com/story/128story_12899_1.html.

scholars of Islam working in North America at well-known universities, and so the sort of situation seen in the case of Hinduism may not play out the same way with Islamic scholars in the United States.[21] Still it will be interesting to see how the encounter between the comparative and the particular will develop. Whether other "non-western" religions will react similarly to "western" scholarship about them remains to be seen. In the meantime, such difficulties call for greater humility on the part of scholars as well as greater efforts at fidelity by all parties involved in investigating ancient sources.

The debate that presently ensues between western academics who situate various religious traditions within larger universal typologies and indigenous scholars articulating their own local traditions replay the debate over translatability versus non-translatability in ancient Israel as well as the disagreement represented by the Greco-Roman histories of Diodorus Siculus and Philo of Byblos: outsider versus insiders, and broad categories versus the unique sensibility for local traditions. For those who identify with a specific religious tradition, a certain reductionism may be apparent when their tradition is analyzed primarily from a comparative perspective.[22] In debates between Christianity and the wider world, theoretical categories become the terms of engagement, and the integrity of local systems and the religious experience that informs them are muted.

Scholars of God, Now and Then

Scholars are part of this situation and are implicated in it. They do not stand above it or to the side. Their books affect the wider cultural discussion and are affected by the general cultural situation. To understand more fully what scholars of the Bible are up to, we may ask how university professors (such as myself), engaged in probing differences between Israel's religious and textual histories, function in comparison with Israel's ancient scribes and their later religious readers. Much modern scholarship reads for polytheism, and in this respect it differs only in perspective from those ancient scribes who sensed polytheism behind Deuteronomy 32:8–9 and Genesis 14:22. The ancient scribes were both historians of religion and biblical exegetes,

---

[21] See Paul Manzoor, "Method against Truth: Orientalism and qur'ānic Studies," *Muslim World Book Review* 7 (1987) 33–47; and Andrew Rippin, "Western Scholarship and the Qur'ān'" in: *The Cambridge Campanion to the Qur'ān* (ed. Jane Dammen McAuliffe; Cambridge, UK/New York: Cambridge University, 2006) 235–51.

[22] This is one of the criticisms that Malhotra has leveled against the work of historians of religion trained under Doniger. See Malhotra, "RISA Lila 1: Wendy Child Syndrome," at http://www.sulekha.com/blogs/blogsisplay.aspx?cid=4489. Note also the reflections on reductionism on the part of religionists offered by Daniel Gold, "The Paradox in Writing on Religion," *HTR* 83 (1990) 332.

albeit informed by their piety; modern scholars return to the same pathways of texts in their capacity as historians of religion, informed by their own scholarly pieties, for example the illusion that their historical critical capabilities and assessments surpass those of ancient authors and tradents. In such an unexpressed supposition, modern scholars may be expressing their own predilections. The ancient scribes attempted to generate a coherent worldview out of the multiple worldviews that they inherited in the texts that they transmitted; they were concerned with the issue of truth. In contrast, we modern critical biblical scholars cannot reconcile (much less, harmonize) our own religious and textual histories. Such are the conditions of the environments in which the two sets of scholars lived and worked. These questions call for a certain self-reflection (if not humility) from modern historians of religion facing the worldviews that informed the creation of the Bible and the emergent worldview of its so-called censors that attempted to read those worldviews as a single whole.

In accordance with these prescriptive considerations, allow me a brief reflection that acknowledges my own "scribal role" in ascertaining the ancient scribal activity in our two cases of censorship. The two cases of biblical censorship that we examined in Chapter Four show how historians of Israelite religion help to highlight the Bible's polytheistic backdrop. This approach can benefit from both textual criticism and from the study of interpreting traditions (in particular, inner-biblical exegesis), in order to mediate the textual and conceptual gaps between polytheistic vestiges and monotheistic understanding. Put differently, history of religion analysis tends to provide background to the religious worldview expressed in biblical texts; textual criticism is sometimes indicative of how these texts were being received and interpreted in the post-biblical context; and inner-biblical exegesis – where available – may provide signals of interpretation of biblical passages in-between during the biblical period. We might say then that inner-biblical exegesis can sometimes bridge the gap between history of religion work and textual criticism. Or, perhaps more fundamentally, traditional history of religion work that tends to examine the backdrop of biblical worldviews is in fact complete when it draws on inner-biblical exegesis and textual criticism, where applicable. University professors retrace the path of ancient scribes, and thus show the ancients' contribution as historians of religion in their own right. To be sure, the ancient scribes were interested in harmonization where Bible scholars read against the grain, but both engaged in history of religion work and exegesis of the texts before them.

As we saw in Chapter Four, censorship whether ancient or modern is not only that which is deliberately removed or altered, overwritten or rewritten by those who know otherwise. In the ancient context, the more substantial cases of biblical censorship reflect the scribes' conviction that what they received and altered was always the case and had always been the case. Even as they were creating such new myths, even ones that are supersessionist, censors asserted that these were not new, but in fact the oldest or "more true" versions. How any reading of Deuteronomy 32:8–9 or Genesis 14:22 could have reconciled the polytheism of the old world of Israel along with the text's claim to monotheism is a sign of the victory of censorship over the audience of the censors and among the censors themselves.

The question is how much better professors do. If we implicate ancient censors in their situation, perhaps we should pursue as well Dominic Boyer's questioning of the academic paradigm of censorship (namely its demonization of censorship as its antipode) and of self-censoring acts performed by modern scholars.[23] Here we may return to a basic insight about culture from Edward T. Hall's book, *The Silent Language*. In his work, Hall suggests: "Culture hides much more than it reveals, and strangely enough what it hides, it hides most effectively from its own participants."[24] For the GDR as for ancient Judea as for modern scholars, Hall's pithy formulation (used as the epigraph for Chapter Four) perhaps expresses the first motivation and final aim of textual censorship: censors perform explicitly what cultures do implicitly, so that what they think at a given point in time or tradition is represented as if it had always been so and should be and hopefully would be in the future. In expressing their beliefs, censors whether in Israel, the GDR or academia, could hope to hide from themselves what they would or did not face. Here in light of Hall's comment, one may entertain – at the risk of sermonizing – a conclusion or two about academic self-censorship in the biblical field.

Generally we academics avoid the question as to whether our own much cherished theory and knowledge may not be nearly as useful or important as we may think, whether in our analytical penetration or for the new information that we may think that we generate. Instead, we place great faith in them. We claim to use paradigms or approaches that allow further claims to superior intellectual achievement (better data, better theories, better insights), but in this operation we may not differ so much from the ancient scribal elites as we may think. In their competing visions, modern academic elites may not be operating so differently compared with ancient religious factions pushing their own agendas. Ancient censors, whose texts that modern scholars analyze but whose ideologies we may oppose, may in fact do a more sophisticated job at reading the ancient data than we do. Moreover,

---

[23] Boyer, *Spirit and System: Media, Intellectuals, and the Dialectic in Modern German Culture* (Chicago/London: University of Chicago, 2005) esp. 275–78. See also Chapter Four.

[24] Hall, *The Silent Language,* 53. See also Holquist, "Corrupt Originals," 15.

the vast majority of modern academics all too often show little concern for the intense atomism of tiny bits of knowledge generated by their work, and here the ancients were arguably superior not only for their vast knowledge, but perhaps also for their aspirations to integration and wisdom.[25] Any more about academic self-censorship, at least by Hall's definition of cultural self-censorship, perhaps we cannot know.

Translation of God in the Ancient and Modern Contexts

A proper intellectual approach to translation (or intersection), in view of both modern contexts for the reception of ancient texts and their own contexts, seems difficult at best. With God and the gods as part of this translation, what may be the risks to understanding divinity? The modern search for God partakes of some of the very same strategies deployed in the Greco-Roman context.[26] On the one hand, religious dialogue, whether in institutional forms or by individuals, seeks neutral or universal terms (such as the very word, "God") and thus would be led to see particular divine names as manifestations of a single divine reality. The field of comparative theology goes considerably farther, in seeking more nuanced and contextualized cross-cultural understandings. This represents a significant advance over the religious ethnography of the Greco-Roman context; what kind of results it yields for traditional religions to address the modern context remains to be seen.

For quite some time now, modern authors have also attempted to "combine science and religion." Several writers especially since the notable Teilhard de Chardin have sought a synthesis of religion and science.[27] These efforts have highlighted the difficulty in preserving a particularly religious voice or perspective in the understanding of divinity within the wider intel-

---

[25] Such criticisms of academia are in fact quite old and rarely, if ever, politically innocent. Cf. the nineteenth century German notion of *Wissenschaft* as "the spirit or internal unity of knowledge," which in the analysis of Dominic Boyer played a political role in the larger agenda of German nation-building (Boyer, *Spirit and System,* 54, 74–75, 85). As this case would suggest, I am also aware that such criticism of atomistic data generated by university scholarship is not new or "objective" in any meaningful sense. As I discussed toward the end of the Introduction, I would characterize my own "agenda" as concerned not only with scholarship and developing habits for thinking, but also with values and meaning, which is in large measure "humanistic" in the older Catholic sense but without a specific concern with theological apologetics or church teaching. My comments here exceed the scope of this discussion in this chapter, but I do not wish to leave such an issue entirely unaddressed and thus left for readers to surmise my stance on their own.

[26] In other ways, it does not. Magical forms play little or no role in translatability in the manner that they did in the Greco-Roman context. There are other differences as well.

[27] For a recent effort to combine evolution and theology in a manner inspired to a degree by Teilhard de Chardin, see Robert Karl Gnuse, *No Other Gods: Emergent Monotheism in Israel* (JSOTSup 241; Sheffield: Sheffield, 1997) 298–345, esp. 309.

lectual context. New cosmologies and the interest in science are perhaps symptomatic of a major shift in paradigm, one that can prove difficult for longstanding religions to negotiate. Again such a shift was part and parcel of the Greco-Roman context,[28] with its combinations of the traditional anthropomorphic deities and natural elements that we noted in Chapter Five. Though operating with rather different languages and worldviews, the intellectual efforts of the modern and Greco-Roman contexts sometimes show strong resemblances.

So are the reactions to such efforts. Then as today, we witness strong responses against such universalizing efforts in order to maintain particular identity. As one reaction to the force of empire and social dislocation, re-ligious life in the west has gravitated toward smaller, personal groups that find common ground in their particular sensibilities. Instead of institutional life characterized by churches and synagogues, many have sought refuge in smaller group settings and movements concerned less with what they regard as dogma (cf. the negative connotation of the word, "dogmatic") and more with what they would call "spirituality."[29] This characterization readily applies also to the situation in the Greco-Roman world. The major challenge before religious traditions in the west includes being able to mediate between the institutional and individual.

Some counter-reactions have issued in some highly political responses, in a desire to foreclose translatability. Like many regional responses to empire in antiquity, regional responses today may see the empire context in which they live as a sign of the evil of our times, whether at home in the United States or abroad. In his closing remarks on cosmic eschatology in the ancient world, John J. Collins comments: "An evil age is caused by the invasion of foreigners, and this is followed by a radical transformation of the earth."[30] Radical eschatology incurs a radical textual rejection of political empire and religious translatability. In order to respond to such a challenge among eschatological groups at home or abroad, traditional religion in North America and Europe needs to understand its own empire context, or at least its perception by such groups that the world seems so dominated by great powers (most especially in our situation, the political and economic power of the United States). As a result, such groups feel they have little

[28] See J. Edward Wright, *The Early History of Heaven* (New York: Oxford University, 2000).
[29] For a recent discussion, see the Baylor Institute for Studies of Religion (ISR) Religion Survey at: http://www.baylor.edu/isreligion/index.php?id=40634; and the 2006 research document generated as a result of the survey, "American Piety in the 21st Century: New Insights to the Depth and Complexity of Religion in the US," available at: http://www.baylor.edu/content/services/document.php/33304.pdf.
[30] Collins, "Cosmology: Time and History," in: *Religions of the Ancient World: A Guide* (ed. Sarah Iles Johnston; Cambridge, MA/London: Belknap, 2004) 70.

capability to effect positive change. Today the powers of the world seem beyond many people, and they seek other means of salvation. Whether the path taken is political withdrawal, social isolation or even violence, these represent some of the very choices made by people in the face of Seleucid or Roman domination.

Historically we tend to think of our religious differences as a result of belonging to different religions. However, the emerging empire-context following the Second World War has yielded a further fault line, one arguably more threatening to the world's well-being. In some quarters, a massive fault line seems to be running through fundamentalist Christianity and its counterparts within other major religions rather than between the religions themselves. In short, the challenge to traditional religions includes facing up to the fact that their very existence has been predicated on empire. Their capacity to respond to the world today will depend in large measure on their ability to return to persuasion and to shed any coercion and appearance of coercion (or complicity), whether religious or political or both, whether in governing their own memberships or communicating beyond their own ranks. (As recent revelations have shown, my own Roman Catholic Church is among the most egregious in this regard.)

At present, the capacity for traditional religions in Europe and the United States to address the economic empire context and its challenges seems sapped by the traumatic events of the twentieth century. Indeed, it has been claimed that the depleted state of the church in Western Europe today can be laid to its failure to cope with the challenge of the Holocaust. Ancient religions likewise struggled in the face of significant disasters, for example Augustine's famous defense of Christianity in *The City of God,* written 413–426 CE/AD in the wake of the fall of Rome to Alaric on August 24, 410.[31] In our time, the very use of God-language is under siege. Some religious leaders facing the full brunt of modernity – or, post-modernity – are prepared to delimit or even drop God-language from preaching, teaching and counseling. Others religious leaders simply continue with traditional God-talk as if there was no problem with the intelligibility of God in the contemporary circumstances; in other words, a retreat into non-translatability of divinity. In these cases, God-language may simply sound like a crutch, one that is unconvincing perhaps even to some of those who use it. Under the massive weight of these circumstances, is God getting lost in translation?

---

[31] See the summary by Julien Ries, "Idolatry," *ER* 7:4361; and the introduction to Augustine, *The City of God Against the Pagans* (ed. R. W. Dyson; Cambridge Texts in the History of Political Thought; Cambridge, UK: Cambridge University, 1998) x–xxix.

Academic Faith and Scholars of God

This is the very question that arguably underlies the tug-of-war between the fields of religion and theology. In the words of Michael Buckley: "But no matter how differently the story of origins [of the field of religion] could have been told, evaluated and employed, I wonder if something far more profound did not get lost in the translation between the Middle Ages and the contemporary understanding and the scientific study of 'religion'. And I wonder if what got lost was 'God' – God as the purpose, and, in this way, the specification of *religio*."[32] Modern scholars of religion might stand a better chance of coping with the current challenges if we were to recognize a fundamental fact of what scholars of God in the different academic fields do. First of all, we do both a great deal and we do quite little. The impact of most research in the fields of theology or religion on the larger world is arguably negligible. However, teachers and writers engage in acts of hope, for as they delve in the past, they also hope for things that they do not see or usually will never see. Indeed, they may affect lives, even change them, often without knowing it. In this respect, modern scholars, whether they are historians of religion, theologians or textual scholars, are quite comparable to their ancient forebears who sought to understand divinity in other cultures and across these cultures. Learned scholars, ancient and modern alike, indulge in a faith in the intellectual life, that what we may have to say is worthwhile not just to the like-minded but also to others in our societies. And sometimes academics have far more impact than they anticipate; and thus they shoulder a tremendous responsibility as their books are published and go out to a public that may read them with little or no guidance. It is hard to anticipate how one's books will be read and interpreted, but it remains an academic responsibility to be concerned with the matter and to make an effort to anticipate problems. The academic tendency to qualify conclusions is not a failure of conviction but key to instructing readers about the limits of our knowledge and insight.

That the academic life is a matter of intellectual faith and not just a matter of ascertaining facts may be highlighted by the faith stance on the part of both theologians and historians of religion. Many theologians, both ancient and modern, reject the operation of studying divinities across cultures; for them, their deity is incommensurate with other deities. As the alter ego of such theologians, some historians of religion see themselves as bracketing their own faith-stances (if they have them), and thus operate without faith.

---

[32] Michael Buckley, SJ, "The Study of Religion and the Rise of Atheism: Conflict or Confirmation?" in: *Fields of Faith: Theology and Religious Studies for the Twenty-First Century* (ed. David F. Ford, Ben Quash and Janet Martin Soskice; Cambridge, UK: Cambridge University, 2005) 22.

Yet in light of critical evaluations by religionists of Mircea Eliade's "latent theological agenda,"[33] it seems that scholars in the field of religion are coping with challenges of personal stance no less than theologians, despite stereotypes to the contrary. Scholars working in the biblical fields find their allegiances divided between the two sides of theology and study of religion, with many of the same issues of academic faith equally in evidence.

Thankfully, the sharp *Auseinandersetzung* of theology and religion may be on the wane, especially as the roots and assumptions of both are subjected to more rigorous scrutiny. With a certain time having passed since their momentous split, the two disciplines may yet turn to what they share in common.[34] In this enterprise, they may be joined in different ways by scholars of the Bible.[35] The question remains as to how, if at all, there can be some translatability, or at least some intersections, concerning divinity among these arenas of research and thought. The academic study of ancient divinity, from whatever quarter, presupposes that its operation can be successful. This really is an act of faith on the part of scholars of God: we engage in a comparative project often lacking in a means of corroboration, apart from amassing a higher stack of facts arrayed according to the current methods accompanied by an appeal to ever improving categories founded on the going theories. Among our most prominent interpreters of culture, the academic situation can look this way.[36]

Whatever our research base and approach, there is a faith in the importance of the study of divinity for our shared humanity. Such an acknowledgement

---

[33] Bryan S. Rennie, "Eliade, Mircea [Further Considerations]," *ER* 4.2757–63, esp. 2761. See also Preus, *Explaining Religion,* xviii–xix; and Daniel Dubuisson's critique of the field of religion in his book, *The Western Construction of Religion: Myth, Knowledge, and Ideology* (trans. William Sayers; Baltimore/London: Johns Hopkins University, 2003). For him, categories of comparative religion represent a particular intellectual privileging (arguably comparable to theology). He is particularly critical of Eliade's privileging the "sacred" as a category.

[34] See the essays in: *Fields of Faith: Theology and Religious Studies for the Twenty-First Century* (ed. David F. Ford, Ben Quash and Janet Martin Soskice; Cambridge, UK: Cambridge University, 2005). Note also the critique of religion as a field from within the field: Dubuisson, *The Western Construction of Religion.* Dubuisson sees the very term religion as religiously or theologically informed; he prefers the term "cosmographic formations" (see especially pp. 36, 180, 198–213).

[35] However, conflict in the field is evident in the recent diatribe against the modern study of the Bible by Hector Avalos, *The End of Biblical Studies* (Amherst, NY: Prometheus, 2007).

[36] Compare the remarks given in a rather personal lecture delivered in 1999 by Clifford Geertz: "I suppose that what I have been doing all these years is piling up learning. But, at the time, it seemed to me that I was trying to figure out what to do next, and hold off a reckoning." Geertz, *A Life of Learning* (Charles Homer Haskins Lecture for 1999; American Council of Learned Societies Occasional Paper, No. 45; np: American Council of Learned Societies, 1999) 1. See also his earlier reflections in: Geertz, *Works and Lives: The Anthropologist as Author* (Stanford, CA: Stanford University, 1988) 1–24.

of scholarly faith should engender humility, open to accepting help from others in various quarters (cf. "another place," Esther 4:14). Interestingly, theologians and historians of religion seem to agree in the great difficulty of translatability. Theologians as well as traditional believers who prize their own traditions or deities over others' are right to think that translation is difficult, arguably impossible. This is true whether for the ancient world or the history of the theological tradition or the wider religious traditions around the world for what they contribute to our larger self-knowledge and awareness. The point applies, too, to the field of religion, according to Jonathan Z. Smith: translation in Smith's characterization is "incorrigible" and "necessarily incomplete."[37] On this point, when it comes to divinity, theologians and historians of religions are perhaps close after all. It is the ultimately impossible job of all scholars of God, believers or not, to translate for the wider world, not just to argue with one another about God or about various data concerning God. As part of the difficult task of translating the wider contexts of our fields, no matter what specific arena we operate in, we need to translate God in our world, today's *ecumene,* just as we need to translate other aspects of our culture across cultural divides. Translatability of divinity is no mere academic task; it is a central task of human self-understanding. Otherwise, in this situation, something of our humanity – and arguably of our divinity – may be lost.

---

[37] Smith, *Relating Religion,* 31. See also his comments on pp. 371–72.

Index of Sources

Sources are arranged in three major divisions: (I) Ancient Near Eastern and Indian texts (Akkadian, Egyptian, Hittite, Hindu, Sumerian, Ugaritic and West Semitic inscriptions); (II) Hebrew Bible, Second Temple Jewish works and later Jewish works; and (III) Classical Texts, the New Testament, and later Christian and Gnostic works.

I. Ancient Near Eastern and Indian Texts: Akkadian, Egyptian, Hittite, Hindu, Ugaritic and West Semitic inscriptions (Aramaic, Hebrew, Moabite, Phoenician, Punic, etc.)

Akkadian Texts

Amarna letters

19	63, 65, 67, 80
20	63
20:79	63
21	63
23	63, 67, 125
24	65, 67
32	66
35	43, 261
45	66
49	43, 66, 261
52	66
55	66, 67
60	66
61	66
68	67
73	67
74	58, 67
74:31	46
74:57	55
75	67
76	67
77	67, 68
78	66, 67
79	67
81	67
83	66, 67
84	67
84:35	55
84:39	46
85	66, 67
86	67
87	67
89	67
92	67
95	67
97	68
100:36	73
100:37	73
100:40	73
108	67, 68, 71, 72
134	67
137	68
141:2	73
141:10	73
141:13	73
141:15	73
141:37	73
141:43	73

II. Hebrew Bible, Second Temple Jewish works and Later Jewish works

III. Classical Texts, the New Testament and
Later Christian and Gnostic Works

Index of Authors

Index of Subjects